Making America

A History of the United States

Brief Edition

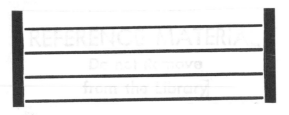

Making America

A History of the United States

Brief Edition

Volume A: To 1877

Carol Berkin
Baruch College, City University of New York

Christopher L. Miller
The University of Texas, Pan American

Robert W. Cherny
San Francisco State University

James L. Gormly
Washington and Jefferson College

and

W. Thomas Mainwaring
Washington and Jefferson College

HOUGHTON MIFFLIN COMPANY
Boston   New York

Sponsoring Editor: Patricia A. Coryell
Senior Associate Editor: Jeffrey Greene
Senior Project Editor: Carol Newman
Senior Production/Design Coordinator: Jill Haber
Senior Manufacturing Coordinator: Marie Barnes

Cover Design: Marc Caleb

Cover Image: John Casper Wild, *Cincinnati Public Landing,* 1835, Cincinnati Historical Society.

Printed in the U.S.A.

Library of Congress Catalog Card Number: 96-76866

ISBN: 0-395-77443-8 (Student Edition)
      0-395-85736-8 (IAE)

2 3 4 5 6 7 8 9-VH-01 00-99 98 97

Brief Contents

Brief Contents

Contents

Maps

Note: Maps listed in boldface type indicate chapter-opening maps.

Features

Preface

Our aim in producing this brief edition has been to be as faithful as possible to the narrative of American history contained in *Making America*. Although the brief edition has reduced the length of *Making America* by one third, we have sacrificed very few sections and none of the features of the long edition. The clear chronology, straightforward narrative, and strong thematic structure remain. In addition, all the learning features, including chapter-opening maps and timelines, chapter outlines with focus questions, and in-text glossaries, have been retained.

Wherever possible, we have cut words and avoided excising larger sections to retain the book's narrative flow. Of necessity, the brief edition provides fewer examples and details. Where there were four examples, this edition may contain only two. We have also followed Mark Twain's advice about the adjective. "When in doubt, strike it out." We trust that in pruning the text severely but with a discerning eye that we have allowed the major themes of *Making America* to stand out clearly.

The brief edition of *Making America* carries the story of American history through the 1996 presidential election. It also includes President Clinton's efforts to promote national healthcare, the Whitewater scandal, the Contract with America, and the confrontation that led to shutdowns of the federal government in 1995 and 1996.

This edition is well suited for use in courses in which additional reading is assigned or where the course is shorter than usual. It is available in a one-volume and two-volume format: Volume A covers American history from prediscovery through Reconstruction, and Volume B covers Reconstruction to the 1996 elections. The chapter on Reconstruction is contained in both volumes.

Approach

Making America follows the course of American history from the earliest human settlements to the present day. This is a remarkable story to tell—and a complex one. A look at the table of contents will show the reader that we have set this story within an explicit political chronology. This structure has the advantage of being basic and familiar to most readers, and is broad enough to accommodate generous attention to social, economic, and diplomatic history. As scholars whose own work focuses on the experience of women, American Indians, political behavior, labor, and international policymakers, we wanted our book to integrate the best new scholarship in these and other important fields. We are confident that the political framework we have chosen allows us to bring all these strands of the American story together over thirty-two chapters.

In *Making America*, we have made a conscious commitment to demonstrate the significance of race, gender, social class, region, ethnic background, age, and religion in shaping the historical experience of Americans. *Making America* does not adopt the perspective of a single group within American society as it narrates our national history. It does not tell the story from the perspective of a single region either. It does not assume that there is one group that makes history and others that simply survive it. *Making America* is built on the premise that all Americans are historically active figures, playing significant roles in creating the history the authors narrate.

This view of history as the product of the ideas and actions of *all* men and women, coupled with our desire to show history as a dynamic process, led to the creation of the ECCO model. ECCO is an acronym for four fundamental aspects of the historical process: Expectations, Constraints, Choices, and Outcomes. As we wrote, it helped the authors to organize the flow of the narrative. In execution, it also functions as an integrated learning aid for the student. In every chapter, *Making America* examines the variety of *expectations* people held about their futures; the *constraints* of time, place, and multiple social and economic factors that these historical figures faced; the *choices* they made, given the circumstances of their lives; and finally, the expected and unexpected *outcomes* produced by their decisions. The ECCO model does not force any historical interpretations upon the student. Instead, it offers a method by which students are able to understand the past as a rich human experience.

Too often, students come away from a textbook with the impression that people in the past behaved very differently from people in the present. Unlike themselves, their friends, their parents, or their nation's leaders, the historical women and men they encounter seem never to be confused by the decisions they face or uncertain about the consequences of their actions. Indeed, a mood of inevitability hangs over the lives of these past generations, as they live out their roles as actors in a drama written for them by destiny. Students find it difficult to relate to these earlier Americans who seem to inhabit a world with too many simple answers and too many clear solutions. Presenting the past in this manner may make it more manageable, but it does not make it good history. *Making America* offers students a way of thinking about history that scholars themselves employ as they research and reconstruct the past. ECCO is a device that will reinforce the reality of history as a dynamic, uncertain process, increase students' empathy for the men and women of the past, and help them to analyze critically and retain what they have read.

Themes

In keeping with our goal of creating a clear and straightforward narrative chronology, a central theme in this text is the political development of the nation. The creation and revision of its federal and local governments, the contests over domestic and diplomatic policies, and the internal and external crises faced by the United States and its political institutions all play a major role in the book's organization. The reader will find this theme of political development throughout the book, for example, in the discussion of events leading to the American Revolution, in the detailed accounts of the constitutional debates of the 1770s and the 1780s, in the analysis of the political tensions and conflicts leading to the Civil War, in the close attention to federal

Indian policy in the nineteenth century, in the examination of the American role in modern world wars, in the contest over the role of the federal government in the Great Depression, and in the economic crises of recent eras.

Political development serves as a broad umbrella for discussion of other significant themes as well. Among these is the understanding of American history as a story of immigrant societies. To do justice to this second theme, *Making America* explores not only English and American immigration, but immigrant communities from Paleolithic times to the present, including Indian societies before European colonization, the creation of African-American culture within slavery, and the great migration from the Pacific rim in recent time.

Making America's third theme recognizes the changing nature of relations between groups—racial, ethnic, class, and gender relations. Thus, *Making America* examines the changing nature of gender roles over several centuries, the way that relations between whites and African-Americans have changed, the development of Anglo-Latino relations (especially in the Southwest), and alterations in the relations between employers and employees. This book focuses on creating understanding about groups, their relation to each other, and the way that some groups have used politics to achieve their goals and define their relations with other groups.

Our fourth theme focuses on the significance of regional economies and cultures. This regional theme is developed, for example, in the discussion of the seventeenth- and eighteenth-century colonies, and in the examination of the striking social and cultural divergences that have existed between the American southwest and the Atlantic coastal region.

A fifth theme is the rise and impact of large social movements, prompted by changing material conditions or by new ideas that challenge the status quo. *Making America* explores movements such as the Great Awakening of the 1740s; the reform efforts of the early nineteenth century, including abolitionism, temperance, and women's rights; the Progressive Era; the emergence of organized labor; third-party organizations; and the rise of a youth culture in the post–World War II era.

The sixth and final theme is the relationship of the United States to other nations, which also fits well within the political framework of the text. *Making America* explores in depth the causes and consequences of this nation's role in world conflict and diplomacy, whether in the eighteenth- and early nineteenth-century struggles for dominance in Europe, the removal of Indian nations from their tribal lands, the impact of American policies of isolationism and interventionism, or the modern role of the United States as a dominant player in world affairs. These are not the only themes students will see threading through the text, but they are themes we believe are useful to identify from the beginning.

Learning Features

Each chapter in *Making America* follows the same format. Before the students are asked to immerse themselves in the past, we provide them with some essential study aids for the task ahead. As they read the narrative, we provide them with a second set of aids, designed both to ensure the best communication between the authors and their readers and to help bridge the gap between women and men of the past and those who are trying to understand them in the present. When the student has finished the chapter, we provide a final set of aids to reinforce what they have learned and to guide them if they want to pursue a topic in greater depth.

Chapter-Opening Features

Each chapter of *Making America* begins by placing historical events in space and in time. First, each chapter begins with a map to set the scene for the most significant events in the narrative to follow. Second, a timeline locates the major political events in the period under discussion within a larger time frame. Third, students are given an outline of new material they will encounter in the chapter. Fourth, several critical thinking questions help students focus on the larger, overarching themes of the material. Following the two pages of chapter-opening material, a chapter introduction demonstrates the dynamic process of history by applying the ECCO model to the subject matter the students will explore.

In-Text Features

As students read they will find a number of features in each chapter designed to make the text more accessible and the people and events it portrays more familiar. First, there are glossaries on each page that define terms and explain their historically specific usage in the narrative. These glossaries are precise and informative. They help students build their vocabularies and review for tests, and they reflect the authors' concern to communicate fully with their student readers. Second, the introductory critical thinking questions reappear at the beginning of each major chapter section. Third, the chapter's illustrations provide an exciting visual connection to the past. The caption for each illustration does more than identify the artist, the scene, or the physical location of the event; it also analyzes the subject of the painting, photograph, or artifact and comments on its significance. Finally, every chapter has an "Individual Choices" feature that helps students understand an important point raised in that chapter. "Individual Choices" provides an intimate portrait of individuals and how they arrived at a decision that shaped their lives. These features dramatically reinforce the essential point that historical events are not inevitable occurrences, but are the result of choices made by real people.

In addition, students are presented with a chance to read the words of Americans of the past as they debate over events or ideas that were critical in their era. This "Voices" feature contains a document relating to a controversial issue and quotations from supporting and opposing voices on that issue. This feature grew out of our conviction that students can learn much from the archival material through which the past speaks for itself.

End-of-Chapter Features

One of the most important obligations of a textbook is to help students reflect on the new information they have encountered and to suggest additional sources for further study. Thus, each chapter contains a summary of the chapter's main topics made dynamic by structuring it according to the ECCO model. The text also provides suggestions for further reading on events and personalities introduced in the chapter. After the last chapter, there is a selected bibliography citing the best scholarship in the field, both old and new, which is provided to assist professors and students who might want to explore the historiographical debates on a topic.

At the heart of *Making America* is the fascinating story of this nation's past. It is told by scholars and instructors who have a genuine enthusiasm for retelling that story to others. Our abiding interest in the experiences of earlier generations of Americans is not lost in an overly abstract style or buried by a narrative designed to impress students rather than inform them. We tell America's story clearly, and people it with women and men who are depicted as individuals rather than representative figures and as complex historical actors rather than simple heroes or villains. *Making America* provides more than a textbook that integrates new scholarship, raises questions about causes and consequences of historical events, and provides analyses of historical developments. The authors know that, above all, a text is a teaching tool, and we have designed *Making America* to be useful in the classrooms of our colleges and universities. Its structure, the themes it emphasizes, and the features it incorporates were chosen to assist our colleagues in their efforts to communicate effectively with students and impart to them a solid knowledge of the American past.

Study and Teaching Aids

A number of useful learning and teaching aids accompany *Making America*. They are designed to help the student get the most from the course and to provide the instructor with some useful teaching tools. The two-volume *Study Guide,* written by Eli Faber of John Jay College of Criminal Justice, City University of New York, provides students with many review exercises and tips on how to study and take tests effectively. Each chapter includes learning objectives, an annotated outline of the chapter, and approximately twenty-five key terms, concepts, and people. The fifteen multiple-choice questions per chapter include a text-page reference and a rejoinder for the correct answer. Also included in each chapter are three to five essay questions with answer guidelines, one analytical question based on an analysis of a primary source, and one map exercise.

A *Computerized Study Guide* is also available for students. It functions as a tutorial providing rejoinders to all multiple-choice questions that explain why the student's response is or is not correct.

The *Instructor's Resource Manual with Test Items,* prepared by Kelly Woestman of Pittsburg State University, begins with a section on how to organize lectures effectively, how to handle large lecture classes efficiently, and provides tips on how to run discussion and activity groups. For every chapter, it includes instructional objectives that are drawn from the textbook's critical thinking questions, a chapter summary and annotated outline, and three lecture topics that include resource material and references to the text. Each chapter also includes discussion questions, answers to the critical thinking questions that follow each main heading in the text, cooperative and individual learning activities, map activities (including activities for the Rand McNally *Atlas of American History*), ideas for paper topics, and a list of audio-visual resources including CD-ROM and videodisc products with addresses of suppliers.

The test items include key terms and definitions, multiple-choice questions, essay questions with answer guidelines, and an analytical exercise to test critical thinking skills per chapter. There is also a section on creating a good testing environment, what constitutes a good test item, and how to construct test questions.

A *Computerized Test Item File* is available for IBM® PC or compatible and Macintosh computers.* This computerized version of the printed *Test Items* file allows professors to create customized tests by editing and adding questions.

There is also a set of over one hundred full-color *Map Transparencies* available on adoption.

A variety of *videos,* documentaries and docudramas by major film producers, is available for use with *Making America.*

Please contact your local Houghton Mifflin representative for more information about the ancillary program or to obtain desk copies.

Acknowledgments

The authors have benefited from the critical reading

*IBM is the registered trademark of International Business Machines Corporation.

of the manuscript by our generous colleagues. We thank the following instructors:

Linda Kelly Alkana, California State University, Long Beach

Gary L. Browne, University of Maryland— Baltimore County

Mark Goldman, Tallahassee Community College

Wendell Griffith, Okaloosa-Walton Community College

Glenn Linden, Southern Methodist University

Edward M. Massey, Bee County College

Elizabeth I. Nybakken, Mississippi State University

Walter Pierce, University of Texas—Brownsville

John C. Willis, The University of the South

William D. Young, Johnson County Community College

W. Thomas Mainwaring, the abridging editor of the Brief Edition of *Making America,* would like to thank his colleague James Gormly at Washington and Jefferson College for suggesting that he take on this task. His thanks also go to John Mark Scott, Jr., professor of Russian at Washington and Jefferson, who read the entire manuscript to ensure that it made sense. Jeff Greene and Carol Newman at Houghton Mifflin did a fine job of turning the manuscript into a book and making sure that everything went smoothly. Finally, he thanks his wife Deborah for her patience during the long hours that went into this project. Amy and Philip were pretty patient as well.

About the Authors

Carol Berkin

Born in Mobile, Alabama, Carol Berkin received her A.B. from Barnard College and her Ph.D. from Columbia University. Her dissertation won the Bancroft Award. She is now professor of history at Baruch College and the Graduate Center of City University of New York. She has written *Jonathan Sewall: Odyssey of an American Loyalist* (1974) and is currently completing *The American Eve: Women in Colonial American Society*. She has edited *Women of America: A History* (with Mary Beth Norton, 1979) and *Women, War, and Revolution* (with Clara M. Lovett, 1980). Her articles have appeared in such collections as *The American Revolution: Changing Perspectives, Around the Square: Greenwich Village, 1830–1890, Portraits of American Women,* and *The Underside of American History*. She was contributing editor on southern women for *The Encyclopedia of Southern Culture.*

Professor Berkin has chaired the Dunning-Beveridge Prize Committee for the American Historical Association and the Columbia University Seminar in Early American History and served on the program committees for both the Society for the History of the Early American Republic and the Organization of American Historians. In addition, she has been a historical consultant for the National Parks Commission and served on the Planning Committee for the Department of Education's National Assessment of Educational Progress.

Christopher L. Miller

Born and raised in Portland, Oregon, Christopher L. Miller received his undergraduate degree from Lewis and Clark College and his Ph.D. from the University of California, Santa Barbara. Before accepting his current position on the faculty of the University of Texas, Pan American, he served as an educational consultant for the Oregon Museum of Science and Industry, was a visiting assistant profes-sor at Rutgers University, and a fellow at the Charles Warren Center for Studies in American History, Harvard University. He is the author of *Prophetic Worlds: Indians and Whites on the Columbian Plateau* (1985), and his articles and reviews have appeared in numerous scholarly journals. In addition to his scholarship in the areas of American West and American Indian history, Professor Miller has been active in projects designed to improve history teaching. He is a charter member of the American Textbook Council and has directed teaching improvement programs funded by the Meadows Foundation, the U.S. Department of Education, and other agencies.

Robert W. Cherny

Born in Marysville, Kansas, and raised in Beatrice, Nebraska, Robert W. Cherny received his B.A. from the University of Nebraska and his M.A. and Ph.D. from Columbia University. He is now professor of history at San Francisco University.

His books include *Populism, Progressivism, and the Transformation of Nebraska Politics, 1885–1915* (1981), *A Righteous Cause: The Life of William Jennings Bryan* (1985, 1994), and *San Francisco, 1865–1932* (with William Issel, 1986). His articles and reviews have appeared in *American Historical Review, Great Plains Quarterly, Journal of American History, Pacific Historical Review, Western Historical Quarterly,* and other journals and anthologies. He has contributed to *The American National Biography, The Reader's Companion to American History, The Dictionary of American Biography,* and other historical encyclope-dias. He has served as a consultant for several documentary films.

He is president of the Society for Historians of the Gilded Age and Progressive Era, and has served on the council of the American Historical Association, Pacific Coast Branch, as president of the Southwest Labor Studies Association, on other professional committees, and on editorial boards.

James L. Gormly

Born in Riverside, California, James L. Gormly received a B.A. from the University of Arizona and his M.A. and Ph.D. from the University of Connecticut. He is now professor of history and chair of the history department at Washington and Jefferson College. He has written *The Collapse of the Grand Alliance* (1970) and *From Potsdam to the Cold War* (1979). His articles and reviews have appeared in *Diplomatic History, The Journal of American History, The American Historical Review, The Historian, The History Teacher,* and *The Journal of Interdisciplinary History.*

W. Thomas Mainwaring

Born in Pittsburgh, Pennsylvania, W. Thomas Mainwaring received his B.A. from Yale University and his M.A. and Ph.D. from the University of North Carolina at Chapel Hill. Currently an associate professor of history at Washington and Jefferson College, he is interested in local and community history. He has edited a collection of essays on the Whiskey Rebellion and has written about a variety of topics on local and community history.

Making America
A History of the United States
Brief Edition

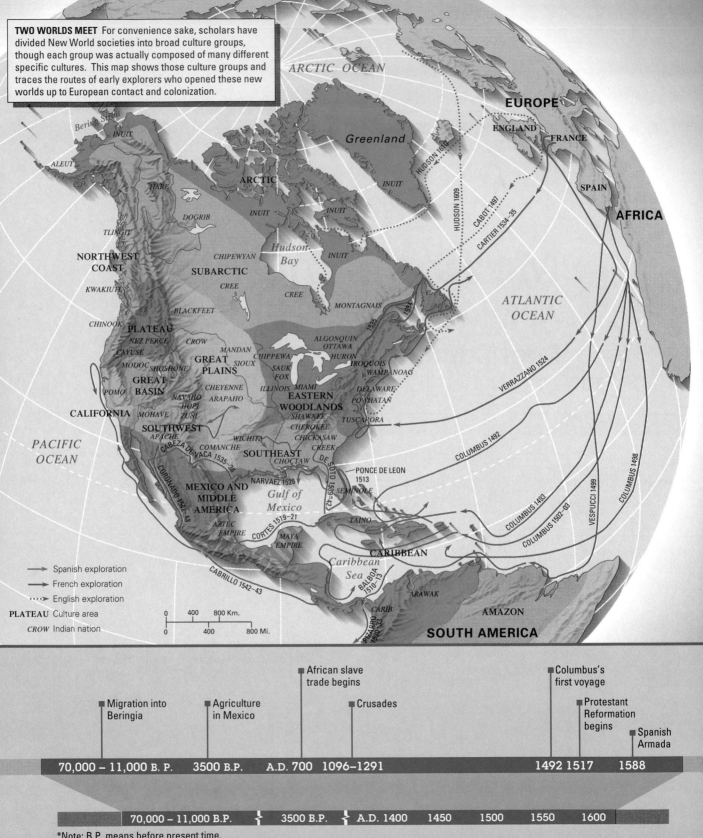

TWO WORLDS MEET For convenience sake, scholars have divided New World societies into broad culture groups, though each group was actually composed of many different specific cultures. This map shows those culture groups and traces the routes of early explorers who opened these new worlds up to European contact and colonization.

ARCTIC OCEAN

EUROPE

ENGLAND

FRANCE

SPAIN

AFRICA

Greenland

Bering Strait

INUIT

ALEUT

HARE

ARCTIC

INUIT

INUIT

HUDSON 1610

CABOT 1497

CARTIER 1534-35

DOGRIB

TLINGIT

CHIPEWYAN

Hudson Bay

INUIT

HUDSON 1609

ATLANTIC OCEAN

NORTHWEST COAST

SUBARCTIC

KWAKIUTL

CREE

CHINOOK

BLACKFEET

CREE

MONTAGNAIS

PLATEAU

NEZ PERCE

CROW

MANDAN

CHIPPEWA

ALGONQUIN

OTTAWA

HURON

1535

1534

CAYUSE

MODOC

SHOSHONE

GREAT PLAINS

SIOUX

SAUK

FOX

IROQUOIS

WAMPANOAG

VERRAZZANO 1524

GREAT BASIN

CHEYENNE

ILLINOIS

MIAMI

DELAWARE

POMO

NAVAHO

ARAPAHO

POWHATAN

HOPI

EASTERN WOODLANDS

CALIFORNIA

ZUNI

MOHAVE

SHAWNEE

TUSCARORA

PACIFIC OCEAN

SOUTHWEST

APACHE

WICHITA

CHEROKEE

COLUMBUS 1492

CABEZA DE VACA 1535-36

COMANCHE

CHICKASAW

SOUTHEAST

CREEK

CORONADO 1542-43

CHOCTAW

DE SOTO 1539-42

PONCE DE LEON 1513

COLUMBUS 1493

VESPUCCI 1499

COLUMBUS 1498

NARVAEZ 1528

MEXICO AND MIDDLE AMERICA

SEMINOLE

COLUMBUS 1502-03

AZTEC EMPIRE

CORTES 1519-21

Gulf of Mexico

TAINO

CABRILLO 1542-43

MAYA EMPIRE

Caribbean Sea

CARIBBEAN

BALBOA 1510-13

ARAWAK

AMAZON

CARIB

SOUTH AMERICA

PIZARRO 1530-33

	Spanish exploration
	French exploration
	English exploration
PLATEAU	Culture area
CROW	Indian nation

0   400   800 Km.
0   400   800 Mi.

■ African slave trade begins

■ Columbus's first voyage

■ Migration into Beringia

■ Agriculture in Mexico

■ Crusades

■ Protestant Reformation begins

■ Spanish Armada

70,000 – 11,000 B. P.   3500 B.P.   A.D. 700   1096–1291   1492 1517   1588

70,000 – 11,000 B.P.   3500 B.P.   A.D. 1400   1450   1500   1550   1600

*Note: B.P. means before present time.

CHAPTER 1

Making a "New" World, to 1588

American Origins

- Before the arrival of Columbus, what *constraints* did native cultures face?
- What kinds of *choices* did they make, and what were the *outcomes* of those *choices* for Indians living in various parts of the continent?

European Outreach and the Age of Exploration

- What *expectations* led Europeans into extensive exploration and outreach?
- What *constraints* stood in their way?
- How did they *choose* to get past those constraints?

The Challenges of Mutual Discovery

- How did American Indians *choose* to respond to European contact?
- How did Europeans *choose* to respond to Indians and Africans?
- What were some *outcomes* of the Columbian Exchange?

The New Europe and the Atlantic World

- What did Europeans *expect* to gain by exploring and subduing North America?
- How did their explorations relate to events in Europe?

INTRODUCTION

E xpectations
C onstraints
C hoices
O utcomes

The first people to come to America *chose* to come here a very long time ago, *expecting* to find improved hunting. These Americans subsequently faced natural, cultural, and economic *constraints* that gave peculiar shape to their societies. As their numbers grew, these hunters were *constrained* by the rapid rise of their own population and the simultaneous decline of the large game animals they depended on for food. Many *chose* to increase their reliance on plants. The *outcome* for these societies was the eventual development of agriculture. Other societies responded differently to the decline and ultimate extinction of big game because of different *constraints* and *expectations*. The overall *outcome* was a broadly diverse cultural universe in North America.

In the meantime, people in Africa, the Middle East, and Europe were making their own *choices*. Muslim traders, following routes first taken by the ancient Egyptians, spread knowledge and goods that presented a new set of *expectations* and *choices* to Africans. One *outcome* was the rise of rich and sophisticated African kingdoms. Another was the establishment of a systematic slave trade by Africans and Muslims.

The influence of Viking and Muslim traders led to changed *expectations* in Europe as well. The wealth of these traders lured Europeans into increasing adventurousness. At first, their neighbors' military strength was a large *constraint*, but gradually Europeans *chose* to challenge Islam's control over large parts of Europe and the Asian and African trade. Italian merchants formed partnerships with their Islamic neighbors, bringing new wealth and knowledge into their cities. Farther west, the Portuguese and then the Spanish swept the Muslims from their lands. They then explored new trade routes to escape the Italian-Muslim monopoly of the Far Eastern and African trade. Their successes led other European nations to *choose* exploration as a way of bringing new riches to their lands.

The *outcome* of these *expectations*, *constraints*, and *choices* was a collision among Europeans, Africans, and American Indians in the Western Hemisphere. This collision of worlds transformed life on both sides of the Atlantic. Thus the story of making America must begin with the first discovery of the New World, long before Columbus, and trace the development of the people who were already here when Columbus arrived. Then we must consider what was happening in the rest of the world so we can understand why others eventually came to this land. Only then will we be prepared to see how the *expectations*, *constraints*, and *choices* made by the people who came together in the New World following Columbus had the particular *outcomes* we call America.

American Origins

• Before the arrival of Columbus, what *constraints* did native cultures face?

• What kinds of *choices* did they make, and what were the *outcomes* of those *choices* for Indians living in various parts of the continent?

The settlement of the **Western Hemisphere** took place fairly recently in human history. Although human culture began about 4 million years ago in what is now northern Tanzania, anthropologists hold that the peopling of the Americas did not begin

> **B.P.**   An abbreviation for "before the present"; 70,000 B.P. means "70,000 years ago."
>
> **Western Hemisphere**   The half of the earth that includes North America, Mexico, Central America, and South America.

CHRONOLOGY

The New World

c. 70,000–11,000 B.P.	Human migration from Asia into Beringia
c. 7000 B.P.	Plant cultivation begins in North America
c. 3500 B.P.	Agriculture begins in central Mexico
c. 300–900 A.D.	Rise of Mayan and Zapotecan cultures
c. 500	Agriculture extends into present-day New Mexico and Arizona
c. 700	Islamic caravans to West Africa and African slave trade begin
800–1100	Vikings extend trade network
c. 500–1000	Rise of Hopewell culture
c. 800–1700	Rise of Mississippian culture
c. 1000	Chichimecs invade Mexico
1096–1291	The Crusades
c. 1325	Aztecs invade central Mexico
1492	Columbus's first voyage
1494	Treaty of Tordesillas
1517	Protestant Reformation begins
1519–1521	Cortés invades Mexico
1527–1535	Henry VIII begins English Reformation
1558	Elizabeth I becomes queen of England
1583	Gilbert's failed attempt at an English colony in North America
1585	English colonize Roanoke Island
1588	English defeat the Spanish Armada
1590	Roanoke found abandoned

until at least 70,000 years ago. Some theorize that this process did not begin until about 20,000 years ago.

The movement of people from Asia to North America is intimately connected to the advance and retreat of glaciers during the Great Ice Age, which began about $2\frac{1}{2}$ million years ago and ended only about 8,000 years ago. During the Wisconsin glaciation, the last major advance of glaciers, a sheet of ice over 8,000 feet thick covered the northern half of both Europe and North America. So much water was frozen into this massive glacier that sea levels dropped as much as 450 feet.

This drop in sea level created a land bridge called **Beringia** between Siberia and Alaska. During the Ice Age, Beringia was a dry, frigid grassland that was free of glaciers. It was a perfect grazing ground for animals such as giant bison and huge-tusked woolly mammoths. Hunters of these animals, including large wolves, saber-toothed cats, and humans, followed them across Beringia into North America.

Geologists believe that sea levels were low enough to expose Beringia between 70,000 and 45,000 years ago, again between 22,000 and 12,500 years ago, and finally between 11,000 and 8,000 years ago. Although evidence is sparse, some archaeologists suspect that people first migrated into Beringia between 70,000 and 45,000 years ago and then into North America. Humans clearly migrated into Beringia when it was exposed between 22,000 and 12,500 years ago. Others

Beringia   An expanse of land between present-day Siberia and Alaska, now covered by water; an avenue for migration between Asia and North America in prehistoric times.

followed when Beringia opened again around 11,000 years ago (see Map 1.1).

About 9,000 years ago, a warming trend began that ended the Ice Age and brought temperatures to what we now consider normal. As temperatures warmed and grasslands disappeared, the gigantic Ice Age creatures that had supplied early hunters with their primary source of meat, clothing, and tools began to die out. The hunters faced the unpleasant prospect of following the large animals into extinction if they kept trying to survive by hunting big game.

Seedtime for Native Cultures in North America

The *constraints* imposed by the changing environment forced the American Indians to make a series of *choices*. The first phase of adaptation, called the **Archaic phase,** lasted until about 3,000 years ago. During this period, people in North America abandoned **nomadic** big-game hunting and began to explore new sources of food, clothing, and tools and new places to live.

Archaic culture emerged at different times in different places. It appears that western North America was hit earliest and hardest by the changing climate. At Fort Rock Cave in southern Oregon, archaeologists have unearthed evidence dating from 9,600 years ago of people abandoning big-game hunting and adapting to local conditions. Three findings at Fort Rock Cave mark it as an important transitional site between the big-game and Archaic cultures. First, investigators found many different tools for grinding seeds. The tools were signs that these people were eating less meat and more local grass seeds, nuts, and other vegetable foods. Second, investigators found baskets, sandals, and clothing woven from grasses and reeds, also indications of a greater reliance on plants. Third, investigators found small spear points and fishing and bird-hunting equipment. These early Indians had apparently stopped chasing after mammoths and had begun to hunt and fish for animals that they could find close by.

Over the next several thousand years, people throughout North America made similar *choices*, differing only in the specific foods and types of materials they employed. In the forests that grew up to cover the eastern half of the continent, Archaic Indians developed finely polished stone tools, which they used to make functional and beautiful implements out of wood, bone, shell, and other materials. There and along the Pacific shore, people hollowed out massive tree trunks to make boats. During this time domesticated dogs were introduced into North America, probably by newly arriving migrants from Asia. With dogs to help carry loads on land and boats for river transportation, Archaic people were able to make the best use of their local environments by moving from camp to camp over the year, perhaps collecting shellfish for several weeks in one spot and then wild strawberries in another.

Such efficient use of local resources caused an enormous increase in population. Nomadic hunting had involved dangerous animals and occasional famines that helped keep human populations small. Archaic life was much safer and food supplies more reliable. Freed from the constant need to track and kill big game for meat, Archaic people also had more spare time. One *outcome* was the continuing invention of new tools and craft skills. Another was the emergence of art, which played a prominent role in the elaborate burial practices that emerged everywhere in North America during this period.

Early Indians left their mark on their local environments. They used fire to clear forests of unwanted scrub and to encourage the growth of berries and other plants that they found valuable. In this way they produced vegetables for themselves and also provided food for browsing animals like deer, which increased in number, while other species, less useful to people, declined.

A significant example of such environmental engineering comes from north-central Mexico. Perhaps 7,000 years ago, humans began cultivating a wild strain of grass. Such cultivation eventually

> **Archaic phase**   In Native American culture, the period when people began to shift away from hunting big game and turn to agriculture and other food sources in local environments.
>
> **nomadic**   Having no fixed home and wandering from place to place in search of food or other resources.

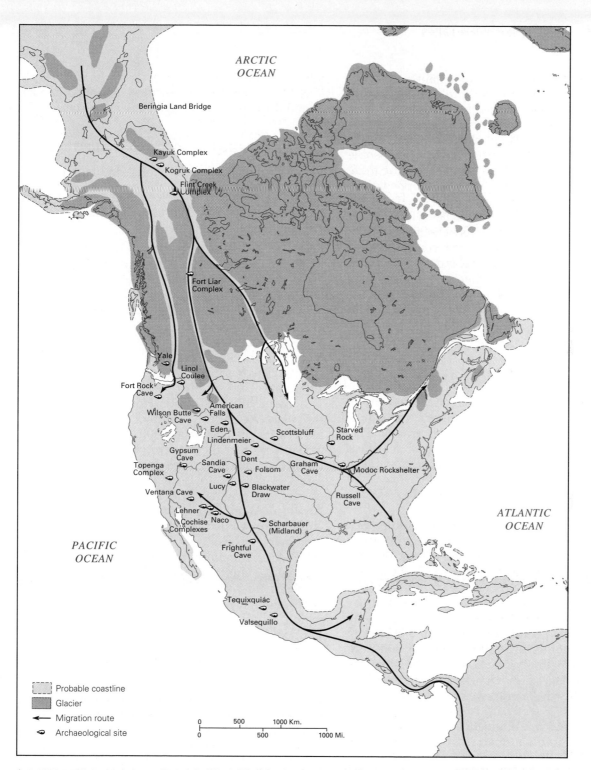

ARCTIC
OCEAN

Beringia Land Bridge

Kayuk Complex

Kogruk Complex

Flint Creek
Complex

Fort Liar
Complex

Yale

Linol
Coulee

Fort Rock
Cave

Wilson Butte
Cave

American
Falls

Eden

Scottsbluff

Starved
Rock

Lindenmeier

Gypsum
Cave

Dent

Topenga
Complex

Sandia
Cave

Folsom

Graham
Cave

Modoc Rockshelter

Ventana Cave

Lucy

Blackwater
Draw

Russell
Cave

Lehner

Naco

Cochise
Complexes

Scharbauer
(Midland)

PACIFIC
OCEAN

Frightful
Cave

ATLANTIC
OCEAN

Tequixquiác

Valsequillo

Probable coastline

Glacier

Migration route

Archaeological site

0	500	1000 Km.
0	500	1000 Mi.

♦ **MAP 1.1 First Americans Enter the New World**   As this map shows, at least two different groups of Asian hunters entered North America during the late Wisconsin Glaciation. The Old Cordilleran group entered to the west of the Rocky Mountains, and the Clovis group entered to the east. Both groups left records of their passing at numerous sites, the most prominent of which are labeled here.

transformed a fairly unproductive plant into **maize,** an enormously nourishing and prolific food crop.

Maize, along with beans, squash, and chilies, formed the basis for an agricultural revolution in America. Although it is not clear how or why this revolution got started, about 3,500 years ago people near what is now Mexico City began planting these vegetables. Shortly thereafter, they stopped their annual round of hunting and gathering. They settled down into villages near their fields and moved away only when these fields were exhausted.

Maize spread like wildfire. From central Mexico, it found its way to New Mexico and Arizona about 1,000 or 2,000 years ago and then spread northward and eastward. Between 500 and 800 years ago, the Woodland Indians of eastern North America, who had been cultivating wild sunflowers and other foods, incorporated maize into their economy.

Culture Areas in Indian America

Although the broad shape of American Indian life was similar throughout North America, vast differences existed among various Indian groups. This variety of Archaic cultures developed in direct response to local environmental conditions. The map at the beginning of the chapter shows the eleven major culture areas that anthropologists have identified.

Lifestyles differed greatly from one culture area to another. The language and technology of Arctic peoples were unlike those anywhere else on the continent. In the eastern half of what is now the United States, Indians were agriculturalists who supplemented their diet of corn, beans, and squash by hunting and fishing. On the Western Plains, an Archaic lifestyle persisted as people traveled from one camp to another on an annual hunting and gathering cycle. On the Pacific coast, Indians lived in permanent villages and harvested the riches of the sea. Clearly North America was socially and culturally complex.

Despite significant linguistic and cultural differences, **pre-Columbian** Americans did not live in isolated tribes. Archaeological research reveals complex trading patterns within and between ecological regions. For example, the Windover Site, an early Archaic burial ground in central Florida, con-

tains beautiful stones from as far away as Alabama and Mississippi. A far-reaching trading network bound the people of North America together.

The Flowering of Indian Civilization

Indians built large, ornate centers in many parts of North America. These centers were generally not residential cities but trading and ceremonial centers where people congregated periodically. Large earthen mounds in the shape of huge animals, pyramids, or geometrical patterns characterize these trading and ceremonial centers. Archaeologists have called these "mound builder" societies. The map of late Archaic America is dotted with such centers (see Map 1.1). Along the Ohio River, a complex of sites known as the Adena culture was constructed about 3,000 years ago. Adena cities were centers of ceremony and trade, as is evidenced by the artifacts from all over North America that have been found at Adena sites.

In the eastern woodlands, **Hopewell culture** took the place of Adena culture. Hopewell culture reached its peak between 1,500 and 1,000 years ago at Cahokia, near the modern city of East St. Louis, Illinois. Archaeologists have found the distinctive forms of pottery, tools, and religious and artistic objects that originated there over much of North America. About 800 years ago, Cahokia and the entire Hopewell complex fell into decline for unknown reasons.

While ceremonial and trading centers declined in the North, their development continued in the southern Mississippi River Valley. Between 1,200 years ago and the time of European entry into the region in the 1700s, peoples speaking Siouan, Caddoan, and Muskogean languages formed a

---

maize   Corn, a tall plant with a solid stem and narrow leaves that bears seeds on large ears; the word *maize* comes from an Indian word for this plant.

pre-Columbian   Existing in the Americas before the arrival of Columbus.

Hopewell culture   An early American Indian culture centered in the Ohio River Valley; it is known for its burial mounds, tools, and pottery.

vibrant agricultural and urban society, which scholars have named the **Mississippian culture.**

Although the Mississippian culture had ties with the earlier Adena and Hopewell cultures, it was more directly influenced by contacts with Mexico. Around 1,500 years ago, two remarkable societies emerged in present-day Mexico: the Mayans on the Atlantic coast and the Zapotecs in the central highlands. From centers such as Tikal in the Yucatán peninsula, the Mayans launched trading ventures that ranged throughout the Gulf of Mexico and into the Mississippi Valley.

The Mississippian culture featured fortified cities such as the one at present-day Natchez. These cities contained gigantic pyramids. Unlike the earlier Hopewell centers, these were true cities in that they housed a large residential population.

As the fortifications at Natchez suggest, war or the prospect of war was a part of Indian life. Evidence from virtually all pre-Columbian Indian sites indicates that some fighting occurred, though warfare seems to have been less common than it was at the same time in Asia, Africa, and Europe. The one glaring exception was in present-day Mexico.

Around A.D. 1000, wandering bands of desert people called Chichimecs from Mexico's northern frontiers began raiding the agricultural centers in the interior. Chichimec invasions finally led to the collapse of the ruling Toltec civilization in the 1170s. A Chichimec group called the **Aztecs** eventually filled the political and military void left by the collapse of the Toltecs.

At the heart of the Aztec Empire stood the city of **Tenochtitlán**—present-day Mexico City. Sitting in the midst of an uninviting lake surrounded by high desert and volcanic mountains, Tenochtitlán made up for the lack of fertile soil in the region by the ingenious use of **chinampas**—platforms of straw and earth that floated on the surface of the lake surrounding Tenochtitlán. These floating gardens were extremely fertile and were a rich source of vegetables.

The Aztecs survived in their hostile environment, however, not because of their agricultural skills but because of their military conquests. They established an empire in which local Indians paid **tribute** to them to avoid invasion. From about 1325 until the arrival of the Spanish in 1519, the Aztecs' tributary empire expanded throughout central Mexico. It extended from the Gulf of Mexico to the Pacific and as far south as Guatemala, perhaps encompassing 6 million people.

Like other native groups throughout North America, the Aztecs practiced human sacrifice, but on a scale that may be unprecedented in world history. Attempting to estimate the number of skulls at the bottom of the grand pyramid in Tenochtitlán, Spanish explorer Andres de Tapia wrote, "We found that there were 136 thousand heads." Bernal Diaz, another early sixteenth-century Spanish explorer, counted more than one hundred thousand skulls in another pyramid.

Human sacrifice played a central role in the Aztecs' religion. The priests and warriors may have eaten the victims' bodies to give themselves spiritual strength (by absorbing the souls of the victims) and physical strength (by adding animal protein to their diet). Not surprisingly, when the Spanish arrived in Mexico in 1519, the Tarascan, Mixtec, and Tlaxcalan peoples who lived nearest the Aztecs willingly allied with the European newcomers against the greatly feared Aztecs.

Despite the Aztecs' grisly blood sacrifices and warfare, Spanish explorers were greatly impressed by Tenochtitlán. The city was cleaner and better kept than any in Europe at the time, and the Spaniards marveled at the Aztecs' sanitation and public works systems. Broad avenues, courtyards, and canals led Europeans to call Tenochtitlán the Venice of the New World.

Mississippian culture   An American Indian culture centered in the southern Mississippi River Valley; influenced by Mexican culture, it is known for its pyramid building and its urban centers.

Aztecs   An Indian group living in central Mexico; the Aztecs used military force to dominate nearby tribes; their civilization was at its peak at the time of the Spanish conquest.

Tenochtitlán   The Aztec capital and site of present-day Mexico City; it was built in the middle of a lake.

chinampa farming   The system of farming used by the Aztecs; crops were planted on floating platforms of straw and earth.

tribute   A payment of money or other valuables that one group makes to another as the price of security.

European Outreach and the Age of Exploration

- What *expectations* led Europeans into extensive exploration?
- What *constraints* stood in their way?
- How did they *choose* to get past those *constraints?*

It might be said that the Spanish discovery of the Venice of the New World originated in Europe's Venice over two hundred years earlier. In 1271, young **Marco Polo** embarked from that Italian city on a voyage that would eventually take him to China. Polo returned home in 1295 and later dictated an account of his adventures. His memoirs fascinated all who read or heard them. At first, only a few adventurous Italian merchants took advantage of the opportunities that Polo described. But as evidence of the wealth available in the mysterious East spread, all of Europe became involved in the search for new economic frontiers.

Crusading, Trading, and the Emergence of Nation-States

Polo's adventures in the thirteenth century were signs of a new restlessness and curiosity among Europeans. Europeans of Polo's generation had gradually been learning about wonders beyond the seas, and increasingly they sought entry into the rich lands they learned about from their neighbors to the north and south.

To the south of Europe was an economic, religious, and political empire controlled by Arabs, Turks, and **Moors,** who practiced the **Islamic** faith. In the north, beginning about 800, the Vikings descended on western Europe, eventually capturing Normandy and the British Isles (see Map 1.2). Another branch of Vikings pushed south simultaneously along Europe's eastern frontier, through Russia, eventually extending their influence all the way to the eastern Mediterranean. They also sailed westward, colonizing Iceland, Greenland, and even North America for a brief time.

Although we tend to think of the Vikings as warriors, they were great traders as well. By the eleventh century they had established a thriving seaborne commerce with northern Africa, the Iberian peninsula, and through their Islamic contacts in the Middle East, they were able to exchange goods with China and India. By 1050 the Viking-Islamic trading network crisscrossed Europe.

The Vikings and the Muslims often made life miserable for Europeans but also eventually benefited them. Both groups helped Europeans expand their knowledge and broaden their culture. Europeans became participants in a trading system that extended from Viking outposts in Greenland to Islamic trading posts in India and China.

In 1096, European Christians launched the first of several **Crusades** designed to sweep the Muslims from their strongholds in the **Holy Land** in the eastern Mediterranean. The Europeans proclaimed that they were seeking to destroy what they claimed was the false religion of Islam, but they also were hoping to break Islamic control of the eastern and African trade. Over the next two centuries, hordes of Crusaders invaded the area, capturing key points, only to be expelled by Muslim counterattacks. In the process, however, the Europeans gained more knowledge, technical skill, and access to trade. By the time the Crusades ended in 1291, families like the Polos had edged their way into the trade between Europe and the East.

The **Reconquista,** or reconquest of the Muslim-held areas of the Iberian peninsula by Christian

---

Marco Polo   Venetian who explored Asia from 1271 to 1295; his account of his travels gave Europe its first description of Southwest Asia.

Moors   The Muslim rulers of the Iberian peninsula.

Islamic   Belonging to the Muslim religion, a monotheistic faith that accepts Mohammed as the chief and last prophet of God.

Iberian peninsula   The peninsula in southwest Europe occupied by Spain and Portugal.

Crusades   Military expeditions undertaken by European Christians in the eleventh through the thirteenth centuries to recover the Holy Land from the Muslims.

Holy Land   The region in which the events in the Old Testament of the Bible took place; it is sacred to Christians, Jews, and Muslims.

Reconquista   The campaign undertaken by European Christians to recapture the Iberian peninsula from the Muslims.

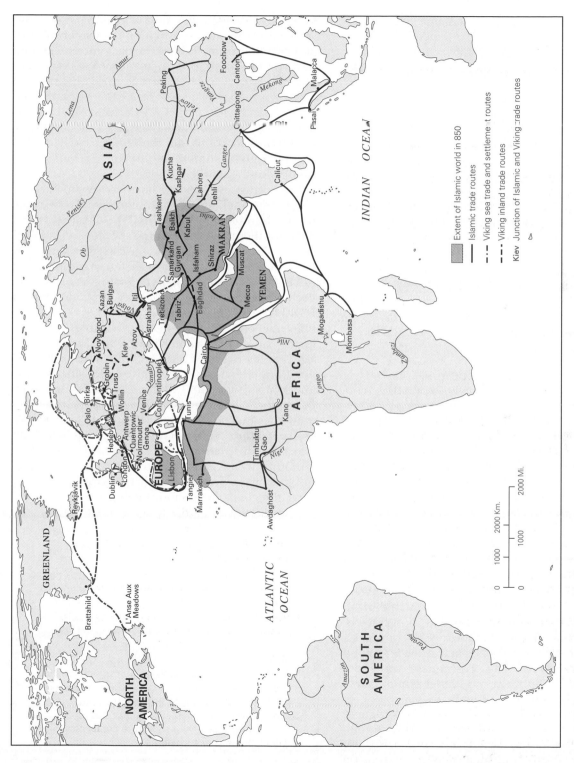

◆ **MAP 1.2 Europe and Its Neighbors, c. 1000 A.D.** Europe was not isolated during Medieval times. As shown here, Viking and Islamic empires surrounded Western Europe, and their trade routes crisscrossed the region.

Europeans, began at about the same time as the Crusades. Portugal attained independence from Islamic rule in 1147, and by 1380, Portugal's King John I had united that country's various principalities under his rule. Spanish unification took much longer because feuding local states could not settle their differences. But in 1469, **Ferdinand and Isabella,** heirs to the rival thrones of Aragon and Castile, married and created a united state in Spain. Twenty-three years later, the Spanish subdued the last Islamic stronghold on the peninsula.

Northern European rulers also attempted to create national states in the face of local and regional rivalries. Consolidation finally occurred in France around 1480, when Louis XI took control of five rival provinces to create a unified kingdom. Five years later, Henry Tudor became king of a unified England when he defeated his rivals in the Wars of the Roses.

Portuguese Exploration, Africa, and the Quest for Asia

Portugal, the first of the European national states, was also the first to contest the hold of Italian merchants and their Islamic trading partners on eastern commerce. **Henry the Navigator,** the son of Portugal's John I, took the decisive step by establishing a school of navigation and ordering expeditions to sail west and south to look for new sources of wealth. By the 1430s, the Portuguese had discovered and taken control of the Azores, the Canaries, and Madeira, islands off the western shore of Africa. Within thirty years, Portuguese captains had pushed their way to sub-Saharan Africa, where they came into contact with the **Songhay Empire.**

The Songhay Empire combined various kingdoms along the Niger River. Timbuktu, the Songhay capital, was a cosmopolitan center where African and Islamic influences met. It was a showplace of art, architecture, and scholarship. From Timbuktu, Muslim traders shipped goods across the Sahara by means of caravans. The Portuguese, however, offered speedier shipment and higher profits, carrying trade goods directly to Europe by sea.

By the end of the fifteenth century, Portuguese navigators had gained control over the flow of gold, ivory, and spices out of West Africa, and Portuguese colonizers were growing sugar and other crops on the newly conquered Azores and Canary Islands. Gradually Portuguese plantation owners borrowed an institution from their former Islamic rulers and their African trading partners: slavery. Slaves had formed a crucial part of Islamic caravans in West Africa since about 700 A.D. From the beginning of the sixteenth century, the Portuguese became increasingly involved in slave trafficking, at first to their own plantations and then to Europe itself. By 1550 Portuguese ships were carrying African slaves throughout the world.

The Portuguese took a major step toward becoming world traders when Bartholomew Dias became the first European to reach the **Cape of Good Hope** at the southern tip of Africa in 1487. Ten years later, Vasco de Gama sailed around the cape and launched the Portuguese exploration of eastern Africa and the Indian Ocean. Eventually, Portuguese sailors reached all the fabled lands that Marco Polo had described in his memoirs.

By the end of the fifteenth century England, Spain, and France were vying with Portugal for access to the riches of the East. Borrowed technologies from China and the Arab world aided these new competitors. From China, Europeans acquired the magnetic compass, which allowed mariners to know the direction in which they were sailing. An Arab invention, the **astrolabe,** allowed navigators to determine their latitude. These inventions, together with improvements in steering mechanisms and in hull design, improved captains' control over their ships' direction, speed, and stability.

Ferdinand and Isabella   Joint rulers of Spain; their marriage in 1469 created a united Spain from the rival kingdoms of Aragon and Castile.

Henry the Navigator   Prince who founded an observatory and school of navigation and directed voyages that helped build Portugal's colonial empire.

Songhay Empire   A large empire in West Africa; its capital was Timbuktu; its rulers accepted Islam in about A.D. 1000.

Cape of Good Hope   A point of land projecting into the ocean at the southern tip of Africa; European mariners had to sail around the cape to pass from the Atlantic to the Indian Ocean.

astrolabe   An instrument that navigators used to measure the height of the sun and stars and calculate their position of latitude.

Columbus's Folly and Exploration Fever

An impoverished but ambitious sailor from the Italian city of Genoa was eager to capitalize on the new technology and knowledge. In 1484, **Christopher Columbus** approached John II of Portugal and asked him to support a risky voyage westward, across the Atlantic, to the East Indies. When John's geographers warned that Columbus had probably underestimated the distance of the trip, the king refused to support the enterprise. Undaunted, Columbus peddled his idea to various European governments over the next several years but found no backers. Finally, in 1492, Ferdinand and Isabella's defeat of the remaining Muslim enclave in Spain provided Columbus with an opportunity.

The Spanish monarchs, eager to break the domination of the Italians and their Arab partners in the east and of the Portuguese in the south and west, agreed to equip three ships and granted Columbus 10 percent of any returns from the voyage. On August 3, 1492, Columbus and some ninety sailors departed on the *Niña, Pinta,* and *Santa Maria* for Asia.

After ten weeks at sea, the three ships finally made landfall on a small island on October 12, 1492. Columbus thought he had reached the Indies, but he really reached the islands that we now call the **Bahamas.** Celebrating his escape from disaster, Columbus named the place *San Salvador* (Holy Savior).

Over the next ten weeks, Columbus sailed around the Caribbean, stopping at Cuba and Hispaniola. He collected spices, coconuts, bits of gold, and some native captives. He called these people "Indians" because he believed that he had reached the Indies. Columbus then returned to Spain, and was welcomed home with great celebration. His account of the trip and the goods he brought back helped gain him backing for three more voyages. Over the next several decades, the Spanish gained a permanent foothold in the region that Columbus had discovered and became aware that the area was not the Indies or Japan but an entirely new world.

Columbus's discovery opened unprecedented opportunities for Europeans. Taking to heart stories of new lands, new goods, new peoples, and new possibilities for acquiring wealth, kings, sailors, and merchants began eyeing the New World with enormous interest. The French and the English soon staked claims to portions of this new land.

The Challenges of Mutual Discovery

- How did American Indians *choose* to respond to European contact?
- How did Europeans *choose* to respond to Indians and Africans?
- What were some *outcomes* of the Columbian Exchange?

It is usually said that Europeans discovered America, but it is also true that America discovered Europeans. The relationship between Europeans and American Indians ran in two directions. Europeans approached the inhabitants of the New World based on what they already knew. American Indians approached Europeans in the same way. Both groups had many of their fundamental assumptions challenged. Mutual discovery in America influenced the *choices* people were to make on a global scale.

A Meeting of Minds in America

Initially most Europeans were content to fit what they found in the New World with their prior *expectations.* Columbus *expected* to find the Indies and Indians, and he believed that was precisely what he had found. Europeans understood only later that America was a new land and that the natives there were a new people.

Europeans were of a divided mind about the people they encountered in America. Columbus's comments about the American Indians set the tone for

Christopher Columbus   Italian explorer in the service of Spain who attempted to reach Asia by sailing west from Europe, thereby discovering America in 1492.

Bahamas   A group of islands in the Atlantic Ocean east of Florida and Cuba.

♦ Europeans had trouble understanding American Indians, sometimes casting them as noble savages and other times casting them as devils. The Brazilian Indian shown in these two works illustrates the conflicting views. In one, the feather-clad Indian is shown as a wise magi paying homage to the Christ-child; in the other, an Indian devil wears the same costume while presiding over the tortures of Hell. *"Adoration of the Magi" by Master of Viseu. Museu de Grao Vasco; "Inferno" anonymous, Portuguese (detail). Giraudon/Art Resource, New York.*

many of those to follow. "They are so **ingenuous** and free with all they have," Columbus wrote, "that no one would believe it who has not seen it. Of anything that they possess, if it be asked of them, they never say no; on the contrary, they invite you to share it and show as much love as if their hearts went with it, and they are content with whatever trifle be given them, whether it be a thing of value or of petty worth." Such writings led to a perception of the Indians as noble savages, men and women free from the temptations and conceits of modern civilization. Many Europeans praised the Indians' apparent ignorance of private property.

Not all Europeans held this view of American Indians. **Amerigo Vespucci,** an Italian explorer who sailed under the Spanish flag, shared the opinion that Indians were savage, but he found them less than noble. "They marry as many wives as they please," he explained. "The son cohabits with mother, brother with sister, male cousin with female, and any man with the first woman he meets. . . . Beyond the fact that they have no church, no religion and are not **idolaters,** what more can I say?"

From the European point of view, the native populations lacked "true" religion. But Columbus was optimistic that this lack could be remedied. "I main-tain," he wrote to Ferdinand and Isabella, "that if they had access to devout religious persons knowing the language, they would all turn Christian." He added, "It appeared to us that these people were very poor in everything." Thus although Indians were savages, they could be made civilized through European religion and trade.

The arrival of Europeans may have been easier for American Indians to understand than the existence of American Indians was for the Europeans. To Indians, Europeans did not appear to be either superhuman or even particularly strange. Their mode of arrival, manners, speech, and dress no doubt seemed odd, but no odder than the language, behavior, and appearance of traders from the Valley of Mexico. Indians accepted Europeans as simply another new group to be added to the already complex social cosmos.

---

ingenuous   Lacking in sophistication; artless.
Amerigo Vespucci   Italian explorer of the South American coast; America was named after him.
idolater   A person who worships idols or false gods.

The Columbian Exchange

Although Europeans and American Indians found some similarities in each other, their natural environments differed greatly. The passage of people, plants, and animals among Europe, Africa, and North America wrought profound changes in all three continents. Historians call this process the **Columbian Exchange.**

Perhaps the most tragic trade among the three continents was in disease. The Indian peoples whom Columbus and other explorers encountered lived in an environment in which contagious diseases that were common in Europe (such as smallpox, measles, and typhus) did not exist. Thus they had no **acquired immunity** to the various bacteria and viruses that Europeans carried. As a result, new diseases spread very rapidly among the native peoples and were much more deadly than they were among Europeans.

Controversy rages over the number of Indians killed by imported European diseases, but most scholars agree that the number was enormous. An estimated 3 to 10 million people lived in America north of Mexico in 1492. Between 90 and 95 percent of this native population appears to have died of European diseases during the first century of contact.

The flow of disease was not just in one direction. At least one disease, **syphilis,** appears to have originated in the Western Hemisphere and migrated eastward.

This exchange of microorganisms created a distinctive pattern of contagion and immunity in North America. American Indians appear to have been less devastated physically by syphilis than other groups were. Africans were largely unaffected by various **malarial** fevers that ravaged both European and native populations. For Europeans measles was a mild childhood disease, but for Africans and Indians it was a mass killer. The march of exchanged diseases across the North American landscape would provide a constant backdrop for the continent's history.

Less immediate effects arose from the exchange of plants, but the long-term consequences were profound. Asian transplants such as bananas, sugar cane, and rice, which came to America by way of Africa, became **cash crops** on New World plantations, as did cotton, **indigo,** and coffee. Wheat, bar-

ley, and millet were readily transplanted to suitable areas in North America. So were grazing grasses and vegetables such as turnips, spinach, and cabbage.

The most important North American plant in the Columbian Exchange was tobacco, a stimulant used widely in North America for ceremonial purposes and broadly adopted by Europeans and Africans as a recreational drug. Another stimulant, cocoa, also enjoyed significant popularity among Old World consumers. New World vegetables helped to revolutionize world food supplies. Maize was remarkably easy to grow and thrived in Europe, the Middle East, and Africa. In addition, the white potato, tomato, manioc, squash, beans, and peas native to the Western Hemisphere were transplanted throughout the world.

The Columbian Exchange also involved animals. Animal populations in North America were very different from those in the Old World. The continent teemed with deer, bison, elk, and moose, but they had to be hunted rather than herded and were useless as draft animals. Europeans brought a full complement of Old World domesticated animals to America. Horses, pigs, cattle, oxen, sheep, goats, and domesticated fowl did well in the new environment.

The exchange of plants and animals altered the natural environments in North America. The transplanting of European grain crops and domesticated

---

Columbian Exchange   The exchange of people, plants, and animals among Europe, Africa, and North America that occurred after Columbus's discovery of the New World.

acquired immunity   Resistance or partial resistance to a disease; it develops in a population over time, after exposure to harmful bacteria and viruses.

syphilis   An infectious disease usually transmitted through sexual contact; if untreated, it can lead to paralysis and death.

malarial   Related to malaria, an infectious disease characterized by chills, fever, and sweating; it is often transmitted through mosquito bites.

cash crop   A crop raised in large quantities for sale rather than for local or home consumption.

indigo   A plant that yielded a blue dye used for coloring textiles; in the mid-eighteenth century it was a staple crop in the lower South.

animals led to the reshaping of the land itself. Clearing trees, plowing, and fencing changed the flow of water, the distribution of seeds, the nesting of birds, and the movement of native animals. Gradually, imported livestock pushed aside native animals, and imported plants choked out native ones.

Probably the most far-reaching environmental impact of the Columbian Exchange was on human populations. Although exchanged diseases killed many millions of Indians and lesser numbers of Africans and Europeans, the transplantation of animals and plants significantly expanded food production in Europe and Africa. The environmental changes that Europeans caused in eastern North America permitted the region to support many more people than it had under Indian cultivation. The result was a population explosion in Europe and Africa that eventually spilled over to repopulate a devastated North America.

New Worlds in Africa and America

The Columbian Exchange did more than redistribute plants, animals, and populations among Europe, Africa, and North America. It permanently altered the history of both hemispheres.

Imported disease had the most devastating influence on the lives of Indians. The survivors of epidemics were often faced with a struggle for survival because too few able bodies were left to perform tasks that had been done cooperatively. Wholesale death by disease sometimes wiped out the elders and storytellers who stored the entire practical, religious, and cultural knowledge of these **nonliterate** societies. The result of this loss was confusion and disorientation among survivors.

The devastation wrought by European diseases also made it easier for Europeans to penetrate the North American continent. Such devastation prompted some Indians to seek alliances with the newcomers. Others adopted European tools, which helped make smaller work forces more productive. Still others turned to European religions for spiritual explanations and possible remedies for the hardships they faced. Together, economic and spiritual forces pushed the Indians into an increasingly tangled alliance with Europeans.

♦ Parties of captured villagers from Africa's interior were bound together and marched to trading centers on the coast, where they were sold to Europeans or Muslims. The slave drivers were heavily influenced by outside contact. One of those shown here is wearing a Muslim-influenced turban, while the clothing of the other is more European. Note, too, he carries both a gun and a traditional African spear. *The Granger Collection, New York.*

The Columbian Exchange also severely disrupted life in Africa. The depopulation of America and the suitability of America for crops such as sugar cane created a huge demand for African slave labor. The Portuguese were well prepared to meet that demand, having taken over much of the African slave trade from North African Muslims in the fifteenth century. They supplied aggressive tribes like the Ashanti with European firearms, thereby enabling coastal tribes to raid deep into the Niger and Congo River regions. These raiders captured millions of prisoners, whom they herded back to the coast and sold to European traders to supply labor for New World mines and plantations.

---

nonliterate   Lacking a system of reading and writing.

It is difficult to determine the number of people sold in the West African slave trade from 1500 to 1800. The most recent estimates suggest that over 9.5 million enslaved Africans arrived in the New World during this period. But these estimates do not include the 10 to 20 percent of the slaves who died on ships, those who died on the march to the African coast, and those who remained as slaves in Africa and elsewhere. Africa sacrificed a great deal to the Columbian Exchange.

A New World in Europe

The discovery of America and the Columbian Exchange also had repercussions on life in Europe. Along with new economic opportunities and food-stuffs, the opening of the Western Hemisphere brought new ideas and demanded new kinds of political and economic organization. The discovery of the New World clearly forced a new and more modern society onto Europeans and in the process, it produced an air of crisis.

Europe's population was already rising when potatoes, maize, and other New World crops began to revolutionize food production. The population of Europe in 1500 was about 81 million. It grew to 100 million by 1600 and 120 million by 1700. This growth occurred despite nearly continuous wars and a flood of thousands of people to the New World each year.

The development of centralized states under leaders like John I of Portugal, Louis XI of France, Ferdinand and Isabella of Spain, and Henry VII of England appeared to offer the most promising avenue for harnessing the riches of the New World while controlling ever-increasing numbers of people at home. The sons and daughters of these monarchs continued the centralization of authority begun by their parents.

They did so even as traditional patterns of authority broke down. Martin Luther, a German monk, dealt a devastating blow to religious authority by preaching that Christians could achieve salvation without the intercession of the Catholic church. Salvation, he said, was God's gift to the faithful. In 1517, Luther attacked the sale of **indulgences** by Catholic priests. He presented ninety-five arguments ("theses") against this practice, maintaining that only individual repentance and the grace of God, not the purchase of a pardon, could save sinners.

Luther's ideas took root among a generation of theologians who were dissatisfied with the corruption that permeated the medieval Catholic church. A Frenchman, John Calvin, further undermined the authority of the Catholic church. Like Luther, Calvin believed that salvation was a gift from God. But Calvin emphasized the belief that God had chosen the souls to be saved and the souls to be damned when he created the world. No human actions could alter God's plan. Although only God knew who was among the saved (**"the elect"**) and who among the damned, Calvin urged Christians to engage in constant meditation, prayer, and scriptural study and to live as though they were among the chosen.

The doctrines of Luther, Calvin, and others who wanted to reform the Catholic church collectively became known as **Protestantism.** Their ideas appealed to a broad audience in the rapidly changing world of the sixteenth century. The new doctrines were most attractive to the middling classes of lawyers, bureaucrats, merchants, and manufacturers, groups that stood to gain from the questioning of entrenched authority. Some in the ruling classes also found the new theology attractive for similar reasons. In Germany, Luther's challenge to the Catholic church led many local princes eager to establish a German national church to question the **divine right** to authority claimed by the ruler of the **Holy Roman Empire.**

---

indulgence   A pardon issued by the pope absolving the purchaser of a particular sin.

the elect   According to Calvinism, the people chosen by God for salvation.

Protestantism   The religion and religious beliefs of Christians who accepted the Bible as the only source of revelation, believed salvation to be God's gift to the faithful, and believed the faithful could form a direct, personal relationship with God.

divine right   The idea that monarchs derive their right to rule directly from God and are accountable only to God.

Holy Roman Empire   A political entity authorized by the Catholic church in 1356 unifying Central Europe under an emperor elected by four princes and three Catholic archbishops.

Similarly, **Henry VIII** of England found Protestantism convenient when he wanted to divorce his wife. Henry VIII was the first undisputed heir to the English throne in several generations, and he was consumed with the desire to have a son who could inherit the crown. When his wife, Catherine of Aragon, daughter of Ferdinand and Isabella of Spain, failed to bear a boy, Henry demanded in 1527 that Pope Clement VII grant him an annulment of his marriage. Fearful of Spanish reprisals on Catherine's behalf, Clement refused. In desperation, Henry launched the English Reformation by seizing the Catholic church in England. By 1535 he had gained complete control of it.

Henry was not a staunch believer in the views aired by Luther and others. But he reluctantly opened the door to Protestant practices in his newly created Church of England to win the support of Protestants. Henry also seized the extensive and valuable lands that the Catholic church owned in England, thereby adding to his wealth and power.

The New Europe and the Atlantic World

• What did Europeans *expect* to gain by exploring and subduing North America?

• How did their explorations relate to events in Europe?

Expansion into the New World aggravated the crisis of authority in Europe. The crisis, however, also helped to promote overseas enterprises. Eager to enlist political allies against Protestant dissenters, popes during this era used land grants in the New World as rewards to faithful monarchs. At the same time, England's Protestant rulers, constantly fearful of being outflanked by Catholic adversaries, promoted the development of a powerful navy and geographical exploration as defensive measures.

The Spanish Empire in America

Spain's Atlantic explorations created a diplomatic crisis with Portugal. In 1493, the pope settled the dispute by drawing a line approximately 300 miles west of Portugal's westernmost holdings in the Atlantic. Spanish exploration was to be confined to areas west of the line (that is, to the New World) and

Portuguese activity to the eastern side (to Africa and India). A year later, Spain and Portugal revised the agreement in the **Treaty of Tordesillas,** which moved the line 1,000 miles westward. This revision unwittingly gave Portugal a claim in the New World because part of Brazil bulged across the line. Most of the Western Hemisphere, however, fell to Spain.

With the pope's blessing, Ferdinand and Isabella in 1493 issued Columbus instructions that set the tone for Spanish colonization in America. They told him to make the conversion of the natives to Catholicism his first priority. In addition, they authorized Columbus to establish a trading center. He would receive one-eighth of the profits, and the rest would go directly to the Spanish crown. Ferdinand and Isabella also told Columbus to continue exploring the Caribbean region for "good things, riches, and more secrets."

Although Columbus was a skillful navigator and sailor, he was not a particularly gifted leader. Spanish officials and settlers could never forget that he was a foreigner, and they gave him only grudging loyalty. Only after Columbus was removed from office did Ferdinand and Isabella's vision of missionary outreach and riches begin to materialize.

Hernando Cortés helped to realize that vision. In 1519, he and an army of six hundred Spanish soldiers landed in Mexico. Within three years Cortés and his small force had conquered the mighty Aztec Empire. Smallpox and other deadly diseases, the Spaniards' armor and guns, and help from numerous native enemies of the Aztecs contributed to this quick and decisive victory. Establishing themselves in Mexico City, the Spanish took over the Aztecs' tributary empire, quickly bringing the Indian groups to the south under their rule.

Henry VIII   King of England (r. 1509–1547); his desire to divorce his first wife led him to break with Catholicism and establish the Church of England.

Treaty of Tordesillas   The treaty, signed by Spain and Portugal in 1494, that moved the line separating Spanish and Portuguese territory in the non-Christian world and gave Portugal a claim to Brazil.

Hernando Cortés   Spanish soldier and explorer who conquered the Aztecs and claimed Mexico for Spain.

The Spanish crown supported many other exploratory ventures. In 1513 and again in 1521, Juan Ponce de León led expeditions to Florida. (For an account of a later expedition to Florida, see Individual Choices: Álvar Nuñez Cabeza de Vaca.) The Spanish sent Hernando de Soto to claim the Mississippi River in 1539. De Soto penetrated into the heart of the mound builders' territory in present-day Louisiana and Mississippi. One year later, Francisco Vásquez de Coronado left Mexico to look for some supposedly very wealthy Indian towns. Coronado crossed what are now New Mexico, Arizona, Colorado, Oklahoma, and Kansas in his unsuccessful quest for these rumored "cities of gold." These explorations were but a few of the ambitious undertakings of Spanish **conquistadors.**

Increasingly, the conquistadors' hunger for riches outstripped the quest for souls or trade. In Bolivia, Colombia, and north-central Mexico, explorers unearthed rich silver deposits. In 1533, **Francisco Pizarro** conquered the **Inca Empire,** an advanced civilization that glittered with gold. Enslaving local Indians to provide labor, Spanish officials moved quickly to rip precious metals out of the ground. Between 1545 and 1660 Indian and African slaves dug over 7 million pounds of silver from these mines—twice the volume of silver held by all of Europe before 1492. In the process, Spain became the richest nation in Europe.

Philip, Elizabeth, and the English Challenge

Spain's early successes in the New World stirred conflict in Europe, particularly with England. Tension between Spain and England had been running high ever since Henry VIII divorced his Spanish wife. That he quit the Catholic church to do so and began permitting Protestant reforms in England deepened the affront. Firmly wedded to the Catholic church, Spain was aggressive in denouncing England. For his part, Henry was concerned primarily with domestic issues and steered away from direct confrontations with Spain.

The Spanish threat could no longer be ignored after Henry VIII's daughter Elizabeth came to the throne in 1558. Relations between Spain and England began to deteriorate when Elizabeth rejected Philip II's offer of marriage. (The Spanish monarch had been married to Elizabeth's half-sister, Mary, a Catholic, who ruled England between 1553 and 1558.) Elizabeth was determined to be her own ruler and to steer England on a Protestant course. That course resulted in a collision when Philip II in 1567 sent an army of twenty thousand soldiers to the Low Countries to crush Protestantism there. To counter Philip's threat just across the English Channel, Elizabeth began providing secret aid to the Dutch Protestants, supporting a revolt against Spanish rule.

She also struck at Philip's New World empire. In 1577, Elizabeth secretly authorized the English **privateer** Francis Drake to attack Spanish ships in the area reserved for Spain under the Treaty of Tordesillas. Drake raided Spanish ships and seized tons of gold and silver during a three-year cruise around the world. Philip demanded that Drake be hanged for piracy, but Elizabeth rewarded the captain on his return in 1580 by knighting him.

The conflict between Elizabeth's England and Philip's Spain escalated during the 1580s. In 1585, Elizabeth incensed the Spanish king by sending an army of six thousand troops across the Channel to aid Dutch rebels. Philip retaliated by supporting a plot within England to have the Catholic Mary Stuart—Mary Queen of Scots—usurp Elizabeth's throne. Elizabeth was outraged when the plot was exposed and executed her cousin for treason. Philip, in turn, was incensed that Elizabeth would behead a legitimate Catholic queen. As tensions increased, so did Drake's piracy. In 1586, Drake not only raided Spanish ships at sea but looted settlements in the New World. By 1586 war between England and Spain loomed on the horizon.

---

conquistadors Spanish soldiers who conquered the Indian civilizations of Mexico, Central America, and Peru.

Francisco Pizarro Spanish soldier and explorer who conquered the Incas and claimed Peru for Spain.

Inca Empire The Indian civilization, based in present-day Peru, that ruled peoples in the lands from northern Ecuador to central Chile until the Spanish conquest.

privateer A ship captain who owned his own boat and hired his own crew and was authorized by his government to attack and capture enemy ships.

Escape and Exploration

Cabeza de Vaca

Captured by Indians along the Gulf Coast of Spanish Florida, Alvar Nuñez Cabeza de Vaca was made a slave. Most of his companions were afraid to resist or run away, but Cabeza de Vaca chose freedom over safety, eventually leading a small party of men all the way back to Mexico. Courtesy Frederick Remington Art Museum. Ogdensburg, NY.

Ever since leaving Spain in June 1527, Álvar Nuñez Cabeza de Vaca had survived one disaster after another. But in November 1528 this heir to a long line of Spanish nobles found himself in a sorrier state than he ever could have imagined: he was a slave belonging to a tribe of Indians along the Gulf Coast of America.

Hardship was nothing new to Nuñez. Like so many others in his generation of young nobles, he had chosen a military career and, during this time of intense competition among European powers, had often been in great danger. Early in his career, he had fought in the Battle of Ravenna, in which twenty thousand men were killed, and he had earned a reputation for bravery and good sense under fire. Since that time he had established such a name for himself that he was made second-in-command of the expedition that was to colonize Florida in 1527. His future appeared bright.

But the expedition seemed cursed from the start. Arriving in the West Indies, the small fleet was hit by a hurricane, and most of the vessels were destroyed. Finally landing somewhere near Tampa Bay in May 1528, the commander, Pánfilo de Narváez, chose to divide his force, leading a small detachment overland in order to explore the country. The unfamiliar and rough

Dreams of an English Eden

Elizabeth was open to whatever ventures might vex her troublesome brother-in-law. New World colonies promised to do precisely that. Like the rest of Europe, sixteenth-century England was experiencing a population boom that put great stress on traditional economic institutions. Farmland was becoming extremely scarce, and there was a clamor for overseas expansion. The English began eyeing the New World for this purpose.

Thus in 1578, Elizabeth granted her friend and political supporter Sir Humphrey Gilbert permission to found a colony in America. In 1583 he set out terrain along the coast made travel difficult, and the Indians the Spaniards met were not friendly. After a series of running battles and hair-raising escapes, the Spanish expedition was all but wiped out, and the survivors were enslaved by their Indian captors.

Escape seemed impossible. The Indians held the few surviving Spaniards at sites distant from each other, eliminating any chance for them to plan a getaway. And the natives' hostility, combined with the unfamiliar terrain, promised certain death to anyone escaping alone. Most of the Spaniards settled dejectedly into life as servants. But not Nuñez. He chose strategy over surrender. He later wrote, "I set to contriving how I might transfer to the forest-dwellers, who looked more propitious [agreeable]." He hit upon the notion of serving as a trader, striving always "to making my traffic profitable so I could get food and good treatment." In this way, he earned a degree of freedom to travel among various tribes, and although he experienced great hardship, he was able to contact other survivors and explore for escape routes.

Nuñez served as a traveling trader among the Gulf Coast Indians for six years. He tried to escape, but his masters chased him down and recaptured him. He needed companions, but other survivors fearfully refused to join him. Finally in 1534 Nuñez encountered Andres Dorantes, Alonso del Castillo, and Castillo's black servant, Estevanico. For six months Nuñez pleaded and planned with these three, but only when the Indians announced they were splitting up and taking their Spanish slaves in different directions did the whole company resolve to escape. "Although the season was late and the prickly pears nearly gone, we still hoped to travel a long distance on acorns which we might find in the woods," Nuñez recalled.

Having made this fateful choice, Nuñez and his companions were forced to see things through. For fourteen months the four Spaniards traveled from village to village, depending on the hospitality of the Indians, exchanging their skills as healers for food, clothing, and other necessities. Finally, in the early spring of 1536, the little party overtook a Spanish exploring and slave-raiding company. "They were dumbfounded at the sight of me, strangely undressed and in company with Indians," Nuñez reported. "They just stood staring for a long time, not thinking to hail me or come closer to ask questions." Over the next several months, Nuñez and his companions rested up and composed a memoir of their experiences, which they presented to the king himself.

The outcome of Nuñez's choice to seek escape was not only his own freedom and that of his companions but a new season of territorial expansion and exploration for Spain. In the course of his travels, he visited places that no other European had ever seen, he saw things that would dazzle those who eventually followed his course, and he heard reports about treasure that prompted generations of Spaniards and others to search for gold, silver, and other riches in the deserts of the American Southwest. Nuñez's stories of vast amounts of gold, silver, and precious gems located just to the north of Spain's New World frontier captured the imagination of a new generation of conquistadors and stirred enormous new interest in America's interior.

with two hundred colonists for what is today Newfoundland. Gilbert and his party were ultimately lost at sea.

Gilbert's vision lived on with his half-brother, **Sir Walter Raleigh,** a great favorite of Queen Elizabeth. Petitioned by Raleigh, the queen gladly gave the dashing young man Gilbert's former land grant. To repay her kindness, Raleigh named the proposed colony Virginia, in honor of the unwed queen.

Sir Walter Raleigh English courtier, soldier, and adventurer who attempted to establish the Virginia Colony.

For his initial settlement, Raleigh chose an island off the coast of present-day North Carolina. He assured potential settlers that **Roanoke Island** was an "American Eden" where the Indians were friendly innocents and "the earth bringeth forth all things in abundance, as in the first Creation, without toile or labour." Encouraged by such rosy promises, 108 settlers sailed to Roanoke in 1585. The venture started out peacefully enough, as the Indians and Europeans labored to understand each other. A dispute over a silver cup, however, led to a series of English raids against Indian villages and an armed confrontation between the two societies. Before the conflict was resolved, trust and friendship had broken down. Thus when Francis Drake visited Roanoke in the late summer of 1586 to warn of a Spanish raid, most of the settlers chose to go back to England with him. Fifteen men remained on the island to protect Raleigh's claim, but none survived.

Despite this loss, Raleigh sent John White, another English courtier, with a new party of settlers in 1587. Remaining only a month, White concluded that his community of ninety-one men, seventeen women, and nine children was safe and well established and set sail for England to get supplies and additional colonists.

The Decline of Spanish Power

While the colony at Roanoke was trying to secure a foothold, Spain's situation was becoming more precarious. Each New World claim asserted by England, France, or some other country represented the loss of a piece of treasure that Spain considered necessary for its continued survival. Philip finally chose to undertake a desperate gamble designed to remove the Protestant threat, rid him of Elizabeth's vexing harassment, and demonstrate to the rest of Europe that Spain intended to exercise absolute authority over the Atlantic world. In the spring of 1585, Philip decided to invade England.

He began massing what was to be the largest marine force the world had ever witnessed. Finally in the spring of 1588 he launched an **armada** of 132 warships carrying over 3,000 cannons and an invasion force of 30,000 men. Arriving off England in July, the Spanish Armada ran up against small, maneuverable English ships commanded by Elizabeth's pirate captains. Drake and his fleet seriously crippled the sluggish Spanish fleet. Then a fierce storm scattered the remaining Spanish ships and destroyed Philip's chance to end English advances into his New World realm.

Delayed by the war with Spain, John White returned to Roanoke in 1590, only to find the colony abandoned. The only clue to what had happened was the word "Croatoan" carved on a doorpost. The Croatoan Indians lived on a neighboring island. The carving led to speculation that the colonists had either gone to live with this tribe or had been attacked by them. Neither theory has ever been confirmed. White returned to England, and colonization efforts were temporarily halted. Although Spain had largely been removed as a threat to English overseas enterprise, only after Elizabeth's death in 1603 did Englishmen return to carry out Raleigh's dream of an English empire in the New World.

> **Roanoke Island**   English colony that Raleigh planted on an island off North Carolina in 1585; the few colonists who did not return to England had disappeared without a trace by 1590.
> **armada**   A fleet of warships.

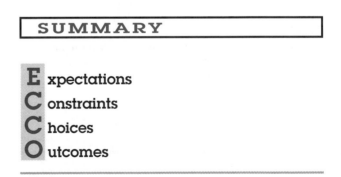

SUMMARY

Expectations
Constraints
Choices
Outcomes

Making America began perhaps as long as 70,000 years ago, when the continent's first human occupants began the long process of adapting to the land. *Expecting* better conditions than they had left behind in Asia, they migrated across Beringia and then overcame or adapted to *constraints* presented by the new environment. Over thousands of years, they continually made *choices* to preserve and enhance their lives. The eventual *outcome* of these *choices* was a rich and flourishing world of different cultures, linked by common religious and economic bonds.

The Atlantic crossing by Europeans presented the natives of America with *constraints* that they had never dreamed of. Disease, then war, and then environmental changes wrought by the Europeans who followed Columbus soon limited the *choices* open to Native Americans.

At the same time, however, Europeans from Cortés to the colonists in Roanoke knew full well that American Indians were an important key to making America. Cortés, after all, could never have succeeded without active Indian assistance. Thus Indians exerted a powerful *constraint* on Europeans' freedom of *choice.*

Influences from the New World accelerated processes that were already changing *expectations* and *constraints* in the Old World. Wealth and food from the New World fostered the growth of population, of powerful kings, and of strong nations, but led in turn to continuing conflict over New World resources. One of these conflicts, between Spain and England, altered the balance of power in Europe, and eventually in North America as well. In Africa, strong coastal states *chose* to raid weaker neighboring tribes, more than doubling the flow of slaves out of Africa. Meanwhile, as disease destroyed millions of Indians, newcomers came pouring in. These newcomers came from a very different physical environment and brought drastic changes to the face of the land. The *outcome* of these continuing interactions among newcomers, and between them and the survivors of America's original people, would be the making of America.

Suggested Readings

Becker, Marvin B. *Civility and Society in Western Europe, 1300–1600* (1988).

A brief but comprehensive look at social conditions in Europe during the period leading up to and out of the exploration of the New World.

Crosby, Alfred W. *The Columbian Exchange: Biological and Cultural Consequences of 1492* (1972).

The landmark book that brought the Columbian impact into focus for the first time. Parts of the book are technical, but the explanations are clear and exciting.

Harris, Marvin. *Cannibals and Kings: The Origin of Cultures* (1977).

Captivating exploration of the rise and development of human cultures by one of the world's leading anthropologists.

Laslett, Peter. *The World We Have Lost Further Explored* (1983).

Updated third edition of the author's well respected characterization of British society before colonization. Highly readable and interesting.

McNeill, William H. *Plagues and Peoples* (1976).

A fascinating history of disease and its impact on people throughout the period of European expansion and New World colonization.

Oliver, Roland, and J. D. Fage. *A Short History of Africa* (1988).

The most concise and understandably written comprehensive history of Africa available.

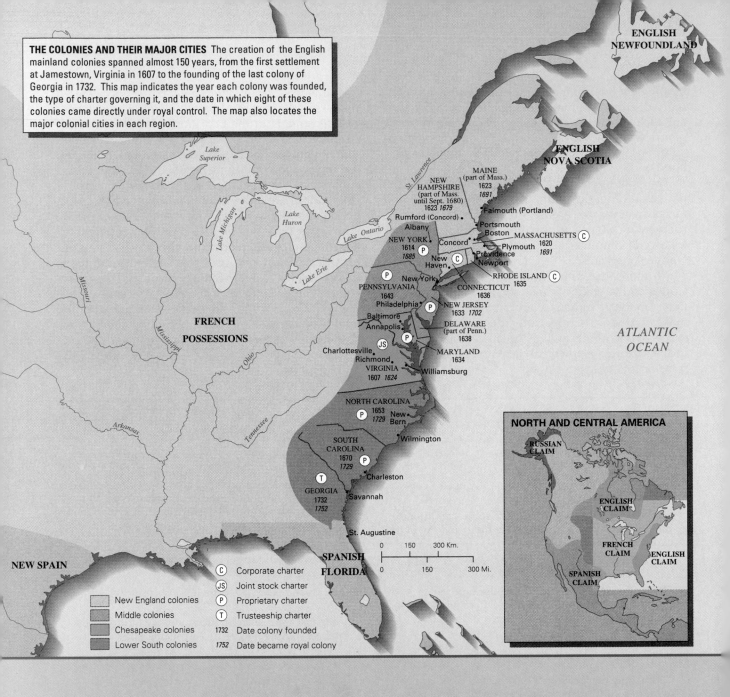

THE COLONIES AND THEIR MAJOR CITIES The creation of the English mainland colonies spanned almost 150 years, from the first settlement at Jamestown, Virginia in 1607 to the founding of the last colony of Georgia in 1732. This map indicates the year each colony was founded, the type of charter governing it, and the date in which eight of these colonies came directly under royal control. The map also locates the major colonial cities in each region.

ENGLISH NEWFOUNDLAND

ENGLISH NOVA SCOTIA

Lake Superior

Lake Michigan

Lake Huron

Lake Ontario

Lake Erie

Missouri

FRENCH POSSESSIONS

Mississippi

Ohio

Tennessee

Arkansas

St. Lawrence

MAINE
(part of Mass.)
1623
1691

NEW HAMPSHIRE
(part of Mass. until Sept. 1680)
1623 *1679*

Falmouth (Portland)

Rumford (Concord)
Albany
Portsmouth
Boston
Concord

NEW YORK
1614
1685 Ⓟ

New Haven Ⓒ

New York Ⓟ

MASSACHUSETTS Ⓒ

Plymouth 1620
1691

Providence
Newport

RHODE ISLAND Ⓒ
1635

CONNECTICUT
1636

PENNSYLVANIA
1643

Philadelphia Ⓟ

NEW JERSEY
1633 *1702*

Baltimore
Annapolis

DELAWARE
(part of Penn.)
1638

Charlottesville Ⓙ̶Ⓢ
Richmond Ⓟ

MARYLAND
1634

VIRGINIA
1607 *1624*

Williamsburg

ATLANTIC OCEAN

NORTH CAROLINA
1653 Ⓟ
1729
New Bern

SOUTH CAROLINA
1670
1729 Ⓟ

Wilmington

Charleston

GEORGIA Ⓣ
1732
1752
Savannah

St. Augustine

0   150   300 Km.
0   150   300 Mi.

NEW SPAIN

SPANISH FLORIDA

Ⓒ   Corporate charter
Ⓙ̶Ⓢ   Joint stock charter
Ⓟ   Proprietary charter
Ⓣ   Trusteeship charter
1732   Date colony founded
1752   Date became royal colony

New England colonies
Middle colonies
Chesapeake colonies
Lower South colonies

NORTH AND CENTRAL AMERICA

RUSSIAN CLAIM

ENGLISH CLAIM

FRENCH CLAIM

ENGLISH CLAIM

SPANISH CLAIM

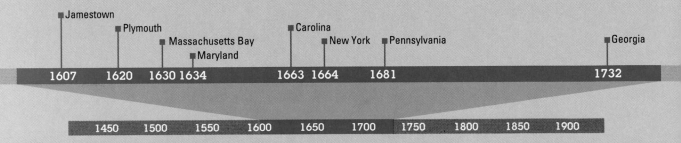

Jamestown	Plymouth	Massachusetts Bay		Carolina	New York	Pennsylvania		Georgia
		Maryland						
1607	**1620**	**1630 1634**		**1663**	**1664**	**1681**		**1732**

1450	1500	1550	1600	1650	1700	1750	1800	1850	1900

English Entry into the New World, 1607–1752

First Footholds

- Compare the earliest settlers at Jamestown and Plymouth in terms of their *expectations*, the *constraints* they faced, and their *choices* regarding their livelihoods.

The Chesapeake Colonies

- What *constraints* did English political and economic developments place on the colonists of the Chesapeake?

- What conflicts arose within each of these colonies, and what were the *outcomes* of these struggles?

The New England Colonies

- What kind of society did the Puritans *expect* to create? What special *constraints* were imposed within their "city upon a hill"?

- How did Puritans *choose* to deal with dissent? What was the *outcome* of dissenters' actions?

The Pluralism of the Middle Colonies

- What were the *expectations* of the many groups who settled in the middle colonies?

- Why were the *expectations* for Pennsylvania so distinctive?

The Colonies of the Lower South

- What economic *constraints* led the colonists of the Carolinas and Georgia to *choose* to establish a slave labor system?

- What kind of society was the *outcome?*

INTRODUCTION

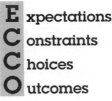

E xpectations
C onstraints
C hoices
O utcomes

Early in the seventeenth century, a group of English men and women *chose* to sail together to America. They had already suffered persecution because of their religious views, endured exile from their homeland, and struggled as refugees in Holland. Their leader, William Bradford, was full of apprehension as he was about to set sail. Even if we survive the hazardous ocean voyage, he wrote, we will be "liable to famine, and nakedness . . . sore sicknesses and grievous diseases." Those who escaped death from starvation or illness, he continued, could *expect* to be "in danger of the savage people, who are cruel, barbarous, and most treacherous."

Throughout the first half of the seventeenth century, other English colonists shared this Pilgrim's *expectations* of danger and disaster. For many, those *expectations* proved true. Mortality rates were high in the first decades of most colonies, and life was difficult. But colonists came because they held positive *expectations*. Some came seeking their fortunes. Some, like the Pilgrims, hoped to find refuge from religious or political persecution. Many were drawn to the colonies because of the opportunity to acquire land, even if they first had to work as servants for other colonists. Those who came involuntarily from Africa, however, *expected* little.

Expectations of a different sort prompted the founders of these English colonies. The earliest colonizers sought glory or gold. Later, men of wealth and power created colonies to test new ways of governing people or to recreate older ways of life that had been lost. Some intended to reform criminals, to assist the poor, or to provide a refuge for members of their own religious faith. Most *expected* to make a profit on their investment.

Whatever their *expectations*, English colonizers and colonists faced significant *constraints*. The earliest settlers lacked important resources to achieve their goals, including survival skills. American Indians resisted the colonists' efforts to clear new lands, and other European nations laid claims to the same lands. Thus militant opposition *constrained* settlement. Finally, colonists were always subject to the *constraints* of the English government's regulations.

Seventeenth-century colonists made an endless series of *choices* about where to settle, how to organize their communities, and how to survive and then prosper. They generally *chose* an aggressive policy toward American Indians and Indian land claims. In some colonies they *chose* to establish slavery so that they could profit from tobacco, rice, and other crops. In most colonies they *chose* to increase population by offering land to new European settlers.

One *outcome* of these fundamental *choices* was the firm establishment of the English presence in North America by 1700. There were other *outcomes* as well. The importation of African slaves meant that English America became a multiracial society. The continuous flow of immigrants from a number of countries meant that English America would be a multicultural society too. The relentless desire for expansion would lead to decades of warfare and diplomacy.

Conflicts between the backcountry and the more settled coastal communities, between rich and poor, between Indians and settlers, and between England and its European rivals prevented seventeenth-century colonial life from being peaceful or secure. But by the eighteenth century, newcomers to the English colonies had no reason to fear the "famine and nakedness" that had so concerned William Bradford.

CHRONOLOGY

Settling the Mainland Colonies

1585	English colonize Roanoke Island
1603	James I becomes king of England
1606	Creation of the Virginia Company
1607	Jamestown founded
1608	Pilgrims flee to Holland from England
1612	Tobacco cultivation begins in Virginia
1619	Virginia House of Burgesses meets
1620	Pilgrims found Plymouth Plantations
1624	Dutch purchase Manhattan Island
1630	Puritans found Massachusetts Bay Colony
1634	First English settlements in Maryland
1636	Roger Williams founds Providence
1637	Anne Hutchinson banished from Massachusetts Pequot War in New England
1642–1648	English Civil War
1649	Charles I executed Cromwell and Puritans come to power in England

1660	Restoration of English monarchy
1662	Half-Way Covenant
1663	Carolina chartered
1664	English capture New Netherland New Jersey chartered
1675	King Philip's War in New England
1676	Bacon's Rebellion in Virginia
1681	Pennsylvania chartered
1685	James II becomes king of England
1686	Dominion of New England established
1688	Glorious Revolution in England
1691	Massachusetts becomes royal colony
1692	Salem witch trials
1732	Georgia chartered

First Footholds

- Compare the earliest settlers at Jamestown and Plymouth in terms of their *expectations,* the *constraints* they faced, and their *choices* regarding their livelihoods.

When Queen Elizabeth died in 1603 without a direct male heir, her nephew James came to the English throne. **James I** was determined to create a colonial empire in America. Happily for James, England's increasingly affluent merchant community was thinking along similar lines.

These merchants had created **joint-stock companies** to distribute the risks and accumulate the money needed to finance large enterprises. If the

James I King of England (r. 1603–1625); his policies encouraged investors to establish colonies in North America and prompted dissenters to leave England.

joint-stock company A business financed through the sale of shares of stock to investors, who hope to make a profit from their investment.

♦ After several winters of starvation and death at Jamestown, the Virginia Company imposed martial law on the colony. A new governor, Sir Thomas Dale, arrived in 1611 and immediately established severe penalties for anyone who failed to work for the security and survival of the colony. A fort and a system of stockades were in place by 1614 when this sketch was drawn. The colonists had also constructed sturdy log houses and a meeting house for religious services. *"Jamestown 1614" (detail) by Sidney King, Colonial National Historical Park.*

venture failed, no single individual would suffer the devastating loss that Sir Walter Raleigh had suffered when his colony at Roanoke failed. If the venture succeeded, profits for all could be dazzling. Sir Francis Drake's raiding spree against the Spanish in 1577 netted a 4,600 percent profit for investors.

In 1606, James granted royal **charters** to two groups of merchants. The Plymouth Company was given the right to colonize a northern area stretching all the way from present-day Maine to Virginia. Its single venture, the Popham Colony in Maine, failed almost immediately in 1607. The wealthier London Company received permission to create settlements from present-day New York to South Carolina.

The Planting of Jamestown

The London Company's investors *expected* a quick profit from their venture because the settlers were instructed to "dig, mine, and search for all Manner of Gold, Silver, and Copper." Many of the 144 initial colonists were gentlemen-adventurers more interested in the excitement of gathering precious metals than in starting life over in a new world.

The exclusively male colonists set sail from England in December 1606. Before land was sighted, sixteen people had died at sea. But **Jamestown,** the camp they established on a small peninsula on the James River, near the Chesapeake Bay, would prove to be more deadly than the transatlantic voyage.

The colonists *chose* the site because it was easy to defend against attack by Spanish ships or local Indians. What they did not realize was that the swampy area around Jamestown was an unhealthy environment. "Swelling Fluxes" and "Burning Fevers" (probably caused by typhoid and dysentery) killed many Englishmen that summer.

By winter, starvation had replaced disease as the primary danger. The English gentlemen in the camp, unaccustomed to working, refused to clear fields or to do any manual labor at all. The personal servants of these gentlemen were inept pioneers as well. By January 1608, only thirty-eight of these helpless settlers were still alive.

Among the survivors of the nightmare winter was a 27-year-old soldier of fortune: **Captain John Smith.** With the settlement in crisis, Smith took charge. He immediately imposed military discipline on the colonists. Smith forced the gentlemen, their servants, and the newcomers who arrived in the spring of 1608 to build, plant, and fish. Even with

---

charter　An official document in which a sovereign or a governing body grants rights or privileges.

Jamestown　The first permanent English settlement in America; it was founded in Virginia in 1607.

Captain John Smith　English colonist at Jamestown who imposed military discipline when disease and famine threatened the settlement.

these sensible efforts, the deaths continued. By October 1608, almost 150 of the original and new Virginia colonists had died.

Terrible as the first winters had been, Virginians remembered 1609 as "the starving time." When new settlers arrived in the spring of 1610, they found only sixty ragged survivors. The Virginia Company, as it was now known, continued to send new colonists annually to replace the dead and the dying. But the survival of the colony remained in doubt.

Tobacco proved to be Virginia's salvation. Since the 1560s, when Indian tobacco was introduced, smoking had become a steady English habit. Native Virginia tobacco was too harsh for English tastes, but colonist John Rolfe experimented successfully with a milder West Indian strain. By 1618 Rolfe and most of his neighbors had begun a mad race to plant and harvest as many acres of tobacco as possible.

Tobacco became the colony's obsession. "Brown gold" grew to dominate every aspect of Virginia life. Colonists dispersed themselves over vast areas, rather than settling in towns or farming communities, because planters needed large tracts of land for a crop that rapidly depleted the soil. Planters fanned out along the Virginia river system because the waterways provided transportation for their tobacco. One *outcome* was a life of isolation rather than a sense of community. Another was improved health, for tobacco drew Virginians away from Jamestown's deadly environment.

"Brown gold" may have made Rolfe and his neighbors prosperous, but the Virginia Company continued to struggle. To cut its expenses, in 1618 the company introduced the **headright system.** Under this system, any man who paid the cost of transporting and supplying a settler—whether himself, a family member, or a servant—had the right to obtain fifty acres per settler for himself. The system shifted the cost of populating and developing the colony to the residents, but it also diminished the company's control over its primary resource: land. The company made other significant concessions to its colonists. The tight military discipline begun by Captain John Smith gave way to civil government. The planters won decision-making powers over local issues in 1619, when the company created an elected, representative lawmaking body called the **House of Burgesses.**

The company made costly errors in its Indian policy. Its governors in Virginia *chose* confrontation rather than compromise or negotiation with the local Powhatan Indians. The *outcome* was a deadly Indian raid on Jamestown on Good Friday in 1622. News of the attack and of other mismanagement prompted King James to revoke the company's charter and to assume control of the colony in 1624.

Founding Plymouth

Protestant reformers in England since the time of Henry VIII had urged a purification of the Church of England. These **Puritans** believed that the Reformation had not gone far enough within the church and that too many Catholic practices and offices remained. They wanted to simplify the worship service and to eliminate much of the church's hierarchy. The Puritans disagreed among themselves, however, on what their stance toward the unreformed church should be. Most Puritans chose to be critics within the Church of England. A small minority known as **Separatists,** however, believed that they should separate themselves completely from a church that they viewed as hopelessly corrupt.

Queen Elizabeth had tolerated Puritans and even Separatists. King James I *chose* to harass them. James was determined to make all dissenters conform to his church, or to "harry them out of this land."

In 1608, a small group of Separatists took this threat to heart and left their homes in Scrooby Village for Holland. These **Pilgrims** went to the city

---

headright system   Virginia Company program under which colonists who paid their own expenses or the expenses of another person got 50 acres of land per settler in return.

House of Burgesses   The representative lawmaking body of Virginia; it was established by the Virginia (London) Company in 1618.

Puritans   English Protestants who wanted to reform the Church of England.

Separatists   English Protestants who chose to leave the Church of England because they believed it was corrupt.

Pilgrims   A small group of Separatists who left England in search of religious freedom and sailed to America on the *Mayflower* in 1620.

of Leyden, where they found religious freedom and prosperity. But **William Bradford,** a leader of the exiles, saw hidden dangers in this comfortable new life. He worried that the Pilgrims were being "drawn away by evil examples into extravagant and dangerous courses." Bradford decided it was time to become a pilgrim once more, this time to America.

In 1620, Bradford led thirty-five supporters back to England. There they joined a second, smaller group of Separatists and set sail for Virginia aboard an old, creaky ship. Nine weeks later, the *Mayflower* delivered them to Cape Cod, hundreds of miles north of their expected destination of Jamestown. Although many of the Pilgrims were disheartened by the captain's faulty piloting and the approach of winter, Bradford saw distinct advantages to the accident that had taken them so far from Virginia. In an isolated settlement, the Pilgrims would be able to pursue their own religious ideas without interference. Bradford's problem was to persuade the loudly complaining passengers to remain where they were.

To prevent a mutiny, Bradford negotiated an unusual contract with all the men aboard the *Mayflower.* The **Mayflower Compact** granted political rights to any man willing to remain and abide by the new colony's laws. Given such an unheard-of opportunity to participate in political decisions, the men *chose* to remain in what came to be called Plymouth Plantations.

Half of the colonists died during that first winter. The colony survived thanks to **Squanto,** a Patuxet Indian who came upon the struggling settlement in the spring of 1621. Squanto became the Pilgrims' teacher and adviser. He taught them how to plant corn, squash, and pumpkins. He acted as translator for William Bradford when he and Massasoit, leader of the local Wampanoag Indians, sat down to negotiate a treaty of friendship. The summer of cooperation between Wampanoags and Pilgrims saved Plymouth Plantations. In the fall of 1621, English settlers and Indians sat down to a harvest feast of thanksgiving.

Over the next decades, Plymouth Plantations grew at a steady, modest pace. When William Bradford died in 1657, after a long career as governor, the colony had over thirteen hundred people. Most colonists lived comfortably by farming, fishing, or cutting timber. A few grew wealthy from the fur trade. Much of the colony's success was probably due to the alliance with the Wampanoags. For forty years, Plymouth Plantations grew peacefully by purchasing land from Massasoit's people. By the time of Bradford's death the intense religious piety of the original Pilgrims had faded. Bradford had recognized the dangers of a comfortable life in Holland but not in America.

The Chesapeake Colonies

- What *constraints* did English political and economic developments place on the colonists of the Chesapeake?
- What conflicts arose within each of these colonies, and what were the *outcomes* of these struggles?

The motives for founding Maryland were quite different from those that had spurred the Virginia Company to plant Jamestown. But the climate and geography of the region were powerful forces in creating a single Chesapeake society.

Creating a Refuge for Catholics

The first Lord Baltimore, George Calvert, was a Catholic who turned his attention to America to accomplish two aims. First, he wanted to create a refuge for English Catholics. Second, he wanted to establish a peaceful, orderly society where aristocrats would rule over respectful commoners much as he believed they had in medieval England. **Charles I,** who had ascended the English throne when James I died in 1625, was happy to oblige his friend's request for a colonial charter.

William Bradford   Pilgrim leader who organized the *Mayflower* journey and became governor of the Plymouth colony.

Mayflower Compact   An agreement drafted in 1620, when the Pilgrims reached Cape Cod, granting political rights to all male colonists willing to abide by the colony's laws.

Squanto   A Patuxet Indian who taught the Pilgrims how to survive in America and acted as a translator.

Charles I   King of England (r. 1625–1649); Protestant armies defeated his forces in the English Civil War, and he was beheaded.

Calvert died before the charter was actually drawn up in 1632. Thus it fell to his son **Cecilius** to realize his father's dreams for Maryland, a vast tract of southern land. The second Lord Baltimore soon discovered, however, that very few of England's remaining Catholics wanted to go to Maryland to become **tenant farmers.** Ironically, most of Maryland's first settlers in 1634 were Protestants from England's middle and lower classes. Few Protestants or Catholics joined the colony subsequently because of the lack of prospects to own land. By 1640, Calvert had to abandon his father's vision in favor of the headright system that Virginia used to attract colonists.

Maryland's colonists immediately turned to tobacco growing. They repeated Virginians' scramble for good riverfront lands and used trickery, threats, or violence to pry acres away from resisting Indians. Virginians did not welcome their new neighbors despite the fact that most were fellow Protestants. They resented the competition of Maryland tobacco planters, and they disliked the constraints on their own acquisition of land that Calvert's colony imposed.

Colonists at War in Maryland

The Catholics who came to Maryland did not find a peaceful haven from religious problems. Both Protestant and Catholic Marylanders brought religious hatreds with them to the New World. When the English Civil War broke out in 1642 between the Puritan-dominated Parliament and King Charles I, the conflict spread to this Catholic colony.

The triumph of the Parliamentary forces, led by Oliver Cromwell, and the subsequent beheading of the king in 1649 spelled trouble for Calvert. In 1654, the militantly Protestant Parliament took Maryland away from the Calvert family and established a Protestant Assembly in the colony. The Assembly began persecuting Catholics and ultimately provoked Catholics to take up arms. At the Battle of Severn River in 1655, a smaller Puritan force routed a Catholic army of two hundred men. When Cromwell died in 1658, the local balance of power shifted once again as the English government returned Maryland to the Calverts. Still no peace followed. Protestants in Maryland organized rebellions in 1659, 1676, 1681, and 1691.

Rebellion in Virginia

Seventeenth-century Virginia also witnessed a revolt, although for different reasons. By the 1670s a planter aristocracy was entrenched in Virginia. Governor William Berkeley ran the colony for the benefit of himself and a group of planter cronies. They faced little opposition until Nathaniel Bacon arrived in the colony. Although Bacon was as well educated and refined as the local elite, he found himself outside the governor's circle of friends. Unable to acquire choice coastal lands, he had no *choice* but to take up land in the backcountry among poor neighbors, who were often freed white servants. Indian resistance to white expansion and high taxes on the backcountry posed serious *constraints* for Bacon and his neighbors.

Bacon's growing anger at the government erupted in 1676 when the Susquehannock Indians retaliated for the settlers' killing of five of their tribe. The Indians killed several dozen colonists, leading western planters to demand protection and reprisals. Governor Berkeley refused to send troops or to permit the westerners to raise an army of their own. Bacon then led a large number of armed planters in a march on Jamestown, threatening to demolish the capital unless the governor changed his mind. Furious but frightened, Berkeley gave in to Bacon's demand for a military commission. As soon as Bacon's army headed west, however, Berkeley revoked the military **commission** he had just given Bacon. He declared Bacon and his men "rebells and traytors" and ordered them to disband at once.

Bacon responded by turning his army around and heading back for Jamestown. Poor farmers, servants, craftsmen, artisans, and black slaves, to whom Bacon promised freedom, swelled the army's ranks as it neared Jamestown. What began as an

---

Cecilius Calvert   Proprietor of Maryland; he hoped to carry out his father's dream of creating a refuge for Catholics.

tenant farmer   A person who farms land owned by someone else and pays rent either in cash or by giving up a share of the crops.

commission   Authorization to carry out a particular task or duty.

uprising by a group of **vigilantes** was rapidly turning into a social revolution against a privileged elite.

Governor Berkeley tried desperately to rally his supporters, but to no avail. When Bacon's army reached Jamestown, even the governor fled. The rebels looted the town and then headed home to fight the Indians. Before Bacon could do so, however, he fell victim to a fatal attack of dysentery.

Without Bacon's leadership, the rebellion fell apart. Berkeley took revenge for all the insults and humiliations he had suffered by executing twenty-three of the rebels. **Bacon's Rebellion** was over, but resistance to the old planter government continued sporadically until 1683, when royal troops flushed the last of Bacon's men out of hiding.

The New England Colonies

- What kind of society did the Puritans *expect* to create? What special *constraints* were imposed within their "city upon a hill"?
- How did Puritans *choose* to deal with dissent? What was the *outcome* of dissenters' actions?

When Charles I came to the throne in 1625, the persecution of religious dissenters became unrelenting. William Laud, whom the king appointed as archbishop of Canterbury, was determined to rid the Church of England of all would-be purifiers. This persecution and a deepening economic depression in England led many Puritans who had opposed the Pilgrims' separatism to reconsider their *choice* to remain critics within the Church of England. The *outcome* was the planting of new colonies in America (see Map 2.1).

The Wilderness Zion

A young Puritan lawyer, **John Winthrop,** agonized over the Puritans' increasingly desperate situation. His solution was to propose that the Puritans leave England yet retain their ties to the Anglican Church. This proposal would free the Puritans from the taint of separatism yet allow them to create a truly godly community far from the prying eyes of the king's officials, especially Archbishop Laud. This ideal Puritan community would serve as a model for others and show England the error of its sinful ways.

◆ **MAP 2.1 New England Settlement in the Seventeenth and Early Eighteenth Centuries** This map shows the major towns and cities of New England and their settlement dates. By the end of the seventeenth century, the region had four colonies. Colonists seeking land moved west and south toward the New York border and north toward French Canada. Those involved in trade, shipping, and crafts migrated to the seaport cities.

King Charles I, who was more than willing to help dissenters leave England, approved the request by Winthrop's Massachusetts Bay Company for a northern colony. The company immediately began to recruit devout Puritan families to join in the religious experiment. Winthrop spoke of the colony in biblical terms, comparing the American "Wilderness Zion" of the Puritans to the desert wilderness in which the Hebrews wandered before

vigilantes People who take the law into their own hands.

Bacon's Rebellion A revolt of backcountry farmers against the colonial government of Virginia; it was triggered by inland taxes and strife with the Indians, and it collapsed after the death of Nathaniel Bacon.

John Winthrop English Puritan who was one of the founders of Massachusetts Bay Colony and served as its first governor.

reaching their "Promised Land." Winthrop's vision and the king's dismissal of Parliament in 1629 produced the **Great Migration** of nearly 20,000 Puritans in the 1630s. Many more Puritans, however, remained in England.

The first years of the Massachusetts Bay Colony stood in sharp contrast to the lean and lonely beginnings of nearby Plymouth Plantations or Jamestown. An advance crew traveled to Massachusetts in early 1629 to prepare shelters and to clear fields for planting. Winthrop and over a thousand more colonists followed in 1630 in seventeen sturdy ships loaded with livestock, tools, supplies, and food. There was no "starving time" in the Wilderness Zion.

Aboard his flagship, the *Arbella,* John Winthrop preached a sermon in which he urged his audience to create a model Protestant community. "We shall be a city upon a hill," he pointed out, observing that "the eyes of all peoples are upon us." God would protect and nurture their settlement if they kept their promises to Him. To falter in their mission, or to forget their purpose, however, would bring punishment from God.

The first government of the colony, called the General Court, consisted of Winthrop and the eleven other stockholders in the Massachusetts Bay Company who had decided to emigrate. No man was permitted to vote or hold office unless he was an acknowledged church member, not simply a churchgoer. To be a church member or **saint,** a person had to testify to an experience of "saving faith"—a moment of intense awareness of God's power that offered an assurance of salvation. Slowly, however, free white males who could not claim sainthood did win the right to vote on local matters, and by the mid-1630s the Puritan saints had wrested important political power from Winthrop and his fellow shareholders with the creation of a representative assembly.

Puritan authorities intended to enforce biblical laws as well as English civil law. A colonist's religious beliefs and practices, style of dress, sexual conduct, and personal behavior were all legally subject to regulation by the community. Every colonist was required to attend church, and the church joined the government in supervising business dealings, parent-child relationships, and marital life. The Puritan desire to create a godly community on earth led the colony's leaders to create standards of behavior that they imposed on every individual.

Despite being victims of persecution, the Puritans did not favor religious toleration. They saw no reason to welcome **Quakers,** Jews, Catholics, or Anglicans into their midst. The Bay Colony dealt harshly with non-Puritans who came to Massachusetts. When Quaker missionaries arrived and attempted to convert the Puritans, they were flogged, beaten, imprisoned, and branded with hot irons. Some persistent Quakers were even hanged.

Dissenters in Zion

Puritan leaders showed just as little tolerance toward fellow Puritans who criticized or challenged them. Winthrop and his cofounders tried to enforce orthodoxy, or religious agreement, by labeling their critics **heretics.**

One of the most powerful challenges came from **Roger Williams,** the assistant minister in the Salem congregation, who was highly critical of every aspect of the colony's life. Williams condemned the government's seizure of Indian lands through intimidation and warfare as a "National Sinne." He insisted that true religious belief was a matter of personal commitment and could not be compelled by the government. "Forced religion," he said bluntly, "stinks in God's nostrils."

Great Migration   The movement of Puritans from England to America in the 1630s; it was caused by political conflict in England and by fear of persecution.

saint   A person who was granted full membership in a Puritan church after testifying to an experience of "saving faith."

Quakers   Members of the Religious Society of Friends, a Protestant sect; Quakers believe in the equality of men and women, refuse to bear arms, and seek divine inspiration from the "inner light" within each individual.

heretic   A person who publicly dissents from an officially accepted doctrine or religion.

Roger Williams   A minister who was banished from Massachusetts for criticizing the Puritan leaders of the colony; in 1636 he founded Providence, a community based on religious freedom.

In 1635, Williams's congregation made him a full minister. Williams's evident popularity and his dissident views, however, led the General Court to banish him from the Bay Colony in the middle of winter. Williams sought refuge with the Narragansett Indians, who lived south of the colony. In the spring, many of his most faithful followers chose to join him in exile. Providence, the community they established, became a magnet for Puritan dissenters, Quakers, and Jews. John Winthrop tolerated Providence, for he saw it as a dumping ground for troublemakers. In 1644, Providence Plantations acquired a colonial charter from England's new Puritan government. This charter clearly established Williams's principle of separation of church and state. The colony later became known as Rhode Island and Providence Plantations.

Another challenge to Winthrop's authority came from **Anne Hutchinson,** who arrived in the Bay Colony with her husband in 1634. Soon after their arrival, the Hutchinsons began to host meetings in their home to discuss their minister's sermons. The meetings were immediately popular. The brilliant Anne Hutchinson, who had been trained by her minister father to interpret the Scriptures, quickly acquired a reputation as a critic of the colony's clergy. She contended that the vast majority of the colony's clergy had slipped into what Calvinists considered a Catholic heresy: the belief that good works earned a person salvation. Hutchinson reemphasized the original Calvinist doctrine that only God's grace, not good behavior or obedience to biblical laws, could save a person's soul. Puritan ministers conceded this point but could not agree with Hutchinson that proper behavior had no place in a Christian community. They feared her thinking might lead to sin and anarchy.

The fact that Hutchinson was a woman made the challenge to Puritan authorities seem worse. Men like John Winthrop believed that women ought to be silent in the church and obedient to the men of their family. To their mind, women had no business criticizing ministers and government officials. A surprising number of Puritans, however, were untroubled by Hutchinson's outspokenness. She developed a strong following among women and among merchants and artisans who were not saints. They appreciated her attacks on men who had political rights that they themselves lacked. Hutchinson also attracted Puritan saints who disliked the tight reins on business, personal, and social life that Winthrop and the clergy maintained.

In the end, however, none of Hutchinson's supporters could protect her (see Individual Choices: Anne Hutchinson). In 1637, she was arrested and brought to trial before the General Court. Although she was in the last stages of a troubled pregnancy, the judges forced her to stand throughout the long, exhausting, repetitive examination. Hutchinson was a clever defendant and seemed to be winning until she made a serious mistake near the end of the trial. In one of her answers she seemed to be claiming direct communication with God. Such a claim was counter to Puritan teachings that God spoke to individuals only through the Bible, and it justified her conviction as a heretic. Triumphantly, Winthrop and his court ruled her "unfit to our society" and banished her from the Bay Colony.

Some Puritans *chose* to leave Massachusetts voluntarily. In 1636, Reverend Thomas Hooker and his entire Newton congregation resettled in the Connecticut River Valley. Other Puritan congregations followed. By 1639, the Connecticut valley towns had drafted their own government, and in 1664, they joined to create the colony of Connecticut. A number of Bay colonists searching for new or better lands made their way north to what later became Maine and New Hampshire. New Hampshire became a separate colony in 1679, but Maine remained part of Massachusetts until 1820.

Puritans in Conflict

The Puritans' commitment to building a godly community did not mean that they were pacifists or that they were always altruistic. Their treatment of the New England Indians offers ample proof that the Puritans were all too often motivated by greed.

In 1637, the Puritans used trumped-up murder charges against Sassacus, the leader of the **Pequots**

Anne Hutchinson   A religious leader who was banished from Massachusetts in 1637 because of her heretical beliefs.

Pequots   An American Indian people inhabiting eastern Connecticut; when the Pequots resisted colonial expansion, the Massachusetts Bay colonists declared war on them.

in Connecticut, as an excuse to declare war on the tribe. The Puritans were often the "savages" in the Pequot War, as is evidenced by their attack on the civilian Indian population at Mystic Village. The Bay Colony's Captain John Underhill noted with satisfaction that there were "about four hundred souls in this fort, and not above five of them escaped out of our hands." The Pequot War did not end until all the men had been killed and the women and children sold into slavery in the Caribbean.

In 1675, the long alliance between the Plymouth colonists and the Wampanoag Indians broke down when colonists encroached on Wampanoag lands. The Narragansetts and other smaller tribes joined Chief Metacomet (known to the English as King Philip) in **King Philip's War.** Indian resistance was dealt a crushing blow when the governor of New York sent Iroquois troops into battle against Metacomet's exhausted army. Metacomet escaped immediate capture, only to be killed in 1676 by an Indian ally of the English.

Metacomet's death ended Indian resistance in New England. Some tribes had been entirely wiped out, or the survivors had been sold into slavery. Indians who escaped death or capture scattered to the north and the west. The *outcome* was a New England virtually depopulated of its original inhabitants.

Religious and Political Change in New England

New England Puritans discovered that the Atlantic Ocean did not free them from the *constraints* of English politics. The start of the English Civil War in 1642, for example, affected New England profoundly. As Puritans seized control of England's government, England itself became a grand Puritan experiment. Massachusetts lost its special place as a "city upon a hill," and the sense of mission among its inhabitants declined.

The war affected New England in mundane ways as well. Population fell as many settlers returned to England to fight beside Oliver Cromwell. The end of the Great Migration dried up the flow of funds and supplies from England. New England's remaining colonists, who had profited by selling livestock and foodstuffs to immigrants, now had to find a new way to pay for the imported goods that they needed. When English fishing fleets could not make their usual voyages to New England's waters because of the war, colonists created local fishing fleets. By the end of the seventeenth century, Bay colonists were actively involved in transatlantic and Caribbean trade, and Boston had grown into the largest of the English mainland colonial cities.

Massachusetts faced new religious problems after the English Civil War. Puritan colonists who had been born in America lacked the religious intensity that marked their parents' sainthood. Perhaps their growing interest in trade and commerce lessened their zeal. Whatever the cause, fewer young Puritans became saints. The declining number of new church members led to the **Half-Way Covenant** of 1662. This allowed children of church members to be baptized even if they could not make a convincing declaration of their salvation. The Half-Way Covenant allowed those baptized to become halfway members of the church and thus to participate in church affairs.

Meanwhile, external political pressures were growing. After the restoration of the monarchy in 1660, King **Charles II** insisted that Anglicans and other Protestants be allowed to settle in New England. A growing number did so. Charles II also pressured Massachusetts to conform to English law. He revoked the colony's charter in 1683 when the colony refused to end its restriction of voting to church members. This marked the beginning of an effort to centralize royal control over the growing American empire.

King James II, who assumed the throne after his brother's death in 1685, took the next step in this process. He revoked the charter of every English mainland colony and combined the New England colonies as well as New Jersey and New York into the Dominion of New England.

King Philip's War   War between settlers and Indians in New England from 1675 through 1676; it ended after the Wampanoag chief Metacomet was killed.

Half-Way Covenant   An agreement that gave partial membership in Puritan churches to the children of church members even if they had not had a "saving faith" experience.

Charles II   King of England (r. 1660–1685); his coronation marked the restoration of the English monarchy, which had been suspended when his father was beheaded.

To Challenge Authority

Anne Hutchinson

Anne Hutchinson challenged the authority of Massachusetts ministers and magistrates and was tried for heresy and treason. She was convicted in 1637 and banished from her Puritan community. Culver Pictures.

In November 1637 Anne Hutchinson was called before the General Court of Massachusetts. The Court accused her of expressing heretical religious beliefs that were a threat to Puritan Massachusetts society. Hutchinson stood before the Court and defended herself energetically for two days. She successfully dodged the theological traps that the examining clergy and magistrates laid for her. Throughout the trial, Hutchinson's knowledge of the Scriptures surprised her male prosecutors and occasionally put them on the defensive. She seemed about to escape conviction when she shocked the courtroom by declaring her belief that individuals could receive revelation directly from God. According to records of the trial kept by John Winthrop, her most determined opponent, Hutchinson insisted that she had discovered God's truth "by an immediate revelation . . . and by the voice of His own spirit in my soul." The claim was her undoing, for it violated the central Puritan belief that no one could ever receive

James *expected* the Dominion would increase the land grants and other political favors that he could distribute to loyal supporters. He also *expected* to increase the royal revenues by imposing duties and taxes on colonial goods. What he may not have *expected* was the strength of popular resistance to his new Dominion and to the man he *chose* to govern it, Sir Edmund Andros.

Andros offended New England's Puritans immediately by establishing the Church of England as the Dominion's official church. Then he alienated the non-Puritans by abolishing the General Court in Massachusetts. Nonsaints had been struggling for inclusion in this representative body, not for its destruction. So when Andros imposed new taxes, many saints and nonsaints refused to pay.

In 1689, when news of James II's downfall in the **Glorious Revolution** reached Boston, New Englanders took their revenge on Andros. They imprisoned him and shipped him back to England

Glorious Revolution   The events in 1688 that resulted in the removal of James II from the throne of England and the crowning of William and Mary as king and queen.

full assurance of God's grace or salvation. Hutchinson might have lightened her punishment by changing her testimony or by admitting she was in error. But she *chose* to remain firm. Winthrop noted that when she was asked again whether she had spoken directly with God, her reply was "yes." The case against her was thus proved. The General Court found her guilty of sedition and immediately banished her from Massachusetts Bay Colony.

Anne Hutchinson was banished from Massachusetts only three years after she, her husband, and their children arrived from England. The Hutchinsons had come to the colony to be near their minister, John Cotton, who preached that the Holy Spirit and salvation were available from God to every believer and not just to a chosen few. At first glance, Anne Hutchinson appeared to be a typical Puritan matron, but she was far from the submissive, retiring wife and mother that Puritan tradition expected all women to be. She was a practicing midwife, a healer, and a spiritual guide to colonists who gathered in her home to discuss both the Scriptures and John Cotton's theology.

As her following grew among men as well as women, Hutchinson grew bolder and began to criticize some members of the local clergy. Bay Colony leaders were shocked by what they called her masculine behavior. At her trial, one judge scolded her, saying, "You have stept out of your place . . . you have rather bine a Husband than a Wife and a preacher than a Hearer; and a Magistrate than a Subject." Her judges declared her "a woman not fit for our society." The church in Boston excommunicated her for preaching a remarkable eighty-two dangerous theological opinions.

The Hutchinsons moved to Narragansett Bay, Rhode Island. In 1642, when her husband died, Anne Hutchinson *chose* to resettle in an isolated area of the nearby Dutch colony, New Netherland. In 1643, an Indian attack killed her and all but one of her children. On hearing the news, Puritan leaders in Massachusetts rejoiced.

for trial as a traitor. Puritans hoped that their new English rulers, William and Mary, would reward them by restoring their charter. But under the new charter of 1691, Massachusetts became a royal colony whose governor was appointed by the Crown. The charter did call for a popularly elected assembly. Potential voters, however, would now have to meet the standard English **property requirement.** Church membership was no longer relevant to the exercise of political rights in New England. The Puritan experiment had largely ended.

The Salem witch trials occurred in the context of these wrenching and bewildering changes in New England life (see Voices: The Salem Witch Trials). In 1692, a group of young women and girls in Salem began to show signs of "bewitchment." They fell into violent fits and their bodies contorted. Under questioning, they named several local women as their tormentors. The conviction that the devil had come to Massachusetts spread quickly, and the number of accused witches grew. By summer, over a

> **property requirement** The limitation of voting rights to people who own certain kinds of property.

The Salem Witch Trials

The Indictment of Martha Carrier

In the sixteenth and seventeenth centuries, the belief in witches was widespread throughout Europe, and thousands of people convicted of witchcraft were executed. In England's North American colonies, an occasional accusation of witchcraft surfaced, but there were no dramatic witch-hunts before the one in Salem Village in 1692. Before that hunt ended, over 150 colonists—young and old, mostly women but some men as well—were arrested, and 19 of them were executed. Testimony that the "shapes," or specters, of the accused had been seen by the bewitched and evidence of suffering if the accused touched the accusers persuaded the judges of their guilt. One man was killed while officials tried to force a plea from him, and even two dogs were hanged by a community convinced the devil had come to Massachusetts. Martha Carrier, whose indictment is provided as a core document, was one of those accused.

Martha Carrier was indicted for the bewitching of certain persons, according to the form usual in such cases pleading not guilty to her indictment. There were first brought in a considerable number of the bewitched persons, who not only made the court sensible to an horrid witchcraft committed upon them, but also deposed that it was Martha Carrier, or her shape, that grievously tormented them by biting, pricking, pinching, and choking of them. It was further deposed that while this Carrier was on her examination before the magistrates, the poor people were so tortured that every one expected their death upon the very spot, but that upon the binding [arrest] of Carrier they were eased. . . .

Before the trial of this prisoner, several of her own children had frankly and fully confessed not only that they were witches themselves, but that this, their mother, had made them so. This confession they made with great shows of repentance, and with much demonstration of truth. They related place, time, occasion; they gave an account of journeys, meetings, and mischiefs by them performed, and were very credible in what they said. . . .

Benjamin Abbot gave in his testimony that . . . this Carrier was very angry with him upon laying out some land near her husband's. Her expressions in this anger were that she "would stick as close to Abbot as the bark stuck to the tree; and that he should repent of it afore seven years came to an end, so as Doctor Prescot should never cure him." . . . Presently after this he was taken with a swelling in his foot, and then with a pain in his side, and exceedingly tormented. It bred into a sore, which was lanced by Doctor Prescot, and several gallons of corruption [pus] ran out of it. For six weeks it continued very bad, and then another sore bred in his groin . . . he was brought unto death's door, and so remained until Carrier was taken and carried away by the constable, from which very day he began to mend and so grew better every day, and is well ever since. . . .

One Foster, who confessed her own share in the witchcraft for which the prisoner stood indicted, affirmed that she had seen the prisoner at some of their witch meetings, and that it was this Carrier who persuaded her to be a witch. She confessed that the devil carried them on a pole to a witch meeting. . . .

Supporters Had This to Say

■ I have indeed set myself to Countermine [combat] the whole Plot of the Devil against New England. . . . Glad should I have been, if I had never known the Name of this man [an accused witch]; or never had this occasion to mention so much as the first Letters of his Name . . . he was Accused by eight of the Confessing Witches, as being a Head Actor at some of the Hellish Randezvouzes, and one who had the promise of being a King in Satan's Kingdom now going to be Erected: he was Accused by nine persons for extraordinary Lifting, in such Feats of Strength, as could not be done without a Diabolical Assistance. . . . And for other such things he was Accused, until about Thirty Testimonies were brought against him; They were enough to fix the Character of a Witch upon him. . . . We cannot but with all Thankfulness acknowledge, the Success which the merciful God has given unto the sedulous and assiduous Endeavors of our honorable Rulers, to detect the abominable Witchcrafts which have been committed in the Country; humbly praying that the discovery of these mysterious and mischievous Wickednesses, may be perfected.
Reverend Cotton Mather, 1692.

Opponents Had This to Say

■ There is no doubt but the Judges and Juries proceeded in their integrity, with a zeal of God against Sin, according to their best light, and according to Law and Evidence; but there is a Question yet unresolved. Whether some of the Laws, Customs and Principles used by the Judges and Juries in the Trials of Witches . . . were not insufficient and unsafe. . . . I have a deep sense of the sad consequences of mistakes in matters Capital; and their impossibility of recovering when compleated. And what grief of heart it brings to a tender conscience, to have been unwittingly encouraging of the Suffering of the innocent. . . . We may hence see ground to fear, that there hath been a great deal of innocent blood shed in the Christian World, by proceeding upon unsafe principles, in condemning persons for Malefick Witchcraft. . . . So that we must beseech the Lord, that if any innocent blood hath been shed, in the hour of temptation, that Lord will not lay it to our charge, but be merciful to his people who he hath redeemed. . . .
Reverend John Hale, 1692.

♦ This mid-nineteenth-century oil painting, *The Trial of George Jacobs,* captures the horrors of the Salem witch-hunts. As the afflicted young women cry out or fall to the floor in agony, the accused attempts to defend himself against charges that he was their tormentor. Jacobs—whose own granddaughter testified against him—was tried and convicted on August 5 and executed two weeks later, along with four neighbors. *"The Trial of George Jacobs, Aug. 5, 1692" by Tompkins Harrison Matteson, 1855. Courtesy, Peabody Essex Museum, Salem, Mass.*

hundred women, men, and even children filled local jails. Testimony of the alleged victims led to the execution of twenty witches, most by hanging, before the new royal governor, Sir William Phips, arrived in Massachusetts and forbade any further arrests. In January 1693, the governor assembled a new court that quickly acquitted the remaining prisoners.

Economic change and local resentments apparently played a role in the Salem witchcraft hysteria as well as uncertainties about the end of Puritan government. Those leveling the accusations typically lived on small farms outside of the town of Salem; those accused of witchcraft were wealthier, and lived in the rising seaport of Salem.

The Pluralism of the Middle Colonies

- What were the *expectations* of the many groups who settled in the middle colonies?
- Why were the *expectations* for Pennsylvania so distinctive?

Between the Chesapeake and New England lay a vast stretch of forests and farmland claimed by the Dutch. In the early seventeenth century, settlers from Holland, Sweden, Germany, and France made **New Netherland** their home. But in the 1660s, the Dutch lost this American empire to England. The English divided the conquered territory into three colonies: New York, New Jersey, and Pennsylvania (see Map 2.2).

From New Amsterdam to New York

The first serious Dutch claim to American territory came in 1609, when **Henry Hudson** explored the Hudson River in search of a water route between the Atlantic and Pacific. The Dutch did little immediately to develop Hudson's claim. As of 1629, only three hundred colonists had spread themselves in a thin ribbon from New Amsterdam on Manhattan Island to Albany on the Hudson River.

In that year, the Dutch West India Company drew up its first serious plans for colonizing New Netherland. The company offered huge estates called **patroonships** resembling medieval manors

New Netherland Territory in present-day New York and New Jersey that was claimed and settled by the Dutch and was seized by the English in 1664.

Henry Hudson English explorer who led English and Dutch expeditions to search for the Northwest Passage; his journey up the Hudson River gave the Dutch their claim to the region.

patroonship A huge grant of land given to Dutchmen who, at their own expense, brought fifty colonists to New Netherland; the colonists became the tenants of the estate owner.

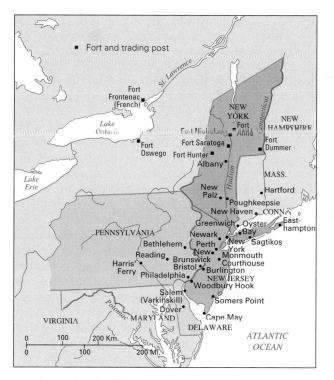

♦ **MAP 2.2 The Middle Colonies** This map shows the major towns, cities, and forts in the colonies of New York, Pennsylvania (including Delaware), and New Jersey. The prosperity of the region was based on the thriving commerce of its largest cities, Philadelphia and New York, and on the commercial production of wheat.

1664 granted New Netherland to his brother James, the duke of York. All James had to do was take this prize from the Dutch.

When the duke's four armed ships arrived in New Amsterdam harbor, the colonists refused to defend the town. The Dutch, after all, had done little for them. Governor Peter Stuyvesant was forced to surrender the colony without a shot being fired, and New Netherland became New York.

New York grew rapidly under James's rule. Its population doubled between 1665 and 1685 and had reached fifteen thousand when James came to the throne in the latter year. The influx of settlers enabled James to adapt the Dutch system of patroonship to his own interests. He gave vast estates to his English friends who, because of growing land shortages, were able to attract tenants and to establish themselves as "lords of the manor." Some of the new settlers were from England, but most were not. Despite the high taxes that James imposed, religious refugees, including French Protestants, English Quakers, and Scottish **Presbyterians,** found New York attractive because it offered religious toleration. The result was a remarkably diverse colonial population.

Diversity did not ensure harmony in the colony. English, Dutch, and German merchants in New York City competed fiercely for control of the colony's trade and for domination of the city's cultural life. Fierce rivalries also existed between New York City's merchants and Albany's fur traders.

New Yorkers were united only in their resentment of James's political control of the colony. Except for a brief period, New York lacked a representative assembly under his rule. Thus when King James II merged New York with the surrounding colonies in his Dominion of New England in 1686, local opposition was as great as it was in Massachusetts. In 1689 news of the Glorious Revolution prompted a revolt in New York City similar to the revolt in Boston. New Yorkers were also successful in deposing the king's officials.

to any man who brought fifty colonists to New Netherland at his own expense. Only one wealthy Dutchman ever did so. Few Dutchmen wanted to become tenants in the New World. They wanted to own their own land. Ignoring the company's plans, settlers created farms and small villages on Long Island, in the Catskill Mountains, and as far east as Connecticut.

When the plan failed, the Dutch West India Company simply neglected New Netherland. New Netherland in 1664 had only about eight thousand people, the majority of whom were not Dutch. The colony grew slowly because it was not very prosperous, thanks largely to the company's poor management.

The company was also unable to defend its colony. Eager to gain an advantage over the Dutch, England's main commercial rival, King Charles II in

> **Presbyterians**   Members of a Calvinist sect that eventually became the established church of Scotland; in the seventeenth century it was sometimes opposed by Scotland's rulers.

The Founding of New Jersey

In 1664 James granted the area west of Manhattan and east of the Delaware River to two loyal supporters. Sir George Carteret and Lord John Berkeley were never able to realize their *expectations* of vast profits from their New Jersey holdings. They did not anticipate the rush of Puritans, Quakers, and Baptists into New Jersey that began as soon as the Dutch surrendered New Netherland. The settlers refused to recognize the authority of the governor appointed by the proprietors or to pay rents. Indeed, New Jersey colonists denied Carteret and Berkeley's right to govern them at all.

Exasperated, Berkeley sold his half-interest in New Jersey to a group of Quaker merchants in 1672. Carteret held on to his half and continued to argue with his colonists over rents and taxes. When he died in 1681, a second group of Quaker merchants acquired the remaining half of the colony. The liberal policies of the Quakers in West Jersey and East Jersey drew great numbers of dissenters to the colony. The Quaker proprietors granted **suffrage** to all male inhabitants and established a representative assembly with broad powers. Colonists were ensured full religious freedom and the right to trial by jury. The Quakers insisted that Indians be paid for all lands deeded to white settlers, and they carefully honored the terms of all contracts with the Indians. The *outcome* of these policies was a thriving and prosperous pair of communities. Quaker attention and resources shifted in the 1680s, however, when **William Penn** created his "holy experiment" in Pennsylvania. In 1702, West Jersey was combined with East Jersey to form the royal colony of New Jersey.

Pennsylvania, Another Holy Experiment

William Penn was eager to create a refuge for his fellow Quakers, who had been persecuted in England. Penn was in a unique position to accomplish this end. His father, Admiral Sir William Penn, who was not a Quaker, had been one of England's naval heroes and one of King Charles II's political advisers. Although Charles II disliked the Quakers, by the 1670s they had become the largest dissenting sect in England, and he wanted their political support in his battles with Parliament. He looked to the younger Penn to secure that support. For a decade Penn combined political loyalty with generous loans to the king just as his father had done. As a reward, in 1681 Charles granted Penn a charter to a huge area west of the Delaware River, which Penn named Pennsylvania ("Penn's Woods"). King Charles gave Penn the same sweeping powers as proprietor that he gave others, but Penn did not intend to govern by whim. He planned a holy experiment based on Quaker values and principles.

Quakers believed that the divine spirit—or "inner light"— resided in every human being. They therefore respected all individuals and maintained a highly egalitarian church structure. The **Quaker meeting** was strikingly simple, without ceremony or ritual. Any congregation member who felt moved to speak was able to participate. Within the meetinghouse, distinctions of wealth and social status were not recognized. Women as well as men were welcome to speak in the meeting. In their plain dress and in their refusal to remove their hats in the presence of their social "betters," Quakers demonstrated their belief that all men and women were equal.

Quaker egalitarianism influenced the political structure of Pennsylvania as well. All free male residents had the right to vote, and the legislature had full governing powers. William Penn, unlike his patron Charles II, did not interfere in the colony's lawmaking process. He honored the legislature's decisions even when they disturbed him. The political quarrels that developed in Pennsylvania's assembly actually shocked Penn, but his only action was to urge political leaders not to be "so noisy, and open, in your dissatisfactions."

Penn's land policy promoted a thriving colony of small, independent, landowning farmers. He wanted no politically powerful landlords and no economically dependent tenant farmers. He insisted that all land be purchased fairly from the Indians,

---

suffrage The right to vote.

William Penn English Quaker who founded the colony of Pennsylvania in 1681.

Quaker meeting A gathering of Quakers for reflection and silent or oral prayer.

and he strived for peaceful coexistence between Indian and English societies. Penn recruited settlers from outside England by publishing pamphlets that stressed the freedom and the economic opportunity available in Pennsylvania. Over eight thousand immigrants poured into the colony in the first four years. Many came from England, but Irish, Scottish, Welsh, French, Scandinavian, and German settlers came as well. To their English neighbors, German newcomers such as the Mennonites and Amish became known as the "Pennsylvania Dutch."

When William Penn died in 1717, he left behind a successful, dynamic colony. Philadelphia had already emerged as a great shipping and commercial center, rivaling Boston and New York City. But this success was achieved at some cost to Penn's original vision and to his Quaker principles. Most of the eighteenth-century settlers were not Quakers and had no strong commitment to egalitarianism, pacifism, or other Quaker principles. Penn's welcome to all immigrants ultimately jeopardized his holy experiment.

The Colonies of the Lower South

- What economic *constraints* led the colonists of the Carolinas and Georgia to *choose* to establish a slave labor system?
- What kind of society was the *outcome*?

In 1663, Charles II granted eight of his favorite supporters several million acres of land south of Virginia and stretching westward to the Pacific. Gratitude certainly influenced Charles's grant, but so did his desire to secure an English foothold in this region that was also claimed by France, Spain, and Holland (see Map 2.3).

The new proprietors named their colony Carolina. Their plan for Carolina was similar to Lord Baltimore's, and to this end the Fundamental Constitution of Carolina sought to create a society of great landowners, yeoman farmers, and serfs. But like the Calverts, the Carolina proprietors found out that few Englishmen and women were willing to travel 3,000 miles to become serfs. The proprietors soon had to abandon their scheme and to adopt the headright system used in Virginia and Maryland.

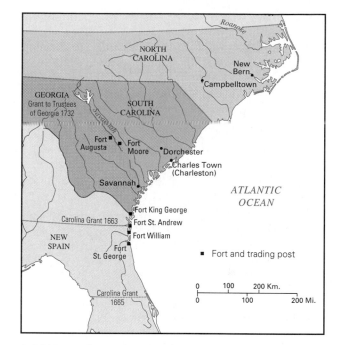

♦ **MAP 2.3 The Settlement of the Lower South**   This map shows the towns and fortifications of North Carolina, South Carolina, and Georgia as well as the overlapping claims by the Spanish and the English to the territory south and west of Fort King George. The many Georgia forts reflect that colony's role as a buffer state between rice-rich South Carolina and the Spanish troops stationed in Florida.

South Carolina

A fine natural harbor, fertile land, and the short distance to England's overcrowded possessions in the West Indies attracted settlers to Charles Town in southeastern Carolina. Charles Town (later Charleston) became the most important city in the southern colonies. The colony supported itself initially by trading with the local Indians for deerskins and for other Indians captured in tribal warfare. The deerskins were shipped to England, and the Indians were shipped to the Caribbean as slaves. Other colonists took advantage of the region's pine forests to produce **naval stores** such as tar, resin, pitch, and

> **naval stores**   Products such as timber, tar, resin, pitch, and turpentine, used in the building of wooden ships.

turpentine, which were used in maintaining wooden ships.

Carolinians tried, but unsuccessfully, to develop sugar cane, tobacco, silk, cotton, ginger, and olives as cash crops. Cattle raising, which the settlers learned from African slaves imported from the West Indies, was successful. Later, rice planting, another African borrowing, proved even more profitable. The rice grown in swampy lowlands by African slaves quickly made Carolina planters the richest English colonists on the mainland. In 1708 African-Americans outnumbered Europeans in the rice region for the first time.

In 1719, the Charleston planter elite wrested control of the southern half of Carolina from the original proprietors. In South Carolina, as it was now called, a small white elite dominated and controlled the lives of thousands of black slaves.

North Carolina

The northern region of Carolina around Albemarle Sound was economically unpromising and isolated. It was bordered by swamps to the north and south. A chain of barrier islands blocked access to ocean-going vessels. Despite all these *constraints*, settlers had begun drifting into the area about 1660. These poor farmers and freed white servants from Virginia were searching for unclaimed land and a fresh start. They grew tobacco and produced naval stores from the pine forests around them.

In 1729 the Albemarle colonists overthrew proprietary rule and officially separated from the southern part of the colony to form North Carolina. The *outcome* of these political changes was the creation of royal colonies in both South Carolina and North Carolina.

Georgia, the Last Colony

In 1732, a group of wealthy English social reformers received a charter for an unusual social experiment. They hoped to reform the lives of thousands of imprisoned English debtors by giving them a new start in America.

James Oglethorpe and his colleagues gave few political rights to their colonists in Georgia. Georgians were not given a representative assembly or a voice in the selection of political or military officers. The reformers established many other restrictions. For example, no Georgian was allowed to buy or sell property in the colony, and slave labor was banned. Clearly, Oglethorpe felt that the ideal colonist was a hardworking farmer of permanently modest means.

Oglethorpe, however, could find few English debtors whom he considered as "deserving poor." Thus Georgia actually filled with South Carolinians searching for new land and with English men and women of the middling ranks. These colonists soon challenged all the land and labor policies imposed on Georgians. They won the right to buy and sell land. They introduced slave labor even though the founders refused to lift the ban on slavery. In 1752, Oglethorpe and his friends abandoned their reform project and turned Georgia over to the king.

> **James Oglethorpe**   Englishman who established the colony of Georgia as an asylum for debtors.

SUMMARY

E xpectations
C onstraints
C hoices
O utcomes

The Virginia Company established Jamestown in *expectation* of profits from gold and silver. But the Virginians found no precious metals. *Constrained* for years by illness and the Powhatan Indians, they *chose* to cultivate tobacco. The *outcome* was a small coastal planter elite that ruled over a struggling frontier population.

Pilgrims sought a refuge from religious persecution. The Pilgrims faced two main *constraints* initially on the New England coast: discontent among the settlers and the cold. They *chose* cooperation by offering political participation to all adult males and by establishing peaceful relations with the local Indians. The *outcome* was a society that attracted other religious dissenters.

Maryland was also intended as a refuge for a religious minority, Catholics, but most of the immigrants were Protestants. Marylanders *chose* to cultivate tobacco through servant and slave labor as Virginians had done. One *outcome* was a tobacco-growing society throughout the Chesapeake.

The Puritan founders of New England *expected* to create a perfect religious society. Colonists were to obey biblical laws, and only church members were to participate in politics. The *outcome* of this experiment was not what the Puritans *expected*. No uniformity existed, and the colony had to exile its dissenters. The Puritan experiment ended in 1691, when King William issued a new Massachusetts charter.

The region between the Chesapeake and New England was colonized by the Dutch and later conquered by the English. Tolerant policies there led a diverse population to *choose* to settle in New York, New Jersey, and Pennsylvania.

In the Lower South, the proprietors of Carolina *expected* to create a medieval society, but settlers would not volunteer to live in such a colony. Carolinians eventually developed a thriving rice economy built on slave labor. The *outcome* in South Carolina was that a small planter elite dominated the culture. Georgia, the last of England's mainland colonies, was founded by philanthropists who *expected* to reform "worthy debtors." In Georgia too, labor supply *constraints* led to a reliance on slavery.

Suggested Readings

Ellis, John Harvard, ed. *The Works of Anne Bradstreet in Prose and Verse* (1867).

> Massachusetts colonist Anne Bradstreet left a rich collection of poems and letters that dealt with love, marriage, and religious faith. They provide an intimate look at family and community life in early New England.

Hawthorne, Nathaniel. *The Scarlet Letter* (1962).

> This novel, set in seventeenth-century Boston, is one of many works by this leading nineteenth-century American novelist that deals with Puritan morality.

Miller, Arthur. "The Crucible," in *Arthur Miller's Collected Plays* (1957).

> This play uses the Salem witch hunts to comment on events during the McCarthy period of the 1950s.

Vaughan, Alden T. *American Genesis: Captain John Smith and the Founding of Virginia* (1975).

> This is a fascinating biography of one of the earliest and most flamboyant English colonists.

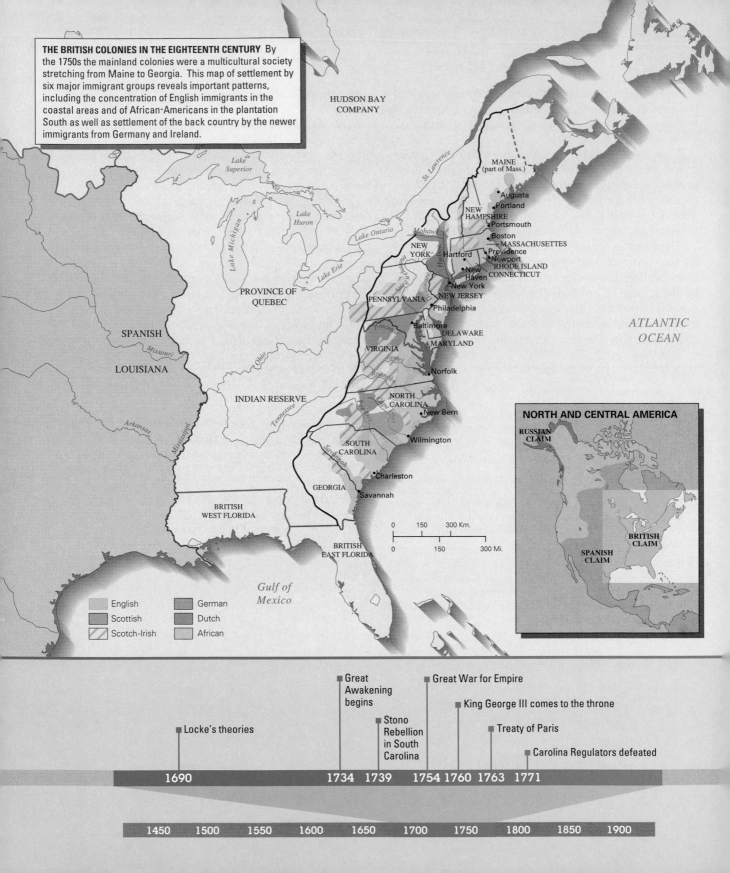

THE BRITISH COLONIES IN THE EIGHTEENTH CENTURY By the 1750s the mainland colonies were a multicultural society stretching from Maine to Georgia. This map of settlement by six major immigrant groups reveals important patterns, including the concentration of English immigrants in the coastal areas and of African-Americans in the plantation South as well as settlement of the back country by the newer immigrants from Germany and Ireland.

HUDSON BAY COMPANY

Lake Superior

Lake Michigan

Lake Huron

Lake Ontario

Lake Erie

St. Lawrence

MAINE (part of Mass.)

- Augusta
- Portland

NEW HAMPSHIRE
- Portsmouth
- Boston
MASSACHUSETTES
- Providence
- Newport
RHODE ISLAND
CONNECTICUT

Mohawk

NEW YORK

Hartford

New Haven

New York

PROVINCE OF QUEBEC

SPANISH

LOUISIANA

Missouri

Ohio

Tennessee

Mississippi

Arkansas

INDIAN RESERVE

PENNSYLVANIA
- Philadelphia

NEW JERSEY

Potomac
- Baltimore
DELAWARE
MARYLAND

VIRGINIA

James

Roanoke
- Norfolk

NORTH CAROLINA
- New Bern

SOUTH CAROLINA
- Wilmington

Savannah

GEORGIA
- Charleston
Savannah

BRITISH WEST FLORIDA

BRITISH EAST FLORIDA

Gulf of Mexico

ATLANTIC OCEAN

0   150   300 Km.
0   150   300 Mi.

NORTH AND CENTRAL AMERICA

RUSSIAN CLAIM

SPANISH CLAIM

BRITISH CLAIM

English
Scottish
Scotch-Irish
German
Dutch
African

Locke's theories

Great Awakening begins

Stono Rebellion in South Carolina

Great War for Empire

King George III comes to the throne

Treaty of Paris

Carolina Regulators defeated

1690   1734 1739   1754 1760 1763 1771

1450   1500   1550   1600   1650   1700   1750   1800   1850   1900

The British Colonies in the Eighteenth Century, 1700–1763

The British Transatlantic Communities of Trade

- What regional differences in commercial activity would someone traveling from Maine to Georgia in the eighteenth century *expect* to find?

- In which region did new immigrants seem to have the best economic *choices?*

Life and Work in Colonial Society

- What *choices* and *constraints* shaped family organization in the Chesapeake and in New England?

- How did the *constraints* indentured servants faced differ from those faced by African-American slaves, and how did each group resist its *constraints?*

Reason and Religion in Eighteenth-Century Colonial Society

- What political and personal *expectations* arose from Enlightenment philosophy?

- What were the significant *outcomes* of the Great Awakening?

Government and Politics in Great Britain's Growing Colonies

- What *constraints* did the governors face in wielding royal power in the colonies?

- What was the *outcome* of the struggle for power between the colonial assemblies and their governors?

The Empires of America

- What *constraints* did the British, French, Spanish, and American Indians place on one another in North America?

- What were the most common *outcomes* of their rivalries?

INTRODUCTION

E xpectations
C onstraints
C hoices
O utcomes

In his *Letters from an American Farmer,* published in 1782, the Frenchman Michel Crèvecoeur wrote that he *expected* America to be a "smiling country" with "fair cities, substantial villages, extensive fields." He was not disappointed after spending a decade in rural New York. In his *Letters,* Crèvecoeur painted a positive portrait of British America's ethnic and racial diversity, its regional economies, its tradition of representative government, and its daily life. Crèvecoeur was enthusiastic about this new society being brought into existence by "the American, this new man."

Crèvecoeur's praise of American society had little impact on the opinions of British citizens, who seldom admired colonial society. On the contrary, members of Parliament *expected* insubordination from colonial legislatures, violations of trade regulations from colonial merchants, and social disruptions from quarrelsome colonists. Most affluent Europeans continued to view the colonists as misfits and hayseeds, struggling to survive on a violent frontier.

Europeans who faced the *constraints* of poverty, religious persecution, or political oppression in their native lands were far more likely to share Crèvecoeur's enthusiasm. Thousands of them *chose* to emigrate to the British mainland colonies. To them, America was a haven.

The America they found was a society with distinct regional economies and local cultures, each shaped by differing *constraints.* In New England, where land and climate limited agriculture, the people had created a commercially oriented, bustling society. Ambitious shopkeepers, wealthy merchants, impoverished widows, and struggling dockworkers filled New England towns and seaport cities. In the more fertile middle colonies, comfortable family farms were the rule, although vast estates with tenant farmers still existed in New York. In the Chesapeake and in the Lower South, a planter aristocracy based on tobacco and rice production dominated. This region's extensive slave population contradicted Crèvecoeur's portrait of boundless opportunity in America. In the backcountry subsistence farmers struggled to feed themselves and fend off American Indians. The *outcome* of these regional differences was visible in everything from the character of the local political and social elites to the daily patterns of work and family life.

These regional differences were also shaped by the *constraints* of Great Britain's imperial policies and rivalries with France and Spain. *Choices* made in the halls of Parliament and in the private chambers of European monarchs had *outcomes* on the docks and on the battlefields of North America. Crèvecoeur's "new man" was, after all, a member of a complex transatlantic community.

The British Transatlantic Communities of Trade

• What regional differences in commercial activity would someone traveling from Maine to Georgia in the eighteenth century *expect* to find?

• In which region did new immigrants seem to have the best economic *choices?*

British America did not have a single, unified economy. The mainland colonies consisted of five distinctive regional economies: four along the Atlantic coast and a **subsistence** society along the western edge of settlement. To the south, the sugar islands of the Caribbean made up a sixth regional economy.

> **subsistence**   Supported by the minimum amount of food and other resources necessary to sustain life.

Regions of Commerce

The sugar-producing islands of the West Indies were the brightest jewels in the British colonial crown. Spain had first laid claim to these islands, but by the eighteenth century the British flag flew over St. Kitts, Barbados, Nevis, Montserrat, and Jamaica. On each island, British plantation owners built fabulous fortunes on the sugar and molasses produced by African slaves. While the absentee planters lived in luxury in England, black slaves lived and died—in staggering numbers—on the islands.

Few mainland colonists enjoyed the wealth of the "Sugar Interest." Still, the planters of South Carolina and Georgia amassed considerable fortunes by growing rice in the coastal lowlands. Planters profited also by growing indigo, which was used to make a blue dye. Like the sugar planters, Carolina and Georgia rice growers made their fortunes from the forced labor of African slaves, but the mainland planters never became permanent **absentee landowners.**

Tobacco continued to dominate the economy of the eighteenth-century Chesapeake. Beginning about 1700, however, overproduction locally and Mediterranean competition caused tobacco prices to fall. Many **tidewater** planters chose crop diversification. They began producing wheat and other grains for export. One *outcome* was a westward shift in tobacco production to the area along the Potomac, the James River Valley, and the **piedmont.** Tobacco remained the biggest export of the mainland colonies.

The New England regional economy depended far less than the Lower South and the Chesapeake did on Britain as an export market. Except in the Connecticut River Valley where tobacco was grown, rocky soil *constrained* New Englanders from large-scale farming. They *chose* therefore to concentrate on fishing, logging, shipbuilding, and trading. These colonists found a market for dried fish and timber in the West Indies, but New England's greatest profits came from its extensive shipping network. New Englanders carried colonial exports across the

---

absentee landowner   An estate owner who collects profits through farming or rent but does not live on the land or help cultivate it.

tidewater area   Low coastal land drained by tidal streams.

piedmont   Land lying at the foot of a mountain range.

Atlantic and distributed foreign goods and British-manufactured products to the colonies. The regional emphasis on shipping made New Englanders the rivals of British merchants rather than useful sources of profit for the mother country.

The middle colonies of New York, New Jersey, and Pennsylvania combined trade and farming. The heart of the region's commerce was wheat production. These colonists benefited from the steady rise of wheat prices during the eighteenth century. Trade was equally important in this mixed regional economy. Ships carried grain and flour as exports and brought back British manufactured goods and luxury items through the region's two major port cities, New York and Philadelphia. By 1775 Philadelphia was the second-largest city in the British empire.

Inland from the coastal farms, towns, and cities of these four established economic regions was a sparsely settled backcountry that was farmed by European immigrants, former servants, or landless sons from older communities. These settlers struggled for survival. Even if they could grow a marketable crop, they lacked the means to get that crop to market. The *outcome* of these *constraints* was a subsistence economy that ran from Maine to inland Carolina.

The Cords of Commercial Empire

Colonists traded with many European nations and their colonies. Salt, wine, and spices reached colonial tables from southern Europe. Sugar, rum, molasses, and cotton came to them from the West Indies. But the deepest and broadest channels in the transatlantic trade were those that connected the mother country and the colonies. The British purchased over half of all the crops and furs that the colonists produced for market and supplied the colonists with 90 percent of their imported goods.

The British mainland colonies were also bound to each other by trade, despite a deserved reputation for endless rivalries. New Englanders might exchange insults with Pennsylvanians, but in the shops and on the wharfs, Pennsylvania flour and Massachusetts mackerel changed hands in a lively and profitable commerce. Domestic trade was greater in volume, although lower in value, than all foreign trade in this eighteenth-century world.

Life and Work in Colonial Society

- What *choices* and *constraints* shaped family organization in the Chesapeake and in New England?
- How did the *constraints* indentured servants faced differ from those faced by African-American slaves?

Visitors to eighteenth-century America might *expect* to see physical differences as they traveled from the carefully laid-out towns of New England into the isolated rural worlds of the plantation South. If they were observant, they would see cultural differences as well. Although political loyalties and economic exchanges linked the colonists, they lived and worked in societies that had some striking differences.

New England Society and Culture

New England was a society of small farms and villages and, increasingly in the eighteenth century, of cities. The early colonists had attempted to recreate the village architecture they had left behind in East Anglia, England. Thus their houses were typically clustered near a village green or common pasture. Most farms and farmhouses were within walking distance of this village center, where the church was built. The design of the New England town put a natural limit on its size. As town population grew, the only farmlands left were those that were a long walk from the village center. The owners of these distant farms often chose to create a new town for themselves, a practice New Englanders called "hiving off."

New England was also a society of families. Its settlers came in family groups, creating a balance between men and women that persisted throughout the colonial period. The temperate climate, the good drinking water, and an adequate diet made early New England an extremely healthy place for Europeans, healthier than England itself. A newly married couple in their early twenties could *expect* to have a family of from five to seven children and to live into their sixties. Life expectancy was shorter for urban New Englanders.

Puritans spoke of the family as a "little commonwealth," a building block out of which the larger society was constructed. Obedience was a central family value. Because Puritans believed that sinfulness and disobedience were the twin results of **Original Sin,** breaking a child's will was a necessary step toward that child's salvation. Puritan society actively reinforced a parent's right to demand respect and a child's duty to obey.

Puritan society exerted considerable pressure on women to marry and produce a family. In marriage, a woman was *expected* to submit willingly to a man's rule. As Puritan clergy counseled, "Wives are part of the House and Family, and ought to be under a Husband's Government: they should Obey their own Husbands." At the same time, a husband should rule without "rigour, haughtiness, harshness, severity; but with the greatest love, gentleness, kindness, tenderness."

A wife was *expected* to be an industrious, economical helpmate to her husband. She was to become skilled at a variety of essential tasks in an agricultural society: spinning yarn, sewing, cooking, baking, picking and preserving fruit, milking cows, churning butter, setting cheeses, slaughtering and butchering farm animals, and curing meat. Throughout the colonial period, New England women shared their work in a neighborly fashion, assisting each other in childbirth or in times of sickness and need.

In New England and elsewhere in the British world, a woman lost most of her legal rights when she married. Under British law she was considered under the guardianship of her husband. She no longer had the right to buy or to sell property, to sue or be sued. She could gain such legal rights only through special contracts made with her husband. Whether married or single, New England women could not vote or hold political office. Although this restriction held throughout the British colonies, the stable, **patriarchal** family of New England made Puritan women more dependent than white women of the colonial Chesapeake.

The growing importance of commerce in New England produced a shift from a Puritan to what became known as a "Yankee" culture in the eighteenth century. Economic competition and the pursuit of wealth replaced older, communal values. Still, certain traditions remained, including the concern for the creation and maintenance of public institutions, such as schools and colleges. As early as 1647, the Massachusetts government had ordered towns with fifteen families or more to support an elementary school through local taxes. Literacy was consequently widespread, even among women. In 1636, in the Bay Colony's first decade of existence, Harvard College was established to educate the sons of the local elite. In 1701, Yale College was established in Connecticut. Whether Puritan or Yankee, New England sustained local newspapers, publishers, and a vibrant intellectual life.

In the eighteenth century, the scarcity of land in the oldest communities sent younger sons whose prospects for inheriting land were slim or nonexistent away from their localities in search of opportunities. They ventured to relatively undeveloped areas of New England such as Maine and New Hampshire, or to the commercial cities of the region. Inequalities of wealth and political power increased, as poor widows and landless young men sought employment and sometimes public charity in Boston or Salem. Aware that good land was scarce, eighteenth-century immigrants generally avoided New England.

Planters, Servants, and Slaves

Tobacco had set the rhythms of work and play in the Chesapeake ever since the time of John Rolfe. Planting, tending, harvesting, and drying tobacco took almost ten months of the year. In the short period between Christmas and the beginning of the new cycle of planting, Chesapeake planters caught up on neglected farm chores and on socializing. These winter weeks often led to quick courtships and marriages.

Tobacco determined where a planter lived and how long he stayed in one spot. As the crop exhausted the soil, the plantation family and its servants moved on to new land. Well into the eighteenth century, few planters placed much stock in building permanent homes or creating social institutions such as schools. They willingly sacrificed community life to the demands of their staple crop.

Original Sin   In Christian doctrine, the condition of sin that is shared by all human beings because of Adam's first act of disobedience in the Garden of Eden.

patriarchal   Ruled by a patriarch—that is, by a man who is the head of a household or a clan.

Choosing Between Prison and Servitude

James Revel

This illustration of a young man shackled in a leg brace and handcuffs in a bare prison cell in 1728 suggests why James Revel chose to serve his sentence as an indentured servant rather than in jail. Marshalsea Prison, 18th-c. print. Fotomas Index Picture Library.

James Revel was one of the thousands of impoverished men and women who made their way to London in the 1690s in search of work. But in the great city, Revel found little that gave him hope. Unemployment was high, competition for wages was fierce, and modest *expectations* of a decent life had given way to a desperate struggle to survive. Many of these landless, homeless, and poverty-stricken people turned to crime. James Revel made the same *choice* and was caught and imprisoned. English authorities offered him one more *choice:* he could sell himself and his labor for several years to a stranger in the colonies, or he could serve his long term in prison.

Revel was only one of thousands who had to make this fateful decision, but the fact that he recorded his *choice*—and that this record has survived—makes him unique. James Revel tells his story in a remarkable autobiographical poem, which he wrote after surviving his term

Cheap and available labor was also sacrificed to tobacco. White **indentured servants** made the sacrifices for most of the seventeenth century. For thousands of landless and jobless Englishmen, Maryland and Virginia held out one last, desperate *choice* (see Individual Choices: James Revel). Anyone who was young, single, and moderately healthy could sign away from four to seven years of his or her life to labor in the Chesapeake tobacco fields. Planters preferred young male adults, but they were willing to take women and children if necessary.

The lure for indentured servants was the chance to own land when their service ended. (Freed ser-

vants were granted fifty acres of land.) Over three-quarters of the Chesapeake immigrant population came as indentured servants. A shocking number did not survive their term of service. Disease, malnutrition, and the grueling work killed four out of every ten who came to the Chesapeake. Planters

> **indentured servant** A person who signed a contract, called an indenture, agreeing to serve an employer for a fixed length of time; when the time was up, the employer released the person and gave him or her some land or money.

as an indentured servant in Virginia. He describes his life of crime, his capture, and his experiences in the Chesapeake tobacco colony. Whatever *expectations* and fears the 17-year-old boy had, nothing appears to have prepared him for the reality of a servant's life in America. He wrote about his arrival in Virginia:

> At length a grim old man unto me came
> He ask'd my trade, and likewise ask'd my Name:
> I told him I a Tin-man was by trade
> And not quite eighteen years of age I said.
> At last to my new master's house I came,
> All the town of Wicoccomoco call'd by name,
> Where my European clothes were took from me,
> Which never after I again could see.
> A canvas shirt and trowsers that they gave,
> With a hop-sack frock in which I was to slave:
> No shoes or stockings had I for to wear,
> Thus dressd into the field I next must go,
> Amongst tobacco plants all day to hoe,
> At day break in the morn our work began,
> And so held to the setting of the Sun.

Revel worked beside African slaves, whom he found more sympathetic and kind than the countryman who was his master. He describes the *constraints* that they shared in common:

> We and the Negroes both alike did fare,
> Of work and food we had an equal share;
> But in a piece of ground we call our own,
> The food we eat first by ourselves were sown,
> Six days we slave for our master's good,
> The seventh day is to produce our food.
> And if we offer for to run away,
> For every hour we must serve a day:
> Much hardships then in deed I did endure,
> No dog was ever nursed so I'm sure,
> More pity the poor negroe slaves bestowed
> Than my inhuman brutal master showed.

Revel was in his thirties when his term of service ended. A free man, he *chose* to return to England rather than remain to seek his fortune in the colonies. He clearly hoped that the *outcome* of his own *choices* in life would serve as a lesson to others:

> At length my fourteen years expired quite,
> Which fill'd my very soul with fine delight
> To think I should no longer there remain,
> But to old England once return again.
> My country men take warning e'er too late,
> Lest you should share my hard unhappy fate;
> Altho' but little crimes you here have done,
> Consider seven or fourteen years to come.

saw no disadvantage in working a servant to death as long as replacements were plentiful.

In the early years, a male servant who survived the years of exhausting labor could *expect* to become a planter himself. A few former servants even joined the ranks of the tobacco elite. But as the century passed, opportunity narrowed. In 1681, Maryland eliminated the grant of land that had been the most desirable part of a servant's "freedom dues." And in both Chesapeake colonies powerful planters owned the best coastal and riverfront lands. Over the years, the sons of these planters married the daughters of the elite, creating a permanent planter class.

One of the most significant *outcomes* of the preference for male workers was an unbalanced sex ratio in the seventeenth-century Chesapeake. In some areas there were six males to every female. Marriage and family were an impossibility for many male colonists.

Family structure was consequently very different in the Chesapeake. Men married late in life if they married at all; women were pressured to marry as soon as possible after they had reached puberty. Few marriages lasted more than a decade, for the average life expectancy of women was 40 years and of men 50 years. The *outcome* of frequent remarriages could be a complex household of stepchildren and half-siblings. In one seventeenth-century family, ten children were the result of marriages among seven adults. Another *outcome* was that women exercised more authority within the family than did white women in other regions. Husbands who did not *expect* to live to see their children grow up frequently left the care and management of their estates to their widows.

A child born in the Chesapeake rarely grew up under the care of both parents. From one-half to three-quarters had lost a father or mother before their twenty-first birthday. By the eighteenth century, conditions of life in the Chesapeake had improved, and the sex ratio had grown more balanced. The *outcome* was the male-headed **nuclear family** familiar to most English men and women.

By the 1680s, improved economic conditions in England halted the steady flow of indentured servants to the Chesapeake tobacco fields. At about the same time, the English established their control over the African slave trade. The *outcome* was a dramatic shift in the tobacco labor force from white servants to enslaved Africans. Although Africans had been brought to Virginia as early as 1619, black workers remained few until late in the seventeenth century. The legal difference between black and white servants was vague until the 1660s. Although some black servants were then being held for life terms, their children were still considered free. In 1662, Virginia made slavery a hereditary condition by declaring that "all children born in this country shall be held bond or free according to the condition of the mother." This natural increase of slaves was supplemented by slaves imported by England's Royal African Company. By 1700, 13 percent of the Chesapeake population was black. At the end of the colonial period, 40 percent of Virginians were of African-American descent.

The African-American culture of the Chesapeake grew slowly during the eighteenth century. Until the 1720s, many slaves worked alone or in small groups of two or three on a tobacco farm. This isolation made both marriage and the creation of a distinctive slave community almost impossible. Even on larger plantations, the steady arrival of newly imported slaves made it difficult for African-Americans to create their own culture during the first decades of the eighteenth century. Slowly, however, these involuntary immigrants from different African societies,

♦ This drawing shows the interior of the slave ship *Vigilante*. On board, 227 male slaves were confined to a 37- by 22-foot room, and 120 female slaves were crowded into a 14- by 19-foot room. The ceilings were less than 5 feet high. Although this is an 1822 slave ship, captured off the coast of Africa by the British navy, the conditions shown here differed little from those described in the eighteenth century by slaves and by commentators on slavery. *Courtesy, American Antiquarian Society.*

speaking different languages, practicing different religions, and surviving under the oppressive conditions of slavery, created a slave community that wove together African and European traditions into an African-American culture.

By the eighteenth century, the Chesapeake colonies were a biracial society in which African-Americans and European-Americans lived with strikingly different *expectations* and *constraints*. Planters with many slaves could *expect* to live well off their tobacco crops. Unable to compete with this planter elite, poorer Virginians and Marylanders moved west. New immigrants, merchants, and skilled craftspeople avoided the Chesapeake because of the lack of opportunities there and competition from slave labor. Few towns or cities developed in the region. The Chesapeake remained a rural society, dominated by a slaveowning class

nuclear family   A family unit consisting of a mother and father and their children.

made prosperous by the labor of African-American men, women, and children.

If tobacco provided a comfortable life for an eighteenth-century planter, rice provided a luxurious one. The Lower South, too, was a plantation society, dominated by the rice growers of coastal Carolina and Georgia. This planter elite concentrated their social life in elegant Charleston, where they moved each summer to avoid the heat, humidity, and unhealthy environment of their lowland plantations. With its beautiful townhouses, theaters, and parks, Charleston was the only truly cosmopolitan city of the South.

By the mid-eighteenth century, 60 percent of the South Carolina population was African-American. These slaves were concentrated on large plantations, where they had limited contact with white society. This isolation allowed them to develop their own creole, or native, culture, including local languages that mixed basic English with a variety of African tongues. On the Sea Islands off the coast of Georgia and South Carolina, the local language of Gullah could be heard until the end of the nineteenth century.

For many slaves, the creation of a distinctive culture represented a form of resistance to slavery. African-Americans also *chose* other ways to show their resistance. Slaves challenged orders, broke tools, pretended sickness, stole supplies, and damaged property. Slaves of all ages ran away to the woods for a day or two or to the slave quarters of a neighboring plantation. African-Americans understood the odds against escape and *chose* actions that undermined the slave system rather than risk the price of rebellion.

Even so, white masters feared slave revolts. Rumors of slave revolts were thick in the 1720s in Virginia and South Carolina, although most of these plots existed only in the planters' imaginations. Despite the odds against success, some rebellions did occur. The most famous, the **Stono Rebellion,** began near the Stono River, just south of Charleston, in 1739. About twenty slaves seized guns and killed several planter families. Other slaves joined the rebels as they headed south toward Spanish Florida and killed other white settlers. The Carolina militias, however, soon caught up to the rebels and surrounded them. Ultimately every rebel was killed or put to death. Although the retaliation against the rebels was quick and bloody, the Stono Rebellion struck deep fear into white planters for a long time thereafter.

The Urban Culture of the Middle Colonies

Small family wheat farms earned Pennsylvania its reputation as the "best poor man's country." Although tenant farmers and hired laborers were not unknown in eastern Pennsylvania, their numbers were much fewer than in neighboring New York, where great estates along the Hudson River monopolized much of the colony's best farmland.

The region's distinguishing feature, however, was the dynamism of its two major cities, New York and Philadelphia. By 1770, Philadelphia's forty thousand residents made it the second-largest city in the British empire, after London. In the same year, twenty-five thousand people crowded onto the tip of Manhattan Island in New York.

The attractions of a colonial city were powerful to a farmer's daughter or son. Cities offered a range of occupations and experiences that simply did not exist in the countryside. Young men could seek training as **apprentices** in scores of trades ranging from blacksmithing to goldsmithing. The poorest might find work on the docks or as servants, or they might go to sea.

Young women had more limited *choices* because few trades were open to them. Some might become dressmakers or **milliners,** but domestic service or prostitution were more likely *choices.* A widow or an unmarried woman who had a little money could open a shop, set up a tavern, or run a boarding house.

Slavery was not common in New England or on the family farms of the middle colonies, but slaves were used on New York City's docks as manual laborers. The city also attracted free African-American men and women who eked out a living as

---

Stono Rebellion   Slave rebellion that occurred in South Carolina in 1739; it prompted the state to pass harsh laws governing the movement of slaves and the capture of runaways.

apprentice   A person bound by legal agreement to work for an employer for a specific length of time in exchange for instruction in a trade, art, or business.

milliner   A maker or designer of hats.

laborers, servants, and sailors. Only perhaps 5 percent of all colonial African-Americans were free.

Life in the Backcountry

The population of the mainland colonies jumped from 225,000 in 1688 to over 2.5 million in 1775 (see chapter opener map). Natural increase accounted for much of this growth, for over half of the colonists were under age 16 in 1775. But almost 650,000 white immigrants risked hunger, thirst, frost, heat, dampness, fear, and misery on the transatlantic voyage to start life over in eighteenth-century America. The majority found their way to the backcountry of the colonies.

The **Scots-Irish** and German Protestants who fled persecution by the tens of thousands in the first half of the eighteenth century saw their best opportunities in western Pennsylvania, Virginia's Shenandoah Valley, and the Carolina backcountry. Those were the favored destinations as well of the younger sons of the tidewater Chesapeake. For descendants of Puritan settlers, western New York and the sparsely settled regions of New Hampshire, Vermont, and Maine beckoned. Many of these settlers were squatters who cleared a few acres of a promising piece of land and lay claim to it by their presence. A backcountry family was likely to move several times before settling down.

Backcountry settlers frequently clashed with American Indians and the established political powers of their own colony over Indian policy. Eighteenth-century colonial governments preferred diplomacy to military action, but western settlers wanted Indians pushed out of the way. Even when there was bloodshed between settlers and Indians, easterners were reluctant to spend tax money to provide protection to the inland region. Consequently, western settlers sometimes took matters into their own hands, as they had in Bacon's Rebellion. The revolt by Pennsylvania's **Paxton Boys** was the most dramatic episode of vigilante action in the eighteenth century.

Pennsylvania's Quaker-dominated government *expected* settlers to live peacefully with local Indian tribes. Scots-Irish settlers did not share this *expectation*. When Indians responded to their provocations, the Scots-Irish demanded but did not get protection from the government. In 1763, frustrated settlers from Paxton, Pennsylvania, attacked a village of Conestoga Indians who had done nothing to these white colonists. Hundreds of colonists from the Pennsylvania frontier chose to join the Paxton Boys' dubious cause and marched on Philadelphia to press their demands for an aggressive Indian policy. The popular Benjamin Franklin met the Paxton Boys on the outskirts of the city and negotiated a truce. As an *outcome* of this vigilante uprising, Pennsylvania's government abandoned its long commitment to peaceful relationships with the Indians and agreed to establish a bounty for Indian scalps.

In South Carolina the conflict between old and new settlements similarly led to vigilante action; in North Carolina it resulted in a brief civil war. South Carolina's lowland planters refused to provide government for the backcountry. Although settlers in western South Carolina paid their taxes, their counties had no courts. The government sent no sheriffs either, allowing outlaws to prey on these communities. In the 1760s, backcountry settlers chose to "regulate" their own affairs. These **Regulators** pursued and punished backcountry outlaws, dispensing justice without the aid of courts or judges.

The Regulator movement in North Carolina was organized against corrupt local officials who had been appointed by the colony's slaveholding elite. These officials awarded contracts for building roads to their friends, charged exorbitant fees to register deeds and surveys, and set high poll taxes on voters. The legislature ignored backcountry demands for the removal of these officials. The *outcome* was a taxpayers' rebellion. The governor squelched this rebellion by leading eastern militiamen into battle near the Alamance River in 1771. The governor's army of twelve hundred easily defeated the two thousand poorly armed Regulators. He subsequently hanged six of the Regulator leaders. The

---

Scots-Irish   Scottish settlers in northern Ireland, many of whom migrated to the colonies in the eighteenth century.

Paxton Boys   Settlers from Paxton, Pennsylvania, who massacred Conestoga Indians in 1763 and then marched on Philadelphia to demand that the colonial government provide better defense against the Indians.

Regulators   Frontier settlers in the Carolinas who protested their lack of representation in the colonial governments; they were suppressed by the government militia in North Carolina in 1771.

conflict between Regulators and colonial governments left a bitter legacy for decades to come.

Reason and Religion in Eighteenth-Century Colonial Society

- What political and personal *expectations* arose from Enlightenment philosophy?
- What were the significant *outcomes* of the Great Awakening?

Trade routes, language, and custom tied the eighteenth-century colonial world to parent societies across the Atlantic. The flow of ideas and religious beliefs helped sustain a transatlantic community.

The Impact of the Enlightenment

At the end of the seventeenth century, a new intellectual movement called the **Enlightenment** arose in Europe. Enlightenment thinkers argued that reason, or rational thinking, rather than divine revelation, tradition, intuition, or established authority, was the true basis for reliable knowledge and human progress. The French thinkers known as *philosophes*—Voltaire, Rousseau, Diderot, Buffon, and Montesquieu, to name a few—were the central figures of the Enlightenment. These philosophers, political theorists, and scientists believed that nature could provide for all human wants and that human nature was basically good rather than flawed by Original Sin. Humans, they insisted, were capable of making progress toward a perfect society if they studied nature, unlocked its secrets, and carefully nurtured the best human qualities in their children. This belief in progress became a central Enlightenment theme.

The colonial elite had the best access to these Enlightenment ideas. They were particularly drawn to the religious philosophy of deism and the political theory of the social contract. **Deism** was the belief that God had created a rational universe that operated in accordance with logical, natural laws. Deists denied the existence of any miracles after Creation and rejected the value of prayer in this rational universe. Deism appealed to Benjamin Franklin, George Washington, Thomas Jefferson,

and other colonists who were intensely interested in science and scientific methods.

The most widely accepted Enlightenment ideas in the colonies were those of the seventeenth-century English political theorist John Locke. In his *Two Treatises on Government* (1690), Locke argued that human beings are born with certain natural rights that cannot be given or taken away. These included the rights of life, liberty, and property. Locke believed that government originated in a **social contract** designed to protect the people's natural rights against the powerful. Government is thus founded by the consent of the people and represents their interests through an elected legislature. Locke went on to say that the people have a right to rebel if government violates their rights.

Religion and Religious Institutions

Eighteenth-century Americans became increasingly tolerant of religious differences as Protestant sects proliferated in the colonies. Colonists began to see religious toleration in a practical light. Toleration did not extend to everyone. No colony, even Maryland, allowed Catholics to vote or to hold elective office. And religious tolerance did not mean the separation of church and state. **Established churches,** supported by public taxes, were the rule in the southern colonies and in Massachusetts and Connecticut.

The Great Awakening

Despite the spread of deism and religious toleration, one of the most notable religious developments in eighteenth-century America was the Great

---

Enlightenment   An eighteenth-century philosophical movement that emphasized the pursuit of knowledge through reason and refused to accept ideas on the strength of religion or tradition alone.

deism   The belief that God created the universe in such a way that no divine intervention was necessary for its continued operation.

social contract   An agreement among members of an organized society or between the government and the governed, which defines and limits the rights and duties of each.

established church   The official church of a nation or state.

♦ The Great Awakening divided congregations, spurred the growth of new churches, sparked heated debate among ministers, and prompted the establishment of several new colleges in the colonies. The revivalists included many persuasive speakers, but the most charismatic of them all was a young English Methodist. George Whitefield moved hundreds of men and women to tears and cries of emotion with every sermon. *"George Whitefield" by John Wollaston, © National Portrait Gallery, London.*

Awakening, a religious revival that swept through the colonies. **Charismatic** preachers denounced the materialism and commercialism they saw growing around them and called for a revival of basic Calvinist belief.

The **Great Awakening** was based on a new approach to preaching. Ministers "awakened" their audiences to the awful condition of their plight as sinners by preaching fiery sermons that vividly depicted the fate of those who were doomed to the fires of hell. These awakeners condemned ministers who delivered dry, literary sermons for their "cold" preaching. This new style of preaching first appeared in New Jersey and Pennsylvania in the 1720s.

Probably the most famous of the awakeners was **Jonathan Edwards,** a Congregational minister who began a local revival in Northampton, Massachusetts, in 1734. He roused terror in his listeners with such powerful sermons as "Sinners in the Hands of an Angry God." Edwards compared mortals to spi-

ders, dangling by a fragile thread over the deadly hellfire. The revival sparked by people like Edwards spread rapidly throughout the colonies, carried from town to town by wandering ministers.

The greatest awakener of all, however, was **George Whitefield,** an Anglican minister who came to the colonies in 1740. Crowds gathered to hear the young preacher wherever he went, from Charleston to Maine. Often the audience grew so large that Whitefield had to finish his service in a nearby field. His impact was electric. "Hearing him preach gave me a heart wound," wrote one colonist. Even Benjamin Franklin, America's most committed deist, was moved by Whitefield's sermons. By the end of a Whitefield sermon his audience was "crying to God for mercy."

The Great Awakening provoked tension and conflict. Many ministers were angered by the criticisms of their preaching and launched a counterattack against the revivalists. Bitter fights within congregations and **denominations** developed over preaching styles and the worship service. Congregations split, and minority groups hurriedly formed new churches. Many awakened believers left their own denominations entirely, joining the Baptists, the Methodists, or the Presbyterians. Antirevivalists sometimes left their strife-ridden churches and became Anglicans. These religious conflicts became intertwined with other, secular issues. For example, poor, "awakened" colonists expressed hostility to their rich neighbors through a religious vocabulary that condemned luxury, dancing, and gambling.

---

charismatic   Having a spiritual power or personal quality that stirs enthusiasm and devotion in large numbers of people.

Great Awakening   Series of religious revivals characterized by fiery preaching that swept over the American colonies during the second quarter of the eighteenth century.

Jonathan Edwards   Congregational minister whose sermons threatening sinners with damnation helped begin the Great Awakening.

George Whitefield   British evangelist in the Great Awakening; he drew huge crowds during his preaching tours through the colonies.

denomination   A group of religious congregations that accept the same doctrines and are united under a single name.

The Great Awakening did produce some positive *outcomes*. The complicated theological arguments between Old Lights (those who opposed the revivalism of the Awakening) and awakeners led the revivalists to found new colleges, including Rutgers, Brown, Princeton, and Dartmouth, to prepare their clergy. One of the most important *outcomes* of the Great Awakening was also one of its least *expected*. All of the debate, argument, and resistance to authority promoted a belief that protest was acceptable, not just in religious matters but in political matters as well.

Government and Politics in Great Britain's Growing Colonies

- What *constraints* did the governors face in wielding royal power in the colonies?
- What was the *outcome* of the struggle for power between the colonial assemblies and their governors?

From a British perspective, colonial governments had been created largely for the convenience of handling the day-to-day affairs of a colony. The real authority for governing still lay in Great Britain. In the eighteenth century, however, colonial assemblies became increasingly powerful at the expense of colonial governors, who represented the king or the proprietor, and increased their control over local matters.

Imperial Institutions and Policies

In 1696, the British government reorganized its colonial administration and formed what became known as the Board of Trade. On paper, the Board of Trade had responsibility for most aspects of colonial administration. In practice, it was simply an advisory board, *expected* to observe and to make recommendations to many offices and agencies. Authority over the colonies thus remained divided. For example, an admiralty board, not the Board of Trade, had the authority to enforce trade regulations.

Parliament's policy for colonial administration in the eighteenth century was largely one of **benign neglect.** This meant that most regulations would be enforced loosely, if at all, as long as the colonies

remained loyal in military and economic matters. As long as colonial raw materials continued to flow into British hands and the colonists continued to rely on British manufactured goods, benign neglect suited the *expectations* of the British government.

Benign neglect did not mean that the colonists were free to do exactly as they pleased. Intense political conflicts had arisen in the first half of the eighteenth century over the *constraints* royal authority placed on the power of the colonial assemblies.

Local Colonial Government

The mainland colonies were strikingly similar in the structure and operation of their governments. Each had a governor, usually appointed by the king or proprietor. (The governor was elected in Connecticut and Rhode Island.) Each colony had a council, usually appointed by the governor, though sometimes elected by the assembly, that served as an advisory body to the governor. Each also had an elected representative assembly with lawmaking and taxing powers.

The governor's powers were impressive in theory. He alone could call the legislature into session, and he had the power to dismiss it. He could veto any act that it passed. He had the sole power to appoint and dismiss all government officials. He made all land grants, oversaw all aspects of colonial trade, and conducted diplomatic negotiations with the Indians. He was commander-in-chief of the colony's military forces. Armed with such extensive powers, the man who sat in the British colonial governor's seat ought to have been obeyed.

On closer look, however, much of the governor's authority evaporated. First, he was not free to act on his own because he was bound by a set of instructions written back in Great Britain by the Board of Trade. Second, the governor's skills and experience were often limited. Few men in the prime of their careers wanted to be sent 3,000 miles from Great Britain to the provinces. Governorships therefore

> **benign neglect**   The British policy of lax enforcement of most regulations on the American colonies as long as the colonies remained loyal and were a source of economic benefit.

often went to **bureaucrats** who were either old and incompetent or young and inexperienced. Third, most governors served too briefly to learn how to govern a particular colony effectively. Often they did not want to be in the colonies and were willing to surrender much of their authority to the local assembly in exchange for a calm, uneventful, and profitable term in office.

Colonial governors also lacked the patronage to grease the wheels of colonial assemblies. The kings of Great Britain had learned that political favors could buy political loyalty in Parliament. By mid-century, over half of Parliament held Crown offices or had received government contracts. Colonial governors had few such favors to hand out.

The greatest *constraint* on the governor, however, was the fact that the assembly paid his salary. Governors who challenged the assembly soon encountered unaccountable delays in the payment of their salaries. Compliant governors were rewarded with cash or land grants.

While the governors realized that their great powers were less than they seemed, assemblies learned how to broaden their powers. They gained the right to elect their own speaker of the assembly and to make their own procedural rules governing the operation of the assembly. They also increased their power of the purse over taxation and the use of revenues.

Colonial political leaders had several advantages besides the governor's weaknesses. They came from a small social and economic elite that was regularly elected to office. Although from 50 to 80 percent of adult free white males in a colony could vote, few met the high property qualifications to hold office. The elite also benefited from the **deference** or respect shown by lesser folks toward the well educated and wealthy. Thus generations of fathers and sons from elite families dominated colonial political officeholding. These men knew each other well. Although they fought among themselves for positions and for power, they could effectively unite against outsiders like a governor.

Conflicting Views of the Assemblies

The king and Parliament *expected* local assemblies to raise taxes, to pay government salaries, and to maintain bridges and roads. To the colonists, this set of *expectations* indicated acceptance of two levels of government. One level was the central government in Great Britain, which created and executed imperial policy. The other level was the various colonial governments, which managed local domestic affairs. The colonists regarded both levels of government as legitimate.

The British did not agree. They saw only one government ruling a vast empire. British leaders did not believe the colonial governments had acquired any share of the British government's sovereign power. They viewed colonial assemblies as inferior to Parliament and as having no real authority.

The Empires of America

- What *constraints* did the British, French, Spanish, and American Indians place on one another in North America?
- What were the most common *outcomes* of their rivalries?

In the eighteenth century, Spain, France, and Great Britain rivaled each other for control of the Americas and for domination of transatlantic trade (see Map 3.1). Their empires differed substantially, but the colonists of these nations shared the experience of enemies at their borders.

The Troubled Spanish Colonial Empire

At the beginning of the century, the Spanish empire stretched from California southward through South America. It also extended into the Caribbean islands and northward into Florida. The problems of governing such a vast empire were enormous. The major problems were corruption and inefficiency in the bureaucracy that Spain had established to administer its colonies. Tensions between colonial administrators, who were typically born in Spain, and the colonists, who had little voice in local government, contributed to these problems. But the

> **bureaucrat** A government official, usually non-elected, who is rigidly devoted to the details of administrative procedure.
>
> **deference** Yielding to the judgment or wishes of another person, usually seen as a social superior.

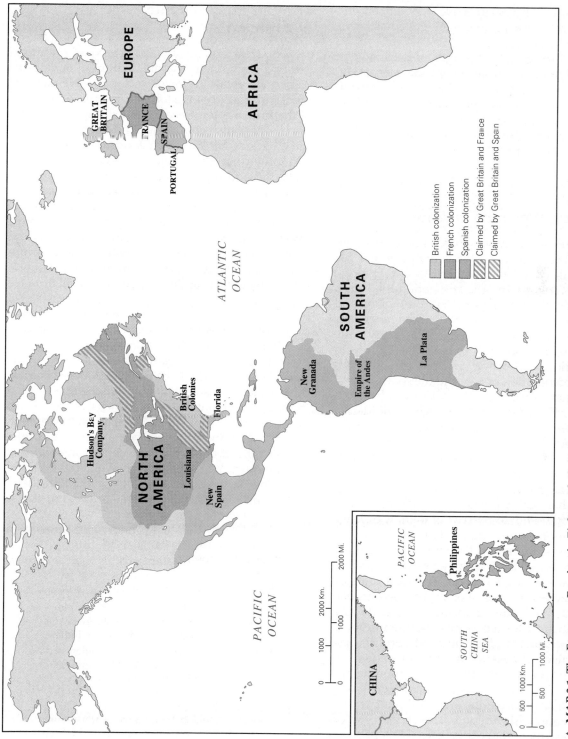

British colonization

French colonization

Spanish colonization

Claimed by Great Britain and France

Claimed by Great Britain and Spain

◆ **MAP 3.1 The European Empires in Eighteenth-Century America** This map shows the colonization of the Americas and the Philippines by three rival powers. It is clear from the map why British colonists felt vulnerable to attack by Britain's archenemies, France and Spain, until British victory in the Great War for Empire in 1763.

wealth produced by Spain's New World empire overshadowed these problems of governance for many decades.

By the eighteenth century signs of decline were evident everywhere within the Spanish empire. Its administration remained unwieldy and corrupt, and the output of its gold, silver, and copper mines was declining. Still, Spain remained a formidable power. Its military presence in Florida cast a long shadow over the British colonies of Georgia and the Carolinas.

The French Presence in America

French Canada since its beginnings in the early seventeenth century had existed largely for the fur trade established by the "father of New France," **Samuel de Champlain.** The fur trade rested on a long-standing alliance with the Huron Indians and on the Hurons' ability to control ample ranges for trapping beaver (see Map 3.2). After 1665, New France maintained an army to assist the Hurons in their struggles for territory against the powerful Iroquois confederation of tribes to the south.

Few French Catholics showed any interest in New France. (French Protestants were forbidden to emigrate.) The practice of making large land grants to a few individuals meant that there were few opportunities in New France for ordinary Frenchmen. The French North American empire had ceased to grow by the eighteenth century. By 1760 fewer than eighty thousand Europeans lived in French Canada, and 20 percent of them were clustered in the towns of Quebec and Montreal.

The fur trade dominated French Canada's culture as well as its economy. It drew young men into the forests to trade with the Indians. These **coureurs de bois,** or runners of the woods, married Indian women and lived among the tribes. **Jesuits** and other religious orders also went into the forests to convert the Indians to Christianity. The French government, however, never found the fur trade profitable enough to balance the cost of running the colony. France's prize possessions in the New World were its sugar islands in the Caribbean: Haiti, Guadeloupe, and Martinique. The French valued Canada primarily because it enhanced France's status and helped prevent the spread of the British empire.

The Differing Colonial Worlds of America

France, Great Britain, and Spain *expected* profit and prestige from their colonial empires. Spain surpassed its rivals in reaping profits. Neither the French fur trade nor the tobacco and rice production of the British colonies could match the wealth produced by Spanish gold, silver, and copper mines. All three nations felt the financial drain of governing and protecting their colonies. Regardless of the costs, these European nations remained willing to go to war to protect or expand their empires.

France and Spain failed to attract many colonists from their own countries. Both barred the most likely candidates for such settlement: religious and political dissenters. Both established land distribution policies that destroyed an important motivation for settlement by ordinary people. Great Britain's colonization effort was much more successful because it tolerated dissenters as colonists, it allowed private colonizing efforts, and it adopted land policies that allowed ordinary colonists to acquire land.

Differences in race relations were striking in the three colonial worlds. Slavery was pervasive in the British and Spanish colonies and in the French West Indies. (It did not develop in French Canada, which had no staple crops.) In both Spanish and British societies African-Americans were considered inferior, but the Spanish Catholic church insisted that African slaves had souls and enjoyed certain rights, including the possibility of gaining their freedom. Slavery in Spanish America was brutal, but it was often *constrained* by the church.

In the British colonies, there was no unified church to speak for the souls and rights of African-Americans. Some Protestant groups tried to convert

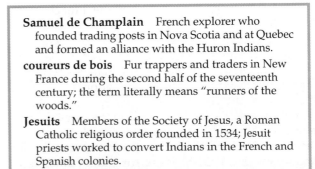

Samuel de Champlain   French explorer who founded trading posts in Nova Scotia and at Quebec and formed an alliance with the Huron Indians.

coureurs de bois   Fur trappers and traders in New France during the second half of the seventeenth century; the term literally means "runners of the woods."

Jesuits   Members of the Society of Jesus, a Roman Catholic religious order founded in 1534; Jesuit priests worked to convert Indians in the French and Spanish colonies.

The Empires of America

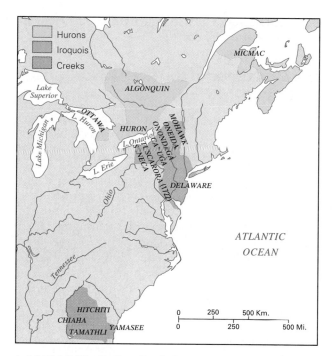

Hurons
Iroquois
Creeks

Lake Superior

MICMAC

ALGONQUIN

OTTAWA
L. Huron
Lake Michigan
HURON
MOHAWK
ONEIDA
ONONDAGA
L. Ontario
CA-UGA
SCARORA (1722)
SENECA
L. Erie
DELAWARE
Ohio

ATLANTIC
OCEAN

Tennessee

HITCHITI
CHIAHA
TAMATHLI YAMASEE

0   250   500 Km.

0   250   500 Mi.

◆ **MAP 3.2 The Indian Confederacies** This map shows the three major Indian military and political coalitions— the Huron, Iroquois, and Creek confederacies. Unlike the squabbling British mainland colonies, these Indian tribes understood the value of military unity in the face of threats to their land and their safety and the importance of diplomatic unity in negotiating with their European allies.

blacks to Christianity, but none was powerful enough to establish its views throughout the colonies. The treatment of slaves remained a private matter in British America. Spanish colonists were allowed to marry African-Americans or American Indians. British America, however, disapproved of interracial marriage, and most colonies prohibited it.

The greatest contrast between the French and British American Colonies centered on relationships with American Indians. The French showed a tolerance and respect for Indian culture that the British never displayed. Many French fur traders and trappers married into Indian tribes, adopted Indian lifestyles, and raised their children as Indians. Although aggressive in pursuing its fur-trading interests, the French government seldom seized Indian lands. The combination of British contempt for Indians and British desire for Indian lands led many tribes to ally with the French.

The Indian Presence in Eastern North America

By 1750, the surviving tribes in the Northeast had formed two major, and opposing, alignments with the European powers. The Hurons, the Algonquins, the Abenakis, the Micmacs, the Ottawas, and several smaller tribes had allied themselves with France. The fur trade and the long-standing hostility between the Hurons and the Iroquois of upper New York shaped this alliance.

The member tribes of the **Iroquois League** cast their lot with the Dutch and later the British. Consisting of the Mohawks, Senecas, Onondagas, Oneidas, Cayugas, and Tuscaroras, the league enjoyed an advantage over other Indians in resisting European expansion because of its strength in numbers and in organization. Both France and Great Britain respected the Iroquois League's strategic importance, for its member tribes were located south of the Great Lakes along routes crucial to the fur trade.

In the South, the **Creek Confederacy** played a role much like the Iroquois League. Initially a profitable trade in deerskins and Indian slaves brought the Creeks and the British colonists into an alliance. The alliance continued until the early eighteenth century, when colonial hunger for Creek lands became insatiable. In 1715, the colonists turned against their former allies and made war on them. The defeated Creeks fled west.

An Age of Imperial Warfare

Between 1688 and 1763, the rivalry between Spain, France, and Great Britain produced five bloody and costly wars. No matter why or where these wars began, colonists could *expect* to be drawn into them. The first four of these wars did little to change the map of Europe. The fifth changed the map of the world.

Iroquois League An American Indian confederacy in New York, originally composed of the Mohawk, Oneida, Onondaga, Cayuga, and Seneca peoples; in 1722 the confederacy was joined by the Tuscaroras.

Creek Confederacy An American Indian confederacy made up of the Creek and various smaller southeast tribes.

The Great War for Empire

In the 1740s, as the population explosion in British America sent thousands of settlers westward, the French began to build trading posts and forts in the Ohio Valley. The neutral zone between the two empires shrank, and in 1754 the fifth and most dramatic war among the European rivals began: the Great War for Empire, known in the colonies as the **French and Indian War.** That year, a young Virginia planter and militia officer, Major George Washington, led an expedition against Fort Duquesne, the newest French garrison in the Ohio Valley. When Washington was badly defeated, colonial leaders attempted to organize a unified defense. The colonial assemblies, however, proved too jealous of their independence to approve this **Albany Plan of Union.**

By 1755, British and French armies were battling in America. The conflict soon involved every major European power and spread to the Caribbean, the Philippines, Africa, and India. The war in North America did not go well for the British initially. Led by General Louis Joseph Montcalm, French and Indian forces by 1757 controlled western and central New York and were threatening Albany and New England.

At that critical juncture William Pitt became Britain's prime minister. Pitt committed the British treasury to the largest war expenditures the nation had ever known and then assembled the largest military force that North America had ever seen: twenty-five thousand colonial troops and twenty-four thousand British regulars. In September 1759, General James Wolfe led this army in a daring attack on Quebec. After scaling the steep cliffs that protected the walled city, Wolfe's army met Montcalm's in front of the city on the Plains of Abraham. Both generals died in this short but decisive battle. Within five days, Quebec had surrendered.

In 1760 Montreal fell to the British. The French governor subsequently surrendered the whole of New France, effectively ending the war in North America. The fighting continued elsewhere until 1763. French hopes had risen briefly when Spain enlisted as their ally in 1761, but British victories in India, the Caribbean, and the Pacific squelched any *expectations* the French had. The **Treaty of Paris** (1763) established the supremacy of the British empire. The reign of George III, which began in 1760, had started in glory.

The Outcomes of the Great War for Empire

At the peace table the map of the world was redrawn. The French empire shriveled. Nothing remained of New France but St. Pierre and St. Miquelon, two tiny islands between Nova Scotia and Newfoundland used by French fishing fleets. The only other remnants of the French empire in the Western Hemisphere were the sugar islands of Guadeloupe, Martinique, and St. Domingue. Great Britain's sugar interest did not want to add these islands to the British empire for they would then be competitors in the British market. Across the Atlantic, France lost trading posts in Africa. On the other side of the world, the French presence in India vanished. The Treaty of Paris dismantled the French empire but left France and its borders intact.

The victorious British did not escape unharmed. Their government was now deeply in debt and faced new problems in managing and protecting its greatly enlarged empire.

The American colonists lit bonfires and staged parades to celebrate their victory. But the war left scars. The British military had been arrogant toward provincial soldiers, had arbitrarily seized colonial goods, and had quartered British soldiers at colonial expense. The resentments were not one-sided. British officials could not understand how the colonists could continue trading with the enemy in wartime. Suspicion, resentment, and a growing sense of difference were the unexpected *outcomes* of a glorious victory.

French and Indian War   A war in North America (1754–1763) that was part of a worldwide struggle between France and Great Britain; it ended with France's defeat.

Albany Plan of Union   A proposal that the colonies form a union with a representative government and an army; Benjamin Franklin drafted it in 1754, but it was never ratified by the colonies.

Treaty of Paris   Treaty that ended the French and Indian War in 1763; it gave all of French Canada and the Spanish Floridas to Great Britain.

SUMMARY

E xpectations
C onstraints
C hoices
O utcomes

Each colonial region developed its own unique culture and society in response to varying regional *constraints.* New England life was centered around the family and community. The men and women of the small farming communities there were *expected* to live godly and harmonious lives. No single religious tradition bound the colonists of the southern or middle regions together. The *choice* to focus on cash crops led to the rise of a planter elite in the Chesapeake and the Lower South. In those regions, *choices* and opportunities were great for those who controlled the labor of others, especially of enslaved African-Americans. The middle colonies developed a lively urban culture. Most people who immigrated to British North America after 1700, however, *chose* to settle in the backcountry, where there were greater opportunities.

Intellectual life in the eighteenth century changed dramatically as Enlightenment ideas encouraged reliance on reason. Colonial elites *chose* to adopt John Locke's theory of natural rights as well as skepticism about religious dogma. The Great Awakening exposed an opposing intellectual current. Revivalist George Whitefield and other evangelicals carried the religious revival throughout the colonies. "Awakeners" challenged all authority except the individual spirit, and many colonists *chose* to embrace those beliefs.

A similar challenge to authority spread to politics and imperial relations. Colonial assemblies *chose* to assert their own claim to power against appointed governors and other British officials. Strains in the relationship between colonial assemblies and imperial officers ran deep.

Rivalries among Spain, France, and Great Britain produced five major wars between 1688 and 1763 whose *outcome* damaged their empires. French power diminished greatly; Spain was put on the defensive. Despite their sweeping victory in the Great War for Empire, the British were forced to go deeply into debt and to face a new challenge to their empire.

Suggested Readings

Berkin, Carol, and Mary Beth Norton, eds. *Women of America: A History* (1980).

In this collection, there are several essays on colonial women, their religious experiences, their legal rights, and their education, as well as an answer to the long-standing question: was the colonial era a "golden age for women"?

de Crèvecoeur, J. Hector St. John (Michel). *Letters from an American Farmer* (1782).

In these essays, the French visitor to the colonies argued that the American character was dramatically different from the European character—an argument that might prompt debate among modern readers.

Lemisch, Jesse, ed. *Benjamin Franklin: The Autobiography and Other Writings* (1961).

In this witty and entertaining classic, the champion of the Enlightenment in America tells his own story. In the process, Franklin also tells the reader much about eighteenth-century science and the religious awakenings that stirred colonial communities.

Mittelberger, Gottlieb. *Journey to Pennsylvania in the Year 1750* (1898).

Mittelberger provides a vivid and disturbing picture of the "middle passage" endured by poor German immigrants on their way to the colonies.

Pollock, John Charles. *George Whitefield and the Great Awakening* (1972).

The author reconstructs the life of this charismatic religious leader who moved his audiences to tears in both the colonies and in Great Britain.

Smith, Venture. *Venture Smith: A Narrative of the Life and Adventures of Venture, a Native of Africa, But Resident Above Sixty Years in the United States of America* (1789).

This account of a young boy, captured, enslaved, and carried to the colonies, sold and resold, and eventually able to win his freedom was probably dictated by Smith to an anonymous author. It, too, offers a first-hand description of a "middle passage," this time from Africa to the colonies.

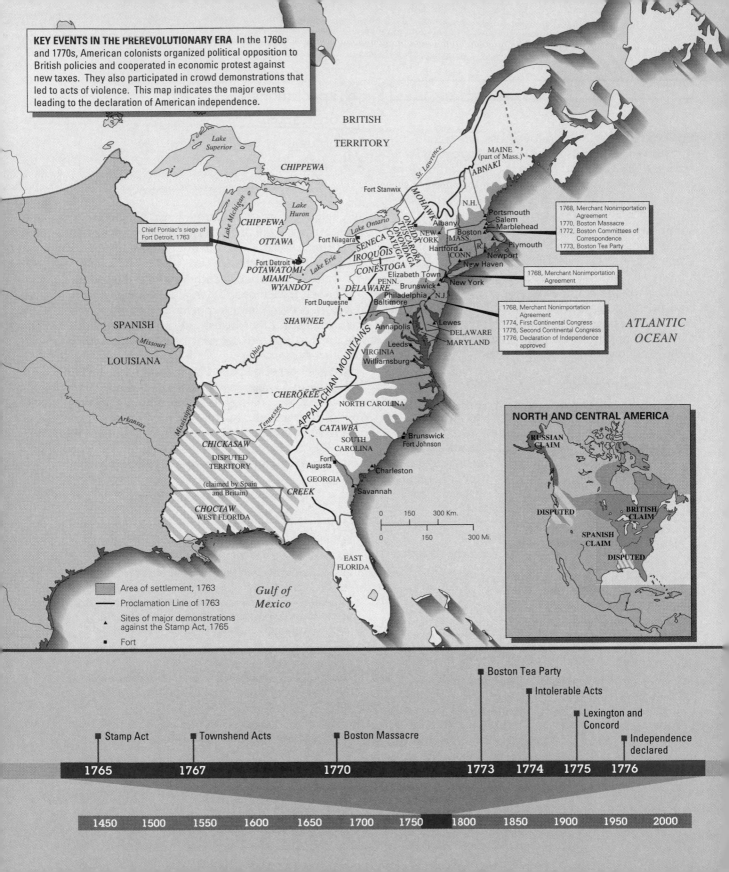

KEY EVENTS IN THE PREREVOLUTIONARY ERA In the 1760s and 1770s, American colonists organized political opposition to British policies and cooperated in economic protest against new taxes. They also participated in crowd demonstrations that led to acts of violence. This map indicates the major events leading to the declaration of American independence.

BRITISH

TERRITORY

Lake Superior

CHIPPEWA

Lake Michigan

Lake Huron

CHIPPEWA

OTTAWA

Fort Niagara

Chief Pontiac's siege of Fort Detroit, 1763

Fort Detroit

POTAWATOMI
MIAMI
WYANDOT

Lake Erie

Lake Ontario

MOHAWK

Fort Stanwix

ONEIDA
TUSCARORA
ONONDAGA
CAYUGA

SENECA

IROQUOIS

CONESTOGA

DELAWARE

Fort Duquesne

SHAWNEE

St. Lawrence

MAINE
(part of Mass.)

ABNAKI

N.H.

Albany

NEW
YORK

Hartford

MASS.
Boston

R.I.
CONN.
New Haven

Portsmouth
Salem
Marblehead

Plymouth

Newport

New York

1768, Merchant Nonimportation Agreement
1770, Boston Massacre
1772, Boston Committees of Correspondence
1773, Boston Tea Party

1768, Merchant Nonimportation Agreement

PENN.
Philadelphia
Baltimore

Elizabeth Town
Brunswick

N.J.

Annapolis

Leeds

VIRGINIA
Williamsburg

Lewes

DELAWARE
MARYLAND

1768, Merchant Nonimportation Agreement
1774, First Continental Congress
1775, Second Continental Congress
1776, Declaration of Independence approved

ATLANTIC
OCEAN

SPANISH

LOUISIANA

Missouri

Ohio

APPALACHIAN MOUNTAINS

CHEROKEE

Tennessee

NORTH CAROLINA

CATAWBA

Arkansas

Mississippi

CHICKASAW
DISPUTED
TERRITORY

(claimed by Spain and Britain)

CHOCTAW
WEST FLORIDA

SOUTH
CAROLINA

Fort
Augusta

GEORGIA

CREEK

Brunswick
Fort Johnson

Charleston

Savannah

0   150   300 Km.
0   150   300 Mi.

NORTH AND CENTRAL AMERICA

RUSSIAN
CLAIM

DISPUTED

SPANISH
CLAIM

BRITISH
CLAIM

DISPUTED

EAST
FLORIDA

Gulf of
Mexico

Area of settlement, 1763
Proclamation Line of 1763
Sites of major demonstrations against the Stamp Act, 1765
Fort

Boston Tea Party

Intolerable Acts

Lexington and Concord

Stamp Act   Townshend Acts   Boston Massacre   Independence declared

1765   1767   1770   1773   1774   1775   1776

1450   1500   1550   1600   1650   1700   1750   1800   1850   1900   1950   2000

Deciding Where Loyalties Lie, 1763–1776

Victory's New Problems

• Why did George Grenville *expect* the colonists to accept part of the burden of financing the British empire in 1764?

• How did the colonists *choose* to respond to direct taxation by Parliament?

Asserting American Rights

• Why did Charles Townshend *expect* his revenue measures to be successful?

• What form of protest did the colonists *choose* in response?

• What was the *outcome* of that protest?

The Crisis Renewed

• What British *choices* led Americans to see a plot against their rights and liberties?

• What *constraints* did the king place on Massachusetts to crush resistance there?

• How did the Continental Congress *choose* to respond?

The Decision for Independence

• Could the Revolutionary War have been avoided?

• What *choices* on both sides might have kept compromise alive?

INTRODUCTION

Expectations
Constraints
Choices
Outcomes

The British victory over France in 1763 raised *expectations* for an era of prosperity and cooperation between mother country and colonies. But less than two years later, Britain's mainland colonists had risen in protest against the *constraints* placed on them by British policies and regulations. Fundamental political differences then emerged between the British government and the colonists. They could not agree on the rights and obligations of the colonists. Americans who had once toasted the king *chose* instead to drink to resistance to tyrants. By 1775, a new *choice* faced the colonists: loyalty or rebellion.

The *outcome* of the troubled years between 1763 and 1775 was the American Revolution. However, the colonists who *chose* to protest taxation in 1765 did not know they were laying the groundwork for a revolution. We can look back on their *expectations*, *constraints*, and *choices* and see that the likely *outcome* was indeed a break with Britain. But the people who made that revolution did not know it was coming.

Events between 1763 and 1776 forced many colonists to *choose* between loyalty to Great Britain or loyalty to colonial independence. The war that resulted set neighbor against neighbor, father against son, and wife against husband. For thousands, the *outcome* of this crisis of loyalty was exile from home and family. For others, it meant death or injury on the battlefield. In 1776, however, the *outcome* was unclear.

Victory's New Problems

- Why did George Grenville *expect* the colonists to accept part of the burden of financing the British empire in 1764?
- How did the colonists *choose* to respond to direct taxation by Parliament?

When **George Grenville** became King George III's chief minister in 1763, he appeared to face a much easier task than William Pitt had confronted six years earlier. The battles of the Great War for Empire had been won, and all that remained to be done was to negotiate a treaty with an exhausted and defeated France.

Grenville soon discovered the costs of glory. Pitt had spent vast sums without hesitation to secure his nation's victory, and he had left the new minister with an enormous war debt. British taxpayers, who had groaned under the wartime burden, were expecting tax relief, not tax increases. There were also serious problems in governing the new Canadian territory because some American Indian tribes were unwilling to pledge their allegiance to King **George III.**

Dealing with Indian Resistance

The former Indian allies of France and Spain were threatened by Britain's recent victory. For decades, they had protected their lands by playing European rivals against each other. Now the French had been ousted from Canada and the Spanish from Florida. The Creeks and the Cherokees of the Southeast had felt the effects of Spanish withdrawal even before the war ended, when settlers from the southern colonies poured into Creek and Cherokee territory. When the Cherokees launched a full-scale war along the southern frontier, the British crushed their rebellion and forced the Cherokees to open up their lands to settlement.

> **George Grenville**   British prime minister who sought to tighten British control over the colonies and impose taxes on colonial trade.
> **George III**   King of Great Britain (r. 1760–1820); his government's policies fed colonial discontent and helped start the American Revolution in 1776.

CHRONOLOGY ▪▪▪▪▪▪▪▪▪▪▪▪▪▪▪

Loyalty or Rebellion?

1763	Treaty of Paris ends French and Indian War
	Pontiac's Rebellion
	Proclamation line
1764	Sugar Act
1765	Stamp Act
	Sons of Liberty organized
	Stamp Act Congress
	Nonimportation of British goods
1766	Repeal of the Stamp Act
	Declaratory Act
1767	Townshend Acts
	John Dickinson's *Letters from a Farmer in Pennsylvania*
	Nonimportation of British goods
1770	Boston Massacre
	Repeal of the Townshend Acts

1772	Burning of the *Gaspée*
1773	Tea Act
	Boston Tea Party
1774	Intolerable Acts
	First Continental Congress
	Declaration of Rights and Grievances
	Suffolk Resolves
1775	Battles of Lexington and Concord
	Second Continental Congress
	Olive Branch Petition
1776	Tom Paine's *Common Sense*
	Declaration of Independence

In 1763, settlers began a similar invasion of Indian territory in the upper Ohio Valley and Great Lakes region. In response, the Ottawa chief, **Pontiac,** created an intertribal alliance known as the **Covenant Chain** to oppose white expansion. Throughout the summer and early fall of 1763, this alliance of Senecas, Ojibwas, Potawatomis, Hurons, Ottawas, Delawares, Shawnees, and Mingos mounted attacks on Fort Detroit and other frontier forts in what became known as Pontiac's Rebellion. The British forts held, however, and by winter Pontiac had to acknowledge British control of the Ohio Valley.

The British recognized that this victory did not ensure permanent peace in the West. Indian resistance would not end as long as settlers continued to pour into Indian territories. Thus in late 1763 Grenville issued a proclamation that temporarily banned settlement west of the Appalachian Mountains (Map 4.1). Colonists in the backcountry were outraged by this **Proclamation Line of 1763.**

The colonists *chose* to overcome this new *constraint* by ignoring it, and they continued to take the land they wanted. The *outcome* was often conflict.

Demanding More from the Colonies

Grenville meanwhile was examining the costs and benefits of the mainland colonies to Britain. It soon became clear to him that something had gone wrong

Pontiac   Ottawa chief and former French ally who organized the Covenant Chain; he mounted an unsuccessful siege of Fort Detroit in 1763.

Covenant Chain   An alliance of American Indian peoples formed to resist colonial settlement in the Northwest and British trading policy.

Proclamation Line of 1763   British policy that banned white settlement west of the Appalachian Mountains; it was intended to reduce conflict between Indians and settlers, but it angered settlers.

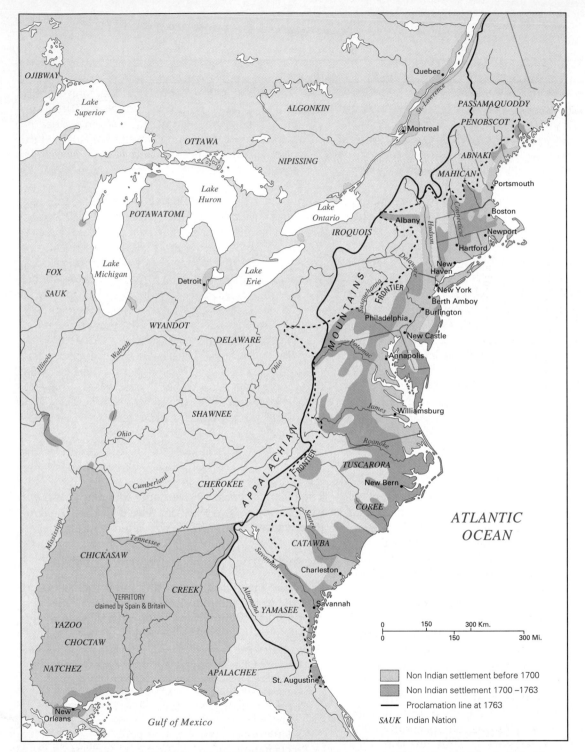

♦ **MAP 4.1 The Proclamation Line of 1763**   This map shows European settlement east of the Appalachian Mountains and the numerous Indian tribes with territorial claims to the lands between the Appalachians and the Mississippi River. The Proclamation Line was the British government's effort to temporarily halt colonial westward expansion and thus to prevent bloodshed between settlers and Indians.

in the economic relationship between mother country and colonies. Grenville singled out illegal colonial trade as the primary reason why the expected benefits of colonies had not materialized. Americans traded for illegal goods with Britain's rivals and avoided paying **import duties** for legal foreign goods whenever they could.

The results of such avoidance were apparent from the imperial trade books. By the 1760s, the Crown was collecting less than £2,000 in customs duties while spending more than £7,000 to collect those duties annually. In 1764, Grenville proposed new policies to correct this problem and thereby ended the long era of benign neglect.

To end American smuggling, Grenville first had to reform the **customs service.** He took steps to stop customs officers from taking bribes from smugglers. He then gave customs men the power to use blanket warrants, or **writs of assistance,** to search ships and warehouses for smuggled goods. Grenville's next step was to reform the import regulations. The 1764 American Revenue Act, known popularly as the **Sugar Act,** showed that Grenville was a practical man. His intent was to make it cheaper to pay the import duties on foreign molasses and sugar than it was to bribe customs officials or to evade the duty by landing a cargo on an isolated beach. The act cut the duty on foreign molasses in half, from six to three pence per gallon but Grenville was determined that this duty be paid.

To ensure that it was, Grenville changed the way smuggling cases were handled in court. Until 1764, a colonist accused of smuggling was brought before a jury of neighbors in a **civil court.** He *expected,* and usually got, a favorable verdict. Grenville now declared that smugglers would be tried in a **vice-admiralty court,** where there were no sympathetic colonial juries. Once smuggling became too costly and too risky, Grenville reasoned, American shippers would bow to the *constraints* of trade regulations and pay the Crown for the privilege of importing French molasses.

The Colonial Response

Grenville's reforms could not have come at a worse time for the colonists. They took effect during the economic **depression** that followed the French and Indian War. The depression was largely the result of an abrupt decline of British military spending in the colonies. Unemployment among artisans, dockworkers, and sailors ran high. Merchants found themselves unable to pay their debts to British suppliers because the merchants' customers had no money to pay their bills. The merchants blamed this situation on Grenville's **Currency Act** of 1764, which outlawed the printing of paper money in the colonies.

Ironically, some colonists welcomed the hard times. They believed that Americans had become overly fond of luxuries, and that this had weakened their spirit, sapped their independence, and corrupted their morals. They warned that moral decay had ruined Britain, where extravagance and corruption infected society. Such colonists appealed to their neighbors to embrace simplicity and to sacrifice by **boycotting** all British manufactured goods.

Colonial newspapers, however, focused on the political dimensions of Grenville's reforms. Those reforms raised disturbing questions about the rights of the colonists and the relationship between Parliament and the colonial governments. But in 1764 Americans were far from agreement over how they should respond to the Sugar Act.

---

import duty   A tax on imported goods.

customs service   A government agency authorized to collect taxes on foreign goods entering a country.

writs of assistance   General search warrants issued to customs officers by colonial courts, giving them the authority to search ships and warehouses for smuggled goods.

Sugar Act   British law (1764) that taxed sugar, molasses, and other colonial imports in order to defray British expenses in protecting the colonies.

civil court   Any court that hears cases regarding the rights of private citizens.

vice-admiralty court   British court that heard cases involving shipping.

depression   A period of drastic economic decline, characterized by decreasing business activity, falling prices, and unemployment.

Currency Act   British law (1764) that banned the printing of paper money in the American colonies.

boycott   An organized protest in which people refuse to buy goods from or otherwise deal with a nation or group of people whose actions they object to.

The Stamp Act

Grenville's next proposal to Parliament startled the colonists even more. He suggested that Parliament approve the first internal or **direct tax** ever levied on the colonies. Until 1765, Parliament had passed many acts regulating colonial trade, some of which taxed imported goods. It had never, however, levied direct taxes on the colonists. Such taxes had previously been approved only by their local assemblies. From a colonial perspective, this proposed tax would change the traditional relationship between the colonial assemblies and Parliament dramatically.

Colonists greeted news of Parliament's approval of the **Stamp Act,** passed in February 1765, with outrage and anger. Come November, when the act went into effect, virtually every free man and woman could *expect* to be affected by this tax that required the use of government "stamped paper" on legal documents, newspapers, pamphlets, and even playing cards. Grenville's Stamp Act united northern merchants and southern planters, rural women and urban workingmen, and it riled the most argumentative of all Americans: lawyers and newspaper publishers.

The Popular Response

Many colonists *chose* to resist the new legislation. During the summer of 1765, a group of Bostonians formed a secret organization called the **Sons of Liberty**. Although one of its founders was the socially prominent, Harvard-educated **Samuel Adams,** most members were artisans and shopkeepers. They had been hit hard by the postwar depression and saw the stamp tax as a further *constraint* on their economic prospects. They took to the streets to make their protests known.

Such protests soon made the position of government stamp agent a hazardous occupation in Boston. On August 14, 1765, the Sons of Liberty paraded an **effigy** of Andrew Oliver, a wealthy merchant and newly appointed stamp agent, through the city. The Sons not only hung the effigy on a tree near Oliver's wharf but destroyed Oliver's warehouse and later broke all the windows in his home. The following day Oliver resigned his position as stamp agent. The Sons of Liberty celebrated by declaring the tree on which they had hanged Oliver's effigy the "liberty tree."

The Sons then harassed other Crown officials living in Boston. **Thomas Hutchinson,** lieutenant governor of Massachusetts, became the chief target of abuse when a false rumor spread that he had written to British officials in support of the Stamp Act. The rumor encouraged a large crowd of artisans and others to trash the lieutenant governor's elegant brick mansion later that August of 1765.

Thomas Hutchinson appears to have been a political and a social target for the working people of Boston. He represented the privilege and power of the few and the well placed. A significant *outcome* of the destruction of his home was that many of Boston's elite merchants withdrew their support from popular protests. They reasoned that the tensions aroused between rich and poor were perhaps more dangerous than the tensions between Parliament and the colonies.

The campaign against stamp agents spread like a brush fire throughout the colonies. Colonists who had agreed to take the position of agent had not *expected* to endure hatred or to suffer harm. They *expected* that a British law would be obeyed. But no stamp agent was safe. When the stamps reached colonial ports that fall, only the young colony of Georgia could produce anyone willing to distribute them.

The British responded to this explosion of violence and political protest by refusing to allow colonial ships to leave port. They hoped that the

---

direct tax   Tax explicitly imposed to raise revenues.

Stamp Act   British law (1765) that levied direct taxes on a large variety of items, including newspapers, almanacs, and legal documents.

Sons of Liberty   A secret organization formed in Boston to oppose the Stamp Act; its leaders included Samuel Adams and Paul Revere.

Samuel Adams   Massachusetts revolutionary leader and propagandist who organized opposition to the Stamp Act and took part in the Boston Tea Party.

effigy   A representation of a hated or despised person.

Thomas Hutchinson   Boston merchant who served as lieutenant governor of Massachusetts and later as governor; his efforts to enforce the Stamp Act prompted a mob to destroy his house.

♦ Eighteenth-century political protest frequently took the form of a public parade in which symbolic figures were used to dramatize a point. Here, a New Hampshire crowd carries a straw figure, or effigy, of a stamp agent. The crowd was likely to burn the effigy as a climax to the demonstration. *The Metropolitan Museum of Art, Bequest of Charles Allen Munn, 1924.* (24.90.1566a)

disruption of trade would force colonial merchants to use their influence to end the resistance. The strategy backfired. Hundreds of angry, unemployed sailors took to the streets to join in the resistance to stamp taxes.

Political Debate

The Stamp Act raised a fundamental issue: whether Parliament had the right to tax the colonists. As the young Virginia lawyer Patrick Henry put it, the Stamp Act was a matter of "liberty or death." A basic British principle held that no citizen could be taxed by a government in which he was not represented. "No taxation without representation" was an *expectation* shared on both sides of the Atlantic. The real question was whether Parliament represented the colonists, even though no colonist sat in that body or voted in parliamentary elections.

To Massachusetts lawyer **James Otis,** the answer to this question was clearly no. Otis took the position that the colonists should be given representation in the House of Commons. Few colonial political leaders took Otis's demand for American representation seriously because they realized that a small contingent of colonists could be easily ignored or defeated in Parliament. Therefore most leaders *chose* instead to declare that taxation was the right of local assemblies and that American rights and liberties were under attack. After much debate, most assemblies issued statements condemning the Stamp Act and demanding its repeal.

The Stamp Act produced the first stirrings of intercolonial unity. Until 1765, the colonies had been more prone to disagree with each other than to cooperate. When Massachusetts called for an intercolonial meeting to discuss the Stamp Act, however, nine colonies sent delegates to New York in the fall of 1765. The **Stamp Act Congress** conceded in a **petition** to the king that Parliament had authority over the colonies but boldly denied that Parliament had a right to impose a direct tax on them. "No taxes," they said, "ever have been, or can be Constitutionally imposed" on the colonies "but by their respective Legislatures." Americans *expected* that tradition to be honored.

Repeal of the Stamp Act

Neither the intimidation of the Sons of Liberty nor the arguments of the Stamp Act Congress prompted the repeal of the stamp tax. But economic pressure did work. American merchants applied this pressure when they announced that as of November 1, 1765, when the Stamp Act went into effect, they would refuse to import any more British manufactured goods. More than patriotic motives were at

---

James Otis   Boston lawyer who argued that writs of assistance violated colonists' rights under British law and who called for colonial representation in Parliament.

Stamp Act Congress   A meeting of colonial delegates in New York in 1765, which drew up a declaration of rights and grievances for presentation to the king and Parliament.

petition   A formal written request to a superior authority.

work here, for the warehouses of these merchants were bulging with unsold goods because of the postwar depression. Economic motives also influenced the *choice* of artisans to support these **nonimportation agreements** wholeheartedly, for their products competed with British goods. Regardless of motive, much of colonial America endorsed a boycott of British goods.

Because the mainland colonies constituted the largest market for goods made in Britain, British exporters consequently saw a huge downturn in their business. Parliament listened to the bitter complaints of these exporters, and talk of repeal grew within the halls of Parliament. The Grenville government had to concede that enforcement of the Stamp Act had failed miserably. Americans continued to sue their neighbors, publish their newspapers, and buy their playing cards as if the Stamp Act did not exist.

By winter's end, a new prime minister, Lord Rockingham, had replaced Grenville. Rockingham had opposed the Stamp Act from the start. For him, the critical issue now was how to repeal the Stamp Act without appearing to cave in to colonial pressures. His solution was to have Parliament repeal the Stamp Act but at the same time pass the **Declaratory Act.** This act reasserted Parliament's absolute right to legislate for and to tax the colonies.

Colonists celebrated news of the repeal with public displays of loyalty to the mother country that were as impressive as their protests had been. There were cannon salutes, bonfires, parades, speeches, and public toasts to the king and Rockingham. The crisis seemed to have passed.

Asserting American Rights

- Why did Charles Townshend *expect* his revenue measures to be successful?
- What form of protest did the colonists *choose* in response?
- What was the *outcome* of that protest?

In their celebrations of repeal, the colonists overlooked the Declaratory Act and its clear assertion of parliamentary power. They soon had to take notice of it. By the summer of 1766, William Pitt had replaced Lord Rockingham. The ailing Pitt, however, could not take firm control of the government.

So the **chancellor of the exchequer,** Charles Townshend, became the effective head of government. By 1767, Townshend had imposed new taxes on the colonies.

The Townshend Acts and Colonial Protest

During the Stamp Act crisis, Pennsylvania's **colonial agent,** Benjamin Franklin, had assured Parliament that American colonists opposed direct taxes (such as stamp taxes) but did not object to indirect taxes (such as import duties). Franklin's hard distinction between direct and indirect taxes was not shared by many colonists. But Charles Townshend took Franklin at his word. The **Townshend Acts** of 1767 placed an import tax on tea, glass, paper, paint, and lead products. These acts differed from previous customs duties in that they were levied on imported British goods instead of on foreign products.

Townshend took every precaution to avoid a repetition of the Stamp Act disaster. He expanded the scope and powers of the customs service. He transferred British troops from the western frontier to the major port cities. He expected the presence of uniformed soldiers, known as "redcoats" because of their scarlet uniforms, to allow customs officers to perform their duties and to keep the peace.

But Townshend made a serious error in accepting Franklin's assurances about taxes on imported

---

nonimportation agreements Colonial policy of refusing to import British goods, undertaken as a protest against the Stamp Act.

Declaratory Act British law (1766) that asserted Parliament's right to make laws for and impose taxes on the American colonies.

chancellor of the exchequer The head of the British government department in charge of collecting taxes; the exchequer is a sort of treasury department.

colonial agent Person chosen by each colonial assembly to represent each colony's interests with Parliament.

Townshend Acts British laws (1767) that required the colonials to pay duties on manufactured goods—such as glass, lead, and tea—imported from England.

goods. When news of the import duties reached the colonies, the response was immediate, determined, and well-organized resistance. The British government was once again trampling on the principle of "no taxation without representation."

John Dickinson, a well-respected landowner and lawyer, laid out the basic American position on taxes in 1767 in his *Letters from a Farmer in Pennsylvania.* Both direct and indirect taxation without representation violated the colonists' rights as British citizens, Dickinson wrote. Parliament did have the right to regulate foreign trade, and thus to levy duties on foreign imports—but not on British goods. An import duty on British products was merely a tax in disguise.

Dickinson also rejected the British argument that Americans were represented in Parliament. According to this argument, the colonists enjoyed **virtual representation** in Parliament because the House of Commons represented the interests of all citizens in the empire, whether they participated directly in elections to the House or not. Dickinson insisted that the colonists were entitled to **actual representation** by men whom they elected to Parliament and who were dedicated to protecting their interests. To Dickinson, virtual representation was only a weak excuse for exploitation. As one American quipped: "Our privileges are all virtual, our sufferings are real."

While political theorists set out the American position in newspaper essays and pamphlets, activists organized popular resistance. Samuel Adams initiated nonimportation agreements of British goods that were to take effect on January 1, 1768. Some colonists again welcomed the chance to "mow down luxury and high living." Economic interests also affected support for the boycott. Underemployed artisans remained enthusiastic about any action that stopped the flow of inexpensive British goods to America. Merchants and shippers who made their living smuggling goods from the West Indies supported the boycott because it cut out competing products. The affluent merchants who had led the nonimportation movement in 1765, however, were reluctant supporters of this new boycott. By 1767, their warehouses no longer overflowed with unsold British stock, and they were not eager to cut off their own livelihoods. Some never signed the new agreements.

The biggest critics of the boycott were colonists in royal offices. These Americans shared their neighbors' attachment to the rights of Englishmen, but they were sworn to uphold and to carry out the policies of the British government. Because their careers and their identities were closely tied to the Crown, they were inclined to accept British policy as a patriotic duty. Despite their prestige and authority, these Crown officers were unable to prevent the boycott.

Just as the Sons of Liberty brought common men into the political arena, the 1768 boycott brought politics more dramatically into the lives of women. By the mid-eighteenth century, any colonial woman with the means bought ready-made British cloth instead of making her own. In 1768, however, British textiles became boycotted goods. Suddenly an old and neglected domestic skill became both a real and a symbolic element in the American political strategy. The Daughters of Liberty staged large public **spinning bees** to support the boycott, boost morale, and pool their resources. Wearing cloth spun at home became a mark of honor. The *outcome* was that politics entered the domestic circle.

The British Humiliated

Townshend faced sustained defiance of British authority in almost every colony, but nowhere else was it as great as in Massachusetts. Enforcers of the boycott roamed the streets of Boston, intimidating pro-British merchants and harassing anyone wearing British-made clothing. Mobs openly threatened customs officials, and the Sons of Liberty protected smuggling operations. Despite more customs officers, the illegal importation of British and foreign goods was thriving. One of the most notorious

---

John Dickinson   Philadelphia lawyer who drafted the Articles of Confederation and argued for the rights of small states.

virtual representation   Parliamentary representation that stems from people's status as citizens, regardless of whether they have directly elected delegates to look out for their specific interests.

actual representation   Parliamentary representation by delegates directly elected to speak for voters' interests.

spinning bee   A meeting of women to compete or work together in spinning thread or yarn.

smugglers, **John Hancock,** seemed to grow more popular each time he unloaded his illegal cargoes of French and Spanish wines or West Indian molasses. Customs officers finally seized his vessel the *Liberty* in June 1768. Their action led mobs to beat up senior customs men and to threaten other royal officials. Governor Francis Bernard sent an urgent plea for help to the British government.

In October 1768 the Crown responded by sending four thousand troops to Boston. These soldiers, many of them young, far from home, and surrounded by a hostile citizenry, worsened the situation. The soldiers passed their idle hours courting local women who would speak to them and pestering those who would not. They angered local dockworkers by moonlighting in the shipyards. In turn, civilians taunted and insulted the soldiers. News of street-corner fights and tavern brawls inflamed feelings on both sides. Samuel Adams and his friends fanned the flames by publishing accounts of confrontations (both real and imagined) between hostile soldiers and innocent townspeople.

These confrontations culminated in what Massachusetts activists called the **"Boston Massacre."** On March 5, 1770, an angry crowd began throwing snowballs at British sentries guarding the customs house. The redcoats issued a frantic call for help. Captain Thomas Preston arrived with troops to rescue the sentries, but he and his men were soon enveloped by the growing crowd. Preston's men panicked and opened fire, killing five colonists.

Accounts of the "Boston Massacre" appeared in colonial newspapers everywhere. Although a jury of colonists later cleared Preston and all but two of his men of the charges against them, nothing that was said at the trial could erase the image of British brutality against British subjects.

On the very day that Captain Preston's men fired on the crowd at Boston, the new British prime minister, **Lord North,** repealed the Townshend Acts. Like Rockingham, North wanted to give no ground on the question of parliamentary control of the colonies. For this reason, he kept the tax on tea.

Success Weakens Colonial Unity

Repeal of the Townshend Acts allowed the colonists to return to their ordinary daily routines. But troubling tensions remained, largely among the colonists themselves. The boycott that began in 1768 exposed growing divisions between the merchant elite and the coalition of small merchants, artisans, and laborers. Despite the boycott, many wealthy merchants had secretly imported and sold British goods whenever possible. When repeal came in 1770, artisans and laborers still faced poor economic prospects and were reluctant to abandon the boycott. But few merchants, large or small, would agree to continue it. The boycott collapsed.

Many elite colonists abandoned the radical **activism** they had shown in the 1760s in favor of social **conservatism.** Their fear of British tyranny dimmed as their fear of the lower classes' demand for political power grew. Artisans and laborers continued to press for broader participation in local politics and for more representative political machinery. "Many of the poorer People," observed one supporter of expanded political participation, "deeply felt the Aristocratic Power, or rather the intolerable Tyranny of the great and opulent." The new political language employed by these common men made their social superiors uneasy. The colonial elite found its impassioned appeals to rights and liberties returning to haunt it.

The Crisis Renewed

- What British *choices* led Americans to see a plot against their rights and liberties?
- What *constraints* did the king place on Massachusetts to crush resistance there?
- How did the Continental Congress *choose* to respond?

John Hancock   Patriot who became president of the First Continental Congress and was the first to sign the Declaration of Independence.

Boston Massacre   Incident in Boston on March 5, 1770, in which British troops fired on a crowd, killing five colonists; it increased colonial resentment of British rule.

Frederick Lord North   British prime minister during the American Revolution.

activism   The assertive use of militant action, such as demonstrations and strikes, to support a controversial position.

conservatism   The desire to maintain the existing or traditional order.

Lord North's government took care not to disturb the calm that followed the repeal of the Townshend Acts. Between 1770 and 1773, North proposed no new taxes on the colonists and made no major changes in colonial policy. American political leaders took equal care not to make any open challenges to British authority. But this political truce had its limits. It certainly did not extend to smugglers and customs men.

Disturbing the Peace of the Early 1770s

Despite the repeal of the Townshend duties, the British effort to crack down on American smuggling continued. Rhode Island merchants were especially angry and frustrated by the highly effective customs operation in their colony. They took their revenge in June 1772 by burning a customs patrol boat, the *Gaspée*, that had run aground as it chased an American vessel.

Rhode Islanders interpreted the burning of the *Gaspée* as an act of political resistance. The British called it vandalism. The British government appointed a royal commission to investigate the raid but could find no witnesses or evidence to support an **indictment.** The British found the conspiracy of silence among the Rhode Islanders appalling.

In turn, American political leaders found the royal commission appalling. They were convinced that the British had intended to take suspects back to Britain for trial and thus deprive them of a jury of their peers. They read this as further evidence of the plot to destroy American liberty.

The *Gaspée* incident convinced leaders of the American resistance that they needed to coordinate their efforts to monitor British moves throughout the colonies. They organized **committees of correspondence** that were instructed to circulate reports of any incidents to the other committees. These committees were also a good mechanism for coordinating protest or resistance. Thus the colonists put in place their first permanent machinery of protest.

The Tea Act and the Tea Party

During the early 1770s, colonial activists worked to keep the political consciousness of the 1760s alive.

They commemorated American victories over British policy and observed the anniversary of the Boston Massacre with solemn speeches and sermons. Without major British provocation, however, any new mass action was unlikely.

In 1773, Parliament provided that provocation when it acted to rescue the East India Tea Company from bankruptcy. To bail the company out, Parliament offered it a government loan and permission to ship tea directly from its warehouses in India to the colonies. This arrangement would bypass British middlemen, cut shipping costs, and allow the company to lower the price of its tea in America. Even with the three-penny tax on tea that remained from the Townshend era, British tea would be cheaper than the Dutch tea smuggled into the colonies. Lord North supported the **Tea Act** when he realized that if Americans *chose* to purchase the cheaper British tea, they would also pay the tea tax and confirm Parliament's right to tax the colonies.

The Tea Act galvanized American protest. Colonists read it as another sign of a conspiracy against their well-being and their liberty. They were troubled that the government had altered its colonial trade policy to suit the needs of a special interest, the East India Tea Company. They feared that the cheaper prices for tea were a temporary measure that would last only until all foreign teas had been driven off the market. And they perceived the snare that Lord North had set for them: if they drank cheap tea, they would be legitimizing Parliament's right to tax them.

Colonists mobilized their resistance in 1773 with the skill acquired from a decade of experience. In many colonies, crowds met the ships carrying the East India Company tea and used violent threats to persuade ship captains to return to Britain with the tea still on board. But in Massachusetts, Governor Thomas Hutchinson refused to allow the tea ships to

---

indictment A formal written statement that charges someone with the commission of a crime.

committees of correspondence Groups formed throughout the colonies on the eve of the Revolution to quickly circulate news of British oppression.

Tea Act British law (1773) that lowered the price of British tea but kept the tax on tea sold to America.

leave Boston harbor without unloading. Boston's activists took him at his word. On December 16, 1773, some sixty men, thinly disguised as Indians, boarded the tea ships. They dumped 342 chests of tea, worth almost £10,000, into Boston harbor.

The Intolerable Acts

The **Boston Tea Party** delighted colonial activists everywhere, especially in New England. The Crown, however, failed to see the humor in this deliberate destruction of valuable private property. Lord North decided to make an example of Boston and Massachusetts. The four harsh acts that Parliament passed in 1774 soon became known in the colonies as the **Intolerable Acts.** The Port Act closed the port of Boston until the city paid for the destroyed tea. The Massachusetts Government Act transferred much of the power of the colony's assembly to the royal governor. The colony's **town meetings,** which had served as forums for anti-British sentiment and protest, also came under the governor's direct control. A third measure, the Justice Act, allowed royal officials charged with **capital crimes** to stand trial in London rather than before local juries. A new Quartering Act gave military commanders the authority to quarter troops in private homes. To see that these laws were enforced, the king named Thomas Gage, commander of the British troops in North America, as the acting governor of Massachusetts.

At the same time that those punitive measures were passed, the British government issued a comprehensive plan for the government of Canada. The timing of the **Quebec Act** may have been a coincidence, but its provisions angered Americans. The Quebec Act granted the French in Canada the right to worship as Catholics, to retain their language, and to keep many of their legal practices. The Quebec Act also expanded the borders of Canada into the Ohio Valley at the expense of the English-speaking colonies' claims. This act seemed to be one more blow in the attack on American liberty that Parliament had launched with the Intolerable Acts.

The king *expected* the harsh punishment of Massachusetts to isolate that colony from its neighbors. But in every colony newspapers urged readers to see Boston's plight as their own. "This horrid attack upon the town of Boston," said the *South*

Carolina Gazette, "we consider not as an attempt upon that town singly, but upon the whole Continent." George Washington, who had become a prominent Virginia planter and militia officer, declared that "the cause of Boston now is and ever will be the cause of America." Indeed the Intolerable Acts produced a wave of sympathy for the beleaguered Bostonians, and relief efforts sprang up across the colonies. The residents of Surry County, Virginia, for example, sent 150 barrels of corn and wheat to their fellow patriots in Boston.

For many colonists, the Intolerable Acts provided conclusive evidence that Great Britain was systematically oppressing them and robbing them of their liberties. Political writers began referring to the British government as the "enemy" and urged the colonists to defend themselves. In Boston, Samuel Adams and his radical followers formed a "solemn league and covenant" when they organized another boycott of British goods. As most Bostonians knew, the words "solemn league" referred to the pact made between Scottish Presbyterians and English Puritans when they challenged royal authority with arms in the 1640s. Adams and his allies had made armed rebellion their *choice.*

Creating a National Forum: The First Continental Congress

On September 5, 1774, delegates from every colony but Georgia gathered in Philadelphia for a continental congress. Few of the delegates thought of themselves as revolutionaries. "We want no revolution,"

Boston Tea Party   Protest against the Tea Act staged by Boston patriots in 1773; they boarded ships carrying British tea and dumped the tea into Boston harbor.

Intolerable Acts   The name colonists gave to four laws that Parliament passed in 1774 to punish Boston for the Boston Tea Party.

town meeting   A legislative assembly of townspeople characteristic of local government in New England.

capital crime   An offense punishable by death.

Quebec Act   British law (1774) that aimed to reform the government of the former French colony of Canada; some of its provisions angered Americans.

a North Carolina delegate bluntly stated. Yet he and other colonists were treading dangerously close to treason. Neither the king nor Parliament had authorized this continental congress that intended to resist acts of Parliament and to defy the king. People had been hanged as traitors for far less.

Radicals such as Samuel Adams wanted the congress to endorse a total boycott of British goods. Conservatives wanted to be more conciliatory and to petition Parliament to pay attention to American grievances. The radicals won this struggle when congress approved a boycott of all British goods to begin on December 1, 1774, and demanded the repeal of the Intolerable Acts.

Still, many delegates hoped for a course in between the radicals and conservatives that would bring a peaceful resolution to the crisis in relations between Crown and colonies. Pennsylvania's Joseph Galloway offered one way out of the existing dilemma by proposing a drastic restructuring of imperial relations. His **Plan of Union** called for a Grand Council, elected by each colonial legislature, that would share with Parliament the right to originate laws for the colonies. The Grand Council and Parliament would have the power to veto or disallow each other's decisions. A governor-general, appointed by the Crown, would oversee the Grand Council and preserve imperial interests.

After much debate, Congress rejected Galloway's compromise by the narrowest of margins. Then it was John Adams's turn to propose a solution. Under his skillful urging and direction, the Congress adopted the **Declaration of Rights and Grievances.** The declaration politely but firmly established the colonial standard for acceptable legislation by Parliament. Colonists, said the declaration, would consent to acts meant to regulate "external commerce." But they absolutely denied the legitimacy of a "taxation, internal or external, for raising a revenue on the subjects of America, without their consent."

To add teeth to Adams's declaration, the delegates endorsed the **Suffolk Resolves.** These resolves, which originated in Suffolk County, Massachusetts, urged citizens to arm themselves and to prepare to resist British military action. Congressional support for these resolutions was a clear message that American leaders were willing to *choose* rebellion if politics failed.

The delegates adjourned and headed home to wait for the Crown's response. When it came, it was electric. "Blows must decide," declared King George III, "whether they are to be subject to this country or independent."

The Decision for Independence

• Could the Revolutionary War have been avoided?

• What *choices* on both sides might have kept compromise alive?

While Americans were waiting for the king's response, a peaceful transfer of political power occurred in most colonies. Americans withdrew their support for royal governments and recognized the authority of anti-British or **patriot** governments. Independent local governments became a reality before any shots were fired.

Taking Charge and Enforcing Policies

The transition from royal to patriot political control was peaceful in communities where anti-British sentiment was strong. Where it was weak or where the community was divided, radicals used persuasion, pressure, and open intimidation to advance the patriot cause. These radicals became increasingly impatient with dissent, disagreement, or even indecision among their neighbors. They *expected* sides to

---

Plan of Union   Joseph Galloway's plan to restructure relations between the colonies and the mother country to give the colonies a greater say about local laws while preserving their basic colonial relationship with Britain.

Declaration of Rights and Grievances   A resolution, passed by the First Continental Congress in 1774, that denied Parliament's right to tax the colonies without their consent.

Suffolk Resolves   Resolutions adopted in 1774 by Boston and other towns in Suffolk County, Massachusetts, calling on the colonists to take up arms against the British.

patriot   An American colonist who opposed British rule and fought for independence.

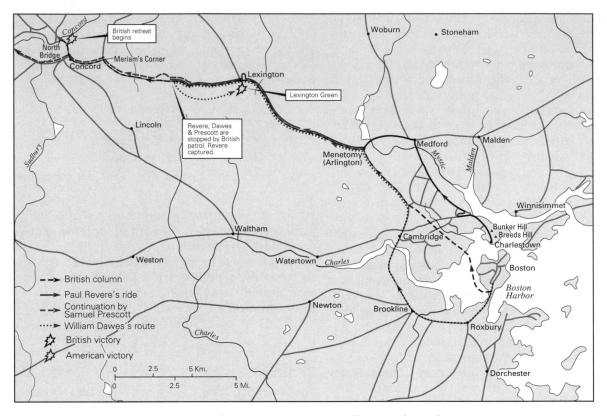

♦ **MAP 4.2 The First Battles in the War for Independence, 1775**   This map shows the British march to Concord and the routes taken by the three Americans who alerted the countryside of the enemy's approach. Although Paul Revere was captured by the British and did not complete his ride, he is the best remembered and most celebrated of these nightriders who spread the alarm.

be *chosen,* and they demanded that loyalties be declared. (See Map 4.2.)

In most colonial cities and towns, patriot committees enforced compliance with the boycott of British goods. These committees published violators' names in local newspapers and called on the community to shun them. If public shaming did not work, most committees were ready to use threats of physical violence and to make good on them.

Suspected British sympathizers were brought before committees and made to swear oaths of support for the patriot cause. Such political pressure often gave way to violence. In New England, many pro-British citizens, or **loyalists,** came to fear for their lives. Hundreds fled to Boston, where they hoped General Gage could protect them.

The Shot Heard Round the World

As the spring of 1775 approached, General Gage decided that it was time to take action against the Massachusetts rebels. Gage planned to dispatch a force of redcoats from Boston to Concord, just twenty miles away, where the patriots had stockpiled arms.

The patriots, however, had anticipated Gage's action. When British troops began to move out of Boston in supposed secret on the night of April 18,

> **loyalist**   An American colonist who supported the British side during the Revolution.

spies in the bell tower of Old North Church signaled that movement to waiting riders. Within moments, Paul Revere and his fellow messengers, William Dawes and Samuel Prescott, galloped off to sound the alarm to the militias in the surrounding countryside.

Around sunrise on April 19, an advance guard of a few hundred redcoats reached Lexington, where they saw about seventy colonial militiamen waiting on the village green. Militia captain John Parker ordered his men to disperse. Some, however, stood their ground. No one ordered the redcoats to fire, but shots rang out, killing eight Americans. Later, Americans would insist that the first musket fired at Lexington sounded a "shot heard round the world."

The British troops marched next to Concord. They searched the nearly deserted town for weapons but found little of military value. At the appropriate moment, the Concord militia launched a surprise attack from their position above the town's North Bridge. The shocked redcoats fled in a panic back toward Boston. The Concord militia followed, gathering more so-called **Minutemen** along the path of pursuit. These American farmers, artisans, servants, and shopkeepers terrorized the young British soldiers, firing on them from behind barns, stone walls, and trees. When the shaken troops reached the British encampment across the Charles River from Boston, 73 of their comrades were dead, 174 were wounded, and 26 were missing. The next day thousands of New England militiamen poured in from the surrounding countryside and laid siege to Boston. The war had begun.

The Second Continental Congress

When the Second Continental Congress convened in Philadelphia in May 1775, it began to ready the colonies for war. It approved the creation of the Continental Army and *chose* George Washington, the Virginia veteran of the French and Indian War, as its commander-in-chief.

Even after Lexington and Concord, some delegates still hoped to find a peaceful solution to the crisis. This sentiment led the Congress to draft the **Olive Branch Petition.** In this petition, the colonists offered to end their armed resistance if the king would withdraw the British military and revoke the Intolerable Acts. Few must have *expected* the king to

do so, for the very next day the Congress issued a public statement in defense of war preparations.

Across the Atlantic, Lord North struggled to find room for negotiations. Before receiving news of Lexington, he had proposed that Parliament suspend its taxation of the colonies if Americans would raise the money to pay for their own defense. North was not willing, however, to concede Parliament's right to tax the colonists.

Americans rejected Lord North's proposals in July 1775. George III rejected the Olive Branch Petition and instead persuaded Parliament to pass the **American Prohibitory Act.** This act instructed the Royal Navy to seize American ships "as if the same were the ships . . . of open enemies." King George III had effectively *chosen* to declare war.

The Impact of *Common Sense*

Although war was now a fact, few Americans called for a complete political break with Britain. Even the most ardent patriots continued to justify their actions as a means to preserve the rights guaranteed to British citizens, not to establish an independent nation.

Few colonists had yet traced the source of their oppression to George III himself. Then, in January 1776, Thomas Paine, an Englishman who had emigrated to Philadelphia several years earlier, published *Common Sense.*

In this pamphlet, Paine attacked the monarchy in the plain language of the common people. He challenged the idea of a hereditary ruler, questioned the

---

Minutemen   Nickname first given to the Concord militia and then applied generally to colonial militia at the time of the Revolution.

Olive Branch Petition   Resolution, adopted by the Second Continental Congress in 1775, that offered to end armed resistance if the king would withdraw his troops and revoke the Intolerable Acts.

American Prohibitory Act   British laws (1775) that authorized the Royal Navy to seize all American ships engaged in trade; it amounted to a declaration of war.

Common Sense   Revolutionary pamphlet written by Thomas Paine and published in 1776; it attacked George III and argued against the monarchial form of government.

Choosing Loyalty

Esther Quincy Sewall

This is the home Esther Sewall chose to leave in 1775 when she accompanied her loyalist husband, Jonathan, to England on the eve of the Revolutionary War. Faced with an uncertain life abroad, she nevertheless chose to stay with her husband rather than remain in Boston and the safety and certainty her friends and family provided. Harvard University Archives.

On November 13, 1790, Esther Quincy Sewall took up her pen to answer a letter from her brother-in-law, the famous patriot John Hancock. Hancock had written, pleading with Esther Sewall to return to her family and friends in their native city, Boston. "I wish it was in my power to accept of your kind invitation," Esther wrote from the isolated loyalist settlement in New Brunswick, Canada; "however this is a pleasure I must post pone for a future day."

Esther Quincy Sewall's exile from her beloved Massachusetts was voluntary. Unlike her husband, Jonathan Sewall, she had not been named a political enemy of the newly independent state. Yet despite the encouragement of her sisters and brothers, she *chose* to continue her exile. For Esther Quincy Sewall the choice was a matter of personal loyalties and commitments as strong as the political ones that shaped her husband's life.

Esther Quincy first met Jonathan Sewall at a boating party in 1759. He was struck by her

value of monarchy as an institution, and criticized the personal character of kings. The common man, Paine insisted, had the ability to be his own king and was surely more deserving of that position than most actual kings. He dismissed George III as a "Royal Brute."

Common Sense sold 120,000 copies in its first three months of publication. Paine's defiance of royal authority and open criticism of the man who wielded it helped many of his readers to discard the last shreds of loyalty to the king and to the empire. The impact of Paine's words could be seen in the taverns and coffeehouses, where ordinary farmers, artisans, shopkeepers, and laborers took up his call for independence and the creation of a republic.

Declaring Independence

The Second Continental Congress had lagged far behind popular sentiment in moving toward independence. Then, on June 7, 1776, Virginia lawyer Richard Henry Lee rose on the floor of the Congress and offered this straightforward motion: "That these United Colonies are, and of right ought to be, beauty and her good humor and placed her immediately in "the rank of the Agreeables." She was, he observed, a woman of "unaffected Modesty," with good judgment, delicate manners, and "real Good sense." Their courtship began at once, but the couple did not marry until 1764, when Jonathan's legal career was better established. Esther's family and friends approved the match, for although Jonathan was from a poor branch of a distinguished family, his talent and ambition led them to predict a good future for the couple. Their predictions were correct. By the eve of the Revolution, Jonathan Sewall held several highly prized positions in the colony's royal government, and Esther lived in quiet elegance with her husband and two sons in their Cambridge home.

The escalating conflicts of 1775 put a sudden end to the life the Sewalls knew. Jonathan Sewall was among the first loyalists to leave America for England in 1775. Esther said goodbye to her patriot relatives and went with him. As the war dragged on, the Sewalls' finances grew strained. They moved from rooming house to rooming house, finally settling in the port city of Bristol.

Exile and the American victory made Jonathan Sewall bitter and psychologically distant. Esther Sewall bore the brunt of his despair. He vented his anger and frustration on his wife, sarcastically wishing her "tyed to the Tail of the Comet of 1668." Esther did not hide her homesickness, and this provoked her husband's anger. He railed against the "deviltry and matrimony" that had ruined his life—and insisted that Esther return to America and leave him in peace.

Despite his accusations and insults, Esther Sewall never considered leaving her physically ailing and depressed husband. She accompanied him to Canada in 1787, joining a small community of loyalist exiles in Nova Scotia. As Sewall's condition deteriorated, Esther became his constant companion and nurse. On September 25, 1796, she began a three-day vigil by his bedside, remaining with him until he died on September 27. Having done her duty as a wife, Esther Sewall felt free to *choose* her own future. After twenty-one years of exile, she packed her few belongings and went home. Whatever her private regrets or satisfactions, she never recorded a word of regret at the *choice* of loyalties that shaped her life.

free and independent States, that they are absolved from all allegiance to the British Crown, and that all political connection between them and the State of Great Britain is, and ought to be, totally dissolved."

Congress *chose* to postpone its final vote until July. The delay would give members time to win over faint-hearted delegates and give the committee appointed to draft a formal declaration of independence time to complete its work.

Four of the men appointed to the committee to draft this declaration were well-known figures: Massachusetts's John Adams, Pennsylvania's Benjamin Franklin, Connecticut's Roger Sherman, and New York's Robert Livingston. But these men delegated the task of writing the document to the fifth and youngest member of the committee, Thomas Jefferson. They *chose* well. The 32-year-old Virginian lacked the reputation of fellow Virginians George Washington and Richard Henry Lee, but he could draw on a deep and broad knowledge of political theory and philosophy. He had read the works of Enlightenment philosophers, classical theorists, and seventeenth-century English revolutionaries. He was also a master of written prose.

Jefferson began the **Declaration of Independence** with a defense of revolution based on "self-evident truths" about humanity's "unalienable rights" to "life, liberty, and the pursuit of happiness." Jefferson argued that these natural rights came from the "Creator" rather than from human law, government, or tradition. Thus they were broader and more sacred than the specific "rights of Englishmen." With this philosophical groundwork in place, Jefferson moved on to list the colonists' grievances, focusing on the king's abuse of power rather than on Parliament's oppressive legislation. All government rested on the consent of the governed, he asserted, and the people had the right to overthrow any government that tyrannized them.

Declaring Loyalties

Delegates to the Second Continental Congress approved the Declaration of Independence in July 1776. Now all Americans had to *choose* their loyalties. For Americans of every region, religion, social class, and even race, this *choice* weighed heavily. Many wavered in the face of such a critical decision. A surprising number clung to neutrality, hoping that the conflict could be resolved without their having to participate or *choose* sides.

Those who did commit themselves based their *choice* on many *constraints, expectations,* and fears (see Individual Choices: Esther Quincy Sewall). For loyalists, tradition and common sense argued for acknowledging parliamentary supremacy and the king's right to rule. Respect for the British government tied these Americans to the empire. The advantages of remaining within the protective circle of the most powerful nation in Europe and the dangers of waging war against it seemed too obvious to debate. Loyalists who were members of the colonial elite also feared that a revolution would unleash the "madness of the multitude."

Economic and social interests brought men and women to the loyalist camp as much as political theory did. Royal officials and merchants who traded with British manufacturers joined the loyalists. Small farmers and tenant farmers from the "multitude" gave their support to the Crown because their foes—the great planters of the South or the manor lords of New York—became patriots. The choosing of sides often hinged on local and economic conflicts rather than on imperial issues.

African-American slaves viewed the conflict in terms of their opportunities for freedom. The royal governor of Virginia, Lord Dunmore, struck a blow against slaveowning patriots when he offered freedom in 1775 to "all indentured Servants, negroes or others . . . able and willing to bear Arms" who escaped their masters. Dunmore's policy had mixed results. It drove many uncommitted southern slaveholders into the revolutionary camp. At the same time, between six hundred and two thousand slaves escaped from their masters in 1775–1776, enough to form an "Ethiopian Regiment" of soldiers. In the long war that followed, perhaps as many as fifty thousand slaves gained their freedom.

Most Indian tribes saw their interests best served by the Crown. Colonial territorial ambitions threatened the Indians along the southern and northwestern frontiers. The Continental Congress knew that Indians were unlikely allies and did little to win their support.

Fewer than half of the colonists sided with the revolutionaries. Among them were people whose economic interests made independence seem worth the risk: artisans and urban laborers, merchants who traded outside the British empire, large and small farmers, and many members of the southern planter elite. Many colonists affected by the Great Awakening's message of egalitarianism *chose* the patriot side. Many who became revolutionaries shared the *expectation* of life under a government that encouraged its citizens to be virtuous and live in simplicity.

As Americans armed themselves or fled from the violence they saw coming, they realized that the conflict was both a war for independence and a civil war. In the South, it pitted master against slave and backcountry farmer against the tidewater elite. In New England, it set neighbor against neighbor, forcing scores of loyalist families to flee. In some families, children were set against parents, and wives against husbands. Whatever the *outcome* of the struggle, Americans knew that it would come at great cost.

> **Declaration of Independence** Document, adopted by the Second Continental Congress in 1776, that listed the rights of man, described the abuses of George III, and declared the American colonies independent of Britain.

SUMMARY

E xpectations
C onstraints
C hoices
O utcomes

Victory in the Great War for Empire made Great Britain the most powerful European nation. The victory also exposed conflicts between British and colonial *expectations* about the colonists' rights and responsibilities. The British had to pay an enormous war debt while maintaining a strong army and navy. Given these *constraints,* the British government *chose* to impose taxes on the colonies. The *outcome* was growing tension between mother country and colonies.

The Sugar Act of 1764 tightened customs collections, the Stamp Act of 1765 taxed legal documents, and the Townshend Acts of 1767 set import taxes on British products such as paint and tea. In response, the colonists *chose* protest. Colonists boycotted British goods, crowds attacked royal officials, and civilians clashed with British troops. American colonists saw Parliament's acts as an abuse of power and as a threat to American liberties.

Protest led to the repeal of the Townshend Acts, but political activists *chose* to prepare themselves for any new crises by creating committees of correspondence. In 1773 the British passed the Tea Act, *expecting* little American opposition. The *outcome* was immediate protest. Activists in Boston dumped tea worth thousands of pounds into the harbor.

The British moved to punish the colonists. They closed the port of Boston to all trade. This action and other Intolerable Acts infuriated the colonists, who decided to take united action in support of Massachusetts. In 1774 the First Continental Congress met to debate the colonies' relationship to Great Britain and to issue united protests. The Congress sent a Declaration of Rights and Grievances to the king. The king *chose* to reject the colonists' appeal for compromise. Instead he declared that "blows must decide."

After the battles at Lexington and Concord, the Second Continental Congress began to prepare for war. Tom Paine's pamphlet *Common Sense* pushed many reluctant colonists into the revolutionary camp. In July 1776 the Congress issued the Declaration of Independence. The Declaration defended the colonists' right to resist the destruction of their liberty by a tyrannical king. In 1776 Americans faced the difficult task of choosing between loyalty to the Crown or revolution. The conflict that followed was both a war for colonial independence and a civil war that divided families and communities across America.

Suggested Readings

Fast, Howard. *Citizen Tom Paine* (1943).
  This novel traces Tom Paine's life from his early English roots to his radical politics during the Revolutionary War.

Flexner, James Thomas. *Washington: The Indispensible Man* (1969).
  This is a spirited biography. An 8 hour miniseries with the same title, produced by CBS, is available on videotape.

Morgan, Edmund and Helen. *The Stamp Act Crisis* (1953).
  This is one of the best and most dramatic accounts of the first explosion of protest in the colonies.

Vidal, Gore. *Burr: A Novel* (1973).
  This novel follows Aaron Burr, a New York political leader and lawyer, through the era of the Revolution to his death in 1836.

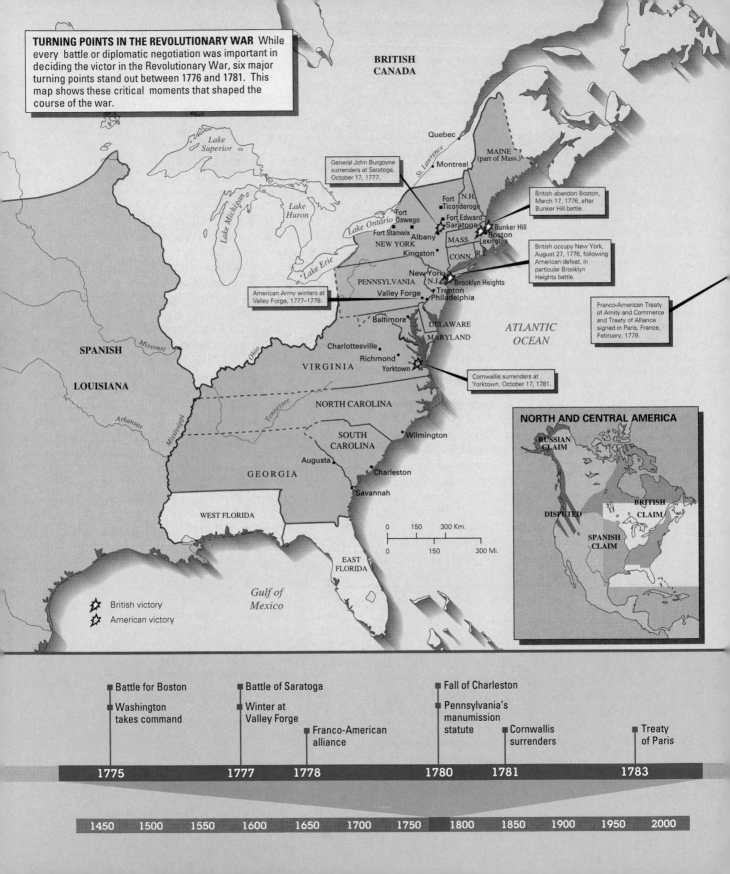

TURNING POINTS IN THE REVOLUTIONARY WAR While every battle or diplomatic negotiation was important in deciding the victor in the Revolutionary War, six major turning points stand out between 1776 and 1781. This map shows these critical moments that shaped the course of the war.

BRITISH CANADA

Quebec

MAINE (part of Mass.)

Montreal

Lake Superior

Lake Michigan

Lake Huron

General John Burgoyne surrenders at Saratoga, October 17, 1777.

British abandon Boston, March 17, 1776, after Bunker Hill battle.

Fort Ticonderoga

N.H.

Fort Oswego

Fort Edward

Saratoga

Bunker Hill

Boston

Lexington

Lake Ontario

Fort Stanwix

Albany

MASS.

Lake Erie

NEW YORK

Kingston

CONN. R.I.

British occupy New York, August 27, 1776, following American defeat, in particular Brooklyn Heights battle.

New York

Brooklyn Heights

PENNSYLVANIA

N.J.

Trenton

American Army winters at Valley Forge, 1777–1778.

Valley Forge

Philadelphia

SPANISH

Missouri

Ohio

Baltimore

DELAWARE

MARYLAND

ATLANTIC OCEAN

Franco-American Treaty of Amity and Commerce and Treaty of Alliance signed in Paris, France, February, 1778.

LOUISIANA

Charlottesville

Richmond

VIRGINIA

Yorktown

Cornwallis surrenders at Yorktown, October 17, 1781.

Arkansas

Tennessee

Mississippi

NORTH CAROLINA

SOUTH CAROLINA

Wilmington

Augusta

Charleston

GEORGIA

Savannah

WEST FLORIDA

0   150   300 Km.

0   150   300 Mi.

NORTH AND CENTRAL AMERICA

RUSSIAN CLAIM

DISPUTED

BRITISH CLAIM

SPANISH CLAIM

EAST FLORIDA

Gulf of Mexico

☆ British victory

✰ American victory

- Battle for Boston
- Washington takes command

- Battle of Saratoga
- Winter at Valley Forge
- Franco-American alliance

- Fall of Charleston
- Pennsylvania's manumission statute
- Cornwallis surrenders

- Treaty of Paris

1775   **1777**   **1778**   **1780**   **1781**   **1783**

1450   1500   1550   1600   1650   1700   1750   1800   1850   1900   1950   2000

Recreating America: Independence and a New Nation, 1775–1783

The First Two Years of War

- What *choices* and *constraints* led to the failure of the British to win the war immediately despite their overwhelming military advantage?

Influences away from the Battlefield

- What *expectations* prompted the French to enter the war?

From Stalemate to Victory

- What different *choices* could the British and Americans have made that might have changed the war's *outcome?*

Republican Expectations in the New Nation

- What *expectations* did the Revolution raise for improvements in the lives of white women and African-Americans, and to what extent were those *expectations* satisfied?

INTRODUCTION

What began as a skirmish at Concord in April 1775 grew into an international war costing millions of pounds and thousands of lives. Great Britain *expected* victory over the colonial rebels, while the Americans' *expectations* were far less confident. Even George Washington frequently expressed his doubts that independence could be won.

To crush the rebellion, Great Britain *chose* to commit vast human and material resources. Between 1775 and 1781, it deployed over fifty thousand British soldiers and hired thirty thousand German mercenaries to fight in North America. The well-trained British troops were assisted and supplied by the most powerful navy in the world. Many Indian tribes, including the Iroquois, *chose* to fight as allies of the British. The Crown harbored *expectations* that thousands of white and black loyalists would fight beside them.

The Americans, in contrast, labored under many *constraints*. The Continental Congress had a nearly empty treasury. The country lacked the foundries and factories to produce arms and ammunition. Through most of the war, American soldiers could *expect* to be underpaid or unpaid, poorly equipped, hungry, and dressed in rags. Unlike the British, these Americans had little military training. Although some officers proved to have a feel for military strategy and tactics, many were just rash young men dreaming of glory. Even the size of this

E xpectations
C onstraints
C hoices
O utcomes

---

poorly equipped and badly prepared American army was uncertain. Washington and his fellow commanders seldom knew how many soldiers would be marching with them on a campaign.

The British advantage was great but not absolute. The Americans were fighting on familiar terrain, and their vast society could not be easily conquered. European rivalries also worked to the Americans' advantage. Holland, France, and Spain supported the rebellion in the *expectation* that Britain's loss would be their gain. When France and Spain *chose* to recognize American independence, the war expanded into an international struggle. French naval support transformed General Washington's strategy. The *outcome* was victory at Yorktown.

Even though the *outcome* of the war was often in doubt, its impact on American men and women was not. No matter which side eighteenth-century Americans supported or what role they played in the war, they shared the experience of extraordinary events and the need to make extraordinary *choices*. In this most personal and immediate sense, the *outcome* was revolutionary.

The First Two Years of War

- What *choices* and *constraints* led to the failure of the British to win the war immediately despite their overwhelming military advantage?

Thomas Gage, the British general who was military governor of Massachusetts, surely wished he were anywhere but Boston in the spring of 1775. The town was unsophisticated by British standards and unfriendly. Gage's army was restless, and his officers were bored. The thousands of colonial **militiamen** gathering on the hills surrounding Boston were

clearly hostile. Yet in 1775 they were still citizens of the British empire rather than foreign invaders or foes. Gage was caught up in the dilemma of an undeclared war.

> **Thomas Gage**   British general who was military governor of Massachusetts; he commanded the British army of occupation at the beginning of the Revolution.
>
> **militiamen**   Soldiers who are not members of a regular army but are ordinary citizens ready to be called out in case of an emergency.

CHRONOLOGY

Rebellion and Independence

1775	Battles of Lexington and Concord Second Continental Congress begins Battle for Boston George Washington takes command of the Continental Army
1776	British campaigns in the middle colonies George Mason's *Declaration of Rights* Thomas Paine publishes *Common Sense* Declaration of Independence
1777	Burgoyne's New York campaign Battle of Saratoga Winter at Valley Forge
1778	Alliance between France and America British begin southern campaign
1780	Fall of Charleston Treason of Benedict Arnold Pennsylvania's manumission statute
1781	Cornwallis surrenders at Yorktown Loyalists leave New York City
1782	British Parliament votes to end war
1783	Treaty of Paris

The Battle for Boston

In early June, Gage proclaimed that all armed colonists were traitors but offered **amnesty** to any rebel who surrendered. The militiamen responded to this offer by expanding their hillside fortifications. Observing this activity, Gage decided it was time to teach the colonials a lesson. He ordered General **William Howe** to take Breed's Hill, across the Charles River from Boston, on June 17, 1775.

Despite the heat and humidity, General Howe ordered his twenty-four hundred soldiers to climb the hill in full dress uniform. Howe also insisted on making a frontal attack on the Americans. The *outcome* was a near massacre of redcoats by Captain William Prescott's militiamen. When the Americans ran out of ammunition, however, the tables turned. Most of Prescott's men fled in confusion. The British bayoneted the few who remained to defend their position.

The British suffered more casualties that June afternoon than they would suffer in any other battle of the war. The Americans, who retreated to the safety of nearby Cambridge, learned the cost of a poor supply system that left fighting men without fresh powder and shot. Little was gained by either side. That the battle was misnamed the **Battle of Bunker Hill** (an adjacent hill) captured perfectly the confusion of the bloody encounter.

On July 3, 1775, **George Washington** arrived to take command of the rebel forces at Cambridge. He could find no signs of military discipline at all. Instead, a carnival atmosphere prevailed. Men fired their muskets at random inside the camp, using their weapons to start fires and to shoot at geese flying overhead. They accidentally wounded and killed themselves and others. The men were dirty, and the camp resembled a pigpen. The general was disturbed but not surprised by what he saw. Many of these country boys were away from home for the first time in their lives. The prevailing chaos resulted from a combination of fear, excitement, boredom, inexperience, and plain homesickness, all brewing

amnesty   A general pardon granted by a government, especially for political offenses.

William Howe   British general in command at the Battle of Bunker Hill; three years later, he was appointed commander-in-chief of British forces in America.

Battle of Bunker Hill   British assault on American troops on Breed's Hill near Boston in June 1775; the British won the battle but suffered heavy losses.

George Washington   Commander-in-chief of the Continental Army; he led the Americans to victory in the Revolutionary War and later became the first president of the United States.

freely under poor leadership. Washington immediately set about to reorganize the militia units and replace incompetent officers.

The siege of Boston ended when cannon captured from the British at Fort Ticonderoga, New York, reached Washington's army after being hauled some 300 miles across country. Once positioned on Dorchester Heights, which overlooked the city, these cannon made Gage's situation hopeless. In March 1776 a fleet of British ships carried Gage, the British army, and almost a thousand loyalist refugees away from Boston and north to Halifax, Nova Scotia. There Gage turned over command to General William Howe.

The British Strategy in 1776

Howe immediately set to work on devising a strategy for subduing the rebellious colonies. The heart of his strategy was to locate areas of loyalist support, to establish a military occupation of these areas with the cooperation of loyalists, and then to expand the British area of influence.

Howe correctly identified New York, New Jersey, Pennsylvania, and the backcountry of the Carolinas as loyalist strongholds. The middle colonies had been slow to take up the cause of independence. In the Carolinas, the coastal planters' support of the revolution had led the majority of backcountry farmers into the loyalist camp. Although the British did make one attempt in 1776 to capture Charleston, South Carolina, Howe *chose* to concentrate his attention on New York.

Escape from New York

Shortly after the American declaration of independence in July 1776, General William Howe and his brother, Admiral **Richard Howe,** sailed into New York harbor with the largest **expeditionary** force of the eighteenth century (see Map 5.1). With thirty thousand men, this British army was larger than the peacetime population of New York City. Washington had anticipated Howe's move and marched his twenty-three thousand troops to defend New York in April 1776.

The British began their advance on August 22, 1776, moving toward the Brooklyn neck of Long Island. Confronted with this large, well-armed British landing force and confused by the sound and the sight of battle, almost all the American troops surrendered or ran. Only Howe's slowness and poor planning prevented a complete fiasco for the Americans. Had Howe stationed ships to guard the East River, Washington's troops would have been trapped on Long Island, and the war might have ended there. But Washington and most of his army escaped to Manhattan and lived to fight another day.

Washington and his army survived primarily by retreating. Howe's troops chased him off Manhattan as well. Watching his men flee in disorder, Washington at one point threw his hat to the ground and shouted, "Are these the men with whom I am to defend America!"

Concerted British pursuit might have put an end to Washington's green and inexperienced army. But after pushing Washington's force out of Manhattan, Howe *chose* to spend a month consolidating his position in New York City. It was October 12 before he engaged Washington again. Howe's haphazard pursuit allowed Washington's army to escape to New Jersey and ultimately across the Delaware River to the safety of Pennsylvania before the arrival of winter.

Winter Quarters and Winter Victories

Following European customs, General Howe established winter quarters before the cold set in. Redcoats and **Hessians** made their camps in the New York area and in Rhode Island that December. Washington did not follow this custom. Enlistment terms in what was left of his army would soon be up, and without some encouraging military success, he *expect*ed that few of his soldiers would reenlist.

Richard Howe   British admiral who commanded British naval forces in America; General William Howe was his brother.

expeditionary   Designed for military operations abroad.

Hessian troops   German mercenaries known as Hessians after the German state of Hesse.

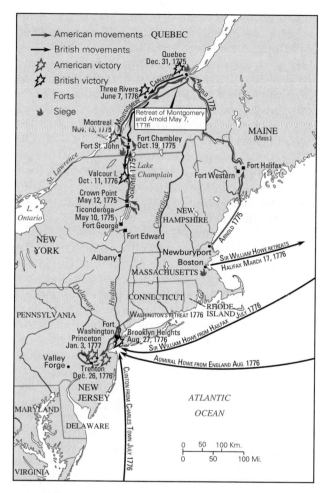

The following labels appear on the map:

→ American movements　QUEBEC

→ British movements

☆ American victory

☆ British victory

■ Forts

🔥 Siege

Quebec Dec. 31, 1775

Three Rivers June 7, 1776

Retreat of Montgomery and Arnold May 7, 1776

Montreal Nov. 13, 1775

Fort Chambley Oct. 19, 1775

Fort St. John

MAINE (Mass.)

Fort Halifax

St. Lawrence

Valcour I. Oct. 11, 1776

Lake Champlain

Fort Western

Crown Point May 12, 1775

Ticonderoga May 10, 1775

Fort George

Fort Edward

L. Ontario

NEW YORK

Albany

NEW HAMPSHIRE

Newburyport

Boston

MASSACHUSETTS

Sir William Howe retreats Halifax March 17, 1776

CONNECTICUT

RHODE ISLAND

Washington's retreat 1776

Sir William Howe from Halifax July 1776

PENNSYLVANIA

Fort Washington

Princeton Jan. 3, 1777

Brooklyn Heights Aug. 27, 1776

Admiral Howe from England Aug. 1776

Valley Forge

Trenton Dec. 26, 1776

NEW JERSEY

ATLANTIC OCEAN

Clinton from Charles Town July 1776

MARYLAND

DELAWARE

VIRGINIA

0　50　100 Km.

0　50　100 Mi.

♦ **MAP 5.1 The War in the North, 1775–1777**　The American attempt to capture Canada and General George Washington's effort to save New York from British occupation were failures, but Washington did manage to stage successful raids in New Jersey before retreating to safety in the winter of 1777. This map details the movements of both British and American troops during the Northern Campaign, and it indicates the victories and defeats for both armies.

Washington *chose* to take a large gamble in his quest for a resounding victory. On Christmas night, in the midst of a howling storm, he and twenty-four hundred troops recrossed the Delaware River and then marched nine miles to Trenton, New Jersey. The hostile weather worked to Washington's ultimate advantage. The several thousand Hessian troops garrisoned near Trenton, never *expecting* anyone to venture out on such a night, drank heavily before falling into their beds. They were in poor

shape to resist when the Americans caught them by surprise the following morning, and quickly surrendered. Washington did not lose a single man in capturing nine hundred prisoners and many badly needed supplies, including six German cannon. Washington then made a rousing appeal to his men to reenlist. The *outcome* proved how correct Washington had been in taking the Christmas night risk, for about half of the soldiers agreed to remain.

Washington enjoyed his next success even more. In early January he again crossed into New Jersey and made his way toward the British garrison at Princeton. En route, his advance guard ran into two British regiments. As both sides lined up for battle, Washington rode back and forth in front of his men, shouting encouragement and urging them to stand firm. His behavior was reckless, for it put him squarely in the line of fire, but it was also effective. When the British turned in retreat, Washington rashly rode after them, delighted to be in pursuit for once.

The Trenton and Princeton victories raised the morale of the Continental Army as it settled into winter quarters near Morristown, New Jersey. Those successes stirred popular support also. Still, the revolutionary forces had done little to stop the Howes, who could be *expected* to march on Philadelphia when warm weather arrived. And neither Washington's polite requests nor angry demands could get Congress to provide the assistance that he needed. The Second Continental Congress met his requests for supplies that winter with "permission" to **commandeer** what was needed from nearby residents. Washington refused, for he knew that seizing civilian property might turn potential patriots into enemies.

Burgoyne's New York Campaign

In July 1777 General William Howe sailed with fifteen thousand men up the Chesapeake Bay toward Philadelphia, causing the Continental Congress to flee. Although the American forces did challenge Howe at Brandywine Creek, they could not stop the British from occupying the capital.

commandeer　To seize for military use.

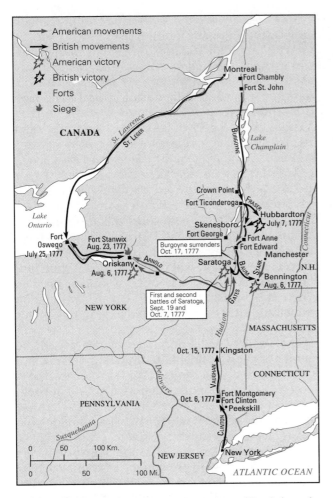

♦ **MAP 5.2 The Burgoyne Campaign, 1777** The defeat of General John Burgoyne and his army at Saratoga was a major turning point in the war. It led to the recognition of American independence by France and later by Spain and to a military alliance with both these European powers. This map shows American and British troop movement and the locations and dates of the Saratoga battles leading to the British surrender.

While Howe was settling in at Philadelphia, a British campaign was getting underway in northern New York. This campaign was part of General **John Burgoyne's** scheme to sever New England from the rest of the American colonies (see Map 5.2). Burgoyne's complex plan called for three British armies to converge on Albany. He would move his army southward from Montreal, while a second army commanded by Colonel Barry St. Leger would head east from Fort Oswego. The third force would march north from New York City. These three armies would isolate New England and provide an opportunity to crush the rebellion.

This daring plan faced serious *constraints*. First, no British official had any knowledge of the American terrain that had to be covered. Second, he badly misjudged Indian support and loyalty. Third, General Howe had not been informed about the plan or his role in it.

Burgoyne's army departed from Montreal in high spirits in June 1777. The troops floated down Lake Champlain in canoes and flatbottom boats. They took Fort Ticonderoga easily. But the subsequent march to Albany proved a nightmare.

In true eighteenth-century British style, Burgoyne *chose* to travel well rather than lightly. The thirty wagons he brought with him contained not only 138 pieces of artillery for the campaign, but Burgoyne's mistress, her personal wardrobe, and a generous supply of champagne. The extra baggage might have been only a minor inconvenience across mild terrain. But after Ticonderoga, the wagons had to travel through swamps and forest, across gullies and ravines. Movement slowed to a snail's pace, and food supplies began to run dangerously low.

The Americans took full advantage of Burgoyne's circumstances. Ethan Allen and the **Green Mountain Boys** harassed the British as they entered what is now Vermont. A confrontation with Allen near Bennington slowed his army even more. When Burgoyne finally reached Albany in mid-September, he was disturbed to discover neither St. Leger nor Howe waiting there.

St. Leger had counted on the support of the entire Iroquois League in his eastward march to Albany. He discovered, however, that some Iroquois had allied with the Americans. St. Leger faced resistance that grew fiercer the closer he got to the rendezvous point. When he learned that Benedict Arnold and an army of a thousand Americans were on their way to challenge him, St. Leger decided to retreat to the safety of Fort Niagara.

> **John Burgoyne** British general who recaptured Fort Ticonderoga but was forced to surrender his entire army at Saratoga in October 1777.
>
> **Green Mountain Boys** Vermont militiamen led by Ethan Allen; together, they and Benedict Arnold captured Fort Ticonderoga in May 1775.

♦ While General Howe's army was enjoying the social life of Philadelphia, Washington's troops made their way to Valley Forge. Seeing the isolated site of this winter camp, one general remarked that either a speculator, a traitor, or a council of idiots must have been responsible for choosing such a location. In fact, Valley Forge was a good tactical choice, for it put Washington's forces between the British army and the Continental Congress, which had fled from Philadelphia to York, Pennsylvania. *"March to Valley Forge" by W. Trego. Courtesy of the Valley Forge Historical Society.*

St. Leger's retreat and William Howe's ignorance of his role in this military operation left Burgoyne stranded. As his supplies dwindled, Burgoyne had few *choices* left by mid-September 1777. He could attempt to break through the American lines and retreat northward to Canada, or he could surrender. On September 19, Burgoyne attacked American forces commanded by Horatio Gates at Saratoga. But "Granny" Gates, as the general was affectionately called, held his ground successfully. He again shut the door on Burgoyne on October 7. On October 17, 1777, Burgoyne had no other *choice* but to surrender.

News of Burgoyne's defeat gave a powerful boost to American confidence and an equally powerful blow to British self-esteem. The stunning victory at Saratoga also raised hopes that France might openly acknowledge American independence and join the war against Britain.

Winter Quarters in 1777

For General Washington, Saratoga was a mixed blessing. The victory fueled *expectations*—which he did not share   that the war was practically at an end. Congress consequently ignored his urgent requests for money to support the Continental Army in its winter quarters some 20 miles from Philadelphia. The *outcome* was a long and dreadful winter at **Valley Forge.**

Rations were a problem from the start. Most soldiers at Valley Forge lived entirely on a diet of fire cakes, made of flour mixed with water and baked in the coals or over the fire on a stick. Keeping warm occupied these soldiers even more than keeping fed, for blankets were scarce, coats were rare, and firewood was precious. They sometimes traded their muskets for the momentary warmth provided by liquor.

The enlisted men at Valley Forge shared a common background. Most were unmarried farm boys, farm laborers, servants, apprentices, artisans, or even former slaves. Although some had wives and children, the majority had few dependents and few hopes of economic advancement. Yet poverty had

Valley Forge   Winter encampment of Washington's army in Pennsylvania (1777–1778), where soldiers were poorly supplied and suffered terribly from cold and hunger.

not driven them into Washington's army. There were other, easier *choices* than soldiering. They could have secured more money, better food, and greater comfort if they had taken up begging. Those who preferred a military life could have served as a substitute for a wealthy man in his local militia unit and been well paid. Instead, they had *chosen* Washington's Continental Army out of their dedication to liberty and independence and intended to see the war to its conclusion.

What these soldiers needed, besides new clothes and hot baths, was professional military training. That is exactly what they got when an unlikely Prussian volunteer arrived at Valley Forge in the spring of 1778. **Friedrich von Steuben** was almost 50 years old, dignified, and elegantly dressed. Although von Steuben was not the grand aristocrat that he claimed to be, he was a talented military drillmaster.

All spring, the baron drilled Washington's troops, alternately shouting in rage and applauding with delight. He *expected* instant obedience, set high standards, and criticized freely. But he also gave lavish praise when it was due and revealed a genuine affection and respect for the men. To Washington, Baron von Steuben was an *unexpected* and invaluable surprise.

The spring of 1778 brought many changes besides a better-trained American army. General William Howe had been called home and replaced by his second-in-command, **Henry Clinton.** The most welcome news to reach Washington was that France had formally recognized the independence of the United States. He immediately declared a day of thanks, ordering cannon to be fired in honor of the new alliance and calling for an inspection of his troops. That day, the officers feasted with their commander, and Washington issued brandy to each enlisted man at Valley Forge.

Influences away from the Battlefield

• What *expectations* prompted the French to enter the war?

The American Revolution, like most other wars, was not confined to the battlefields. Diplomacy in foreign capitals played a crucial role in its *outcome*. So did American popular support for the revolutionary government. In the end, diplomatic and political concerns could not be separated from the fate of the armies on the battlefield.

The Long Road to Formal Recognition

In 1776, Great Britain's rivals in Europe *expected* the American Revolution to fail. Thus France, Spain, and the Netherlands were willing to provide aid secretly to the colonial rebels but unwilling to risk war with Britain by formally recognizing American independence. Even **Benjamin Franklin,** the American minister to France who had charmed everyone in Paris, could not produce a diplomatic miracle of this magnitude. Burgoyne's surrender changed everything.

After Saratoga, the French government immediately reassessed its diplomatic position. The comte de Vergennes, the chief minister of King Louis XVI, suspected that the British would quickly send a peace commission to America. France would gain nothing if the American Congress agreed to a compromise ending the rebellion. But if France gave Americans reason to hope for total victory, perhaps it could recoup some of the territory and prestige that had been lost to Britain in the Great War for Empire. This meant, of course, recognizing the United States and entering a war against Britain. The comte wavered.

Meanwhile, the British government was indeed preparing a new peace offer. George III believed that he was offering the Americans two great concessions. First, Parliament would renounce all intentions of ever taxing the colonies again. Second, Parliament would repeal the Intolerable Acts, the

---

Friedrich von Steuben   Prussian military officer who volunteered to drill Washington's army at Valley Forge, giving the Continental troops much-needed military training at a pivotal period in the war.

Henry Clinton   General who replaced William Howe as commander of the British forces in America in 1778; the change of command was in response to the British defeat at Saratoga.

Benjamin Franklin   American writer, inventor, and diplomat who successfully negotiated French support for the American Revolution in 1778.

Tea Act, and any other objectionable legislation passed since 1763. For the American government, these concessions were too late in coming. By 1778 a voluntary return to colonial status was unthinkable.

Benjamin Franklin knew that Congress would reject the king's offer, but the comte de Vergennes did not. Franklin shrewdly played upon the comte's fears of compromise. He secured French recognition of American independence and a military alliance. Spain followed with recognition in 1779, and the Netherlands in 1780.

War and the American Public

In America, the most striking consequence of the treaty with France was an orgy of spending. Conditions were ripe for this in 1778. The value of government-issued paper money was dropping steadily, and spending rather than saving seemed more sensible. The profits that some farmers and civilians were making from supplying the American armies meant that there were more Americans with money to spend. Finally, some of the credit that American diplomats negotiated with European allies went to purchase foreign manufactured goods. Fear of a long and unsuccessful war had kept Americans wary of spending. When the treaty spurred new confidence that victory was on the way, the combination of optimism, **cheap money,** and the availability of foreign goods led to a wartime spending spree.

Many of these goods were actually made in Britain. Such products often found their way into American hands by way of British-occupied New York City, where imports had reached their prewar levels by 1780. American consumers apparently saw no contradiction between patriotism and the purchase of enemy products.

The spirit of self-indulgence infected the government and the military. Corruption and **graft** were common, especially in the department of the **quartermaster** and in the **commissaries.** Administrators in these divisions sold government supplies for their own profit or charged the army excessive rates for shoddy goods and services. Civilians cheated the government too. Soldiers became accustomed to defective weapons, shoes, and ammunition. They were not immune to the lure of easy money. Some soldiers sold army-issued supplies to any buyers they could find.

Although American *expectations* of victory rose after Saratoga, victory itself remained out of reach. By 1778, the war effort was in financial crisis. Both Congress and the states had exhausted their meager sources of hard currency, leaving the Continental Army in desperate straits. Congress and the state governments met the crisis with the only *choice* they had: printing more paper money. The result was a further lowering of the value of paper currency and complaints from soldiers that they were being cheated out of their pay. Congress acknowledged the justice of these complaints by giving soldiers pay raises in the form of certificates that could be redeemed after the war.

From Stalemate to Victory

• What different *choices* could the British and Americans have made that might have changed the war's *outcome?*

The entrance of France into the war did not immediately alter the strategies of British or American military leaders. After Burgoyne's surrender at Saratoga, British generals continued to be cautious. Washington, who was waiting for help from the French navy, was unwilling to take risks either. The result was a stalemate.

The War Stalls in the North

Sir Henry Clinton, William Howe's successor as British military commander in America, was painfully aware that the French fleet could pose a serious problem for his army. Philadelphia was an easy target for a naval blockade. Clinton accordingly decided to abandon Philadelphia and to return to the safety of New York. By the spring of 1778, Clinton's army was marching east toward New York.

---

cheap money   Loans obtainable at a low rate of interest.

graft   Unscrupulous use of one's position to derive profit or advantage.

quartermaster   An officer responsible for purchasing the food, clothing, and equipment used by troops.

commissary   A supplier of food and other essentials to the continental army. Members of a commissary received a commission for their services.

Washington decided that the retreating British forces, with their long and cumbersome supply lines, were a ripe target. But **Charles Lee,** the American who commanded this attack, called for a retreat almost as soon as the enemy began to return fire. Only Washington's personal intervention rallied the retreating Americans. Trained by von Steuben, the men responded well. They held their lines and then drove the redcoats back. The **Battle of Monmouth** was not the decisive victory Washington had dreamed of, but it was a fine recovery after what appeared to be certain defeat.

The sense of missed opportunity at Monmouth was followed by others. An early joint operation with the French was particularly upsetting. In August 1778, a combined French and American force landed to attack the large British base at Newport, Rhode Island. The French commander, Admiral D'Estaing, lost his nerve, abruptly gathered up his own men, and sailed to safety on the open seas. The Americans were left stranded, forced to retreat as best they could.

General Washington could hardly contain his frustration with the new allies. He was eager to map out a joint strategy using American military strengths and French naval resources to their best advantage. But no French admiral contacted him. All Washington could do was wait.

He did that as patiently as he could through the summer of 1779. That fall he learned that D'Estaing and his fleet had sailed for the West Indies to protect French possessions and perhaps to acquire new islands from the British. Washington understood the French priorities, but he was discouraged. D'Estaing's departure meant more months of inactivity for the general and his restless troops.

The War Moves South

By 1778 it had become apparent to the British that their campaigns in the northern colonies were a failure. Although they could occupy any port that they selected, the countryside remained in patriot hands. And when British troops ceased their occupation of places such as Philadelphia, the rebels quickly resumed control. The British had little to show for three years of fighting in the North. General Henry Clinton decided to shift his attention to the South, where he hoped to find a stronger base of loyalists.

The southern campaign began in earnest with an assault on Savannah, Georgia, in the fall of 1778 (see Map 5.3). When Savannah fell that December, all resistance in Georgia collapsed. For once the British controlled the countryside. Clinton's next target was Charleston. Clinton sailed for Charleston, accompanied by eight thousand troops, in late 1779. After a month-long bombardment, Charleston fell in May 1780. The loss of Charleston was the costliest one for the Americans of the entire war: the whole garrison of fifty-four hundred soldiers surrendered.

Clinton then returned to New York, leaving the ambitious and able general **Charles Cornwallis** in charge. Cornwallis and his regular army were joined by loyalist militias who were eager to take revenge on their enemies. Since 1776, small, roving bands of loyalist guerrillas had kept alive resistance to the Revolution. After the British victory at Charleston, these guerrillas increased their attacks, and a bloody civil war of ambush, arson, and brutality on both sides resulted. By the summer of 1780, the *outcome* was a reversal of fortunes: the revolutionaries were now the resistance, and the loyalists were in control.

The revolutionary resistance produced legendary guerrilla leaders. None of these men was more loved, or feared, than Francis Marion, known as the "Swamp Fox." Marion recruited both blacks and whites to his raiding bands. They steadily harassed Cornwallis's army and effectively cut British lines of communication between Charleston and the interior of South Carolina.

When guerrillas and loyalists met in battle, few rules of war were honored. In October 1780, for example, in the **Battle of King's Mountain,** revolu-

Charles Lee   Revolutionary general who was envious of Washington and allowed his egotism to dictate his decisions on the battlefield; he was eventually dismissed from service.

Battle of Monmouth   Battle fought in New Jersey in June 1778, in which the American retreat ordered by Charles Lee was stopped by General Washington.

Charles Cornwallis   British general who was second-in-command to Henry Clinton; his surrender at Yorktown in 1781 brought the Revolutionary War to a close.

Battle of King's Mountain   Battle fought in October 1780 on the border between the Carolinas; revolutionary troops forced the British to retreat to South Carolina.

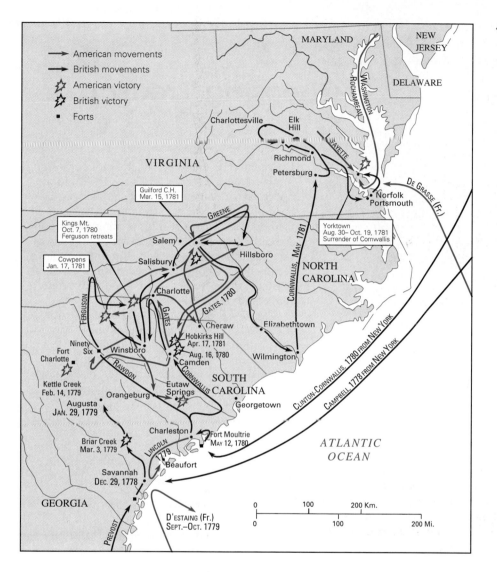

◆ **MAP 5.3 The Southern Campaign, 1778–1781** This map of the British attempt to crush the rebellion in the South shows the many battles waged in the Lower South before Cornwallis's encampment at Yorktown and his surrender there. This decisive southern campaign involved all the military resources of the combatants, including British, loyalist, French, and American ground forces and British and French naval fleets.

tionaries surrounded loyalist troops and picked them off one by one. As this bitter civil war continued, civilians were terrorized and their farms and homes plundered. Outlaws posing as soldiers often did the worst damage.

The regular American army, under the command of the Saratoga hero, "Granny" Gates, enjoyed little success against Cornwallis. In August 1780, Gates suffered a crushing defeat at Camden, South Carolina. Washington ordered Gates's removal that fall, replacing him with **Nathanael Greene**, a younger, more energetic officer from Rhode Island.

Greene was shocked when he arrived in South Carolina. Not only were his fourteen hundred troops tired, hungry, and poorly clothed, but they were "without discipline and so addicted to plundering that the utmost exertions of the officers cannot restrain them." Under these *constraints*, Greene realized that conventional military strategies were pointless. He *chose* to improvise instead.

Greene's most effective move turned out to be his most unorthodox. He boldly split his military force

Nathanael Greene   American general who took command of the Carolinas campaign in 1780.

Choosing Treason

Benedict Arnold

From 1775 until 1779, Benedict Arnold was a military hero, devoted to the patriot cause. But in 1779, he chose to become a traitor, plotting to turn over West Point to the enemy. He escaped to England when the plot was uncovered and died there in 1801. Courtesy of the John Carter Brown Library at Brown University. Photo by Richard Hurley.

Everyone who knew Benedict Arnold admired him as a natural leader and a fearless fighter, but those who knew him best said he was also argumentative and temperamental. General George Washington seemed willing to overlook Arnold's temper and took an active and kindly interest in the younger man's progress. When a serious leg wound threatened to end Arnold's military career, Washington chose to appoint him commandant of Philadelphia.

The move to Philadelphia changed Arnold's life—and almost changed the course of the Revolutionary War. He met and fell in love with the beautiful, vain, and very rich Peggy Shippen. Her wealth far surpassed his, and her political sympathies for the British made her a questionable choice for the wife of a patriot hero. Yet Arnold *chose* to pursue Peggy Shippen, even though he had to take up embezzlement and graft to keep pace with her elegant lifestyle. Peggy tried to convince Benedict that the revolutionary cause was hopeless and that his

in half, sending six hundred soldiers to western South Carolina under the able command of Virginian Daniel Morgan. Cornwallis countered by sending Lieutenant Colonel Banastre Tarleton in pursuit. Morgan led the British officer on a hectic chase across rugged terrain. By the time Tarleton's men cornered the Americans on an open meadow called Cowpens, the British were tired and frustrated. When the smaller American force *chose* to stand its ground, it inflicted heavy casualties on the

British and took six hundred prisoners. Morgan and his soldiers then reunited with General Greene.

Cornwallis subsequently took the offensive against Greene's half of the army. But the American general repeated Morgan's strategy and led the British commander on a long, exhausting chase, retreating into North Carolina. In March 1781, Greene decided it was time to stop running and to fight. Although the Americans withdrew from the Battle of Guilford Courthouse in North Carolina,

expectations for advancement and recognition would never be met by the rebels. A man of his stature, she insisted, could expect far better treatment from the British than from the struggling Americans. At first, Benedict was uncertain. But after they were married, her influence on him increased.

While Peggy was urging her husband to reconsider his *choices,* the American military was investigating his criminal activities. He was charged, tried, and convicted of graft and embezzlement. Again, however, General Washington intervened, and Arnold got off with a slight reprimand. Soon after, Arnold pleaded for one more favor from the general: an appointment as commander of the New York fort at West Point which commanded the Hudson River, a transportation route crucial to the American war effort. Washington was puzzled by the request but eventually agreed.

What was Benedict Arnold up to? The young officer had made his fateful *choice* to switch sides and *expected* to defect in spectacular fashion. The British would get not only a famous revolutionary but control of the Hudson River. Benedict Arnold planned to turn over to the enemy the strategic fort at West Point.

At the last moment, unexpected complications arose. On September 25, 1780, General Washington *chose* to pay a social call on Benedict and Peggy Arnold just as the treasonous plan was set in motion. As a patient Washington sat down to dinner alone—his host nowhere in sight—American soldiers rushed in with secret papers taken from a captured British spy. When the commander-in-chief read the papers, he cried out: "Arnold has betrayed us! Whom can we trust now?"

Benedict Arnold escaped to British lines. Although West Point was saved, Americans mourned that the man who had once been "his Country's Idol" was "now her horror."

British losses were so great that Cornwallis was compelled to retreat to coastal Wilmington, where he could obtain fresh supplies and troops. Cornwallis then headed north into Virginia.

Treason and Triumph

If Washington sometimes wished for a diversion from months of military inactivity, he would not have *chosen* the one that came in the fall of 1780: the treason of **Benedict Arnold** (see Individual Choices: Benedict Arnold). Arnold was both a popular military hero and a particular favorite of Washington. Washington had appointed him commandant at Philadelphia and even protected him from serious

> **Benedict Arnold**   American military leader who helped capture Fort Ticonderoga in 1775; he plotted to hand over West Point to the British in 1780.

punishment when the young officer was convicted of misusing military funds. Arnold repaid the general's kindnesses by plotting to turn **West Point,** a key fort on the Hudson, over to the British. Arnold's plot failed, but his treason shook American morale and caused Washington a deep personal loss.

In May 1781, Washington's gloom was suddenly dispelled when the long-awaited war council with the French materialized at last. Meeting with the French naval commander, the comte de Rochambeau, Washington pressed his case for an attack on New York. Rochambeau, however, had already decided to move against Cornwallis in Virginia and ordered Admiral de Grasse's fleet to Chesapeake Bay. Washington had little *choice* but to concur with Rochambeau's plan. On July 6, 1781, a French army joined Washington's forces just north of Manhattan for the long march to Virginia.

General Cornwallis, unaware that a combined army was marching toward him, busied himself fighting skirmishes with local Virginia militia units. His first clue that trouble lay ahead came when a force of regulars, led by Baron von Steuben and the **marquis de Lafayette,** appeared in Virginia. Soon afterward, Cornwallis *chose* to settle his army at the peninsula port of **Yorktown** and to prepare for more serious battles ahead.

By September 1781, French and American troops coming from New York had joined forces with von Steuben's and Lafayette's men to surround Cornwallis. Meanwhile, Admiral de Grasse's twenty-seven ships had arrived in Chesapeake Bay to seal the trap. General Clinton, still in New York, had been slow to realize what the enemy intended. He could send only a small number of ships from New York to rescue the trapped Cornwallis because most of the British fleet was in the Caribbean.

Admiral de Grasse had little trouble fending off Clinton's rescue squad. Then he and Washington turned their guns on the redcoats. For Cornwallis, there was no escape. On October 17, 1781, he admitted the hopelessness of his situation and surrendered. It was an *outcome* few had *expected*.

Despite the surrender at Yorktown, loyalists and patriots continued to fight each other in the South for another year. Indian warfare continued in the backcountry. The British occupation of Charleston, Savannah, and New York continued. But after Yorktown the British gave up all *expectation* of military victory against the revolutionaries. On March 4,

1782, Parliament voted to cease "the further prosecution of offensive war on the Continent of North America, for the purpose of reducing the Colonies to obedience by force." The war for independence had been won.

Winning Diplomatic Independence

European political leaders *expected* American diplomats to fare badly against the more experienced British and French diplomats in peace discussions held at Paris. But Benjamin Franklin, John Jay, and John Adams were far from naive. Each was a veteran of wartime negotiations with European governments. They knew that their chief ally, France, had its own agenda and that Great Britain still wavered about the degree of independence America was to enjoy.

Despite firm orders from Congress to rely on France at every phase of the negotiations, the American diplomats quickly put their own agenda on the table. They issued a direct challenge to Britain: you must recognize American independence as a precondition to negotiations. The British commissioner reluctantly agreed.

In the **Treaty of Paris** of 1783 the Americans emerged with two clear victories. First, the boundaries of the new nation were to be extensive, going all the way to the Mississippi River. The British did not, however, give up Canada as the Americans had hoped. Second, the treaty granted the United States unlimited access to the fisheries off Newfoundland, a particular concern of New Englander John Adams. But the treaty was vague about many other matters. For example, Britain ceded the Northwest to the United States, but the treaty set no timetable for

---

West Point Site of a fort above the Hudson River north of New York City.

Marquis de Lafayette French aristocrat who served on Washington's staff during the Revolution.

Yorktown Port town in Virginia on the York River near Chesapeake Bay; its location on a peninsula allowed American and French forces to trap the British in their encampment there.

Treaty of Paris Treaty that ended the Revolutionary War in 1783; it gave the Northwest to the United States, set boundaries between the United States and Canada, and called for the payment of prewar debts.

British evacuation of this territory. In some cases, the vague language worked to the Americans' advantage. The treaty contained only the most general promise that the American government would not interfere with Britain's efforts to receive payment for the large prewar debts owed to British merchants. The promise to urge the states to return confiscated property to loyalists was equally vague. The American peacemakers were aware of the treaty's lack of clarity on some issues. But they had gained their major objectives and were willing to accept vagueness as the cost of avoiding stalemate.

Republican Expectations in the New Nation

- What *expectations* did the Revolution raise for improvements in the lives of white women and African-Americans, and to what extent were those *expectations* satisfied?

As an old man, John Adams reminisced about the American Revolution with his family and friends. The Revolution, Adams said, took place "in the hearts and the minds of the people." What he meant was that changes in American social values and political ideas were as critical as artillery, swords, and battlefield strategies in the making of the new nation. Significant changes certainly did take place in American thought and behavior during the war years. Many of these changes reflected the growing identification of the new American nation as a **republic**—that is, a nation in which supreme power rests in the people, not kings or aristocrats. Republican values could be seen in the emphasis on individual rights, in the establishment of representative and **limited government,** and in the ideals of civic-mindedness, patriotism, and a simple, unpretentious lifestyle.

The Protection of Individual Rights

After 1763, the debates over British colonial policy brought about a new emphasis on individual rights. By 1776, many Americans *expected* their government to protect fundamental rights such as life, liberty, and property. Americans also *expected* the power of a government to be limited. No government, they believed, had the authority to abuse or threaten their fundamental rights. Whatever form Americans *chose*

for their new, independent government, they would demand that it protect their rights.

The emphasis on individual rights opened the door to a reform of laws affecting religion. Although individual dissenters such as Roger Williams in the seventeenth century had *chosen* to risk their lives for freedom of conscience, most colonists did not question the value of established churches until the Revolutionary Era.

In 1776, the Virginia House of Burgesses approved George Mason's Declaration of Rights, which ensured Virginians of the right to "the free exercise of religion." Virginia, however, continued to use tax monies to support the Anglican Church. Not until the passage of the Statute of Religious Freedom in 1786 did the state sever its ties with the Anglican Church and allow for complete freedom of conscience, even for atheists. Other southern states followed Virginia's lead.

New Englanders proved more resistant to **disestablishment.** Many wished to continue government support of the Congregational church. Others wished to retain the principle of an established church. As a compromise, the New England states allowed some towns to decide which denomination would be the established church. New England did not separate church and state entirely until the nineteenth century.

Protection of Property Rights

The American revolutionaries were very vocal about the importance of private property. They *expected* government to protect people's rights to own property. In the decade before the Revolution, much of the protest against British policy had focused on this issue. For property holders and aspiring property holders, life, liberty, and happiness were interwoven with the right of ownership.

---

republic A nation in which supreme power resides in the citizens who elect representatives to govern them.

limited government Government that guarantees the security and freedom of the people and interferes as little as possible with their lives.

disestablishment Depriving a church of official government support.

The property rights of some, however, *constrained* the freedoms of others. Slavery's reduction of human beings to private property produced a stark contradiction in values. *Constraints* were also evident in the control that masters wielded over the lives of indentured servants, including the power to forbid a servant to marry or to bear children. *Constraints* could be seen in the white community's denial of Indian claims to the land. Laws placed *constraints* on women's property rights as well. Unless special contracts were drafted before marriage, a woman's property, including her clothing and personal items, fell under the control of her husband.

Although all free white males had the right to own property, not all of them were able to acquire it. When the Revolution began, at least one-fifth of the American people lived in poverty or depended on public charity. The uneven distribution of wealth among white colonists was obvious on the streets of colonial Boston and in the rise in **almshouses** in Philadelphia.

Social Equality

Despite wide variations in wealth, American republicans did believe in social equality. In particular, they aimed to create a society free of artificial privileges that benefited a few at the expense of the many. They eliminated **primogeniture** and **entail** for this reason. In Britain, primogeniture and entail together had created a landed aristocracy. Although the danger of the formation of a similarly privileged aristocracy in the United States was small, the revolutionaries repealed these laws nevertheless.

The passion for social equality extended to national heroes. George Washington and his fellow Revolutionary War officers ran afoul of public opinion when they organized the Society of the Cincinnati in 1783 to sustain wartime friendships. Critics warned that the Society's hereditary memberships, which were to pass from officer fathers to their eldest sons, would create a military aristocracy and pose a threat to republican government. Washington and his comrades were forced to revise the offending Society bylaws.

In some states, the principle of social equality had concrete political consequences. Pennsylvania and Georgia eliminated all property qualifications for voting among free white males. Other states lowered their property requirements for voters but refused to go as far as universal manhood suffrage.

Women in the New Republic

American women would remember the war years as a time of shortages, worry, harassment, and difficult responsibilities. Men going off to war left women and children to manage the farm or the shop, to cope with shortages of food and supplies, and to survive on meager budgets. Many women faced these new circumstances with great anxiety. After the war, however, they remembered with satisfaction how well they had adapted to new roles. They expressed their sense of accomplishment in letters to husbands that spoke no longer of "your farm" and "your crop" but of "our farm" and even "my crop."

What struck many women most vividly was their sudden independence from men. Even women whose circumstances were difficult experienced a new sense of freedom. Grace Galloway, wife of loyalist exile Joseph Galloway of Pennsylvania, remained in America during the war in an effort to preserve her family property. Reduced from wealth to painful poverty, Grace Galloway nevertheless confided to her diary that "Ye liberty of doing as I please Makes even Poverty more agreeable than any time I ever spent since I married."

Galloway's new self-confidence and her newfound liberty were unanticipated *outcomes* of wartime experiences. Not all women were so fortunate. For the victims of rape and physical attack by soldiers on either side, the war meant age-old experiences of vulnerability.

For women, the war meant adapting traditional behavior and skills to new circumstances. Women who joined husbands or fathers in army camps took up the familiar domestic chores of cooking, cleaning, laundering, and providing nursing care. On some occasions, however, they crossed gender boundaries dramatically. Women such as Mary Ludwig Hays (better known as "Molly Pitcher") carried water and ammunition to their husbands and

---

almshouse   A public shelter for the poor.

primogeniture   The legal right of the eldest son to inherit the entire estate of his father.

entail   A legal limitation that prevents property from being divided, sold, or given away.

took up the men's guns when they fell wounded. After the war, a number of these women applied to the government for pensions, citing evidence of wounds they had received in battle.

Both loyalist and patriot women served as spies, sheltered soldiers, and hid weapons in their basements. Sometimes they burned their crops or destroyed their homes to prevent the enemy from using them. These were conscious acts of patriotism rather than wifely duties. The same was true of the small number of women who disguised themselves as men and fought in the military.

The *outcome* of such novel experiences was a new role for women in the family and in a republican society. This new role of **republican motherhood** called for women to be involved actively in the preservation of a republican society. Republican motherhood stressed the importance of women as educators of the next generation of republicans. Republican motherhood did not arise solely from women's wartime experience. It had roots in the growth during colonial times of a prosperous urban class that could purchase many household necessities. These prosperous urban wives and mothers had more time to devote to raising children. Yet the Revolution did give republican motherhood its particular qualities. The republican woman was *expected* to possess an independence of mind and an ability to survive in times of crisis and disaster.

This new civic role for American mothers had profound implications for education. Women could not raise proper republican citizens if they themselves were ignorant and uneducated. It suddenly became important to teach women not just domestic skills but geography, philosophy, and history as well. By the 1780s, public education had come to include girls, and private academies had opened to educate the daughters of wealthy American families.

The War's Impact on Slaves and Slavery

The protection of liberty and the fear of enslavement were major themes of the Revolution. The denial of liberty was a central *constraint* in the lives of most African-Americans. Ironically, the desire for freedom set many slaves against the Revolution. Of the fifty thousand or so slaves who won their freedom in the war, half did so by escaping to the British

army. Only about five thousand African-American men joined the Continental Army. In both armies, however, African-American troops were paid less than white soldiers.

Slaves found other routes to freedom besides military service during the war. They escaped from farms and plantations to the cities, where they passed as free people. Or they fled to the frontier, where they joined sympathetic Indian tribes.

The long war affected the lives of those who remained in slavery. Control and discipline broke down when the southern campaigns disrupted work routines. Slave masters complained loudly and bitterly that their slaves "all do now what they please every where" or that slaves "pay no attention to the orders of the overseer."

In the northern states, the revolutionaries' demand for liberty undermined black slavery. Loyalists taunted patriots, asking, "How is it that we hear the loudest yelps for liberty among the drivers of negroes?" The question made the contradiction between revolutionary ideals and American reality painfully clear. In Boston, a young African-born slave named **Phillis Wheatley,** whose literary talents were encouraged by her master, called on the revolutionaries to acknowledge the universality of the wish for freedom. "In every human breast," Wheatley wrote, "God had implanted a Principle, which we call love of freedom; it is impatient of Oppression, and pants for Deliverance."

Free black Americans joined with white reformers to mobilize antislavery campaigns in Pennsylvania, Massachusetts, Rhode Island, and Connecticut. The broadly based antislavery sentiment in these states was not entirely a matter of moral commitment, however, for the region had few slaves outside New York City (see Figure 5.1).

Manumission increased during the 1770s, especially in the North. In 1780, Pennsylvania became the first state to pass an emancipation statute.

---

republican motherhood   A role for women that stressed the importance of instructing children in republican virtues such as patriotism and honor.

Phillis Wheatley   African-born poet who became the first widely recognized black writer in America.

manumission   The legal act of giving a slave freedom.

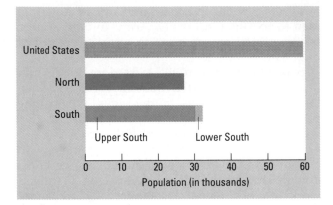

♦ **FIGURE 5.1 Free Black Population, 1790**   This graph shows the number of free African-Americans in the United States in 1790 as well as their regional distribution. These almost 60,000 free people were less than 10 percent of the African-American population of the nation. Although 40 percent of northern blacks were members of this free community, only about 5.5 percent of the Upper South African-Americans and less than 2 percent of the Lower South lived outside the bounds of slavery.

Pennsylvania lawmakers, however, compromised on a gradual rather than an immediate end to slavery. Only persons born after 1780 were to be free, and only after they had served a twenty-eight-year term of indenture. By 1804, all northern states except Delaware had committed themselves to a slow end to slavery.

Slavery was far more deeply embedded in the South. In the Lower South, white Americans ignored the debate over slavery and continued to maintain the institution as if nothing had changed. Manumission did occur in the Upper South, where planters debated the morality of slavery in a republic. They did not all reach the same conclusions. George Washington *chose* to free all his slaves when he died. Patrick Henry in 1765 had stirred the souls of his fellow Virginia legislators by shouting, "Give me liberty or give me death!" But after the war he justified his *choice* to continue slavery with blunt honesty. Freeing his slaves, he said, would be inconvenient.

The Fate of the Loyalists

After 1775, Americans loyal to the Crown flocked to the safety of British-occupied cities—first Boston, and later, New York City and Philadelphia. When the British left an area, most of the loyalists went with them. Over a thousand Massachusetts loyalists boarded British ships when the British abandoned Boston in 1776. Fifteen thousand sailed out of New York in 1781 when the fighting ended. As many as a hundred thousand men, women, and children left America to take up new lives in Great Britain, Canada, and the West Indies.

Wealth often determined a loyalist's destination. Rich and influential men like Thomas Hutchinson of Massachusetts took refuge in Great Britain. But even wealthy colonials discovered that the cost of living there was so great that they could not live comfortably. Some were reduced to passing their days in seedy boarding houses. Even those who fared better lost their status and prestige. Ironically, many loyalists in Britain grew homesick.

When the war ended, most loyalists in Britain departed for Nova Scotia, New Brunswick, or the Caribbean. Some were specifically forbidden to return to the United States, while others had no desire to return. Those who did return to the United States adjusted slowly. Less prosperous loyalists, and especially those who had served in the loyalist battalions during the war, went to Canada after 1781. The separation from family and friends at first caused depression and despair in some exiles. One woman who had bravely endured the war and its deprivations cried when she landed at Nova Scotia. Like the revolutionaries, these men and women had based their political loyalty on a mixture of principled and self-interested *expectations*. Unlike the revolutionaries, they had *chosen* the losing side. They would live with the consequences for the rest of their lives.

Although the revolutionaries were spared homesickness and the task of rebuilding their lives, they still faced serious problems. They faced the task of creating governments to meet republican *expectations* and postwar realities. They confronted a widespread economic depression. The British remained a presence in the Northwest despite the Treaty of Paris, and independence did not ensure the American republic respect in the Atlantic community of nations. *Expectations* were high, but *outcomes* were uncertain.

SUMMARY

E xpectations
C onstraints
C hoices
O utcomes

At the start of the American Revolution, both sides had *expectations* that proved incorrect. The British *expected* a short war from the inexperienced Americans. The Americans *expected* the British to abandon a war fought so far from home. The war, however, dragged on for seven years.

The British *chose* initially to invade New York, *expecting* to find strong loyalist support there. But the British were unable to deliver a crushing blow, and Washington's retreat across the Delaware saved the Americans from surrender.

A dramatic turning point in the war came in 1777, when British general John Burgoyne was forced to surrender at Saratoga, New York. The *outcome* of this American victory was an alliance between France and the United States that expanded the war into an international conflict. When the British *chose* to invade the South in 1778, their campaign ended in disaster. French and American forces together defeated General Cornwallis at Yorktown, Virginia, in October 1781. Fighting continued for a time, but in March 1782, the British Parliament *chose* to end the conflict. The war for American independence had been won.

Independence from British rule was not the only *outcome* of the war. Victory led to transformations in American society. Individual rights were strengthened for free white men. Many white women developed a new sense of the importance of their domestic role as "republican mothers." Black Americans also made some gains. Fifty thousand slaves won their freedom during the war. Some northerners moved to outlaw slavery, but southern slaveholders *chose* to preserve the institution. Loyalists, having made their political *choices*, had to live with the consequences of defeat. The *outcome* for most was exile. Most loyalists *chose* to resettle in Nova Scotia, New Brunswick, or the Caribbean.

Suggested Readings

Freneau, Philip. *The Poems of Philip Freneau Written Chiefly During the Late War* (1786).

This volume of poetry is one of the earliest signs of literary independence from English tradition by an eyewitness to the Revolution.

Nelson, William. *The American Tory* (1961).

A readable history of those who chose to align themselves with the British during the war.

Revolution

This feature-length film, starring Al Pacino, is available in most well-stocked video stores. Although it is a romance, the film captures some of the mood and spirit of the revolutionary era.

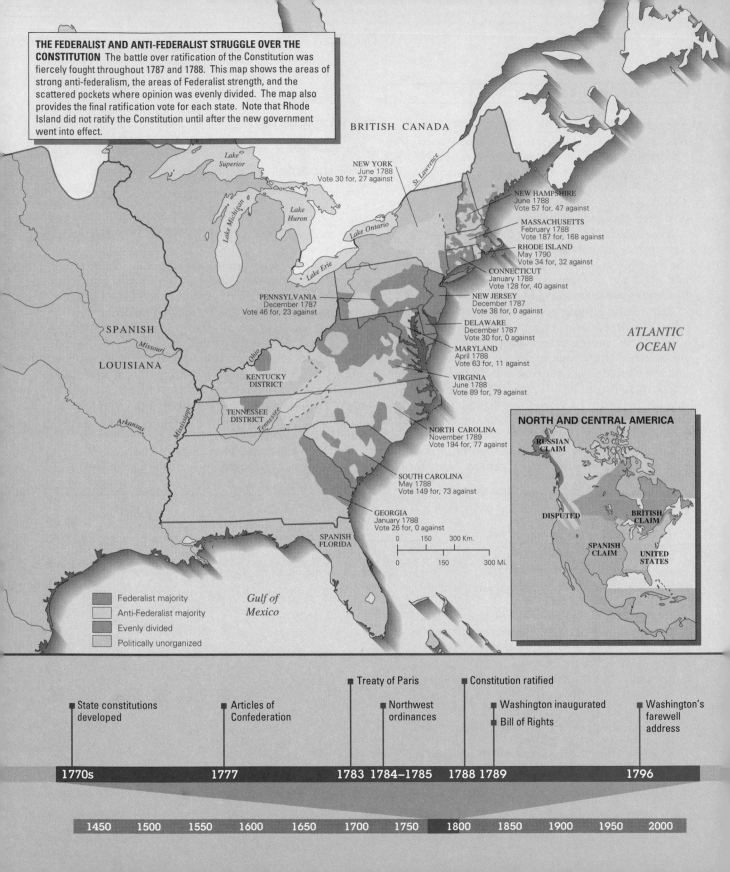

THE FEDERALIST AND ANTI-FEDERALIST STRUGGLE OVER THE CONSTITUTION The battle over ratification of the Constitution was fiercely fought throughout 1787 and 1788. This map shows the areas of strong anti-federalism, the areas of Federalist strength, and the scattered pockets where opinion was evenly divided. The map also provides the final ratification vote for each state. Note that Rhode Island did not ratify the Constitution until after the new government went into effect.

BRITISH CANADA

Lake Superior

Lake Michigan

Lake Huron

Lake Ontario

Lake Erie

St. Lawrence

NEW YORK
June 1788
Vote 30 for, 27 against

NEW HAMPSHIRE
June 1788
Vote 57 for, 47 against

MASSACHUSETTS
February 1788
Vote 187 for, 168 against

RHODE ISLAND
May 1790
Vote 34 for, 32 against

CONNECTICUT
January 1788
Vote 128 for, 40 against

NEW JERSEY
December 1787
Vote 38 for, 0 against

DELAWARE
December 1787
Vote 30 for, 0 against

MARYLAND
April 1788
Vote 63 for, 11 against

VIRGINIA
June 1788
Vote 89 for, 79 against

PENNSYLVANIA
December 1787
Vote 46 for, 23 against

SPANISH

LOUISIANA

Missouri

Ohio

KENTUCKY
DISTRICT

TENNESSEE
DISTRICT

Tennessee

Arkansas

Mississippi

ATLANTIC
OCEAN

NORTH CAROLINA
November 1789
Vote 194 for, 77 against

SOUTH CAROLINA
May 1788
Vote 149 for, 73 against

GEORGIA
January 1788
Vote 26 for, 0 against

SPANISH
FLORIDA

Gulf of Mexico

0   150   300 Km.

0   150   300 Mi.

NORTH AND CENTRAL AMERICA

RUSSIAN
CLAIM

DISPUTED

BRITISH
CLAIM

SPANISH
CLAIM

UNITED
STATES

Federalist majority
Anti-Federalist majority
Evenly divided
Politically unorganized

Treaty of Paris

Constitution ratified

State constitutions
developed

Articles of
Confederation

Northwest
ordinances

Washington inaugurated

Bill of Rights

Washington's
farewell
address

1770s   1777   1783 1784–1785   1788 1789   1796

1450   1500   1550   1600   1650   1700   1750   1800   1850   1900   1950   2000

Competing Visions of a Virtuous Republic, 1776–1796

What Kind of Republic?

- What definitions of a republic were held by eighteenth-century Americans?
- How did these different definitions influence political *expectations* and *choices* as constitutions were written?

Challenges to the Confederation

- How did some political leaders feel the Confederation *constrained* national growth and prosperity?
- What alternatives did they *choose* to propose?

Creating a New Government

- What critical *choices* made by the Constitution's framers reflected the long struggle over the central government's power and scope?

Resolving the Conflict of Vision

- What arguments did the Antifederalists *choose* to stress in opposing ratification of the Constitution?
- What arguments did the Federalists use most effectively to support ratification?

Competing Visions Re-emerge

- What were the major differences between Jefferson's and Hamilton's visions of a republic?
- What was the *outcome* of Hamilton's dominance in the Washington administrations?

INTRODUCTION

E xpectations
C onstraints
C hoices
O utcomes

Most Americans of the revolutionary generation rejected monarchy and *expected* to live in a republic. They disagreed, however, on what form of republic best suited their new nation. As a consequence, the transition from revolution to nationhood was neither smooth nor uncontested.

In the great political contests that occurred during this transition, fundamental *choices* were made about how power should be divided between local and national governments, how laws should be made and by whom, and who should administer those laws. Americans also had to *choose* the best way to protect their unalienable individual rights.

Americans made these political *choices* within the context of serious postwar *constraints*. After the Revolution, the nation struggled with economic depression, unpaid war debts, and vanishing credit. There were rivalries among the states over trade and territory, diplomatic problems with foreign nations and Indians, and disputes among Americans that sometimes erupted into violence.

The first national government, established by the Articles of Confederation, guided Americans through the last years of the war and the peace negotiations. The Articles, however, did not survive the decade of postwar adjustment. The nation *chose* to replace them with the Constitution. The Constitution greatly strengthened and expanded the role of the central government in such matters as regulating trade. The Constitution also provided the central government with powers that the Confederation government had lacked, including the right to levy taxes.

The creation of a new federal government was controversial. Its opponents, the Antifederalists, argued that the Constitution rejected basic revolutionary ideals such as the commitment to local representative government and the guarantee of protection from the dangers of centralized authority. Its supporters, the Federalists, argued that it would save America from economic disaster, international scorn, and domestic unrest. Leading patriots of the 1760s and 1770s could be found on both sides of this debate, but the Federalists carried the day.

The framers of the Constitution knew they had left many problems unresolved. Tensions remained between northern and southern states and between people who supported an active, strong central government and those who believed strong local governments offered the best protection of their liberties. The framers knew also that the nation was seriously divided over foreign policy. But when President George Washington said his farewells to public life in 1796, many Americans believed their young nation would survive.

What Kind of Republic?

- What definitions of a republic were held by eighteenth-century Americans?
- How did these different definitions influence political *expectations* and *choices* as constitutions were written?

To late eighteenth-century Americans, a republic had three basic elements. First and most important, political power rested with the people rather than with a monarch. Second, the people elected those who governed them. Finally, officeholders were *expected* to represent the people's interests and to protect individual rights. While there was broad agreement on these basics, Americans disputed much else about republican government.

Creating Republican Governments: The State Constitutions

The drafting of state constitutions after 1776 offers a revealing look at the many differences in how Americans defined republican government. The states were a laboratory for republican experiments. They came up with many different answers to such

CHRONOLOGY

From Revolution to Nationhood

1770s	State constitutions developed
1775	Battles of Lexington and Concord
1776	New Jersey constitution gives women the right to vote Declaration of Independence
1777	Articles of Confederation adopted by Congress
1780	Massachusetts constitution establishes bicameral legislature
1781	Articles of Confederation ratified Surrender of Yorktown
1783	Treaty of Paris
1784–1785	Northwest Ordinances developed
1786	Annapolis conference
1786–1787	Shays's Rebellion in Massachusetts
1787	Constitutional Convention Northwest Ordinances enacted
1788	Constitution ratified First congressional elections
1789	Washington becomes first president Judiciary Act Bill of Rights adopted by Congress French Revolution begins
1791	Hamilton's *Report on Manufactures* First Bank of the United States chartered Bill of Rights ratified
1793	Genêt affair Jefferson resigns as secretary of state
1794	Whiskey Rebellion in Pennsylvania
1795	Jay's Treaty
1796	Washington's Farewell Address

fundamental questions as who should be allowed to vote, who should be allowed to hold office, and what the structure of a republican government should be.

Pennsylvania passed the most democratic of the state constitutions. Its constitution abolished all property qualifications and granted the vote to all white males. Maryland, in contrast, continued to link property ownership to voting and required officeholders to possess considerable property.

The state constitutions also reflected disagreements over how political power should be distributed in a republic. Pennsylvania's constitution concentrated all power in a **unicameral** assembly. Pennsylvania had neither a governor nor an upper house in the legislature. To ensure that the assembly remained responsive to popular will, the constitution required the annual election of all legislators. Maryland *chose* to divide power among a governor, an upper house requiring high property qualifications for its members, and a lower house. In this manner, Maryland ensured a voice for its elite.

Pennsylvania and Maryland represent two ends of the democratic spectrum. The remaining states fell somewhere between them. New Hampshire, North Carolina, and Georgia followed the democratic tendencies of Pennsylvania. New York, South Carolina, and Virginia *chose* Maryland's more conservative approach. New Jersey and Delaware took the middle ground. New Jersey's constitution was unusual in extending **suffrage** to white women who met modest property qualifications. New Jersey rescinded this right in 1807.

---

unicameral   Consisting of a single legislative house.
suffrage   The right to vote.

♦ The men who drafted the New Jersey constitution took care to include a property qualification for voting but forgot to specify the sex of an eligible voter. Thus women who owned property had the right to vote from 1776 to 1807, when the "error" was corrected. New Jersey did not choose to grant women the vote again for over a century. *The Bettmann Archive, Inc.*

A state's history as a colony was likely to influence its constitution. New Hampshire, South Carolina, Virginia, and North Carolina had all been dominated by coastal elites. Their first state constitutions corrected this injustice by giving more representation to small farmers in the interior. In Massachusetts, the memory of high-handed colonial governors and elitist upper houses led citizens to demand limited powers for their new government.

Revisions of the state constitutions in the 1780s generally expanded the powers of the state governments and curbed democratic tendencies. The Massachusetts constitution of 1780 became a model for these constitutional reforms. It called for a system of **checks and balances** among the legislative, judicial, and executive branches and for a **bicameral** legislature. Wealth returned as a qualification to govern in these revised constitutions, but the wealthy were not allowed to tamper with the basic individual rights of citizens. In seven states, this protection was ensured by a **bill of rights,** which guaranteed freedom of speech, religion, the press, and other rights.

Creating the Government of the Republic: The Articles of Confederation

Almost six years after the Second Continental Congress had declared independence, the first representatives to the new national government arrived in Philadelphia in March 1781. Congress had adopted the first national framework of government, the **Articles of Confederation,** in 1777, and submitted the plan to the state governments for their approval. But ratification of the Articles by the states turned out to be a long and difficult process.

Although Pennsylvania's John Dickinson had proposed a strong national government, the Continental Congress ultimately approved a plan for a **confederation** of states. This confederation was a limited union that preserved the rights and privileges of the states and that had few powers. This arrangement reflected the revolutionaries' fears that a strong central government was the enemy of liberty.

The Confederation government consisted of a unicameral legislature. It had no executive branch and no separate **judiciary.** Democrats such as Tom Paine and Samuel Adams praised this concentration of powers in the hands of an elected assembly. John Adams, however, thought it "too democratical."

The Confederation government had no power to tax. The states retained this crucial power. Thus the Confederation government had to rely on the states

---

checks and balances   The separation of the powers of government into executive, legislative, and judicial branches, each of which is intended to prevent the others from getting out of control.

bicameral   Consisting of two legislative houses.

bill of rights   A formal summary of essential rights and liberties.

Articles of Confederation   The first constitution of the United States; it created a central government with limited powers and was replaced by the Constitution in 1788.

confederation   An association of states or nations united for joint action in matters that affect them all.

judiciary   A system of courts of law for the administration of justice.

◆ **MAP 6.1 Western Land Claims After American Independence** This map indicates the claims made by several of the thirteen original states to land west of the Appalachian Mountains and in the New England region. The states based their claims on the colonial charters that governed them before independence. Until this land was ceded to the federal government, new states could not be created here as they were in the Northwest Territory.

for funds. It had no legal right to compel states to provide funds and no practical means of forcing them to contribute.

Voting in the Confederation Congress was to be done by states. Each state, whether large or small, had one vote. This jealous protection of state sovereignty also determined the amendment process for the Articles of Confederation. An amendment required the consent of all the states.

Fierce arguments developed over how each state's share of the federal budget was to be determined. Proposals that everyone in a state be counted brought southern political leaders to their feet, for their states had large slave populations. If slaves were included, southern whites would have to shoulder a heavier tax burden. Congress ultimately decided to count slaves for tax purposes.

The biggest delay in ratifying the Articles of Confederation, however, was caused by the battle over western land claims. Based on their colonial charters, Virginia, Massachusetts, and Connecticut claimed the Pacific as their western boundary (see Map 6.1). Consequently they could assert rights to the Northwest Territory, the region north of the Ohio and east of the Mississippi rivers. States with fixed western boundaries such as Maryland feared that they would be dwarfed by their neighbors that claimed western lands for expansion. Maryland advocated that western lands be set aside as part of a national domain controlled by Congress, not by the individual states. Although most states without western claims reluctantly ratified the Articles, Maryland would not endorse them without the establishment of a national domain.

To avoid further delays in ratification, Virginia ceded all of its claims to Congress. The other states with western claims followed suit. In 1781, Maryland became the thirteenth and final state to ratify the Articles.

Challenges to the Confederation

- How did some political leaders feel the Confederation *constrained* national growth and prosperity?
- What alternatives did they *choose* to propose?

Members of the first Confederation Congress had barely taken their seats when Lord Cornwallis surrendered at Yorktown in 1781. Even the most optimistic could see, however, that the new nation faced monumental challenges. The physical, psychological, and economic damage caused by the long and brutal war was extensive. New York and Charleston had been burned. Communities in New Jersey and Pennsylvania bore the scars of rape and looting by the British armies. In the South, where civil war had raged, plantations had been destroyed and slaves had fled. A steady stream of refugees filled the cities.

Depression and Financial Crisis

Americans were hard hit by a postwar depression. By the time peace was declared, small farmers who had lost barns and livestock and planters who had lost slaves or seen their tobacco warehouses go up in smoke were desperate. Wages plummeted in the 1780s for urban workers and farm laborers. Soldiers waited without hope for their back pay.

Financial problems also plagued wealthy Americans. Many merchants feared ruin because they had overextended their credit to import foreign goods after the war. Land speculators had borrowed too heavily in order to grab up confiscated loyalist lands or secure claims in the Northwest Territory. Independence hurt those who had once lived well by supplying British markets. Rice planters saw the demand for their crop fall dramatically after the war.

British policy also hurt the economy. Parliament banned the sale of American farm products in the West Indies and limited the rights of American ships to carry goods to and from Caribbean ports. These restrictions hit New England shipbuilders so hard that whole communities faced poverty.

This economic depression made it extremely difficult for the Confederation government to pay its debts. To finance the war, the Continental Congress had printed over $240 million in paper money backed by "good faith" rather than by gold and silver. As *expectations* that the national government would ever **redeem** the paper for hard currency fell, the value of the paper money declined rapidly. The phrase "Not worth a Continental" was coined to indicate the low regard Americans had for this paper money. Congress was equally embarrassed by substantial debts to foreign nations that it could not repay.

Congress appointed Robert Morris, a Philadelphia merchant who had earned a reputation during the war for his financial genius, to raise money to pay these debts. Morris knew from experience that he could not rely on the states for contributions. Instead, he asked the states for permission to impose a 5 percent federal **tariff** on imported goods. The states, however, refused to give their unanimous permission in 1782, 1783, and again in 1784. Morris resigned in disgust in 1784.

The Northwest Ordinances

The Confederation Congress turned next to western land sales as a way to raise money. Here at least Congress was not *constrained* by the need for state approval. It had the exclusive authority to set policy for the settlement and governance of national territory.

National land policy took shape in three **Northwest Ordinances** enacted in 1784, 1785, and

---

redeem To pay a specified sum in return for something.

tariff A tax on imported or exported goods.

Northwest Ordinances Three laws (1784, 1785, 1787) that dealt with the sale of public lands in the Northwest Territory and established a plan for the admission of new states to the Union.

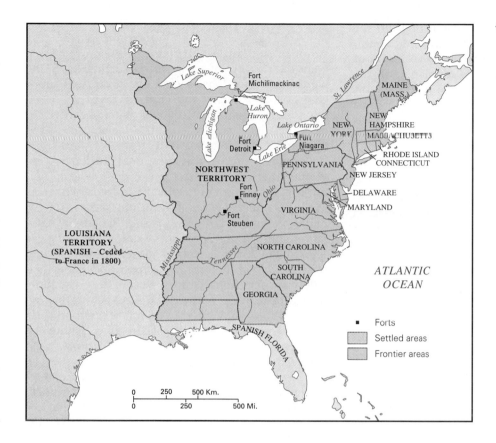

♦ **MAP 6.2 The United States in 1787**   This map shows the extent of American westward settlement in 1787 and the limits placed on that settlement by French and Spanish claims west of the Mississippi and in Florida. Plans for the creation of three to five states in the Northwest Territory were approved by Congress in 1787, ensuring that the settlers in this region would enjoy the same political rights as the citizens of the original thirteen states.

1787. These ordinances had a significance far beyond their role in raising money. They guaranteed that men and women who moved west would not be colonial dependents of the original states. The 1784 ordinance prescribed that five new states would be carved out of the region and that each new state would be equal in status to the original thirteen. Settlers in the region could *expect* to acquire the rights of self-government quickly. Initially each territory would have a governor appointed by Congress. As soon as there were enough voters, settlers were entitled to a representative assembly. Finally, the territory's voters would draft a state constitution and elect representatives to the Confederation Congress. Ohio, Illinois, Indiana, Michigan, and Wisconsin followed this path to statehood (see Map 6.2).

The ordinance of 1785 spelled out the terms for the sale of government land. It called for Congress to auction off 640 acre plots to individual settlers at a minimum price of a dollar per acre. When the original price proved too high for the average farm family, Congress lowered the price but also began to sell to wealthy speculators.

The ordinance of 1787 specified that any territory with sixty thousand white males could apply for admission as a state. Thomas Jefferson, who drafted this ordinance, took care to protect the liberties of the settlers with a bill of rights and to ban slavery forever north of the Ohio River.

Diplomatic Problems

Despite the Treaty of Paris, diplomatic relations between the new nation and former mother country remained sour. The British refused to evacuate their western forts until the Americans repaid their war debts and allowed loyalists to recover confiscated property. Meanwhile, the British supported Indian resistance to American settlement in the Ohio Valley by providing a steady supply of weapons to the Shawnees, the Miamis, the Delawares, and other tribes that refused to recognize the 1784 **Treaty of Fort Stanwix.** Made with the remnants of the Iroquois League, the treaty opened up all Iroquois lands to white settlement, according to Americans. Tribes that were not party to the treaty disagreed and, with British assistance, waged warfare along the frontier for a decade.

The Americans got little satisfaction from the British on this or other issues. John Adams, the American minister to Britain, was unable to persuade the British to abandon their northwestern forts, to stop their aid to Indians, or to open up their markets to American goods.

The United States also experienced difficulties with its former allies. When Spain saw a steady stream of Americans heading into Kentucky and Tennessee, it became alarmed that Americans might soon threaten its interests west of the Mississippi. Aware that the Mississippi provided the only practical way for Americans west of the mountains to export their surplus goods, Spain *chose* to ban all American traffic on the Mississippi. This move was intended to discourage migration into the trans-Appalachian area. When American negotiator **John Jay** reported that talks with Spain produced no promise of access to the Mississippi, southern states moved as a bloc to prevent any further negotiations.

The Confederation's failures in dealing with the **Barbary pirates** were military rather than diplomatic in nature. For many years, rulers along the Barbary coast of North Africa had attacked ships engaged in Mediterranean trade. Although most European nations paid blackmail to these pirates, the British provided naval escorts for their ships. Ships flying the American flag now traveled at their own risk.

In 1785 the Barbary pirates captured an American ship, seized its cargo, and sold its crew into slavery. Despite outcries, the Confederation Congress could do nothing. It had no navy and no authority to create one. It could not even raise enough money to ransom the enslaved crew.

Lack of resources and authority thus plagued the Confederation government in its efforts to conduct foreign affairs. It was a frustrating fact that the Confederation could make few effective *choices* in its diplomacy.

A Farmers' Revolt

Among those hardest hit by the postwar depression were the farmers of western Massachusetts. Many were deeply in debt to creditors who held mortgages on their farms and lands. When they asked the state government for debt relief, however, it turned a deaf ear. Instead, the legislature raised taxes to pay the state's war debts.

Farmers protested this additional burden by petitioning the legislature to lower their taxes. Their protests again went unheeded. Hundreds of farmers led by Daniel Shays, a 39-year-old veteran of the Battle of Bunker Hill, then turned to armed resistance in the western part of the state.

In 1786, Shays's Rebels closed down several courts in which debtors were tried and freed their fellow farmers from debtors' prison. Fear of a widespread uprising prompted the Massachusetts government to order General William Sheperd and six hundred men to Springfield. There, over a thousand farmers, most of them armed with pitchforks, had gathered to close the local courthouse. Sheperd let loose a cannon barrage that killed four rebels and set the rest to flight. In February 1787, a government force surprised the remaining rebels in the village of Petersham. Daniel Shays managed to escape, but the revolt was over.

Shays's Rebellion revealed the temper of the times. When the government did not respond to their needs, the farmers *chose* to act as they had in the years before the Revolution. They organized; they protested; and when their *expectations* were not met, they took up arms. Across the country, many

---

Treaty of Fort Stanwix   Treaty signed in 1784 that opened all Iroquois lands to white settlement.

John Jay   New York lawyer and diplomat who negotiated with Great Britain and Spain on behalf of the Confederation; he later became the first chief justice of the Supreme Court.

Barbary pirates   Pirates along the Barbary coast of North Africa who attacked European and American vessels engaged in Mediterranean trade.

Shays's Rebellion   Uprising by farmers in western Massachusetts who wanted to protest the indifference of the state legislature to the plight of farmers; the rebellion was suppressed by the state militia in 1787.

Americans sympathized with those *expectations* and the actions that followed.

But many did not. Among the southern planter elite and the prosperous commercial class of the North, the revolt raised the fear that other local insurrections would follow. Rebellions by slaves, pitched battles between debtors and creditors, and wars between the haves and have-nots could easily be imagined. Such anxieties led many Americans to wonder if their state and national governments were strong enough to preserve the rule of law.

The Revolt of the "Better Sort"

Even before Shays's Rebellion, many Americans had come to believe that a crisis was enveloping their young nation. They pointed to the Confederation's lack of power to solve critical problems as a major cause of this crisis. In the words of George Washington, "I predict the worst consequences from a half-starved, limping government, always moving upon crutches and tottering at every step."

To Washington, the solution was clear: a stronger national government. Support for a revision of the Articles grew in the key states of Virginia, Massachusetts, and New York, especially among the elite. They urged that the central government be given taxing powers and that some legal means of enforcing national government policies be instituted. These reforms would help improve the young republic's diplomatic and trade relations with foreign countries. But these reforms would also create a national government able to protect their property and to preserve their peace of mind.

The **nationalists'** agenda began to take shape in 1786 when they obtained approval from the Congress for a conference at Annapolis, Maryland. Their stated purpose was to discuss trade restrictions and conflicts among the states. But the organizers also meant to test support for revising the nation's constitution. Although only a third of the states participated, the nationalists were convinced that they had strong support. They asked Congress to call a convention for the following year in Philadelphia to discuss remedies for the Confederation's problems. News of Shays's Rebellion convinced doubters of the need for a convention. Leaders of the "better sort" thus won an

opportunity to reopen debate on the nature of the republic.

Creating a New Government

• What critical *choices* made by the Constitution's framers reflected the long struggle over the central government's power and scope?

Late in May 1787, George Washington welcomed delegates from twelve of the thirteen states to the Constitutional Convention. Rhode Island had declined to attend, declaring that this was a meeting to revise the Articles masquerading as a discussion of interstate trade. The accusation was correct. The fifty-five men in attendance *expected* to consider significant changes in their national government. The seriousness of their task explained their willingness to meet in a tightly closed room in the sweltering heat of a Philadelphia summer.

Revise or Replace?

Most of the delegates were nationalists, but they did not agree about whether to revise or to abandon the Articles of Confederation. For five days the Convention debated this issue. Then Edmund Randolph of Virginia presented a plan that essentially scrapped the Articles of Confederation.

Although Randolph introduced the **Virginia Plan, James Madison** was its guiding spirit. The plan reflected the 36-year-old Madison's deep consideration of the following question: what kind of government was best for a republic? He concluded that a strong central government could serve a republic well. Fear of tyranny should not be an overpowering *constraint* against a powerful national

> **nationalist** A person devoted to the interests of a particular nation and favoring a strong central government.
>
> **Virginia Plan** A plan for a federal government submitted by the Virginia delegation; it gave states representation in a bicameral legislature in proportion to their population.
>
> **James Madison** Virginia planter and political theorist who supported ratification of the Constitution; he later became the fourth president.

government. Abuse of power could be avoided, Madison believed, if internal checks and balances were built into the government's structure.

The Virginia Plan embodied this conviction. It called for a government with three distinct branches: legislative, executive, and judicial. The Confederation Congress had performed all three of these functions. By dividing power, Madison intended to ensure that no group or individual could wield too much authority. And by allowing each branch of government some means to check the other branches, Madison intended to protect the interests of citizens.

Although the delegates supported the broad principles of the Virginia Plan, they were in sharp disagreement over many specific issues. The greatest controversy centered on representation in the legislative branch. Madison had proposed that membership in each house of the bicameral legislature be based on proportional representation. Large states supported the plan, for representation based on population was to their advantage. Small states objected that the Virginia Plan would leave them helpless in a federal government dominated by large states. They supported the **New Jersey Plan,** which proposed that every state have an equal voice within a unicameral legislature.

The hopeless deadlock over the Virginia and New Jersey plans threatened to destroy the convention. Roger Sherman of Connecticut then introduced the **Great Compromise.** It called for **proportional representation** in the lower house (the House of Representatives) and equal representation in the upper house (the Senate).

The Great Compromise resolved the first major controversy at the convention. Another compromise settled the issue of how representatives were to be *chosen.* State legislatures would select senators, and a state's eligible voters would elect members of the House of Representatives.

The final stumbling block over representation was the question of who was to be counted in determining a state's population. Southern delegates argued that slaves should be counted for the purposes of representation but not for the purposes of taxation. Northern delegates countered that slaves should be considered property, and not people, for both purposes. The **Three-fifths Compromise** settled this issue. It stipulated that three-fifths of the slave population be included in a state's critical head count.

Drafting an Acceptable Document

The Three-fifths Compromise ended the long, exhausting debate over representation. No other issue provoked such controversy, and the Constitutional Convention proceeded calmly to implement the principle of checks and balances. For example, the president was named commander-in-chief of the armed forces and given primary responsibility for the conduct of foreign affairs. To balance the president's executive powers, the rights to declare war and to raise an army were given to Congress. Congress was also given the critical power to tax, but this power was checked by the president's power to veto congressional legislation. Congress in turn could override a presidential veto by the vote of a two-thirds majority.

The procedure for electing a president reflected the delegates' fears that the ordinary people could not be trusted to perform such an important task. Their solution was to elect the president indirectly, through the **Electoral College.** This body consisted of electors *chosen* by the states to vote for presidential candidates. Each state was entitled to as many electors as it had senators and representatives in

---

New Jersey Plan   A plan for a federal government giving all states equal representation in a unicameral legislature.

Great Compromise   A plan for a federal government that set up a bicameral legislature, with one house providing equal representation to all states and the other providing proportional representation based on population.

proportional representation   Representation in the legislature based on population; it gives large states more power than small states.

Three-fifths Compromise   An agreement to count three-fifths of a state's slaves for purposes of determining a state's representation in the House of Representatives.

Electoral College   A body of electors chosen by the states to elect the president and vice president; each state gets a number of electors equal to the number of its senators and representatives in Congress.

Congress. (No one serving in Congress was eligible to be an elector.) If two candidates received the same number of votes in the Electoral College, or if no candidate received a majority of the Electoral College votes, the House of Representatives would *choose* the new president.

The *outcome* of the Constitutional Convention was a new plan for a national government. The plan won near unanimous support from the delegates. A weary George Washington at last declared the convention adjourned on September 17, 1787.

Resolving the Conflict of Vision

• What arguments did the Antifederalists *choose* to stress in opposing ratification of the Constitution?
• What arguments did the Federalists use most effectively to support ratification?

For the new Constitution to go into effect, special state ratifying conventions had to approve of the proposed change of government. The framers of the Constitution argued that these conventions would give citizens a more direct role in making this important political decision. This procedure also gave the framers two advantages. First, it allowed them to bypass the state legislatures, which stood to lose power under the new government and were thus likely to oppose it. Second, it allowed the framers to nominate their supporters and to campaign for their election to the state conventions. The framers added to their advantage by declaring that the approval of only nine states was necessary for ratification. Fortunately, the Confederation Congress agreed to all these terms and procedures. By the end of September 1787, Congress had passed the proposed Constitution on to the states, triggering the next debate over America's political future.

The Ratification Controversy

The framers were leading figures in their states. These men of wealth, political experience, and frequently great persuasive powers put their skills to the task of ratifying the Constitution. But many revolutionary heroes and political leaders strongly opposed the Constitution, most notably Patrick Henry and Samuel Adams. Leadership on both sides of the issue was drawn from the political elite of the revolutionary generation.

Pro-Constitution forces won an early and important victory by calling themselves **Federalists.** This name had originally been associated with those who supported strong state governments and a limited national government. This shrewd tactic robbed opponents of the Constitution of their rightful name. The pro-Constitution forces then dubbed their opponents **Antifederalists.**

Although the philosophical debate over the best form of government for a republic was important, voters considered practical factors in choosing a Federalist or an Antifederalist position. Voters in states with a stable economy were likely to oppose the Constitution because the Confederation system gave their state greater independent powers. Voters in small states, in contrast, were likely to favor a strong central government that could protect them from their competitive neighbors. Thus the small states of Delaware and Connecticut ratified the Constitution quickly.

To some degree, the split between Federalists and Antifederalists matched the divisions between the urban, market-oriented communities of the Atlantic coast and rural, inland communities. For example, the backcountry of North and South Carolina saw little benefit in a strong central government that might tax them. However, commercial centers such as Boston, New York City, and Charleston were eager to see an aggressive national policy regarding foreign and interstate trade. Artisans, shopkeepers, and even laborers in these urban centers joined forces with wealthy merchants and shippers to support the Constitution.

Antifederalists developed a number of arguments against the proposed Constitution. They rejected the claim that the nation was facing economic and political collapse. As one New Yorker put it: "I deny that we are in immediate danger of anarchy and commotions." Antifederalists struck hard

---

Federalists Supporters of ratification of the Constitution; they believed in a strong central government.
Antifederalists Opponents of ratification of the Constitution; they feared that a strong central government would be an instrument of tyranny.

as well against the dangerous **elitism** that they saw in the Constitution. They portrayed the Federalists as a privileged minority, ready to oppress the people if a powerful national government were ratified.

The Antifederalists' most convincing evidence of their opponents' potential for tyranny was that the Constitution lacked any bill of rights. Unlike many of the state constitutions, the Constitution did not contain written guarantees of the people's rights. Antifederalists asked what this glaring omission revealed about the intentions of the framers. The only conclusion, Antifederalists argued, was that the Constitution was a threat to republican principles of representative government, a vehicle for elite rule, and a document unconcerned with the protection of individual liberties.

The Federalists' strategy was to portray America in crisis. They pointed to the stagnation of the American economy, to the potential for revolt and social anarchy, and to the contempt that other nations showed toward the young republic. They also argued that the Constitution could preserve the republican ideals of the Revolution far better than the Articles of Confederation.

That was the primary argument of the *Federalist Papers,* a series of essays that appeared in New York newspapers. Signed by "Publius," they were actually written by **Alexander Hamilton,** James Madison, and John Jay in an effort to persuade New Yorkers of the merits of ratification. The essays linked American prosperity and a strong central government. They countered Antifederalist claims that a strong central government would endanger individual liberties by arguing that a system of checks and balances would protect those liberties. And as Madison pointed out in *The Federalist,* No. 10, a large republic with an effective national government offered far better protection against tyranny than the state governments, where it was far easier to form a permanent majority.

The Federalist Victory

Practical politics influenced the decision of most state ratifying conventions. Delaware, New Jersey, Georgia, and Connecticut—all states with small populations—quickly approved the Constitution. Although there was more opposition in Pennsylvania, Federalists won a quick victory there

as well. In the remaining states, the two sides were more evenly matched.

Antifederalists had the majority initially in the Massachusetts convention. Many delegates were small farmers from the western counties, more than twenty of whom had participated in Shays's Rebellion. The Federalist strategy in Massachusetts was to woo key Antifederalists such as Samuel Adams and John Hancock with promises that a bill of rights would be added to the Constitution. This strategy yielded the Federalists a narrow 19-vote margin of victory out of the more than 350 votes cast.

After Massachusetts ratified, the Federalists in New Hampshire carried the day by a small majority. Rhode Island, true to its history of opposition to strong central authority, refused to hold a convention. But Maryland and South Carolina ratified. Thus as of June 1788 the requisite number of nine states had given their assent to the new plan of government. But this new government could not function effectively in the absence of such large and populous states as New York and Virginia. In Virginia, Antifederalist leaders Richard Henry Lee, Patrick Henry, and James Monroe focused on the absence of a bill of rights in the proposed Constitution. Edmund Randolph, James Madison, and George Washington directed the Federalist counterattack. In the end, Washington's presence and promises of a bill of rights proved decisive. Virginians *expected* this war hero to be the first president of the United States if the Constitution went into effect. Virginia became the tenth state to ratify the new government. Realizing that the new government had already become a reality, New York's strongly Antifederalist convention followed Vir-

---

elitism The belief that certain people deserve favored treatment because of their social, intellectual, or financial status.

Federalist Papers Essays written by Alexander Hamilton, James Madison, and John Jay in defense of the Constitution; they helped establish the basic principles of American government.

Alexander Hamilton New York lawyer and political theorist who worked to win ratification of the Constitution; he later became the first U.S. secretary of the treasury.

ginia's course. North Carolina ratified the Constitution in 1789, and a reluctant Rhode Island followed suit in 1790.

President George Washington

George Washington's unanimous selection by the Electoral College to become the nation's first president took no one by surprise. He was the hero of the Revolution. The celebrations surrounding Washington's inauguration in the temporary capital of New York in April 1789 bore witness to the genuine affection Americans of all classes and regions felt for the Virginian.

Washington's popularity served the new government well, for it softened general suspicion of executive power. The new president understood that he symbolized a new national experiment in government and that his behavior in office would be watched carefully. Because he was the first person to hold the presidency, every action he took had the potential to set a precedent for those who followed.

The early debate over Washington's public title showed the importance of precedents. Vice President John Adams urged that Washington be called "His Highness, the President of the United States of America, and Protector of their Liberties." Several senators proposed similar titles, each meant to rival the titles of foreign monarchs. Antifederalists, who had refused to run for office in the first Congress of 1788, were quick to note the unrepublican quality of these suggestions. In the end, Washington *chose* the solidly republican title "Mr. President" as the appropriate term of address.

Washington was a cautious and deliberate man. Sensitivity to his precedent-setting role made him especially deliberate as he staffed the executive branch. He took particular care in *choosing* the men to head the four executive departments—Treasury, War, Attorney General, and State—created with approval from Congress. Naming his **protégé** Alexander Hamilton to head the Treasury Department was probably Washington's easiest decision. He asked Henry Knox of Massachusetts to head the War Department and fellow Virginians Edmund Randolph to serve as attorney general and Thomas Jefferson as secretary of state. Over time, the president established a pattern of meeting with these advisers regularly to discuss policy. Thus,

although the Constitution made no provision for a **cabinet,** Washington established the precedent of cabinet meetings with the department heads and the vice president.

Competing Visions Re-emerge

- What were the major differences between Jefferson's and Hamilton's visions of a republic?
- What was the *outcome* of Hamilton's dominance in the Washington administrations?

A remarkable spirit of unity marked the early days of Washington's administration. Federalists had won the overwhelming majority of seats in the new Congress, and this success enabled them to work quickly and efficiently. This unity also proved to be fragile. As the government debated foreign policy and domestic affairs, two distinct groups slowly emerged. Alexander Hamilton's vision for America guided one; Thomas Jefferson's guided another.

Unity's Achievements

One of the first Congress's major accomplishments was the creation of a federal judiciary. The **Judiciary Act of 1789** established a Supreme Court, thirteen district courts, and three circuit courts. It also empowered the Supreme Court to review the decisions of state courts and to nullify state laws that violated either the Constitution or any treaty made by the federal government. Washington *chose* John Jay to serve as the first chief justice of the Supreme Court.

The spirit of cooperation during Washington's first term enabled Congress to break the stalemate

---

protégé   One whose welfare or career is promoted by an influential person.

cabinet   A body of officials appointed by the president to run the executive departments of the government and to act as his advisers.

Judiciary Act of 1789   Law establishing the Supreme Court and the lower federal courts; it gave the Supreme Court the right to review state laws and state court decisions to determine constitutionality.

on the tariff issue. Discussion of tariffs had previously become snarled by regional interests. But James Madison was able to negotiate an import tax on items such as rum, cocoa, and coffee that was acceptable to northerners and southerners.

Madison also prodded Congress to draft the promised bill of rights. He gathered eighty suggested amendments and honed them down to nineteen for Congress to consider. Congress narrowed these to ten amendments and submitted them to the states for ratification. The required approval by three-fourths of the states came quickly, and by December 1791 the **Bill of Rights** had become part of the Constitution. Eight of these amendments spelled out the government's commitment to protect the **civil liberties** of individuals such as free speech and freedom of religion. The Ninth Amendment made clear that the inclusion of these rights did not imply the exclusion of others. The Tenth stated that any powers not given to the federal government or denied to the states belonged solely to the states or the people.

Hamilton's and Jefferson's Differences

Alexander Hamilton dreamed of transforming an agricultural America into a manufacturing society that would rival Great Britain. His blueprint for achieving this goal included tariffs designed to protect developing American industry and government **subsidies** for new enterprises. It also called for close economic and diplomatic ties with Great Britain.

Thomas Jefferson and his ally James Madison had a different vision for America's future. They hoped America would remain a prosperous agrarian society. They favored a national policy of **free trade** rather than one employing protective tariffs. Jefferson was willing to tolerate commerce and industry as long as they complemented agrarian society. A dominant commercial society constituted a threat, because it could exploit citizens or lead to the love of luxury, which every republican knew was bad.

Hamilton's group spoke of themselves as true **Federalists.** Those who agreed with Jefferson and Madison spoke of themselves as **Republicans.** The emergence of these two political camps troubled even the men who helped create them. The revolu-

tionary generation had been taught that **factions** or parties were great political evils.

Hamilton's Economic Plan

As secretary of the treasury, Alexander Hamilton was responsible for solving the young republic's **fiscal** problems, particularly its foreign and domestic debts. For Hamilton, these problems were as much an opportunity as a challenge. His solutions, however, bitterly divided Congress in the early 1790s.

In January 1790 Hamilton submitted a *Report on Public Credit* to the Congress. In it, he argued that the public debt fell into three categories:

1. Foreign debts, owed primarily to France

2. State debts, incurred by the individual states to finance their war efforts

3. A national debt in the form of government notes (the notorious paper Continentals) that the Second Continental Congress had issued to finance the war

To establish its credit and trustworthiness, Hamilton said, the nation must find a way to pay

---

Bill of Rights   The first ten amendments to the U.S. Constitution, added in 1791 to protect certain basic rights of American citizens.

civil liberties   Fundamental individual rights such as freedom of speech and religion, protected by law against interference by the government.

subsidy   Financial assistance granted by a government in support of an enterprise regarded as being in the public interest.

free trade   Trade between nations without protective tariffs.

Federalists   Political group led by Alexander Hamilton that formed during Washington's first administration; they favored commercial growth and a strong central government.

Republicans   Political group led by Thomas Jefferson that favored limited government and envisioned the United States as a nation of independent farmers.

faction   A group of people with shared opinions and goals who split off from a larger group.

fiscal   Relating to government finances.

♦ Both Charles Wilson Peale, who painted this portrait, and his son Rembrandt Peale, preferred to portray Jefferson as a man of noble character rather than power and wealth. Jefferson undoubtedly approved. As a young man Jefferson preferred to read science and philosophy rather than join in the gambling and drinking common to the Virginia planter elite. When his papers and library were destroyed in a fire in 1770, Jefferson sighed, "Would to God it had been the money." *Courtesy Independence National Historic Park Collection.*

each type of debt. Hamilton proposed that the federal government assume responsibility for all three types. He insisted that the Continentals be redeemed at their face value, which was much greater than their current market value. And he proposed that the current holders of Continentals should receive that payment. These recommendations raised a storm of debate within Congress.

Before Hamilton's *Report*, James Madison had been the voice of unity in Congress. Now, Madison leaped to his feet in protest. The government's debt, he argued, was not to the current holders of the Continentals but to the original bondholders. Many of the original holders were ordinary citizens and Continental soldiers who had sold their bonds to speculators at a tremendous loss during the postwar depression. If Hamilton's plan were adopted, Madison warned, these speculators rather than the nation's true patriots would reap enormous profits.

Hamilton responded by pointing out the difficulty of identifying and finding the original holders of the Continentals. Madison's solution was simply impractical. With some misgivings, Congress *chose* to support Hamilton.

Madison was still not prepared to accept Hamilton's proposal that the federal government assume, or take over, the states' debts. A fierce nationalist, Hamilton wanted to concentrate political and economic power in the federal government. He knew that creditors, who included America's wealthiest citizens, would take a particular interest in the welfare and success of any government that owed them money. Hamilton intended to tie the material interests of America's elite to the federal government.

Maryland and Virginia led the fight against assumption. These states pointed out that they had already paid all their war debts. If the national government assumed state debts and raised taxes to repay them, then the citizens of Maryland and Virginia would have to be burdened with debts that other states had not paid.

The Senate approved assumption, but the House deferred action. To ensure success, Hamilton conducted some behind-the-scenes negotiations with Madison and Jefferson. Hamilton's bargaining chip was the location of the national capital. Although the new government had made New York its temporary home in 1789, a permanent site for the national capital had not yet been decided upon. Hamilton was willing to put the capital in Madison's and Jefferson's backyard in exchange for their support of federal assumption of state debts. The bargain appealed to the two Virginians, and they threw their support behind assumption. The future capital was to be located on a site between Maryland and Virginia.

Hamilton made still another proposal in 1791 to further his vision for America. This time he proposed chartering a national bank. The bank, modeled on the Bank of England, would serve as fiscal agent for the federal government, although it would not be an exclusively public institution. The bank would be funded by the government and by private sources in a partnership that would further tie national prosperity to the interests of private wealth.

Although James Madison questioned the constitutionality of this proposal, Congress nevertheless passed the legislation. Madison's argument did cause President Washington to consult Secretary of State Jefferson and Treasury Secretary Hamilton for their views on the constitutionality of the Bank of the United States before signing the bill.

Jefferson, like Madison, was a **strict constructionist** in his interpretation of the Constitution. Jefferson argued that there were grave dangers in interpreting the government's powers broadly: "To take a single step beyond the boundaries . . . specifically drawn around the powers of Congress is to take possession of a boundless field of power." Hamilton saw no such danger in the proposed bank. A **broad constructionist,** Hamilton countered with an argument based on Article I, Section 8, of the Constitution. This section granted Congress the right to "make all Laws which shall be necessary and proper" to exercise its legitimate powers. Hamilton believed that this language "ought to be construed liberally in advancement of the public good." Since the bank would serve a useful purpose in tax collections, Hamilton believed there could be no reasonable constitutional objection to it. Hamilton's argument persuaded the president.

Hamilton outlined the next phase of his economic development program for the United States in his *Report on Manufactures* in 1791. This report called for protective tariffs, government subsidies, and other policies that would make the country into an industrial power. These proposals, however, were too extreme for Congress. Still, Hamilton had done much to realize his dream of a commercial and manufacturing republic. The Bank of the United States and the establishment of sound national credit did much to create and to attract **capital** for new enterprises.

Foreign Affairs and Deepening Divisions

The first signs of division in American politics had appeared in response to Hamilton's economic program. Those divisions hardened into permanent political parties when Americans were forced to

choose how to respond to the **French Revolution** and to its international repercussions. When the French Revolution broke out in 1789, Americans had almost universally applauded it. The American Revolution and the French Revolution seemed close cousins in their shared political rhetoric and ideals. Like most other Americans, Washington was pleased to be identified with this newest struggle for the "rights of man."

By 1793, however, American public opinion had begun to divide sharply on the French Revolution. Popular support weakened when the revolution's most radical party, the **Jacobins,** imprisoned and then executed the king and queen. Shocked Americans denounced the revolution when the Jacobins began the **Reign of Terror** against their opponents.

Meanwhile, France had become involved in a war with Great Britain, Spain, Austria, and Prussia. France *expected* the Americans to honor the terms of the 1778 alliance, which bound the United States to protect French possessions in the West Indies. Since the British were most likely to strike these possessions, a second war between Britain and the United States loomed as a possibility.

American opinion about such a war was contradictory and complex. Some thought American

---

strict constructionist   A person who believes the government has only those powers that the Constitution specifically grants to it.

broad constructionist   A person who believes the government has not only the powers specifically listed in the Constitution but whatever implied powers are in keeping with the spirit of the Constitution.

capital   Money needed to start a commercial enterprise.

French Revolution   Political upheaval against the French monarchy and aristocratic privileges; it began in 1789 and ended ten years later; its republican ideals gradually gave way to violence and disorder.

Jacobins   Radical republican party during the French Revolution.

Reign of Terror   The period from 1793 to 1794 in the French Revolution during which thousands of people were executed because the revolutionary government considered them to be enemies of the state.

honor dictated that the United States should aid France, its Revolutionary War ally. Others, including Thomas Jefferson, did not want the United States to become embroiled in a European war. Hamilton favored maintaining close ties with the British. While Americans struggled with these contradictory views, the French decided to mobilize American support directly.

In 1793, the French republic sent a diplomatic minister to the United States. When Citizen **Edmond Genêt** arrived in Charleston, he did not present his credentials as an official representative from France. Instead he launched a campaign to recruit Americans for the war effort. Genêt's flagrant disregard for formal procedures infuriated Washington. But popular support for the colorful Genêt was strong. Prominent citizens welcomed and entertained him when he arrived in Philadelphia, the new temporary capital.

Genêt may have believed he had outmaneuvered Washington, but he was wrong. The president skillfully finessed his nation's obligations to France under the 1778 treaty. On April 22, 1793, Washington issued a proclamation that declared American **neutrality** without actually using that term. Thus he avoided a formal **repudiation** of the alliance with France but made it clear that the United States would not give the French military support (see Voices: Washington's Policy of Neutrality in 1793). When Genêt ignored the proclamation and commissioned several Americans as officers in the French army, even Jefferson thought that he had gone too far. Genêt's influence declined rapidly and the Genêt affair was over.

The diplomatic crisis was far from over. The British began seizing American vessels that were trading with France. These seizures prompted a new outburst of popular support for war against Great Britain. Anti-British emotions ran even higher when the governor of Canada encouraged Indian violence against American settlers in the Northwest. Such emotions led Congress to debate trade restrictions against the British and to divide between supporters and opponents of the Washington administration's largely pro-British policies. Washington's unanimous re-election as president in the fall of 1793 did not reflect this increasingly bitter divide. Jefferson's resignation as secretary of state in late 1793 was a better gauge of political unity.

Washington's response to the growing diplomatic crisis was to send Supreme Court Chief Justice John Jay to Britain as his special **envoy** early in 1794. The treaty that Jay negotiated was not a great victory for American diplomacy. True, it did resolve some old, nagging issues. The British agreed to evacuate the western forts and to grant some small trade concessions in the West Indies. The United States in return agreed to see that all prewar debts to British merchants were at last paid. But Jay was forced to abandon America's demand for freedom of the seas and conceded the Royal Navy's right to remove French property from any neutral ship. Jay returned home to face strong public criticism and very little praise. The Federalists credited **Jay's Treaty** with preserving the peace, but the Republicans condemned it. Jay's Treaty squeaked through the Senate in 1795. Neutrality, compromised and shaky, continued to be the nation's policy.

The Washington administration did far better in military and diplomatic affairs in the West. In August 1794, at the **Battle of Fallen Timbers,** General "Mad" Anthony Wayne's army decisively defeated Indians from several tribes in the Northwest Territory. In the **Treaty of Greenville** in August 1795, the Indians ceded most of the land that

---

Edmond Genêt   French diplomat whom the French revolutionary government sent to the United States to try to draw the United States into France's war against Britain and Spain.

neutrality   The policy of not favoring either side in a conflict but treating both sides in the same way.

repudiation   The act of rejecting the validity or authority of something.

envoy   A government representative who is sent on a special diplomatic mission.

Jay's Treaty   Treaty between the United States and Britain negotiated in 1794 by John Jay; it addressed such issues as British refusal to evacuate forts in the Northwest and British seizures of American ships.

Battle of Fallen Timbers   Battle in August 1794 in which Kentucky riflemen defeated Indians of several tribes, hastening the end of Indian resistance in the Northwest.

Treaty of Greenville   Treaty of 1795 under which Northwest Indians were paid about $10,000 to cede land that later became the state of Ohio.

Washington's Policy of Neutrality in 1793

Proclamation of Neutrality

On April 22, 1793, President George Washington announced that the United States would maintain a "friendly and impartial" relationship with the warring nations of France and Great Britain. The choice to remain neutral came after heated debate in the press and in the government between supporters and opponents of the French Revolution. Even though the excesses of French radicals had disturbed pro-French groups, they argued that the 1778 treaty of alliance between France and America committed the United States to support the French in the current European war. Alexander Hamilton and other opponents believed the outcome of American involvement in the conflict would be disaster. Washington's decision to issue the neutrality proclamation was motivated in part by the actions of Edmond Genêt and by the rise of "Democratic Societies"—groups supposedly organized to support the French Revolution, but devoted to criticizing the president and his Federalist policies and programs.

Whereas it appears that a state of war exists between Austria, Prussia, Sardinia, Great Britain, and the United Netherlands on the one part, and France on the other, and the duty and interest of the United States require that they should with sincerity and good faith adopt and pursue a conduct friendly and impartial toward the belligerent powers:

I have therefore thought fit by these presents to declare the disposition of the United States to observe the conduct aforesaid toward those powers respectively, and to exhort and warn the citizens of the United States carefully to avoid all acts and proceedings whatsoever which may in any manner tend to contravene such disposition.

And I do hereby also make known that whosoever of the citizens of the United States shall render himself liable to punishment or forfeiture under the law of nations by committing, aiding, or abetting hostilities against any of the said powers, or by carrying to any of them those articles which are deemed contraband by the modern usage of nations, will not receive the protection of the United States against such punishment or forfeiture; and further, that I have given instructions to those officers to whom it belongs to cause prosecutions to be instituted against all persons who shall, within the cognizance of the courts of the United States, violate the law of nations with respect to the powers at war, or any of them.

Supporters Had This to Say

■ In respect to foreign politics, the views of [the pro-French faction] are, in my judgment, equally unsound and dangerous. They have a womanish attachment to France and a womanish resentment against Great Britain. They would draw us into the closest embrace of the former, and involve us in all the consequences of her politics; and they would risk the peace of the country in their endeavors to keep us at the greatest possible distance from the latter. The neutral and the pacific policy appears to me to mark the true path to the United States. *Alexander Hamilton to Edward Carrington, 1793.*

■ I have no doubt, that the sense of this Country [Virginia] is for a perfect neutrality, if it can possibly be had. My own sentiments are, that the French, from having commenced one of the noblest causes that ever presented itself in any country, have lost themselves in the wildest quixotism: My wish is, that they may recover their reason, and establish for themselves a good Government, leaving other Countries to judge for themselves. If they do this, they need not fear the combinations of their Enemies. *Edward Carrington to Alexander Hamilton, April 26, 1793.*

Opponents Had This to Say

■ Had you, sir [President Washington], before you ventured to issue a proclamation which appears to have given much uneasiness, consulted the general sentiments of your fellow citizens, you would have found them, from one extremity of the Union to the other, firmly attached to the cause of France. You would not have found them disposed to consider it as a "duty" to forget their debt of gratitude to the French nation . . . Even had no written treaty existed between France and the United States, still would the strongest ties of amity have united the people of both nations. National Gazette *(Philadelphia), June 5, 1793.*

■ Should the glorious efforts of France be defeated, we have reason to presume that this country, the only remaining depository of liberty, will not long be permitted to enjoy in peace the honors of an independent and the happiness of a republican government. The seeds of luxury appear to have taken root in our domestic society, and the jealous eye of patriotism already regards the spirit of freedom and equality as eclipsed by the pride of wealth and the arrogance of power. *The Democratic Society of Pennsylvania, July 1793.*

To Crush a Revolt

Alexander Hamilton

Alexander Hamilton was an ardent advocate of a strong central government. He chose to crush a poorly armed group of men rebelling against a tax imposed on whiskey in 1794, rather than retract the tax, which in his view, would signal a weakened government. "Alexander Hamilton" by Charles Wilson Peale. Courtesy Independence National Historical Park.

In his meteoric rise from poverty and obscurity, Alexander Hamilton was an American success story. Yet Hamilton had little interest in wealth or social status. Instead, he burned with the desire to shape his adopted nation's future. Politics was his life, and he worked hard to achieve his goal of creating a dynamic and internationally respected nation.

As secretary of the treasury, Hamilton labored to establish sound national credit, a banking system, and programs to stimulate economic growth and expansion. He *expected* criticism of his actions and always *chose* to ignore it. He cared little for what the public thought of him or his policies, he said, for he had "long since learned to hold public opinion of no value." Thus, when news came in 1794 that farmers in western Pennsylvania had revolted against his whiskey tax, Hamilton wasted little time *choosing* a course of action.

Other cabinet members saw the Whiskey Rebellion as justified civil disobedience to harsh or unfair legislation. But Hamilton disagreed. He admitted that the tax—which was his brain-

later became Ohio. Soon after, Thomas Pinckney, U.S. envoy to Spain, negotiated a treaty with Spain that won for the United States the right of free navigation on the Mississippi.

Another Farmers' Revolt

In domestic matters, President Washington demonstrated the new government's willingness and abil-

ity to enforce its laws. In 1794, farmers in western Pennsylvania revolted against a steep federal excise tax on whiskey (see Individual Choices: Alexander Hamilton). Political opponents of the tax saw it as an example of the dangers of a strong central government. The grain farmers saw it as a sign that the new government was blind to their interests. But Washington, haunted by the memory of Shays's Rebellion and troubled by the radical spirit of the child—was a high one, requiring a 25 percent charge on all production of liquor. And he knew that distilling was a critical home industry for many grain farmers whose crops might rot before reaching the market unless they were converted into whiskey. Yet Hamilton cast the issue in dramatic political terms, arguing that the rebellion challenged the authority of the new constitutional government. "Shall the majority govern or be governed?" was the critical question for Hamilton. "Shall the general will prevail, or the will of a faction? Shall there be government or no government?" In such a crisis, the federal government's only *choice* was swift, effective military action.

Hamilton's sense of urgency could not be explained entirely by the danger to national security. In truth, the whiskey rebels were few in number and poorly armed. Their resistance, however, was a direct threat to Hamilton's plan for national economic expansion. If one group of citizens *chose* to oppose government taxes by force and succeeded, he reasoned, their success would set a dangerous precedent for other discontented groups. As an active participant in the prerevolutionary protests, Hamilton knew where such protest could lead.

Hamilton's arguments helped persuade the president. George Washington chose to ride at the head of the army sent to crush the rebellion. With him were thirteen thousand men, a force larger than the one he had commanded during the American Revolution. The *outcome* of this confrontation between farmers and soldiers was never in doubt. When the rebels saw the huge army marching against them, they quickly dispersed, and their leaders fled to safety.

Thomas Jefferson reprimanded the treasury secretary for pursuing his "favorite purpose of strengthening government" at the expense of ordinary Americans. While Hamilton *chose* to be "so patient of the kicks and scoffs of our [foreign] enemies," Jefferson observed, at home Hamilton was a terror, "rising at a feather against our friends." If Hamilton was affected by this criticism, he did not show it. The ardent nationalist did not stop working for a more prosperous, more powerful nation until another political enemy, Aaron Burr, killed him in a duel on a summer day in 1804.

French Revolution spreading throughout America, sent thirteen thousand troops to western Pennsylvania to crush the **Whiskey Rebellion.**

Washington's Farewell

The bitter political fight over Jay's Treaty, nagging press criticism of his policies, and the hardening of party lines between Federalists and Republicans helped George Washington decide not to seek a third term as president. In 1796 he retired to Mount

> **Whiskey Rebellion**   An uprising by grain farmers in western Pennsylvania in 1794 over a federal tax on whiskey; Washington led militias from nearby states to quell the rebellion.

GENERAL GEORGE WASHINGTON.
Reviewing the Western army at Fort Cumberland the 18th of October 1794

♦ President Washington donned his Continental Army uniform when he led thirteen thousand troops against the western Pennsylvania farmers who dared to resist the federal government's excise tax on whiskey. At the sight of such a massive army—larger than the Continental force Washington had commanded during the Revolution—the whiskey rebels wisely fled to safety. *"General George Washington Reviewing the Western Army" by Kemmelmeyer. Courtesy, Winterthur Museum.*

Vernon, his beloved Virginia home, and resumed the life of a gentleman planter.

When Washington retired, he left behind a nation very different from the one whose independence he had helped win. The postwar economic depression was over. The economy of the United States had moved decisively in the direction that Alexander Hamilton had envisioned. The pursuit of profit and of individual success had captured the imagination of many white Americans. Hamilton's policies as secretary of the treasury had promoted the expansion of trade, the growth of markets, and the development of American manufacturing and industry. In its political life, the republic had seen the relationships between the states and the central government redefined. America's political leadership, taught that factions were dangerous, had nevertheless created and begun to work within an evolving party system.

In his **Farewell Address** to the public, Washington reflected on these changes. Washington spoke against political parties, urging the nation to return to nonpartisan cooperation. Washington also warned America not to "entangle our peace and prosperity in the toils of European ambition." An honorable country must "observe good faith and justice toward all nations," said the aging Virginian, but not let any alliance draw the nation into a foreign war.

Farewell Address   Speech that George Washington made at the end of his second term as president; in it he called for nonpartisan cooperation and warned against entanglements with foreign nations.

SUMMARY

After winning independence, Americans faced the challenge of creating a new nation out of thirteen distinct states. *Constrained* by enormous debt and still surrounded by real and potential enemies, the United States appeared dangerously vulnerable. To many Americans and foreigners, *expectations* for its survival seemed doubtful.

During the Revolution and immediately after, the states drafted their own constitutions. Some *chose* relatively democratic forms of government. Others *chose* to retain less democratic features such as high property qualifications for voting. A major *constraint* on state cooperation was the Articles of Confederation. The Articles guaranteed state representatives the right to withhold important powers from the national governing body. The *outcome* of this weak central government was continuing financial crises and debt.

The Confederation *chose* the sale of western lands as one solution to its financial problems. The *outcome* was conflict with the British, Indians, and Spanish. Farmers, too, felt the *constraints* of economic depression and indebtedness, and Massachusetts farmers rose in revolt during Shays's Rebellion. The continuing national crisis convinced many of the nation's elite that critical *choices* had to be made about revising the system of government.

In the summer of 1787 experienced political leaders met in Philadelphia to draft the Constitution of the United States. This document steered a middle course between a central government that was too powerful and one that was too weak. The states ratified the Constitution after a vigorous battle between Federalists and Antifederalists. George Washington was elected the nation's first president.

Although harmony prevailed initially, sharp differences in political opinion soon emerged between Alexander Hamilton's Federalists and Thomas Jefferson's Republicans. Federalists wanted an industrial nation and opposed the French Revolution. Republicans *expected* the United States to remain agrarian and generally supported the Revolution. The *outcome* was deeper divisions between these two political groups. The United States remained neutral, however, when France and Britain went to war.

By the end of Washington's second term, the United States had expanded its borders, negotiated with Spain for access to the Mississippi River, and established a national bank that promoted economic growth. The departing Washington warned Americans not to allow competing visions of America's future to harm their republic.

E xpectations
C onstraints
C hoices
O utcomes

Suggested Readings

Butterfield, Lyman, et al. *The Book of Abigail and John: Selected Letters of the Adams Family, 1762–1784* (1975).

The editors of the Adams Papers have collected part of the extensive correspondence between John and Abigail Adams during the critical decades of the independence movement.

Morris, Richard B. *Witness at the Creation* (1985).

A distinguished scholar recreates the drama of the constitutional convention by focusing on the personalities and motives of the framers.

Slaughter, Thomas P. *The Whiskey Rebellion* (1986).

This is a vivid account of the major challenge to the Washington government.

Wills, Gary. *Cincinnatus: George Washington and the Enlightenment* (1984).

This is a beautifully written biography of our first president and his times.

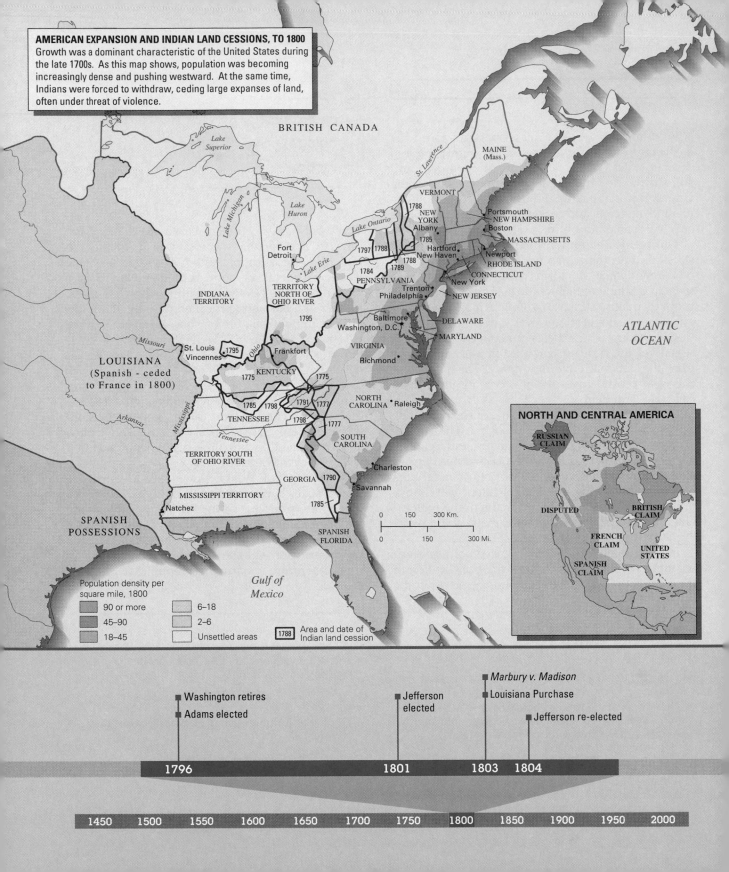

AMERICAN EXPANSION AND INDIAN LAND CESSIONS, TO 1800
Growth was a dominant characteristic of the United States during the late 1700s. As this map shows, population was becoming increasingly dense and pushing westward. At the same time, Indians were forced to withdraw, ceding large expanses of land, often under threat of violence.

BRITISH CANADA

Lake Superior

Lake Michigan

Lake Huron

Fort Detroit

Lake Ontario

Lake Erie

St. Lawrence

MAINE (Mass.)

VERMONT

1788

NEW YORK
Albany

Portsmouth
NEW HAMPSHIRE
Boston
MASSACHUSETTS

1785

Hartford
New Haven

Newport
RHODE ISLAND
CONNECTICUT

1797 1788

1784

1788
1789

TERRITORY NORTH OF OHIO RIVER

INDIANA TERRITORY

PENNSYLVANIA

Trenton
Philadelphia

New York

NEW JERSEY

1795

Baltimore
Washington, D.C.

DELAWARE
MARYLAND

Missouri

St. Louis
Vincennes

1795

Ohio

Frankfort

VIRGINIA
Richmond

ATLANTIC OCEAN

LOUISIANA
(Spanish - ceded to France in 1800)

Arkansas

KENTUCKY

1775

1775

1785 1798

1791

1777

NORTH CAROLINA
Raleigh

Mississippi

TENNESSEE

1798

1777

Tennessee

SOUTH CAROLINA

TERRITORY SOUTH OF OHIO RIVER

Charleston

MISSISSIPPI TERRITORY

Natchez

GEORGIA

1790

Savannah

1785

SPANISH POSSESSIONS

SPANISH FLORIDA

Gulf of Mexico

0   150   300 Km.
0   150   300 Mi.

Population density per square mile, 1800
- 90 or more
- 45–90
- 18–45
- 6–18
- 2–6
- Unsettled areas

1788 Area and date of Indian land cession

NORTH AND CENTRAL AMERICA

RUSSIAN CLAIM

DISPUTED

FRENCH CLAIM

SPANISH CLAIM

BRITISH CLAIM

UNITED STATES

■ *Marbury v. Madison*

■ Washington retires

■ Adams elected

■ Jefferson elected

■ Louisiana Purchase

■ Jefferson re-elected

1796   **1801**   **1803 1804**

1450 1500 1550 1600 1650 1700 1750 1800 1850 1900 1950 2000

The Early Republic, 1796–1804

Conflict in the Adams Administration

- What did Federalists *expect* to accomplish by *choosing* to wage a limited war against France in 1798?

- How did Republicans respond to *constraints* imposed by Federalists during the Quasi-War?

The "Revolution of 1800"

- What did Thomas Jefferson mean when he said that "every difference of opinion is not a difference of principles"?

- How did Federalists *choose* to respond to the ideas behind Jefferson's statement?

Republicanism in Action

- What were Jefferson's *expectations* for American development?

- What policies did he *choose* to meet those *expectations*?

Challenge and Uncertainty in Jefferson's America

- What were the *outcomes* of Jefferson's expansion policies for most Americans and for the Indians?

INTRODUCTION

E xpectations
C onstraints
C hoices
O utcomes

The end of George Washington's second presidential term came at a critical time in the nation's political development. Despite the general's personal dislike for partisan politics, quarreling factions seemed poised to tear the nation apart. Issues such as the national debt, the Bank of the United States, and the Whiskey Rebellion had led to enduring hatreds between the followers of Thomas Jefferson and of Alexander Hamilton. Disputes over the proper role of the United States in international affairs also fueled conflict. The nation had to pick its way through a complicated diplomatic maze of conflicting *constraints* imposed by the continuing war between France and Great Britain. Republicans favored France, which Federalists regarded as excessively democratic. Federalists *chose* Britain, which Republicans regarded as excessively aristocratic.

In domestic politics, Americans had conflicting *expectations*. Federalists *expected* disaster if they lost political control and intended to retain it at any cost. They were willing to destroy democracy before allowing disorder to run rampant. They turned to the courts to destroy political opposition to their policies. On the international front, Federalist policies pushed the United States to the brink of war with France. For their part, Republicans *expected* that if Federalists maintained power, the nation would soon become a satellite of Great Britain, with a similarly aristocratic government. *Constrained* by Federalist aggression, they *chose* to oppose centralized power by seeking support from state governments.

The *outcome* of Federalist efforts to maintain power at any cost was the loss of voter support. In 1800, voters *chose* to remove Federalists from office, turning the government over to Thomas Jefferson. But enough people remained faithful to the Federalist position to maintain that faction's existence and to ensure that it would act as a continuing *constraint* on Republican political activity.

Although Jefferson claimed that he distrusted and disapproved of federal power, he used his power as president to pursue his policy goals. Jefferson purchased the Louisiana Territory despite the fact that there was no constitutional provision permitting such a purchase.

The entire direction of national development changed during Jefferson's presidency. The Louisiana Purchase and the elimination of internal taxes indicated that the days of eastern-dominated mercantilism were at an end. Now the nation's future would be tied to the West. Most Americans saw significant improvement in their *expectations*, and the nation became increasingly optimistic. Some, however, saw little or no improvement in their daily lives. The very success enjoyed by Republicans put greater *constraints* on American Indians and Federalists. The *outcome* of Jefferson's policies was the making of a new kind of politics and of a new kind of nation.

Conflict in the Adams Administration

- What did Federalists *expect* to accomplish by *choosing* to wage a limited war against France in 1798?
- How did Republicans respond to *constraints* imposed by Federalists during the Quasi-War?

Retiring president George Washington warned of "the baneful effects of the spirit of party" in his Farewell Address in 1796. But few in the newly organized political parties listened to him. The Republicans were eager to unseat the politicians responsible for causing the Whiskey Rebellion and for tying the United States diplomatically to Britain. For their part, Federalists were eager to rid the nation of those who might pull down Hamilton's carefully designed economy and the philosophy of government by the well-to-do.

CHRONOLOGY

Partisan Tension and Jeffersonian Optimism

1796	Washington's farewell address
	First contested presidential election:
	    John Adams elected president;
	    Thomas Jefferson vice president

1797	XYZ affair
1798	Alien and Sedition Acts Kentucky and Virginia Resolutions
1799	Fries's Rebellion Napoleon seizes control in France Convention of Mortefontaine
1800	Jefferson and Aaron Burr tie in the Electoral College
1801	Jefferson elected president in the House of Representatives; Burr vice president Judiciary Act of 1801 John Marshall becomes chief justice

	American navy ships fight the Barbary
	    pirates
	Outdoor revival meeting at Cane Ridge,
	    Kentucky

1802	Congress repeals all internal taxes Congress repeals Judiciary Act of 1801 French invade Santo Domingo
1803	*Marbury v. Madison* Impeachment of justices John Pickering and Samuel Chase Louisiana Purchase
1804	Twelfth Amendment ratified Jefferson re-elected
1804–1806	Lewis and Clark expedition
1816	African Methodist Episcopal church (Bethel) formed in Philadelphia

The Split Election of 1796

Thomas Jefferson was the Republican party's logical *choice* to represent the party in the presidential election in 1796. **Aaron Burr,** a brilliant young New York attorney and member of the U.S. Senate, was *chosen* to balance the ticket. Both Jefferson and Burr were veterans of the revolutionary struggles in 1776 and outspoken champions of democracy.

The unity of the Republicans contrasted sharply with the Federalists. The Federalists were deeply divided over the candidacies of **Thomas Pinckney** of South Carolina and John Adams of Massachusetts. Pinckney, the younger son of a prestigious South Carolina planter, had been a prominent military figure during the Revolution and became governor of South Carolina during the late 1780s. His diplomatic success with Spain in opening the Mississippi River to American commerce won Pinckney the unreserved admiration of southerners and westerners (see page 126). Alexander Hamilton, the leader of the Federalists, supported Pinckney's

candidacy because Pinckney was more conservative than Adams and because Hamilton felt he could exercise more influence over the mild-mannered South Carolinian than he could over the stiff-necked Yankee. Hamilton himself was not a candidate because of his illegitimate birth and his outspoken belief that "the rich and the well-born" should govern.

Most Federalists aligned behind the old warhorse from Massachusetts. Many old revolutionaries viewed Adams, like Washington, as a **statesman**

Aaron Burr New York lawyer who became Thomas Jefferson's vice president after the House of Representatives broke a deadlock in the Electoral College.

Thomas Pinckney South Carolina politician and diplomat who was an unsuccessful Federalist candidate for president in 1796.

statesman A political leader who acts out of concern for the public good and not out of self-interest.

above politics whose conscience would help the new nation avoid the pitfalls of party.

Hamilton's scheming nearly lost the election for the Federalists. He was counting on a peculiarity in the election process. According to Article II, Section 1, of the Constitution, each member of the Electoral College could vote for two candidates. The highest vote getter (regardless of party) became president, and the runner-up (again regardless of party) became vice president. Hamilton urged Pinckney supporters to withhold votes from Adams so that Pinckney would win more votes than the former vice president. Adams's supporters learned of the plot, however, withheld their votes from Pinckney, and gave them to Jefferson. Jefferson ended up with more votes than Pinckney. The first truly contested presidential election thus produced a president and vice president who belonged to different factions and held opposing political philosophies.

Never known for charm, subtlety, or willingness to compromise, Adams was ill suited to lead a deeply divided nation. The new president did little to put Republicans' fears to rest. He retained Secretary of Treasury Oliver Wolcott, Secretary of War James McHenry, and Secretary of State Timothy Pickering from Washington's cabinet—all Hamilton men. Republicans had hoped Hamilton's influence would wane now that he had retired from government service to practice law, but the selection of these ardent Federalists dashed that hope.

XYZ: The Power of Patriotism

Since the signing of the pro-British Jay Treaty in 1795, the revolutionary government in France had been angry with the Federalists. During the election of 1796, France actively favored the Republican candidates, threatening to close diplomatic relations if the vocally anti-French Federalists won. True to its word, France broke off relations with the United States as soon as Adams was elected.

In 1797 an angry Adams recalled the American minister to France, James Monroe, who was sympathetic to the French, and replaced him with a devout Federalist, **Charles Cotesworth Pinckney**, the older brother of Thomas Pinckney. The French refused to acknowledge Pinckney as ambassador and began seizing American shipping. Faced with this diplomatic crisis, Adams wisely *chose* to pursue two courses simultaneously. Asserting that the United States would not be "humiliated under a colonial spirit of fear and a sense of inferiority," he pressed Congress to build up America's military defenses. At the same time, he dispatched John Marshall of Virginia and Elbridge Gerry of Massachusetts to join Pinckney in Paris to arrange a peaceful settlement of differences.

French foreign minister Talleyrand declined to receive Pinckney and the peace delegation. As weeks passed, three Parisian businessmen suggested a way to meet with Talleyrand. If the Americans were willing to pay a bribe to key members of the French government and to guarantee an American loan of several million dollars to France, the businessmen would be able to get them a hearing. Offended at such treatment, Pinckney reportedly responded, "No, no, not a sixpence." In relating the affair to President Adams, Pinckney refused to name the three businessmen, calling them only "X," "Y," and "Z."

Americans' response to the **XYZ affair** was overwhelming. In Philadelphia, people paraded in the streets to protest France's arrogance, chanting Pinckney's response to X, Y, and Z. "Millions for defense but not a cent for tribute!" became the rallying cry of the American people. The president vowed not to resume diplomatic relations with France until the U.S. envoy was "received, respected and honored as a representative of a great, free, powerful and independent nation."

The patriotic response to the XYZ affair overcame the divisions that had plagued the Adams administration, giving the president a virtually unified Congress and country. Adams pressed for increased military forces, and in short order Congress created the Department of the Navy, appropriated the money to build a fleet of warships, and authorized a

---

Charles Cotesworth Pinckney   Federalist politician and brother of Thomas Pinckney; he was sent on a diplomatic mission to Paris in 1796 during a period of unfriendly relations between France and the United States.

XYZ affair   A diplomatic incident in which American envoys to France were told that the United States would have to loan France money and bribe government officials as a condition for negotiation.

standing army of twenty thousand troops. Washington came out of retirement to lead the new army. Although the old general saw no action, running sea battles between French and American ships resulted in the sinking or capture of many vessels. This undeclared war became known as the Quasi-War.

Despite the combat, Adams stopped short of asking Congress for a declaration of war and continued to press for a peaceful solution. In doing so, he clashed with Hamilton's wing of the party, which wanted desperately to declare war. Hamilton and his supporters dreamed of crushing the French revolutionary state, which they regarded as the evil fruit of democracy. Hamilton also saw war with France as a way to destroy the Jeffersonian opposition, which had been sympathetic to the French Revolution.

The War at Home

The Quasi-War led the Federalists to identify the Republican party as an enemy nearly as great as France. The Federalists attacked foreigners living in the United States (especially those from Ireland and France, who detested the Federalists' pro-British stance) and the Jeffersonian press, which showed little restraint in attacking the Adams administration.

In 1798 Federalists in Congress passed three acts designed to counter the influence of immigrants. The Naturalization Act extended the residency requirement for citizenship from five to fourteen years. The **Alien Act** authorized the president to deport any foreigner he judged "dangerous to the peace and safety of the United States." Another bill, the Alien Enemies Act, permitted the president to imprison or to banish any foreigner he considered dangerous during a national emergency. The Naturalization Act was designed to prevent recent immigrants from supporting the Republican cause. The other two acts served as a constant reminder that the president could arbitrarily imprison or deport any resident alien who stepped out of line.

Later in 1798, the Federalist Congress passed the **Sedition Act** to silence the Jeffersonian press. The Sedition Act outlawed the publication or utterance of any criticism of the government that might be regarded as "false, scandalous and malicious" or that would bring the government "into contempt or disrepute." In the words of one Federalist newspaper, "it is patriotism to write in favour of our government, it is **sedition** to write against it." Federalists brandished the law against criticism directed toward the government or the president. Not surprisingly, most of the defendants were prominent Republican newspaper editors.

One case involved a Republican journalist named James Thompson Callender, a notorious radical who had been forced to flee Britain in 1793. In the United States, he wielded his pen in support of Jefferson and became widely disliked by the Federalists. In 1798, Callender was arrested for writing a pamphlet that attacked Adams and the Federalists. Federalist judge Samuel Chase fined Callender $200, sentenced him to nine months in jail, and ordered him to post a bond of $1,200 to ensure his continued compliance with the Sedition Act.

Republicans complained that the Alien and Sedition Acts violated the Bill of Rights, but the Federalist Congress and judiciary paid no attention. Jefferson and Madison had little *choice* but to take their case to the states. In 1798, Madison submitted a resolution to the Virginia legislature, and Jefferson submitted one in Kentucky.

The **Virginia and Kentucky Resolutions** argued that the national government was simply a compact that the individual states had created and that the states could declare inappropriate federal laws null and void. In the Virginia Resolution, Madison asserted that the collective will of the states should overrule federal authority. Jefferson went further in the Kentucky Resolution, arguing that each individual state had the "natural right" to interpose its own authority to protect the rights of its citizens.

Alien Act   Law passed by Congress in 1798 authorizing the president to order out of the United States any alien regarded as dangerous to the public peace or safety.

Sedition Act   Law passed by Congress in 1798 outlawing any criticism of the U.S. government that might bring the government into disrepute; the law was enforced mainly against Republicans.

sedition   Conduct or language inciting rebellion against the authority of a state.

Virginia and Kentucky Resolutions   Statements issued by the Virginia and Kentucky legislatures in 1798 asserting their right to declare the Alien and Sedition Acts unconstitutional.

Choosing Peace

George Logan

The United States was caught up in a wave of patriotism when the French slighted President Adams's ambassadors in the XYZ affair. Federalists promoted war, but George Logan chose to resist emotionalism and Federalist pressure by going to France to iron out the two nations' difficulties, thus ending the threat of war. "George Logan" by Gilbert Stuart. The Historical Society of Pennsylvania.

The very idea of the United States fighting a war presented a serious personal dilemma for George Logan. He was a loyal American with deep roots in the nation's history—his grandfather James Logan had been one of the first generation of pioneers in Pennsylvania. Like many descendants of Pennsylvania's first families, George was a Quaker and was morally opposed to war. His father, a conscientious objector during the Revolutionary War, had sent him to study medicine in Scotland and Paris while the war continued. Returning to the United States in 1780, George learned that his family was dead and much of the considerable Logan estate had been destroyed.

Some of the family's landholdings had survived, but, Logan noted, his primary inheritance consisted of "piles of utterly depreciated paper currency." He turned to farming to support himself and then, in 1785, to politics, winning a seat in the Pennsylvania assembly. Ever a critic of Federalist economic and diplomatic strategies, he followed his friend Thomas Jefferson as the Republican faction became an opposition party. His became a prominent voice for Republican principles in the Pennsylvania legislature.

By 1798, Logan seemed well on his way to recovering the fortune and prominence that

The Virginia and Kentucky Resolutions passed in the respective state legislatures in 1798, but no other states followed suit. Nevertheless, the resolutions brought the disputed relationship between federal law and **states' rights** into national prominence. This relationship would be a major bone of contention in the decades to come.

Another bone of contention was the methods used to finance the Quasi-War with France.

Although tariffs and **excises** were the primary sources of revenue, the Federalists also imposed a tax on land, hitting cash-poor farmers especially

> **states' rights** Favoring limited federal powers and the greatest possible autonomy for the states.
> **excise** A tax on the production, sale, or consumption of a commodity or the use of a service.

war had robbed him of. But then President John Adams's peace delegation to France was rebuffed, and as news of the XYZ affair spread, it appeared that war again was inevitable. Recalling his father's frustration as the colonies were drawn into war in 1776, Logan made a fateful choice: he would risk his property, his reputation, even his life, to prevent another war.

Quietly Logan began selling off some of his land, accumulating cash to support a private peace effort. He then went to his friend Jefferson, who gave him letters of introduction to important people in France. Federalist agents learned of Logan's aims and put him under surveillance, but they could not prevent him from sailing for Hamburg, Germany, during the summer of 1798. There he met with Lafayette, who used his influence to get Logan into France and arrange an audience with French foreign minister Talleyrand.

Locked into a war with Great Britain, the last thing Talleyrand wanted was to alienate the only other revolutionary and democratic nation in the world. Meeting with Talleyrand and other French officials in early August, Logan capitalized on this fact. He told them that most Americans supported democracy in France but warned that French seizure of American ships and especially the XYZ affair were undermining that support. If the French released the American sailors they were holding and ended the embargo placed on American ships, he assured them, American popular support would turn back to France and force the Federalist government to end the Quasi-War.

Returning from Paris, Logan received a warm welcome from his fellow Republicans and, surprisingly, from President Adams, who ignored his party's advice and immediately sought peace with France. Within a year, William Vans Murray and Napoleon had solidified the peace Logan had negotiated. Thus Logan succeeded. *Choosing* to risk all for peace, he overcame official *constraints* and averted a war.

The "Logan Act" passed by the outraged Federalists in Congress imposed a fine of $5,000 and a three-year prison term on any American citizen who conducted a private diplomatic mission to a foreign government. Passed after Logan's meetings with Talleyrand, the Logan Act could not be used to punish the courageous Quaker from Pennsylvania for his interference in 1798. In fact, Logan emerged from the whole affair with his reputation and position firmer than ever. He joined the U.S. Senate in 1801, where he remained a Republican force until he retired in 1807.

Logan's principles were to be tested yet again, however. In part because of his success in winning peace between the United States and France, relations with Great Britain began to deteriorate. By 1810 war with Great Britain was looming large. Again, Logan risked all for peace. He sailed to Great Britain in an effort to get that nation to recognize American neutrality, but this time he failed. Returning to the United States, he might have been prosecuted under the Logan Act, but no charges were brought against him. He retired to his farm in Philadelphia, his name immortalized only in the federal law designed to punish the moral integrity he personified so well.

hard. In 1799, farmers in Northampton County, Pennsylvania, used the tactics employed during the Whiskey Rebellion to avoid paying the land tax. After several tax resisters had been arrested and jailed, John Fries raised an armed force to break them out of jail. The federal troops sent by Adams to subdue Fries's Rebellion arrested Fries and two of his associates. The three were tried in federal court, found guilty of treason, and condemned to death.

Settlement with France

Shortly after the XYZ affair, George Logan, a Quaker friend of Jefferson, secretly departed for France, where he sought to open the way for a peaceful solution to the diplomatic crisis (see Individual Choices: George Logan). Logan gained quick admission to see Foreign Minister Talleyrand, who told him that France would gladly receive an American peace

overture. When Logan returned to America, Adams ignored his party's advice and met with him. Soon thereafter, without consulting his cabinet, Adams instructed the American minister to the Netherlands, William Vans Murray, to lead a delegation to Paris.

Hamilton and his supporters were furious, and the fissure that had opened between Adams and Hamilton during the 1796 election widened. Adams responded to his Federalist critics by firing Hamilton's supporters in the cabinet. In addition, he pardoned the Pennsylvanians who had been condemned after Fries's Rebellion.

Adams's diplomatic appeal to France was well timed. On November 9, 1799, **Napoleon Bonaparte** overthrew the government that was responsible for the XYZ affair. Napoleon was more interested in establishing an empire in Europe than in continuing a conflict with the United States. Murray and Napoleon negotiated the Convention of Mortefontaine, which ended the Quasi-War. All prisoners captured during the conflict were released. French restrictions on trade with the United States were removed, and France was forgiven for seizing American property worth $20 million.

The "Revolution of 1800"

- What did Thomas Jefferson mean when he said that "every difference of opinion is not a difference of principles"?
- How did Federalists *choose* to respond to the ideas behind Jefferson's statement?

The partisan press portrayed the election of 1800 in terms of stark contrasts. The Republican press characterized Adams as a monarchist who planned to rob citizens of their freedom and to turn the United States back into a British colony. In contrast, Federalist newspapers painted Vice President Jefferson as a dangerous, atheistic radical who shared French tastes for violent politics and loose sexual morals.

The Lesser of Republican Evils

As the election of 1800 approached, the split within the Federalist Party widened further. Disgusted by the president's failure to declare war on France,

Hamilton schemed to elevate Charles Cotesworth Pinckney, hero of the XYZ affair and a stalwart Federalist, to the presidency over Adams. Hamilton's methods backfired. They drove southern Federalists into supporting Jefferson and helped the Republicans win the election.

Still, it was not clear who would be the next president. Jefferson and his running mate, Aaron Burr, emerged with the same number of electoral votes, thereby throwing the election into the House of Representatives. The majority of the House consisted of hard-line Federalists elected during the Quasi-War hysteria in 1798. These Federalists were forced to *choose* between two men, both of whom they regarded as dangerous radicals. Neither Jefferson nor Burr could win a clear majority of House votes. Burr could have ended the deadlock at any time by withdrawing, but he sat silent.

Hamilton helped to break the deadlock by convincing several Federalists that, despite his dangerous rhetoric, Jefferson was a gentleman of property and integrity. Another development that tipped the scales in Jefferson's favor was the mobilization of the Virginia and Pennsylvania militias. These states feared that the Federalists might attempt to steal the election from Jefferson. As Delaware senator James Bayard described the situation, Federalists had to admit "that we must risk the Constitution and a Civil War or take Mr. Jefferson." Finally, on the thirty-sixth ballot, Jefferson emerged with a clear majority.

The Jefferson-Burr deadlock of 1801 led to the passage of the **Twelfth Amendment.** Ratified in 1804, this amendment separated balloting in the Electoral College for president and vice president and thereby eliminated the confusion that had nearly wrecked the nation in 1800.

---

overture   A proposal or the actions that lead up to a proposal.

Napoleon Bonaparte   General who took control of the French government at the end of the revolutionary period and eventually proclaimed himself emperor of France.

Twelfth Amendment   Constitutional amendment, ratified in 1804, that provides for separate balloting in the Electoral College for president and vice president.

♦ This portrait of the young John Marshall, painted in 1801 as he assumed the Chief Justiceship, conveys the vibrancy and wilful resolve that would make him the nation's primary legal authority for the next thirty years. *"Chief Justice John Marshall" by Ferret de Saint Memin 1801. Duke University Archives.*

Federalist Defenses and Party Acceptance

The Federalists were not about to leave office without erecting some defenses for themselves. The judiciary offered the strongest bulwark against the Republicans. During its last days in office, the Federalist Congress passed the **Judiciary Act of 1801,** which created sixteen new federal judgeships, six additional circuit courts, and many federal marshalships and clerkships. President Adams then filled all these positions with loyal Federalists, signing appointments right up to midnight on his last day in office. **John Marshall,** Adams's secretary of state, was unable to deliver all the appointment letters before his term ran out. But Marshall did deliver one letter promptly: the one addressed to himself, making him chief justice of the Supreme Court.

Despite these last-minute Federalist appointments, Jefferson's inaugural address was conciliatory. "We are all Republicans; we are all Federalists," Jefferson said. In his mind, all Americans shared the same fundamental principles established in 1776. Yet even Jefferson considered the election of 1800 "a revolution in the principles of our government."

Jefferson sought to restore the republic envisioned by revolutionaries twenty-five years before. Unlike the Federalists, Jefferson was unalterably opposed to sedition acts or other government restraints directed against political opponents. The Republican Congress endorsed Jefferson's commitment to free speech by letting the Sedition Act and the Alien Acts expire. Congress also repealed the Naturalization Act, replacing its fourteen-year naturalization period with one of five years.

Jefferson's **conciliatory** policies and tone led Americans to see political parties in a new light. Many concluded that people in opposite political camps could hold different positions and not be enemies. As Jefferson observed, "Every difference of opinion is not a difference of principles." Even extreme Federalists like Fisher Ames of Massachusetts came to realize that a "party is an association of honest men for honest purposes." Such realizations marked the beginnings of accepting political parties in the United States.

Madison Versus the Midnight Appointments

The power of the judicial branch to interpret and to enforce federal law became a major issue during Jefferson's first administration. His secretary of state, James Madison, had held back the appointment letters that John Marshall had been unable to deliver before the expiration of his term. One jilted appointee was William Marbury, who was to have been justice of the peace for the newly created District of Columbia. Marbury filed suit in the Supreme Court, claiming the Judiciary Act of 1789 gave the Court the power to demand that Madison deliver Marbury's appointment letter.

Judiciary Act of 1801   Law that the Federalist Congress passed to increase the number of federal courts and judicial positions; President Adams rushed to fill these positions with Federalists before his term ended.

John Marshall   Virginia lawyer and politician made chief justice of the Supreme Court by President Adams; his legal decisions helped shape the role of the Supreme Court in American government.

conciliatory   Striving to overcome distrust or to regain someone's good will.

In considering *Marbury v. Madison,* Chief Justice Marshall believed that the Judiciary Act did require Madison to deliver the letter. He was keenly aware, however, that the Court had no power to enforce its orders. Ordering Madison to appoint Marbury justice of the peace could lead to a confrontation between the executive and judicial branches, a confrontation that Marshall was sure that the Court would lose. He thus ruled in 1803 that the Constitution contained no provision for the Supreme Court to issue orders such as the Judiciary Act of 1789 required. Therefore the 1789 act was unconstitutional.

Jefferson and Madison accepted Marshall's decision because it meant they did not have to place Adams's handpicked men in powerful judicial positions. But it also meant that they would have to acknowledge that the Supreme Court, not the individual states or the branches of the federal government, had the right to determine the **constitutionality** of federal laws. Most Republicans endorsed Marshall's decision, which asserted the principle of **judicial review** over acts of Congress. Because of their experience with the Alien and Sedition acts, however, many southerners continued to assert that states had the fundamental right to determine the constitutionality of the laws.

The War on the Courts

Although the Jefferson administration appealed for unity, it could act in extremely partisan ways. It was not beneath targeting Federalist judges for removal for political reasons. The Republicans' first target was John Pickering, a district judge from New Hampshire. An alcoholic who suffered from mental illness, Pickering was an easy choice. No one, not even staunch Federalists, doubted that he was incompetent. The Constitution, however, specified that a judge could be **impeached** only for committing "high crimes and misdemeanors." Whether Pickering had or not, the Senate found him guilty and removed him from office.

Republicans next took on a much more challenging opponent, Supreme Court justice Samuel Chase. Chase was notorious for making partisan decisions such as convicting Republican journalist James Callender under the Sedition Act. He also used the bench as a soapbox from which to rant against

Republican ideas. Although Chase was neither an incompetent nor a criminal, many Republicans thought that the Senate would convict and remove him, opening the way for the removal of any fiercely anti-Republican judge. Vice President Burr, however, surprised everyone by conducting an impartial trial and giving Chase every opportunity to defend himself. Both Federalists and the majority of Republicans voted to dismiss the charges against Chase. Efforts to impeach other Federalist judges were subsequently dropped.

Republicanism in Action

- What were Jefferson's *expectations* for American development?
- What policies did he *choose* to meet those *expectations?*

When Jefferson assumed office, he ushered a new spirit into national politics and the presidency. He was the first president to be inaugurated in the new national capital of Washington City. He led a much simpler life than his predecessors in office had. He refused, for example, to ride in a carriage, *choosing* to go by horseback through Washington's muddy and rutted streets. He abandoned the fashion of wearing a wig, letting his red hair stand out.

Jefferson's Vision for America

Jefferson had a strong, positive vision for the nation that was guided by his fears and hopes for the American experiment in republican government. The greatest dangers to a republic, he believed, were high population density and the concentration of

---

Marbury v. Madison   Supreme Court decision (1803) declaring part of the Judiciary Act of 1789 unconstitutional and thus establishing the principle of judicial review.

constitutionality   Agreement with the principles or provisions of the Constitution.

judicial review   The power of the Supreme Court to review the constitutionality of laws passed by Congress and by the states.

impeach   To charge a public official with improper conduct in office.

money in the hands of a few. These led to corruption and the rise of tyrants like George III. Accordingly, Jefferson wanted to steer America away from the large, publicly supported industries that Hamilton advocated. Jefferson wanted America to be a nation of farmers who owned their own land, produced their own food, and were beholden to no one. Such yeoman farmers, Jefferson believed, could make political decisions based solely on reason and good sense.

Jefferson did not want Americans to be deprived of the benefits of industry and commerce. But he did want to preserve American independence and freedom from corruption. His solution was simple: America's vast surpluses of food should be traded for European manufactures.

Jefferson was also an advocate of free trade. He believed that businesses should make their own decisions and succeed or fail in a marketplace free of government interference. This belief contrasted with the mercantilist theory that governments should control prices and restrict trade to benefit the nation-state.

Responsibility for implementing this economic policy fell to Treasury Secretary **Albert Gallatin.** Gallatin's first goal was to make the United States free of debt by 1817. Gallatin cut the budget drastically, even closing several American embassies. At home, he pared administrative costs by reducing staff and putting an end to fancy receptions and balls. The administration reduced the army from four thousand to twenty-five hundred men and the navy from twenty-five ships to a mere seven. In making these cuts, Gallatin subtly weakened the central government's economic presence, putting more responsibilities back onto the states, where he thought they belonged.

Gallatin's plan also called for a significant change in how the government raised revenue. In 1802, the Republican Congress repealed all internal taxes, leaving customs duties and the sale of western lands as the sole sources of federal revenue. With this one gesture, Gallatin struck a major blow for Jefferson's economic vision by tying the nation's financial future to westward expansion and foreign trade.

The success of Jefferson's economic policy depended greatly on his handling of foreign affairs. During Jefferson's presidency, two foreign issues loomed large. One was the need to improve naviga-tion on North America's inland waterways. The other was the need to ensure free navigation of the open seas. France and Spain posed a major challenge to the first of these, and pirates threatened the other.

War in the Mediterranean

The challenge to free navigation came from pirates who patrolled the northern coast of Africa from Tangier to Tripoli (see Map 7.1). Ever since the 1790s, the United States had paid the Barbary pirates not to attack American ships. By 1800, fully a fifth of the federal budget was earmarked for this purpose. Gallatin wanted to eliminate this expense. For Jefferson, the principle of free navigation of the seas was just as important. Noting that "tribute or war is the usual alternative of these Barbary pirates," Jefferson decided on war and dispatched navy ships to the Mediterranean in 1801.

The war that followed was far from successful. The American navy suffered a major defeat when the warship *Philadelphia* and its entire crew were captured. Lieutenant Stephen Decatur, Jr.'s bold raid left the *Philadelphia* in ashes so it could not be used by the ruler of Tripoli, but the ship's crew remained in captivity. The United States finally negotiated peace terms in 1805, paying $60,000 for the release of the hostages, while Tripoli promised to halt pirate raids on American shipping.

Crisis in America's Interior

As settlers continued to pour into the region west of the Appalachian Mountains, the commercial importance of the Mississippi River increased. Whoever controlled the mouth of the Mississippi would have the power to make or break the economy of the interior.

In Pinckney's treaty of 1795 (see page 126), Spain had granted American farmers the right to ship cargoes down the Mississippi. In 1800, however, Napoleon had exchanged some French holdings in

Albert Gallatin Treasury secretary in Jefferson's administration; he favored limited government and reduced the federal debt by cutting spending.

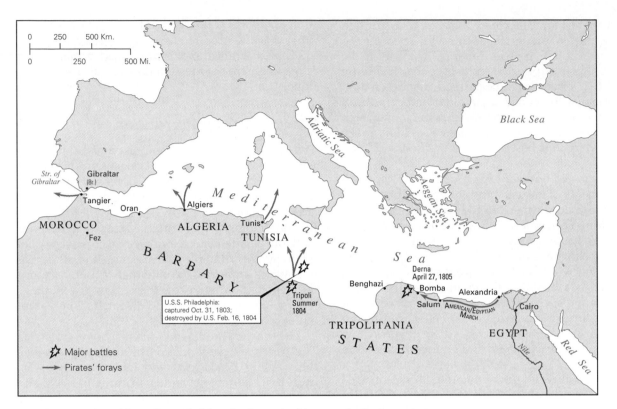

♦ **MAP 7.1 Barbary Pirate Strongholds**   As shown in this map, the Barbary pirates controlled important routes throughout the Mediterranean Sea. In 1801, President Jefferson sent American forces to the area to stop pirate interference with American shipping. After the inconclusive battles shown here, both sides agreed to a truce in 1805.

southern Europe for Spain's land in North America. Because the United States had no agreement with France concerning navigation on the Mississippi, the deal between Spain and France threatened to scuttle American commerce on the river. Such fears took on substance when Spanish officials suspended free trade in New Orleans.

Jefferson responded by dispatching James Monroe to talk with the British about a military alliance. He also had Monroe instruct the American minister to France, Robert Livingston, to purchase New Orleans and as much adjacent real estate as he could get for $2 million.

Napoleon may have been considering the creation of a North American empire when he acquired Louisiana from Spain. **Santo Domingo,** a French colony in the Caribbean, would likely have been the hub for such an empire. But Napoleon's invasion force that was sent in 1802 to reclaim Santo

Domingo from rebellious slaves fell victim to the military skills of rebel leader **Toussaint L'Ouverture** and disease.

Meanwhile, Napoleon began to contemplate further conquests in Europe and his need for considerable money. By the time James Monroe and Robert Livingston entered into negotiations with the French, Napoleon had instructed Foreign Minister Talleyrand to sell the whole of Louisiana for $15 million.

Santo Domingo   Island shared by the modern nations of Haiti and the Dominican Republic.

François Dominique Toussaint L'Ouverture   Black revolutionary who with the help of the French led a force that expelled the British and Spanish from the island of Santo Domingo in 1798.

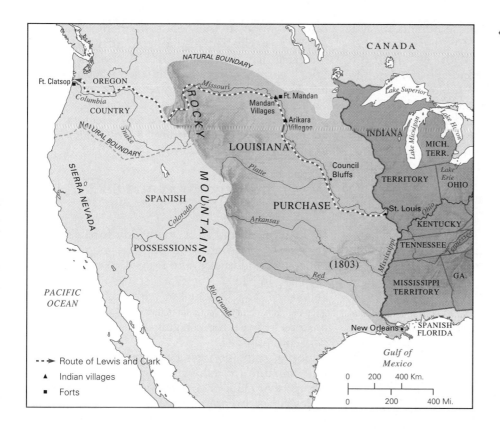

◆ **MAP 7.2 Louisiana Purchase and the Lewis and Clark Expedition** As this map shows, President Jefferson added an enormous tract of land to the United States when he purchased Louisiana from France in 1803. Even before the purchase, Jefferson and his secretary, Meriwether Lewis, had decided to send a spy mission into the region to explore and win over resident Indian tribes. In 1804 Lewis and his companion William Clark led an expedition all the way to the Pacific, returning in 1806.

The Louisiana Purchase

Although Livingston and Monroe had been authorized to spend only $2 million, they jumped at the deal. The president not only approved of their action but was overjoyed. The deal offered three important benefits. It saved him from having to ally the United States with Britain. It secured the Mississippi River for shipments of American agricultural products to Europe. And it doubled the size of the United States, opening up uncharted new expanses for settlement by yeoman farmers. The Senate approved the **Louisiana Purchase** overwhelmingly in November 1803.

Even before the negotiations with Napoleon, Jefferson had begun preparations to send a small party to explore this area (see Map 7.2). **Meriwether Lewis,** Jefferson's private secretary, and his co-commander, Indian fighter **William Clark,** were to note the numbers of French, Spanish, and Indians in the area, and to chart major waterways and other important strategic sites. They were also to undermine the Indians' relations with the Spanish and French.

The expedition set out by boat in the spring of 1804, arriving among the Mandan Indians in present-day North Dakota in the late fall. The explorers spent the winter there, gathering information from the Mandans and from French Canadian fur traders.

Louisiana Purchase The U.S. purchase of Louisiana from France for $15 million in 1803; the Lousiana Territory extended from the Mississippi River to the Rocky Mountains.

Meriwether Lewis Jefferson aide who was sent to explore the Louisiana Territory in 1803; he later served as its governor.

William Clark Soldier and explorer who joined Meriwether Lewis on the expedition to explore the Louisiana Territory; he was responsible for map-making.

Next spring they set out across the mountains, led by a French trapper named Charbono and his Shoshone wife, **Sacajawea.** With the help of Sacajawea's people and other Indians, the expedition reached the Pacific Ocean in November 1805, wintering near the mouth of the Columbia River. When spring came, the party retraced its steps eastward. Finally, after nearly three years, Lewis and Clark arrived back in the United States carrying the information they had been asked to gather. They had also obtained promises from many Indian tribes to join in friendship with the new American republic.

Challenge and Uncertainty in Jefferson's America

• What were the *outcomes* of Jefferson's expansion policies for most Americans and for the Indians?

Jefferson's policies brought a new spirit into the land. The Virginian's commitment to opportunity and progress, to openness and frugality, offered a stark contrast to the policies of his predecessors. Nevertheless, some disturbing social and intellectual developments began to surface. In particular, rapid westward expansion strained conventional social institutions.

The Heritage of Partisan Politics

The popularity of Jefferson's party was abundantly clear by the 1804 election. His Republican party had virtually eclipsed the Federalists in the congressional elections of 1802, and by 1804 the Federalists were in disarray. Prominent Federalists such as Fisher Ames and John Jay had withdrawn from public life altogether.

The Federalists *chose* Charles Cotesworth Pinckney to head the ticket in 1804. The Federalists' primary campaign issue became the Louisiana Purchase. They charged that Jefferson purchased the Louisiana Territory despite the absence of a constitutional provision permitting such a purchase.

Such charges did little to challenge Jefferson's strong record in office. Jefferson had eliminated internal taxes, encouraged westward migration, eliminated the hated Alien and Sedition Acts, and

fostered hope in the hearts of many disaffected Americans. He had also proved that he was no threat to national commerce. America's international earnings grew at the same pace during Jefferson's tenure in office as they had in the 1790s. This substantial record won Jefferson a resounding victory in 1804. He captured 162 electoral votes to Pinckney's 14, carrying every state except Connecticut and Delaware.

Westward Expansion and Social Stress

By 1810 vast numbers of young adults had grabbed at Jefferson's frontier vision. The population of Ohio, for example, grew from 45,000 in 1800 to 231,000 in 1810. Similar spurts occurred in Tennessee and Kentucky. Although such rapid growth was a source of pride, it was also a source of anxiety to westerners trying to establish order in new communities.

Social instability was common in the West. The odd mixture of ethnic, religious, and national groups that made their way west did little to bring cohesiveness to community life. Most of the population consisted of young men. There were few women or older people to encourage stable behavior.

The expansion of the American West had an unsettling effect on communities in the East as well. During the eighteenth century, older people had maintained their authority by controlling the distribution of land to their children. Sons and daughters lived with and worked for their parents until their elders saw fit to deed property over to them. As a result, children living in the East generally did not marry or operate their own farms and businesses until they were in their thirties. Economic opportunities on the frontier lessened young people's need to rely on their parents for support and lowered the age at which they began to break away from their parents.

During the early nineteenth century, the age at which children attained independence fell steadily.

Sacajawea Shoshone woman who served as guide and interpreter on the Lewis and Clark expedition.

By the 1820s, children were marrying in their early to mid-twenties. Breathing the new air of independence, intrepid young people moved out of their parents' homes, migrating westward to find land and new opportunities.

The Religious Response to Social Change

The changes taking place in the young republic stirred conflicting religious currents. One was **rationalism** in religious thought. The other was a new **evangelicalism.**

Jefferson, Franklin, Paine, and many others of the revolutionary generation had embraced the deism of the Enlightenment (see page 58). They viewed God as a vague "first cause" whose universe was a perfectly crafted machine that had been left to run itself according to rational laws. Religion had to be plain, reasonable, and verifiable to be acceptable to such rationalists. Jefferson, for example, edited his own version of the Bible, keeping only the moral principles and the solid historical facts and discarding anything that he regarded as supernatural. Thomas Paine rejected Christianity altogether, calling it the "strangest religion ever set up."

Rationalism also permeated some mainstream denominations during the revolutionary era. Some New England Congregationalists began to question predestination and to emphasize instead the individual's role in salvation, especially the significance of reason in that pursuit. Like Jefferson, these rationalist reformers rejected much of the mystery in Christian faith, including the ideas of the **Trinity** and Christ's divinity. Unitarianism, as this form of Christian worship came to be called, grew by leaps and bounds during and after the Revolution.

Unitarianism held great appeal for the young generation in fast-growing port cities like Boston, New York, and Baltimore. In a nation where young people were carving out economic lives for themselves in the worlds of commerce and manufacturing, the notion that they were powerless to effect their own salvation seemed increasingly ridiculous.

While deism and Unitarianism were gaining footholds in eastern cities, a very different kind of religious response was taking shape in the West. There, Methodists, Baptists, and Presbyterians emphasized the centrality of conversion in the life of a Christian. Conversion was that emotional moment during which one realizes that one is damned and can be saved only by the grace of God. Typically conversions were brought about by spirited preaching. These denominations concentrated on training a new, young ministry and sending it to preach in every corner of the nation. The *outcome* was the Second Great Awakening, which began in Cane Ridge, Kentucky, in 1801, and spread throughout the country.

Like the rationalist sects, the evangelicals stressed individuals' roles in their own salvation and de-emphasized predestination. However, the new awakeners breathed new life into the old Puritan notion of God's plan for the world and the role that Americans were to play in this plan.

Presbyterian, Baptist, and Methodist churches provided ideological underpinnings for the expansive behavior of westerners and a sense of mission to ease the insecurities produced by venturing into the unknown. They also provided some stability for communities in which traditional controls were lacking. These attractive features helped evangelicalism to sweep across the West.

Nonwhites in Jefferson's Republic

Jefferson's policies enabled many Americans to benefit from the nation's development, but they certainly did not help everyone. Neither Indians nor blacks had much of a role in Jefferson's America.

A slaveholder, Jefferson doubted the capabilities of blacks. In his *Notes on the State of Virginia* (1785) Jefferson asserted that blacks were "inferior to whites in the endowments both of body and mind." Although Phillis Wheatley had won acclaim for her poetry (see page 103), Jefferson dismissed her work as "below the dignity of criticism." He similarly refused to accept the accomplishments of the black

---

rationalism   The theory that the exercise of reason, rather than the acceptance of authority or spiritual revelation, is the only valid basis for belief and the best source of spiritual truth.

evangelicalism   Protestant movements that stress personal conversion and salvation by faith.

Trinity   The Christian belief that God consists of three divine persons: Father, Son, and Holy Spirit.

mathematician, astronomer, and engineer **Benjamin Banneker** as proof that blacks were the intellectual equals of whites.

Throughout the Jeffersonian era, the great majority of blacks in America were slaves in the southern states. From the 1790s onward, the number of free blacks increased steadily. Emancipation did not bring equality, however, even in northern states that had mandated the gradual abolition of slavery (see page 104). Many states did not permit free blacks to testify in court, to vote, or to exercise other fundamental freedoms accorded to whites. Public schools often refused admission to black children. Even churches were often closed to blacks.

Free blacks began to respond to systematic exclusion by forming their own institutions. In Philadelphia, tension between white and free black Methodists led former slave Richard Allen to form the Bethel Church for Negro Methodists in 1793. Ongoing tension with the white Methodist hierarchy eventually led Allen to secede from the church and to form his own **African Methodist Episcopal church** (Bethel) in 1816. Similar controversies in New York led James Varick to found the African Methodist Episcopal church (Zion) in 1821.

The African Methodist Episcopal (AME) church grew rapidly. Besides providing places of worship and centers for cultural and social activities, AME churches joined with other black churches to provide schools and other services withheld by whites. Bishop Allen's organization launched the first black magazine in America and eventually founded its own college, Wilberforce University.

The place of Indians in Jeffersonian thought was somewhat paradoxical. Jefferson considered Indians to be savages but was not convinced that they were biologically inferior to Europeans. Jefferson attributed the differences between Indians and Europeans to the Indians' cultural retardation. He argued that harsh economic conditions and lack of a written language had kept the Indians in a condition of "barbarism." Jefferson was confident that whites could help lift Indians out of their uncivilized state.

Jefferson's Indian policy reflected this attitude. As president, he created government-owned trading posts at which Indians were offered goods at cheap prices. He believed that Indians who were exposed to white manufactures would recognize the superiority of white culture and adopt that culture. Until this process was complete, the Indians, like children, were to be protected from those who would take advantage of them. Also like children, the Indians were not to be given the full rights and responsibilities of citizenship. What rights they had were to be protected not by the Constitution but were to be subject to the whims of the Senate.

The chief problem for Jeffersonian Indian policy was not the Indians' supposed cultural retardation but their rapid progress and acculturation. This was particularly true of the Cherokees and Creeks. Alexander McGillivray of the Creeks, for example, deftly played American, French, and Spanish interests off against each other while building a strong economic base founded on both communal and privately owned plantations. In similar fashion, the Cherokee elite in 1794 established a centralized government that brought the Cherokees wealth and power.

The Indians' white neighbors generally did not think that this represented the right kind of progress. From their perspective, the Indians' destiny was to vanish along with the receding wilderness. Eyeing Cherokee lands, Georgia contended that Indians within its borders were no concern of the federal government. Jefferson insisted, however, that federal authority over Indian affairs was essential for maintaining peace and ensuring the Indians' future welfare.

Jefferson nonetheless feared that an all-out war between the states and the Indians might develop. He accordingly suggested that large reserves in the Louisiana Territory be created for Indians. This would remove Indians from state jurisdictions and from the corrupting influence of the baser elements of white society. He made many efforts, largely unsuccessful, to convince the Indians to exchange traditional lands for new lands west of the Mississippi.

Benjamin Banneker African-American mathematician and astronomer who published an almanac that calculated the movements of stars and planets.

African Methodist Episcopal church African-American branch of Methodism established in Philadelphia in 1816 and in New York in 1821.

SUMMARY

E xpectations
C onstraints
C hoices
O utcomes

Americans faced the difficult *choice* in 1796 of continuing with the Federalist John Adams or of moving in a new direction with the Republican Thomas Jefferson. Electoral quirks led to Adams's election as president and Jefferson's as vice president. The Federalists subsequently used every excuse to make war on their political opponents. Diplomatically, they let relations with France sour to the point that the two nations were at war in all but name. At home, they used the Alien and Sedition Acts to silence opponents, and they imposed tariffs and taxes that were hateful to many. Rebelling against heavy-handed Federalist policies, the American people in 1800 *chose* to give Jefferson a chance.

Although Jefferson would call the election "the revolution of 1800," even Hamilton did not think that the general direction in government would change. Just to be safe, however, Federalists stacked the court system so that Republicans would have to face insurmountable *constraints* if they tried to change government too much.

Jefferson's inaugural address in 1801 seemed to announce an end to partisan warfare, but the Republicans attempted to restrict Federalist power in the courts. Jefferson envisioned a future in which Americans could own enough land to produce life's basic necessities for themselves and would be free to vote their consciences. To attain this end, Jefferson ordered reductions in the size of government, the elimination of internal taxes, and the purchase of Louisiana. For many the *outcome* was excitement and optimism, but some were unsure and fearful of this new order.

Not all were free to share in the bounty that Jefferson envisioned. For American Indians, the very success of Jefferson's expansion policy meant contraction of their lands and *constraints* on their freedom. African-Americans found that equality was not intended for them.

Suggested Readings

DeConde, Alexander. *This Affair of Louisiana* (1976).
An excellent and readable account by one of America's premier diplomatic historians.

Hofstadter, Richard. *The Idea of a Party System* (1969).
The classic account of the rise of legitimate opposition in the American party system.

McCoy, Drew. *The Elusive Republic* (1980).
The best summary of Jefferson's agrarian vision; engagingly written and forcefully argued.

Miller, John C. *The Wolf by the Ears: Thomas Jefferson and Slavery* (1977).
A master historian confronts the dichotomy between Jefferson's attitudes about race and the actuality of slavery.

Nash, Gary B. *Forging Freedom: The Formation of Philadelphia's Black Community, 1720–1840* (1990).
A brilliant and exciting exploration of how African-Americans in early Philadelphia created their own urban community.

Ronda, James. *Lewis and Clark Among the Indians* (1984).
A bold retelling of the expedition's story, showcasing the Indian role in both Lewis and Clark's and the nation's successful expansion into Louisiana.

Sheehan, Bernard W. *Seeds of Extinction: Jeffersonian Philanthropy and the American Indian* (1973).
An evaluation of Jefferson's attitudes toward Indians and his Indian policy, beautifully written by one of the nation's best Indian policy historians.

Smith, James Morton. *Freedom's Fetters* (1956).
Dated, but excellent discussion of the Alien and Sedition Acts and their relationship to American principles.

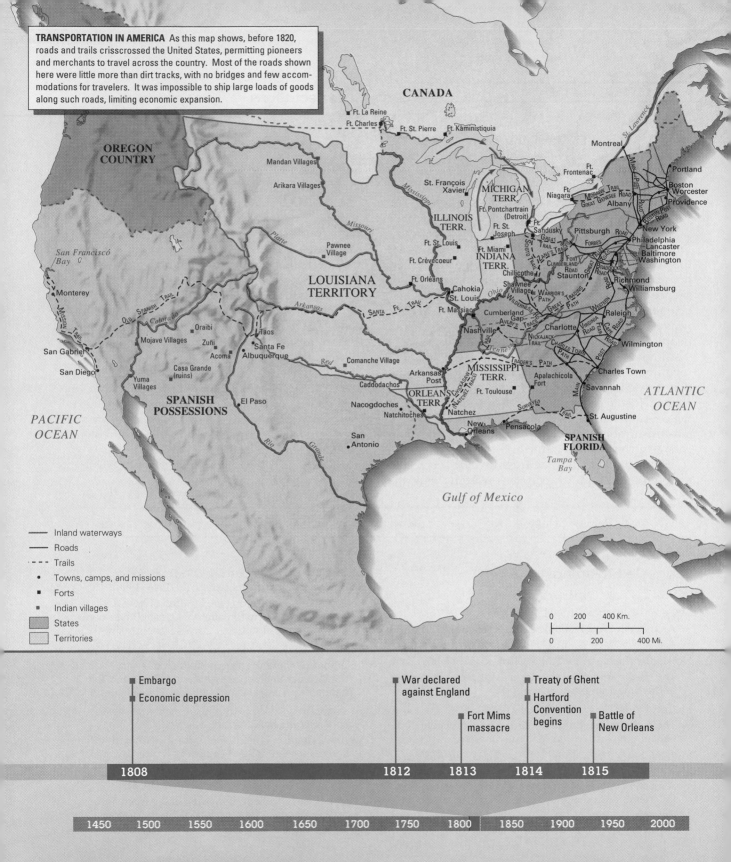

TRANSPORTATION IN AMERICA As this map shows, before 1820, roads and trails crisscrossed the United States, permitting pioneers and merchants to travel across the country. Most of the roads shown here were little more than dirt tracks, with no bridges and few accommodations for travelers. It was impossible to ship large loads of goods along such roads, limiting economic expansion.

CANADA

OREGON COUNTRY

PACIFIC OCEAN

San Francisco Bay

Monterey

San Gabriel

San Diego

Yuma Villages

Mojave Villages

Oraibi

Zuñi

Acoma

Casa Grande (ruins)

Santa Fe
Albuquerque

El Paso

SPANISH POSSESSIONS

San Antonio

Rio Grande

Nacogdoches

Natchitoches

Caddodachos

Arkansas Post

Comanche Village

Red

Ft. La Reine
Ft. Charles
Ft. St. Pierre
Ft. Kaministiquia

Mandan Villages

Arikara Villages

Missouri

Platte

Colorado

Arkansas

Santa Fe Trail

Old Spanish Trail

Mission Trail

Pawnee Village

LOUISIANA TERRITORY

St. François Xavier

Mississippi

Ft. St. Louis

Ft. Crèvecoeur

Ft. Orleans

Cahokia
St. Louis

Ft. Massiac

MICHIGAN TERR.

Ft. Pontchartrain (Detroit)

ILLINOIS TERR.

Ft. St. Joseph

Ft. Miami

INDIANA TERR.

Ohio

Chillicothe

Shawnee Village

Cumberland Gap

Avery's Trace

Nashville

Tennessee

MISSISSIPPI TERR.

Natchez Trace

ORLEANS TERR.

Natchez

New Orleans

Ft. Toulouse

Apalachicola Fort

Pensacola

SPANISH FLORIDA

Tampa Bay

St. Augustine

Gulf of Mexico

Montreal

St. Lawrence

Ft. Frontenac

Ft. Niagara

Portland

Boston
Worcester
Providence

Albany

Pittsburgh

New York

Philadelphia
Lancaster
Baltimore
Washington

Staunton

Richmond
Williamsburg

Raleigh

Charlotte

Wilmington

Charles Town

Savannah

ATLANTIC OCEAN

Legend:
- Inland waterways
- Roads
- Trails
- • Towns, camps, and missions
- ■ Forts
- ■ Indian villages
- States
- Territories

0   200   400 Km.
0   200   400 Mi.

Embargo
Economic depression

War declared against England

Fort Mims massacre

Treaty of Ghent
Hartford Convention begins

Battle of New Orleans

1808   **1812**   **1813**   **1814**   **1815**

1450 1500 1550 1600 1650 1700 1750 1800 1850 1900 1950 2000

Renewing Independence, 1805–1814

Troubling Currents in Jefferson's America

- How did changing relations among Europe and the various regions of the United States *constrain* Jefferson's political and economic *expectations*?

Crises in the Nation

- What *constraints* arose from Jefferson's economic and Indian policies?

- How did they affect easterners?

- How did they encourage westerners to *choose* a prowar position?

The Second War for Independence

- What developments finally convinced the United States to *choose* war against Great Britain in 1812?

- How did the conduct of the war reveal the Americans' true aims?

The War's Strange Conclusion

- What *constraints* on American national development did the *outcome* of the War of 1812 remove?

- How did the war change Americans' *expectations* about politics, economics, and national expansion?

INTRODUCTION

E xpectations
C onstraints
C hoices
O utcomes

Jefferson's first term in office was an unqualified success. The president's supporters had *expected* a revolution in the spirit of government in 1800 and had gotten one. Federalists had *expected* political and financial collapse when the red-headed radical assumed the presidency, but they were wrong. The hard feelings of 1800 had apparently been forgiven and forgotten. The *outcome* was a new sense of unity in the nation's politics. And the *outcome* of the Republicans' frugal financial management was a thriving economy. A new spirit was alive in the land, and Americans grew confident that their future would be glorious.

Jefferson's greatest accomplishments, however, had stemmed from continuing crises in world affairs. His successful acquisition of Louisiana, for example, had come as the result of tension between Great Britain, France, and Spain. The vibrant economy was also a product of international problems rather than of Jefferson's *choices*. The nearly constant war in the Old World allowed Americans to make money by selling grain to Europeans. National security and economic prosperity depended on Jefferson's ability to keep America a neutral player on the world stage, a role that became harder to sustain in his second term.

After 1804, increasing *constraints* on American trade forced Jefferson, and then his successor, James

Madison, to make hard *choices*. Believing that Europe needed American food more than America needed European manufactures, Republicans *chose* to prohibit American ships from trading with Europe. The *outcome* was economic depression in the United States. Adding to the problem were widening cracks in Jefferson's party support. Some Republicans thought Jefferson had overstepped his bounds in *choosing* to make the Louisiana Purchase. Federalists too were upset, especially in the Northeast. They believed that Jefferson had *chosen* to serve southern and western interests exclusively.

The *expectations* and *choices* of others played havoc with Jefferson's hopes for a peaceful and prosperous nation. French and British policymakers *chose* not to respect American neutrality. American politicians of various stripes *chose* to oppose the president. In the West, whites seeking land for expansion *expected* that war against the Indians and the British would best serve their ends, while Indians increasingly *chose* to stop retreating. The *outcome* of these *choices* was another war with Great Britain in 1812.

Troubling Currents in Jefferson's America

- How did changing relations among Europe and the various regions of the United States *constrain* Jefferson's political and economic *expectations*?

Jefferson's successes through the 1804 election seemed to ensure the Republicans absolute control over the nation's political reins. But factions that would challenge Jefferson's control were forming. A small but vocal coalition of disgruntled Federalists threatened to **secede** from the Union. Even within his own party, voices were raised against Jefferson.

Diplomatic problems were also to trouble Jefferson's second administration.

Emerging Factions in American Politics

The Federalists' failure in the election of 1804 nearly spelled their demise. With the West and the South

secede   To withdraw formally from membership in an alliance or association.

CHRONOLOGY

Domestic Expansion and International Crisis

1803	Louisiana Purchase
	Renewal of war between France and Britain
1804	Jefferson re-elected
	Britain steps up impressment
	Duel between Alexander Hamilton and Aaron Burr
1805	Beginning of Shawnee religious revival
	Battles of Trafalgar and Austerlitz
1806	Napoleon issues Berlin Decree
1807	Burr conspiracy trial
	Founding of Prophetstown
	Chesapeake affair
1808	Embargo goes into effect
	Economic depression begins
	James Madison elected president
1809	Fort Wayne Treaty
	Non-Intercourse Act
1810	Macon's Bill No. 2
	Formation of the War Hawks
1811	United States breaks trade relations with Britain
	Invasion and destruction of Prophetstown
1812	United States declares war against Britain
	United States invades Canada
	James Madison re-elected
1813	Fort Mims massacre
	Battle of Put-in-Bay
	Embargo of 1813
	Battle of the Thames
1814	Battle of Horseshoe Bend
	Napoleon defeated
	Battle of Plattsburgh
	British capture and burn Washington, D.C.
	Treaty of Ghent
	Hartford Convention begins
1815	Battle of New Orleans

firmly in Jefferson's camp, New England Federalists found themselves powerless. Federalist leader Timothy Pickering was so disgruntled that he advocated the secession of the northeastern states from the Union. He formed a political coalition called the **Essex Junto** to carry out this scheme, which came to nothing at this time.

Rifts appeared in Jefferson's party as well. Throughout Jefferson's first administration, some southerners had criticized the president for expanding federal power and interfering with states' rights. One of Jefferson's most vocal critics was his cousin, congressman **John Randolph** of Roanoke. Randolph considered himself the last true Republican, and he opposed any legislation that violated his principles.

The tension between the two Virginia Republicans came to a head in 1804 over the **Yazoo affair,** a scandal stemming from Georgia's sale of most of

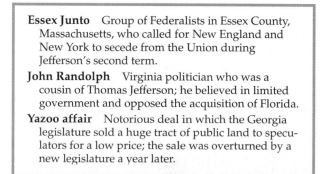

Essex Junto Group of Federalists in Essex County, Massachusetts, who called for New England and New York to secede from the Union during Jefferson's second term.

John Randolph Virginia politician who was a cousin of Thomas Jefferson; he believed in limited government and opposed the acquisition of Florida.

Yazoo affair Notorious deal in which the Georgia legislature sold a huge tract of public land to speculators for a low price; the sale was overturned by a new legislature a year later.

present-day Alabama and Mississippi to political insiders in 1795. Outraged voters forced the Georgia legislature to overturn the sale in the following year, but lawsuits were still pending when Georgia ceded the area to the United States in 1802. Jefferson advocated federal compensation for those who had lost money because of the overturned sale. Randolph claimed that would violate Republican principles and plain morality, and he used his power in Congress to block Jefferson's efforts.

A similar conflict in 1806 led Randolph to break with Jefferson altogether. Seeking to acquire Spanish Florida, Jefferson asked Congress for $2 million designed to win French influence in convincing Spain to part with Florida. Randolph bristled at what he regarded as open bribery. He formed a third party, the **Tertium Quids,** fracturing Jefferson's united political front.

A second fissure in the party opened over Vice President Aaron Burr. Burr's failure to renounce the presidency in the election of 1800 had deeply angered Jefferson. Jefferson snubbed Burr throughout his first term and then dropped him from the ticket in 1804. Burr then ran for governor of New York in 1804 with the support of the Essex Junto, which was scheming to have New York join a northern confederacy. Alexander Hamilton was furious when he perceived Burr's intentions and loudly denounced Burr as "a dangerous man . . . who ought not to be trusted with the reins of government." Burr lost the election in a landslide.

Steaming with resentment, Burr blamed Hamilton for his defeat and challenged him to a duel. Although Hamilton hated dueling, he still accepted Burr's challenge. The vice president wounded Hamilton mortally in July 1804. Burr found himself indicted for murder and fled. While in hiding, he hatched a plot with James Wilkinson, a Revolutionary War commander who had become something of a soldier of fortune. The nature of this plot remains obscure. Whatever they had in mind, Burr managed to get Wilkinson appointed governor of the Louisiana Territory when the indictments against him were torn up, and he resumed his role as vice president of the United States.

When Burr left office in 1805, he sailed down the Mississippi recruiting associates. Rumors that Burr and Wilkinson intended to seize Louisiana soon surfaced. Federal authorities began investigating when

they received a letter from Wilkinson in December 1806 warning of a "deep, dark, wicked, and widespread conspiracy" against America. Playing innocent, Wilkinson implicated Burr. Learning that Wilkinson had turned him in, Burr tried to reach Spanish Florida but was captured early in 1807 and put on trial for treason. Chief Justice John Marshall instructed the jury that treason, according to the Constitution, consisted of "levying war against the United States or adhering to their enemies." Because Burr had not waged war and because neither Spain nor Britain was then an enemy of the United States, the jury acquitted the former vice president.

The Problem of American Neutrality

Jefferson found the task of maintaining American neutrality much more difficult in his second administration. Great Britain and France put major *constraints* on American trade, thereby forcing him to make *choices* that violated his republican principles.

Impressment was a major *constraint* on American neutrality and trade after the European war resumed in 1803 following a brief peace. Great Britain, strapped for mariners by renewed warfare and by thousands of desertions, pursued a vigorous policy of reclaiming British sailors, even if they were on neutral American ships and, more provocatively, even if they had become naturalized American citizens. The British abducted as many as eight thousand sailors from American ships between 1803 and 1812. The loss of so many seamen hurt American shippers, but it wounded American pride even more. Like the XYZ affair, impressment insulted national honor.

Pressure on American neutrality increased after 1805, when the British won a decisive naval victory at Trafalgar (off the Spanish coast) and the French an equally decisive land victory at Austerlitz (in Austria). A military deadlock followed, with Britain supreme at sea and France in control of continental Europe. Both sides used whatever resources were available to gain an advantage. Thus the war

---

Tertium Quids Republican faction formed by John Randolph in protest against Jefferson's plan for acquiring Florida from Spain.

♦ The impressment of sailors into the British navy from American ships was one of the more prominent causes of the War of 1812. This nineteenth-century engraving shows an American sailor being seized at gunpoint while those who might try to assist him are elbowed aside. *Library of Congress.*

changed from one of military campaigning to one of diplomatic and economic maneuvering.

Napoleon made the first move by issuing the **Berlin Decree** in November 1806. Seeking to shut off foreign supplies to Britain, the order barred ships that had anchored at British harbors from entering ports controlled by France. It also declared that all British-made items found on neutral ships would be subject to confiscation by French authorities. The British Parliament responded to the Berlin Decree by issuing orders that virtually blockaded Europe. Neutral ships were permitted to sail to Europe only if they first called at a British port to pay a transit tax. It was thus impossible for a neutral ship to follow the laws of either nation without violating the laws of the other.

Toward Economic War

The escalating economic warfare quickly involved Americans. A pivotal event occurred in June 1807. A British frigate fired on the American warship *Chesapeake* inside American territorial waters when the latter refused to hand over any British sailors. The British **broadsides** crippled the American vessel, killing three men. The British then boarded the *Chesapeake* and dragged off four men, three of them naturalized American citizens. Americans were outraged.

Napoleon responded to more aggressive British enforcement by declaring economic war against neutrals. In the **Milan Decree,** he vowed to seize any neutral ship that even carried licenses to trade with Britain. Ships that had been boarded by the British would be subject to immediate French capture.

Many Americans viewed the escalating French and British sanctions as extremely insulting. The *Washington Federalist* observed, "We have never, on any occasion, witnessed . . . such a thirst for revenge." If Congress had been in session, it would have called for war. But Jefferson stayed calm. War would bring his whole political program to a crashing halt. He had insisted on inexpensive government, lobbied for American neutrality, and hoped for renewed prosperity through continuing trade with Europe. War would destroy all those things. Doing nothing, however, put them all in great peril.

Believing that Europeans were far more dependent on American goods than Americans were on European manufactures, Jefferson *chose* to violate one of his cardinal principles. The U.S. government would interfere in the economy to force Europeans to recognize American neutral rights. In December 1807, the president issued an **embargo**—an absolute ban—on all American trade with Europe. It went into effect at the beginning of 1808.

Berlin Decree   Napoleon's order declaring the British Isles under blockade and authorizing the confiscation of British goods from any ship found carrying them.

broadside   The simultaneous discharge of all the guns on one side of a warship.

Milan Decree   Napoleon's order authorizing the capture of any neutral vessels sailing from British ports or submitting to British searches.

embargo   A government order that bans trade with another nation or group of nations.

Crises in the Nation

• What *constraints* arose from Jefferson's economic and Indian policies?

• How did they affect easterners?

• How did they encourage westerners to *choose* a prowar position?

While impressment, blockade, and embargo plagued America's Atlantic frontier, a combination of European and Indian hostility along the western frontier added to the air of national emergency. The resulting series of domestic crises played havoc with Jefferson's vision of a peaceful, prosperous nation.

The Depression of 1808

Jefferson's embargo resulted in the worst economic depression since the founding of the American colonies. Trade slumped disastrously. American exports fell from $109 million to $22 million, and net earnings from shipping plummeted by almost 50 percent. During 1808, earnings from legitimate business enterprise in America declined to less than a quarter of their value in 1807.

The depression shattered economic and social life in many eastern towns. Some thirty thousand sailors were thrown out of work. In New York City alone, 120 businesses went bankrupt, and twelve hundred New Yorkers were imprisoned for debt in 1808. New England, where the economy had become almost entirely dependent on foreign trade, was hit harder still. The Federalists enjoyed a comeback, not in spite of but because of their rhetoric calling for disobedience to federal law and the possibility of secession.

New Englanders screamed loudest about the embargo, but southerners and westerners were just as seriously hurt by it. The economy of the South had depended on the export of staple crops like tobacco since colonial times. Embargo meant near-death to all legitimate trade. The loss of foreign markets caused tobacco prices to fall from $6.75 per hundredweight to $3.25, and cotton from 21 to 13 cents per pound. In the West, wholesale prices for agricultural products spiraled downward also. The prices of farm products were 16 percent lower between 1807 and 1811 than they had been between 1791 and 1801. At the same time, the price of consumer items went up. For example, the price of building materials rose 11 percent during the same period, and the price of textiles jumped 20 percent. Only food did not go up in price, and that was the one thing farmers did not need to buy.

Although trading interests in New England suffered during the depression, a new avenue of economic expansion opened there as the result of the embargo. Cut off from European manufactured goods, Americans started to make more textiles and other items for themselves. The expansion in cotton spinning is a case in point. Prior to 1808, only fifteen cotton mills had been built in the United States. Between the passage of the embargo and the end of 1809, eighty-seven additional mills sprang up, mostly in New England.

The Rise of the Prophet

The crisis along the Atlantic frontier was echoed by a problem along the nation's western frontier. Relations with Indians in the West had been peaceful since the Battle of Fallen Timbers in Ohio in 1794, but only because the Indians had been crushed into submission. The Shawnees and other groups had been thrown off their traditional homelands in Ohio by the Treaty of Greenville and forced to move to new lands in Indiana. There, food shortages, disease, and continuing encroachment by settlers caused many young Indians to lose faith in their traditional beliefs and in themselves as human beings. A growing number turned to alcohol to escape feelings of helplessness and hopelessness. No native could see any way to halt the drowning tide of white expansion.

In the midst of the crisis, one disheartened, diseased alcoholic rose above his sickness to lead the Indians into a brief new era of hope. A young Shawnee named Lalawathika claimed that he remembered dying and meeting the Master of Life, who showed him the way to lead his people out of degradation. He then returned to the world of the living and awoke, cured of his illness. He immediately adopted the name Tenskwatawa ("The Way") and launched a revival to teach the ways revealed to him by the Master of Life. Whites called him "the Prophet."

The Prophet preached a message of ethnic pride, nonviolence, and passive resistance. Blaming the decline of his people on their adoption of white ways, the Prophet taught them to discard whites' clothing, religion, and especially alcohol and to live as their ancestors had. Whites, he said, were dangerous witches, and Indians must avoid them. He also urged his followers to unify against the white exploiters and to hold on to what remained of their lands. If they followed his teachings, the Indians would regain control of their lives and their lands, and the whites would vanish from their world.

In 1807, the Prophet established a new community, Prophetstown, on the banks of Tippecanoe Creek, in Indiana. This community was to serve as a model for revitalized Indian life. Liquor, guns, and other white goods were banned from the settlement. The residents of Prophetstown worked together, using traditional forms of agriculture, hunting, and gathering.

The Prophet's message of passive resistance underwent a significant change in the face of continuing white opposition. He began to advocate more forceful solutions to the Indians' problems. In April 1807, the Prophet first suggested that warriors unite to resist white expansion. Although he did not urge his followers to attack the whites, he claimed that the Master of Life would protect his followers in the event of war. This development frightened white settlers. But the residents of Prophetstown continued to live together peacefully for a number of years, giving anxious whites no excuse to destroy the settlement.

Tecumseh and the Western War Advocates

While the Prophet continued to stress spiritual means for stopping white aggression, his older brother **Tecumseh** advocated a political course of action. A brave fighter and a persuasive political orator, Tecumseh traveled the western frontier working out alliances with other Indian tribes. Although he did not want to start a war against white settlers, Tecumseh exhorted Indians to defend every inch of land that remained to them.

Tecumseh's success in organizing Indian groups caused confusion among whites. British authorities in Canada were convinced that the Prophet and Tecumseh were French agents trying to divert British attention from the war in Europe. Americans in the West were equally convinced that the brothers were British agents. Both the British and the Americans were wrong. Like many other gifted Indian leaders, Tecumseh played whites off against each other to gain what he wanted for his people. He did go to Canada in 1807 and secured promises of British support, but he did not become a British agent. Rather, Tecumseh wanted the Americans to believe that he had a powerful ally. He wanted to avoid war at all costs.

To many westerners, however, war was attractive. Anything that stood in the way of American control of all of North America deserved to be brushed aside. Thus war with Britain and its supposed Indian allies was an attractive option for at least three reasons.

First, a war with Britain could justify Americans' invading and seizing Canada. Taking Canada from the British would open up rich timber, fur, and agricultural lands for Americans. More important, it would secure American control of the Great Lakes and Saint Lawrence River, the primary shipping route for agricultural produce from upper New York, northern Ohio, and the newly opening areas of the Old Northwest.

Second, many believed that the British in Canada stirred up Indian conflict on America's frontiers. A war could remove this source of trouble and remove obstacles to American expansion. It would further provide an excuse to attack the Shawnees and break up their emerging confederacy.

Finally, frontiersmen, like other Americans, blamed Britain for the economic depression that began in 1808. They believed that eliminating

---

The Prophet Shawnee religious visionary who called for a return to Indian traditions and founded the community of Prophetstown on Tippecanoe Creek in Indiana.

Tecumseh Shawnee leader and brother of the Prophet; he tried to establish an Indian confederacy along the frontier as a barrier to white expansion.

♦ Although they were half-brothers and shared a common vision concerning the future for American Indians, Tecumseh *(left)* and the Prophet *(right)* had very different personal styles. The portrait of Tecumseh shows a determined man whose dress conveys a comfortable acquaintanceship with European ways of doing things. The Prophet, on the other hand, appears much more traditional, in keeping with his teaching that white ways were a form of evil witchcraft. *"Tecumseh." Field Museum of Natural History FMNH Neg #A993851; "The Prophet, Tenskwatawa" by Henry Inmen after Charles Bird King. National Portrait Gallery, Smithsonian Institution/Art Resource, NY.*

British interference would restore a boom economy for western farmers. Thus westerners banded together to raise their voices in favor of American patriotism and war against Britain.

The Second War for Independence

- What developments finally convinced the United States to *choose* war against Great Britain in 1812?
- How did the conduct of the war reveal the Americans' true aims?

In 1808, Jefferson *chose* to follow Washington's lead and left the presidency after two terms. In the national elections that year, the **consensus** was for peace. But the Federalists and factions within the Republican party clamored against Jefferson's policy of economic warfare. As the political fractures widened after 1808, pressure for war grew stronger.

The Misleading Election of 1808

When Jefferson stepped down from the presidency, he pegged James Madison as his successor. Madison was a man of few words, but of piercing intellect and unflinching conviction. Madison easily defeated his Federalist opponent, Charles Cotesworth Pinckney. But the one-sided election disguised deep political divisions in the nation. Federalist criticism of Jefferson's embargo found a growing audience as the depression deepened, and the Republicans lost twenty-four congressional seats to Federalists.

Significant divisions also split the Republican ranks. Dissatisfied with Jefferson's policies, both southern and northeastern party members had contested Madison's succession. John Randolph's dissident Tertium Quids had tried unsuccessfully to secure the nomination for **James Monroe**. Northeasterners, stung by the embargo, had nominated their own presidential candidate, New Yorker George Clinton. Although Clinton polled only six electoral votes for the presidency, his nomination showed how deeply divided the Republican party was over the problems that the United States faced in 1808.

---

consensus   An opinion about which there is general agreement.

James Monroe   Republican politican from Virginia who served in diplomatic posts under Thomas Jefferson and later became the fifth president of the United States.

These dissident factions in the Republican party gained strength in the 1810 election, which saw unprecedented turnover. In that election sixty-three incumbent congressmen were swept out of office. The newcomers who replaced them belonged to Madison's party but did not agree with his conciliatory policy toward the British. Their increasingly strident demands for aggressive action against Britain earned them the nickname **War Hawks.**

Renewed Tension and Coming to Blows

Henry Clay and **John C. Calhoun** quickly assumed the leadership of the War Hawks, who were mostly young southerners and westerners. Clay was the dominant voice among the younger representatives. Born in Virginia in 1777, Clay at the age of 20 had moved to the wilds of Kentucky to practice law and carve out a career in politics. He became Speaker of the Kentucky state assembly when he was only 30 years old and won a seat in the House of Representatives four years later.

Only 29 years old when he was elected to the House of Representatives, John C. Calhoun of South Carolina was a dedicated nationalist who wanted to break Britain's stranglehold on the American agricultural economy. Together, he and Clay called for aggressive action against British provocations. Events soon played into their hands.

In 1809, Congress revoked the Embargo Act and replaced it with the **Non-Intercourse Act,** which forbade trade only with Britain and France. Even though this act was much less restrictive than the embargo, American merchants were relieved when it expired in 1810. Congress then passed an even more liberal boycott, **Macon's Bill No. 2**. Under this new law, merchants could trade even with the combatants if they wanted to take the risk. Also, if either France or Britain lifted its blockade, the United States would stop trading with the other.

Napoleon responded to Macon's Bill in August by promising to suspend French restrictions on American shipping. (The French emperor had no intentions of living up to this promise.) Madison sought to use the French peace overture as a lever. He instructed the American mission in London to tell the British that France's action would force the president to close down trade with Britain unless Britain ended its trade restrictions. Sure that Napoleon was lying, the British refused. In February 1811 the provisions of Macon's Bill forced Madison to end trading with Britain.

Another clash between American and British naval vessels shortly thereafter added to the crisis. In May 1811 the American warship *President* attacked a smaller British ship, killing nine sailors. The British press immediately demanded revenge while American papers celebrated just retribution for the *Chesapeake* incident.

Events in the West added the final element to the unfolding diplomatic crisis. In the fall of 1809, U.S. government agents met at Fort Wayne in Indiana with representatives of three tribes that had not joined Tecumseh's coalition. In return for an outright bribe of $5,200 and individual **annuities** ranging from $250 to $500, tribal leaders sold over 3 million acres of Indian land in Indiana and Illinois. Tecumseh repudiated the Fort Wayne Treaty, claiming it was fraudulent because the three tribes had no right to sell this land.

In August 1810, Tecumseh and a delegation conveyed that message to Governor **William Henry Harrison** in a meeting at Vincennes, Indiana. From

---

War Hawks   Members of Congress from the West and South who campaigned for war with Britain in the hopes of stimulating the economy and annexing new territory.

Henry Clay   Congressman from Kentucky who was a leader of the War Hawks; he helped negotiate the treaty ending the War of 1812.

John C. Calhoun   Congressman from South Carolina who was a leader of the War Hawks; he later became an advocate of states' rights.

Non-Intercourse Act   Law passed by the Congress in 1809 reopening trade with all nations except France and Britain and authorizing the president to reopen trade with them if they lifted restrictions on American shipping.

Macon's Bill No. 2   Law passed by Congress in 1810 that offered exclusive trading rights to France or Britain, whichever recognized American neutral rights first.

annuity   An allowance or income paid annually.

William Henry Harrison   Indiana governor who led U.S. forces in the battle at Tippecanoe; he later became the ninth president of the United States.

the outset, the air between Harrison and Tecumseh crackled with antagonism. Harrison insisted that the Fort Wayne Treaty was legitimate. Tecumseh countered that "bad consequences" would follow if whites attempted to settle in the disputed lands. The meeting resulted in a complete stalemate.

The Vincennes meeting convinced the Indians that they must prepare for a white attack. The Prophet increasingly preached the Master of Life's commitment to support the faithful in battle against the whites. Tecumseh traveled the frontier to enlist additional allies for his confederacy.

Convinced that war was imminent, Harrison determined to attack the Indians before they could unite. He got his chance in the fall of 1811 when Potawatomis raided a village in Illinois. Harrison assembled over a thousand soldiers and militiamen to march on Prophetstown, even though Indians there had had nothing to do with the raid. Arriving near Tippecanoe Creek on November 6, Harrison's force was met by a party of Shawnees, who told Harrison that the Prophet wanted to discuss a settlement the next day. Harrison agreed to the meeting but instructed his men to be ready for an attack.

The Prophet ignored his older brother's advice to avoid confrontation and unleashed restless, young Indians on Harrison's army. Prepared for the assault, the white soldiers routed the attackers and made a mockery of the Prophet's assurance that the Master of Life would make the Indians victorious. Disheartened, most of the warriors from Prophetstown deserted the settlement. The enraged frontiersmen burned the village.

Tecumseh was away trying to win southwestern Indians over to his cause when Harrison's men burned Prophetstown. When he learned that hope for a peaceful settlement had vanished, he gathered an army of Indian allies to defend Indian territory. Harrison immediately called on the federal government for military support against what he portrayed as a unified Indian and British declaration of war. He had no doubt that the British stood behind Tecumseh.

Declaring War: The Disastrous First Year

The **Battle of Tippecanoe** provided the War Hawks with the excuse they had been looking for. John C.

Calhoun declared that Great Britain had left Americans with the *choice* only between "the base surrender of their rights, and a manly vindication of them." Calhoun was out to vindicate American rights, and he introduced a war bill in Congress in 1812. His bill declaring war on Great Britain passed by a vote of 79 to 49 in the House and 19 to 13 in the Senate. Representatives from heavily Federalist regions that depended the most on overseas trade— Massachusetts, Connecticut, and New York—voted against war. Republican western and southern representatives voted in favor.

In line with War Hawk ambitions, the first military campaign was a three-pronged drive toward Canada (see Map 8.1). Harrison's force was successful in raiding undefended Indian villages but was unable to make any gains against British troops. Farther east, Major General Stephen Van Rensselaer's force was defeated by a small British and Indian army. Meanwhile, Henry Dearborn's troops lunged at Montreal but withdrew into U.S. territory after an inconclusive battle.

American sailors fared much better. Leading the war effort at sea were the *Constitution* (popularly known as **Old Ironsides**), the *President*, and the *United States*. In mid-August, the *Constitution* outmaneuvered a British **frigate** and sank it. The *United States* enjoyed a similar victory.

The biggest threat to British seafaring, however, came from armed American privateers. During the first six months of the war, privateers captured 450 British merchant ships valued in the millions. American naval victories were all that kept the nation's morale alive in 1812. One observer commented, "But for the gallantry of our noble Tar's [sailors], we should be covered with shame and disgrace." Vowing to reverse the situation, Congress

---

Battle of Tippecanoe   Battle near Prophetstown in Indiana Territory in 1811, where American forces led by William Henry Harrison defeated Shawnee followers of the Prophet.

Old Ironsides   Nickname of the *Constitution*, the 44-gun American frigate whose victory over the *Guerrière* bolstered sagging national morale in the War of 1812.

frigate   A very fast warship, rigged with square sails, usually carrying thirty guns on its gun deck.

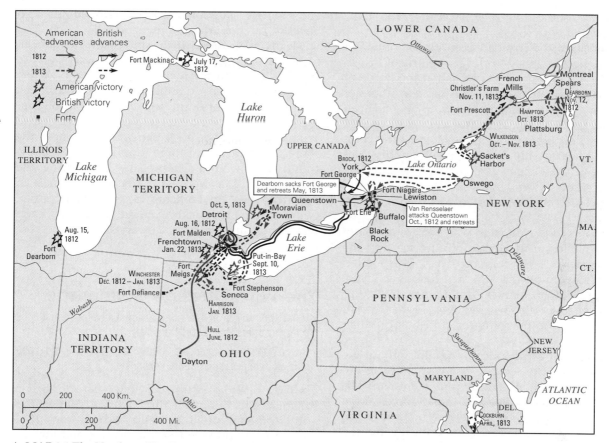

♦ **MAP 8.1 The Northern War Front, 1812–1813**   The heaviest action during the first two years of the War of 1812 lay along the U.S./Canadian border. This map shows the attempted American invasion of Canada and the major battles that took place along the northern frontier. Cockburn's 1813 raid against the Chesapeake was an isolated event, but foreshadowed an offensive to come in the following year.

increased the size of the army to 57,000 men and offered a $16 bonus to encourage enlistments.

Madison thus stood for re-election at a time when the nation's military fate appeared uncertain and his own leadership seemed shaky. Although the majority of his party's congressional caucus supported him for re-election, nearly a third of the Republican congressmen—mostly those from New York and New England—rallied around New Yorker DeWitt Clinton, nephew of Madison's former challenger George Clinton. Like his uncle, DeWitt Clinton was a Republican who favored Federalist economic policies and agreed that the war was unnecessary. Most Federalists supported Clinton and did not field a candidate of their own.

The *outcome* of the election was nearly the same as the *outcome* of the congressional vote on the war bill earlier in 1812. New York and New England rallied behind Clinton. The South and West supported Madison, the Republicans, and war. Madison won, but his share of electoral votes fell from 72 percent in 1808 to 59 percent. The Republicans also lost strength in the House and the Senate.

The War's Fruitless Second Year

In the spring of 1813, American forces challenged British control of the Great Lakes and the uninterrupted supply line those lakes afforded. On Lake

Ontario the Americans met frustration; on Lake Erie, they met with success.

Oliver Hazard Perry had been given command of a small fleet assigned to clear Lake Erie of British ships. Perry's ships met the British at the Battle of Put-in-Bay in September 1813. After two hours of cannon fire, Perry's **flagship,** the *Lawrence,* had been nearly destroyed. Still, Perry refused to surrender. He slipped off his damaged vessel and took command of a nearby ship. What remained of his command then cut the enemy to pieces and captured six British vessels. "We have met the enemy and they are ours," Perry reported to William Henry Harrison.

Harrison's land campaign was not going nearly so well. In the spring of 1813, Tecumseh and the British general Henry Procter had surrounded Harrison's camp on the Maumee Rapids in Ohio. Finally, on May 5, Kentucky militiamen arrived to drive the enemy off. However, they lost nearly half of their number in pursuing the British and Indian force.

After harassing American forces throughout the summer of 1813, Procter and Tecumseh withdrew to Canada in the fall. Harrison pursued them. His army surprised the British and Indian forces at the Thames River, about 50 miles east of Detroit, on October 5. The British surrendered quickly, but the Indians abandoned the fight only after Tecumseh was killed. His body was torn apart by the victorious Americans following the Battle of the Thames.

Another war front opened up during 1813. Although the Creek Confederacy as a whole remained neutral, the Red Stick faction had allied with Tecumseh in 1812. When war broke out, the Red Sticks raided settlements in what are now Alabama and Mississippi. Alexander McGillivray's heir, William Weatherford, led a Red Stick army against Fort Mims, 40 miles north of Mobile (see Individual Choices: William Weatherford). The attackers overran the fort, killing all but about thirty of the more than three hundred people there.

The Fort Mims massacre enraged whites in the Southeast. In Tennessee, twenty-five hundred militiamen enlisted under the command of **Andrew Jackson.** Nicknamed "Old Hickory" because of his toughness, Jackson promised that "the blood of our women & children shall not call for vengeance in vain." Along with other volunteers from Tennessee

and Georgia, Jackson's troops hounded the Red Sticks throughout the summer and fall.

Meanwhile, the British shut down American forces at sea. Embarrassed by the success of *Old Ironsides* and other American frigates, the British sent sufficient ships to bottle up the American fleet and merchant marine in port. British control over the Atlantic was so complete that they decided to bring the war home to Americans living near the shore. Admiral Sir George Cockburn raided the countryside around Chesapeake Bay during the spring of 1813. In Maryland, Cockburn burned an American fleet in Frenchtown, and then burned Georgetown, Fredericktown, and Havre de Grace. The Americans seemed powerless against these raids.

The War's Strange Conclusion

- What *constraints* on American national development did the *outcome* of the War of 1812 remove?
- How did the war change Americans' *expectations* about politics, economics, and national expansion?

The War of 1812 assumed a new character when Britain and its European allies defeated Napoleon's army in the fall of 1813. By the end of March 1814 they had forced Napoleon's abdication and imprisoned him on Elba. Napoleon's defeat left the United States as Great Britain's sole military target. Republican Joseph Nicholson expressed a common lament when he said, "We should have to fight hereafter not for 'free Trade and sailors rights,' not for the Conquest of the Canadas, but for our national Existence."

The Politics of Waging War

American *choices* in the war were complicated by the British offer in December 1813 to open peace negoti-

---

Oliver Hazard Perry American naval officer who led the fleet that defeated the British in the Battle of Put-in-Bay during the War of 1812.

flagship The ship that carries the fleet commander and bears the commander's flag.

Andrew Jackson General in the War of 1812 who defeated the British at New Orleans in 1815; he later became the seventh president of the United States.

ations. President Madison responded by forming an American peace commission. The British peace overture made the unruly Congress even more difficult to deal with. Federalist William Gaston of North Carolina proclaimed it "inexpedient to prosecute military operations against the Canadas" while negotiations were pending. Fellow Federalists joined him in supporting bills to limit American military operations to "the defence of the territories and frontiers of the United States." Madison's supporters objected. John C. Calhoun proclaimed that the entire war was "defensive."

While this debate was going on, Madison turned his attention to diplomacy. He proposed another embargo to hasten negotiations with the British. Madison had two objectives in mind: (1) to stop the flow of American flour and other supplies to British military commissaries in Canada and (2) to stop the drain of American currency from the country. He asked and obtained Congress's approval to prohibit American ships and goods from leaving port and to ban British imports.

The **Embargo of 1813** was the most far-reaching trade restriction bill ever passed by the American Congress. It had a devastating economic impact. The embargo virtually shut down the economies of New England and New York and crippled the economy of nearly every other state.

A Stumbling British Offensive

As combat-hardened British veterans began arriving in North America after Napoleon's fall, the survival of the United States was in jeopardy (see Map 8.2). By September 1814, the British had thirty thousand troops in Canada. From this position of strength, the British prepared three offensives to bring the war to a quick end.

The main thrust of the British offensive in the North was against eastern New York. Sir George Prevost, governor-general of Canada, massed ten thousand troops for an attack against Plattsburgh, New York. Prevost's plans were upset when a small American fleet shredded British naval forces on Lake Champlain on September 11. Prevost broke off his attack when he learned about the fate of the British lake fleet and ordered a retreat. The New Yorkers gave chase and turned the retreat into a rout. Prevost's failure in the Battle of Plattsburgh

marked the end of the major fighting on the Canadian frontier.

The British opened a second front farther south in August 1814. It began when twenty British warships and several troop transports, commanded by Cockburn, sailed up the Chesapeake Bay. The British landed a force outside Washington, D.C., on August 24. Some seven thousand Maryland militia men held off the experienced British regulars for several hours, but when they ran out of ammunition, the British broke their defensive line and seized the capital.

The defenders did stop the British long enough to allow most of the civilians in the capital, including the president, to escape. Dolly Madison, the president's wife, managed to save a number of treasures from the presidential mansion, as well as important cabinet documents. Department clerks succeeded in moving most of the government's vital papers. Even so, much of value was lost. Cockburn and his men looted many buildings, including the White House, and then torched most of the structures, including the Capitol, which housed the Library of Congress. The British finally abandoned the ruins of Washington on August 25, marching toward Baltimore.

At Baltimore, the British navy had to knock out Fort McHenry and control the harbor before they could take the city. On September 12, British ships armed with heavy **mortars** and rockets attacked the fort. During a twenty-five-hour bombardment, the British fired more than fifteen hundred rounds at the American post. Despite the pounding, the American flag continued to wave over Fort McHenry. The sight moved a young volunteer named **Francis Scott Key,** who had watched the shelling as a prisoner aboard a British ship, to record the event in a verse that later became the national anthem of the United States.

Embargo of 1813   An absolute embargo on all American trade and British imports.

mortar   A portable, muzzle-loading cannon.

Francis Scott Key   Author of "The Star-Spangled Banner," which chronicles the British bombardment of Fort McHenry at Baltimore in the War of 1812; it became the official U.S. national anthem in 1916.

Choice in Civil War

William Weatherford

Tecumseh's effort to unite all Indians into a single political and military alliance split the Creek Confederacy into two warring factions. At first, William Weatherford tried to mediate between the two, but he finally chose to lead the "red stick" faction into war against the United States. Tennessee State Library & Archives.

William Weatherford had the potential to be the most powerful man in the Creek Nation. Like his maternal uncle Alexander McGillivray, Weatherford was part white and part Indian. But among the Creeks, family roots were traced back only through the mother's line, making him fully Creek in the tribe's eyes. The Creek tradition also marked him to inherit McGillivray's position as the dominant chief in the confederacy. But by 1800, historical pressures on the Creeks had eroded traditional ways of doing things, and Weatherford's position was far from secure. In 1812, he found himself facing a difficult *choice:* he had to *choose* sides in a Creek nation split in two by civil war.

The Creek Nation was a confederacy consisting of a variety of Indian groups that spoke a variety of languages, had different customs, and practiced quite different economies. Over time, these groups had aligned themselves into two large organizations: the Lower Towns—villages in the low-lying southern portion of the Creek territory in modern day Georgia and Alabama—and the Upper Towns—villages in the more mountainous and heavily wooded northern part of the region. Geographical and cultural diversity, in fact, was part of what held the Creek confederacy together: the many different resources controlled by different Creek member villages led them to depend on each other.

By the end of the eighteenth century, the mutually dependent economy that had kept the Creek towns aligned had given way to greater dependence on the Europeans. In the Upper Towns, where Weatherford was born, the fur trade distracted hunters from providing meat and other necessities to the confederacy. In the Lower Towns, the lure of growing cotton and tobacco for sale to the whites distracted the people from providing corn. In many villages, essential commodities now had to be purchased outside the confederacy.

The economic separation between the two areas became a source of major conflict after 1808, when President Jefferson's embargo triggered a depression. Suddenly, Creeks in the Upper Towns had no market for their furs. Blaming whites for their dependency on the fur trade, and the fur trade for their dire economic situation, many in the Upper Towns found the Prophet's message of turning away from white ways appealing. More appealing still was Tecumseh's suggestion of empowerment through joint action. Not surprisingly, then, when Tecumseh visited the Creeks in 1811, he was well received in the Upper Towns. Many *chose* to follow Tecumseh's red war stick.

It appears that Weatherford was leery of Tecumseh, but the response by the Lower Towns to Tecumseh's visit forced Weatherford's hand. Allied by common economic interests with southern white planters, Creeks in the Lower Towns feared that rumors of an alliance between Creeks in the Upper Towns and the Shawnees might ruin their economy further and, more important, close off avenues of improvement through political cooperation with their white neighbors. Creeks in the Lower Towns began putting enormous pressure on the Upper Towns to turn away from Tecumseh's message. Weatherford and other responsible leaders tried to keep the peace, but when war broke out between the Americans and the British in 1812, that became hard to do. In February 1813 rogue bands of Red Sticks went on forays against settlements, aiming to punish whites for attacks or rumored attacks on Indians.

Bent on preventing war with the Americans, the Creeks in the Lower Towns sent an armed party against the Upper Towns to put an end to Red Stick violence but only worsened the situation. Determined to defend themselves, the Upper Towns sent a party under Red Stick leader Peter McQueen to the Spanish post at Pensacola to buy guns and ammunition.

Though not yet committed to the Red Stick position, Weatherford accompanied this party, possibly hoping to prevent further outbreaks. A combined force of white militiamen and Creeks from the Lower Towns stumbled on them at midday on July 27, attacking them while they ate lunch. Most of McQueen's party was able to escape, but the bodies of the twenty men who were killed in the surprise attack were brutally defiled. For Weatherford, that was the last straw. An honorable peace no longer seemed possible, and he *chose* war.

A little over a month later, Weatherford led about seven hundred Red Sticks on a raid against Fort Mims, a post jointly occupied by Creeks from the Lower Towns and by white militiamen with their families. Weatherford and his force launched their assault as the lunch bell rang at noon on August 30. Within moments they swept into the surprised post, and a general melee began. When the fighting stopped, between three hundred and five hundred people lay dead, and the fort was in flames. Major Joseph P. Kennedy, who arrived at the fort ten days after the battle, reported, "Indians, negroes, white men, women, and children lay in one promiscuous ruin."

Though he preferred peace and was no convert to the teachings of Tecumseh and the Prophet, Weatherford had seen his *choices* narrow as differing interests among the Creeks pulled the confederacy apart. Pushed finally into making a *choice,* his decision forever altered the Creek Nation's future. After the massacre at Fort Mims, there was no going back: the destiny of the Creeks would depend on the *outcome* of Tecumseh's plan and British military success.

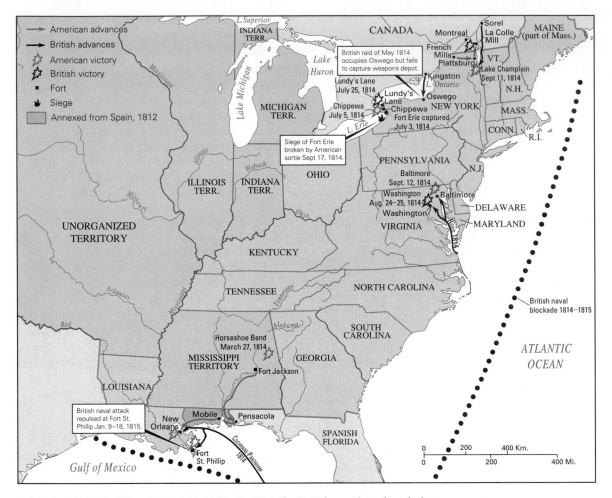

♦ **MAP 8.2 British Offensives, 1814–1815** In 1814, the British sought to knock the United States out of the war by staging three offensives. As this map shows, one came along the northern frontier at Plattsburgh, New York; one followed Cockburn's earlier route into the Chesapeake; and the third was directed at the Mississippi River at New Orleans. All three offensives failed.

The Gulf Coast Campaign

On the third front, the British pressed an offensive against the Gulf Coast designed to take pressure off Canada and to close the Mississippi River. The campaign began in May 1814 when the British occupied the Spanish port city of Pensacola, Florida. From there the British began working their way toward New Orleans and the Mississippi.

The defense of the Gulf Coast fell to Andrew Jackson and his Tennessee volunteers. Having spent

the winter raising troops and collecting supplies, Jackson's army of four thousand resumed its mission in March 1814 to punish the Red Sticks. At the Battle of **Horseshoe Bend** on the Tallapoosa River in

---

Horseshoe Bend Site of a battle in 1814 between Tennessee militia and Creek Indians in Alabama; the American victory marked the end of Indian power in the South.

Alabama, Jackson's forces killed nearly eight hundred Red Sticks, destroying the tribe's power.

Jackson then moved on the British depot at Pensacola. Although ordered to stay out of Florida to avoid war with Spain, he ignored the order. He attacked Pensacola on November 7, 1814. The Spanish did nothing, and the overmatched British withdrew.

Jackson immediately left Pensacola and raced with his army to New Orleans, where the main British force was closing in. When he arrived on December 1, he found the city ill prepared to defend itself. The local militia, consisting mostly of French and Spanish residents, would not obey American officers. Local banks and businesses refused to support government efforts, fearing a collapse in the nation's economy.

A man of forceful action, Jackson permitted no opposition or apathy. "Those who are not for us are against us, and will be dealt with accordingly," he proclaimed. Through the example of his own energy and enthusiasm he transformed the community. "General Jackson electrified all hearts," one observer said. Soon volunteers flooded to the general's assistance. Free blacks in the city formed a regular army corps, and Jackson created a special unit of black refugees from Santo Domingo. Proper white citizens protested when Jackson armed runaway slaves and when he accepted a company of Baratarian pirates under the command of **Jean Laffite,** but Jackson ignored them. The pirate commander became Jackson's constant companion during the campaign.

Having pulled his ragtag force together, Jackson settled in to wait for the British attack. On January 7, 1815, it came. Jackson's men waited until the British were only five hundred yards away before they fired their cannon. When the British got to within three hundred yards, riflemen opened fire. And when the British were within one hundred yards, those of Jackson's men armed with muskets began to shoot. One British veteran said that it was "the most murderous fire I have ever beheld before or since." General Edward Pakenham tried to keep his men from running but was cut in half by a cannon ball. General John Lambert, who took over command, raised a white flag immediately.

The **Battle of New Orleans** was by far the most successful battle fought by Americans during the War of 1812. The British lost over two thousand men in the battle; the Americans, only seventy. Ironically, the war was already officially over before the battle began.

The Treaty of Ghent

While the British were closing in on Washington in August 1814, treaty negotiations were beginning in Ghent, Belgium. Confident of victory, the British refused to enter meaningful negotiations. They declined to discuss impressment and insisted that the security of Canada be ensured by the formation of an Indian buffer state between Canada and the United States.

The Americans, however, were anxious for a peaceful settlement. Madison ordered the delegation to drop impressment as an issue. He justified this decision by saying that the end of the war in Europe had so greatly reduced Britain's need for sailors that impressment was no longer an important issue. Far more important was the British plan for an Indian buffer state.

When Prevost lost the Battle of Plattsburgh and the Lake Champlain fleet, however, the British demand for an Indian buffer zone suddenly became negotiable. The sticking point then became what territories each country would retain when the war ended. The British proposed that each nation keep whatever land it held when hostilities stopped. The Americans rejected this because it would require giving up much of Maine, some territory around the Great Lakes, and perhaps even New Orleans and the nation's capital.

At that point, domestic politics in Britain intervened. After two decades at arms, the British people were weary of war and wartime taxes. The failure at

Jean Laffite   Leader of a band of pirates off Barataria Bay in southeast Louisiana; he offered to fight for the Americans at New Orleans in return for the pardon of his men.

Battle of New Orleans   Battle in the War of 1812 in which American troops commanded by Andrew Jackson repulsed the British attempt to seize New Orleans.

Plattsburgh made it appear that the war would drag on endlessly. Moreover, the American war interfered with Britain's European diplomacy. Still trying to arrive at a peace settlement for Europe at the Congress of Vienna, a British official commented, "We do not think the Continental Powers will continue in good humour with our Blockade of the whole Coast of America." Like the proposed Indian buffer state, British territorial demands fell before practical considerations.

In the end, the **Treaty of Ghent,** completed on December 24, 1814, restored diplomatic relations between Britain and the United States to what they had been before the war. The treaty said nothing about impressment, blockades, or neutral trading rights. It left Canada in British hands. Although Americans had not fulfilled any of the initial goals for which the war was fought, they still considered it a victory. They had secured national survival against the world's most formidable military power and could point to the Battle of New Orleans with justifiable pride.

The War of 1812 also proved to be a pivotal experience in American history. First, the conflict entirely discredited Jefferson's plan for an agricultural nation that would exchange raw materials for European manufactures. Americans now meant to steer clear of entanglement in European affairs and tried to become more self-sufficient. Pioneering developments in American manufacturing during the embargo of 1808 helped make this course possible. The pace of industrialization quickened considerably during the war. The number of people employed in industry increased from four thousand in 1809 to perhaps as many as a hundred thousand in 1816. In the years to come, factories in New England and elsewhere would supply more and more of America's consumer goods. Industrial areas in turn offered an enlarging market for the nation's harvests. In an economic sense, the War of 1812 truly was a second war of independence.

Second, relations between the United States and the Indian nations changed profoundly. When Harrison's soldiers burned Prophetstown and later killed Tecumseh, they wiped out all hopes for a pan-Indian confederacy. Jackson's victories against the Red Sticks destroyed the power of the Creeks and the other southern tribes. As a result, no serious Indian resistance occurred for decades. During that time white settlers occupied most of the eastern half of the continent.

Third, the failure to take Canada and its water routes convinced Americans that they had to improve inland transportation. British control of the Great Lakes had demonstrated how poor American transportation was. The lack of roads and resulting shortage of men and equipment in the interior had ruled out any significant American victories on the Canadian front. In coming decades Americans built canals, national roads, and other transportation links to tie the expanding West to the rest of the nation.

Finally, the war's conclusion helped bring an end to political factionalism. As the war dragged on, the Essex Junto grew in strength. From mid-December 1814 until January 5, 1815, New England Federalists met in Hartford, Connecticut. At the Hartford Convention, party members finally went public with their threat to secede. If Madison did not repeal the Embargo of 1813 and submit constitutional amendments that protected New England's minority rights, New England was ready to leave the Union. News of the Treaty of Ghent and Battle of New Orleans, however, made the Federalists appear to be traitors. Madison and the Republicans were able to drive their political opponents into retreat. Federalists managed to hold on in hard-core areas of New England until the 1820s, but the party as a whole was on a steepening decline. They vanished altogether in 1825.

Thus, after 1815 a new surge of hopefulness and national pride engulfed Americans. The United States had fought the greatest military power in the world to a standstill and in the process had launched new ventures in manufacturing, swept away Indian resistance, and restored political unity.

Treaty of Ghent   Treaty ending the War of 1812, signed in Belgium in 1814; it restored peace but was silent on the issues over which the United States and Britain had clashed.

SUMMARY

After Jefferson's triumphal first four years in office, factional disputes at home and diplomatic problems began to *constrain* Jefferson and the Republicans. Although the Federalists were in full retreat, many within Jefferson's own party *chose* to oppose some of his policies. When Jefferson stepped down in 1808, tapping James Madison as his successor, Republicans in both Virginia and New York bucked the president and supported other candidates.

To a large extent, the Republicans' problems were the *outcome* of external stresses. On the Atlantic frontier, the United States tried to remain neutral in the wars that engulfed Europe. On the western frontier, Tecumseh was successfully unifying dispossessed Indians into a single nation devoted to stopping U.S. expansion. Jefferson *chose* to use federal and executive power to meet these *constraints* and settle disputes, and his enemies rose up in protest.

Jefferson's use of economic sanctions created the worst depression since the beginnings of English colonization. The embargo strangled the economy in port cities and threatened bankruptcy to southern and western farmers.

The combination of economic and diplomatic *constraints* brought aggressive politicians into power. Men like William Henry Harrison, Henry Clay, and John C. Calhoun *expected* that war with Britain would finally secure the independence of the United States by gaining freedom of the seas, eliminating Indian hostility, and conquering the rest of North America. Southern and western interests finally pushed the nation into the *choice* for war with Britain.

Although there were moments of glory for the Americans, the war was mostly disastrous. Americans were saved when the British people *chose* to demand peace. When their offensive failed in 1814, the British *chose* to sign the Treaty of Ghent. The treaty restored diplomatic relations to what they had been before 1812. Nevertheless, the *outcome* of the war provoked strong feelings among Americans of national pride, confidence, and unity. The clouds that had begun gathering a decade before seemed to have lifted, and Americans were ready for a springtime of good feelings.

E xpectations
C onstraints
C hoices
O utcomes

Suggested Readings

Edmunds, R. David. *The Shawnee Prophet* (1983); *Tecumseh and the Quest for Indian Leadership* (1984).

Each of these biographies is a masterpiece, but taken together they present the most complete recounting of the lives and accomplishments of these two fascinating Shawnee brothers and their historical world.

Fowler, William F., Jr. *Jack Tars and Commodores* (1984).

A look at one of the more interesting aspects of the War of 1812: the sea battles and the men who fought them.

Hickey, Donald. *The War of 1812: A Forgotten Conflict* (1989).

Arguably the best single-volume history of the war, encyclopedic in content, but so colorfully written that it will hold anyone's attention.

McCoy, Drew. *The Last of the Fathers: James Madison and the Republican Legacy* (1989).

Hailed by most critics as the best treatment yet written on Madison and his role in making the early republic.

Rutland, Robert A. *Madison's Alternatives: The Jeffersonian Republicans and the Coming of War, 1805–1812* (1975).

An interesting review of the events leading up to the outbreak of war in 1812 and the various alternatives Jefferson and Madison had to choose from in facing the evolving diplomatic and political crises.

Stagg, J. C. A. *Mr. Madison's War: Politics, Diplomacy, and Warfare in the Early American Republic, 1783–1830* (1983).

An excellent view of the politics and diplomacy surrounding the War of 1812.

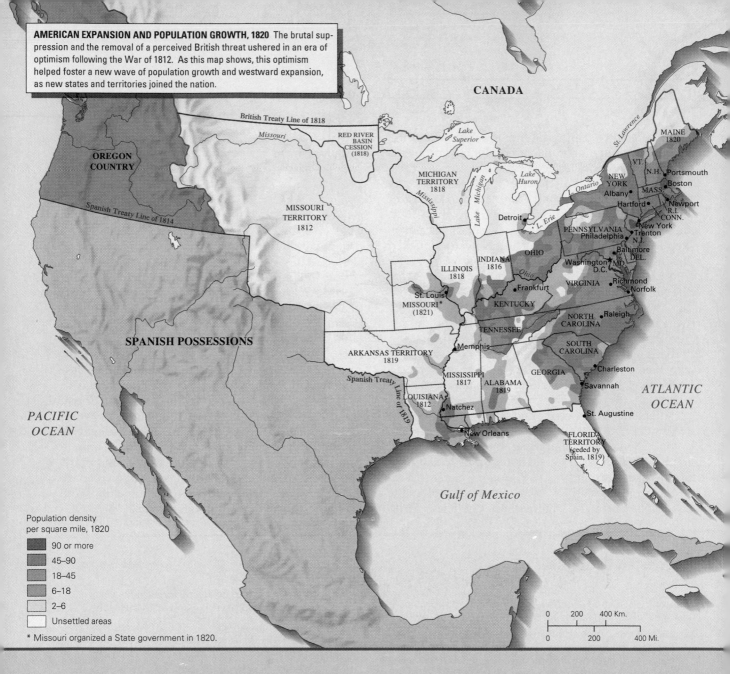

AMERICAN EXPANSION AND POPULATION GROWTH, 1820 The brutal suppression and the removal of a perceived British threat ushered in an era of optimism following the War of 1812. As this map shows, this optimism helped foster a new wave of population growth and westward expansion, as new states and territories joined the nation.

CANADA

British Treaty Line of 1818

OREGON COUNTRY

RED RIVER BASIN CESSION (1818)

Missouri

Lake Superior

MICHIGAN TERRITORY 1818

Spanish Treaty Line of 1814

MISSOURI TERRITORY 1812

Lake Michigan

Lake Huron

Mississippi

Detroit

L. Ontario

Lake Erie

MAINE 1820

VT.

N.H.

NEW YORK

Portsmouth
Boston

MASS.

Albany

Hartford

Newport
R.I.
CONN.

ILLINOIS 1818

INDIANA 1816

OHIO

Ohio

PENNSYLVANIA

Philadelphia

New York

Trenton

N.J.

Baltimore

DEL.

St. Louis

MISSOURI* (1821)

Frankfort

Washington D.C.

MD.

VIRGINIA

Richmond

Norfolk

KENTUCKY

TENNESSEE

NORTH CAROLINA

Raleigh

ARKANSAS TERRITORY 1819

Memphis

SOUTH CAROLINA

Spanish Treaty Line of 1819

MISSISSIPPI 1817

ALABAMA 1819

GEORGIA

Charleston

SPANISH POSSESSIONS

LOUISIANA 1812

Natchez

Savannah

ATLANTIC OCEAN

PACIFIC OCEAN

New Orleans

St. Augustine

FLORIDA TERRITORY (ceded by Spain, 1819)

Gulf of Mexico

Population density per square mile, 1820

- 90 or more
- 45–90
- 18–45
- 6–18
- 2–6
- Unsettled areas

* Missouri organized a State government in 1820.

0   200   400 Km.

0   200   400 Mi.

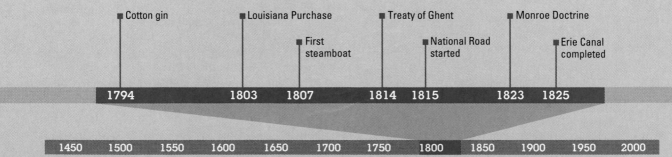

■ Cotton gin   ■ Louisiana Purchase   ■ Treaty of Ghent   ■ Monroe Doctrine

■ First steamboat   ■ National Road started   ■ Erie Canal completed

1794   1803   1807   1814   1815   1823   1825

1450   1500   1550   1600   1650   1700   1750   1800   1850   1900   1950   2000

The Rise of a New Nation, 1815–1819

Politics and Diplomacy in an "Era of Good Feelings"

- What new *expectations* did Americans have as they emerged from the War of 1812?

- What diplomatic and economic *constraints* did they seek to overcome, and how did they *choose* to overcome them?

The Emergence of the Old South

- How did the *expectations* of southerners change after 1815?

- How did they *choose* to respond to new opportunities, and what new *constraints* did they create in the process?

Slaves and King Cotton

- What was the *outcome* for southern blacks, especially for slaves, of white southerners' *choices* concerning economic progress during the period following the War of 1812?

The Transportation Revolution

- What geographical *constraints* prevented economic and political development in the North and West before the transportation revolution?

- How did specific *choices* help to overcome those *constraints*?

INTRODUCTION

E xpectations
C onstraints
C hoices
O utcomes

The United States emerged from the War of 1812 with new confidence. "The veterans of Wellington attest the prowess of our troops," one Protestant preacher declared at war's end, "and the world is astonished at the facility with which our naval heroes have conquered . . . those who have conquered all other nations." The United States had finally become a nation to be reckoned with, and nationalism emerged as the dominant force in domestic and international affairs.

Confident *expectations* led to *choices* that would greatly influence the country's future. Both James Madison and his successor, James Monroe, sought to develop a national market economy. Nationalists like Henry Clay and John C. Calhoun steered bills through Congress designed to expand transportation systems, strengthen the nation's currency, and encourage economic development. Others, like John Quincy Adams and Andrew Jackson, expanded the boundaries of the nation itself.

Expanding economic opportunities, too, created optimistic *expectations*. Many Americans *chose* to invest in transportation systems and in new forms of manufacturing and agriculture. Initial *constraints* were brushed aside as a confident generation developed new technologies, new systems of engineering, and organizational innovations. The South specialized as many farmers and planters *chose* cot-

ton as the crop most likely to generate a profit. The *outcome* was a peculiar economy and culture that eventually placed the South at odds with the rest of the nation.

Another profound *outcome* of southern *choices* was the development of a unique culture among its slaves. Descendants of transported Africans overcame *constraints* on their freedom by *choosing* strategies that made a difficult life more acceptable and meaningful. Family structure, religion, and folklore formed the basis for a vibrant African-American culture able to withstand decades of blunted *expectations* and *constrained choices*.

Other regions framed their own *expectations* and *choices* under the Republicans' optimistic agenda. New York leaped to develop transportation and communication systems, and the entire country began to feel the pressure to modernize. For the moment, the optimistic *expectations* of most Americans produced a spirit of cooperation in politics. But in the long run, regional economic specialization created regional political interests that pulled the nation apart even as technology drew it closer together.

Politics and Diplomacy in an "Era of Good Feelings"

• What new *expectations* did Americans have as they emerged from the War of 1812?

• What diplomatic and economic *constraints* did they seek to overcome, and how did they *choose* to overcome them?

The nationalism that arose after the War of 1812 caused the Federalists to be seen as traitors or fools, and they disappeared from politics. For the first time since Washington's administration, the air was free of party politics, prompting a Boston newspaper to proclaim the dawn of an **"Era of Good Feelings."** Capitalizing on this harmony, President

Madison seized the initiative to inaugurate vigorous new programs in the diplomatic and domestic spheres.

Madison's Agenda for the Nation

Shortly after the war with Britain ended, Madison launched an aggressive diplomacy against the

Era of Good Feelings   The period from 1816 to 1823, when the decline of the Federalist party and the end of the War of 1812 gave rise to a time of political cooperation.

CHRONOLOGY

Expanding Horizons and Slavery

1794	Eli Whitney patents the cotton gin
1800	Jefferson elected Prosser's Rebellion in Richmond, Virginia
1803	Louisiana Purchase
1807	Robert Fulton tests the *Clermont*
1814	Treaty of Ghent ends War of 1812
1815	Government funding for the Cumberland Road Stephen Decatur defeats the Barbary pirates
1816	Tariff of 1816 First successful steamboat run from Pittsburgh to New Orleans James Monroe elected president
1817	Second Bank of the United States opens for business

	Rush-Bagot Agreement Construction of the Erie Canal begins
1818	Convention of 1818 Andrew Jackson invades Spanish Florida
1819	*Dartmouth College v. Woodward* *McCulloch v. Maryland* Adams-Onís Treaty
1823	Monroe Doctrine
1824	*Gibbons v. Ogden*
1830	Defeat of steam locomotive by a stage-coach horse
1831	Nat Turner's Rebellion in Southampton County, Virginia

Barbary pirates, who had resumed their raids against American shipping during the conflict (see page 141). In June 1815, Madison ordered a military force to the Mediterranean. Naval hero Stephen Decatur captured two Algerian pirate vessels and then threatened to level the city of Algiers if the pirates did not stop their raids. Faced with a superior force, the Algerians and the rest of the Barbary pirates signed treaties promising to cease such activities.

In December 1815, Madison urged Congress to address the economic ills that had helped propel the nation into war. Madison called for the resurrection of the national bank, increased military spending, and a system of **protective tariffs.** He also encouraged the states to invest in the nation's future by sponsoring transportation systems and making other internal improvements. Former critics DeWitt Clinton, Henry Clay, and John C. Calhoun quickly rallied behind the president's nationalistic economic and political agenda.

The "American System" and New Economic Direction

The nationalism that characterized the Era of Good Feelings was evident in the Republican economic plan, which Henry Clay called the **American System.** The American System depended on three essential developments. First, a national bank was needed to promote the country's economic growth. Although Republicans had opposed Alexander

---

protective tariff   Tax on imported goods intended to make them more expensive than similar domestic goods, thus protecting the market for goods produced at home.

American System   An economic plan sponsored by nationalists in Congress; it was intended to spur U.S. economic growth and the domestic production of goods previously bought from foreign manufacturers.

Hamilton's Bank of the United States, they came to appreciate the need for a national bank after the difficulties of financing the recent war. In 1816, the overwhelmingly Republican Congress chartered the Second Bank of the United States for twenty years. The Second Bank, which opened in Philadelphia in 1817, had many of the same powers and responsibilities as Hamilton's bank. Congress provided $7 million of its initial $35 million capital and appointed one-fifth of its board of directors.

Second, the war had shown that improvements in communication and transportation were needed. Poor lines of supply and communication had spelled disaster for American military efforts. Although Congress approved legislation to finance a national transportation program, Madison vetoed the bill. The president contended that the Constitution did not authorize federal spending on projects designed to benefit the states. Instead, Madison advocated that the states either pass a constitutional amendment authorizing such federal spending or that they carry out the task of building roads and canals themselves.

Finally, Republicans advocated protective tariffs to help the fledgling industries that had hatched during the war. Incubated by trade restrictions, American cotton-spinning plants had mushroomed between 1808 and 1815. But with the reopening of trade at war's end, British merchants dumped accumulated inventories of cotton cloth below cost, hampering further American development. Although most southerners and westerners remained leery of tariffs, Clay and Calhoun were able to gain enough support to pass the Tariff of 1816.

The American System was designed to create a national **market economy.** Since colonial times local market economies had existed in the trading centers of the Northeast. Individuals in these areas produced items for cash sale and used the cash they earned to purchase goods produced by others. Economic specialization was the natural *outcome.* Farmers, for example, *chose* to grow only one or two crops and sell the whole harvest for cash, which they used to buy goods that they had once grown or made for themselves.

But outside of such centers people generally **bartered** goods and labor. Families tried to make or grow as much of what they needed as they could and exchanged some surplus goods for sugar, tea, metal goods, and other items they could not produce. Little cash changed hands in this economic world.

Advocates of the American System envisioned a time when whole regions would specialize in producing commodities for which they were most suited. Agricultural regions in the West, for example, would produce food for the industrializing Northeast and the fiber-producing South. The North would depend on the South for cotton, and both the South and the West would look to the Northeast for manufactured goods. Improved transportation systems would make this flow of goods possible, and a strong national currency would ensure orderly trade. Advocates of the American System were confident that regional specialization would free the nation from economic dependence on manufacturing centers in Europe.

The popularity of Madison's programs was apparent in the *outcome* of the 1816 elections. His handpicked successor, fellow Virginian James Monroe, won 184 electoral votes to Federalist Rufus King's 34. Congressional Republicans swept over three-fourths of the seats in both the House of Representatives and the Senate. Presented with such a powerful mandate, Republicans immediately set about expanding Madison's agenda for the nation.

James Monroe and the Nationalist Agenda

The new president turned his diplomatic skills to the task of calming political disputes. He was the first president since Washington to take a national goodwill tour, and he persistently urged political factions to forget their differences.

Monroe's first diplomatic goal was to solve important issues not settled by the Treaty of Ghent, which ended the War of 1812. He assigned this task

---

market economy   An economic system based on the buying and selling of goods and services, with money as the primary medium of exchange and in which the forces of supply and demand are allowed to set prices.

barter   To trade goods or services without the exchange of money.

♦ This portrait of James Monroe, painted as he entered the White House in 1816 by artist John Vanderlyn, captures the president's conservative bearing. His clothing, for example, is much more typical of the revolutionary years than the nineteenth century. His conservatism endeared him to many who were tired of political strife. *"James Monroe" by John Vanderlyn. National Portrait Gallery, Smithsonian Institution/Art Resource, NY.*

to Secretary of State John Quincy Adams. Adams first helped establish peaceful borders with British Canada. In the 1817 Rush-Bagot Agreement, both nations agreed to cut back their Great Lakes naval fleets to a few vessels. A year later, the two nations drew up the Convention of 1818. The British agreed to honor American fishing rights in the Atlantic, to recognize a boundary between the Louisiana Territory and Canada at the 49th parallel, and to occupy the Oregon Territory jointly with the United States.

With these northern border issues settled, Adams set his sights on defining the nation's southern and southwestern frontiers. Conditions in Spanish Florida had been extremely unsettled since Napoleon had deposed the king of Spain in 1808. Pirates, runaway slaves, and Indians used Florida as a base for launching raids against American settle-

ments and shipping. By December 1817, matters in Florida seemed critical. General Andrew Jackson urged the president to take possession of Spanish Florida by invading it.

A short time later, Secretary of War John C. Calhoun ordered Jackson and his troops to patrol Georgia's border with Spanish territory. Claiming that he had received secret authorization from Monroe to invade Florida, Jackson crossed into Spanish territory, where his troops brutally destroyed peaceful Seminole villages. He then invaded the Spanish capital at Pensacola on May 24, 1818, forcing the governor to flee to Cuba. The zealous general capped his already reckless venture by executing two British citizens for conspiring with the Indians.

In response to Spanish and British protests, Calhoun and others recommended privately that the general be severely disciplined. Adams, however, saw Jackson's raid as an opportunity to settle the Florida border issue. Jackson's raid, he claimed, was an act of self-defense, and warned that it would be repeated unless Spain could police the area adequately. Fully aware that Spain could not do that, Adams proposed that Spain give up Florida. Understanding his country's precarious position, Spanish minister Don Luis de Onís ceded Florida in the Adams-Onís Treaty of 1819. The United States in return released Spain from $5 million in damage claims resulting from pirate and Indian raids.

The Monroe Doctrine

Spain's declining power posed a more general diplomatic problem. Many of its colonies in Latin America had rebelled and established themselves as independent republics. Fearful that their own colonists might follow this example, Austria, France, Prussia, Russia, and other European powers considered helping Spain reclaim its overseas empire.

Neither Great Britain nor the United States wanted European intervention in the Western Hemisphere. The British had developed a thriving trade with the new Latin American republics. Americans supported Latin American independence for various reasons. Some hoped the new countries would follow in American footsteps and move toward greater democracy. Others favored an independent Latin America as a fertile ground for American expansion.

In 1823, British Foreign Minister George Canning proposed that the United States and Britain form an alliance to end European meddling in Latin America. Most of Monroe's cabinet supported this proposal, but Adams, who disliked the British intensely, protested that America would be reduced to a "cock-boat in the wake of the British man-of-war." In other words, Adams feared that the United States would always be following the British lead. Instead, he suggested that the United States should act **unilaterally** in declaring the Western Hemisphere off-limits to "future colonization by any European power."

Monroe ultimately supported Adams's position. In December 1823 he announced that the United States would regard any effort by European countries "to extend their system to any portion of this hemisphere as dangerous to our peace and safety." European intervention in the hemisphere would be seen as an act of war against the United States.

The **Monroe Doctrine,** as this statement was later called, announced the arrival of the United States on the international scene as a nation to be contended with. Both Europeans and Latin Americans, however, thought it was a meaningless statement. Despite proud assertions, the policy depended on the British navy and on Britain's informal commitment to New World autonomy.

The Emergence of the Old South

- How did the *expectations* of southerners change after 1815?
- How did they *choose* to respond to new opportunities, and what new *constraints* did they create in the process?

Before the War of 1812, the southern economy had been sluggish, and the future of the region's single-crop agricultural system doubtful. Tobacco was no longer the glorious profit maker it had been during the colonial period. Sea Island cotton, rice, sugar, and other products continued to find markets, but they could be grown only in limited areas. Now, though, postwar technological and economic changes pumped new energy into the South's economy. In only a few decades, an entirely new South

emerged, one that became known to history as "the Old South."

The Birth and Growth of King Cotton

Although southern planters had grown cotton since colonial times, the demand for it was small until the **mechanization** of the British textile industry in the late 1700s. The production of cotton cloth rapidly increased, and the need for raw cotton fiber grew.

Planters along the Carolina coast had responded by growing long-staple or Sea Island cotton for the British market. This variety could be grown, however, only in warm, wet, semitropical climates like that of the Carolina Sea Islands. Short-staple cotton could be grown throughout much of the South, but the difficulty of separating sticky seeds from its fibers made it unprofitable. A world-wide shortage of cotton threatened Britain's textile industry.

Eli Whitney, a 1792 graduate of Yale College, found a solution. In 1793, while a guest at a Georgia plantation, he learned about the difficulty of removing the seeds from short-staple cotton. In a matter of weeks, Whitney designed a machine that quickly combed out the seeds without damaging the fibers. He obtained a **patent** for the cotton gin (short for "engine") in 1794.

Whitney's inventiveness allowed short-staple cotton to spread rapidly throughout inland South Carolina and Georgia. From there it spread westward into Alabama and Mississippi and then into Arkansas, northern Louisiana, and east Texas.

---

unilateral Undertaken or issued by only one side and thus not involving an agreement made with others.

Monroe Doctrine President Monroe's 1823 statement declaring the Americas closed to further European colonization and discouraging European interference in the affairs of the Western Hemisphere.

mechanization The substitution of machinery for hand labor.

Eli Whitney American inventor and manufacturer; his invention of the cotton gin revolutionized the cotton industry.

patent A government grant that gives the creator of an invention the sole right to produce, use, or sell that invention for a set period of time.

Between 1790 and 1840, the South's annual cotton crop grew from about three thousand bales to nearly 1.5 million bales.

Most of the South's cotton was exported initially to Britain, but a significant and growing amount went to New England's textile factories (see pages 194–198). Cotton from the South thus helped spur industrialization in the North. Northern demand in turn encouraged southern suppliers to plant more cotton. This dynamic interaction between North and South pushed their regional economies in different directions. Although both remained predominantly rural, the North moved toward mechanization and urbanization, and the South depended more and more on the labor of people rather than on the power of machines.

A New Planter Aristocracy

Few other images have persisted in American history longer than that of courtly southern planters in the years before the Civil War. Songs and stories have immortalized the myth of a southern aristocracy of enormous wealth and polished manners upholding a culture of romantic chivalry. Charming though this image of the **antebellum South** is, it is not accurate.

Statistics indicate that the great planters of popular myth were few and far between. In the early nineteenth century, only about a third of all southerners owned slaves. Large-scale planters were a tiny minority of these. Nearly three-fourths of these slaveholders were small farmers who owned fewer than ten slaves. Another 15 percent of slaveholders owned between ten and twenty slaves. The true planters, who possessed more than twenty slaves, constituted just 12 percent of all slaveholders. Only the very wealthy—less than 1 percent—owned more than one hundred slaves.

Even among true southern planters, the aristocratic manners and trappings of the idealized plantation were rare. King Cotton brought a new sort of man to the forefront. These new aristocrats were generally not related to the old colonial plantation gentry. Most had begun their careers as land speculators, financiers, and rough-and-tumble yeoman farmers. They had parlayed ruthlessness, good luck, and dealings in the burgeoning cotton market into large landholdings and armies of slaves.

The wives of these planters bore little resemblance to their counterparts in popular fiction. Far from being frail, helpless creatures, southern plantation mistresses carried a heavy burden of responsibility. A planter's wife supervised large staffs of slaves, organized and ran schools for the white children on the plantation, looked out for the health of everyone on the plantation, and managed the plantation in the absence of her husband.

All those duties were complicated by a sex code that relegated southern women to a peculiar position in the plantation hierarchy. On one hand, white women were *expected* to exercise absolute authority over their slaves. On the other, they were to be absolutely obedient to white men. "He is master of the house," said Mary Boykin Chesnut about her husband. "To hear [him] is to obey."

This is not to say that the image of grand plantations and aristocratic living is entirely false. Enormous profits from cotton in the 1840s and 1850s permitted some planters to build elegant mansions and to affect the lifestyle that they had read about in romantic literature. Planters assumed what they imagined were the ways of medieval knights, adopting courtly manners and the nobleman's **paternalistic** obligation to look out for their social inferiors, both black and white. Women decked out in the latest gowns flocked to formal balls and weekend parties. Young men were sent to academies where they could learn the aristocratic virtues of militarism and honor. Courtship became highly ritualized, a modern imitation of imagined medieval court manners.

Plain Folk in the South

Another enduring myth about the South holds that society there was sharply divided between two kinds of people: slaveholders and slaves. If the planter myth is only partially true, this myth is totally false.

---

antebellum South   The South in the decades before the Civil War, the period from 1815 to 1860; *antebellum* means "before the war."

paternalistic   Treating social dependents as a father treats his children, providing for their needs without allowing them rights or responsibilities.

Fully two-thirds of southern white families owned no slaves. A small number of these families owned stores, craft shops, and other businesses in Charleston, New Orleans, Atlanta, and other southern cities. The great majority, however, were proud and independent small farmers.

Often tarred with the label "poor white trash," most of these yeomen were actually productive stock raisers and farmers. They concentrated on growing and producing what they needed to live, but all aspired to produce small surpluses of grain, meat, and other commodities that they could sell. Many grew small crops of cotton to raise cash. Whatever money they made was usually spent on needed manufactured goods, land, and, if possible, slaves.

These small farmers had a troubled relationship with white planters. On the one hand, many yeoman farmers yearned to join the ranks of the great planters. On the other, they resented the aristocracy and envied the planters' exalted status and power.

Free Blacks in the South

Free blacks are entirely absent from the myth of the South. The Lower South did have very few free blacks, but in states such as Virginia free blacks amounted to 10 percent of the black population. Some could trace their origins back to the earliest colonial times, when blacks had served limited terms of indenture. The majority, however, had been freed since the late 1700s. Most worked for white employers as day laborers.

Some opportunities were available to free blacks. In the Upper South they could become master carpenters, coopers, painters, brick masons, blacksmiths, boatmen, bakers, and barbers. Black women had few opportunities as skilled laborers. Some became seamstresses, washers, and cooks. A few grew up to run small groceries, taverns, and restaurants. Folk healing and **midwifery** might also lead to economic independence for black women. Some resorted to prostitution.

Mounting restrictions on free blacks during the first half of the nineteenth century limited their freedom of movement, their economic freedom, and their legal rights. Skin color left them open to abuses and forced them to be extremely careful in their dealings with whites.

Slaves and King Cotton

- What was the *outcome* for southern blacks, especially for slaves, of white southerners' *choices* concerning economic progress during the period following the War of 1812?

Before the emergence of King Cotton, many southerners questioned slavery. In 1782 Virginia made it legal for individual masters to free their slaves, and many did so. In 1784 Thomas Jefferson proposed an ordinance that would have prohibited slavery in all of the nation's territories after 1800. Some southern leaders advocated abolishing slavery and transporting freed blacks to Africa. But the cotton boom after the War of 1812 required the expansion of slavery, not its elimination.

A New Birth for the Slavery System

The rapid expansion of cotton production revived the slave system. A map showing cotton production and one showing slave population would appear nearly identical (see Map 9.1). In the 1820s, when cotton was most heavily concentrated in South Carolina and Georgia, the greatest density of slaves occurred in the same area. As cotton spread west, so did slavery. By 1860, both cotton growing and slavery would appear as a continuous belt stretching from the Carolinas to the Brazos River in Texas.

Although a majority of slaves—58 percent of men and 69 percent of women—were employed as **field hands,** slaves did much more than just pick cotton. Two percent of slave men and 17 percent of the women were employed as **house slaves.** The remaining 14 percent of slave women were employed in occupations like sewing, weaving, and food processing. Seventeen percent of slave men drove wagons, piloted riverboats, and herded cattle.

The remaining 23 percent of the male slaves on plantations were managers and craftsmen. This percentage was even higher in cities, where slave artisans such as carpenters were often allowed to hire

---

midwifery   Assistance in childbirth.
field hands   People who did agricultural work such as planting, weeding, and harvesting.
house slaves   People who did domestic work such as cleaning and cooking.

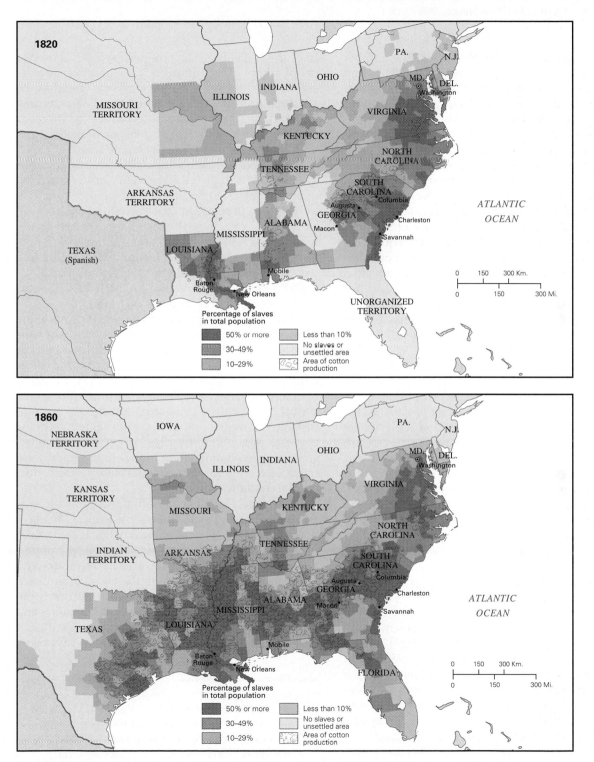

♦ **MAP 9.1 Cotton Agriculture and Slave Population**   Between 1820 and 1860, the expansion of cotton agriculture and the extension of slavery went hand in hand. As these maps show, cotton production was an isolated activity in 1820, and slavery remained isolated as well. By 1860, both had extended westward.

themselves out on the open job market. The number of slave artisans declined during the 1840s and 1850s due to pressure from white craftsmen. Nevertheless, they remained a significant proportion of the slave population.

The owners of cotton plantations made an excellent living from slave labor. Although they often complained of debt and poor markets, large-scale planters could *expect* an annual **return on capital** of between 8 and 10 percent—the equivalent of what the most successful northern industrialists were making. Agricultural profits in noncotton areas were significantly lower. Outside of the **Cotton Belt,** tobacco, rice, and sugar growers earned considerable money selling off slaves that were not essential to their operations. The enormous demand for workers in the Cotton Belt created a profitable interstate slave trade. Thus even planters who did not grow cotton came to have a significant stake in its cultivation.

Slaves were a major capital investment. In the 1850s, a healthy male field hand in his mid-twenties sold for an average of $1,800, a skilled craftsman for $2,500. Even a male child too young to work in the fields or a man in his fifties would cost anywhere from $250 to $500. The price for female slaves was more variable. A female field hand did less heavy work than a healthy male of the same age and thus cost proportionately less. A particularly beautiful young woman might bring as much as $5,000 at auction. Such women generally became the mistresses of the men who bought them.

Living Conditions for Southern Slaves

Slaveowners' enormous economic investment in their human property played a significant role in their treatment of slaves. Damaging or killing a healthy slave resulted in a large financial loss even if **slave codes** allowed an owner to do anything to his property. A delicate balance between power and profit shaped planters' policies toward slaves and set the tone for slave life.

Housing for slaves was seldom more than adequate. Generally slaves lived in one-room log cabins with dirt floors and a fireplace or stove. The cabins were usually about 16 by 18 feet square and housed five or six people. Slaveowners seldom crowded people into slave quarters. As one slaveowner explained, "In no case should two families be allowed to occupy the same house. The crowding [of] a number into one house is unhealthy. It breeds contention; is destructive of delicacy of feeling, and it promotes immorality between the sexes."

Slave quarters were not particularly comfortable. The windows had only wooden shutters and no glass, so they let in flies in summer and cold in winter. An open fireplace or stove provided light as well as heat for cooking. The need for a cooking fire required slaves to build fires even at the hottest time of year. Furnishings were usually crude. Bedding consisted of straw pallets stacked on the floor. Equally simple rough-hewn wooden benches and plank tables could sometimes be found.

Clothing too was basic. "The proper and usual quantity of clothes for plantation hands is two suits of cotton for spring and summer, and two suits of woolen for winter; four pair of shoes and three hats," a Georgia planter observed in 1854. On many plantations, slave women made a durable but rough cotton fabric called osnaburg, which was uncomfortable to wear. One slave complained that the material was "like needles when it was new." Children often went naked in the summer and were fitted with long, loose-hanging osnaburg shirts during the colder months.

Slave diet, like slave clothing and housing, was adequate but not particularly pleasing. One slave noted that there was "plenty to eat sich as it was." The average slave diet was actually rich by comparison with the diet of many other Americans and many people in the rest of the world. Southern slaves ate significantly more meat than contemporary workers in the urban North or in Germany and Italy. In addition to meat, slaves consumed milk and corn, potatoes, peas and beans, molasses, and fish.

---

return on capital   The yield on money that has been invested in an enterprise or product.

Cotton Belt   The region in the southeastern United States in which cotton is grown (see Map 9.1).

slave codes   Laws that established the status of slaves, denying them basic rights and classifying them as the property of slaveowners.

◆ This early photograph, taken on a South Carolina plantation before the Civil War, gives us a view of what slave cabins looked like, how they were arranged, how slaves dressed, and how they spent what little leisure time they had. *Collection of William Gladstone.*

Diet-related diseases nevertheless plagued slave communities. These diseases, however, were probably no more common among slaves than among their owners, who also lived on meals consisting mostly of corn and pork. Such a diet often led to diseases such as pellagra that were caused by vitamin deficiencies. Because of the lack of proper sanitation, slaves did suffer from dysentery and cholera more than southern whites.

With the possible exception of sexual exploitation, no other aspect of slavery has generated more controversy than violence. The image of sadistic white men beating slaves permeates the dark side of the southern myth. Such behavior was not unknown, but it was far from typical. Slaves represented money, and damaging slaves was expensive. Still, given the need to keep up production, slaveowners were not shy about using measured force. "When picking cotton I never put on more than 20 stripes [lashes with a whip] and verry frequently not more than 10 or 15," one plantation owner observed. But not all owners were so practical when it came to discipline.

The significant number of slaves who lived on small farms probably did not live much better than plantation slaves. Owners of such farms saw slaves as vehicles for social and economic advancement and were willing to overwork or sell their slaves if it would benefit themselves. When all was going well, slaves might be treated like members of the farmer's family. But when conditions were bad, slaves were the first victims.

Slave Culture in the South

Slaves fashioned a rich culture that helped them survive and maintain their humanity under inhumane conditions. The degree to which African practices endured in America is remarkable considering that slaves seldom came to the South directly from Africa. The passing of many African practices from one generation to another demonstrates the strength of slave families, religion, and folklore.

Traces of African heritage were visible in slaves' clothing, entertainment, and folkways. Colorful head scarves similar to those worn in Africa compensated for the plainness of the garments that masters provided. Hairstyles often resembled those of African tribes. Music, dancing, and other forms of public entertainment also showed strong African roots. Musical instruments were copies of traditional ones. Healers used African ceremonies and both imported and native herbs to effect cures. These survivals and adaptations of African traditions provided a strong base on which blacks erected an African-American culture.

Strong family ties helped to make possible this cultural continuity. Slave families endured despite a highly precarious life. Husbands and wives could be sold to different owners or be separated at the whim of a master, and children could be taken away from their parents. Families that remained intact, however, remained stable. When families did suffer separation, the **extended family** of grandparents, uncles, aunts, and other relatives offered emotional support and helped to maintain continuity.

Slave religion was another means of preserving unique African-American traits. White churches had ignored the slaves until the Great Awakening,

extended family   A family group consisting of various close relatives as well as the parents and children.

Choosing Freedom

Frederick Douglass

Although he was a skilled craftsman, arranging his own work contracts and setting his own schedule, Frederick Douglass despised the fact that he was a slave. Even though he had no assurance that he could make as good a living as a free man, he chose to run away from slavery and seek a new life in the North. National Portrait Gallery, Smithsonian Institution/Art Resource, NY.

Although he was born a slave, Frederick Douglass thought a lot about freedom while growing up in Baltimore, Maryland, during the 1820s. As a young boy he cultivated white friends, both for their companionship and because they were willing to teach him to read and write, but he was struck by the difference in their status. He would tell them, " 'You will be free as soon as you are twenty-one, *but I am a slave for life!'* "

Escaping, however, was not an easy thing to do, as he learned in 1834. He and two other slaves devised a plan to steal a canoe and paddle into Chesapeake Bay, heading out of Maryland and into freedom. But their plan was betrayed, and Douglass and his companions were arrested and jailed. Douglass was sure that he would be gravely punished for trying to escape—his master threatened to sell him to a cotton plantation owner in Alabama—but instead, he was made an apprentice ship caulker.

Working as an apprentice, Douglass observed that he was "kept in such a perpetual whirl of excitement, I could think of nothing, scarcely, but my life; and in thinking of my life, I almost forgot my liberty." He soon became a master caulker, earning the highest wages in the yard.

when **evangelicals** carried the Christian message to slaves. The Christianity that slaves practiced both resembled and differed from the religion practiced by southern whites. Slave preachers often equated Christian and African religious figures. Ceremonies combined African practices like group dancing with Christian prayer. The joining of African musical forms with Christian lyrics gave rise to a new form of Christian music, the **spiritual.** Masters often encouraged worship, thinking that the Christian emphasis on obedience and meekness would make for better servants. Some, however, discouraged religion for fear that large congregations of slaves

> **evangelicals** Members of Protestant groups that emphasized the sole authority of the Bible and the necessity of actively striving to convert others.
>
> **spiritual** A religious folk song originated by African-Americans, often expressing the longing for deliverance from the constraints and hardships of their lives.

"I was now of some importance to my master," Douglass recalled. "I was bringing him from six to seven dollars per week." His productivity earned him a great deal of freedom: he made his own contracts, set his own work schedule, and collected his own earnings. But he also remembered his liberty: "I have observed this in my experience of slavery that whenever my condition was improved, instead of its increasing my contentment, it only increased my desire to be free."

In 1838 Douglass decided that he would again try to escape. He chose not to contact any of the white organizations that helped slaves escape to the North because he believed that in seeking recognition, such organizations undermined their purpose. "The underground railroad . . . by their open declarations, has been made most emphatically the 'upper-ground railroad,'" Douglass observed, pointing out that by publicizing what they did, they actually made it easier for masters to track runaway slaves. He chose instead to depend on friends for help. He had become engaged to a free black woman named Anna Murray, who sold a featherbed and other property to finance his escape. He also contacted a retired black sailor from whom he secured seaman's protection papers, legal documents entitling black sailors to pass unmolested through slave territory.

Bearing cash and the borrowed papers, Douglass disguised himself as a sailor and boarded a train heading north out of Baltimore on September 3, 1838. Switching from train to ferry boat, ferry boat to steamship, steamship back to train, and finally from train back to ferry boat, Douglass made his way northward, arriving in New York City early on the morning of September 4. Although he came close to being caught—he ran into two men who knew he was not a sailor, one of whom apparently did not notice him and another who chose not to turn him in—Douglass's escape had succeeded.

Douglass now had what the white boys he had known in his younger days also enjoyed—freedom. But the color of his skin still deprived him of equality. Moving to New Bedford, Massachusetts, where he hoped to earn a living in the boat yards, Douglass found that "such was the strength of prejudice against color, among the white caulkers, that they refused to work with me, and of course I could get no employment." For three years he was forced to do odd jobs to keep himself and his wife alive. "There was no work too hard—none too dirty," he recalled.

But in 1841 Douglass found a new profession and a new life. Attending an antislavery conference in Nantucket, Massachusetts, Douglass was encouraged by a white abolitionist to speak about his experiences. "It was a severe cross," Douglass recalled, "but I took it up reluctantly." Famed abolitionist William Lloyd Garrison heard Douglass's speech, declaring that "Patrick Henry, of revolutionary fame, never made a speech more eloquent in the cause of liberty." Garrison was so moved that he offered to support Douglass as a lecturer in the antislavery cause. Douglass accepted, lending a thundering voice to the cause of racial equality for the next fifty years.

---

might rebel. Slaves facing such *constraints* often met secretly.

Resistance and Rebellion Among Southern Slaves

Despite the hopes of white masters, slaves did resist and rebel, sometimes subtly and sometimes quite openly and violently. Slaves adopted clever strategies for getting extra food, clothing, and other supplies and developed sly techniques for manipulating their masters. Slaves often stole food simply to fluster their masters. Farm animals disappeared mysteriously, tools broke in puzzling ways, and people fell ill from unknown diseases.

The importance of clever resistance is evident in the tales that slaves told among themselves. Perhaps the best known are the stories of Br'er Rabbit (Brother Rabbit), the physically weak but shrewd character who uses deceit to get what he wants. One particularly revealing tale tells of Br'er Rabbit's being caught by Br'er Fox. Unable to get a fire started to cook the helpless rabbit, Fox threatens Rabbit with all sorts of horrible tortures. Rabbit replies that Fox can do anything he wants so long as he does not throw him into the nearby briar patch. Seizing on Rabbit's apparent fear, Fox pitches him deep into the briar patch, *expecting* to see the rabbit die amid the thorns. But Br'er Rabbit had been raised in a briar patch, and so he scampers away, laughing at how he had tricked Br'er Fox into doing exactly what he wanted him to do. Such stories taught slaves how to deal with powerful adversaries.

Not all slave resistance took covert forms. Perhaps the most common form of active resistance was running away. An average of about a thousand slaves made their way to freedom each year between 1840 and 1860. Most of them lived in the **border states** or Texas, where freedom lay not far away. Most were also young male slaves between the ages of 16 and 35. Artisans and other slaves with special skills became fugitive slaves more frequently than other slaves.

Runaway slaves left few documents explaining why they were willing to face hounds, patrollers, hunger, and other dangers. Frederick Douglass, who became a famous abolitionist leader, ran away because he grew tired of turning his wages over to his master (see Individual Choices: Frederick Douglass). Many ran away to be with wives who had been sold. But contemporary observers thought that fear of punishment was the most common motivation for running away. One former slave disagreed with this explanation: "They didn't do something and run. They run before they did it, 'cause they knew that if they struck a white man there wasn't going to be a nigger."

To southerners, the most frightening form of slave resistance was armed revolt. The nineteenth-century South saw very few actual rebellions, although a number of planned uprisings were betrayed before they could take place. Such was the fate of Gabriel Prosser's rebellion in Richmond, Virginia, in 1800, and the Denmark Vesey conspiracy in Charleston in 1822.

Nat Turner, a black preacher, carried out the most serious and violent of the antebellum slave revolts. In 1831 Turner led about seventy slaves in a predawn raid against the slaveholding households in Southampton County, Virginia. During the four days of Nat Turner's Rebellion, the slaves slaughtered fifty-five white men, women, and children. Angry whites finally captured and executed Turner and sixteen of his followers.

In the wake of such frightening revolts, southern courts and legislatures clapped stricter controls on slaves and free blacks. In most areas, free blacks were denied the right to own guns, to buy liquor, and to hold public assemblies. Slaves were forbidden to attend unsupervised worship services and to learn reading and writing. The new laws virtually eliminated slaves as unsupervised urban craftsmen after 1840.

Fear of slave revolts reached paranoid levels in areas where slaves outnumbered whites. Whites felt justified in passing strong restrictions and using harsh methods to enforce them. White citizens formed local **vigilance committees,** which rode armed through the countryside to intimidate slaves. Local authorities pressed court clerks and ship captains to limit the freedom of blacks. White critics of slavery, who had been numerous and well respected before the birth of King Cotton, were harassed and sometimes beaten into silence. Increasingly, the extension of slavery limited the freedoms of both whites and blacks.

The Transportation Revolution

- What geographical *constraints* prevented economic and political development in the North and West before the transportation revolution?
- How did specific *choices* help to overcome those *constraints*?

The development of the cotton South triggered demands for improved transportation. Although the Mississippi and its tributaries drained much of the Cotton Belt, they did not serve all of it. Also,

---

border states The slave states of Delaware, Maryland, Kentucky, and Missouri, which shared a border with states in which slavery was illegal.

vigilance committees Groups of armed private citizens who use the threat of mob violence to enforce their own interpretation of the law.

river traffic could not flow upstream. Travel along existing roads was uncomfortable, undependable, and expensive. Without some coordination by the federal government, neither roads nor rivers could tie together the national economy. What was called for was a transportation revolution (see Map 9.2).

Building National Roads

Before the War of 1812, travel on the nation's roads was a wearying, bone-rattling experience. Those who could afford to travel by stagecoach were bounced along over muddy, rutted roads at the pace of 4 miles per hour. The enjoyment of such dubious luxury cost the equivalent of a pint of good whiskey for each mile traveled.

Although some private **turnpikes** had existed since the 1790s, the road-building business took on new energy after the War of 1812, when the federal and state governments began financing road improvements. The federal commitment began in 1815 when President Madison supported the government-funded national road between Cumberland, Maryland, and Wheeling, Virginia. Such a road was a military and postal necessity, Madison declared, and therefore permissible under the Constitution. By 1838, the government had spent in excess of $7 million on the **Cumberland Road,** extending it all the way to Vandalia, Illinois.

New roads helped to alleviate the transportation problems faced by the growing nation, but they hardly solved them. Some small manufactured goods could be hauled west along the new roads, and relatively lightweight items like whiskey could move the other way. But heavy, bulky products were still difficult and expensive to move. At a minimum, hauling a ton of **freight** along the nation's roads cost 15 cents per mile.

A Network of Canals

Water transportation remained the most economical means for shipping large loads. Unfortunately, navigable rivers and lakes seldom formed usable transportation networks. Holland and other European countries had solved this problem by digging canals. After the War of 1812, the state and federal governments opened an era of canal building.

New York State was most successful at canal development. In 1817, the state started work on a canal that would run more than 350 miles from Lake Erie at Buffalo to the Hudson River at Albany. The Erie Canal revolutionized shipping when completed in 1825. The cost of shipping a ton of oats from Buffalo to Albany fell more than 80 percent, and the transit time dropped from twenty days to eight. The canal enabled a flood of goods from America's interior to reach New York and made that city the nation's commercial center.

The spectacular success of the **Erie Canal** prompted state governments to offer all manner of financial incentives to canal-building companies. The result was an explosion in canal building that lasted through the 1830s.

Pennsylvania's experiences were typical. Jealous of New York's success, Pennsylvania proposed a system of canals and roads that would make it the commercial hub of the Western Hemisphere. At the center of this system was the Main Line Canal connecting Philadelphia and Pittsburgh. The problem was that the two cities were separated by mountains over two thousand feet high. Using **locks** to raise boats over this height was a technological impossibility. Engineers finally designed a **portage** railroad over the Allegheny Mountains.

The Allegheny Portage Railroad permitted passengers and cargo to make the trip across the mountains on land but without leaving canal boats. The

---

turnpike A highway on which tolls are collected at barriers set up along the way; companies that hoped to make a profit from the tolls built the first turnpikes.

Cumberland Road A national highway built with federal funds; it eventually stretched from Cumberland, Maryland, to Vandalia, Illinois, and beyond.

freight Any goods or cargo carried in commercial transport.

Erie Canal A 350-mile canal stretching from Buffalo to Albany; it revolutionized shipping in New York.

lock An enclosed section of a canal, with gates at each end, used to raise or lower boats from one level to another by admitting or releasing water; locks allow canals to compensate for changes in terrain.

portage The carrying of boats or supplies overland between two waterways.

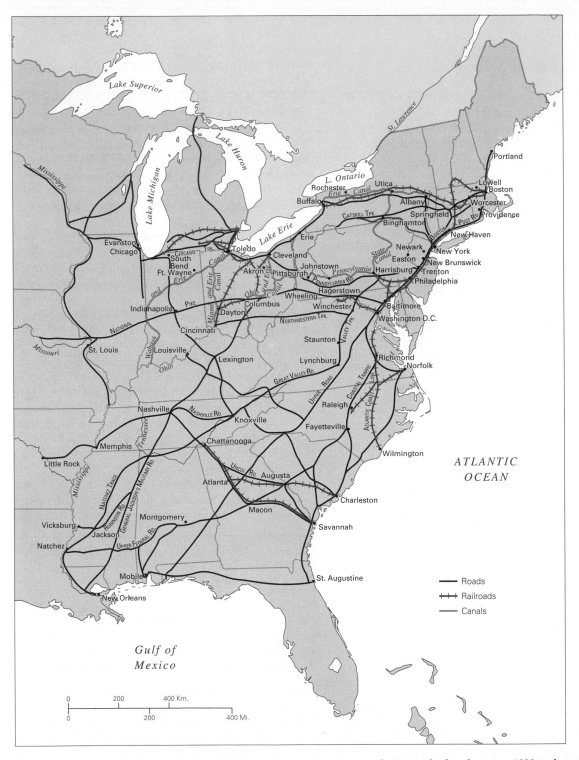

Lake Superior

Lake Huron

Lake Michigan

Mississippi

L. Ontario

St. Lawrence

Portland

Rochester   Utica   Lowell
Erie Canal   Albany   Boston
Buffalo   Worcester
Catskill Tpk.   Springfield   Providence
Erie   Binghamton   Boston Post Rd.   New Haven
State Canal   Newark   New York
Evanston   Toledo   Cleveland   Easton   New Brunswick
Chicago   Chicago Tpk.   Johnstown   Harrisburg   Trenton
South Bend   Akron   Pittsburgh   Pennsylvania Rd.   Philadelphia
Ft. Wayne   Erie   Ohio and Erie Canal   Hagerstown
    Wheeling   Baltimore
Indianapolis   Pike   Columbus   Winchester   Washington D.C.
    Dayton   Northwestern Tpk.
Cincinnati   Staunton   Valley Tpk.
National   Lexington   Richmond
St. Louis   Louisville   Great Valley Rd.   Norfolk
Missouri   Wabash   Ohio
    Lynchburg

Lake Erie
Erie

Miami and Erie Canal

Pennsylvania

Nashville   Nashville Rd.   Raleigh   Upper Road   Atlantic Coast Line
Knoxville   Fayetteville
Memphis   Chattanooga
Little Rock   Unicoi Rd.   Augusta   Wilmington
Mississippi   Atlanta   Charleston
Natchez Trace   Macon
Vicksburg   Robinson Rd.   Montgomery   Savannah
Jackson   General Jackson's Military Rd.
Natchez   Upper Federal Rd.   St. Augustine

ATLANTIC
OCEAN

Mobile
New Orleans

Gulf of
Mexico

─── Roads
┼┼┼ Railroads
─── Canals

0   200   400 Km.
0   200   400 Mi.

♦ **MAP 9.2 Roads, Canals, and Railways in 1850**   A transportation revolution took place between 1820 and 1850, as roads, canals, and rails reached out to bind the many parts of the nation together economically. This map shows the major transportation routes developed in America by 1850.

canal boats were lifted out of the water and placed on railcars. Steam power was then used to pull the railcars, which were attached to a cable, up a series of inclined planes. After being pulled up five steep inclines, the railcars began the descent to the canal at the other side of the mountains. At the bottom of the last incline, the boats were unloaded and placed in the canal to continue the trip to Philadelphia or Pittsburgh.

The portage railroad was an engineering marvel. The completion of the Main Line system allowed a family to travel relatively quickly and comfortably all the way from Philadelphia to Pittsburgh. The tolls alone, however, cost as much as six acres of prime farmland. In the long run, the Main Line Canal was a dismal financial failure, never earning investors one cent of profit.

Despite Pennsylvania's experience, nearly every state in the North and West undertook some canal building between 1820 and 1840. States and private individuals invested over $100 million on nearly 3,500 miles of canals during the heyday of canal building. Nearly all experienced the same sad financial fate as Pennsylvania's Main Line Canal.

Steam Power

Canals solved one problem of water transportation but did not address the issue of how to move people and goods upstream on America's great rivers. While a barge could make it downstream from Pittsburgh to New Orleans in about a month, the return trip took over four months, if it could be made at all. As a result, most shippers barged their freight downriver, sold the barges for lumber in New Orleans, and walked back home along the **Natchez Trace.**

In 1807, Robert Fulton perfected a design that made steam-powered shipping practical. His *Clermont* used steam-driven wheels mounted on the sides of the vessel to push it up the Hudson River from New York City to Albany. Unfortunately, the *Clermont* was not well suited to most of America's waterways. Heavy and narrow-beamed, Fulton's ship needed deep water to carry a limited **payload.** Only after the War of 1812 did engineers design broader-beamed, lighter vessels that could carry heavy loads in shallow western rivers.

Steam power took canal building's impact on inland transportation a revolutionary step further.

Between 1816 and 1840, the cost of shipping a ton of goods down American rivers fell from an average of $1\frac{1}{4}$ cents per mile to less than half a cent. The cost of upstream transport fell from over 10 cents per mile to about half a cent. In addition, steamboats could carry bulky and heavy objects that could not be hauled upstream for any price by any other means. Dependable river transportation drew cotton cultivation farther into the nation's interior and allowed fur trappers and traders to press up the Missouri River.

Only the development of steam railroads would ultimately have a greater impact on nineteenth-century transportation. Merchants from cities without extensive navigable rivers such as Baltimore took the lead in developing this new technology. In 1828, the state chartered the Baltimore and Ohio Railroad (B&O). The B&O soon demonstrated its potential when inventor Peter Cooper's steam locomotive *Tom Thumb* sped 13 miles along B&O track. Ironically the B&O abandoned steam power and replaced it with horses when a stagecoach horse beat the Tom Thumb in a widely publicized race held in 1830.

Despite this race, South Carolina *chose* to invest in steam technology and chartered a 136-mile rail line from Charleston to Hamburg. Here, the first full-size American-built locomotive was used to pull cars. Even the explosion of this engine did not deter the Charleston and Hamburg Railroad from continuing to use steam engines.

Rail transport could not rival water-based transportation systems during this early period. By 1850 individual companies had laid approximately 9,000 miles of track, but not in any coherent network. Also, the distance between tracks varied from company to company. As a result, cargoes had to be unloaded from the cars of one company's trains at line's end, lugged to the railhead of another line, and re-loaded onto the other company's cars. There

---

Natchez Trace　A road connecting Natchez, Mississippi, with Nashville, Tennessee; it evolved from a series of Indian trails and had commercial and military importance in the late eighteenth and early nineteenth centuries.

payload　The part of a cargo that generates revenue, as opposed to the part needed to fire the boiler or supply the crew.

were other problems too. Boiler explosions, fires, and derailments were common. Entrenched interest groups used their power in state legislatures to limit the extension of railroads. These obstacles prevented railroads from becoming a major factor in American life until the 1850s.

Information Revolution

Migrants, adventurers, and goods were not the only cargoes carried by the new transportation systems. Information was another important payload.

Since the nation's founding, American leaders had feared that the sheer size of the country would make true federal democracy impractical. During the 1790s, it took a week for a letter to travel from Virginia to New York City and three weeks from Cincinnati to the Atlantic coast. Thomas Jefferson speculated that the continent would become a series of allied republics, each small enough to operate efficiently given the slow speed of communication. The transportation revolution, however, made quite a difference in how quickly news got around.

The Erie Canal enabled letters posted in Buffalo to reach New York City within six days and New Orleans in about two weeks. The increased flow of information caused an explosion in the number of newspapers and magazines published in the country. In 1790, the 92 American newspapers had a total **circulation** of around 4 million. By 1835, the number of periodicals had risen to 1,258, and circulation had surpassed 90 million.

Transportation, Business, and the Law

Before wholesale changes could take place in American transportation and business, some thorny legal issues needed to be resolved. The American System made questions of authority over finance and interstate commerce increasingly important. In three landmark legal cases, John Marshall, chief justice of the U.S. Supreme Court, resolved such questions and cleared the way for the expansion of interstate trade.

If businesses were going to build and operate large enterprises, they had to have confidence in the sanctity of legal contracts. In the case of *Dartmouth College v. Woodward* (1819), the Supreme Court made contracts secure. The 1769 charter for Dartmouth

College specified that the college's board of trustees would be self-perpetuating. In 1816, to gain control over the college, the New Hampshire legislature passed a bill allowing the state's governor to appoint board members. The board sued, claiming that the charter was a legal contract that the legislature had no right to alter. Marshall concurred that the Constitution protected the sanctity of contracts and that state legislatures could not interfere with them.

In *McCulloch v. Maryland* (1819), Marshall established the superiority of the federal government over state authorities in matters of finance. The case involved the cashier of the Baltimore branch of the Bank of the United States who refused to put state revenue stamps on federal bank notes as required by Maryland law. McCulloch (the cashier) was **indicted** by the state but appealed to federal authorities. Marshall ruled that the states could not impose taxes on federal institutions and that McCulloch was right in refusing to comply with Maryland's law. As he wrote, "The Constitution and the laws made in pursuance thereof are supreme."

The supremacy of federal authority was demonstrated again in *Gibbons v. Ogden* (1824). This case involved a New York charter given to Robert Fulton and Robert Livingston that granted them exclusive rights to run steamboats on rivers in that state. Thomas Gibbons also operated a steamboat service in the same area, but under the authority of the federal Coasting Act. When a conflict between the two companies ended up in court, Marshall ruled in favor of Gibbons, arguing that the **monopoly** that New York had granted conflicted with federal authority and was therefore invalid.

Those three cases helped ease the way for the development of new businesses. With contracts free from state and local meddling and the superiority of Congress in banking and interstate commerce established, businesses had the security they needed to turn Clay's dream of a national market economy into a reality.

---

circulation The number of copies of a publication sold or distributed.

indict To make a formal accusation against someone.

monopoly The right to exclusive control over a commercial activity; it may be granted by the government.

SUMMARY

E xpectations
C onstraints
C hoices
O utcomes

With the end of the War of 1812, President Madison and the Republicans *chose* to promote an agenda for an expansive America. They championed a national market economy and passed federal legislation to create a national bank and to protect American industry. Madison gave free rein to nationalists such as John Quincy Adams and Andrew Jackson, who expanded the nation's sphere of influence.

The South was the first region where the new economic direction drastically altered *expectations*. The cotton gin gave agricultural specialization in the South new life. Southerners *chose* cotton growing and an expanded slavery system to provide the necessary labor. The *outcome* was a peculiar social, political, and economic hierarchy. A small planter aristocracy held sway at the top. A mass of slave laborers occupied the bottom. Caught in the middle were small white and free black farmers, artisans, and merchants.

For slaves, uncomfortable homes, plain food, and rough clothing added to the demeaning character of lives devoid of freedom. In the face of hardship, slaves crafted a unique culture consisting of retained African practices and customs borrowed from whites. Fear of rebellion increasingly *constrained* the freedom of whites.

The North and West experienced *constraints* because they lacked a coherent transportation system. Madison's agenda called for the states to address the problem. *Expecting* quick and enormous profits, New York, Pennsylvania, and others *chose* to respond. The Erie Canal was the first successful link between the increasingly urban and manufacturing East and the rural, agricultural West.

In the years to come, canals, roads, and rivers tied the nation's three sections firmly together, promoting the regional specialization envisioned by advocates of the American System. The *outcome* of such specialization, however, was increasing tension among regions.

Suggested Readings

Berlin, Ira. *Slaves Without Masters* (1975).

A masterful study of a forgotten population: free blacks in the Old South. Lively and informative.

Dangerfield, George. *The Era of Good Feelings* (1952).

An older book, but so well written and informative that it deserves its status as a classic. All students will enjoy this grand overview.

Fox-Genovese, Elizabeth. *Within the Plantation Household* (1988).

A look at the lives of black and white women in the antebellum South. This study is quite long, but is well written and very informative.

Haley, Arthur. *Roots* (1976).

A fascinating reconstruction of slave life from African beginnings through emancipation and beyond by a man seeking his cultural and family heritage. A television miniseries made from the book is widely available as well.

Mitchell, Margaret. *Gone with the Wind* (1936).

Arguably the most influential book in conveying a stereotyped vision of antebellum southern life. The film version, directed by Victor Fleming in 1939, was even more influential.

Owsley, Frank. *Plain Folk in the Old South* (1949).

A truly phenomenal study by a scholar whose methods and outlook were forty years ahead of their time.

Taylor, George Rogers. *The Transportation Revolution, 1815–1860* (1951).

The only comprehensive treatment of changes in transportation during the antebellum period and their economic impact. Nicely written and comprehensive in treating the topic.

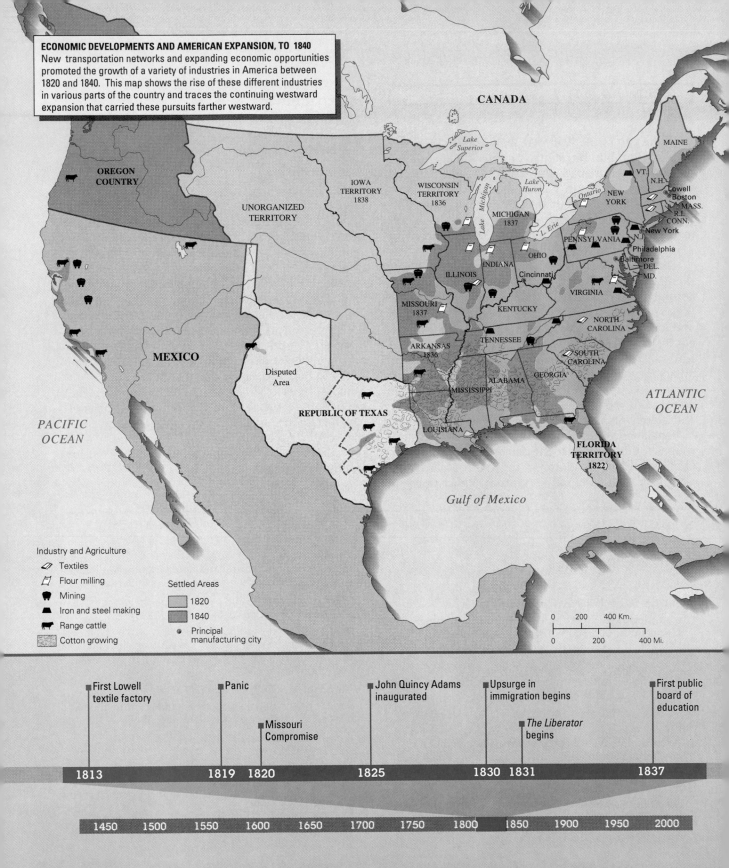

ECONOMIC DEVELOPMENTS AND AMERICAN EXPANSION, TO 1840
New transportation networks and expanding economic opportunities promoted the growth of a variety of industries in America between 1820 and 1840. This map shows the rise of these different industries in various parts of the country and traces the continuing westward expansion that carried these pursuits farther westward.

CANADA

OREGON COUNTRY

MEXICO

PACIFIC OCEAN

Lake Superior

Lake Michigan

Lake Huron

L. Ontario

L. Erie

IOWA TERRITORY 1838

UNORGANIZED TERRITORY

WISCONSIN TERRITORY 1836

MICHIGAN 1837

MAINE

VT.

N.H.

Lowell

Boston

MASS.

R.I.

CONN.

NEW YORK

New York

PENNSYLVANIA

Philadelphia

Baltimore

N.J.

DEL.

MD.

ILLINOIS

INDIANA

OHIO

Cincinnati

MISSOURI 1837

KENTUCKY

VIRGINIA

NORTH CAROLINA

ARKANSAS 1836

TENNESSEE

SOUTH CAROLINA

Disputed Area

REPUBLIC OF TEXAS

MISSISSIPPI

ALABAMA

GEORGIA

LOUISIANA

ATLANTIC OCEAN

FLORIDA TERRITORY 1822

Gulf of Mexico

Industry and Agriculture
- Textiles
- Flour milling
- Mining
- Iron and steel making
- Range cattle
- Cotton growing

Settled Areas
- 1820
- 1840
- Principal manufacturing city

0   200   400 Km.

0   200   400 Mi.

First Lowell textile factory

Panic

Missouri Compromise

John Quincy Adams inaugurated

Upsurge in immigration begins

The Liberator begins

First public board of education

1813   1819   1820   1825   1830   1831   1837

1450   1500   1550   1600   1650   1700   1750   1800   1850   1900   1950   2000

Dynamic Growth and Its Consequences, 1820–1827

Dynamic Growth and Political Consequences

- How did the *expectation* of prosperity and economic growth help lead to economic panic in 1819?

- Why were increased sectional conflict and political contention an *outcome* of growth and panic?

The Mechanization of Northern Society

- How did new manufacturing techniques following the War of 1812 change the nature of work and the *expectations* of artisans, elites, and middle-class Americans?

Immigration and Working-Class America

- How did industrialization and massive immigration to America produce a working-class culture?

- How did working people respond to changing conditions?

Reactions to Dynamic Growth and Failure

- How did the Second Great Awakening affect *expectations* and *choices* for different social classes and geographic regions?

INTRODUCTION

Madison's and Monroe's economic policies had ushered in a new era of national confidence. As transportation systems expanded and markets opened for American goods worldwide, the country embarked on a course of dynamic growth. Americans came to *expect* a quick return on investments, and they *chose* to leap into opportunity.

But the *choices* attending dynamic growth had unforeseen *outcomes*. Politicians *chose* to manipulate land and credit policies to win votes. The *outcome* was a credit balloon, inflated by speculative hot air. When the American economy faced unexpected *constraints* imposed by changing market conditions in Europe, Congress, banks, and speculators *chose* to constrict credit, causing the credit balloon to collapse. The *outcome* was six years of crippling economic depression.

At the same time, the manufacturing revolution that began before the War of 1812 left its mark on the northeastern section of the nation. The area's political leaders *chose* to demand specific political and economic policies to give the Northeast a competitive edge in both domestic and foreign markets. The *outcome* was competition between the Northeast and the South for control over the nation's institutions. Political contention, seemingly put to rest during the Era of Good Feelings, suddenly emerged again in a new and threatening form. Economic disputes among regions found a new focus on the issue of slavery expansion, and sectional rivalry revealed its potential to destroy the Union.

Contraction in the European economy had another *outcome* as well. *Expecting* to find better

E xpectations
C onstraints
C hoices
O utcomes

working and living conditions in America, farmers and artisans from Ireland, the German states, and elsewhere *chose* to relocate to the New World. In port cities like New York, Philadelphia, and Boston, immigrants found themselves *constrained* by economic and cultural forces. Increasingly they were pushed into low-paying manufacturing jobs. The *outcome* was the formation of a distinct working class in the Northeast.

Economic specialization and immigration created other unexpected changes in the Northeast. Mechanization changed the nature of work, the workplace, and the lives of both workers and supervisors. The *outcome* was the breakdown of traditional community organization, which left many in the region feeling lost, angry, or frightened. As workers *chose* to protest their plight, middle-class and genteel folk attempted to stabilize the rapidly changing society through reform movements that reflected middle-class and evangelical Protestant values. A modern America was being born in the North, one increasingly out of tune with the rural capitalism of the South and with the traditional farming society of the West. Thomas Jefferson envisioned a disastrous *outcome* for these regional differences, but Americans plunged on, *expecting* to make a better nation and a better world.

Dynamic Growth and Political Consequences

- How did the *expectation* of prosperity and economic growth help lead to economic panic in 1819?

- Why were increased sectional conflict and political contention an *outcome* of growth and panic?

During the **Napoleonic wars,** massive armies had drained Europe's manpower, laid waste to crops,

and tied up ships, making European nations dependent on America. Although those wars ended in 1815, a war-torn Europe continued to need American food and manufactures. Encouraged by a ready European market and easy credit, southern

Napoleonic wars   Wars in Europe waged by or against Napoleon between 1803 and 1815.

CHRONOLOGY

Dynamic Growth

1794	Cotton gin patented
1803	Louisiana Purchase
1806	Journeyman shoemakers' strike in New York City
1807	Congress outlaws the importation of slaves
1813	Francis Cabot Lowell and partners build textile factory in Waltham, Massachusetts
1814	Treaty of Ghent
1817	Congress suspends installment payments on public land purchases Formation of the American Colonization Society
1819	Missouri Territory applies for statehood Panic of 1819
1820	James Monroe re-elected president Missouri Compromise Northeastern congressmen propose protective tariffs, reduction of public land prices
1821	Charles G. Finney experiences a religious conversion
1822	Lowell's partners open textile mill in Lowell, Massachusetts Northeastern congressmen propose federal spending to extend the Cumberland Road farther west
1824	Western congressmen join northeastern congressmen to pass increased protective tariffs
	John H. Hall uses interchangeable parts in rifles Andrew Jackson wins electoral plurality and popular majority in the presidential election
1825	House of Representatives elects John Quincy Adams president
1828	Weavers protest and riot in New York City
1830	Upsurge in immigration from Ireland and Germany
1831	William Lloyd Garrison begins publishing *The Liberator*
1834	Riot in Charlestown, Massachusetts, leads to the destruction of a Catholic convent National Trades' Union formed
1835	Five Points Riot in New York City
1836	Congress passes the gag rule
1837	Horace Mann heads the first public board of education Panic of 1837
1842	*Commonwealth v. Hunt*
1843	Dorothea Dix advocates state-funded asylums for the insane

planters, northern manufacturers, and western farmers embarked on a frenzy of speculation. They rushed to borrow money to buy equipment, land, and slaves for what they were sure was a golden future.

Entrepreneurs in the North, West, and South, however, had different ideas about the best course for the American economy. As the American System drew the regions together into increasing mutual dependency, the tensions among them began to swell. As long as economic conditions remained good, there was little reason for conflict, but when the speculative boom collapsed, sectional tensions increased dramatically.

The Panic of 1819

Liberal federal land policies helped to inflate the speculative balloon. After 1804 Americans could buy a minimum of 160 acres from the national government in **installments.** Lowering the minimum purchase and extending credit encouraged purchasers to buy farms that they could barely afford.

Land speculators complicated the problem by buying land on credit. Unlike farmers, speculators never intended to put the land into production. They hoped to subdivide and sell it to people who could not afford to buy 160-acre lots directly from the government. Speculators extended credit to buyers, thereby adding to the existing tower of debt. Banks, too, extended credit to farmers to purchase equipment, seed, building materials, and other necessities. Farmers thus had acreage and tools, but an enormous debt.

Developments in Europe undermined the foundation of this tower of debt. When Europe began to recover several years after the Napoleonic Wars, its demand for American products, particularly foodstuffs, dropped rapidly. The bottom fell out of the international market that had fueled speculation in the United States.

Congress tried to head off disaster by tightening credit. In 1817, it stopped installment payments on new land purchases and demanded that land be paid for in hard currency. The Second Bank of the United States in 1818 tightened credit further by demanding immediate repayment of loans in either gold or silver. State banks and land speculators followed suit. Instead of curing the problem, however, tightening credit and recalling loans burst the speculative balloon, creating the **Panic of 1819.**

Six years of economic depression followed. As prices declined, individual farmers and manufacturers, unable to repay loans for land and equipment, faced **repossession** and imprisonment for debt. Bankruptcy sales were a daily occurrence. Factories fell idle, and the ranks of the unemployed grew steadily. The number of paupers in New York more than doubled between 1819 and 1820.

Although the financial panic was the result of Americans' own reckless speculation, they tended to point the finger of blame elsewhere. Many blamed the national bank and called for the destruction of this "Monster." Some understood that controlling credit was the only way to prevent similar crises, but the Second Bank's critics prevented any meaningful financial reforms.

Economic Woes and Political Sectionalism

The Panic of 1819 drove a wedge between the nation's geographical sections. The depression touched each region differently, and for several years the halls of Congress rang with debates rooted in sectional economic needs.

The issue that pitted section against section more violently than any other was protective tariffs. Before 1816, the tariffs enacted by Congress were designed to produce tax revenue. The goal of President Madison's **Tariff of 1816,** however, was the protection of American industry. As the Panic of 1819 spread economic devastation throughout the country, the coal, iron, and textile industries began clamoring for more protection against foreign competition.

Farmers were split on the issue. Small farmers favored a free market that would keep the price of manufactures low. In contrast, commercial farmers who specialized in cash crops such as wheat and wool joined industrialists, factory managers, and industrial workers in supporting protection against the foreign dumping of such products. Southern cotton and tobacco farmers did not favor protection.

After supporting the Tariff of 1816, John C. Calhoun and other southerners became firm opponents of tariffs. Cotton growing had slowed the development of industry in the South, so protection offered small benefit to southerners. Also, Britain,

---

installment Partial payment of a debt to be made at regular intervals until the entire debt is repaid.

Panic of 1819 A financial panic that began when the Second Bank of the United States tightened credit and recalled government loans.

repossession The reclaiming of land or goods by the seller after the purchaser fails to pay installments due.

Tarriff of 1816 First protective tariff in U.S. history; its purpose was to protect America's fledgling textile industry.

not the United States, was the South's main supplier of manufactured goods and its primary market for raw cotton. Protective tariffs raised the price of the former and might cause Britain to enact a tariff on southern cotton. If that happened, southerners would pay more for manufactures but receive less for cotton.

In 1820, northern congressmen proposed a major increase in the tariff. Small farmers in the West and cotton growers defeated the measure. Northerners then wooed western congressmen by supporting bills favorable to westerners. These bills lowered the minimum price of public land from $2 to $1.25 per acre and authorized the extension of the Cumberland Road into the West. Western congressmen reciprocated in 1824 by favoring a greatly increased tariff.

The Missouri Compromise

As all three regions sought solutions to the nation's economic woes, the regional balance of power in Congress became a matter of crucial importance. The delicate balance in Congress began to tip when the Missouri Territory applied for statehood in 1819. New York congressman James Tallmadge, Jr., provoked the crisis when he proposed that no new slaves be taken into Missouri and that those already in the territory be emancipated gradually. His amendment generated a moral and political debate that nearly led to national collapse.

The political issue in the Missouri controversy was straightforward. If Missouri was admitted as a slave state, its congressional **bloc** would undoubtedly support the southern position on tariffs and other key issues. But if Missouri was admitted as a free state, its congressmen would be inclined to support the position taken by representatives from the Old Northwest.

Both sides in the debate about Missouri were deeply entrenched. In 1820, Henry Clay suggested a compromise. He proposed that Missouri be admitted as a slave state and that Maine, which had separated from Massachusetts in 1819, be admitted as a free state. Clay also proposed that slavery be banned in the rest of the Louisiana Territory above 36°30' north latitude, the line that formed Missouri's southern border (see Map 10.1). Congress approved

the **Missouri Compromise,** and the issue of slavery in the territories quieted down for a while.

New Politics and the End of Good Feelings

Conducted in the midst of the Missouri crisis, the presidential election of 1820 went as smoothly as could be *expected*. Monroe faced no meaningful political opposition. The people's faith in Jefferson's party and his handpicked successors remained firm. As the election of 1824 approached, however, it became clear that the Panic of 1819 and the Missouri crisis had broken Republican unity.

In 1824, the southern-dominated Republican caucus named Georgia states' rights advocate William Crawford as its presidential candidate. As nationalists, Henry Clay and John Quincy Adams were so disappointed with this selection that each defied party discipline by deciding to run without the approval of the caucus. The Tennessee legislature then named its own candidate, Andrew Jackson.

The 1824 election brought home how deeply divided the nation had become. Northern political leaders rallied behind Adams, southerners supported Crawford, and northwestern commercial farmers and other supporters of the American System lined up behind Clay. Many independent yeoman farmers, traditional craftsmen, and immigrants supported the hero of New Orleans.

The Tennessean said little during the campaign, but his reputation as the hero of the Battle of New Orleans spoke louder than words. Jackson won the most popular votes, capturing 153,544 to Adams's 108,740, Clay's 47,136, and Crawford's 46,618. Jackson also received more electoral votes than any other candidate, but he did not have the majority needed to win the election. The Constitution specifies in such cases that a list of the top three vote getters be passed to the House of Representatives for a final decision.

---

bloc   A group of people united for common action.

Missouri Compromise   Law proposed by Henry Clay in 1820 admitting Missouri to the Union as a slave state and Maine as a free state and banning slavery in the Louisiana Territory north of latitude 36°30'.

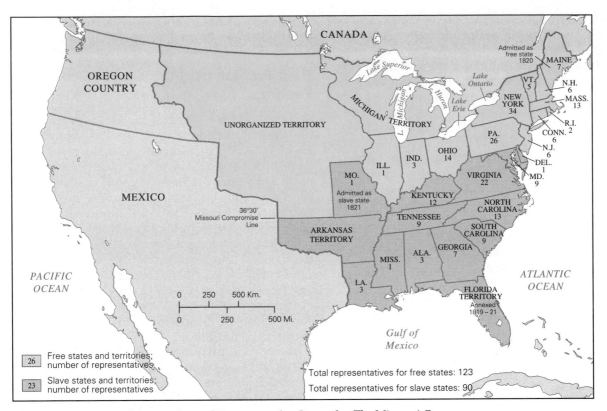

♦ **MAP 10.1 Missouri Compromise and Representative Strength**   The Missouri Compromise fixed the boundary between free and slave territories at 36°30'. This map shows the result both in geographical and political terms. While each section emerged from the Compromise with the same number of senators (24), the balance in the House of Representatives and Electoral College tilted toward the North.

By the time the House convened to settle the election, Crawford had suffered a disabling stroke, and was no longer a contender. Clay's name was not put before the House because he had finished fourth. As Speaker of the House, however, he had considerable influence over the *outcome* of the election. Backers of both candidates asked him for support. Seeing himself as the leading spokesman for western interests, Clay viewed Jackson as a rival rather than as a kindred spirit. Although Clay had no great love for the New Englander either, their views on tariffs, manufacturing, and foreign affairs were quite compatible. Clay therefore threw his support to Adams, who won the House election and in 1825 became the nation's sixth president.

Adams subsequently named Clay as his secretary of state, the position that had been the springboard to the presidency for every past Republican who

had held it. Although Adams had done nothing illegal, Jacksonians accused Adams of having made a "corrupt bargain" with Clay, whom they dubbed the "Judas of the West." In anger and disgust, Jackson supporters withdrew from the party of Jefferson, bringing an end to the Era of Good Feelings.

The Mechanization of Northern Society

• How did new manufacturing techniques following the War of 1812 change the nature of work and the *expectations* of artisans, elites, and middle-class Americans?

During the early nineteenth century, most manufacturing in America took place in the home. Before the 1820s, over 60 percent of American clothing had been spun from raw fibers and sewn by women in their own homes. Master craftsmen who produced furniture, clocks, and tools also usually worked in their homes. From 1820 onward, manufacturing increasingly moved out of the home and into factories.

The Birth of the Factory System

At first, mechanized production played only a small part in the manufacturing of textiles. Samuel Slater, a British immigrant, had introduced the use of machines for spinning cotton thread to the United States. But even he depended on the **putting-out system** to finish the manufacturing process. In this system, manufacturers provided thread and other materials to women artisans, who then wove, dyed, and sewed the final products at home. During slack times in the agricultural year, entire families participated in this home industry. When the householders had used all the thread, they took the finished goods to the manufacturer and were paid for their work.

A radical departure in cloth manufacturing took place in 1813, when the Boston Manufacturing Company built a weaving factory in Waltham, Massachusetts. The company mechanized all the stages in the production of finished cloth, bringing the entire process under one roof. By 1822, the factory's success led the company to build a larger one in Lowell, Massachusetts, a town named after one of the company's founders, Francis Cabot Lowell.

The design of the Lowell factory was widely copied during the 1820s and 1830s. Spinning and weaving on machines located in one building cut the time and the cost of manufacturing significantly. **Quality control** became easier because employees were under constant supervision. As a result, the putting-out system for turning thread into cloth went into serious decline, as did home production of clothes for family use. Ready-made clothing became standard wearing apparel in the 1830s and 1840s.

A major technological revolution helped to push factory production into other areas of manufacturing during these same years. In traditional manufacturing, individual artisans crafted each item one at a time. A clockmaker, for example, either cast or carved individually by hand all the gears, levers, and wheels. As a result, the innards of a clock worked together only in the clock for which they

had been made. If that clock ever needed repair, new parts had to be custom-made for it. The lack of **interchangeable parts** made manufacturing extremely slow and repairs difficult.

Eli Whitney, inventor of the cotton gin (see page 174), was the first American to propose the large-scale use of interchangeable parts to manufacture guns in 1798. Whitney's efforts failed because of a lack of start-up money and precision machine tools. But his former partner, John H. Hall, proved that manufacturing guns from interchangeable parts was practical at the federal armory in Harpers Ferry, Virginia, in 1824. This "American system of manufacturing" spread to the Springfield Armory in Massachusetts and then to private gun manufacturers like Samuel Colt. Within twenty years, products ranging from sewing machines to farm implements were being made from interchangeable parts.

The use of interchangeable parts speeded up the manufacture of important products and improved their dependability. The new technology also made repairing guns and other standardized mechanisms easy and relatively cheap. Like the textile mills, factories assembling interchangeable parts slashed the production costs. The use of interchangeable parts allowed employers to hire unskilled workers to assemble those parts. Extensive training became irrelevant. A gunsmith with years of experience was likely to find himself working on equal terms alongside a youngster or recent immigrant with no craft experience at all.

Toward a New Labor System

Moving manufacturing from the home to the factory changed the nature of work and altered the traditional relationship between employers and employees. To attract workers, some entrepreneurs

---

putting-out system   A system of production in which manufacturers provided artisans with materials such as thread and dye for use in producing goods at home.

quality control   The effort to ensure that all goods produced meet consistent standards of quality.

interchangeable parts   Parts that are identical and can be substituted for each other.

Choosing Mill Work

Susan Miller

After her father's death, Susan Miller faced a choice between watching her family be dishonored and possibly dispossessed for debt or accepting work in the new textile factories. Like many in her generation, she choose to abandon tradition and the farm to become a mill girl. University of Lowell.

Susan Miller* greeted her father's death with mixed feelings. He had not been an evil man, but he was a weak one, and his death after years of wrestling with alcohol could be seen as a blessing. The years of her father's idleness had put a terrible burden on the family. The Millers were in debt and had no way to pay off the mortgage on their farm. Susan's mother was worn out by years of caring for her sinful husband and dependent children, and Susan's brother and sisters were too young to help out. The future of the family depended entirely on Susan.

On a beautiful May afternoon, Susan set out from her home to the spacious farmhouse owned by Deacon Rand, the owner of the farm on which she and her family lived. "I wish to know," she asked her landlord, "whether you intend to turn us all out of doors, as you have a perfect right to do—or suffer us still to remain, with a slight hope that we may sometime pay you the debt for which our farm is mortgaged."

"How in the name of common sense, and charity, and religion, could I turn a widow and her fatherless children out of their house and home," the Deacon replied. "But you spake about sometime paying me; pray, how do you hope to do it?"

"I am going to Lowell," said Susan quietly, "to work in the Factory."

developed **company towns.** Families recruited from the economically depressed New England countryside were installed in neat row houses, each with its own small vegetable garden. Each family member was employed by the company. Women worked on the production line. Men ran heavy machinery and worked as **millwrights,** carpenters, haulers, or day

company town   A town built and owned by a single company; its residents depend on the company not only for jobs but for stores, schools, and housing.

millwright   A person who designs, builds, or repairs mills or mill machinery.

"I do not approve of it," blustered the deacon. "I do not think it is right for a young girl like you, to put herself in the way of all sorts of temptation."

But Susan would not be deterred. "I have never seen but one factory girl," she responded, "and that was my cousin Esther. . . . I do not believe there is a better girl in the world than she is; and I cannot think she would be so contented and cheerful among such a set of wretches as some folks think factory girls must be."

As for the noise, living conditions, and supposed dangers, Susan had thought them all through. "I know the noise of the Mills must be unpleasant at first," she acknowledged, "but I shall get used to that; and as to my health, I know that I have as good a constitution to begin with, as any girl could wish, and no predisposition to . . . any of those diseases which a factory life might otherwise bring upon me. I do not expect all the comforts which are common to country farmers; but I am not afraid of starving.

"I know there is danger," she went on, "among so much machinery; but those who meet with accidents are but a very small number, in proportion to the whole; and if I am careful, I need not fear any injury.

"You know that I must do something," Susan told the deacon, "and I have made up my mind what it shall be." She departed the very next day for the mills.

At first Susan found the situation dispiriting. The loom was hard to manage, and she was not used to being observed at her work every minute. The sights and sounds, both at work and in her sleeping quarters, were strange and disturbing. But, she told herself, "It won't seem so always."

Eventually Susan became used to the routine on the factory floor and came to enjoy the company of her colleagues in the boarding house, with whom she found common cause.

Every morning the bells pealed forth the same clangor, and every night brought the same feeling of fatigue. But Susan felt, as all factory girls feel, that she could bear it for a while. There are few who look upon factory labor as a pursuit for life. It is but a temporary vocation; and most of the girls resolve to quit the Mill when some favorite design is accomplished. Money is their object—not for itself, but for what it can perform; and pay-days are the landmarks which cheer all hearts, by assuring them of their progress to the wished-for goal.

For Susan, the goal was the quarterly cash payment she sent to Deacon Rand. She visited home from time to time, "longed to go, never to leave it; but she conquered the desire, and remained in Lowell more than a year after the last dollar had been forwarded to Deacon Rand." Her sisters, who eventually joined her in the factories, both married and settled in Lowell. Susan, however, moved back home, where she became a guest in the household she had saved from debt, which was now her brother's farm.

*Susan Miller is probably a fictional name. It was adopted for use in a biographical sketch written by an anonymous mill girl now identifiable only by her initials: F. G. A. The sketch was published in the *Lowell Offering* in 1841 and is quoted here.

laborers. Children did light work in the factories and tended gardens at home.

Lowell's company developed another system. Hard-pressed to find enough families to work in the factories, it recruited unmarried farm girls (see Individual Choices: Susan Miller). Because most of the girls saw factory work as a transitional stage between girlhood and marriage, the company assured them and their families that the moral atmosphere in its dormitories would be strictly controlled to maintain the girls' reputations.

In New York, Philadelphia, and other cities, enterprising manufacturers found an alternative source of labor in the immigrant slums. In the shoe industry, for example, they assigned one family to make soles, another to make heels, and so forth. Making shoes this way was not as efficient as making them in a factory, but it did have advantages. Such manufacturers did not have to build factories and could pay rock-bottom wages to desperate slum dwellers.

Machine production and the growing pool of labor proved economically devastating to the working class. No longer was the employer a master craftsman who felt some responsibility toward his workers. Factory owners had obligations to investors and bankers, but not to their workers. Owners kept wages low, regardless of the workers' cost of living. As the supply of labor swelled and wages declined, increasing numbers of working people faced poverty and squalor.

Large-scale manufacturing also introduced demands for a new class of skilled managerial and clerical employees. The Boston Manufacturing Company employed teams of young men as clerks who kept accounts, wrote orders, and drafted correspondence, all in longhand. As manufacturers became involved in building new factories, pursuing investors, and entering new markets, professional managers increasingly supervised clerical and manufacturing employees. These men had either risen through the ranks of the company or had been master craftsmen who had been overwhelmed by the breakneck speed of industrialization.

Social Life for a Genteel Class

The factory system also altered the daily lives of manufacturers. In earlier years, **journeymen** and apprentices had lived with master craftsmen and their families. Craftsmen exercised great authority over their workers but felt obligated to care for them almost as parents would. Such working arrangements blurred the distinction between employee and employer. The factory system ended this relationship. The movement of workers out of owners' homes permitted the emerging elite class to develop a genteel lifestyle that set them apart from the rest of the population.

Genteel families aimed at the complete separation of their private and public lives. Men in the elite class spent their leisure time socializing with each other in private clubs and organizations instead of drinking and eating with their employees. The lives of genteel wives also changed. The wife of a traditional craftsman had been responsible for important tasks in the operation of the business. Genteel women, in contrast, were *expected* to leave business dealings to men. They became immersed in what is called the **cult of domesticity,** which encouraged women to focus their lives completely on their homes and children. Women who did so believed they were performing an important duty for God and country and fulfilling their natural calling.

Motherhood consumed genteel women during the antebellum period. The new magazines and advice manuals of the 1820s and 1830s urged mothers to nurture rather than punish their children. Influential author Bronson Alcott helped to convince an entire generation of the need for a gentle and supporting hand and for a departure from harsh, Puritan methods of child rearing.

Despite the demands of motherhood, many genteel women found themselves isolated with time on their hands. They sought activities that would provide a sense of accomplishment without imperiling their genteel status. Many found outlets in fancy needlework, reading, and art appreciation societies. But some wished for more challenging activities. As Sarah Huntington Smith complained in 1833, "To make and receive visits, exchange friendly salutations, attend to one's wardrobe, cultivate a garden, read good and entertaining books, and even attend religious meetings for one's own enjoyment; all this does not satisfy me." Smith *chose* to become a missionary. Other genteel women during the 1830s and 1840s used their nurturing and purifying talents to reform what appeared to be a chaotic and immoral society by involving themselves in crusades against alcohol and slavery.

---

journeyman   A person who has finished an apprenticeship in a trade or craft and is a qualified worker in the employ of another.

cult of domesticity   The belief that women's proper role lay in domestic pursuits.

Life and Culture Among the New Middle Class

The new class of clerks, bookkeepers, and managers sought to find their own cultural level. This middle class had many of the same prejudices and ideals as the elite class. They read the same advice magazines, often attended the same churches, and sometimes belonged to the same civic and reform societies. Nevertheless, the lives of these two classes were different in many respects.

One distinguishing characteristic of the new middle class was its relative youth. These young people had flocked from the countryside to newly emerging cities in pursuit of formal education and employment. While middle-class men found employment as clerks, bookkeepers, and managers, middle-class women parlayed their education and perceived gift for nurturing children into work as teachers. It became acceptable for women to work as teachers for several years before marriage. Some avoided marriage altogether to pursue their hard-won careers.

Middle-class men and women tended to put off marriage until they had established themselves socially and economically. They also tended to have fewer children than their parents had. Because middle-class children were sent to school to prepare them to pursue careers, they were an economic liability rather than an asset. Late marriage and birth control kept middle-class families small.

Middle-class city life cut people off from the comforting sociability of farm families and the church-centered communities that shaped and directed rural life. Many unmarried men and women seeking their fortunes in town boarded in private homes or rooming houses. After marriage, they emulated the closely knit isolation of the elite. Accordingly, these couples looked to each other for companionship and guidance.

Like the elite class, this new group sought bonds in voluntary associations. College students formed discussion groups, preprofessional clubs, and benevolent societies. For those out of school, groups like the Odd Fellows and the Masons brought people together for companionship. Such organizations helped enforce traditional values through rigid membership standards stressing moral character, upright behavior, and, above all, order.

Immigration and Working-Class America

- How did industrialization and massive immigration to America produce a working-class culture?
- How did working people respond to changing conditions?

The elite and middle classes banded together in private enclaves in part because the social scene around them was changing in disturbing ways. Between 1820 and 1830, slightly more than 151,000 people immigrated to the United States. In the following decade, that number increased to nearly 600,000; between 1840 and 1850, it soared to more than a million and a half people (see Map 10.2). This enormous increase in immigration changed the cultural and economic face of the nation. Immigrants flocked to the port and manufacturing cities of the Northeast, where they joined Americans fleeing the countryside after the Panic of 1819. Former master craftsmen, journeymen, and apprentices combined with immigrants and refugees from the farm to form a new social class and culture in America.

Changing Patterns in Immigration

Eighteenth-century immigrants were seldom truly poor. With the exception of indentured servants, they had a small stake of money or at least some marketable skills. During the early nineteenth century, however, this pattern changed. Nearly half of all immigrants to the United States between 1820 and 1860 came from Ireland, a nation beset with poverty, political strife, and, after the potato blight appeared in 1841, starvation. Few Irish had marketable skills or more money than the voyage to America cost. They arrived penniless and virtually unemployable. Many of them spoke not English but Gaelic.

The same was true of many Germans, the second most numerous immigrant group. Radical economic change and political upheaval put peasants and skilled craftsmen into flight. Like Irish peasants, German farmers arrived in America destitute and void of opportunities. Trained German craftsmen had a better chance at finding employment, but mechanization threatened their livelihoods as well.

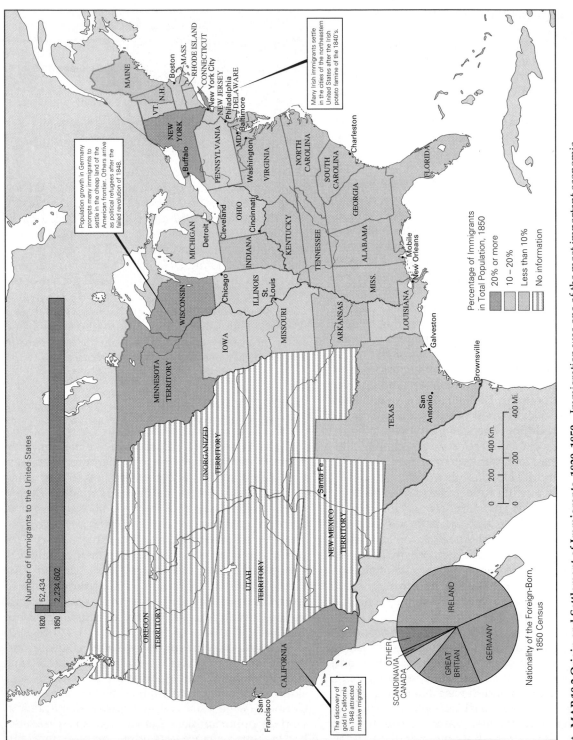

Many Irish immigrants settle in the cities of the northeastern United States after the Irish potato famine of the 1840's.

Population growth in Germany prompts many immigrants to settle in the cheap land of the American frontier. Others arrive as political refugees after the failed revolution of 1848.

The discovery of gold in California in 1848 attracted massive migration.

Percentage of Immigrants in Total Population, 1850
- 20% or more
- 10 – 20%
- Less than 10%
- No information

Number of Immigrants to the United States
- 1820 — 52,434
- 1850 — 2,234,602

Nationality of the Foreign-Born, 1850 Census

IRELAND
GERMANY
GREAT BRITAIN
CANADA
SCANDINAVIA
OTHER

◆ **MAP 10.2 Origin and Settlement of Immigrants, 1820–1850** Immigration was one of the most important economic, political, and social factors in American life during the antebellum period. As this map shows, with the exception of Louisiana, immigration was confined almost exclusively to areas where slavery was not permitted. This gave the North, Northwest, and California a different cultural flavor than the rest of the country, and also affected the political balance between those areas and the South.

Adding to their difficulties was their lack of fluency in English.

Not only were the new immigrants poor and unskilled, but most were culturally different from native-born Americans. Catholicism separated most from the vast majority of Americans, who were Protestants. In religion, language, dress, eating and drinking habits, and social values, the new immigrants were very different from the people whose culture dominated American society.

Poverty, cultural distinctiveness, and the desire to live among fellow immigrants created ethnic neighborhoods in New York, Philadelphia, and other cities. Here, people with the same culture and religion built churches, stores, pubs, beer halls, and other familiar institutions to help themselves cope with the shock of transplantation and to adapt to life in the United States. They started fraternal organizations and clubs to overcome loneliness and isolation. Living conditions were crowded, uncomfortable, and unsanitary.

Desperate for work, the new immigrants were willing to do nearly anything to earn money. For manufacturers, they were the perfect work force. As immigration increased, the traditional labor shortage in America was replaced by a **labor glut,** and the social and economic status of all workers declined accordingly.

Working Conditions in Industrializing America

Working conditions for factory workers reflected the labor supply, the manufacturing company's capital, and the personal philosophy of the factory owner. Girls at Lowell's factories described an environment of familiar paternalism. Factory managers and boarding-house keepers supervised every aspect of their lives. As for the work itself, one mill girl commented that it was "not half so hard as . . . attending the dairy, washing, cleaning house, and cooking." What bothered her most was the repetitive work and the resulting boredom.

Boredom could have disastrous consequences. Inattentive factory workers were likely to lose fingers, hands, arms, or even lives to whirring, pounding, slashing mechanisms. Some owners tried to make the workplace safe, but investors discouraged many from buying safety devices. Samuel Slater

♦ Working-class neighborhoods like the infamous Five Points District in New York, shown in this anonymous 1829 picture, were filthy, unhealthy, and crime-ridden. Reformers sought to help by changing workers' habits and morals, but seldom addressed their economic plight. *"Five Points District," artist unknown. c. 1829. Courtesy of Mr. and Mrs. Screven Lorillard, photo by Josh Nefsky.*

complained bitterly to investors after a child was chewed up in a factory machine. "You call for yarn," he declared, "but think little about the means by which it is to be made."

Such concern became increasingly rare as factory owners withdrew from overseeing daily operations. The influx of laborers from the countryside and foreign lands wiped out the decent wages and living conditions that manufacturing pioneers had offered. Laborers were increasingly *expected* to provide their own housing, food, and entertainment.

Large areas in cities became working-class neighborhoods. Factory workers, journeymen, and day laborers crammed into the boxlike rooms of tenements. Large houses formerly occupied by domestic manufacturers and their apprentices were broken up into tiny apartments and were rented to laborers. In some working-class areas of New York City, laborers were crowded fifty to a house. Sewage disposal, drinking water, and trash removal were sorely neglected in such areas.

---

labor glut Oversupply of labor in relation to the number of jobs available.

The Beginnings of Working-Class Culture

Wretched living conditions and dispiriting poverty caused working-class people to *choose* social and cultural outlets that were very different from those of upper- and middle-class Americans. Drinking was the social distraction of *choice* among working people. Whiskey was cheap at 25 cents a gallon during the 1820s and 1830s as western farmers used the new roads and canals to ship distilled spirits to urban markets.

Working-class entertainment tended to revolve around drinking. Theaters that catered to working-men by staging **minstrel shows** or popular plays sold cheap drinks in the lobby or in basement pubs. Alcohol was usually also sold at sporting events such as bare-knuckle boxing contests that drew large working-class audiences.

Working-class women experienced the same dull but dangerous working conditions and dismal living circumstances as working-class men, but their lives were even harder. Single women were paid significantly less than men but had to pay as much for living quarters, food, and clothing. Marriage could reduce a woman's personal expenses, but at a cost. While men congregated in the barbershop or pub during their leisure hours, married women were stuck in tiny apartments caring for children and doing household chores. Social convention banned women from many activities that provided their husbands, boyfriends, and sons with some relief.

Protest and Resistance

In view of their working and living conditions, it is not surprising that some manufacturing workers began to organize in protest. Skilled journeymen took the lead in making their dissatisfaction known to factory owners.

Journeyman shoemakers staged the first labor strike in America in 1806 to protest the hiring of unskilled workers to perform work that the journeymen had been doing. The strike failed, but it set the precedent for labor actions for the next half-century. The replacement of skilled workers remained a major cause of labor unrest in the 1820s and 1830s. Journeymen bemoaned the decline in craftsmanship and their loss of power to set hours, conditions, and wages. Industrialization was costing journeymen their independence and forcing some to become wage laborers.

Instead of attacking or even criticizing industrialization, however, journeymen simply asked for decent wages and working conditions. To achieve these goals, they banded together in **trade unions**, which were groups of skilled workers in a specific occupation. During the 1830s, trade unions from different towns formed the beginnings of a national trade union movement. In this way, house carpenters, shoemakers, handloom weavers, printers, and comb makers attempted to enforce national wage standards in their industries. In 1834, many of these merged to form the **National Trades' Union**, which was the first labor union in the nation's history to represent many different crafts.

The trade union movement accomplished little during the antebellum period. Factory owners, bankers, and others who wanted to keep labor cheap used every device available to prevent unions from gaining the upper hand. Employers formed their own associations to resist union activity. They also used the courts to keep unions from disrupting business. A series of local court decisions upheld employers and threatened labor's right to organize.

A breakthrough for trade unions finally came in 1842. The Massachusetts Supreme Court decided in *Commonwealth v. Hunt* that Boston's journeymen bootmakers had the right to organize and to call strikes. By that time, however, the Panic of 1837, which threw many people out of work for long periods of time, had so undermined the labor movement that legal protection became somewhat meaningless.

Not all labor protests were peaceful. In 1828, for example, immigrant weavers protested the low wages paid by Alexander Knox, New York City's

---

minstrel show   A variety show in which white actors made up as blacks presented jokes, songs, dances, and comic skits.

trade union   A labor organization whose members work in a specific trade or craft.

National Trades' Union   The first national association of trade unions in the United States; it was formed in 1834.

leading textile employer. Demanding higher pay, they stormed and vandalized his home. The weavers then marched to the homes of weavers who had not joined the protest and destroyed their looms.

More frequently, however, working men took out their frustrations not on their employers but on other ethnic groups. Ethnic riots shook New York, Philadelphia, and Boston during the late 1820s and 1830s. In 1834, rumors that innocent girls were being held captive and tortured in a Catholic convent near Boston led a Protestant mob to burn the convent to the ground. A year later, as many as five hundred native-born Protestants and immigrant Irish Catholics clashed in the streets of New York. These ethnic tensions were the direct result of declining economic power and terrible living conditions. Native-born journeymen blamed immigrants for lowered wages and loss of status. Immigrants hated being treated like dirt.

Apart from drinking and fighting among themselves, working people in America during the early nineteenth century did little to protest their fate. Why were American workers so unresponsive? One reason may be that as poor as conditions were, life was better than in Ireland and Germany. Another reason is that workers did not see themselves staying poor. As one English observer commented, women in America's factories were willing to endure boring twelve-hour days because "none of them consider it as their permanent condition." Men *expected* to "accumulate enough to go off to the West, and buy an estate at $1\frac{1}{4}$ dollar an acre, or set up in some small way of business at home."

Reactions to Dynamic Growth and Failure

- How did the Second Great Awakening affect *expectations* and *choices* for different social classes and geographic regions?

In the grasping, competitive conditions that were emerging in America, an individual's status, reputation, and welfare seemed to depend exclusively on economic position. But economic position proved to be highly precarious. Desperate for some stability, many Americans pushed for reforms to bring the fast-spinning world under control.

A Second Great Awakening

Popular religion was a major counterbalance to rapid change. Beginning in the 1790s, Protestant theologians sought to create a new Protestant creed that would maintain Christian community in an era of increasing individualism and competition.

Mirroring tendencies in society, Protestant thinking during the early nineteenth century emphasized the role of the individual. Traditional Puritanism had emphasized **predestination,** the idea that individuals can do nothing to win salvation. Nathaniel Taylor of Yale College created a theology that was consistent with the new secular creed of individualism. According to Taylor, God offered salvation to all who sought it. Thus the individual had "free will" to *choose* or not *choose* salvation. Taylor's ideas struck a responsive chord in a restless and expanding America. Hundreds of ministers carried his message of a democratic God.

Most prominent among the evangelists of the **Second Great Awakening** was Charles Grandison Finney. A former schoolteacher and lawyer, Finney experienced a soul-shattering religious conversion in 1821 at the age of 29. Finney performed on the pulpit as a spirited attorney might argue a case in court. Seating those most likely to be converted on a special "anxious bench," Finney focused his whole attention on them. The *outcome* was likely to be dramatic emotional scenes. Many of those on the anxious bench fainted, experienced bodily spasms, or cried out in hysteria. Such dramatic results brought Finney enormous publicity, which he and an army of imitators used to gain access to communities all over the West and Northeast. The result was a nearly continuous season of religious revival. It spread across rural America like a wildfire until Finney carried it into Boston and New York in the 1830s.

---

predestination   The doctrine that God has predetermined everything that happens, including the final salvation or damnation of each person.

Second Great Awakening   Series of religious revivals that began around 1800 and were characterized by emotional public meetings and conversions.

Revival meetings were remarkable affairs. Usually beginning on a Thursday and continuing until the following Tuesday, they drew crowds of up to twenty-five thousand people. Those attending listened to spirited preaching in the evenings and engaged in religious study during the daylight hours.

The revivals led to the breakdown of traditional church organizations and the creation of various Christian denominations. The Presbyterians, Baptists, and Methodists split between those who supported the new theology and those who clung to more traditional notions. Such fragmentation worried all denominations that state support of any one church might give that denomination an advantage in the continuing competition for souls. Oddly, those most fervent in their Christian beliefs joined deists and other Enlightenment-influenced thinkers in arguing for even more stringent separation of church and state.

Although religious conversion had become an individual matter, revivalists did not ignore the notion of community. At revival meetings, for example, when individuals were overcome by the power of the spirit, those already saved began "surrounding them with melodious songs, or fervent prayers for their happy resurrection, in the love of Christ." Finney put great emphasis on creating a single Christian community to stand in opposition to sin. As he observed, "Christians of every denomination generally seemed to make common cause, and went to work with a will, to pull sinners out of the fire."

The intimacy forged during revivals gave a generation of isolated individuals a sense of community and a sense of duty. According to the new theology, it was each convert's obligation to carry the message of salvation to the multitudes still in darkness. New congregations, missionary societies, and a thousand other **benevolent** groups rose up to lead America in the continuing battle against sin.

The Middle Class and Moral Reform

The missionary activism that accompanied the Second Great Awakening dovetailed with the inclination toward reform among genteel and middle-class people. The Christian benevolence movement gave rise to voluntary societies that aimed to outlaw alcohol and a hundred other evils. These organizations provided both genteel and middle-class men and women with a purpose missing from their lives. Such activism drew them together in common causes and served as an antidote to the alienation and loneliness common in early nineteenth-century America.

As traditional family and village life broke down, voluntary societies pressed for public intervention to address social problems. The new theology emphasized that even the most depraved might be saved if proper means were applied. This idea had immediate application to crime and punishment. Criminals were no longer characterized as evil but were seen as lost and in need of divine guidance.

Mental illness underwent a similar change in definition. Rather than being viewed as hopeless cases suffering an innate spiritual flaw, the mentally ill were now spoken of as lost souls in need of help. **Dorothea Dix,** a young, compassionate, and reform-minded teacher, learned firsthand about the plight of the mentally ill when she taught a Sunday school class in a Boston-area prison. "I tell what I have seen," she said to the Massachusetts legislature in 1843. "Insane persons confined within the Commonwealth, in cages, closets, cellars, stalls, pens! Chained, naked, beaten with rods, and lashed into obedience!" For the balance of the century, Dix toured the country pleading the cause of the mentally ill.

Middle-class Protestant activists targeted many other areas for reform. They insisted on stopping mail delivery and closing canals on Sundays. Others joined Bible and tract societies that distributed Christian literature. They founded Sunday schools or opened domestic missions to win the **irreligious** and Roman Catholics to what they regarded as the true religion.

---

revival meeting   A meeting for the purpose of reawakening religious faith, often characterized by impassioned preaching and emotional public testimony by converted sinners.

benevolent   Concerned with doing good or organized for the benefit of charity.

Dorothea Dix   Philanthropist, reformer, and educator who was a pioneer in the movement for specialized treatment of the mentally ill.

irreligious   Hostile or indifferent to religion.

♦ After seeing the conditions under which the mentally ill lived in antebellum Massachusetts, Dorothea Dix, shown in this early photograph, campaigned for special asylums where they could receive special care and treatment. *Boston Athenaeum.*

Moral Reform and Social Control

Many white-collar reformers were genuinely interested in forging a new social welfare system. A number of their programs, however, appear to have been aimed more at achieving control over others than social reform. Such reformers often tried to force people to conform to a middle-class standard of behavior. Reformers believed that immigrants should willingly discard their traditional customs and learn American ways. Immigrants who clung to familiar ways were suspected of disloyalty. Social control was particularly prominent in public education and **temperance.**

Some communities, like Puritan Boston, had always emphasized compulsory education for children. Most communities, however, did not require children to attend school. The apprenticeship system rather than schools often provided the rudiments of reading, writing, and figuring. But as the complexity of life increased during the early nineteenth century, **Horace Mann** and others came out in favor of formal schooling.

Mann, like Charles Finney, was trained as a lawyer. But Mann believed that ignorance, not sin, lay at the heart of the nation's problems. Mann, a Bostonian, became the nation's leading advocate of publicly funded education for all children. "If we do not prepare children to become good citizens," Mann proclaimed, "if we do not enrich their minds with knowledge, then our republic must go down to destruction, as others have gone before it."

Massachusetts took the lead in formalizing schooling in 1837 when the state founded the country's first public board of education. Appointed head of the board, Mann extended the school year to a minimum of six months and increased teachers' salaries. Gradually the state board changed the curriculum in Massachusetts schools, replacing classical learning and ministerial training with courses like arithmetic, practical geography, and physical science.

Education reformers were interested in more than knowledge. Mann and others were equally concerned that new immigrants and the urban poor be trained in Protestant values and middle-class habits. Thus school books emphasized promptness, persistence, discipline, and obedience to authority. In cities with numerous Roman Catholics, Catholic parents resisted the Protestant-dominated school boards by establishing **parochial schools.**

Social control was also evident in the crusade against alcohol. Before the early nineteenth century, the consumption of alcohol was not broadly perceived as a significant social problem. Two factors contributed to a new perception. One was the increasing visibility of drinking and its consequence, drunkenness, as populations became more concentrated in cities. Rochester, New York, by the mid-1820s had nearly a hundred drinking establishments that included groceries, barbershops, and even candy stores.

---

temperance   Avoidance of alcoholic drinks.

Horace Mann   Educator who called for publicly funded education for all children and was head of the first public board of education in the United States.

parochial school   A school supported by a church parish.

The changing taste of genteel and middle-class people was the second factor that contributed to a new view of alcohol. As alternatives to alcohol such as clean water and coffee became available or affordable, these people reduced their consumption of alcohol and disapproved of those who did not. By 1829, the middle class saw strong drink as "the cause of almost all of the crime and almost all of the misery that flesh is heir to." Drinking made self-control impossible and endangered morality and industry. Thus behavior that had been acceptable in the late eighteenth century was judged to be a social problem in the nineteenth.

Drunkenness earned special condemnation from reawakened Protestants, who believed that people besotted by alcohol could not possibly gain salvation. Christian reformers believed that stopping the drinking of alcohol was necessary not only to preserve the nation but to save people's souls.

The religious appeal of temperance was enhanced by a powerful economic appeal. Factory owners recognized that workers who drank heavily threatened the quantity and quality of production. They rallied around temperance as a way of policing their employees in and out of the factory. By promoting temperance, reformers believed they could increase production and turn the raucous lower classes into clean-living, self-controlled, peaceful workers.

The Rise of Abolitionism

Another reform movement that had profound influence in antebellum America was **abolitionism.** Although Quakers had long opposed slavery, there was little organized opposition to it before the American Revolution. During the Revolution, many Americans saw the contradiction between asserting the "unalienable rights" of "life, liberty, and the pursuit of happiness" and holding slaves (see page 103). By the end of the Revolution, Massachusetts and Pennsylvania had taken steps to abolish slavery. And by the mid-1780s, most states, including those in the South, had active antislavery societies. In 1807, when Congress voted to outlaw the importation of slaves, little was said in defense of slavery. But by 1815, the morality of slavery had begun to emerge as a national issue.

The **American Colonization Society,** founded in 1817, reflected public feeling about slavery. Humanitarian concern for slaves' well-being was not the only reason for the society's existence. Many members believed that the black and white races could not live together and advocated that emancipated slaves be sent back to Africa. Although the American Colonization Society began in the South, its policies were particularly popular in the Northeast and West. In eastern cities, workers feared that free blacks would lower their wages and take their jobs. Western farmers similarly feared economic competition.

Most evangelical preachers supported colonization, but a few individuals advocated more radical reforms. The most vocal leader was **William Lloyd Garrison.** A Christian reformer from Massachusetts, Garrison in 1831 founded the nation's first prominent abolitionist newspaper, *The Liberator.* In it he advocated immediate emancipation for blacks and no compensation for slaveholders. Garrison founded the American Anti-Slavery Society in 1833.

At first, Garrison had few followers. Some Christian reformers joined his cause, but the majority supported colonization. At this early date, radical abolitionists were almost universally ignored or, worse, attacked. Throughout the 1830s, riots often accompanied abolitionist rallies as angry mobs stormed stages and pulpits to silence abolitionist speakers. Still, support for the movement gradually grew. In 1836, petitions flooded into Congress demanding an end to the slave trade in the District of Columbia. Congress responded by passing a **gag rule,** which lasted until 1844, to avoid any discussion of the issue. But the issue of slavery would not go away.

---

abolitionism   A reform movement favoring the immediate freeing of all slaves.

American Colonization Society   Organization established in 1817 to send free blacks from the United States to Africa; it used government money to buy land in Africa and found the colony of Liberia.

William Lloyd Garrison   Abolitionist leader who founded and published *The Liberator,* an antislavery newspaper.

gag rule   A rule that limits or prevents debate on an issue.

SUMMARY

E xpectations

C onstraints

C hoices

O utcomes

An age that began with optimism closed in a tangle of conflict and ill will. Optimistic *expectations* ultimately produced economic panic in 1819 and a collapse in the speculative economy as their *outcomes*. Economic hard times, in turn, triggered increased competition among the nation's geographical sections. Supporters of the American System tried to craft a solution, but their compromise did not satisfy anyone entirely. In the contention surrounding the Missouri Compromise, the Era of Good Feelings collapsed.

Rapid economic change in the Northeast worsened the tension among the nation's sections. Northeasterners *chose* to engage in large-scale manufacturing, combining European machines with American ingenuity. *Expecting* to enrich themselves and the nation, men like Francis Cabot Lowell and John Hall invented new forms of industrialism that would revolutionize their region and eventually the world. An unexpected *outcome* was that northeastern society began to divide into three distinct social and economic classes, each with its own cultural values.

Adding to the distinctiveness of the Northeast was an ever-increasing flow of Irish and German immigrants who brought their own cultural values with them. The *outcome* was a distinctive working-class society and culture growing out of the mixture of foreign and native-born workers.

To many, it seemed that the world was spinning out of control. Religion was one response to the turmoil. From 1800 onward, Americans enjoyed a persistent season of religious enthusiasm that ignited backcountry farmer and urban worker alike. Elite and middle-class Americans captured the rhetoric of perfectionism flowing out of the new theology and applied it to moral, social, cultural, and political reform. They *chose* to emphasize two primary targets for reform: (1) immigrants and other workers, who were to be made into productive citizens through public education, imposed sobriety, and strict time management, and (2) southerners, who were to be saved from sin by the elimination of slavery.

Suggested Readings

Cott, Nancy M. *The Bonds of Womanhood: "Woman's Sphere" in New England, 1780–1835* (1977).

A pioneering work on the ties that held the woman's world together, but collectively bound them into a secondary position in American life.

Dublin, Thomas. *Women at Work: The Transformation of Work and Community in Lowell, Massachusetts, 1826–1860* (1979).

An interesting look at the way in which the nature of work changed and the sorts of changes that were brought to one manufacturing community.

Eisler, Benita, ed. *The Lowell Offering: Writings by New England Mill Women, 1840–1845* (1977).

First-hand accounts of factory life and changing social conditions written by the young women who worked at Lowell's various factories.

Pessen, Edward. *Most Uncommon Jacksonians: The Radical Leaders of the Early Labor Movement* (1967).

A look at early labor movements and reform by one of America's leading radical scholars.

Ryan, Mary P. *Cradle of the Middle Class: The Family in Oneida County, New York, 1790–1865* (1981).

A marvelous synthesis of materials focusing on the emergence of a new social and economic class in the midst of the change from a traditional to a modern society.

Walters, Ronald G. *American Reformers, 1815–1860* (1978).

The best overview of the reform movements and key personalities who guided them during this difficult period in American history.

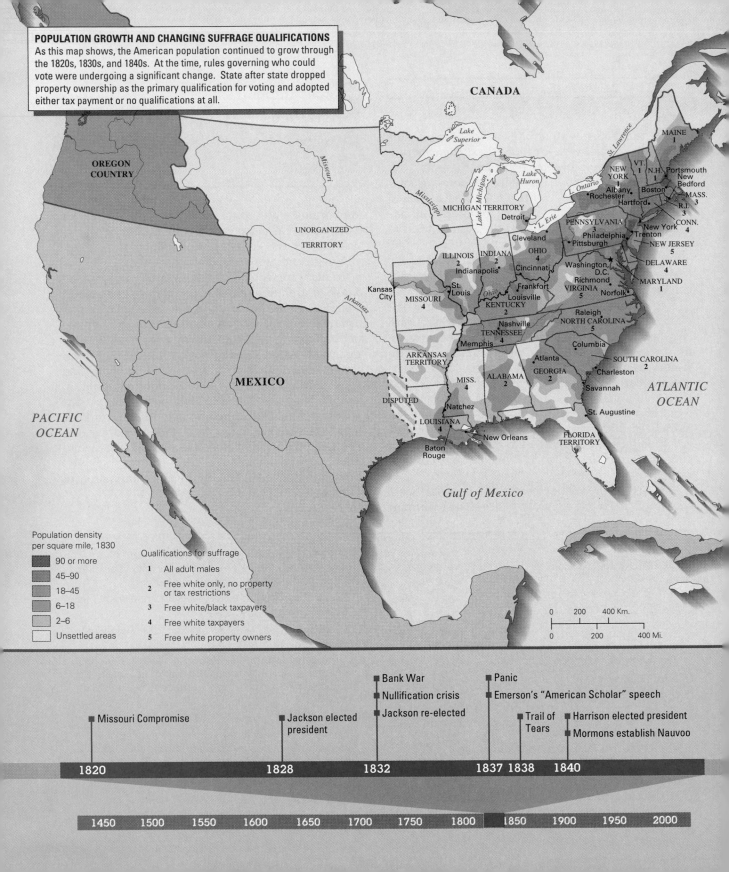

POPULATION GROWTH AND CHANGING SUFFRAGE QUALIFICATIONS
As this map shows, the American population continued to grow through the 1820s, 1830s, and 1840s. At the time, rules governing who could vote were undergoing a significant change. State after state dropped property ownership as the primary qualification for voting and adopted either tax payment or no qualifications at all.

CANADA

Lake Superior

Missouri

MICHIGAN TERRITORY

Lake Michigan

Lake Huron

OREGON COUNTRY

UNORGANIZED TERRITORY

Detroit

L. Erie

MAINE
1

VT.
1

N.H.
1

Portsmouth
New Bedford

NEW YORK
1

L. Ontario

Albany

Rochester

Boston

MASS.
3

Hartford

R.I.
1

CONN.
4

Cleveland

PENNSYLVANIA
3

New York

NEW JERSEY

Philadelphia
Pittsburgh

Trenton

DELAWARE
4

ILLINOIS
2

INDIANA
2

OHIO
4

Cincinnati

Indianapolis

Kansas City

St. Louis

MISSOURI
4

Ohio

Frankfort

Louisville

KENTUCKY

Washington, D.C.

Richmond

VIRGINIA
5

Norfolk

MARYLAND
1

Arkansas

Nashville

TENNESSEE
4

Memphis

Raleigh

NORTH CAROLINA
5

ARKANSAS TERRITORY

Columbia

SOUTH CAROLINA
2

Atlanta

GEORGIA
2

Charleston

MISS.
4

ALABAMA
2

MEXICO

DISPUTED

Natchez

LOUISIANA
4

New Orleans

Savannah

St. Augustine

FLORIDA TERRITORY

PACIFIC OCEAN

Baton Rouge

Gulf of Mexico

ATLANTIC OCEAN

Population density per square mile, 1830
- 90 or more
- 45–90
- 18–45
- 6–18
- 2–6
- Unsettled areas

Qualifications for suffrage
1. All adult males
2. Free white only, no property or tax restrictions
3. Free white/black taxpayers
4. Free white taxpayers
5. Free white property owners

0   200   400 Km.
0   200   400 Mi.

		Bank War		Panic	
Missouri Compromise		Nullification crisis		Emerson's "American Scholar" speech	
	Jackson elected president	Jackson re-elected		Trail of Tears	Harrison elected president
					Mormons establish Nauvoo

1820   **1828**   **1832**   **1837 1838**   **1840**

1450 1500 1550 1600 1650 1700 1750 1800 1850 1900 1950 2000

Politics and Change in Jackson's America, 1828–1840

The "New Man" in Politics

- How did Americans' political *expectations* change between John Quincy Adams's election in 1824 and Andrew Jackson's election in 1828?

- How did Jackson create those *expectations*?

Jackson in Power

- In what ways were the crises that affected Jackson's administration natural *outcomes* of the *choices* Jackson and his supporters made?

The Whig Alternative to Jacksonian Democracy

- What *expectations* did Jackson's opponents have when they built their coalition to oppose the Democrats?

- Was the *outcome* what they *expected*?

Toward an American Culture

- What *choices* did Americans make in dealing with the stresses created by rapid change during the Jacksonian era?

- What was the cultural *outcome*?

```
┌─────────────────────────────────┐
│ INTRODUCTION                    │
└─────────────────────────────────┘
```

E xpectations
C onstraints
C hoices
O utcomes

Americans wrestled to adjust their *expectations* in the 1820s. They lived in an unsettling time. In the brief period since the War of 1812, the transformation of the economy had sent waves of change through American society. In the resulting climate of ferment, Americans sought new political, religious, and cultural solutions to the disorder affecting their lives.

Republican political rhetoric dating back to Jefferson's time had led Americans to *expect* that they should have a voice in public affairs. Two *constraints* limited their participation in the political process in the 1820s. First, many educated, wage-earning Americans had long been prohibited from voting because they did not own land. Second, small farmers, artisans, and others of modest means who owned property and voted felt that they were not represented as they watched the presidency pass from one member of the eastern elite to another. They also watched federal, state, and local government jobs pass from one political insider to another. Thus a host of disgruntled citizens demanded that the political process be opened up. The *outcome* was a new style of politics in the United States.

John Quincy Adams was the first president to confront the rapidly changing face of American politics. Old-fashioned and paternalistic, Adams alienated much of the nation. His *expectation* that he could govern as a dignified statesman ran headlong into the *expectations* of newly politicized Americans who were demanding a rapid increase in political and economic opportunities.

In the election of 1828, voters swept out the old gentlemanly style of politics and brought into power a new and exciting figure: Andrew Jackson. Although Jackson had the overwhelming affection and political support of most Americans, sectional tension that had been growing since the crisis over slavery in Missouri made his job difficult. Each region *expected* to have its particular economic problems solved and found the demands of other regions *constraining* and frustrating. The Northeast, for example, believed that higher tariffs and strict economic controls were necessary for its welfare. But westerners and southerners saw such policies as unfair to their own region's interests, and they lobbied hard for quite different solutions to the nation's ills. The *outcome* of sectional *choices* was continued political turmoil.

Personal turmoil mirrored political turmoil. Traditional communities were breaking down everywhere, leaving individuals isolated and alone. Americans were divided in their response to this development. Some celebrated the freedom of the newly liberated individual, personified by Andrew Jackson, the frontier orphan who became president. Others longed for the comfort and security they had known in the rural communities that were quickly disappearing in the face of a modernizing economy.

As economic and political stress intensified during the 1820s and 1830s, it spilled into more and more people's innermost lives. Frightened, often angry, and feeling confused and *constrained* in spirit, many people *chose* to seek relief in various religious and cultural outlets. Religious revivalism and a commitment to reforming society along Christian lines continued to seem a reasonable *choice* for some. Others explored less traditional options, ranging from free love to absolute celibacy, from egalitarian communes to highly ordered communities. But nothing seemed able to overcome the unrest and tension in society. It was a highly experimental and exciting time, but the cultural *outcomes*, like the political and economic ones, were often very different from what people *expected*.

CHRONOLOGY

Era of Growth and Anxiety

1820	Missouri Compromise
1823	James Fenimore Cooper publishes *The Pioneers*
1824–1828	Suffrage reform triples the number of voters
1825	John Quincy Adams elected president Hudson River school of painting begun by Thomas Cole Robert Owen establishes community at New Harmony, Indiana
1826	Shakers have eighteen communities in eight states Disappearance of William Morgan and beginning of the Antimasons
1827	Ratification of Cherokee constitution
1828	Tariff of Abominations Publication of *The South Carolina Exposition and Protest* First issue of the *Cherokee Phoenix* Andrew Jackson elected president
1830	Webster-Hayne debate Joseph Smith publishes the Book of Mormon and founds the Church of Jesus Christ of Latter-Day Saints

1831	Federal removal of Choctaws *Cherokee Nation v. Georgia*
1832	*Worcester v. Georgia* Bank War Nullification crisis Black Hawk War Seminole War begins Jackson re-elected
1836	Martin Van Buren elected president
1836–1838	Federal removal of Creeks, Chickasaws, and Cherokees
1837	Panic of 1837 Ralph Waldo Emerson's "The American Scholar" speech
1838	Emerson articulates transcendentalism
1840	Log Cabin campaign William Henry Harrison elected president Mormons establish Nauvoo, Illinois
1841	Brook Farm founded

The "New Man" in Politics

- How did Americans' political *expectations* change between John Quincy Adams's election in 1824 and Andrew Jackson's in 1828?
- How did Jackson create those *expectations*?

Since Washington's day Americans had *expected* their presidents to be gentlemen. The social changes unleashed after the War of 1812, however, altered those *expectations*. New voters with radically vary-ing political and economic views began making political demands. Many felt isolated from a political system that permitted the presidency to pass from one propertied gentleman to another. Clearly, changing times called for political change.

Adams's Troubled Administration

John Quincy Adams may have been the best pre-pared man ever to assume the office of president. The son of a former president, John Quincy by the time of his election in 1825 had been a diplomat, a U.S. senator, a Harvard professor, and an exceptionally effective secretary of state. But he was singularly lacking in the personal warmth and political skill that might have made him a successful chief executive.

Rigidly idealistic, the new president believed himself to be above partisan politics. Apart from his appointment of Henry Clay as secretary of state, he refused to distribute political favors, and so he had few political followers. Adams was thereby exposed to the constant sniping of his critics, and his administration floundered.

Adams's policies also alienated many. He proposed increased tariffs to protect American manufacturers and wanted the Second Bank of the United States to provide ample loans to finance new manufacturing ventures. Southerners opposed these measures because they feared the increase in federal power that Adams's policies implied and because they disliked tariffs.

The **Tariff of Abominations,** passed in 1828, illustrates Adams's difficulties as president. Manufacturers insisted on raising the tariff even higher than Adams had recommended. Some of Adams's opponents also supported the bill so that it would pass and thereby discredit Adams in the fall election. Only southerners universally opposed the proposed legislation.

Democratic Styles and Political Structure

Adams's political style added to his problems. The detached style appropriate to his father's era became a liability in his own. The easy informality of Adams's archrival, Andrew Jackson, was better suited to an increasingly democratic age than Adams's stiff reserve.

Adams's demeanor would not have been so damaging if a huge increase in voter turnout had not framed his presidency. In the election of 1824, 356,038 people cast votes for the presidency. In 1828, over three times that number voted. These numbers reflect the mobilization of a new **electorate.** Voting rights in the early republic had been restricted to landowners. This restriction had raised no controversy earlier because a majority of white Americans owned land. The expansion of a commercial and industrial economy, however, meant that an increas-

ing number of people did not own land and were therefore not entitled to vote. The emerging middle class clamored for suffrage reform. In 1800, only three of the sixteen states had no qualifications for voting. Three other states permitted taxpayers who were not landowners to vote. By 1830, only six of the twenty-four states continued to demand property qualifications. Nine others required tax payment only, and the remaining nine had no qualifications. As a result, the number of voters grew enormously and rapidly. The United States was evolving from a republic into a democracy in which all white males could vote.

Changes in the structure of politics accompanied this expansion of the electorate. Among the most important was the popular selection of members of the Electoral College. By 1828 only two states continued to name electors. Another important change was that government jobs that had been appointive became elective. States increasingly dropped property qualifications for officeholding, opening new fields for political participation.

Opportunists quickly took advantage of the new situation. Men like New Yorker **Martin Van Buren** organized political factions into tightly disciplined local and statewide units. A long-time opponent of Governor DeWitt Clinton, Van Buren molded disaffected Republicans into the so-called Bucktail faction. In 1820, the Bucktails' charges that the Clintonians were corrupt and aristocratic swept Clinton out of office. The new politics practiced by the Bucktails had clearly triumphed. This new politics combined political patronage and fiery speeches to draw newly qualified voters into the political process.

These new voters were often frustrated that their voting had little impact. The "corrupt bargain" that had denied the presidency to Andrew Jackson in 1824 was a prime example. Secret, elite societies

---

Tariff of Abominations   Tariff, passed by Congress in 1828, that outraged the southern states by placing high duties on raw materials.

electorate   The portion of the population that is qualified to vote.

Martin Van Buren   New York politician known for his skillful handling of party politics; he helped found the Democratic party and later became eighth president of the United States.

such as the **Masons** also appeared to thwart the popular will. The most notorious case of Masonic influence concerned William Morgan, a New York bricklayer and Mason who mysteriously disappeared in 1826 after threatening to publish some Masonic secrets. Morgan's presumed murder caused an outcry. When an investigation turned up no clues, many suspected that the Masons had used their political clout to suppress the facts. Within a year, young politicians such as New Yorkers Thurlow Weed and William Seward and Pennsylvanian Thaddeus Stevens had exploited the Morgan case to form a new political organization. Based on the resentments felt by craftsmen, small farmers, and others, the **Antimasonic party** had no platform beyond a disapproval of politics as usual.

New York typified political developments throughout the country. As the party of Jefferson dissolved, a rash of political factions broke out. It was Van Buren who forged an alliance that would fundamentally alter American politics.

The Rise of Andrew Jackson

By 1826, Van Buren had brought together political outsiders and dissidents from all over the country into a new political party, the Democratic-Republicans, or the **Democrats.** The Democrats in some ways looked to the past. They denounced the National Republicans by calling for a return to Jeffersonian simplicity, states' rights, and democratic principles. But they relied on the modern political tactics and organization that Van Buren had perfected in New York. The appeal to Jeffersonian verities and the use of tight party discipline attracted new voters and political outsiders. In the congressional elections of 1826, Van Buren's coalition gained a majority in the House of Representatives and in the Senate.

Perhaps the key to the Democrats' electoral success was their use of Andrew Jackson's name. Jackson became synonymous with the new party. Thus voters who identified with him identified with the new party. In many ways, Jackson was a perfect reflection of the new voters. He had been born into humble circumstances and had lost his family as a youngster. Jackson epitomized the self-made man who, through sheer will and hard work, had risen far above his modest beginnings. Voters did not begrudge the fact that by the 1820s Jackson had become one of the wealthiest men in Tennessee and owned over two hundred slaves. They admired him for his accomplishments and hoped to emulate his example. Despite fame and fortune, Jackson remained a common man with the common touch. He had become a man of substance without becoming a snob. Jackson was also a military hero. His exploits along the southern frontier during the War of 1812, culminating in the Battle of New Orleans, had become legendary (see page 165).

The images of Jackson and Adams, not substantive issues, dominated the election of 1828. Jackson forces accused Adams of diverting public funds to buy personal luxuries, providing the Russian tsar with a young American mistress to win his diplomatic support, and bowing to **special interests** in defining his tariff and land policies. Adams's supporters charged Jackson with being a dueler, an insubordinate military adventurer, and a rustic backwoodsman who had lived with a married woman before she had divorced her first husband.

The charges of corruption were entirely untrue. The charges against Jackson were all too true, but voters saw them as irrelevant. Rather than damaging Jackson's image, such talk made him appear romantic and daring. The Tennessean polled a hundred thousand more popular votes than did the New Englander and won the majority of states, taking every one in the South and the West (see Map 11.1).

Jackson's inauguration on March 4, 1829, gave cause for celebration among his supporters and for contempt among his detractors. A crowd of ten thousand well-wishers packed the capital to witness

---

Masons   An international fraternal organization with many socially and politically prominent members, including a number of U.S. presidents.

Antimasonic party   Political party formed in 1827 to capitalize on popular anxiety about the influence of the Masons; it opposed politics as usual without offering any particular substitute.

Democrats   Political party that brought Andrew Jackson into office; it harked back to Jeffersonian principles of limited government and drew its support from farmers and small businessmen.

special interest   A person or organization that attempts to influence legislators to support one particular interest or issue.

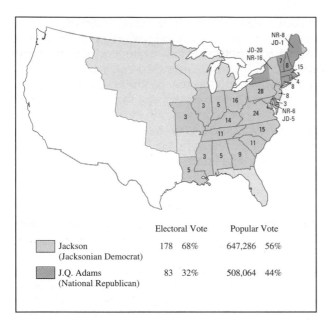

	Electoral Vote		Popular Vote	
Jackson (Jacksonian Democrat)	178	68%	647,286	56%
J.Q. Adams (National Republican)	83	32%	508,064	44%

♦ **MAP 11.1 Presidential Election, 1828**   This map shows how the political coalition between Andrew Jackson and Martin Van Buren turned the tables in the election of 1828. Jackson's Democratic Party won every region except Adams's native New England.

Jackson take the oath of office. Boisterous supporters then followed Jackson into the presidential mansion, where they climbed over furniture, broke glassware, and generally frolicked. The new president was finally forced to flee the near-riot by climbing out a back window. A new spirit was alive in the nation's politics.

Launching Jacksonian Politics

Jackson had courted public support with the implied promise that he would run the nation for the benefit of the people against the manipulations of the privileged. He had pulled together a coalition from all three sections of the nation, but keeping the coalition together was not easy in a time of increasing sectional tension.

Jackson faced a novel problem in that he suspected he could not trust the ten thousand **civil servants** his Republican predecessors had appointed. Jackson's supporters also claimed that many of these government employees were incompetent and had been retained only because of their political connections. Jackson's solution was to introduce the

principle of rotation in office for federal officials. Appointments in his administration, he promised, would last only four years. After that, civil servants would have to return to "making a living as other people do."

Rotation in office was intended to accomplish several goals. First, it would rid the government of entrenched bureaucrats and replace them with honest, publicly minded men. The average citizen, Jackson believed, was fully capable of carrying out public responsibilities. Such duties were "so plain and simple that men of intelligence may readily qualify themselves for their performance." Second, rotation in office opened up many federal jobs. The Jacksonian adage became, "To the victor belong the **spoils."** The Jacksonian practice of distributing government jobs to loyal party members became known as the spoils system.

Patronage appointments extended to the highest levels of government. Jackson selected cabinet members not for their experience but for their political loyalty. The president abandoned his predecessors' practice of holding regular cabinet meetings and of giving cabinet members a vote on major issues. Jackson called virtually no meetings and seldom asked for his cabinet's opinion. Instead, he surrounded himself with an informal network of friends and advisers known as the **Kitchen Cabinet.**

Jackson conducted himself in office unlike any of his predecessors. He raged, pouted, and stormed at those who disagreed with him. Earlier presidents had at least pretended to believe in the equal distribution of power among the three branches of government. Jackson, however, believed that the executive should be supreme because the president was the only member of the government elected by all the people. (This belief conveniently ignored the fact that the Electoral College actually elected the president.) The president was to be the people's advocate in the face of entrenched interests, whether

---

civil servants   Workers in government administration, excluding the courts, the legislature, and the military; they are usually appointed rather than elected.

spoils   Jobs and other rewards for political support.

Kitchen Cabinet   President Jackson's informal advisers, who helped him shape both national and Democratic party policy.

in banks, factories, or the halls of Congress. One sign of his testy relationship with the legislative branch was that he vetoed twelve bills while in office, three more than all his predecessors combined. Through his policies and his style, Jackson changed the presidency profoundly.

Jackson in Power

- In what ways were the crises that affected Jackson's administration natural *outcomes* of the *choices* Jackson and his supporters made?

Jackson had promised the voters "retrenchment and reform." He gave them retrenchment, but reform was more difficult to manage. Jackson tried to reform (1) Indian affairs, (2) internal improvements and public land policy, (3) the collection of revenue and enforcement of federal law, and (4) the nation's banking and financial system. The steps that he took appealed to some of his supporters and alienated others. Jackson's efforts to reform the nation nearly tore it apart.

Jackson and the Indians

Immediately after the War of 1812, the federal government began pressuring eastern tribes to give up their lands and to resettle west of the Mississippi River. Between 1815 and 1820 a number of smaller northern tribes exchanged their land for reservations west of the Mississippi. During the 1820s many other tribes, plied with money from the federal government, followed suit. Factions within the tribes, however, often fought to stay on ancestral lands.

The **Five Civilized Tribes**—the Cherokees, Choctaws, Seminoles, Creeks, and Chickasaws—were also pressured to relocate. They were able to resist the lure of money more successfully than their smaller northern neighbors. These more powerful southern tribes numbered nearly seventy-five thousand people and occupied large areas of Georgia, North and South Carolina, Alabama, Mississippi, and Tennessee. Although these tribes had made significant strides in becoming acculturated to European ways, most southern whites saw them merely as obstacles to obtaining rich cotton lands.

John Quincy Adams had at least paid lip-service to honest dealings with the Indians, and on one occasion he even overturned a fraudulent treaty.

Jackson, however, had never been troubled by such niceties. "I have long viewed treaties with the Indians an absurdity not to be reconciled to the principles of our government," he proclaimed in 1817. Indians were subjects of the United States, he said, and there was no point in negotiating treaties with them. His policy was to remove all the eastern Indians west of the Mississippi (see Map 11.2). If persuasion did not accomplish this goal, Jackson advocated the use of force. Congress gave Jackson this authority when it passed the **Indian Removal Act** in 1830.

The case of the Cherokees provides an excellent illustration of the new, more aggressive Indian policy. By 1830 the Cherokees had shown considerable progress in following Jefferson's advice to become as much like white Americans as possible. They had created a formal government with a bicameral legislature and a court system. They ratified their written constitution, modeled on the U.S. Constitution, in 1827. The next year they began publication of a newspaper, the *Cherokee Phoenix,* written in English and in the eighty-six character Cherokee alphabet invented by tribal member **George Guess (Sequoyah).**

None of these accomplishments won the acceptance of their white neighbors. From the frontiersmen's point of view, Indians were supposed to be dying out, not flourishing. The Georgia legislature responded by **annulling** the Cherokee constitution in 1828 and, when gold was found on Cherokee land in 1829, ordering all tribal lands seized.

Subsequently Georgia passed a series of laws to make life as difficult as possible for the Cherokees. When Christian missionaries living with the tribe

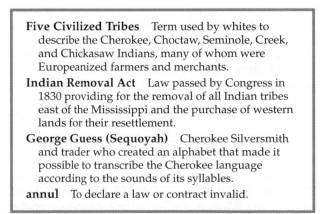

Five Civilized Tribes   Term used by whites to describe the Cherokee, Choctaw, Seminole, Creek, and Chickasaw Indians, many of whom were Europeanized farmers and merchants.

Indian Removal Act   Law passed by Congress in 1830 providing for the removal of all Indian tribes east of the Mississippi and the purchase of western lands for their resettlement.

George Guess (Sequoyah)   Cherokee Silversmith and trader who created an alphabet that made it possible to transcribe the Cherokee language according to the sounds of its syllables.

annul   To declare a law or contract invalid.

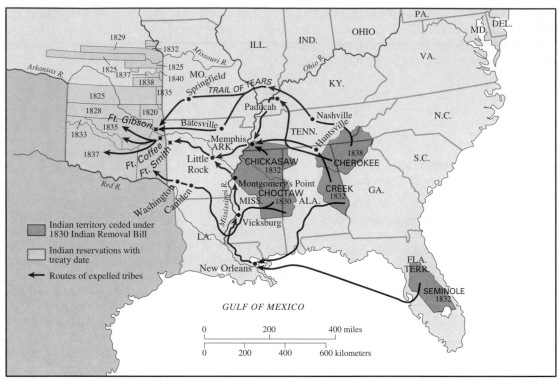

♦ **MAP 11.2 Indian Removal**   The outcome of Andrew Jackson's Indian policy appears clearly on this map. Between 1830 and 1838, all of the Civilized Tribes except Osceola's faction of Seminoles were forced to relocate west of the Mississippi River. Thousands died in the process. *"Removal of Native Americans from the South, 1820–1840" from* American History Atlas *by Martin Gilbert. Copyright ©Routledge Limited. Used with permission.*

encouraged the Cherokees to seek federal assistance, Georgia passed a law that required teachers among the Indians to obtain state licenses. When Samuel Austin Worcester and Elizar Butler refused to apply for the licenses, a company of Georgia militia invaded the Cherokee country and arrested them.

Two notable lawsuits came out of these arrests. In *Cherokee Nation v. Georgia* (1831), the Cherokees claimed that Georgia's enforcement of a state law within Cherokee territory was entirely illegal because they were a sovereign nation. The U.S. Supreme Court refused to hear this case on grounds that the Cherokee Nation was not sovereign. As American citizens, however, Worcester and Butler did have a standing in federal law. In 1832, Chief Justice John Marshall held that Georgia did not have legitimate power to pass laws regulating Indian behavior or to invade Indian land. The court thus declared that all the laws Georgia passed to harass

the Cherokees null and void and ordered Georgia to release Worcester and Butler from jail (see Individual Choices: Reverend Samuel Austin Worcester).

The Cherokees' joy was brief. When Jackson heard the *outcome* of *Worcester v. Georgia,* he refused to use federal troops to carry out Marshall's order. Jackson reportedly fumed, "John Marshall has made his decision, now let him enforce it."

Cherokee Nation v. Georgia   Supreme Court case (1831) concerning Georgia's annulment of all Cherokee laws; Chief Justice John Marshall ruled that Indian tribes did not have the right to appeal to the Supreme Court.

Worcester v. Georgia   Supreme Court case (1832) concerning the arrest of two missionaries to the Cherokees in Georgia; the Court found that Georgia had no right to rule in Cherokee territory.

♦ Realizing that literacy had given whites as advantage in their dealings with Indians, George Guess (also known as Sequoyah) invented a writing system for his native language. This 1838 lithograph shows Guess and his alphabet. *Princeton University Libraries.*

Jackson's refusal to act broke the back of tribal unity. Most Cherokees stood fast with their leader, John Ross. But another faction advocated relocation. Federal Indian agents named this faction as the true representative of the tribe and convinced it to sign the **Treaty of New Echota** (1835), which sold the last 8 million acres of Cherokee land in the East for $5 million.

A similar combination of pressure, manipulation, and outright fraud led to the dispossession of the other Civilized Tribes. During the winter of 1831–1832, the Choctaws were removed forcibly from their lands in Mississippi and Alabama to Indian Territory in what is now Oklahoma. They were joined by the Creeks in 1836 and by the Chickasaws in 1837. In 1838, President Martin Van Buren ordered federal troops to round up the entire Cherokee tribe, nearly twenty thousand people, and force-march them to Indian Territory. The Cherokees suffered terribly in the course of the long trek known as the **Trail of Tears** (see Map 11.2). Nearly a fourth of the Cherokees died of disease, exhaustion, or heartbreak on this march.

The only Civilized Tribe to adopt a policy of military resistance was the Seminoles. Like the other tribes, the Seminoles were deeply divided. Some *chose* peaceful relocation. But after the conciliatory majority signed the Treaty of Payne's Landing in 1832, a group led by **Osceola** declared war on the protreaty group and on the United States. After years of guerrilla swamp fighting, Osceola was finally captured in 1837. The antitreaty faction fought on until 1842, when, after losing fifteen hundred men, the United States withdrew its troops. Eventually, even Osceola's followers agreed to move west, though a small faction of the Seminoles remained in Florida's swamps.

Jackson and the West

Jackson's Indian policy enhanced his popularity in the West, but two other western demands proved troublesome for Old Hickory. The demand for federally funded internal improvements clashed with his notions of small and frugal government, and the demand for more liberal public land policies endangered government revenues and Jackson's relationship with supporters outside the West.

Jackson's views on federal spending for roads, canals, and other internal improvements were influenced more by political than by regional considerations. For example, Jackson vetoed a bill appropriating money to build a road from Maysville, Kentucky, on the Ohio border, to Lexington. He claimed that it would benefit only one state and was therefore unconstitutional. But political considerations clearly influenced this decision. Party loyalists in places like Pennsylvania and New York opposed federal aid to western states. Lexington was also the hub of Henry Clay's political district, and Jackson wanted to do nothing that

---

Treaty of New Echota   Treaty in 1835 that gave all Cherokee lands east of the Mississippi to the U.S. government in return for $5 million and land in the Indian Territory.

Trail of Tears   Forced march of the Cherokee people from Georgia to Indian Territory in the winter of 1838, during which thousands of Cherokees died.

Osceola   Seminole leader in Florida who opposed removal of his people to the West and led resistance to U.S. troops; he was captured by treachery while bearing a flag of truce.

Choosing Justice or Union

Samuel Austin Worcester

Samuel Austin Worcester chose to help the Cherokee Indians when Georgia passed a series of discriminatory laws. This aid led to Worcester's imprisonment. He took his case all the way to the Supreme Court, and the court sided with him. But he chose to back away from his position when it became clear that civil war would be the result of defending Cherokee rights. From *Cherokee Messenger* by Althea Bass, University of Oklahoma Press.

During the waning days of 1830, two very different groups met in Georgia to discuss the impact of the Indian Removal Act. One, the Georgia state legislature, was flush with victory: when enforced, the new federal law would sweep the Cherokees out of western Georgia, freeing up the tribe's rich lands. The other was a group of missionaries. At its head was the frail-looking and scholarly heir to seven generations of New England ministers, Reverend Samuel A. Worcester, who, with his associates, vowed to resist Cherokee removal.

Announcing their vow in the *Cherokee Phoenix,* Worcester stated that Andrew Jackson's Indian policy had moral as well as political implications "inasmuch as it involves the maintenance or violation of the faith of our country." Moreover, the American Board of Commissioners for Foreign Missions had declared in 1810 that it would bring about the Christian conversion of the entire world within a single generation, and removing the Cherokees would delay their conversion and imperil the board's agenda.

For their part, the Georgia state legislators had spent years attempting to drive the Cherokees out of the state, and they regarded missionary support for the Indians as an irritation. Now, with victory nearly at hand, the

would aid his rival. In this case, Jackson's constitutional scruples coincided with his political interests.

The issue of public land policy proved more difficult for Jackson. Many aspiring farmers could not afford to pay $1.25 per acre for public land and clamored for a price reduction. Jackson's response was to propose that federal lands be offered for sale at what it cost to **survey** the land and process the sale. This

proposal represented a departure from previous land policy, which assumed that land sales should profit the government. Easterners and southerners

> **survey** To determine the area and boundaries of land through measurement and mathematical calculation.

legislators wanted to cut off missionary assistance. They passed a new law ordering the missionaries to sign a loyalty oath to the state promising to comply with Georgia law. If they signed the oath, Georgia could legally order them to stop helping the Indians. If they did not sign the oath, they would be imprisoned.

The new law became effective on March 1, 1831, and shortly thereafter Worcester and his colleagues were arrested. Because Worcester was the federal postmaster for the community of New Echota, a Georgia judge released him. But on May 15, Worcester received notice from Georgia governor George R. Gilmer that politicians had pulled strings in Washington to have his postmaster's commission suspended. The governor told Worcester that he had ten days to sign the oath, leave the state, or face arrest. Writing back to the governor, Worcester asserted that he did not believe the state of Georgia had the authority to enforce its will within the Cherokee Nation. Even if it did, he said, he was answerable to a Higher Law.

On July 7, Worcester was arrested again. He posted a bond and regained his freedom, but threats of further harassment forced him to move to neighboring Tennessee, leaving his ailing wife and baby at the mission in New Echota. On August 14, his baby daughter died, and when he rushed home to be with his family, he was arrested. When the court learned why he had returned to Georgia, he was released but was forced to return to exile in Tennessee.

Worcester thus lived like a fugitive, separated from his family and subject to legal harassment, until his case finally came to trial on September 16. The facts were clear. Worcester's own letter to the governor had declared his guilt, and the jury quickly made it official. Samuel Worcester and ten other missionaries were sentenced to four years at hard labor in the Georgia state penitentiary.

After refusing to hear the case of *Cherokee Nation v. Georgia,* Chief Justice John Marshall informed Cherokee tribal lawyers that he was eager for them to bring a stronger case. Worcester's case filled the bill, and the Cherokee Nation and the American Board jointly appealed Worcester's conviction before the Supreme Court. The Court agreed to hear the case, and in a landmark decision ordered Worcester and his co-defendants released, declaring all the laws passed to harass the Cherokees null and void.

Technically, Worcester should have been a free man, but President Jackson refused to acknowledge Marshall's decision and would not order Georgia to release him. The American Board's attorneys had to return to Marshall and ask for a federal court order instructing Jackson to force Worcester's release. In the meantime, however, the Bank War and the nullification crisis had hit the nation with full force, threatening the fabric of the Union itself. Hoping to avoid yet another blow, newly elected Georgia governor Wilson Lumpkin told Worcester and his associates that he would grant them a pardon if they chose not to press their case. The American Board instructed the missionaries to accept the pardon and end the legal struggle. Given the *constraints* surrounding them, their decision to follow the board's instruction is understandable, but there is truth to the charge leveled by historian William G. McLoughlin that Worcester and the American Board *chose* to "sacrifice the Cherokees to save the Union."

were alarmed at proposals to sell federal land at cost. They feared that migration would drain their population and give the West an even bigger voice in the nation's economics and politics. Southerners were also concerned that Congress would replace revenues lost from the sale of public land by raising tariffs. Northern employers were afraid that westward migration would drive up the price of labor.

The result was nearly three years of debate in Congress that hinted at the difficulties that sectionalized politics could cause.

The Nullification Crisis

Southern concerns about rising tariffs were felt most keenly in South Carolina. Soil exhaustion and declining agricultural prices left many planters in the state in an economic pinch. South Carolina had protested loudly in 1828 when Congress passed the Tariff of Abominations. Calhoun, who had turned away from Clay's nationalist program to support southern interests and states' rights as the economy turned sour in 1819, led the protest.

In 1828, Calhoun wrote an anonymous pamphlet, *The South Carolina Exposition and Protest.* In it he argued that tariffs benefited only one part of the country rather than the nation at large and should be considered unconstitutional. More important, Calhoun echoed the Virginia and Kentucky Resolutions of 1798 in asserting that the states were the ultimate judge of the national government's legitimate power. The states had given up none of their sovereignty when they signed the Constitution. It was thus reserved for the states, not the Supreme Court, to judge the constitutionality of any law.

This reasoning led Calhoun to assert that the Tariff of Abominations could not be imposed on a state that believed it unjust. Such a state had the right to call a popular convention to consider a disputed law. If the state convention decided against the law, the law would not be binding within the state. In other words, a state had the right to declare the law invalid within the state's jurisdiction. This idea came to be called **nullification.**

As Calhoun's pamphlet circulated, nationalists like Clay and Jackson became more anxious about the potential threat to federal power. The first test came in 1830, when Senator Robert Y. Hayne of South Carolina and Senator **Daniel Webster** of Massachusetts debated Calhoun's ideas. Hayne supported Calhoun's ideas completely. Webster countered with one of the most stirring orations ever delivered in the Senate. Webster concluded his speech by proclaiming, "Liberty and Union, now and for ever, one and inseparable!"

Jackson soon made his position clear. At a political banquet, he offered a toast: "Our Federal Union—it must be preserved." Calhoun then rose and countered Jackson's toast with one of his own: "The Union—next to our liberty most dear. May we always remember that it can only be preserved by distributing evenly the benefits and burthens of the Union." These toasts marked a complete rift between Jackson and Calhoun, who had been elected as Jackson's vice president in 1828.

Two years passed before the crisis finally came to a head. In 1832, Jackson sought to enhance his re-election prospects by asking Congress to lower tariff rates. (Jackson dropped Calhoun as his running mate in favor of Martin Van Buren.) It gladly complied. This action still did not satisfy the nullifiers in South Carolina. They called for a special convention to consider the matter of the tariff. The convention met in November 1832 and voted overwhelmingly to nullify the tariff.

Jackson quickly proved true to his toast of two years before. Bristling that nullification violated the Constitution, Jackson immediately reinforced federal forts in South Carolina and sent warships to enforce the collection of the tariff. He also asked Congress to pass a "force bill" giving him the power to invade the rebellious state if necessary. In hopes of placating southerners and winning popular support in the upcoming election, Clay proposed and Congress passed a lowered tariff, but it also voted to give Jackson the power he asked for.

Passage of these measures prompted South Carolina to repeal its nullification of the tariff. But it then nullified the force bill. Although Jackson ignored this action, the problem was not resolved. The issue of federal versus states' rights continued to fester throughout the antebellum period.

Jackson and the Bank War

Jackson faced another major crisis related to federal power in 1832, this one involving the Second Bank of the United States. Casting about for an issue that might dampen Jackson's popularity in an election year, Webster and Clay seized on the bank. Although the bank's twenty-year charter was not due for renewal until 1836, several considerations led Jackson's political enemies to press for renewal on the eve of the 1832 election. First, Jackson was a known opponent of the bank. Second, the country was prosperous at the time, and the bank was apparently popular. Many attributed this prosperity

---

nullification   Refusal of a state to recognize or enforce a federal law within its boundaries.

Daniel Webster   Massachusetts senator and lawyer who was known for his forceful speeches and considered nullification a threat to the Union.

to the economic stability provided by the bank under the leadership of **Nicholas Biddle,** who had been its president since 1823. Proponents of the bank reasoned that Democratic unity might break down if Jackson opposed renewing the bank's charter.

Jackson's opponents were partially right. Congress passed the renewal bill and Jackson vetoed it, but the envisioned rift between Jackson and congressional Democrats did not open. The president stole the day by delivering a powerful veto message. Jackson denounced the Second Bank as an example of vested privilege and monopoly power that served the interests of "the few at the expense of the many" and injured "humbler members of society— the farmers, the mechanics, and laborers—who have neither the time nor the means of securing like favors to themselves." Jackson further asserted that foreign interests, many of which were seen as enemies to American rights, had used the bank to amass large blocks of American securities.

Although the charter was not renewed, the Second Bank could operate for four more years on its existing charter. Jackson, however, wanted to kill the bank immediately. His strategy was to withdraw federal funds from the bank and redeposit the money in state banks.

Powerless to stop the withdrawal of federal funds, Biddle sought to replace dwindling assets by calling in loans owed by state banks and by raising interest rates. In this way, the banker believed, he would not only head off the Second Bank's collapse, but would trigger a business panic that might force the government to reverse its course.

The Whig Alternative to Jacksonian Democracy

- What *expectations* did Jackson's opponents have when they built their coalition to oppose the Democrats?

- Was the *outcome* what they *expected*?

Although Jackson was perhaps the most popular president since George Washington, not all Americans agreed with his philosophy, policies, or political style. Men like Henry Clay and Daniel Webster opposed Jackson in and out of Congress. Gradually, anger over Jackson's policies and anxiety about the changing character of the nation convinced dissidents to combine into a new national party.

The End of the Old Party Structure

Jackson's enemies were deeply divided among themselves. Henry Clay had started the **Bank War** to rally Jackson's opponents behind a political cause. Southern politicians like Calhoun, however, feared and hated Clay's nationalistic policies as much as they did Jackson's assertions of federal power. And political outsiders like the Antimasons distrusted all political organizations.

The Antimasons kicked off the anti-Jackson campaign in September 1831 when they held a national nominating convention in Baltimore. The convention drew a wide range of people who were disgusted with politics as usual. Thurlow Weed cajoled the convention into nominating William Wirt, a respected lawyer from Maryland, as its presidential candidate. Weed fully *expected* that the Republicans would later rubber-stamp the Antimasonic nomination and present a united front against Jackson. But the Republicans, fearful of the Antimasons' odd combination of **machine politics** and antiparty philosophy, nominated Clay for president.

Even having two anti-Jackson parties in the running did not satisfy some. Distrustful of the Antimasons and hating Clay's nationalist philosophy, some southerners refused to support any of the announced candidates. They backed nullification advocate John Floyd of Virginia.

Lack of unity spelled disaster for Jackson's opponents. The president received 219 electoral votes to Clay's 49, Wirt's 7, and Floyd's 11. Despite unsettling changes in the land and continuing political chaos, the people still wanted the hero of New Orleans as their leader.

Nicholas Biddle   President of the Second Bank of the United States; he struggled to keep the bank functioning when President Jackson tried to undermine its powers.

Bank War   The political conflict that occurred when Andrew Jackson tried to destroy the Second Bank of the United States, which he thought represented special interests at the expense of the common man.

machine politics   The aggressive use of influence, favors, and tradeoffs by a political organization, or "machine," to mobilize support among its followers.

The New Political Coalition

If one lesson emerged clearly from the election of 1832, it was that Jackson's opponents needed to unite if they *expected* to challenge the Democrats successfully. By 1834 the various factions opposing Jackson had formed the **Whig Party.** The term "Whig" referred to the party in opposition to the British king. In adopting it, Clay and his associates delighted in calling attention to Jackson's growing power and what they saw as his monarchical pretensions. They took to calling Jackson "King Andrew."

Clay's supporters formed the heart of the Whigs. The nullifiers, however, quickly came around. Late in 1832, Clay and Calhoun joined forces in opposing Jackson's appointment of Van Buren as American minister to Britain. The Antimasons joined the Whig coalition prior to the 1834 congressional elections. Not only was Jackson a Mason, but his use of patronage and back-alley politics disgusted the Antimasons sufficiently to overcome their distrust of Clay's party philosophy. Christian reformers who wanted to eliminate alcohol, violations of the Sabbath, and dozens of other perceived evils also joined the Whigs. Evangelicals disapproved of Jackson's lifestyle and his views on issues ranging from slavery to alcohol.

The new Whig coalition proved its ability to challenge Jacksonian Democrats in the 1834 elections. In their first electoral contest, the Whigs won nearly 40 percent of the seats in the House and over 48 percent in the Senate.

Van Buren in the White House

Jackson had seemed to be a tower of strength when he was first elected to the presidency in 1828, but he was aging and ill by the end of his second term. Nearly 70 years old and plagued by various ailments, Old Hickory decided not to run for a third term. Instead, he did all that was within his power to ensure that Martin Van Buren would win the Democratic presidential nomination.

Meanwhile, Clay and the Whigs were hatching a novel strategy. Rather than holding a national convention and nominating one candidate, the Whigs let each region's party organization nominate its own candidates. As a result, four **favorite sons** ran on the Whig ticket: Daniel Webster of Massachusetts, Hugh Lawson White of Tennessee, W. P. Mangum of South Carolina, and William Henry Harrison of Ohio. Whig leaders hoped the large number of candidates would confuse voters and throw the election into the House of Representatives. This strategy failed narrowly. Van Buren squeaked by in the Electoral College, winning by a margin of less than 1 percent.

Van Buren's entire presidency was colored by the economic collapse that occurred just weeks after he took office. Although the Panic of 1837 was a direct *outcome* of the Bank War and Jackson's money policies, Van Buren bore the blame. The crisis had begun with Nicholas Biddle's manipulation of credit and interest rates in an effort to have the Second Bank rechartered. Jackson had added to the problem by issuing the **Specie Circular** on August 15, 1836. The intent of the Specie Circular was to make it more difficult for speculators to obtain public lands by requiring payment in specie for all public lands. The effect was to remove paper money from the economy.

The contraction in credit and currency had the same impact in 1837 as in 1819: the national economy collapsed. By May 1837, New York banks were no longer accepting any paper currency, a policy soon followed by all other banks. Hundreds of businesses, plantations, farms, factories, canals, and other enterprises were thrown into bankruptcy by the end of the year. Over a third of the population lost their jobs. Those fortunate enough to keep their jobs found their pay reduced by as much as 50 percent. The nation sank into an economic and an emotional depression.

As credit continued to collapse through 1838 and 1839, President Van Buren tried to address the problems but only made them worse. His first mistake was to continue Jackson's hard-money policy of accepting payment only in specie. The *outcome* was more contraction in the economy. Then, to keep the

---

Whig party   Political party that came into being in 1834 as an anti-Jackson coalition and that charged "King Andrew" with executive tyranny.

favorite son   A candidate nominated for office by delegates from his or her own region or state.

Specie Circular   Order issued by President Jackson in 1836 stating that the federal government would accept only gold and silver as payment for public land.

government solvent, Van Buren cut federal spending to the bone, accelerating the downward economic spiral. The public began referring to him as Martin Van Ruin.

Log-Cabin and Hard-Cider Campaign of 1840

The Whigs had learned their lesson in 1836: only a party united behind one candidate could possibly beat the Democrats. For that candidate, they *chose* William Henry Harrison, the hero of Tippecanoe. The general had a distinguished military record and few enemies. **John Tyler,** a Virginian who had bolted from the Democrats during the Bank War, was *chosen* as his running mate.

Although the economy was in bad shape, the Whigs avoided addressing any serious issues. Instead, they launched a smear campaign against Van Buren. The Whig press portrayed Van Buren, the son of a tavernkeeper, as an aristocrat with expensive tastes in clothes, food, and furniture. Harrison, in contrast, had been born into the Virginia aristocracy, but the Whigs characterized him as a simple frontiersman who had risen to greatness through his own efforts. Whig claims were so extravagant that the Democratic press soon satirized Harrison in political cartoons as a rustic hick rocking on the porch of a log cabin and swilling hard cider. The satire backfired. Whig newspapers and speechmakers sold Harrison, the long-time political insider, as a simple man of the people who truly lived in a log cabin. At campaign rallies, Whigs passed out cider to voters while they chanted, "Van, Van, Van, Oh! Van is a used-up man."

Unfortunately for Van Buren, the slogan was on target. By the time the cider had been drunk and the votes counted, Harrison was swept out of his log cabin and into the White House.

Toward an American Culture

- What *choices* did Americans make in dealing with the stresses created by rapid change during the Jacksonian era?
- What was the cultural *outcome*?

The profound political, social, and economic changes of the early nineteenth century gave birth to a distinctively American culture during Jackson's era. One of the distinguishing characteristics of this culture was a widely shared commitment to individualism. Americans came to believe that the individual was responsible for his or her destiny. They stressed the power of the individual self, not fate or accidents of birth. The popularity of Andrew Jackson, the quintessential self-made man, reflected Americans' beliefs in individualism.

Romanticism, a European import, was another major ingredient in the shaping of contemporary American culture. The Romantics in Europe rebelled against Enlightenment rationalism, stressing the heart over the mind, the wild over the controlled, the mystical over the rational. The combination of romanticism and individualism gave American writers and artists a new vocabulary for portraying the American experience.

The Transcendentalist Mood

Romanticism and individualism had their earliest and perhaps greatest impact in the religious realm, and their greatest spokesman in **Ralph Waldo Emerson.** Emerson by 1829 had become pastor of the prestigious Second Unitarian Church in Boston. He was thrown into a religious crisis, however, when his young wife, Ellen Louisa, died in 1831 after only two years of marriage.

Emerson could find no consolation in the rationalism of **Unitarianism.** He sought alternatives in

---

John Tyler   Virginia senator who left the Democratic party after conflicts with Andrew Jackson; he was elected vice president in 1840 and became president when Harrison died.

Romanticism   Artistic and intellectual movement characterized by interest in nature, emphasis on emotion and imagination, and rebellion against social conventions.

Ralph Waldo Emerson   Philosopher, writer, and poet whose essays and poems made him a central figure in the transcendentalist movement and an important figure in the development of literary expression in America.

Unitarianism   Christian religious association that considers God alone to be divine; it holds that all people are granted salvation and that faith should be based on reason and conscience.

Europe, where he met the famous Romantic poets William Wordsworth and Thomas Carlyle. They taught Emerson to seek truth in nature and spirit rather than in reason and order. Building from their insights, Emerson created a new philosophy and religion called **Transcendentalism.** Recovered from his grief, he returned to the United States to begin a new career as an essayist and lecturer.

The problem with historical Christianity, Emerson told students at the Harvard Divinity School in 1838, is that it treated revelation as "long ago given and done, as if God were dead." Emerson, however, believed that revelation could happen at any time and that God was everywhere. Only through direct contact with the **transcendent** power in the universe could men and women know the truth. "It cannot be received at second hand," Emerson insisted, but only through the independent working of the liberated mind.

Although Emerson emphasized **nonconformity** and dissent in his writings, his ideas were in tune with the economic currents of his day. In celebrating the individual, Emerson validated the surging individualism of Jacksonian America. Rather than condemning the "selfish cupidity" that French visitor Alexis de Tocqueville said characterized Jacksonian America, Emerson stated that money represented the "prose of life." Little wonder, then, that Emerson's ideas found a wide following among young people of means in the Northeast.

American Scenes in Art and Literature

Emerson's declaration of literary independence from European models in an 1837 address entitled "The American Scholar" set a bold new direction for American literature. During the next twenty years, Henry David Thoreau, Walt Whitman, Henry Wadsworth Longfellow, and others spread the Transcendentalist message, emphasizing the uniqueness of the individual and the role of literature as a vehicle for self-discovery. "I celebrate myself, and sing myself," Whitman proclaimed in *Leaves of Grass,* published in 1855. Like the Romantics, the Transcendentalists celebrated the primitive and the common. Longfellow wrote of the legendary Indian chief Hiawatha and sang the praises of the village blacksmith. In "I Hear America Singing," Whitman made poetry of the everyday speech of mechanics, carpenters, and other common folk.

Perhaps the most radical of the Transcendentalists was Emerson's good friend **Henry David Thoreau.** Emerson advocated self-reliance, but Thoreau embodied it. He lived for several years at Walden Pond near Concord, Massachusetts, where he did his best to live independently of the rapidly modernizing market economy. "I went to the woods because I wished to live deliberately," Thoreau wrote, "and not, when I came to die, discover that I had not lived."

James Fenimore Cooper, Herman Melville, Nathaniel Hawthorne, and Edgar Allan Poe pushed American literature in a romantic direction. Even before Emerson's "American Scholar," Cooper had launched a new sort of American novel and American hero. In *The Pioneers* (1823), Cooper introduced Natty Bumppo, a frontiersman whose honesty, independent-mindedness, and skill as a marksman represented the rough-hewn virtues so beloved by romantics. Altogether, Cooper wrote five novels featuring the plucky Bumppo.

Like Cooper, Herman Melville emphasized primitive scenes and noble savages in his adventure novels. Beginning with *Typee* (1846), Melville's semi-autobiographical accounts of an American seaman among the natives of the South Pacific became overnight bestsellers. Melville followed these with his most famous novel, *Moby Dick* (1851), an **allegorical** tale of a good man turned bad by his obsession for revenge against a whale he believed to be evil. Literary critics and the public hated *Moby Dick.*

Transcendentalism   A philosophical and literary movement asserting the existence of God within human beings and in nature and the belief that intuition is the highest source of knowledge.

transcendent   Lying beyond the normal range of experience.

nonconformity   Refusal to accept or conform to the beliefs and practices of the majority.

Henry David Thoreau   Writer and naturalist and friend of Ralph Waldo Emerson; his best-known work is *Walden* (1854).

allegorical   Having the characteristics of an allegory, a literary device in which characters and events stand for abstract ideas.

Nathaniel Hawthorne had more financial success than Melville in exploring the contest between good and evil. In his first famous work, *Twice-Told Tales* (1837), Hawthorne presented readers with a collection of moral allegories stressing the evils of pride, selfishness, and secret guilt. He brought these themes to fruition in his 1850 novel *The Scarlet Letter*, in which adulteress Hester Prynne overcomes shame to gain redemption and her secret lover, Puritan minister Arthur Dimmesdale, is destroyed by his hidden sins.

Edgar Allan Poe excelled in telling **Gothic** tales of pure terror. For Poe, the purpose of writing was to stir the passions of the reader. Poe tried to instill fear, which he believed was the strongest emotion. Haunting short stories like "The Tell-Tale Heart," "Masque of the Red Death," and "Pit and the Pendulum" did precisely that.

The drive to celebrate America and American uniqueness also influenced the visual arts during this period. Greek and Roman themes had dominated American art through the first decades of the nineteenth century. Horatio Greenough's statue of George Washington, for example, depicted the nation's first president wrapped in a toga.

After 1825, however, American scenes gradually replaced classical ones. Thomas Cole, a British immigrant painter, was the dominant force in this movement. Cole fell in love with the landscapes he saw in New York's Hudson River Valley. The refreshing naturalness and Americanness of Cole's paintings created a large following known as the **Hudson River school**, who lived in and painted landscapes of this valley.

George Caleb Bingham started a different artistic trend in his realistic pictures of common people engaged in everyday activities. He departed from traditional portrait artists, who painted the well-to-do posed in their finery. The flatboatmen, marketplace dwellers, and electioneering politicians in Bingham's paintings were artistic testimony to the emerging democratic style of America in the Jacksonian period.

Radical Attempts to Regain Community

Some religious groups and thinkers tried to ward off the excesses of Jacksonian individualism by forming communities that experimented with various living arrangements and ideological commitments. Nearly all of these experiments were in the North, where the unsettling effects of a market-driven economy were felt most acutely. Those who joined these communes hoped to strike a new balance between self-sufficiency and community support.

Brook Farm, a commune near Boston founded by transcendentalist George Ripley in 1841, was such a community. Ripley's goal in establishing Brook Farm was to "permit a more wholesome and simple life than can be led amidst the pressure of our competitive institutions." Each member of the community was *expected* to work on the farm to make the group self-sufficient. Brook Farm attracted few residents during its first few years. The adoption in 1844 of the **socialist** ideas of Frenchman Charles Fourier, however, attracted numerous artisans and farmers. **Fourierism** emphasized community self-sufficiency but also called for the equal sharing of earnings among members of the community. A disastrous fire in 1845 cut the experiment short. Brook Farm was one of nearly a hundred Fourierist communities founded during this period from Massachusetts to Michigan. All ended in failure.

Gothic   A style of fiction that emphasizes mystery, horror, and the supernatural; it is so named because the action often takes place in gloomy, ghost-infested castles built in the medieval Gothic style of architecture.

Hudson River school   The first native school of landscape painting in the United States (1825–1875); it attracted artists rebelling against the neoclassical tradition.

Brook Farm   An experimental farm based on cooperative living; established in 1841, it first attracted transcendentalists and then serious farmers before fire destroyed it in 1845.

socialist   Someone who believes in the public ownership of manufacturing, farming, and other forms of production so that they benefit society rather than create individual profit.

Fourierism   Social system advanced by Charles Fourier, who argued that people were capable of living in perfect harmony under the right conditions, which included communal life and republican government.

So did Robert Owen's community at New Harmony, Indiana. Owen, a wealthy Welsh industrialist, believed that the solution to poverty was to collect the unemployed into self-contained and self-supporting villages. In 1825, Owen attempted to put his ideas into practice when he purchased an existing agricultural commune. At **New Harmony,** Owen opened a textile factory in which ownership was held communally and decisions were made by group consensus. Despite such innovations, internal dissent and economic difficulties forced New Harmony to close in 1827.

Communal experiments based on religious ideas fared much better than those founded on secular theories. The **Oneida Community,** established in central New York in 1848, reflected the religious ideas of its founder, John Humphrey Noyes. No church was willing to ordain him because of his beliefs that Christ had already returned to earth and had commanded his followers to live communally and to practice group marriage. Unlike Brook Farm and New Harmony, the Oneida Community was financially successful, establishing thriving logging, farming, and manufacturing businesses. It finally disbanded in 1881 because of local outcries about the "free love" practiced by its members.

The **Shakers** avoided the Oneida Community's problems by banning sex altogether. Called the "Shaking Quakers" because of the ecstatic dances they performed as part of their worship services, or more simply the "Shakers," they grew steadily after their founder, Ann Lee, emigrated from Great Britain in 1774. By 1826 there were eighteen Shaker communities in eight states. The Shakers at one time claimed nearly six thousand members. The Shakers' emphasis on celibacy stemmed from their belief that sexuality promoted selfishness and sinfulness. Farming activities and the manufacture and sale of widely admired furniture and handicrafts brought them success. After 1860, however, recruiting new members became difficult. The Shakers' rules of celibacy ultimately spelled their demise.

By far the most successful of these communal groups were the Mormons. They harnessed the religious fervor of the Second Great Awakening, the Romantics' appeal to the primitive, and the inclination to communal living displayed by the Shakers and other groups. This peculiarly American movement was founded by **Joseph Smith, Jr.,** a New York farmer. Smith claimed in 1827 that an angel had led him to a set of golden plates inscribed in a strange hieroglyphic language. Smith's translation of these plates resulted in the Book of Mormon, printed in 1830.

Smith then founded the Church of Jesus Christ of Latter-Day Saints, also called the Mormon church, after the prophet Mormon, who had written the golden plates. A revelation inspired Smith in 1831 to lead his congregation out of New York to Kirtland, Ohio. Stressing community, faith, and hard work, the **Mormons** thrived there for a while. More traditional Protestants, however, regarded Smith's followers with suspicion, envy, and hostility. Their misgivings increased markedly after 1840, when Smith and other elders in the church began to practice **polygamy.** Increasing persecution convinced Smith to lead his followers farther west into Missouri.

The Mormons found Missouri frontiersmen no less resentful than easterners. Smith then decided to lead his congregation to Illinois, founding the city of Nauvoo in 1840. Continuing conversions to the new faith brought a flood of Mormons to Smith's Zion in Illinois. In 1844, Nauvoo, with a population of fifteen thousand Mormons, dwarfed every other Illinois city.

New Harmony   Utopian community that Robert Owen established in Indiana in 1825; economic problems and discord among members led to its failure two years later.

Oneida Community   A religious community established in central New York in 1848; its members shared property, practiced group marriage, and reared children under communal care.

Shakers   A mid-eighteenth-century offshoot of the Quakers, Shakers practiced communal living and strict celibacy; they gained members only by conversion.

Joseph Smith, Jr.   Founder of the Church of Jesus Christ of Latter-Day Saints, also known as the Mormon church; he led his congregation westward from New York to Illinois, where he was murdered by an anti-Mormon mob.

Mormons   Members of the church founded by Joseph Smith in 1830; Mormon doctrines are based on the Bible, the Book of Mormon, and revelations made to church leaders.

polygamy   The practice of having more than one husband or wife at a time.

SUMMARY

E xpectations
C onstraints
C hoices
O utcomes

Choices that politicians and their constituents made during the 1820s changed American politics in profound ways. As traditional *constraints* on political participation were removed, Americans basked in the *expectation* that they would control their own affairs.

Americans' *choice* of Andrew Jackson as president in 1828 promised to fulfill their *expectations* for more political responsiveness. Jackson soon encountered *constraints*. His need to satisfy regional constituencies on financial matters, the tariff, and Indian policy ended up satisfying no one. The *outcome* was a series of regional crises—the Bank War, nullification, and Indian removal—that alienated each region and together constituted a crisis of national proportions.

American optimism weakened under the weight of these *constraints* and hit rock bottom during the Panic of 1837. Exploiting disappointed *expectations*, the Whigs formed a national coalition to challenge Jackson's party. The political *outcome* was the nation's first "modern" presidential election in 1840. In it, hullabaloo and image-making eclipsed issues as the central concern.

Alienated by political posturing, competitive individualism, and the breakdown of traditional community, many Americans looked for alternative sources of inspiration. Some *chose* to join farming communes like Brook Farm. Others slipped into the radical lifestyles advocated by John Humphrey Noyes and the Shakers. Some *chose* to adapt their lives to the preaching of the Second Great Awakening exhorters. Others followed Joseph Smith. Still others celebrated the chaos, *choosing* to embrace individualism and romanticism and, like Walt Whitman, sing of themselves. The *outcome* of all this social and cultural experimentation was increasing rather than decreasing tension. Change was begetting change in every aspect of American life.

SUGGESTED READINGS

Rogin, Michael Paul. *Fathers and Children: Andrew Jackson and the Subjugation of the American Indian* (1975).

A controversial and enjoyable psychoanalysis of Andrew Jackson. Focuses on his Indian policy but gives an interesting view of his entire personality.

Ward, John William. *Andrew Jackson: Symbol for an Age* (1955).

A classic and fascinating view of Jackson: how he was shaped as a man and reasons for his dramatic hold on the American imagination.

The Last of the Mohicans (1993).

A truly transcendental film rendition of James Fenimore Cooper's novel. Captures Cooper's romantic flair and Thomas Cole's vision of Hudson River scenery.

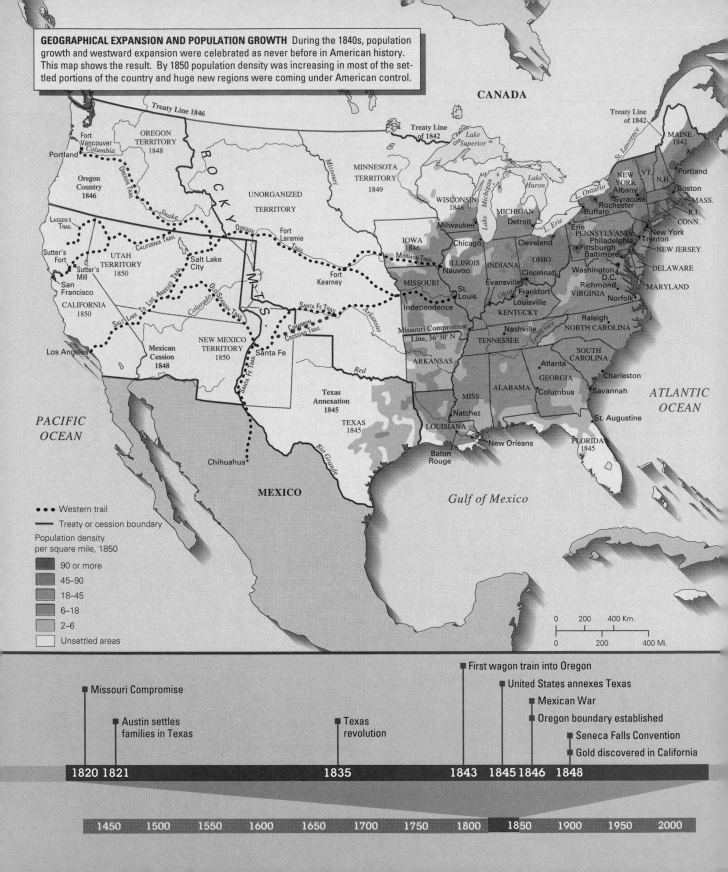

GEOGRAPHICAL EXPANSION AND POPULATION GROWTH During the 1840s, population growth and westward expansion were celebrated as never before in American history. This map shows the result. By 1850 population density was increasing in most of the settled portions of the country and huge new regions were coming under American control.

CANADA

Treaty Line 1846

Treaty Line of 1842

OREGON TERRITORY 1848

Fort Vancouver
Columbia
Portland

Oregon Country 1846

R O C K Y

MINNESOTA TERRITORY 1849

Missouri

Treaty Line of 1842

Lake Superior

Treaty Line of 1842

MAINE 1842

LASSEN'S TRAIL

Sutter's Fort

UTAH TERRITORY 1850

Salt Lake City

Fort Laramie

Snake

OREGON TRAIL

CALIFORNIA TRAIL

M T S.

Fort Kearney

WISCONSIN 1848

Lake Michigan

MICHIGAN
Detroit

Lake Huron

Milwaukee

Chicago

Cleveland

L. Ontario

L. Erie

Erie

Buffalo

Rochester

Syracuse

Albany

VT

N.H.

Portland

Boston

MASS.

R.I.
CONN.

NEW YORK

Sutter's Mill

San Francisco

CALIFORNIA 1850

SALT LAKE TO LOS ANGELES TRAIL

OLD SPANISH TRAIL

Colorado

Santa Fe Trail

CIMARRON CROSSING TRAIL

IOWA 1846

MORMON TRAIL

ILLINOIS
Nauvoo

MISSOURI

St. Louis

Independence

Missouri Compromise Line, 36°30' N

INDIANA

OHIO

Cincinnati

Evansville

Ohio

Frankfort
Louisville

KENTUCKY

Nashville

PENNSYLVANIA
Pittsburgh

Washington, D.C.

Richmond

VIRGINIA

Norfolk

Philadelphia

Baltimore

NEW JERSEY

DELAWARE

MARYLAND

New York
Trenton

Los Angeles

Mexican Cession 1848

NEW MEXICO TERRITORY 1850

SANTA FE TRAIL

Santa Fe

Arkansas

ARKANSAS

Red

TENNESSEE

Tennessee

Raleigh

NORTH CAROLINA

SOUTH CAROLINA

Atlanta

GEORGIA

Charleston

Columbus

Savannah

Texas Annexation 1845

TEXAS 1845

MISS.

ALABAMA

Natchez

LOUISIANA

Baton Rouge

New Orleans

St. Augustine

FLORIDA 1845

Chihuahua

Rio Grande

MEXICO

Gulf of Mexico

PACIFIC OCEAN

ATLANTIC OCEAN

• • • Western trail

—— Treaty or cession boundary

Population density per square mile, 1850

90 or more
45–90
18–45
6–18
2–6
Unsettled areas

0   200   400 Km.
0   200   400 Mi.

First wagon train into Oregon

United States annexes Texas

Missouri Compromise

Mexican War

Oregon boundary established

Austin settles families in Texas

Texas revolution

Seneca Falls Convention

Gold discovered in California

1820 1821   1835   1843 1845 1846 1848

1450 1500 1550 1600 1650 1700 1750 1800 1850 1900 1950 2000

Westward Expansion and Manifest Destiny, 1841–1849

The Explosion Westward

- What *expectations* pulled Americans westward between 1820 and 1848?

The Social Fabric in the West

- To what extent did people in the West *expect* to create new and different societies in that region?

- What sorts of cultures emerged in response to western *constraints*?

The Triumph of "Manifest Destiny"

- What political *expectations* did Americans have when they pushed forcefully beyond the Mississippi River?

- Did their *choices* result in the *outcomes* they *expected*?

Expansion and Sectional Crisis

- How did the slavery issue and differing economic values interact with various Americans' *expectations* to create a crisis in the 1840s?

INTRODUCTION

E xpectations
C onstraints
C hoices
O utcomes

The election of frontier hero William Henry Harrison to the presidency in 1840 was but one milestone in a progressive westward tilt in the nation's political and cultural focus. As transportation systems extended the American frontier and as industrialization generated new capital, speculators invested in the newly opened West. Americans looking for economic opportunities, places to transplant particular religious or political beliefs, or simply adventure followed those entrepreneurs. They *expected* to find a wide-open land of opportunity.

But men and women moving into the West faced many *constraints*. The land itself was often not what they *expected*. Water was frequently in short supply, and wild animals were a constant threat to crops and livestock. In addition, most of the land in the West was already claimed by Indians, the Spanish, or the British.

Environmental and cultural *constraints* forced change on pioneers and led to the creation of new societies. Mormon farmers in the Utah deserts, for example, had to learn to cooperate with each other in building irrigation systems. Pioneers in the Southwest had to learn about the Spanish language and culture.

Westward expansion brought great pressure to bear on the nation's political and economic institutions. Easterners disagreed about what institutions should be planted in the new territories. Southerners *expected* to spread cotton agriculture. Northerners were equally convinced that a diversified entrepreneurial economy was the wave of the future. And each region had specific notions about tariffs, taxes, the money supply, and the role of the federal government in the economy.

Each section *chose* to push for its own vision of westward expansion, but each met *constraints*. The United States fought a war with Mexico and then faced a national crisis over what to do with newly acquired territories. The *outcome* was a political dispute that rocked the halls of Congress and moved some to call for outright civil disobedience.

At the core of the debate lay the issue of slavery. Although only a few Americans were disturbed about its moral implications, slavery symbolized the cultural, economic, and political differences between northerners and southerners. Independent farmers and businessmen feared the *constraint* of competition from wealthy southern planters. Workers, too, wondered how they could compete successfully against slave laborers. While more and more people in the North and Old Northwest *chose* to raise their voices against the expansion of slavery, southerners worked all the harder to ensure their freedom to take slaves anywhere they *chose*.

As the debate over slavery and expansion broadened, another group of Americans chafed under discrimination. Evangelical women had *chosen* to join a wide variety of reform movements, including abolitionism, but they found that their sex was a major *constraint* to their participation. Few men were willing to give them the political and economic voice they believed they needed to carry out their mission. Increasing frustration was the *outcome* for such women.

The Explosion Westward

• What *expectations* pulled Americans westward between 1820 and 1848?

Western pioneers seldom sought to create new lifestyles for themselves, but the physical and cultural environments in the West shaped their society in peculiar ways. The cultures that emerged in the West contrasted sharply with those in the industrializing North and the plantation South.

Early Western Pioneers

As canal systems, steamboat lines, improved roads, and early railroads extended the American frontier,

CHRONOLOGY

Expansion and Crisis

1820	Missouri Compromise
1821	Stephen F. Austin settles Americans in Texas
1828	Jackson elected
1834	Mexican government begins seizure of California mission lands
1835	Texas Revolution begins
1836	Rebellion against Mexican rule in California
1838	Senate rejects annexation of Texas Armed confrontation between Maine and New Brunswick Trail of Tears
1839	John Sutter founds New Helvetia
1840	Log Cabin campaign
1841	John Tyler becomes president Congress passes pre-emption bill
1842	Elijah White named federal Indian agent for Oregon
1843	First wagon train into Oregon First Organic Laws adopted in Oregon
1844	James K. Polk elected president Murder of Joseph Smith
1845	United States annexes Texas John L. O'Sullivan articulates "manifest destiny"
1846	Mexican War begins Oregon boundary established; United States and Britain end joint occupation California declares itself a republic
1847	Whitman Massacre Mormons arrive in Utah
1848	Gold discovered in California Zachary Taylor elected president Seneca Falls Convention Treaty of Guadalupe Hidalgo
1855	Indians in the Pacific Northwest settled on reservations

adventurous speculators viewed the West as a source of new wealth. Fur-trapping mountain men, land speculators, and gold seekers flowed into the **Far West** seeking their fortunes and opened the region for the farmers and shopkeepers who would follow.

The image of the lone trapper braving a hostile environment and even more hostile Indians is the stuff of American adventure novels and movies. Although characters like Christopher ("Kit") Carson and Jeremiah ("Crow Killer") Johnson really did exist, what is missing from the fur trade legend are the merchant-capitalists who financed this industry and reaped enormous rewards.

John Jacob Astor, a German immigrant, led the way. Astor established a string of trading posts from St. Louis to the Pacific. Although he instructed his employees to treat Indian trappers well, his intention was to get them into debt, thereby obliging them to trade only at his posts. The key to Astor's fur empire was the post he built at the mouth of the Columbia River in 1811. From there, Astor shipped furs directly to Asia, where rival British companies were not permitted to trade. In Asia, the furs were exchanged for tea, spices, silks, and other goods. His fur business and Asia trade did so well that when he

> **Far West** In North America, the lands west of the Mississippi River.

died in 1848, John Jacob Astor was the richest man in the United States.

Auguste Chouteau's vision of the fur business was less panoramic. A French frontiersman, Chouteau had helped to found the town of St. Louis and to establish France's fur ventures in the Southwest. He and his brother Pierre employed an extensive kinship network that included French, Spanish, and Indian connections. The Chouteau brothers were able to extend their reach deep into the Missouri region and as far as Spanish Santa Fe. Like Astor, Auguste Chouteau depended on Indians to provide the labor in hunting furs.

A former Astor employee and one-time partner of Chouteau, William Henry Ashley broke the tradition of depending exclusively on Indian labor. In 1825, he set up the highly successful **rendezvous system** for collecting pelts. Under this arrangement, individual trappers like Kit Carson combed the upper Missouri for furs. Once each year Ashley conducted a fur rendezvous in the mountains, where the trappers brought their furs and exchanged them for goods.

Ashley's, Chouteau's, and Astor's strategies for extracting wealth from the Far West made these men extremely rich and important. But the success of their business inadvertently led to its decline. Astor's Asia trade opened the way for vast silk imports. Soon silk hats became a fashion rage in both America and Europe, replacing beaver hats that had sustained the fur trade. In addition, the efficiency of these enterprises virtually wiped out beaver populations in the Rocky Mountains. By the 1830s the beaver business had slowed to a near standstill.

Many beaver hunters stayed in the West to become founding members of new communities. As early as 1840, fur trapper Robert ("Doc") Newell reportedly told his companion Joe Meek, "Come, we are all done with this life in the mountains—done with wading in Beaver-dams, and freezing or starving alternately—done with Indian trading and Indian fighting. The fur trade is dead in the Rocky Mountains, and it is no place for us now, if ever it was." The two men then headed to the Willamette Valley in Oregon to become settlers.

Often the first to join the former fur trappers in the West were not rugged yeoman farmers but highly organized and well-financed land specula-

tors. Liberalization of the land laws during the first half of the nineteenth century had put smaller tracts within reach of more citizens, but speculators continued to play a role in land distribution by offering even smaller tracts and more liberal credit.

A third group of expectant fortune hunters was lured into the Far West by the discovery of gold. Most fortune hunters did not find gold, but many stayed to establish trading businesses, banks, and farms. Others moved on, still seeking their fortunes. But usually they too eventually settled down to become shopkeepers, farmers, and entrepreneurs.

The Attraction of the West

The underlying cause for westward migration was the hope of economic opportunity. The promise of cheap land was especially enticing after the panics of 1819 and 1837.

Although the promise of economic opportunity pulled most people westward, some were pushed westward, particularly New Englanders. Two sources of land pressure combined to uproot these descendants of Puritans. First, the New England tradition of dividing family holdings equally among adult children had created a shortage of workable farms in the region. Second, innovations in spinning and weaving wool had created a sheep-raising craze in New England after 1824. Sheep required little labor but a lot of land. Between 1825 and 1840 sheep displaced people throughout much of the New England countryside as smaller, poorer farmers sold out.

Thus young people in New England faced a *choice* between moving into cities or heading west. Those who opted to migrate westward sought an environment friendly to their moral and religious outlook in areas like upper New York, Michigan, and Oregon, where Protestant missionaries were establishing little New Englands in the wilderness.

> **rendezvous system**   A system in which trappers gathered furs independently in their own territories and met traders once a year to exchange the furs for goods.

The Westward Migration

The image of the independent farmer fleeing the restrictions of civilized life and hewing out a living on the frontier is a persistent myth in American history. Although a few antisocial sorts moved to the frontier to escape neighbors, most went west as part of a larger community.

Most migrants to Texas in the 1820s and 1830s came in large groups under the direction of men like **Stephen F. Austin.** Beginning in 1821, the Spanish government in Mexico gave these **empresarios** land grants and the right to assess fees in exchange for encouraging settlement in its northern colony. Spanish authorities stipulated that all of the families had to be Roman Catholic or be willing to convert.

Austin offered families land for a filing fee of only 12½ cents per acre and had no trouble finding willing settlers. He led his first overland party from Louisiana into Texas in 1821. After Mexico became independent of Spain in 1822, Austin convinced the Mexican government to extend his license.

The first permanent agricultural settlements in the Pacific Northwest were begun by Protestant missionaries to the Indians. These missionaries encouraged mass migration to the new territory. Their calls appealed to people eager for economic opportunity in familiar cultural surroundings. When the Methodist church issued a call for a "great reinforcement" for its mission in Oregon, it received a flood of applications. Three separate reinforcements arrived in Oregon by ship in 1840. But it was not until 1843 that large-scale immigration began.

Beginning in the spring of 1843 and every spring thereafter for decades, families from all over the East gathered in Missouri to start the overland trek by wagon train. Although trail life was novel for most of the Oregon-bound emigrants, the division in domestic labor remained much as it was at home. "Everybody was supposed to rise at daylight, and while the women were preparing breakfast, the men rounded up the cattle, took down the tents, yoked the oxen to the wagons and made everything ready for an immediate start after the morning meal was finished," one young pioneer woman remembered. Even social customs remained the same. "We were expected to visit our neighbors when we paused for rest," the same woman noted. "If we did not, we were designated as 'high-toned' or 'stuck-up.'"

And so life went on during the six months it took to cross the more than 2,000 miles to the **Oregon Country.** Families arriving in Oregon tended to settle in rings around the existing missions, which soon became the hubs for transplanted New England–style villages.

The Mormons established another migration pattern into the **Great Basin.** After Joseph Smith was murdered by a mob in Carthage, Illinois, in 1844, the remaining church leaders concluded that the Mormons would never be safe until they moved far from mainstream American civilization. **Brigham Young,** Smith's successor, led sixteen hundred Mormons beyond the Rocky Mountains in search of a refuge. On July 24, 1847, Young's advance party finally pushed into the valley of the **Great Salt Lake.**

Despite their differences, pioneers shared the fundamental problem of being short of hard cash. Western farmers barely made ends meet when conditions were good and fell into debt when weather or other hazards interrupted farming. Still, those who were lucky and exercised careful management could carve out excellent livings. Strongly centralized authority and a deeply felt sense of community helped the Mormons to prosper. Many in other communities, however, had their land repossessed or had to sell out to pay off creditors.

Stephen F. Austin   American colonizer in Texas who was imprisoned by the Mexican government on suspicion of revolutionary sympathies and who later took part in the Texas Revolution.

empresario   In the Spanish colonies, a person who organized and led a group of settlers in exchange for land grants and the right to assess fees.

Oregon Country   The region to the north of Spanish California extending from the crest of the Rocky Mountains to the Pacific Coast.

Great Basin   A desert region including most of present-day Nevada and parts of Utah, California, Idaho, Wyoming, and Oregon.

Brigham Young   Mormon leader who took over in 1844 after Joseph Smith's death and guided the Mormons from Illinois to Utah, where they established a permanent home for the church.

Great Salt Lake   A shallow, salty lake in the Great Basin, about 83 miles long and 51 miles wide; the Mormons established a permanent settlement near it in 1847.

Many pioneers had no legal claim to their farms. People often settled wherever they could find unoccupied land. Thousands of squatters living on unsold federal lands were a problem for the national government when the time came to sell off the public domain. Western politicians frequently advocated bills guaranteeing "squatter rights." They finally maneuvered the passage of a **pre-emption bill** in 1841 that gave squatters the right to settle on unsurveyed federal land. Squatters still had to buy the land once it came up for sale.

The Social Fabric in the West

- To what extent did people in the West *expect* to create new and different societies in that region?
- What sorts of cultures emerged in response to western *constraints*?

Migrants to Texas, Oregon, and Utah seldom intended to create a new social order in the West. Rather, they intended to recreate the society they were leaving behind. The physical and cultural environments into which they moved, however, forced change on them. Pioneers had to accommodate themselves to the geography and people they found there. Thus some significant differences in the culture and society of the Far West emerged.

The New Cotton Country

Migrants to cotton country in Texas and Arkansas often started out as landless herders. These families carved out claims beyond the **frontier line** and worked as herders until they could put the land into production. Frequently they did not have to clear land because Indians had already done so.

Although some areas were cleared and extremely fertile, others were swampy, rocky, and unproductive. Differences in the quality of land helped to recreate the southern class system in the new lands. Those fortunate enough to get profitable lands might become great planters; those less fortunate had to settle for lesser prosperity.

Southern pioneers devoted most of their time to the tasks necessary for survival. Even their social and recreational life tended to center on practical tasks. House building, planting, and harvesting were often done in cooperation with neighbors. On such occasions plenty of food and homemade whiskey were consumed. Women gathered together separately for large-scale projects like group quilting. Another community event for southwestern settlers was the periodic religious revival, which might last for days. Here they could make new acquaintances, court sweethearts, and discuss the common failings in their souls and on their farms.

Westering Yankees

The frontier experience for migrants to Michigan and Oregon differed from that of southwesterners. In the Old Northwest, as Indians such as the Winnebagos were pushed out, pioneers snatched up their deserted farms. Settlers quickly established villages like those left behind in New England. Law courts, churches, and schools were likely to be the first institutions brought into being in northwestern towns. These institutions and the similarity of this region to New England helped to prevent the growth of class distinctions that had developed so quickly along the southern frontier.

Conditions in the Oregon Country resembled those farther east in most respects, but some significant differences did exist. Most important, the Indians in the Oregon Country had never practiced agriculture. Their environment was so rich in fish, meat, and wild vegetables that farming was unnecessary. Large, open prairies flanking the Columbia, Willamette, and other rivers provided fertile farmland.

Much like the Indians in colonial New England, the Nez Percés, Cayuses, and Kalapuyas made whites welcome. In 1831, the Nez Percés and the Flatheads even issued an appeal for whites to come live among them. Although occasional tensions arose between white settlers and Indians, no serious conflict took place until 1847, when a disillusioned group of Cayuse Indians killed missionaries Marcus

pre-emption bill A temporary law that gave squatters the right to buy land they had settled on before it was offered for sale at public auction.

frontier line The outer limit of agricultural settlement bordering on the wilderness.

and Narcissa Whitman. The Whitman Massacre triggered the Cayuse War and a concerted effort by white Americans to confine all the northwestern tribes to reservations. By 1855 this effort had succeeded.

California and the Southwest

Frontier life in California was unique in many ways. One major reason was that the Spanish left a lasting cultural imprint on California. Spanish exploration into what is now California did not begin until 1769. Prompted by Russian expansion into North America, the Spanish established garrisons at San Diego and Monterey. Eventually Franciscan monks established twenty-one missions, each placed one day's travel from the next, extending from San Diego to the town of Sonoma, north of San Francisco.

The mission system provided a skeleton for Spanish settlement in California. The missions were soon surrounded by groves, vineyards, and lush farms, all tended by California Indians, who often became virtual slaves. Although the death rate among the mission Indians was terrible, their labor turned California's coastal plain into a vast and productive garden.

The Franciscans continued to control these missions after Mexico won its independence from Spain. Between 1834 and 1840, however, the Mexican government seized the California missions and sold them off to private citizens. An elite class of Spanish-speaking Californians snatched up the rich lands. Never numbering more than about a thousand people, this Hispanic elite eventually owned some 15 million acres of California's richest land. In 1836, the **Californios** and non-Hispanic newcomers together rebelled against Mexico to place Californio Juan Bautista Alvarado in the governorship of California. The landholding elite never ended California's official relationship with Mexico but nevertheless ran the region's government.

At first, the Californios welcomed outsiders as neighbors and trading partners. Ships from the United States called at California ports regularly, picking up cargoes of beef **tallow** and cow hides. The settlers they brought were given generous grants and assistance to open up new lands and businesses. **John Sutter,** for example, a Swiss immi-

♦ Using Indian labor, Franciscan missionaries transformed the dry California coastal plain into a blooming garden and built beautiful missions in which to celebrate their religion. This early nineteenth-century painting by Oriana Day shows the Carmel Mission at the peak of its prosperity. "Mission San Carlos Borromeo de Carmelo" *by Oriana Day, oil on canvas 20" x 30". The Fine Art Museum of San Francisco. Gift of Mrs. Eleanor Martin 87566.*

grant, was given a grant of land in the Sacramento Valley, where he established a colony called New Helvetia in 1839. This settlement drew trappers, traders, Indians, and other settlers like a magnet.

In New Helvetia, San Francisco, and other centers in northern California, a cosmopolitan society developed. Farther south, however, in the heartland of Spanish California, the Hispanic landholding elite resented intrusions by lower-class Mexicans and other newcomers. Governor Alvarado had a number of American and British citizens arrested on the suspicion that they were plotting to overthrow his government.

A more harmonious pattern of interracial cooperation existed in Santa Fe, where an elite class

---

Californios Spanish colonists in California in the eighteenth and early nineteenth centuries.

tallow Hard fat obtained from the bodies of cattle and other animals and used to make candles and soap.

John Sutter Swiss immigrant who founded a colony in California; in 1848 the discovery of gold on his property attracted hordes of miners who seized his land, leaving him financially ruined.

emerged from the intermingled fortunes and inter-marriages among Indian, European, and American populations. Thus the Hispanic leaders of New Mexico, unlike those of California, consistently worked with their kinsmen.

In Texas, the economic desperation of impover-ished southern frontiersmen combined with cul-tural insensitivity and misunderstanding to create the sort of tensions that were rare in New Mexico. **Texians** (non-Hispanic settlers) tended to cling to their own ways, and **Tejanos** (migrants from Mexico) did the same.

The Mormon Community

Physical conditions in the Great Basin led to a com-pletely different social and cultural order in that area. Utah is a high desert plateau where water is scarce and survival depends on its careful manage-ment. The tightly knit community of Mormons was perfectly suited to that hostile environment.

Mormons followed the principle that "land belongs to the Lord, and his Saints are to use so much as they can work profitably." The church mea-sured off plots of up to 40 acres and assigned them to settlers on the basis of need. Thus a man with sev-eral wives, many children, and enough wealth to hire help might receive a grant of 40 acres, but a man with one wife, few children, and little capital might receive only 10. Receiving a larger land grant meant that the recipient was under greater obligation to support community efforts. A man who had been granted 40 acres had to provide four times the amount of labor than one who had been granted 10. Community work parties among the Mormons were more rigidly controlled and formal than in other settlements.

Because of their bad experiences in Missouri and Illinois, the Mormons were unaccepting of strangers. The **General Authorities** of the church made every effort to keep Utah an exclusively Mormon society. The one exception was American Indians. Because Indians occupied a central place in Mormon sacred literature, the Mormons practiced an accepting and gentle Indian policy. The Mormon hierarchy used its enormous power in Utah to prevent private violence against Indians whenever possible.

The Triumph of "Manifest Destiny"

- What political *expectations* did Americans have when they pushed forcefully beyond the Mississippi River?
- Did their *choices* result in the *outcomes* they *expected*?

Economic opportunity was the primary reason for westward movement before the Civil War erupted in 1861, but it was not the only reason people ven-tured west. Cultural and religious issues also pushed people west. So did the idea of **manifest destiny.**

The Rise of Manifest Destiny

To some extent, manifest destiny was as old as the Puritan idea of a "wilderness Zion" (see page 32). Like John Winthrop, many early nineteenth-century Americans believed they had a mission to go into new lands. During the antebellum period, romantic nationalism, land hunger, and the Second Great Awakening shaped this sense of divine mission into a powerful incentive to westward expansion.

Evangelical Protestants came to believe that the westward movement was part of a divine plan for North America and the rest of the world. The earli-est and most aggressive proponents of expansion were Christian missionary organizations, whose many magazines, newsletters, and reports were the first to give it formal voice. Politicians were not far behind. Democrat Thomas Hart Benton of Missouri quickly adopted the missionary rhetoric in promot-ing liberal land policies, territorial acquisition, and overseas expansion. By 1845, when journalist John

Texians Non-Hispanic settlers in Texas in the nine-teenth century.

Tejanos Mexican settlers in Texas in the nineteenth century.

General Authorities Leaders in the Mormon church hierarchy; the prophet, his two assistants, twelve apostles, and several full-time administra-tors.

manifest destiny Term first used in the 1840s to describe the inevitability of the continued west-ward expansion of the United States.

L. O'Sullivan coined the expression "manifest destiny," the idea that the United States should occupy all of North America was already an established one.

Expansion to the North and West

One major obstacle to manifest destiny was that Spain, Britain, Russia, and other countries already owned large parts of North America. The continued presence of the British proved to be a constant irritation.

The disputed border between Maine and Canada threatened to lead to a major confrontation in 1838, when Canadian loggers moved into the disputed region and began cutting trees. Fighting broke out when American lumberjacks attempted to drive them away. The Canadian province of New Brunswick and the state of Maine then mobilized their militias; Congress called up fifty thousand men; and President Van Buren ordered General Winfield Scott to the scene. Scott arranged a truce, but tensions continued to run high.

Another source of conflict with Britain was the **Oregon Question.** At the close of the War of 1812, the two countries had been unable to settle their claims and had agreed to joint occupation of Oregon for ten years. This arrangement was extended indefinitely in 1827.

Joint occupation began to be undermined when American settlers in the Willamette Valley held a series of meetings in 1843 to create a civil government. A constitutional convention was called for May 2. Although the British tried to prevent the convention, the assembly passed the First Organic Laws of Oregon on July 5, 1843, making Oregon an independent republic in all but name. Independence, however, was not the settlers' long-term goal. They desired **annexation** to the United States of America.

Revolution in Texas

Unlike the situation in Maine and the Oregon Country, the ownership of the Southwest was fairly clear. Present-day Texas, New Mexico, Arizona, California, Nevada, and portions of Colorado, Oklahoma, Kansas, and Wyoming belonged to Spain prior to Mexico's successful revolution in 1821. After that revolution, title presumably passed to Mexico. But owning this vast region and controlling it were two different matters. The distance between the capital in Mexico City and the northern provinces made governing the region difficult.

Anglo-American settlers in the Southwest generally ignored Mexican customs, including their pledge to practice Roman Catholicism. The distant and politically unstable Mexican government could do little to enforce laws and customs. In addition, many Tejanos desired greater autonomy from Mexico City as much as their American counterparts did.

In an effort to forge a peaceful settlement with the Mexican government, Stephen F. Austin went to Mexico City in 1833. While Austin was there, **Antonio López de Santa Anna** seized power. A key figure in the adoption of a republican constitution in 1824, Santa Anna had come to the conclusion that Mexico was not ready for democracy. He suspended the constitution, dismissed congress, and declared himself the "Napoleon of the West."

Austin pressed several petitions advocating reforms and greater self-government in Texas upon the Mexican president. Believing that Santa Anna agreed with him, Austin departed for home, only to be arrested and dragged back to Mexico City in chains on charges of advocating revolution in Texas. Although finally cleared of all charges in 1835, Austin had decided by the time he arrived back in Texas that "war is our only recourse." In early September, he called for a convention of delegates from all over Texas to discuss what should be done.

By the time this convention met in November 1835, the first shots of the **Texas Revolution** had

---

Oregon Question   The question of the national ownership of the Pacific Northwest; the United States and Great Britain renegotiated the boundary in 1846, establishing it at 49° north latitude.

annexation   The incorporation of a territory into an existing political unit such as a neighboring country.

Antonio López de Santa Anna   Mexican general who was president of Mexico when he led an attack on the Alamo in 1836.

Texas Revolution   A revolt by American colonists in Texas against Mexican rule; it began in 1835 and ended with the establishment of the Republic of Texas in 1836.

Legend:
- Area claimed by Texas and Mexico
- Land grant
- Texan movements
- Mexican movements
- Texan victory
- Mexican victory

♦ MAP 12.1 Texas Revolution   This map shows troop movements and the major battles in the Texas Revolution, as well as the conflicting boundary claims made by Texans and the Mexican government. The Battle of San Jacinto ended the war, but the conflicting land claims continued.

including former congressman and frontier celebrity Davy Crockett.

Texas rebels elsewhere were consolidating the revolution. On March 2, a convention met at Washington-on-the-Brazos and issued a declaration of independence. The convention also ratified a constitution, based largely on the Constitution of the United States, on March 16. It elected David G. Burnet president of the new republic and Lorenzo de Zavala, one of the many Tejanos who had joined the rebellion, as vice president (see Individual Choices: Lorenzo de Zavala). **Sam Houston** had earlier been named commander of the army.

Despite the loss at the Alamo, Texans continued to underestimate Santa Anna's strength. On March 18 a large Mexican detachment under General José Urrea captured the town of Goliad and its defenders. Over the next several days, Urrea scoured the countryside for additional prisoners. On Palm Sunday in 1836, Urrea ordered all 445 able-bodied prisoners to be marched out of town, where their guards shot and killed them.

Vengeance came on April 21 after Santa Anna had ordered his troops to pause at the San Jacinto River. Arriving in the vicinity undetected, Houston's force of just over nine hundred formed up quietly. Shouting "Remember the Alamo" and "Remember Goliad," the Texans stormed the unsuspecting Mexican camp. In just eighteen minutes, 630 Mexican soldiers lay dead. Santa Anna attempted to escape but was captured. In exchange for his release, the Mexican president signed the **Treaty of Velasco,** in which he agreed to withdraw his troops south of the Rio Grande.

already been fired. The convention formed itself into a provisional government but refrained from declaring its independence from Mexico.

The first major confrontation of the rebellion occurred at San Antonio (see Map 12.1). Santa Anna personally led the Mexican army against that city, which had been captured by the rebels. Knowing that Santa Anna was on his way, Texas commander William Travis moved his troops into a former mission called the **Alamo.** On March 6 Santa Anna ordered an all-out assault on the Alamo. Storming the walls, the Mexican army sustained staggering casualties but captured it nevertheless. Most of the post's defenders were killed in the assault. Santa Anna executed those who survived the battle,

---

Alamo   A Franciscan mission that the Mexican commander at San Antonio fortified to resist Colonel Burleson's attack on the city; rebellious Texas colonists were besieged there by Santa Anna's forces in 1836.

Sam Houston   American general and politician who fought in the struggle for Texas's independence from Mexico and became president of the Republic of Texas.

Treaty of Velasco   Treaty signed by Santa Anna in May 1836 after his capture at the San Jacinto River; it granted recognition to the Republic of Texas but was later rejected by the Mexican congress.

Many leaders in Texas hoped for annexation by the United States. In 1838, Houston, by then president of the Republic of Texas, invited the United States to annex Texas. He was forced to withdraw the invitation when John Quincy Adams, elected to Congress after his loss in the presidential election of 1828, **filibustered** in the House of Representatives for three weeks against the acquisition of such a big bloc of potentially slave territory.

The Politics of Manifest Destiny

Adams certainly did not speak for the majority of Whigs on the topic of national expansion. The party of manufacturing, revivalism, and social reform inclined naturally toward manifest destiny. William Henry Harrison, the party's first national candidate, had been a prominent War Hawk and Indian fighter, and his political campaign in 1840 had celebrated the virtues of frontier life. When Harrison died only a month after taking office in 1841, his vice president, John Tyler, picked up the torch of American expansionism.

Tyler was an atypical Whig. A Virginian and a states' rights advocate, he had been a staunch Democrat until the nullification crisis. Although he had objected to Jackson's use of presidential power, Tyler as president was as unyielding as Old Hickory where political principles were concerned. He vetoed high protective tariffs, internal improvement bills, and attempts to revive the Second Bank of the United States. Tyler's refusal to promote Whig economic policies led to a general crisis in government in 1843, when his entire cabinet resigned over his veto of a bank bill.

Tyler did share his party's desire for expansion. He assigned Secretary of State Daniel Webster to settle the Maine border dispute with Britain. The resulting **Webster-Ashburton Treaty** (1842) gave over half of the disputed territory to the United States and finally established the nation's northeastern border with Canada. Tyler adopted an aggressive stance on the Oregon Question by appointing Elijah White as the federal Indian agent for the region in 1842. This action flew in the face of the mutual occupation agreement between the United States and Great Britain. Historians have speculated that Tyler also encouraged emigration to Oregon to strengthen the U.S. claim to the region.

Tyler similarly pushed a forceful policy toward Texas and the Southwest. He opened negotiations with Sam Houston that led to a proposed treaty of annexation in 1844. Proslavery and antislavery forces in the Senate fiercely debated the treaty, however, and failed to ratify it. The issue of Texas annexation then joined the Oregon Question as a major campaign issue in the presidential election of 1844.

The issue of expansion put the two leading political figures of the day, Democrat Martin Van Buren and Whig Henry Clay, in an uncomfortable position. Van Buren had opposed the extension of slavery and was therefore against the annexation of Texas. Clay, a slaveholder, was opposed to any form of expansion that would fan sectional tensions. Both candidates stated that they favored annexation only if Mexico agreed.

Despite Clay's stance on expansion, President Tyler's constant refusal to support the larger Whig political agenda led the party to nominate Clay. Van Buren was not so lucky. The strong southern wing of the Democratic party was so put off by Van Buren's position on slavery that it nominated Tennessee congressman **James K. Polk.**

The Democrats proclaimed in their platform that they stood for "the re-occupation of Oregon and the re-annexation of Texas at the earliest practicable period." Polk vowed to stand up to the British by claiming the entire Oregon Country up to 54°40' north latitude and to defend the territorial claims of Texas. The Democrats appealed to the expansionist sentiments of northerners and southerners. Clay ignored expansionism, emphasizing economic policies instead.

The temper of the people was evident in the election's *outcome.* Clay was a national figure, well

---

filibuster   To use obstructionist tactics, especially prolonged speechmaking, in order to delay legislative action.

Webster-Ashburton Treaty   Treaty, negotiated by Secretary of State Daniel Webster and the British minister Lord Ashburton in 1842, that established the present border between Canada and northeastern Maine.

James K. Polk   Tennessee congressman who was a leader of the Democratic party and the dark-horse winner of the presidential campaign in 1844.

Choosing Texas and Independence

Lorenzo de Zavala

Lorenzo de Zavala fought against tyranny in his native Mexico. When the government he helped establish after a successful revolution against Spain refused to create a democracy, de Zavala moved to Texas. In 1835 he chose to join the Texas revolution against Mexico and was elected vice president of the Republic of Texas. Lorenzo de Zavala *by C. E. Proctor. Archives Division. Texas State Library. Photo by Eric Beggs.*

Although Lorenzo de Zavala was a physician by training, his heart persistently pulled him into politics. An ardent liberal and federalist, he was elected to the Merida city council in his native Yucatán, in southern Mexico, when he was only 23 years old. Then in 1814 he was elected a delegate to the Spanish parliament, though he never assumed his seat. The young liberal was imprisoned by Spain's king Ferdinand VII for anti-monarchial sentiments. Gaining his release in 1817, de Zavala returned to Yucatán.

De Zavala chafed at Spanish rule, and as revolutionary movements broke out in all parts of Mexico in 1820, he again entered politics, winning election as the secretary of the Yucatán assembly. From this position, he assisted the Mexican independence movement. Shortly after it succeeded in 1821, he was elected to the Mexican constituent congress, serving there and in the national senate until 1827, when he was made governor of the province of Mexico.

By 1829, de Zavala was having doubts about how things were going in Mexico. The independent government had proved far from stable, and the ruling authorities seemed just as reactionary as the Spaniards. The liberals' demand to allocate farmland to peasants, for example, was continually refused by the gov-

respected and regarded as one of the nation's leading statesmen. Polk was barely known outside Tennessee. Even so, Polk captured the presidency by sixty-five electoral votes.

Outgoing president Tyler accomplished one of the Democrats' platform goals before Polk assumed the presidency. In a special message to Congress in December 1844, Tyler proposed a **joint resolution**

annexing Texas. Congressmen who had opposed annexation could not ignore the clear mandate

> **joint resolution** A special resolution adopted by both houses of Congress and subject to approval by the president; if approved, it has the force of law.

ernment. Seeking some way to help the peasants, de Zavala resigned his governorship and secured an empresario grant to settle five hundred poor Mexican families in Texas.

For the next several years, de Zavala traveled and wrote a history of the revolutionary movement in Mexico, which he published in 1831. Then, finding himself in Paris, de Zavala accepted a post as Mexico's ambassador to France in 1833, returning to public service and politics. In 1834, Antonio López de Santa Anna pushed his way into power, suspending the constitution, dissolving the national congress, and assuming dictatorial control. Watching events unfold from his post in Paris, de Zavala became increasingly disaffected by Santa Anna. In 1835 he resigned as ambassador and sailed for Texas, where, he believed, he might join with others to oppose Santa Anna and restore the constitution. When Stephen F. Austin called for a "general consultation of the people" in the fall of 1835, de Zavala sought and won a seat.

Like many settlers in Texas—whether they were originally from the United States, Europe, or Mexico—de Zavala wanted reform, but not necessarily independence. Thus he agreed with the consultation's decision in November 1835 to form a provisional government using the Mexican constitution of 1824—a document he had helped write—as a legal foundation. But when Santa Anna declared all members of the consultation traitors and ordered troops into Texas, de Zavala gave up hope of a peaceful settlement. On March 2, 1836, he *chose* to join his colleagues in signing a declaration of independence and then threw himself into the task of writing a constitution for Texas. The resulting document was an interesting hybrid: a mixture of de Zavala's and James Madison's views concerning liberal federalism.

The Texas consultation ratified the new constitution on March 16, 1836. Then, in recognition of de Zavala's strong political voice and the significant role he had played in helping to launch the revolution, the consultation unanimously elected him vice president of the Republic of Texas.

The revolution and the establishment of the Texas republic represented a victory for views that de Zavala and many Mexican-born Texans had held for a lifetime. Throughout his political career, de Zavala had fought for reform in Mexico, helping to win independence from Spain and pushing for liberal federalism. His *expectations* had been dashed by the harsh *constraints* imposed by self-interested political factions, which had created such instability that Santa Anna had bullied his way to the top and ended liberal government. For de Zavala and many others, the *choice* was clear: if Mexico could not be reformed, they would throw their lot in with a new state where their views might be brought into reality. The Republic of Texas became the seat for their dreams.

given to manifest destiny in the presidential election. The bill to annex Texas passed in February 1845, just as Tyler was about to leave the White House.

Often called "Young Hickory" because of his political resemblance to Andrew Jackson, Polk promoted expansion by asking Congress to end the joint occupation of Oregon and by negotiating with Mexico to purchase much of the Southwest. The president urged Congress to pursue exclusive control over the Oregon Country and to obtain the Southwest even if doing so meant war.

Neither the United States nor Britain intended to go to war over Oregon. The only issue was where the border would be. Polk insisted on 54°40'. The British lobbied for the Columbia River, but their position softened quickly. The fur trade along the Columbia had become unprofitable by the early 1840s. As a result, in the spring of 1846, the British foreign secretary offered Polk a compromise boundary at the 49th parallel. The Senate recommended that Polk accept the offer, and a treaty settling the Oregon issue was ratified on June 15, 1846.

Expansion and Sectional Crisis

• How did the slavery issue and differing economic values interact with various Americans' *expectations* to create a crisis in the 1840s?

Significant political controversy accompanied the extension of the nation's borders. At the heart of the matter lay slavery. Although only a few radicals were totally opposed to southern slavery, many people in the North and West were strongly opposed to its expansion. For them this was less a moral than an economic issue. The expansion of slavery meant economic competition with slaves or slaveholders for jobs and profits. Southerners, in contrast, demanded that slavery be allowed to expand as far as economic opportunity permitted. Not surprisingly, southerners believed the nation should expand into areas where cotton would grow and slavery would be profitable. Given these strong economic motives, the debate over expansion turned into a debate over slavery.

The Texas Crisis and Sectional Conflict

In annexing Texas, the United States had offended Mexico. Mexico immediately severed diplomatic relations with the United States and threatened war. The Mexican government held that Texas was still a province of Mexico, not an independent republic, and that Texas's southern boundary was the Nueces River, not the Rio Grande. Polk responded by blustering that the entire Southwest should be annexed.

Polk sought his objectives peacefully but was prepared to use force. Late in 1845, he dispatched John Slidell to Mexico City to negotiate the boundary dispute, authorizing Slidell to purchase New Mexico and California. He also sent American troops to Louisiana, ready to strike if Mexico resisted Slidell's

offers. And he notified the American consul in California that American naval ships had orders to seize California ports if war broke out with Mexico.

The Mexican government refused to receive Slidell. In January 1846 Slidell reported that his mission was a failure. Polk then ordered **Zachary Taylor** to lead troops into the disputed area between the Nueces River and the Rio Grande. Shortly thereafter, an American military exploration party led by **John C. Frémont** violated Mexican territory by crossing the mountains into California's Salinas Valley.

On April 22, Mexico declared war. Two days later, Mexican troops engaged a detachment of Taylor's army at Matamoros on the Rio Grande, killing 11 and capturing the rest. When news of this action reached Washington on May 9, Polk asked Congress for a declaration of war, charging that Mexico had "invaded our territory, and shed American blood upon American soil." Although the nation was far from united, Congress declared war on May 13, 1846 (see Map 12.2).

The outbreak of war disturbed many Americans. In New England, protest ran high. Henry David Thoreau *chose* to be jailed rather than to pay taxes that would support the war. The United States had lost its reputation as a "refuge of liberty," he wrote, when it held a sixth of its population as slaves and engaged in an unjust war with Mexico.

Other protesters also made the connection between the war with Mexico and slavery. Although antislavery sentiments were not widespread among the American people during the 1840s, antislavery voices were getting louder. Despite strong and sometimes violent opposition, the abolition movement had continued to grow, especially among the privileged and educated classes in the Northeast. Throughout the 1830s, evangelicals increasingly stressed the sinful nature of slavery and broke away

---

Zachary Taylor   American general whose defeat of Santa Anna at Buena Vista in 1847 made him a national hero and the Whig choice for president in 1848.

John C. Frémont   Explorer, soldier, and politician who explored and mapped much of the American West and Northwest; he later ran unsuccessfully for president.

♦ **MAP 12.2 The Southwest and the Mexican War**   When the United States acquired Texas, it inherited the Texans' boundary disputes with Mexico. This map shows the outcome: war with Mexico in 1846 and the acquisition of the disputed territories in Texas and most of Arizona, New Mexico, and California through the Treaty of Guadalupe Hidalgo.

from the **gradualism** of the American Colonization Society to demand the immediate, uncompensated liberation of slaves.

The annexation of Texas brought slavery to the attention of the American people like nothing before. To southerners, this land represented economic and political power. Proslavery constitutions in these newly acquired territories would ensure the immigration of friendly voters and the strengthening of the South's interests in Congress. Northerners saw something much more alarming in the southern expansion movement. Since the Missouri Compromise in 1820, some northerners had come to believe that a slaveholding **oligarchy** controlled life and politics in the South. Abolitionists warned that this "Slave Power" sought to expand its reach until it controlled every aspect of American life. Many viewed Congress's adoption of the gag rule in 1836 and the drive to annex Texas as evidence of the Slave

Power's influence. Thus debates over Texas pitted two regions of the country against each other in what champions of both sides viewed as mortal combat.

The contenders joined battle in earnest over appropriations for the war effort. In August 1846, David Wilmot, a Democratic representative from Pennsylvania, proposed an amendment to a military appropriations bill specifying that "neither slavery nor involuntary servitude shall ever exist" in any territory gained in the Mexican War. The

---

gradualism   The belief that slavery in the United States should be abolished gradually, by methods such as placing territorial limits on slavery or settling free blacks in Africa.

oligarchy   Government by a small group of people or families.

Wilmot Proviso passed in the House of Representatives but failed in the Senate. The vote on the proviso was an ominous one, for it followed sectional and not party lines. After several more efforts to pass the proviso, the House finally decided in April 1847 to appropriate money for the war without stipulating whether slavery would be permitted in territories acquired from Mexico.

War with Mexico

Americans quickly took control of the Southwest from Mexico. In California, American settlers in the Sacramento Valley captured the town of Sonoma in June 1846 and declared themselves independent. They crafted a flag depicting a grizzly bear and announced the birth of the Republic of California, also called the Bear Flag Republic. Frémont's force joined the Bear Flag rebels and marched south toward Monterey. There they found that the American navy had already seized the city. The Mexican forces were in full flight southward.

Polk had also ordered Colonel Stephen Kearney to invade New Mexico on May 15. After leading his men across 800 miles of desert to Santa Fe, Kearney found a less-than-hostile enemy force facing him. The interracial upper class of Santa Fe, which had already expressed interest in joining the United States, surrendered without firing a shot.

Within a short time, all of New Mexico and California were securely in the hands of U.S. forces. Zachary Taylor faced more serious opposition in Mexico. After marching across the Rio Grande, Taylor captured the Mexican city of Monterrey in September 1846, but then allowed the enemy garrison to retreat through his lines. From Monterrey, Taylor planned to turn southward toward Mexico City, but politics intervened.

After Taylor's victory at Monterrey, Polk feared that Taylor might use his military success to challenge him for the presidency. That Taylor had allowed the Mexican garrison to escape also convinced the president that Taylor was not aggressive enough to win the war quickly. Thus Polk ordered General **Winfield Scott** to lead American troops in the assault against Mexico City.

Polk complicated the military situation by plotting with deposed Mexican president Santa Anna, who had been exiled to Cuba after his defeat at San Jacinto. Santa Anna promised that he would help end the war in America's favor if Polk would help him return to Mexico. The American president agreed, and Santa Anna soon resumed the presidency of Mexico. To Polk's dismay, however, Santa Anna vowed to resist American expansion. Thus Mexico's most able general resumed command and *chose* to strike.

Santa Anna and his numerically superior army encountered Taylor at Buena Vista in February 1847. Tired from marching across the desert, the Mexican army was in no shape to fight, but Santa Anna ordered an attack anyway. Although the **Battle of Buena Vista** was a draw, Santa Anna's force was compelled to withdraw into the interior of Mexico.

Scott's forces captured the port of Vera Cruz on March 9 and then moved relentlessly toward Mexico City where Scott's army could not be stopped. An ambush at Cerro Gordo turned into a disaster for Santa Anna. Scott's forces captured three thousand Mexican troops, most of Santa Anna's equipment and provisions, and even the president's personal effects. By May 15, however, Scott had run into trouble. Nearly a third of his army went home when their twelve-month enlistments expired on that date.

Finally, after three months of waiting, Scott received reinforcements and resumed his march on Mexico City. Leading a brilliant assault, Scott and his force routed the Mexican defenders, capturing the city on September 13, 1847.

Scott's enormous success caused Santa Anna's government to collapse, leaving no one to negotiate with American peace commissioner Nicholas Trist.

Wilmot Proviso   Amendment to an appropriations bill in 1846 proposing that any territory acquired from Mexico be closed to slavery; it was defeated in the Senate.

Winfield Scott   Virginia soldier and statesman who led troops in the War of 1812 and the war with Mexico; he was still serving as a general at the start of the Civil War.

Battle of Buena Vista   Battle in February 1847 during which U.S. troops led by Zachary Taylor forced Santa Anna's forces to withdraw into the interior of Mexico.

After a month had passed with no settlement, Polk concluded that Trist was not pressing hard enough and removed him as peace commissioner. But by the time Polk's orders arrived, the Mexican government had elected a new president and had told Trist that Mexico was ready to begin negotiations. Trist *chose* to ignore Polk's orders and pressed on with negotiations. On February 2, 1848, Trist and the Mexican delegation signed the **Treaty of Guadalupe Hidalgo,** granting the United States all the territory between the Nueces River and the Rio Grande and all the territory between there and the Pacific. In exchange, the United States would pay Mexico $15 million and all claims made by Texans for war damages.

Polk was very angry when he heard the terms of the treaty. He felt that Scott's sweeping victory at Mexico City should have gained the United States more territory for less money. Political realities in Washington, however, prevented Polk from trying to get a more aggressive treaty ratified by the Senate. Although the president had strong support for annexing all of Mexico, antislavery voices loudly protested the acquisition of so much land south of the Missouri Compromise line. Others opposed the annexation of Mexico because they feared that the largely Roman Catholic population of Mexico might threaten Protestant institutions in the United States. Still others had moral objections to taking any territory by force. Congress was also unwilling to appropriate more money for war if peace was within reach. Thus Polk submitted the treaty Trist had negotiated, and the Senate approved it by a vote of 38 to 14.

Issues in the Election of 1848

The presidential election in 1848 came along at the peak of national tension. Sectional differences were reaching crisis proportions. Rather than offering solutions, however, both major parties continued to practice the politics of avoidance.

In poor health, Polk declined to run for a second term. The Democrats *chose* Lewis Cass of Michigan, a long-time moderate on slavery issues, as their candidate. The Whigs hoped to ride a wave of nationalism following the Mexican War by running military hero Zachary Taylor, a Louisianan and a slaveholder, for president. During the campaign, Cass tried to avoid offending anyone by advocating the policy of **popular sovereignty.** Under this policy, territories would *choose* for themselves whether to admit slavery. Taylor echoed Calhoun's opinion that Congress did not have the authority to control slavery in the territories.

A third party cut to the heart of the issues at hand. A number of northern Democrats and northern Whigs joined forces with members of the former **Liberty party** to form the **Free-Soil party.** The party acquired this name because it wanted to exclude slavery from the territories. It named Martin Van Buren as its candidate.

Although the Free Soilers won 10 percent of the votes cast in the election, Taylor emerged as the victor. Congress remained split between Whigs and Democrats. Sectional issues had not yet fragmented the political system, but large cracks were showing.

These fissures widened noticeably when the question of admitting California to the Union arose. During the winter of 1847–1848, workmen had discovered gold while digging a ditch for John Sutter. Word soon reached San Francisco that huge gold deposits had been discovered at New Helvetia. By mid-May 1848, prospectors were swarming into the Sacramento Valley from all over California and Oregon. By September, the news had reached the East. Over a hundred thousand **forty-niners** took up residence in California the next year.

The twin issues of expansion and slavery were raised once again. Southerners wanted California to be open for slavery. But northerners were not about to turn the richest source of gold yet discovered over

---

Treaty of Guadalupe Hidalgo   Treaty, signed in 1848, under which Mexico gave up Texas above the Rio Grande and ceded New Mexico and California to the United States in return for $15 million.

popular sovereignty   The doctrine that the people of a territory had the right to determine whether slavery would exist within their territory.

Liberty party   The first antislavery political party; it was formed in Albany, New York, in 1840.

Free-Soil party   A political party that opposed the extension of slavery into any of the territories newly acquired from Mexico.

forty-niners   Prospectors who streamed into California in 1849, after the discovery of gold at New Helvetia in 1848.

The Seneca Falls Convention

The Declaration of Sentiments

During the 1830s and 1840s, women played a prominent role in encouraging American reform. Beginning in churches—considered extensions of the woman's domestic universe—women began working in orphanages, brothels, prisons, and other seemingly polluted realms. Responding to solicitations by leaders like William Lloyd Garrison, they also rallied around the anti-slavery cause.

But reforming women found themselves frustrated at every turn. Two such women— Elizabeth Cady Stanton and Lucretia Mott—accompanied Garrison to London to attend the World's Anti-Slavery Convention in 1840, but were turned away and forced to sit silently behind a curtain while men conducted the convention's business. This and similar slights led Stanton and Mott to join with other women in 1848 to call for a series of conventions to advocate women's rights. The first of these conventions convened on July 19, 1848. The women discussed many issues they believed important and issued a "Declaration of Sentiments" expressing their shared perception of their actual and their desired position in American society.

The history of mankind is a history of repeated injuries and usurpations on the part of man toward woman, having in direct object the establishment of an absolute tyranny over her. To prove this, let the facts be submitted to a candid world.

He has never permitted her to exercise her inalienable right to the elective franchise.

He has compelled her to submit to laws, in the formation of which she had no voice.

He has withheld from her rights which are given to the most ignorant and degraded men—both natives and foreigners. . . .

He has made her, if married, in the eyes of the law, civilly dead.

He has taken from her all right in property, even to the wages she earns.

He has made her, morally, an irresponsible being, as she can commit many crimes with impunity, provided they be done in the presence of her husband. In the covenant of marriage, she is compelled to promise obedience to her husband, he becoming, to all intents and purposes, her master. . . .

He has so framed the laws of divorce, as to what shall be the proper causes, and in case of separation, to whom the guardianship to the children shall be given, as to be totally regardless of the happiness of the woman. . . .

After depriving her of all rights as a married woman, if single, and the owner of property, he has taxed her to support a government which recognizes her only when her property can be made profitable to it.

He has monopolized nearly all the profitable employments, and from those she is permitted to follow, she receives but a scanty remuneration. He closes against her all avenues to wealth and distinction which he considers most honorable to himself. As a teacher of theology, medicine, or law, she is not known.

He has denied her the facilities for obtaining a thorough education, all colleges being closed against her.

He has created a false public sentiment by giving to the world a different code of morals for men and women, by which moral delinquencies which exclude women from society, are not only tolerated, but deemed of little account in man.

He has usurped the prerogative of Jehovah himself, claiming it as his right to assign for her a sphere of action, when that belongs to her conscience and to her God.

He has endeavored, in every way that he could, to destroy her confidence in her own powers, to lessen her self-respect, and to make her willing to lead a dependent and abject life.

Supporters Had This to Say

■ We are not insensible that the bare mention of this truly important subject [woman's rights] in any other than terms of contemptuous ridicule and scornful disfavor, is likely to excite against us the fury of bigotry and the folly of prejudice. A discussion of the rights of animals would be regarded with far more complacency by many of what are called the wise and the good for our land, than would a discussion of the rights of women. It is, in their estimation, to be guilty of evil thoughts, to think that woman is entitled to equal rights with man. Many who have at last made the discovery that the Negroes have some rights as well as other members of the human family, have yet to be convinced that women are entitled to any. . . . *Frederick Douglass in* The North Star, *July 28, 1848*

■ There is no danger of the Woman Question dying for want of notice . . . But one might suppose from the articles in some papers, that . . . the chief object of these recent conventions was to seat every lord at the foot of the cradle, and to clothe every woman in her lord's attire. . . . We did not meet to discuss fashion, customs, or dress, the rights of men or the propriety of the sexes changing positions, but simply our own inalienable rights. . . . *Elizabeth Cady Stanton to the Editor, (Rochester)* National Reformer, *September 14, 1848*

Opponents Had This to Say

■ The New York girls aspire to mount the rostrum, to do all the voting, and we suppose, all the fighting too. . . . Women have enough influence over human affairs without being politicians. Is not everything managed by female influence? Mothers, grandmothers, aunts, sweethearts manage everything. . . . Their rule is absolute; their power unbounded. Under such a system men have no claim to rights, especially "equal rights."

A woman is nothing. A wife is everything. A pretty girl is equal to ten thousand men, and a mother is, next to God, all-powerful. *(Philadelphia)* Public Ledger and Daily Transcript, *July–August 1848*

■ The women who attend these meetings, no doubt at the expense of their more appropriate duties, . . . affirm, as among their rights, that of unrestricted franchise. . . . Now, it requires no argument to prove that this is unwomanly, and that to be practically carried out, the males must change their position in society to the same extent in the opposite direction. . . . Society would have to be radically remodeled in order to accommodate itself to so great a change in the most vital part of the compact of the social relations of life; and the order of things established at the creation of mankind, and continued six thousand years, would be completely broken up. *(Albany)* Mechanic's Advocate, *July–August 1848*

♦ Elizabeth Cady Stanton was one of William Lloyd Garrison's supporters during the 1830s and early 1840s, but she and associates like Lucretia Mott became disenchanted by their second-class treatment by male abolitionists. This rare photograph shows Stanton with her child in 1856, eight years after she helped sponsor the "Declaration of Sentiments" at Seneca Falls, New York. *From the Archives of the Seneca Falls Historical Society.*

to the Slave Power. Thus although the discovery of gold in California seemed to announce God's approval of American expansionism, it drove an enormous wedge into an already cracking political system.

Women and the Politics of Avoidance

While Congress debated expansion and slavery, women were becoming impatient. Having assumed the burden of eliminating sin from the world, many evangelical women rallied around William Lloyd Garrison and abolitionism.

Women's growing prominence in the abolition movement led Garrison to insist that they play a more equal role. In 1840 he proposed that a woman be elected to the executive committee of the American Anti-Slavery Society. Later that year women were members of Garrison's delegation to the first World's Anti-Slavery Convention in London. British antislavery advocates, like many of their American counterparts, considered the presence of women inappropriate and refused to seat them. Garrison's group walked out in protest. Such slights made female abolitionists aware of a similarity between their condition and that of the slaves they hoped to free. Many women backed away from the male-dominated abolitionist cause and began advancing their own cause.

In 1848, two women who had been excluded from the World's Anti-Slavery Convention, Lucretia Mott and Elizabeth Cady Stanton, called women to a convention at Seneca Falls, New York, to discuss their common problems. At **Seneca Falls,** they presented a "Declaration of Sentiments" based on the Declaration of Independence, citing "the history of repeated injuries and usurpations on the part of man toward woman." The convention adopted eleven resolutions relating to equality under the law, rights to control property, and other prominent issues. A twelfth resolution, calling for the right to vote, failed to receive unanimous endorsement (see Voices: The Seneca Falls Convention).

Despite this effort, women made few immediate strides toward attaining legal equality or political rights. Traditionalists both inside and outside the reform movement resisted women's call for change, and even among themselves, women differed in their perceptions of how to lead more meaningful lives. Many continued to steep themselves in the cult of domesticity (see page 198). Only a minority *chose* to struggle for equality.

Seneca Falls Site in New York in 1848 of the first convention for women's rights, organized by reformers Lucretia Mott and Elizabeth Cady Stanton.

SUMMARY

E xpectations
C onstraints
C hoices
O utcomes

During the first half of the nineteenth century, the westward movement of Americans steadily gained momentum. Successful fur traders like John Jacob Astor, Auguste Chouteau, and William Henry Ashley made enormous profits from their *choice* to move west. Land speculators and gold seekers, too, helped open areas to settlement.

Communities in Texas, Oregon, California, Utah, and elsewhere in the West sprang up like weeds. One *outcome* was the development of a variety of cultures and economies, which evolved from the interplay of old habits, new ideals, and environmental *constraints*.

Conflicting *expectations* about the country's manifest destiny promoted an air of crisis in the nation at large. Northerners wanted a West that would be free for diversified economic development. Southerners wanted the West to be open to slavery and staple crops. And people from each region *chose* to use expansion to add to their power in Congress.

Slavery began to eclipse all other issues in symbolizing the differing demands made by North and South. For northerners, the idea of going to war to win Oregon was acceptable because the Missouri Compromise prohibited slavery there, but the idea of going to war to acquire Texas was quite another matter. The possibility of many new southern senators and representatives filled northerners with dread. Nevertheless, the nation *chose* to fight a war with Mexico between 1846 and 1848. It thereby gained California and vast territories in the Southwest. The discovery of gold in California in 1848 made that region a new bone of contention in the sectional debate.

Meanwhile, radical abolitionists like William Lloyd Garrison still labored for acceptance. What made Garrison's message hard for many to accept was his insistence on an equal role for women. But severely discriminatory conditions *constrained* the many women who participated in abolition and other reform movements. One *outcome* was the Seneca Falls conference in 1848, where politically active women called for greater equality with men.

SUGGESTED READINGS

Billington, Ray Allen. *America's Frontier Heritage* (1966).
A broad overview of America's western experience from a Turnerian point of view.

Hietala, Thomas R. *Manifest Design* (1985).
An interesting and well-written interpretation of the Mexican-American War and the events leading up to it.

Limerick, Patricia Nelson. *The Legacy of Conquest* (1988).
Considered by many to be the Bible of the New Western History, this wonderfully written interpretation of events in the West challenges many assumptions and stereotypes.

Meinig, Donald W. *Imperial Texas* (1969).
A fascinating look at Texas history by a leading historical geographer.

Miller, Christopher L. *Prophetic Worlds* (1985).
Critics have called this a seductive reinterpretation of the history of Indians and whites in the Oregon Country.

Paul, Rodman. *California Gold* (1947; reprint 1965).
A classic, but still the best account of the Gold Rush and its impact on life in California.

Stegner, Wallace E. *The Gathering of Zion* (1964).
A masterfully written history of the Mormon Trail by one of the West's leading literary figures.

Unruh, John David. *The Plains Across* (1979).
Arguably the best one-volume account of the overland passage to Oregon. The author captures the adventure of the Oregon Trail.

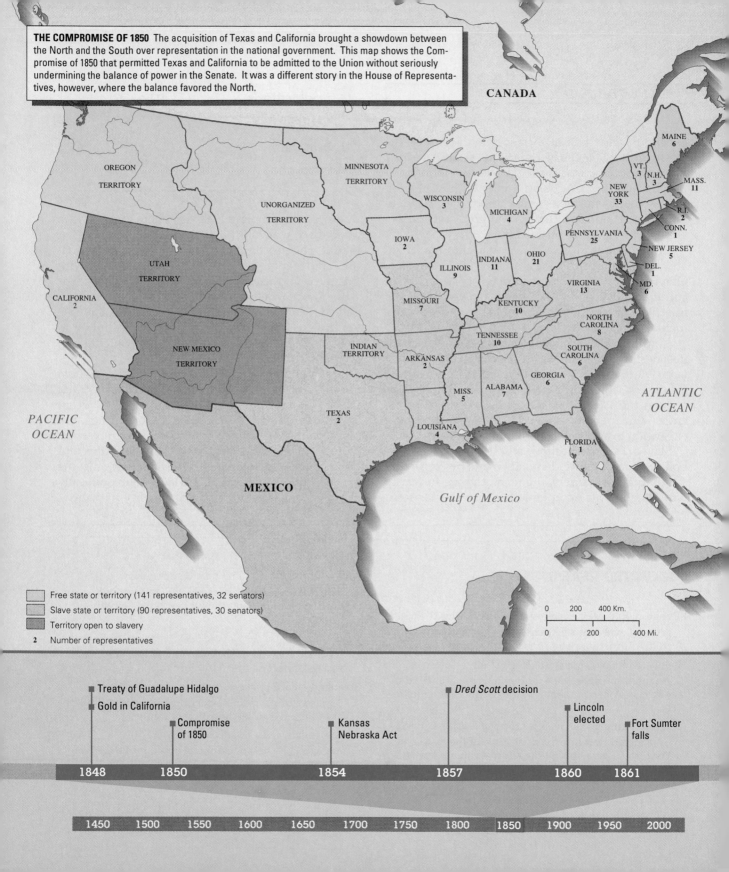

THE COMPROMISE OF 1850 The acquisition of Texas and California brought a showdown between the North and the South over representation in the national government. This map shows the Compromise of 1850 that permitted Texas and California to be admitted to the Union without seriously undermining the balance of power in the Senate. It was a different story in the House of Representatives, however, where the balance favored the North.

CANADA

OREGON TERRITORY

MINNESOTA TERRITORY

UNORGANIZED TERRITORY

WISCONSIN 3

MICHIGAN 4

MAINE 6

VT. 3

N.H. 3

MASS. 11

NEW YORK 33

R.I. 2

CONN. 1

PENNSYLVANIA 25

NEW JERSEY 5

DEL. 1

MD. 6

UTAH TERRITORY

IOWA 2

ILLINOIS 9

INDIANA 11

OHIO 21

CALIFORNIA 2

MISSOURI 7

KENTUCKY 10

VIRGINIA 13

NORTH CAROLINA 8

NEW MEXICO TERRITORY

INDIAN TERRITORY

ARKANSAS 2

TENNESSEE 10

SOUTH CAROLINA 6

GEORGIA 6

PACIFIC OCEAN

TEXAS 2

MISS. 5

ALABAMA 7

ATLANTIC OCEAN

LOUISIANA 4

FLORIDA 1

MEXICO

Gulf of Mexico

☐ Free state or territory (141 representatives, 32 senators)

☐ Slave state or territory (90 representatives, 30 senators)

☐ Territory open to slavery

2 Number of representatives

0   200   400 Km.

0   200   400 Mi.

■ Treaty of Guadalupe Hidalgo

■ *Dred Scott* decision

■ Gold in California

■ Lincoln elected

■ Compromise of 1850

■ Kansas Nebraska Act

■ Fort Sumter falls

1848   **1850**   **1854**   **1857**   **1860**   **1861**

1450   1500   1550   1600   1650   1700   1750   1800   **1850**   1900   1950   2000

CHAPTER 13

Sectional Conflict and Shattered Union, 1850–1861

New Political Choices

- What *constraints* convinced voters to make new political *choices* during the 1850s?
- What *expectations* did voters have for the *outcome* of those *choices*?

Toward a House Divided

- What did Stephen A. Douglas *expect* when he proposed to organize Nebraska Territory?
- Was the *outcome* what he envisioned?
- What *choices* and *constraints* influenced the *outcome*?

The Divided Nation

- What did northerners and southerners *expect* to happen as the result of the presidential election in 1860?
- What *choices* did they make as a result, and what was the *outcome*?

The Nation Dissolved

- What *choices* were available to Abraham Lincoln and Jefferson Davis in March 1861?
- How did events *constrain* their *choices*?

INTRODUCTION

E xpectations
C onstraints
C hoices
O utcomes

The United States entered a period of major growth and transition during the 1850s. Wealth and population grew dramatically as technology and industry continued to advance rapidly. After the successful military adventure against Mexico, the future seemed to hold infinite promise. Many Americans *expected* that their nation's growing wealth and vitality would open great opportunities for themselves. The nation simply needed to chart a correct course to claim its destiny.

But achieving the national destiny meant *choosing* particular goals and specific methods. Sharp disagreements *constrained* Americans seeking the correct national course. Most agreed that railroad development was good, but not everyone agreed on where the rail lines should run, how development should be funded, or what should be carried on the rails. Technological advances and industrial development brought new *constraints*, altering the nation's social structure and adding to disagreement. Social disruption occurred as unskilled immigrant factory laborers displaced native-born artisans. Disruption also occurred as commercial cotton growing and slave labor expanded farther into the American continent.

These problems quickly became the subject of political debate. Old-line northeastern and southern political interests continued to clash over traditional matters like tariffs and currency control. But rising immigration and westward migration brought new voters and new interests into play, particularly regarding the expansion of slavery. Reformers continued in their efforts to restore order and virtue, creating political blocs to fight for moral reform. All

of these voter groups had extremely diverse *expectations* about the correct course for the nation.

The *outcome* of these diverse *expectations* was a changing political environment. Both the Whigs and the Democrats attempted to direct and exploit the events of the 1850s. But both faced new *constraints* in the changing social, economic, and political climate. The total number of voters grew significantly, but so did the diversity of the electorate. Building a coalition strong enough to win a national election became increasingly difficult as regional, ethnic, and social distinctions influenced voters.

In this fragmented climate, the expansion of slavery into the territories became the dominant political issue. Political leaders *chose* either to seek compromise or to ignore the slavery question. In reality, they could do neither. Through all the debates, political platforms, and confrontations, two separate societies attempted to control the course of national destiny.

As the nation's leaders wrestled with a host of new issues amid political fragmentation, the confrontation between those two societies peaked. Although many people wanted peace and favored reconciliation, the political structure thwarted that desire. *Constrained* by the regional interests that had given birth to them, the new political coalitions proved incapable of compromise. The *outcome* was the end of the Union.

New Political Choices

- What *constraints* convinced voters to make new political *choices* during the 1850s?

- What *expectations* did voters have for the *outcome* of those *choices*?

The presidential election in 1848 had celebrated American expansion and nationalism, but the flow

of Americans into California soon created a crisis. It began when newly elected president Zachary Taylor ordered Californians to draw up a state constitution and apply for statehood. California produced a document that barred slavery in the state. Taylor then recommended that California be admitted as a free state and that Utah and New Mexico be organized as territories without reference to slavery.

CHRONOLOGY

Toward a Shattered Union

1848	Zachary Taylor elected president Immigration to the United States exceeds 100,000 for the first time Treaty of Guadalupe Hidalgo Gold discovered in California
1850	Compromise of 1850
1852	First railroad line completed to Chicago Publication of *Uncle Tom's Cabin* by Harriet Beecher Stowe Franklin Pierce elected president Destruction of the Whig party American party emerges
1853	Gadsden Purchase
1854	Kansas-Nebraska Act Ostend Manifesto Formation of the Republican party
1855	Sack of Lawrence, Kansas Pottawatomie Massacre
1856	James Buchanan elected president
1857	*Dred Scott* decision Pro-slavery Lecompton constitution adopted in Kansas
1858	Lincoln-Douglas debates
1859	Oregon admitted to the Union John Brown's raid on Harpers Ferry
1860	Abraham Lincoln elected president Crittenden compromise fails
1861	Formation of the Confederate States of America Shelling of Fort Sumter

Taylor's proposal frightened and angered southerners, for they had assumed that California would be open to slavery. Southerners also contended that another free state would unbalance sectional representation in the Senate. John C. Calhoun stated, "I trust we shall persist in our resistance until restoration of all our rights, or disunion, one or the other, is the consequence."

The Politics of Compromise

Henry Clay, who had crafted the Missouri Compromise, believed that any successful agreement would have to address all sides of the issue. He proposed an **omnibus** bill—a package of separate proposals—to the Senate early in 1850. California would enter the Union as a free state, but the slavery question would be left to popular sovereignty in all other territories acquired from Mexico. Clay then called for an end to the slave trade in the District of Columbia to appease abolitionists and for a new, more effective **fugitive slave law** to ensure southern support of his proposed legislation.

Congress debated the bill for six months, then finally defeated it in July 1850. However, **Stephen A. Douglas** of Illinois revived the compromise by submitting each component of Clay's omnibus package as a separate bill. Using persuasion and backroom political arm twisting, he steered each bill through

---

omnibus   Including or covering many things.

fugitive slave law   Law providing for the return of escaped slaves to their owners; a 1793 law was replaced with a stiffer version as part of the Compromise of 1850.

Stephen A. Douglas   Illinois senator who tried to reconcile northern and southern differences over slavery through the Compromise of 1850 and sponsor of the Kansas-Nebraska Act.

♦ This painting shows Henry Clay attempting to convince his fellow senators to support his omnibus compromise bill in 1850. Clay failed, but Illinois senator Stephen Douglas was able to get the compromise passed by breaking up the complicated bill, calling for a vote on each separate provision. *Library of Congress.*

Congress. President Taylor's sudden death on July 9 also made passage of the compromise package easier because his successor, **Millard Fillmore,** obtained northern Whig support for the bills. Finally in September Congress passed the Compromise of 1850.

The **Compromise of 1850** did little to settle underlying regional differences. Many northerners resented the fact that slaveowners could pursue runaway slaves into northern states and return them back into slavery. Nor did southerners find reason to celebrate. They had lost the balance of power in the Senate and gained no protection for slavery, either in the territories or at home. Still, the compromise created a brief respite from the slavery-extension question.

The compromise soon took its toll on the political system, particularly the Whigs. They passed over Millard Fillmore in 1852 in favor of Mexican War hero General Winfield Scott as their presidential nominee. The Democrats tapped the virtually unknown **Franklin Pierce** of New Hampshire. Despite the fact that Scott was a national figure and a distinguished military hero, he was overwhelmed by Pierce. Pierce gathered 254 electoral votes to Scott's 42. Although no one knew it at the time, the election of 1852 marked the end of the Whig

party. It was the casualty of a changing political environment.

A Changing Political Environment

During the 1850s industrial growth accelerated. By 1860 fewer than half of all northern workers made a living from agriculture. Steam began to replace water as the primary power source, and factories were no longer limited to locations along rivers and streams. The use of interchangeable parts became more sophisticated and intricate. For example, in 1851, Isaac Singer began mass-producing sewing

Millard Fillmore   Vice President who succeeded Zachary Taylor when he died in office and who tried to occupy a middle ground on slavery.

Compromise of 1850   Plan intended to reconcile North and South on the issue of slavery; it recognized the principle of popular sovereignty and included a strong fugitive slave law.

Franklin Pierce   New Hampshire lawyer and politician who was *chosen* as a compromise candidate at the 1852 Democratic convention and became the fourteenth president of the United States.

machines. As industry expanded, the North became more reliant on the West and South for raw materials and for the food that northeastern factory workers consumed.

Railroad development stimulated economic and industrial growth. Between 1850 and 1860, American railroad trackage jumped from 9,000 to more than 30,000 miles. Most of these lines linked the Northeast with the Midwest, carrying produce to eastern markets and eastern manufactures to western consumers. In 1852, the Michigan Southern Railroad completed the first line into Chicago from the East, and by 1855 that city had become a major transportation hub.

Railroads quickly reshaped the expanding American economy. Western farmers, who had previously shipped their products downriver to New Orleans on slow and undependable barges and boats, now sent them much more rapidly by rail to eastern industrial centers. Warehouses and **grain elevators** sprang up to accommodate such shipments. Reliable transportation and storage facilities induced farmers to cultivate more land. Mining boomed, particularly the iron industry, as the rail lines not only transported ore but became a major consumer.

Government actively supported railroad development and expansion, particularly in sparsely settled areas where returns on investment were *expected* to be meager. State and local governments loaned money directly to rail companies, financed them indirectly by purchasing stock, or extended state tax exemptions. The most crucial aid to railroads, however, was federal land grants. These were given to railroad developers who then leased or sold plots along the proposed route to finance construction. In 1850, a 2.6-million-acre land grant went to a railroad between Chicago and Mobile. Congress also invested $150,000 in 1853 to survey routes for a transcontinental railroad.

Railroads and improved farm technology opened up many parts of the Midwest to commercial farming. The steel plow, devised in 1837 by **John Deere,** allowed farmers to cultivate more acres with greater ease, and the mechanical reaper, invented in 1841 by **Cyrus McCormick,** could harvest more than fourteen field hands could. The combination of greater production and speedy transportation prompted westerners to increase farm size and concentrate on cash crops. It also greatly increased the economic and political power of the West.

The Midwest developed as America's bread basket as food shortages and poverty were driving millions from Europe. Beginning in the 1840s, a potato blight in Ireland caused extensive crop failures and increasing numbers to flee. Total immigration to the United States exceeded 100,000 for the first time in 1848. In 1851, 221,000 immigrants arrived from Ireland alone. Crop failures and political upheavals also pushed large numbers of Germans toward the United States. In 1852, German immigrants reached 145,000. Many newcomers, particularly the Irish, were unskilled and settled in the industrial cities of the Northeast. The concentration of immigrants there played a significant role in the unraveling of antebellum American politics.

Decline of the Whigs

During the 1850s many unemployed artisans were forced to accept factory work at a time when the flood of immigrants was driving wages down. Such artisans wanted a political party that would address their most pressing problems: loss of status, income, and jobs.

The Whig party had been their voice in politics during the party's glory days. During the elections in 1848, however, the Whigs had tried to win Catholic and immigrant voters away from the Democrats. Not only did the Whigs fail to attract immigrant voters, they alienated two groups of supporters. One group was artisans, who saw immigrants as the main source of their economic and social woes. The other was Protestant evangelicals, to whom Roman Catholic immigrants symbolized all that was threatening to the American republic. As

---

grain elevator   A building equipped with mechanical lifting devices and used for storing grain.

John Deere   American industrialist who pioneered the manufacture of steel plows especially suited for working prairie soil.

Cyrus McCormick   Virginia inventor and manufacturer who developed a machine for harvesting crops in 1831 and built a factory to mass-produce the McCormick reaper in 1847.

a result, increasing numbers abandoned the Whig party to form coalitions more in tune with voters' hopes and fears. Between 1852 and 1856, the Whig party dissolved and was replaced by two emerging parties: the Know-Nothing, or American, party, and the Republican party.

The anti-Catholic, anti-immigrant, **Know-Nothings** traced their origins back to secret **nativist** societies that had come into existence during the 1830s. These secret fraternal organizations entered politics by endorsing candidates who shared their views about immigration. They told their members to say "I know nothing" if they were questioned about the organization or its political intrigues, hence the name Know-Nothings. After the election of 1852, the societies began nominating and voting for their own candidates under the banner of the American party. The party charged that immigrants were part of a Catholic plot to overthrow democracy in the United States. The party advocated a twenty-one-year naturalization period, a ban against naturalized citizens' holding public office, and the use of the Protestant Bible in the public schools.

Know-Nothings disagreed about many issues, but they agreed that the Whig and Democratic parties were corrupt and that the only hope for the nation lay in scrapping traditional politics. As Ohio governor Rutherford B. Hayes noted, the people were expressing a "general disgust with the powers that be."

Local antislavery coalitions also deserted the Whigs. Sectional tensions doomed all Whig attempts to formulate a national policy. Those tensions were heightened in 1852 with the publication of *Uncle Tom's Cabin* by **Harriet Beecher Stowe.** Stowe portrayed the darkest inhumanities of southern slavery in the first American novel to include blacks as central characters. *Uncle Tom's Cabin* sold three hundred thousand copies in its first year and became one of the most popular plays of the period. It drew attention to the new Fugitive Slave Law and its harsh provisions for individuals caught helping runaway slaves. The work of Stowe and the lectures of people like **Harriet Tubman,** a former slave who rescued hundreds from slavery, made northerners increasingly aware of the plight of slaves (see Individual Choices: Harriet Tubman). When Free-Soilers and "conscience" (antislavery) Whigs saw that the party was incapable of addressing the slav-

ery question, they began to look for other political options.

Increasing Tension under Pierce

The Democrats were not immune to the problems caused by a changing electorate and by the issue of slavery. In May 1853, only two months after assuming office, Franklin Pierce inflamed antislavery forces by sending James Gadsden, a southern railroad developer, to Mexico to purchase a strip of land lying south of the Arizona and New Mexico territories. Pierce and his southern supporters wanted to buy this land because any southern transcontinental rail route would have to pass through it to go to California. The **Gadsden Purchase,** ratified by Congress in 1853, added 29,640 square miles to the United States for a cost of $10 million and set the southwestern border of the United States.

The Gadsden Purchase led to a more serious sectional crisis. It prompted advocates of a southern transcontinental railroad to push for government sponsorship of the project. They found themselves blocked, however, by Illinois senator Stephen A. Douglas.

A consummate politician, Douglas wanted a national railroad that would pass through Chicago and the Midwest, strengthening that region's economic and political strength and furthering his own career. Using his position as chairman of the

---

Know-Nothings   Members of secret organizations that aimed to exclude Catholics and "foreigners" from public office; members' "I know nothing" response to questions about the organizations produced their nickname.

nativist   Favoring native-born inhabitants of a country over immigrants.

Harriet Beecher Stowe   American novelist and abolitionist whose novel *Uncle Tom's Cabin* fanned antislavery sentiment in the North.

Harriet Tubman   Antislavery activist who had escaped from slavery and led many others to freedom on the Underground Railroad.

Gadsden Purchase   A strip of land in present-day Arizona and New Mexico that the United States bought from Mexico in 1853 in order to secure a southern route for a transcontinental railroad.

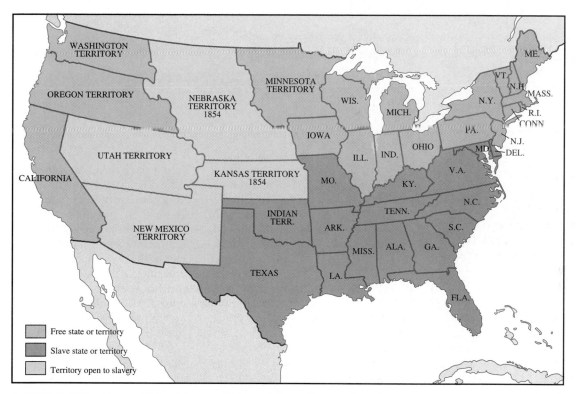

♦ **MAP 13.1 The Kansas-Nebraska Act**   This map shows Stephen Douglas's proposed compromise to the dilemma of organizing the vast territory separating the settled part of the United States from California and Oregon. His solution, designed to win profitable rail connections for his home district in Illinois, stirred a political crisis by repealing the Missouri Compromise and replacing it with popular sovereignty.

Senate's Committee on Territories, Douglas thwarted efforts to build a southern transcontinental railroad. Because the northern route that Douglas favored would have to pass through territory that had not yet been organized, Douglas introduced a bill in January 1854 that called for incorporating the Nebraska Territory.

Douglas knew that he would need northern and southern support to get his bill through Congress. Hoping to avoid yet another debate over slavery, Douglas proposed that the issue of slavery be settled by popular sovereignty within the territory. Southerners pointed out, however, that Congress might prohibit popular sovereignty in Nebraska because the territory was north of the Missouri Compromise line. Douglas finally supported an amendment to his original bill that divided the territory in half: Nebraska in the north and Kansas in the south (see Map 13.1). He assumed that popular

sovereignty would lead to slavery in Kansas and a system of free labor in Nebraska.

Toward a House Divided

- What did Stephen A. Douglas *expect* when he proposed to organize Nebraska Territory?
- Was the *outcome* what he envisioned?
- What *choices* and *constraints* influenced the *outcome*?

The Kansas-Nebraska bill angered northern Democrats, "conscience" Whigs, and Free-Soil advocates. All of them feared that without the Missouri Compromise limitations, slavery would spread throughout the territories. Once again slavery threatened national political stability. In the North, opponents of the bill formed local coalitions to challenge its passage. On January 24, 1854, a group calling itself the Independent Democrats,

To Free Others

Harriet Tubman

Fearful of being torn from her family in Maryland and sold to a cotton plantation in the Deep South, Harriet Tubman chose to run away from slavery. Seeking to reunite her family, she returned to the South to help them escape. Despite personal danger to herself, she chose to continue her efforts, finally conducting as many as 300 slaves along the Underground Railroad to freedom. She is seen here (on the left) with some of the slaves she helped free. Sophia Smith Collection.

Resisting slavery seemed second nature to Harriet Tubman. Born a slave on a Maryland plantation in 1820, she quickly developed a fiery spirit and was not shy about protesting bad treatment. One such incident so angered the plantation overseer that he hit her over the head with a lead weight, inflicting a permanent brain injury that would cause her to suddenly lose consciousness several times a day for the rest of her life. To overcome this disability, she worked on building herself up physically, becoming an uncommonly strong woman. It was said that she could single-handedly haul a boat fully loaded with stones, a feat deemed impossible for all but the strongest men.

Although Tubman dreamed about freedom after learning of Nat Turner's Rebellion in 1831, her disability and fear of being caught prevented her from acting. But in 1849, all that changed when the owner of her plantation died. Rumors began circulating that the man's estate was going to be liquidated and that the slaves were to be sold "down the river" to cotton plantations in the Deep South. The thought of being taken so far away from any avenue to freedom forced Tubman to *choose.*

Leaving the plantation, she slowly made her way northward by land, stopping at places she had heard about where free blacks or sympathetic whites would provide food and shelter. After a harrowing flight, she finally arrived in

who included Salmon P. Chase, Gerrit Smith, Joshua Giddings, and Charles Sumner, denounced the bill as an "atrocious plot" to make Nebraska a "dreary region of despotism, inhabited by masters and slaves." On February 28, other opponents of the bill met in Ripon, Wisconsin, and recommended the formation of a new political party. Similar meetings elsewhere in the North led to the emergence of the **Republican party.**

Republican party   Political party that arose in the 1850s and opposed the extension of slavery into the western territories.

Philadelphia. She was free but was not content with winning freedom just for herself. Tubman had left a large family behind in Maryland and would not be happy until she had won their freedom as well.

Soon after arriving in Pennsylvania, Tubman met William Still, a black clerk for the Pennsylvania Anti-Slavery Society. Still had worked since 1847 as a "conductor" on the Underground Railroad. Every so often, he and others like him made their way secretly into the South, contacted slaves who wanted to escape, and led them northward, stopping at pre-arranged stations—homes and businesses owned by free blacks or white abolitionists—for food and shelter. With the passage of the Fugitive Slave Act in 1850, Tubman decided that the only way she could win freedom for her family was to become a conductor herself. She chose to risk her freedom—even her life—to bring her parents, her brother and his family, and her own two children out of slavery.

It took Tubman several trips into the slave South to accomplish her aim of reuniting her family. In the course of her adventure, what began as a commitment to her immediate kin became a mission to her entire people. In all, Tubman made nineteen trips back into the slave South between 1850 and the outbreak of civil war in 1861, and it was said that she was personally responsible for conducting three hundred slaves to freedom. In between trips she, like Frederick Douglass, Sojourner Truth, and other escaped slaves, told her story to northern audiences, seeking support for her efforts to free individual slaves and for the larger effort to free all slaves. Her activities as a speaker and as an underground agent brought her acclaim and notoriety. John Brown consulted her while planning his raid on Harpers Ferry, and authorities in the South acknowledged her impact by posting a $40,000 reward for her capture.

Tubman continued her activities after war broke out in 1861. Like other black women who had either been born into or had won freedom, she again volunteered to go into the South with Union forces to serve as a nurse and cook and to help evacuate slaves from areas won by federal troops. She also continued speaking out in the interest of her people. To beat the South, she admonished, President Lincoln must set the slaves free.

A Shattered Compromise

Despite strong opposition, Douglas and Pierce secured passage of the **Kansas-Nebraska Act** in 1854. Its passage crystallized northern antislavery sentiment. As Senator William Seward of New York stated, "We will engage in competition for the virgin soil of Kansas, and God give the victory to the side which is stronger in numbers as it is in right."

> **Kansas-Nebraska Act** Law, passed by Congress in 1854, that allowed residents of Kansas and Nebraska territories to decide whether to allow slavery.

Southerners were determined to prevail in this struggle. They had come to believe that the expansion of slavery was necessary to prevent northern domination. They saw northern industrial and commercial power as a threat to reduce the South to a "colony" controlled by northern bankers and industrialists. The South needed to expand to survive.

Some southerners attempted to expand slavery by mounting private expeditions into the Caribbean and Central America. They believed that places such as Cuba and Nicaragua could be added to the list of slaveowning states. Although these expeditions were the work of a few power-hungry individuals, many northerners believed them to be part of the Slave Power conspiracy.

Bleeding Kansas

Meanwhile frictions were producing sparks in the Kansas Territory. In April 1854, Eli Thayer of Worcester, Massachusetts, organized the New England Emigrant Aid Society to encourage antislavery supporters to move to Kansas. He hoped to "save" the region from slavery by flooding it with right-minded emigrants. The society eventually sent two thousand settlers to Kansas and equipped them with rifles and ammunition. Proslavery southerners, particularly those in Missouri, also encouraged settlement of the territory. Like their northern counterparts, these southerners came armed and ready to fight for their cause.

As proslavery and abolitionist settlers vied for control of Kansas, the region became a testing ground for popular sovereignty. When the vote came on March 30, 1855, armed slavery supporters from Missouri—so-called border ruffians—crossed into Kansas and cast ballots. These unlawful ballots gave proslavery supporters a large majority in the legislature. They promptly expelled all antislavery legislators and passed laws meant to drive all antislavery forces out of the territory. Antislavery advocates, however, refused to acknowledge the validity of the election or the laws. They organized their own free-state government at Lawrence and drew up an alternative constitution.

Bloodshed soon followed when a proslavery judge, Samuel LeCompte, sent a **posse** of about eight hundred armed men to Lawrence. There they "arrested" the antislavery forces and sacked the town. With that, civil war erupted in Kansas. **John Brown,** an antislavery zealot, took his four sons and three others to exact "an eye for an eye" for the five antislavery settlers who had been killed in Kansas. Brown murdered five proslavery men living along the Pottawatomie River. (The victims had not been involved in the sack of Lawrence.) The Pottawatomie Massacre triggered a series of reprisals that killed over two hundred men.

The Kansas issue also led to violence in Congress. During the debates over the admission of the territory, **Charles Sumner,** a senator from Massachusetts, delivered an abusive speech against the proslavery elements in Congress. In "The Crime Against Kansas," he insulted South Carolina senator Andrew Butler by contending that Butler was a "Don Quixote" who had "made his vows" to "the harlot, slavery." Three days later, Representative Preston Brooks, Butler's nephew, beat Sumner unconscious with a cane to avenge his uncle's honor. Sumner was badly hurt and needed almost three years to recover. Though **censured** by the House of Representatives, Brooks was overwhelmingly re-elected and openly praised by his constituents for his actions. He received canes as gifts from admirers all over the South. Northerners were appalled by Brooks's action and by southern responses to it.

As the presidential election of 1856 approached, Kansas and slavery dominated the agenda. The Know-Nothings had split over slavery at their initial national convention in 1855. Disagreement over the Kansas-Nebraska Act caused most northerners to bolt from the convention and to join Republican coalitions. In 1856, the remaining Know-Nothings nominated former president Millard Fillmore as the American party's standard-bearer.

posse A group of people usually summoned by a sheriff to aid in law enforcement.

John Brown Abolitionist who fought proslavery settlers in Kansas in 1855; he was hanged after seizing the U.S. arsenal at Harpers Ferry in 1859 as part of an effort to liberate southern slaves.

Charles Sumner Massachusetts senator who was brutally beaten by a southern congressman in 1856 after delivering a speech attacking the South.

censure To issue an official rebuke, as by a legislature to one of its members.

John C. Frémont, a moderate abolitionist who had achieved fame as the liberator of California, got the Republican nomination. The few remaining Whigs endorsed Fillmore at their convention. The Democrats rejected both Pierce and Douglas and nominated **James Buchanan** from Pennsylvania, believing that he would be less controversial than the other two.

The election became a contest for the right to challenge Democratic occupancy of the office of president rather than a national referendum on slavery. Buchanan received 45 percent of the popular vote and 163 electoral votes. Frémont finished second with 33 percent of the popular vote and 114 electoral votes. Fillmore received 21 percent of the popular vote but only 8 electoral votes. Frémont's surprising showing demonstrated the appeal of the newly formed Republican coalition to northern voters. The Know-Nothings, fragmented over slavery, disappeared.

Bringing Slavery Home to the North

Two days after Buchanan assumed office in March 1857, the Supreme Court issued a ruling that sent shock waves through the already troubled nation. **Dred Scott,** a slave owned by John Emerson, resided in Missouri, a slave state. But Emerson, an army surgeon, had lived for two years in Illinois, where slavery was illegal, and had served in Wisconsin Territory, where the Missouri Compromise banned the practice. Scott's attorney argued that living in Illinois and Wisconsin had made Scott a free man. When Missouri courts rejected this argument, Scott, with the help of abolitionist lawyers, appealed to the Supreme Court.

In a 7-to-2 decision, the Court ruled against Scott. Chief Justice Roger B. Taney, a Maryland slaveowner, argued that slaves were not people but property, could not be citizens of the United States, and had no right to petition the Court. Taney then ignited a political powder keg by stating that Congress had no constitutional authority to limit slavery in a federal territory, thus totally negating the Missouri Compromise.

Antislavery forces and northern evangelical leaders called the *Dred Scott* decision a mockery of justice. Some radical abolitionists, harking back to the Hartford Convention's threat of secession (see page 166), argued that the North should separate from the Union. Others advocated impeaching the Supreme Court. Antislavery leaders contended that the next move of the Slave Power would be to get the Supreme Court to strike down antislavery laws in northern states.

While debates raged over the *Dred Scott* decision, the Kansas issue simmered. Although very few slaveholders had actually moved into the territory, proslavery leaders meeting in Lecompton in June 1857 drafted a state constitution favoring slavery. Antislavery forces protested by refusing to vote on this constitution, so it was easily ratified. But when the constitution was submitted to Congress for approval, northern Democrats such as Stephen Douglas joined Republicans in denouncing it. Congress ultimately returned the **Lecompton constitution** to Kansas for another vote. This time Free-Soilers participated in the election and defeated the proposed constitution. Kansas remained a territory.

The Kansas controversy and the *Dred Scott* case figured prominently in the 1858 contest for the Senate between Douglas and **Abraham Lincoln,** a small-town lawyer and moderate antislavery Republican. Born in Kentucky in 1809, Lincoln as a young man had worked odd jobs as a farm worker, ferryman, flatboatman, surveyor, and store clerk. In 1834, he was elected to the Illinois legislature and began a serious study of law. Lincoln had steered a middle course between the "cotton" and "conscience" wings of the Whig party. He acknowledged that slavery was evil but contended that it was the consequence of black racial inferiority. The only way

---

James Buchanan   Pennsylvania senator who was elected president in 1856 after gaining the Democratic nomination as a compromise candidate.

Dred Scott   Slave who sued for his liberty in the Missouri courts, arguing that four years on free soil had made him free; in 1857 the Supreme Court ruled against him.

Lecompton constitution   State constitution written for Kansas in 1857 at a convention dominated by proslavery forces, which tried to slant the document in favor of slavery; Kansas voters rejected it in 1858.

Abraham Lincoln   Illinois lawyer and politician who argued against popular sovereignty in his debates with Stephen Douglas in 1858; he lost the senatorial election to Douglas but was elected president in 1860.

to escape the evil, he believed, was to prevent the expansion of slavery into the territories.

Lincoln challenged Douglas to a series of seven debates about slavery that were to be held throughout Illinois. During the debate at Freeport, Lincoln asked Douglas to explain how the people of a territory could exclude slavery in the light of the *Dred Scott* ruling. Douglas's reply became known as the **Freeport Doctrine.** Slavery, he said, needed the protection of "local police regulations." In any territory, citizens could elect representatives who would "by unfriendly legislation" prevent the introduction of slavery "into their midst." Voters apparently found Douglas's position more attractive than Lincoln's. They elected a majority of Douglas supporters to the state legislature, which then returned Douglas to his senate seat.

Radical Responses to Abolitionism and Slavery

Southerners reacted with fear to the threat of limitations on the extension of slavery. Because intensive agriculture had depleted the soil in the South, expansion seemed necessary for economic survival. Although Republican leaders maintained that they had no intention of outlawing slavery where it already existed, their commitment against expansion appeared to sentence slavery to death.

Southern apologists defended their system against northern charges that it was immoral and evil. Charles C. Jones and other southern evangelicals offered a religious defense of slavery. They claimed that the Bible condoned slavery, pointing out that the Israelites practiced slavery and that Jesus walked among slaves but never mentioned freedom. The apostle Paul even commanded slaves to obey their masters.

Northern radicals such as John Brown, however, were developing plans that called for slaves to overthrow their masters. In 1857 Brown came east to convince prominent antislavery leaders to finance a daring plan to raise an army of slaves against their masters. Brown and twenty-one followers, including four free blacks, attacked the federal arsenal at **Harpers Ferry,** Virginia, on October 16, 1859, attempting to seize weapons.

Brown's force seized the arsenal but could not convince any slaves to join the uprising. Local

♦ Seeing himself as an avenging angel, John Brown, shown here in an 1856 photograph, used the same terrorist tactics employed by border ruffians in Kansas. Three years after this picture was taken, Brown attempted to set off a civil war by raiding the federal armory at Harpers Ferry, Virginia. He was hanged for treason in 1859. *Boston Athenaeum.*

citizens surrounded the building until federal troops, commanded by Colonel Robert E. Lee, arrived. On October 18, Lee's forces battered down the barricaded entrance and arrested Brown. He was tried, convicted of treason, and hanged on December 2, 1859.

John Brown's raid on Harpers Ferry captured the imagination of radical abolitionists and terrified southerners. Republican leaders denounced it, but

---

Freeport Doctrine   Stephen Douglas's belief, stated at Freeport, Illinois, that a territory could exclude slavery by writing local laws or regulations that made slavery impossible to enforce.

Harpers Ferry   Town in present-day West Virginia and site of the U.S. arsenal that John Brown briefly seized in 1859.

other northerners proclaimed Brown a martyr. Church bells tolled in many northern cities on the day of his execution, and radical evangelicals offered eulogies to Brown's cause. Brown's raid and the perception that Republicans had secretly sponsored it caused many moderate southerners to consider **secession.** The Alabama, Mississippi, and Florida legislatures resolved that a Republican victory in the upcoming presidential election would provide justification for such action.

The Divided Nation

- What did northerners and southerners *expect* to happen as the result of the presidential election in 1860?
- What *choices* did they make as a result, and what was the *outcome*?

The Republicans were a new phenomenon on the American political scene: a purely regional political party. The party drew its strength and ideas almost entirely from the North. The Republican platform— "Free Soil, Free Labor, and Free Men"—stressed the defilement of white labor by slavery. By taking up a cry against "Rum, Romanism, and Slavery," the Republicans drew former Know-Nothings and temperance advocates alike into their ranks.

Democratic Divisions and Nominating Conventions

During the Buchanan administration, Democrats found it increasingly difficult to achieve national party unity. Northern Democrats realized that any commitment to slavery would cost them votes at home. Southern Democrats, however, believed that protecting slavery was absolutely necessary. In April 1860 these conflicting views on slavery met when the party convened in Charleston, South Carolina.

The fight began over the party platform. Douglas's supporters championed a popular sovereignty position. Southern radicals countered by demanding the legal protection of slavery in the territories. After heated debates, the Douglas forces carried the day on this issue. Disgusted delegates from eight southern states walked out of the convention, thereby denying Douglas the two-thirds

majority required for nomination. Shocked, the remaining delegates adjourned the convention and reconvened in Baltimore in June. A boycott by most southern delegates allowed Douglas to win the presidential nomination easily. The party's final platform supported popular sovereignty and emphasized allegiance to the Union, hoping to attract moderate voters from both North and South.

The southern Democratic contingent met one week later and nominated John C. Breckinridge of Kentucky as its presidential candidate. The southern Democrats' platform vowed support for the Union but called for federal protection of the right to own slaves in the territories and for the preservation of slavery where it already existed.

In May 1860, a group of former Whigs, Know-Nothings, and some disaffected Democrats formed the **Constitutional Union party.** They nominated John Bell, a wealthy slaveholder from Tennessee, for president. This group had no hope of winning but believed it could gather enough support to throw the election into the House of Representatives. The party resolved to take no stand on the sectional controversy and pledged to uphold the Constitution and the Union.

The front runner for the Republican nomination was William Seward of New York. A former Whig, Seward had actively opposed the extension of slavery. Abraham Lincoln emerged as Seward's main challenger at the party's Chicago convention. Many delegates considered Seward too radical and doubted his honesty. Lincoln, in contrast, had a reputation for integrity and had not alienated any of the Republican factions. Lincoln won the nomination on the third ballot.

The Election of 1860

The 1860 presidential campaign began as two separate contests. Lincoln and Douglas competed for northern votes, and Breckinridge and Bell vied for

---

> **secession**   Withdrawal from the United States.
>
> **Constitutional Union party**   Political party that organized on the eve of the Civil War with no platform other than the preservation of the Constitution, the Union, and the law.

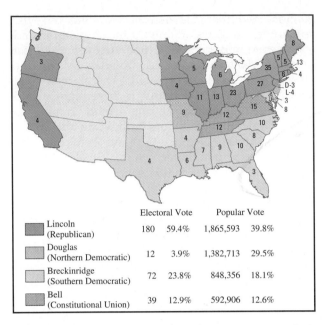

	Electoral Vote		Popular Vote	
Lincoln (Republican)	180	59.4%	1,865,593	39.8%
Douglas (Northern Democratic)	12	3.9%	1,382,713	29.5%
Breckinridge (Southern Democratic)	72	23.8%	848,356	18.1%
Bell (Constitutional Union)	39	12.9%	592,906	12.6%

♦ **MAP 13.2 Election of 1860** The election of 1860 verified the worst fears expressed by concerned Union supporters during the 1850s: changes in the nation's population made it possible for one section to dominate national politics. As this map shows, the Republican and Southern Democratic parties virtually split the nation, and the Republicans were able to seize the presidency.

the South. The Republicans were not even on the ballot in the **Deep South.** Breckinridge and the southern Democrats *expected* no support in the North. Douglas proclaimed himself the only national candidate. Bell and the Constitutional Unionists attempted to campaign in both regions but attracted mostly southern voters who wanted to avoid the crisis of disunion.

Sensing that Lincoln would win the North, Douglas launched a last-ditch effort to hold the Union together by campaigning in the South. Douglas tried unsuccessfully to form a coalition between moderate Democrats and Constitutional Unionists. Already in poor health, he exhausted himself trying to prevent disunion.

As the election drew near, rumors of slave uprisings incited by Yankee strangers led to hysteria in the South. Reports of violence, arson, and rape in faraway places filled southern newspapers. Although supported by no hard evidence, these rumors contributed to the climate of gloom in the South. Even moderate southerners started to believe that the Republicans intended to crush their way of life.

To improve the party's image, Republican leaders forged a platform promising not to interfere with slavery in areas where it already existed but opposing its expansion. Particularly in the Midwest, party leaders worked hard to portray themselves as "the white man's party" rather than as "black Republicans," as their opponents contemptuously called them. These tactics alienated a few abolitionists but appealed to many northerners and westerners.

On November 6, 1860, Abraham Lincoln was elected president of the United States with a clear majority of the electoral votes but only 40 percent of the popular vote. He carried all the northern states, California, and Oregon (see Map 13.2). Douglas finished second with 29 percent of the popular vote but only 12 electoral votes. Bell won in Virginia, Kentucky, and Tennessee. Breckinridge carried the Deep South but won only 72 electoral votes and 18 percent of the popular vote nationwide. For the first time in American history, a purely regional party held the presidency. The Republicans also swept congressional races in the North and had a large majority in Congress for the upcoming term.

The First Wave of Secession

After the Republican victory, southern sentiment for secession snowballed, especially in the Deep South. The Republicans were a "party founded on a single sentiment," stated the *Richmond Examiner:* "hatred of African slavery." The *New Orleans Delta* agreed, calling the Republicans "essentially a revolutionary party." To a growing number of southerners, the Republican victory was proof that secession was the only alternative to political domination.

Most Republicans did not believe that the South would actually leave the Union. Calls for secession

Deep South The region of the South farthest from the North; usually said to comprise the states of Alabama, Florida, Georgia, Louisiana, Mississippi, and South Carolina.

had been heard in the South for a decade. Seward had ridiculed threats of secession as an attempt "to terrify or alarm" the northern people. Lincoln himself believed that the "people of the South" had "too much sense" to launch an "attempt to ruin the government." He continued to urge moderation.

In a last-ditch attempt at compromise, **John J. Crittenden** of Kentucky introduced several proposals in the Senate on December 18, 1860. He suggested extending the Missouri Compromise line westward across the continent. Crittenden's plan also called for compensation to slaveowners who were unable to recover fugitive slaves from northern states.

Lincoln did not like Crittenden's plan. The extension of the Missouri Compromise line, he warned, would "lose us everything we gained by the election." He let senators and congressmen know that he wanted no "compromise in regard to the extension of slavery." The Senate defeated Crittenden's proposals by a vote of 25 to 23.

Meanwhile, on December 20, 1860, delegates in South Carolina voted 169 to 0 to dissolve their ties with the United States. Seceding from the Union, they proclaimed, was the sovereign right of a state. Other southern states followed South Carolina's lead. During January 1861, Mississippi, Florida, Alabama, Georgia, and Louisiana voted to secede from the Union.

On February 4, 1861, delegates from the six seceding states met in Montgomery, Alabama, and formed the **Confederate States of America,** or the Confederacy. Shortly afterward, Texans voted to leave the Union and join the Confederacy. The Confederate congress drafted a constitution, and the Confederate states ratified it on March 11, 1861. The Confederate constitution created a government modeled on the government of the United States— but with a few notable differences. It emphasized the "sovereign and independent character" of the states and guaranteed the protection of slavery in any new territories. The document limited the president and vice president to a single six-year term. A bicameral legislative body and six executive departments whose heads served as the cabinet rounded out the government. The U.S. Constitution, excluding provisions in conflict with the Confederate constitution, would remain in force in the Confederacy.

Responses to Disunion

Even as late as March 1861, not all southerners favored secession. John Bell and Stephen Douglas together had received over 50 percent of southern votes in 1860, winning support from southerners who desired compromise and had only limited stakes in upholding slavery. Nonslaveholders constituted the majority in many southern states. The border states, which had numerous ties with the North, were not strongly inclined toward secession. In February, Virginia had even called for a peace conference in Washington. Like Crittenden's efforts, this attempt failed.

The division in southern sentiments was a major stumbling block to the election of a president of the Confederacy. Many moderate delegates to the constitutional convention refused to support radical secessionists. The convention remained deadlocked until Mississippi moderate **Jefferson Davis** was put forward as a compromise candidate.

Davis appeared to be the ideal *choice*. A West Point graduate, he had served during the Mexican War and as secretary of war under Franklin Pierce. He had twice been elected to the Senate, resigning immediately after Lincoln's victory in 1860. Although Davis had long championed southern interests, he was no romantic, fire-eating secessionist. Before 1860 he had been a strong Unionist. He had supported the Compromise of 1850. Like many of his contemporaries, however, Davis had become increasingly alarmed as he watched the South's political power decline.

John J. Crittenden Kentucky senator who made an unsuccessful attempt to prevent the Civil War by proposing a series of constitutional amendments protecting slavery south of the Missouri Compromise line.

Confederate States of America Political entity formed by the seceding states of South Carolina, Georgia, Florida, Alabama, Mississippi, and Louisiana in February 1861.

Jefferson Davis Former U.S. army officer, secretary of war, and senator from Mississippi who resigned from Congress when Mississippi seceded and became president of the Confederacy.

To moderates like Davis, the presidential election of 1860 demonstrated that the South could no longer control its own affairs. It had no other option than to withdraw from the nation. Shortly after his inauguration as president of the Confederate States of America on February 9, 1861, Davis asserted: "The time for compromise has now passed. The South is determined to maintain her position, and make all who oppose her smell Southern powder and feel Southern steel."

Northern Democrats and Republicans alike watched developments in the South with dismay. Lame-duck President Buchanan argued that any state leaving the Union did so unlawfully. But he also believed that the federal government had no constitutional power to "coerce a State" to remain in the Union. Buchanan accepted no responsibility for the situation and did little to alleviate the tension.

During the four months between the election and Lincoln's inauguration, the Republicans could do nothing about secession. But Lincoln quickly defined his position: "My opinion is that no state can, in any way, lawfully get out of the Union, without the consent of the others." He tried to reassure southerners that his administration would not interfere with their slaves, but he refused to consider any compromise on the extension of slavery.

Black abolitionist Frederick Douglass assessed the crisis this way: "Much as I value the current apparent hostility to Slavery, I plainly see that it is less the outgrowth of high and moral conviction against Slavery, as such, than because of the trouble its friends have brought upon the country." Many northerners, as Douglass correctly perceived, were much more concerned about the breakup of the nation than they ever had been about slavery.

The Nation Dissolved

- What *choices* were available to Abraham Lincoln and Jefferson Davis in March 1861?
- How did events *constrain* their *choices*?

Lincoln's inaugural address on March 4, 1861, repeated themes that he had been stressing since the election: no interference with slavery in existing states, no extension of slavery into the territories, and no tolerance of secession. "The Union," he contended, was "perpetual," and no state could withdraw from it. Lincoln pledged "that the laws of the Union be faithfully executed in all the States." This policy, he continued, necessitated "no bloodshed or violence, and there shall be none, unless it is forced upon the national authority."

Lincoln, Sumter, and War

Lincoln's first presidential address drew mixed reactions. Most Republicans found it firm and reasonable. Union advocates in both North and South thought the speech held promise for the future. Even former rival Stephen Douglas stated, "I am with him." Moderate southerners believed the speech was all "any reasonable Southern man" could have *expected*. Confederates, however, branded the speech a "Declaration of War." Lincoln had hoped the address would foster a climate of reconciliation, but it did not.

Even before Lincoln assumed office, South Carolina officials had ordered the state militia to seize two federal forts and the federal arsenal at Charleston. In response, Major Robert Anderson moved all federal troops from Charleston to **Fort Sumter,** an island stronghold in Charleston harbor. The Confederate congress demanded that President Buchanan remove all federal troops from Confederate territory. Despite his sympathy for the southern cause, Buchanan announced that Fort Sumter would be defended "against all hostile attacks." On January 3, 1861, a Charleston harbor **battery** fired on a supply ship as it attempted to reach the fort. Buchanan denounced the action but did nothing.

Immediately after taking office, Lincoln received a report from Fort Sumter that supplies were running low. Under great pressure from northern public opinion to do something without starting a war,

> **Fort Sumter**   Fort at the mouth of the harbor of Charleston, South Carolina; it was the scene of the opening engagement of the Civil War in April 1861.
>
> **battery**   An army artillery unit, usually supplied with heavy guns.

he informed South Carolina governor Francis Pickens of his peaceful intention to send unarmed boats to resupply the besieged fort. Lincoln thus placed the Confederacy in the position of either accepting the resupply of federal forts and losing face or firing on the unarmed supply ships and starting a war. From Lincoln's perspective, the plan could not fail. If no shots were fired, he would achieve his objective by holding the fort. But if armed conflict evolved, he could blame the Confederates for starting it.

Confederate officials determined not to allow Sumter to be resupplied. Jefferson Davis ordered the Confederate commander at Charleston, General P. G. T. Beauregard, to demand the evacuation of Sumter and if the Federals refused, to "proceed, in such a manner as you may determine, to reduce it." On April 12, Beauregard demanded that Anderson surrender. When Anderson refused, shore batteries opened fire. After a thirty-four-hour artillery battle, Anderson surrendered. Neither side had inflicted casualties on the other, but civil war had officially begun.

Public outcry over the shelling of Fort Sumter was deafening. Newspapers across the North rallied behind the Union cause. In New York, where southern sympathizers had once vehemently criticized abolitionist actions, a million people attended a Union rally. Even northern Democrats rallied behind the Republican president. Stephen Douglas proclaimed, "There can be no neutrals in this war, only patriots—or traitors." Spurred by the public outcry, Lincoln called for seventy-five thousand militiamen to save the Union. Northern states responded immediately and enthusiastically. Across the Upper South and the border regions, however, the call to arms meant that a *choice* had to be made between the Union and the Confederacy.

Choosing Sides in the Upper South

As of April 12, 1861, seven slaveholding states had seceded, but eight remained in the Union. The Upper South, consisting of Virginia, North Carolina, and Tennessee, and the Border States of Missouri, Kentucky, Maryland, and Delaware were critical to the hopes of the Confederacy, for they contained over two-thirds of the South's white population and possessed most of its industrial capacity. If the Confederacy were to have any chance, the human and physical resources of the Upper South were essential.

After Lincoln's call to mobilize the militia, Virginia initiated a second wave of secession. On May 23 the state's voters overwhelmingly ratified an ordinance of secession. The Confederate congress accepted Virginia's offer of **Richmond** as the new Confederate capital. Not all Virginians were flattered by becoming the seat for the Confederacy. Residents of the western portion of the state had strong Union ties and long-standing political differences with their neighbors east of the Allegheny Mountains. They called mass **Unionist** meetings to protest the state's secession, and in a June convention at Wheeling, elected their own governor and drew up a constitution.

For many individuals in the Upper South, the decision to support the Confederacy was not an easy one. No one typified this dilemma more than Virginian **Robert E. Lee,** the son of Revolutionary War hero Henry ("Light Horse Harry") Lee. Lee had strong ties to the Union. A West Point graduate and career officer in the U.S. Army, he had a distinguished record in the Mexican War and as superintendent of West Point. General Winfield Scott, commander of the Union forces, called Lee "the best soldier I ever saw in the field." Recognizing his military skill, Lincoln offered Lee field command of the Union armies. Lee agonized over the decision but told a friend, "I cannot raise my hand against my birthplace, my home, my children." He resigned his U.S. Army commission and accepted command of Virginia's defenses in April 1861.

Influenced by the Virginia convention and by the events at Fort Sumter, North Carolina and

---

Richmond Port city on the James River in Virginia; it was already the state capital and became the capital of the Confederacy.

Unionist Loyal to the United States of America during the Civil War.

Robert E. Lee A Virginian with a distinguished career in the U.S. Army who resigned from that army to assume command of the army of the Confederate States of America.

Tennessee joined the Confederacy. Tennessee, the eleventh and final state to join the Confederacy, remained divided between eastern residents, who favored the Union, and westerners who favored the Confederacy. East Tennesseans attempted to divide the state much as West Virginians had done, but Davis ordered Confederate troops to occupy the region, thwarting the effort.

Trouble in the Border States

The start of hostilities brought political and military confrontation in three of the four slave states that remained in the Union. Delaware, which had few slaveholders, quietly stayed in the Union. Maryland, Missouri, and Kentucky, however, each contained large, vocal secessionist minorities and appeared poised to bolt to the Confederacy.

Maryland was particularly vital to the Union, for it enclosed Washington, D.C., on three sides. If Maryland had seceded, the Union might have been forced to move its capital. Because southern sympathizers controlled the legislature, Governor Thomas Hicks, a Unionist, refused to call a special legislative session to consider secession.

Even without a secession ordinance, prosouthern Marylanders caused trouble. On April 6, a mob attacked a Massachusetts regiment that was passing through Baltimore on its way to the capital. The soldiers returned fire. When the violence subsided, twelve Baltimore residents and four soldiers lay dead. Secessionists subsequently destroyed railroad bridges to keep additional northern troops out of the state and effectively cut Washington, D.C., off from the North.

Lincoln ordered the military occupation of Baltimore and declared **martial law.** He then had the army arrest suspected southern sympathizers and hold them without formal hearings or charges. When the legislature met again and appeared to be planning secession, Lincoln ordered the army to surround Frederick, the legislative seat. With southern sympathizers suppressed, new state elections were held that resulted in an overwhelmingly Unionist legislature.

Kentucky had important economic ties to the South but was strongly nationalistic. Kentuckian Henry Clay had engineered compromises between the regions, and John Crittenden had made the only significant attempt to resolve the current crisis. Most Kentuckians favored compromise. The governor refused to honor Lincoln's call for troops, but the state legislature voted to remain neutral. Both North and South honored that neutrality. Kentucky's own militia, however, split into two factions, and the state became a bloody battleground of brother against brother. In Missouri, Governor Claiborne F. Jackson, a former border ruffian, pushed for secession. When Unionists frustrated the secession movement, Jackson's forces seized the federal arsenal at Liberty. Union sympathizers fielded their own forces and fought Jackson at every turn. Jackson's secessionist movement sent representatives to the Confederate congress, but Union forces controlled the state and drove prosouthern leaders into exile.

> **martial law**   Temporary rule by military authorities, imposed on a civilian population in time of war or when civil authority has broken down.

SUMMARY

E xpectations
C onstraints
C hoices
O utcomes

As social and economic change heightened Americans' *expectations* during the 1850s, individuals made a variety of *choices*, creating a new political environment. New political allegiances changed party composition and platforms. As the Compromise of 1850 failed to alleviate regional tension, the Whig party disintegrated. Two completely new groups, the American and Republican parties, replaced the Whigs. Events such as the Kansas-Nebraska Act and the *Dred Scott* decision intensified regional polarization, and radicals on both sides fanned the flames of sectional rivalry.

The *constraints* imposed by regional interests left the new parties with far less ability to achieve compromise than their more nationally oriented predecessors. Even the Democratic party could not hold together, splitting into northern and southern wings. By 1859, the young Republican party, committed to containing slavery, seemed poised to gain control of the federal government. Southerners *expected* that a Republican victory would doom their way of life.

With the election of Abraham Lincoln in 1860, seven southern states *chose* to withdraw from the Union. Last-minute efforts at compromise failed, and on April 12, 1861, five weeks after Lincoln's inauguration, Confederate forces fired on federal troops at Fort Sumter in Charleston Harbor.

Lincoln's call to arms forced wavering states to *choose* sides. Virginia, Tennessee, Maryland, Kentucky, and Missouri had to make painful *choices* that frequently brought violence and military action. A second wave of secession and conflict over the border states solidified the lines between the two competing societies. The sides were quickly drawn, the stakes were set, the division was completed. The nation would now face the bloodiest war in its history.

SUGGESTED READINGS

Fehrenbacker, Don E. *Prelude to Greatness* (1962).

A well-written and interesting account of Lincoln's early career.

Fehrenbacher, Don E. *Slavery, Law, and Politics: The Dred Scott Case in Historical Perspective* (1981).

An excellent interpretive account of this landmark antebellum legal decision, placing it firmly into historical context.

Gienapp, William E., et al. *Essays in American Antebellum Politics, 1840–1860* (1982).

A collection of essays by the rising generation of new political scholars. Exciting and challenging reading.

Holt, Michael F. *The Political Crisis of the 1850s* (1978).

Arguably the best single-volume discussion of the political problems besetting the nation during this critical decade.

Oates, Stephen B. *To Purge This Land with Blood* (1984).

The best biography to date on John Brown, focusing on his role in the emerging sectional crisis during the 1850s.

Potter, David. *The Impending Crisis, 1848–1861* (1976).

An extremely long and detailed work but beautifully written and informative.

Rawley, James. *Race and Politics: "Bleeding Kansas" and the Coming of the Civil War* (1969).

An interesting look at the conflicts in Kansas, centering around racial attitudes in the West. Insightful and captivating reading.

Stowe, Harriet Beecher. *Uncle Tom's Cabin* (1852; reprint, 1982).

This reprint includes notes and chronology by noted social historian Kathryn Kish Sklar, making it especially informative. See also the one-hour film version produced by the Program for Culture at Play, available on videocassette from Films for the Humanities.

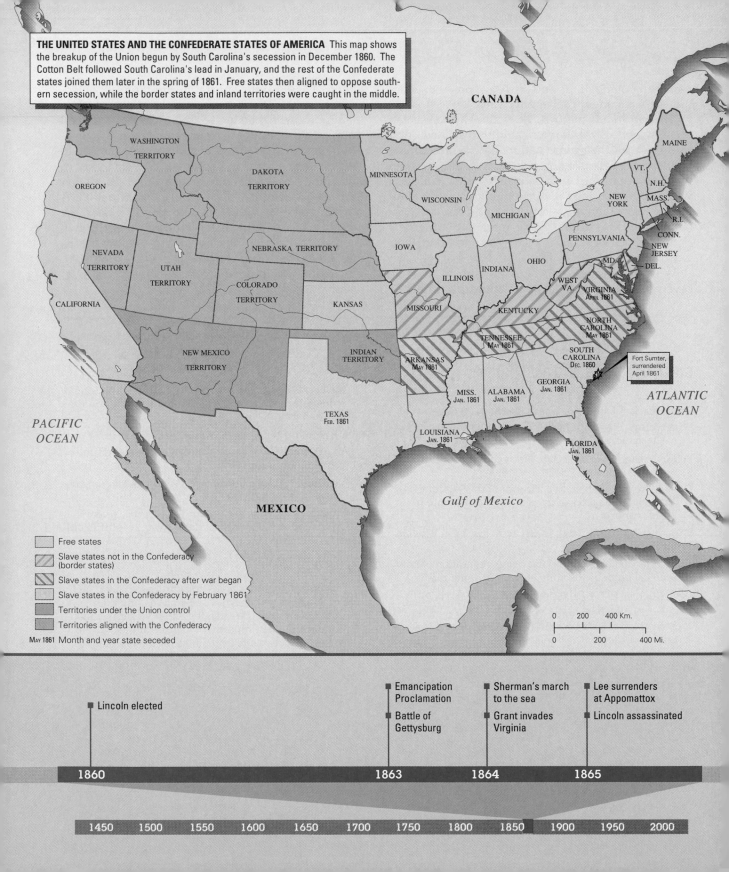

THE UNITED STATES AND THE CONFEDERATE STATES OF AMERICA This map shows the breakup of the Union begun by South Carolina's secession in December 1860. The Cotton Belt followed South Carolina's lead in January, and the rest of the Confederate states joined them later in the spring of 1861. Free states then aligned to oppose southern secession, while the border states and inland territories were caught in the middle.

CANADA

MAINE

WASHINGTON TERRITORY

OREGON

DAKOTA TERRITORY

MINNESOTA

VT.
N.H.
NEW YORK
MASS.
R.I.
CONN.

WISCONSIN

MICHIGAN

PENNSYLVANIA
NEW JERSEY
DEL.
MD.

NEVADA TERRITORY

UTAH TERRITORY

NEBRASKA TERRITORY

IOWA

ILLINOIS

INDIANA

OHIO

WEST VA.

VIRGINIA
April 1861

CALIFORNIA

COLORADO TERRITORY

KANSAS

MISSOURI

KENTUCKY

NORTH CAROLINA
May 1861

NEW MEXICO TERRITORY

INDIAN TERRITORY

ARKANSAS
May 1861

TENNESSEE
May 1861

SOUTH CAROLINA
Dec. 1860

Fort Sumter, surrendered April 1861

MISS.
Jan. 1861

ALABAMA
Jan. 1861

GEORGIA
Jan. 1861

ATLANTIC OCEAN

PACIFIC OCEAN

TEXAS
Feb. 1861

LOUISIANA
Jan. 1861

FLORIDA
Jan. 1861

MEXICO

Gulf of Mexico

Free states

Slave states not in the Confederacy (border states)

Slave states in the Confederacy after war began

Slave states in the Confederacy by February 1861

Territories under the Union control

Territories aligned with the Confederacy

May 1861 Month and year state seceded

0   200   400 Km.

0   200   400 Mi.

Lincoln elected

Emancipation Proclamation

Battle of Gettysburg

Sherman's march to the sea

Grant invades Virginia

Lee surrenders at Appomattox

Lincoln assassinated

1860   1863   1864   1865

1450   1500   1550   1600   1650   1700   1750   1800   1850   1900   1950   2000

A Violent Solution: Civil War, 1861–1865

The Politics of War

- What *constraints* did Abraham Lincoln and Jefferson Davis face as they led their respective nations into war?

- How did they *choose* to deal with those *constraints*?

From Bull Run to Antietam

- How did military action during the opening years of the war affect the *expectations* of people in the North and South?

- How did the Emancipation Proclamation change *expectations* for the war's *outcome*?

Social Consequences of War

- How did *constraints* created by the war affect society during the course of the fighting?

- What *choices* did individuals and governments make to meet those *constraints*?

Waging Total War

- What *expectations* contributed to military *choices* on both sides after 1862?

- What were the *outcomes* of those *choices*?

INTRODUCTION

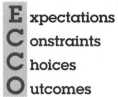

E xpectations
C onstraints
C hoices
O utcomes

Union president Abraham Lincoln and Confederate president Jefferson Davis faced serious political, economic, and military *constraints* as they mobilized for war. Lincoln felt *constrained* by an aged army, a tiny navy, and a sluggish economy, yet even that was more than Davis had to work with. Both presidents also had to contend with political disagreements and demands. These *constraints* combined to shape their *expectations* and *choices*. Davis *chose* to pursue a defensive strategy, *expecting* that the North would soon tire of war. Lincoln, blessed with superior manpower, manufacturing capability, and natural resources, *chose* to use the military to squeeze the South economically, *expecting* that the Confederacy would soon sue for peace. When disastrous losses early in the war and political pressure from radicals in the Republican party upset Lincoln's plan, he *chose* a more aggressive approach. Davis was forced to *choose* a more aggressive course also. The *outcome* was total war as Union and Confederate armies clashed across the better part of a continent.

The economy in the North actually grew as industry moved into high gear to supply the troops. The Union Army kept Confederates from disrupting northern production, and the Union Navy kept international commerce flowing. Meanwhile, the southern economy deteriorated. *Expecting* sales of cotton overseas to keep money flowing in for the war effort, southerners were disappointed when Britain stopped buying cotton and remained neutral. Southerners also had to face the unpleasant reality of invading troops' marching across their land and pitched battles being fought where corn, beans, and cotton once grew. The *outcome* was economic chaos. Many southern people—black as well as white, loyal as well as rebel—went hungry; some even starved.

In the fall of 1862, Lincoln boldly *chose* to change the direction of the war by announcing the Emancipation Proclamation. Knowing that the South would not sue for peace after that development, Lincoln pressed his generals to deal a death blow to southern resistance. In the summer of 1864, Ulysses S. Grant and William Tecumseh Sherman *chose* military strategies that took a terrible human toll. While Sherman slashed his way through the Deep South, Grant sacrificed tens of thousands of his men's lives to contain the Confederate forces under Robert E. Lee. The *outcome* was Lee's surrender on April 9, 1865.

Lincoln then began planning how to bring the defeated South back into the Union. But the man who had led the nation through the war did not survive to pursue his plans for peace. Lincoln was shot by an actor sympathetic to the South. The president died, leaving the nation in mourning, uncertain what the final *outcome* would be.

The Politics of War

• What *constraints* did Abraham Lincoln and Jefferson Davis face as they led their respective nations into war?

• How did they *choose* to deal with those *constraints*?

Running the war posed complex problems for both Abraham Lincoln and Jefferson Davis. At the outset, neither side had the experience, soldiers, or supplies to wage an effective war. Foreign diplomacy and foreign trade were vital to both sides. The Union needed to convince the rest of the world that this conflict was a **rebellion** against legitimate authority,

---

rebellion   Open, armed, and organized resistance to a legally constituted government.

CHRONOLOGY

War Between the States

1860	Lincoln elected

1861 Ft. Sumter falls
Lincoln takes office and runs the Union by
  executive authority until July
Battle of Bull Run
George McClellan organizes the Union
  Army
Union naval blockade begins

1862 Grant's victories in the Mississippi Valley
U.S. Navy captures New Orleans
Battle of Shiloh
Peninsular Campaign
Battle of Antietam
African-Americans permitted in Union Army

1863 Emancipation Proclamation takes effect
Union enacts conscription

Battle of Chancellorsville and death of
  Stonewall Jackson
Union victories at Gettysburg and Vicksburg
Draft riots in New York City

1864 Grant invades Virginia
Sherman captures Atlanta
Lincoln re-elected
Sherman's March to the Sea

1865 Sherman's march through the Carolinas
Lee abandons Petersburg and Richmond
Lee surrenders at Appomattox
Lincoln proposes a gentle reconstruction
  policy
Lincoln is assassinated

the Confederacy that this was a war between nations. The distinction was important. International law permitted neutral nations to trade, negotiate, and communicate with nations engaged in a war. International law forbade neutrals from having any dealings with rebels against a legally constituted government.

Perhaps the biggest challenge confronting both Davis and Lincoln, however, was internal politics. Lincoln had to contend not only with northern Democrats and with **Copperheads**—northerners who sympathized with the South—but also with divisions in his own party. Davis too faced internal political problems. The Confederate constitution guaranteed considerable autonomy to the Confederate states, and each state had a different opinion about war strategy.

Union Policies and Objectives

Lincoln's first objective was to rebuild an army that was in disarray. When hostilities broke out, the Union had only sixteen thousand men in uniform. Nearly one-third of the officers had resigned to support the Confederacy. The remaining military leadership was aged: General-in-Chief Winfield Scott was 74 years old. The only two Union officers who had ever commanded a brigade were in their seventies. Weapons were old, supplies were low, and personnel was limited. On May 3, acting on his executive authority because Congress was not in session, Lincoln called for regular army recruits to meet the crisis.

Lincoln then ordered the U.S. Navy to stop all incoming supplies to the states in rebellion. In 1861, the Union Navy had few resources, but Navy Secretary Gideon Welles quickly turned that situation around. Starting with almost nothing, he built

Copperheads   Derogatory term (the name of a poisonous snake) applied to northerners who supported the South during the Civil War.

an effective navy that could both blockade the South and support land forces. By 1862, the Union Navy had 260 warships on the seas and a hundred more under construction.

Winfield Scott drafted the initial Union military strategy. He advised that the blockade of southern ports be combined with a strong Union thrust down the Mississippi River. This strategy would split the Confederacy in two, separating Confederate states and territories west of the river from the rest of the Confederacy. It also would cut the Confederacy off from trade with the outside world. Scott believed that economic pressure would bring southern moderates forward to negotiate a return to the Union. The northern press sneered at this **anaconda plan,** noting that Scott intended to "squeeze the South to military death." A passive strategy did not appeal to war-fevered northerners who hungered for complete victory.

When Congress convened in a special session on July 4, 1861, Lincoln explained the actions he had taken in Congress's absence and outlined his plans. He said that he had no intention of abolishing slavery. Rebellion, not slavery, had caused the war, he said, and the seceding states must be brought back into the Union. On July 22 and 25, 1861, Congress passed resolutions validating Lincoln's actions.

This seemingly unified front lasted only briefly. **Radical Republicans** regarded vengeance as the primary objective of the war. Radical leader **Thaddeus Stevens** of Pennsylvania pressed for and got a law promoting severe penalties against individuals in rebellion. Treason was punishable by death, and anyone aiding the rebellion was to be punished with imprisonment, confiscation of property, and the emancipation of slaves. All persons living in the eleven seceding states, whether loyal to the Union or not, were declared enemies of the Union.

The Radicals splintered any consensus Lincoln might have achieved in his own party, and northern Democrats railed against his accumulation of power. Lincoln attempted to appease both factions and used military appointments to smooth political feathers. Still, his attitudes frequently enraged radical abolitionists. Lincoln maintained his calm in the face of their criticism. Nevertheless, ongoing divisiveness hindered efforts to run the war.

Confederate Policies and Objectives

At the start of the war, the Confederacy had no army, no navy, no war supplies, no government structure, and no foreign alliances. It had less than half the people of the Union (nine million as opposed to twenty-three million) and almost none of the Union's manufacturing capabilities. After the attack on Fort Sumter, the Confederate government's main task was amassing supplies, troops, ships, and war materials.

The Union naval blockade posed an immediate problem. The Confederacy had no navy and no capacity to build ships. Nevertheless, Secretary of the Navy Stephen Mallory converted river steamboats, tugboats, and **revenue cutters** into harbor patrol gunboats. He also developed explosive mines that were placed at the entrance to southern harbors and rivers. Commander James D. Bulloch purchased boats from the British. On one occasion, he bought a fast merchant ship, loaded it with military supplies, maneuvered through the Union blockade at Savannah, and then equipped the vessel to ram Union vessels. The *C.S.S. Sumter* captured or burned eighteen Union ships during the first months of the war.

Confederates pinned their main hope of winning the war on the army. Southerners strongly believed they could "lick the Yankees" despite being outnumbered. Southern boys rushed to enlist to fight the northern "popinjays." By the time Lincoln issued his call for seventy-five thousand militiamen,

---

anaconda plan   Winfield Scott's plan (named after a snake that smothers prey in its coils) to blockade southern ports and take control of the Mississippi River, thus splitting the Confederacy, cutting off southern trade, and causing an economic collapse.

Radical Republicans   Republican faction that tried to limit presidential power and enhance congressional authority during the Civil War.

Thaddeus Stevens   Pennsylvania congressman who was a leader of the Radical Republicans, hated the South, and wanted to abolish slavery.

revenue cutter   A small, lightly armed boat used by government customs agents to look for merchant ships violating customs laws.

the Confederates already had sixty thousand men in uniform.

Despite this rush of fighting men, the South faced major handicaps. Even with the addition of the four Upper South states, Confederate industrial capacity and transportation systems were still outstripped by the North. The southern states built only 3 percent of all firearms manufactured in the United States in 1860. The North produced almost all of the country's cloth, **pig iron,** boots, and shoes. Early in the war, the South produced enough food but lacked the means to transport it where it was needed.

Josiah Gorgas worked miracles as the Confederate chief of **ordnance.** Gorgas purchased arms from Europe while his ordnance officers bought or stole copper stills to make **percussion caps,** bronze church bells to make cannon, and lead to make bullets. He built factories and foundries to manufacture small arms. But despite all his skill, he could not supply all of the Confederate troops. In 1861, more than half of the enlistees were turned away because of lack of equipment.

Internal politics also plagued the Davis administration. Despite the shortage of arms, state governors hoarded weapons seized from federal arsenals for their own state militias. Powerful state politicians with little military experience such as Henry A. Wise of Virginia received appointments as generals. Davis contributed to the political problems by constantly interfering with the war department and squabbling with everyone.

Davis favored a defensive war. He thought that by counterattacking and yielding territory, the Confederacy could prolong the war and make it so costly that the Union would finally relent. State leaders, however, demanded that their state's borders be protected. In any case, most southerners preferred an aggressive policy. As one editor put it, "Waiting for blows, instead of inflicting them is altogether unsuited to the genius of our people."

The Diplomatic Front

Perhaps the biggest challenge facing the Confederacy was gaining international recognition and foreign aid. The primary focus of Confederate foreign policy was Great Britain. For years, the South had been exporting large amounts of cotton to Britain.

Many southerners felt that Britain would recognize the Confederacy immediately following the organization of a government. Such was not the case. Although the British allowed southern agents to purchase ships and goods, they remained neutral and did not recognize the Confederacy. Not convinced that the Confederacy could make good on its bid for independence, the British steered a safe course. The British pronouncement set the tone for other European responses.

Lincoln had to take care not to provoke the British while preventing aid to the Confederacy. Despite his best efforts, an incident at sea nearly scuttled British-American relations. In November 1861 the U.S. warship *San Jacinto* stopped the *Trent,* a British merchant ship carrying two Confederate diplomats. The Confederates were then taken to Boston for confinement.

The British were not pleased. They viewed the Trent Affair as a violation of international law. President Lincoln calmed the British by arguing that the *San Jacinto*'s captain had acted without orders. He ordered the release of the prisoners and apologized to the British.

The Union's First Attack

Confident that the Union could end the war quickly, General Irvin McDowell moved his troops into Virginia in July 1861 (see Map 14.1). McDowell's poorly trained troops ambled along as though they were on a country outing. Their dawdling allowed Confederate General P. G. T. Beauregard enough time to defend a vital rail center near Manassas Junction along a creek called **Bull Run.**

---

pig iron Crude iron, direct from a blast furnace, that is cast into rectangular molds called pigs in preparation for conversion into steel, cast iron, or wrought iron.

ordnance Weapons, ammunition, and other military equipment.

percussion cap A thin metal cap containing gunpowder that explodes when struck.

Bull Run A creek in Virginia not far from Washington, D.C., where Confederate soldiers forced federal troops to retreat in the first major battle of the Civil War, fought in July 1861.

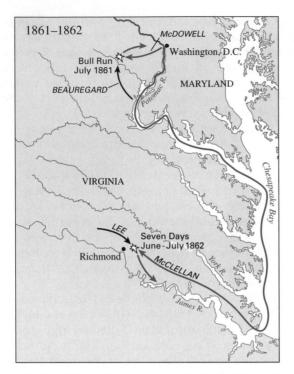

♦ MAP 14.1 Union Offensives into Virginia, 1861–1862
This map shows two failed Union attempts to invade Virginia: the Battle of Bull Run (July 1861) and the Peninsular Campaign (April–July 1862). Confederate victories embarrassed the richer and more populous Union.

McDowell attacked on Sunday, July 21. He seemed poised to overrun the Confederates until southern reinforcements under **Thomas J. Jackson** took a position on a hill and, fighting furiously, stalled the Union advance. Jackson's stand at Bull Run turned the tide for the Confederacy and earned him the nickname "Stonewall." Under intense cannon fire, Union troops panicked and began retreating pell-mell toward Washington. The Confederates were also in disarray, and they made no attempt to pursue the fleeing Union forces.

This battle profoundly affected both sides. In the South, the victory stirred confidence that the war would be short. Northerners, disillusioned and embarrassed, pledged that no similar retreats would occur. Lincoln replaced General Scott with **George B. McClellan.**

General McClellan's strengths were in organizing and in inspiring his troops. Both were sorely needed. After Bull Run, the army's confidence was badly shaken. Under McClellan, months of training turned the 185,000-man army into a well-drilled and efficient unit. Calls to attack Richmond began anew, but McClellan continued to drill the troops and remained in the capital.

The new year began with Lincoln's taking a much more aggressive stance. On January 27, 1862, he called for a broad offensive, but McClellan ignored the order. Completely frustrated, Lincoln removed McClellan as general-in-chief on March 11 but left him in command of the Army of the Potomac.

From Bull Run to Antietam

- How did military action during the opening years of the war affect the *expectations* of people in the North and South?
- How did the Emancipation Proclamation change *expectations* for the war's *outcome*?

After Bull Run it was clear that the war would be neither short nor glorious. Military, political, and diplomatic strategies became increasingly entangled as both the North and the South struggled for ways to end the war.

The War in the West

Both the United States and the Confederacy coveted the western territories. In 1861 Confederate Henry Hopkins Sibley led an expedition in an attempt to gain control of New Mexico and Arizona. Sibley recruited thirty-seven hundred Texans and marched into New Mexico. Although he defeated a Union

---

Thomas J. Jackson　Confederate general nicknamed "Stonewall," who commanded troops at both battles of Bull Run and who was mortally wounded by his own troops at Chancellorsville in 1863.

George B. McClellan　U.S. general who replaced Winfield Scott as general-in-chief of Union forces; a skillful organizer, he was slow and indecisive as a strategist.

force at Valverde and Santa Fe, lack of provisions forced Sibley and his troops to retreat to Texas.

Confederate leaders also sought to gain western territory by making alliances with Indian tribes, particularly those in the newly settled Indian Territory south of Kansas. Indians who had endured the Trail of Tears had no particular love for the Union. If these Indian tribes aligned with the Confederacy, they not only could supply troops but could form a buffer between Union forces in Kansas and the thinly spread Confederate defenses west of the Mississippi.

Although one Cherokee leader, Stand Watie, became a Confederate general and distinguished himself in battle, Confederate Indian troops never provided the kind of assistance hoped for. They disliked army discipline and became disgusted when promised supplies failed to materialize. Many Indian troops defected when ordered to attack other Indians. Still, several battles, such as the 1862 Battle of Pea Ridge in Arkansas, pitted Indian troops on each side against each other. The divisions between Indian groups allied with the North and with the South often reflected long-standing tribal animosities.

Struggle for the Mississippi

While McClellan stalled in the East, one Union general finally had some success in the western theater. **Ulysses S. Grant** moved against southern strongholds in the Mississippi Valley in 1862. On February 6, he took Fort Henry along the Tennessee River and ten days later captured Fort Donelson on the Cumberland River (see Map 14.2). Grant's army suffered few casualties and took more than fifteen thousand prisoners of war. As Union forces approached Nashville, the Confederates retreated to Corinth, Mississippi. In this one stroke, Grant brought Kentucky and most of Tennessee under federal control.

At Corinth, Confederate general Albert Sidney Johnston finally reorganized the retreating southern troops. Early on April 6, to Grant's surprise, Johnston attacked at Pittsburg Landing, Tennessee, near a small country meetinghouse called Shiloh Church. Union forces under General **William Tecumseh Sherman** were driven back, but the Confederate attack soon lost momentum. The **Battle of Shiloh** raged until midafternoon, when Johnston was mortally wounded. General Beauregard, now in command, forced over two thousand Union soldiers to surrender. Believing the enemy defeated, he ended the action. Union reinforcements who arrived during the night enabled Grant to counterattack the next morning and to push the Confederates back to Corinth.

Losses on both sides were staggering, by far the heaviest to date in the war. The Union had 13,047 men killed, wounded, or captured, while the Confederacy suffered a loss of 10,694 men. The Battle of Shiloh made the reality of war apparent to everyone. After Shiloh, one Confederate wrote: "Death in every awful form, if it really be death, is a pleasant sight in comparison to the fearfully and mortally wounded." The number of casualties at Shiloh stunned people in the North and South alike.

Farther south, Admiral David G. Farragut's fleet of U.S. Navy gunboats captured New Orleans on April 25. Farragut then sailed up the Mississippi. He scored several victories until he reached Port Hudson, Louisiana, where Confederate defenses and shallow water forced him to halt. Meanwhile, on June 6, Union gunboats destroyed a Confederate fleet at Memphis, Tennessee, and brought the upper Mississippi under Union control. **Vicksburg,** Mississippi, remained the only major obstacle to Union control of the entire river (see Map 14.2).

Grant launched two attacks against Vicksburg in December 1862. But Confederate cavalry and the

---

Ulysses S. Grant   U.S. general who became commander-in-chief of the Union Army in 1864 after the Vicksburg campaign; he later became president of the United States.

William Tecumseh Sherman   U.S. general who captured Atlanta in 1864 and led a destructive march to the Atlantic coast.

Battle of Shiloh   Battle in Tennessee in April 1862 that ended with an unpursued Confederate withdrawal; both sides suffered heavy casualties for the first time, and neither side gained ground.

Vicksburg   Confederate-held city on the Mississippi River that surrendered on July 4, 1863, after a siege by Grant's forces.

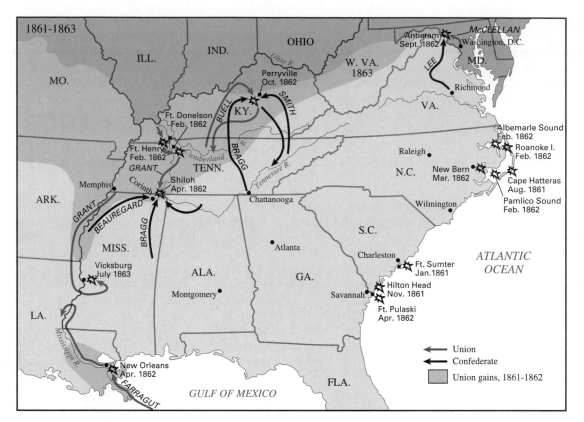

♦ **MAP 14.2 The Anaconda Plan and the Battle of Antietam** This map illustrates the anaconda plan at work. The Union Navy closed southern harbors while Grant's troops worked to seal the northern end of the Mississippi River. It also shows the Battle of Antietam (September 1862), in which Confederate troops under Robert E. Lee were finally halted by a Union army under General George McClellan.

cannon defending Vicksburg thwarted his offensives. Grant had to come up with a new strategy for taking the city. Union efforts along the Mississippi now stalled. But Union forces had wrenched control of the upper and lower ends of the river away from the Confederacy.

Lee's Aggressive Defense of Virginia

Winfield Scott's anaconda plan was well on its way to cutting the Confederacy in two. But the northern public thought that the path to victory led to Richmond, the Confederate capital. To maintain public support for the war, Lincoln needed victories

over the Confederates in the East. Confederate leaders responded by making the defense of Richmond the South's primary military goal. More supplies and men were assigned to Virginia than to defending Confederate borders elsewhere.

A naval battle early in 1862 cleared the way for a Union offensive against Richmond. Early in the war, Confederate forces had captured a Union ship, the *Merrimac*. Hoping to break the Union naval blockade around Norfolk, Virginia, Confederate naval architects redesigned the *Merrimac*. They encased the entire ship in iron plates and renamed it the *Virginia*. Operating out of Norfolk, the Confederate ironclad sunk several Union blockaders in a single day. The Union Navy countered with the *Monitor,* a low-decked ironclad vessel with a revolving gun turret. In March the *Virginia* and the *Monitor* shelled each other for five hours. Both were badly damaged but still afloat when the *Virginia* withdrew, limping back to Norfolk, never to leave harbor again.

Taking advantage of the *Monitor*'s success and Union naval superiority, McClellan transported the entire **Army of the Potomac** by ship to Fort Monroe, Virginia. The army then marched up the peninsula between the York and James rivers to begin what became known as the Peninsular Campaign. McClellan *expected* to surprise the Confederates by attacking Richmond from the south. (see Map 14.1). In typical fashion, he proceeded cautiously. The outnumbered Confederate forces bluffed McClellan into thinking that he was facing a whole army and slowly retreated to Richmond. On May 31, General Joseph E. Johnston, commander of the Confederate Army of Northern Virginia, attacked at Seven Pines, hoping to surprise his opponent. Johnston was severely wounded, forcing Jefferson Davis to find a replacement.

Davis named Robert E. Lee as that replacement. Lee had previously advised Davis and helped organize the defense of the Atlantic coast. Daring, bold, and tactically aggressive, he enjoyed combat, pushed his troops to the maximum, and was well liked by those serving under him. Lee had an uncanny ability to read the character of his opponents, predict their maneuvers, and turn their mistakes to his advantage.

As McClellan worked his way toward Richmond, Stonewall Jackson staged a brilliant diversionary thrust up the Shenandoah Valley toward Washington. Jackson seemed to be everywhere at once. In thirty days, he and his men marched 350 miles, defeated three Union armies in five battles, captured a fortune in provisions and equipment, inflicted twice as many casualties as they received, and confused and immobilized Union forces in the region.

Following Jackson's brilliant campaign, Lee launched a series of attacks to drive McClellan away from the Confederate capital. Over a seven-day period in late June and early July, he forced McClellan to abandon the Peninsular Campaign. Fed up with McClellan, Lincoln gave command of the Army of the Potomac to General John Pope. In the **Second Battle of Bull Run,** Lee soundly defeated Lincoln's new general. Thoroughly disappointed with Pope's performance and not knowing whom else to turn to, Lincoln once again named McClellan commander of the Army of the Potomac.

Lee's Invasion of Maryland

Feeling confident after the victory at Bull Run, Lee devised a bold offensive against Maryland. His plan had three objectives: (1) to move the fighting out of wartorn Virginia so that farmers could harvest food, (2) to acquire volunteers from Maryland, and (3) to gain diplomatic recognition of the Confederacy from Europe. He hoped to force the Union to sue for peace. On September 4, Lee crossed the Potomac into Maryland, dividing his army into three separate attack wings. McClellan learned of Lee's plans when Union soldiers found a copy of Lee's detailed instructions wrapped around some cigars.

If McClellan had acted swiftly on this intelligence, he could have crushed Lee's army piece by piece, but he waited sixteen hours before advancing. By then Lee had learned of the missing orders. After bitter fighting at Fox's Gap, Lee reunited some of his forces at Sharpsburg, Maryland, near **Antietam Creek** (see Map 14.2). There, on September 17, the Army of the Potomac and the Army of Northern Virginia engaged in the bloodiest single-day battle of the Civil War.

The casualties in this one battle were more than double those suffered in the War of 1812 and the Mexican War combined. One Union soldier said of the Battle of Antietam, "The whole landscape turned red." Both armies were exhausted by the

---

Army of the Potomac   Army created to guard the U.S. capital after the Battle of Bull Run in 1861; it became the main Union army in the East.

Second Battle of Bull Run   Union defeat near Bull Run in August 1862; Union troops led by John Pope were outmaneuvered by Lee.

Antietam Creek   Site of a battle that occurred in September 1862 when Lee's forces invaded Maryland; both sides suffered heavy losses, and Lee retreated into Virginia.

♦ No one could doubt the bloody reality of war after the Battle of Antietam on September 17, 1862. In a single day of fighting, there were more than twice the number of casualties than in the War of 1812 and the Mexican War combined. This photograph shows one group of Confederate artillerymen laid out near their cannons after the battle was over. *Confederate dead at Antietam. Photo by Alexander Gardner. US Army Military History Institute.*

bitter fighting. After a day of rest, Lee retreated across the Potomac. For the first time, Lee had experienced defeat.

Nevertheless, Lincoln was totally displeased with the performance of his army's leadership. He felt that Lee's force could have been destroyed if McClellan had attacked earlier or pursued the fleeing Confederate army. He fired McClellan again, this time for good, and placed Ambrose E. Burnside in command of the Army of the Potomac.

Burnside moved the Army of the Potomac to the east bank of the Rappahannock River overlooking **Fredericksburg,** Virginia (see Map 14.3). On December 13, in one of the worst mistakes of the war, Burnside ordered a day-long frontal assault against Lee's heavily fortified positions. Federal troops suffered tremendous casualties, and once again the Army of the Potomac retreated to Washington.

Diplomacy and the Politics of Emancipation

The year 1862 ended with mixed results for both sides. Union forces in the West had scored major victories, taking Memphis and New Orleans. But the failure of the Army of the Potomac outweighed the Union's success in the West. Lee's victories, however, carried heavy casualties. A long, drawn-out conflict favored the Union unless Jefferson Davis could secure help for the Confederacy from abroad.

The Confederacy still *expected* British aid. But nothing seemed to shake Britain's commitment to neutrality. The brilliant diplomacy of Charles Francis Adams, Lincoln's ambassador in London, and the fact that Britain possessed a surplus of cotton helped prevent British recognition of the Confederacy. Any prospects the Confederacy had of recognition disappeared with Lee's failure at Antietam.

Five days after the battle, Lincoln unveiled the **Emancipation Proclamation.** The proclamation,

---

Fredericksburg Site in Virginia of a Union defeat in December 1862, which demonstrated the incompetence of the new Union commander, Ambrose E. Burnside.

Emancipation Proclamation Lincoln's order abolishing slavery in states "in rebellion" but not in border territories still loyal to the Union, as of January 1, 1863.

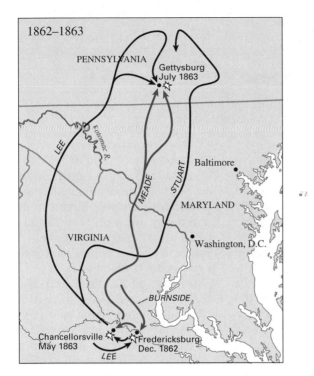

1862–1863

PENNSYLVANIA

Gettysburg
July 1863

LEE

Potomac R.

MEADE

STUART

Baltimore

MARYLAND

VIRGINIA

Washington, D.C.

BURNSIDE

Chancellorsville
May 1863

Fredericksburg
Dec. 1862

LEE

◆ **MAP 14.3 Fredericksburg, Chancellorsville, and Gettysburg** This map shows the campaigns that took place during the winter of 1862 and spring of 1863, culminating in the Battle of Gettysburg (July 1863). General Meade's victory at Gettysburg may have been the critical turning point in the war.

which went into effect on January 1, 1863, abolished slavery in rebellious areas (see Voices: Emancipation Proclamation). Ironically, the proclamation actually freed no slaves. The four slave states that remained in the Union and Confederate territory under federal control were exempt from its terms. Moreover, Lincoln had no power to enforce emancipation in areas still controlled by the Confederacy. Lincoln's wording of the proclamation, however, was quite deliberate. He knew that he could not afford to antagonize the slaveholding border states and drive them into the Confederacy. For that reason, the proclamation was not a resounding moral denunciation of slavery.

Still, some northerners considered it a monumental step forward. Frederick Douglass wrote, "We shout for joy that we live to record this righteous decree." Others, however, thought it carried little

significance. Confederate leaders argued that the Proclamation merely demonstrated Lincoln's hypocrisy. Conservative British newspapers pointed to the paradox of the Proclamation: it declared an end to slavery in areas where Lincoln could not enforce it, but it had no effect on slavery in areas under Lincoln's control. British abolitionists, however, applauded the document.

Lincoln's new general-in-chief, Henry Halleck, understood the underlying significance of the Proclamation. He explained to Grant that the "character of the war has very much changed within the last year. There is now no possible hope of reconciliation." As Lincoln told one member of his cabinet, the war would now be "one of subjugation."

Social Consequences of War

- How did *constraints* created by the war affect society during the course of the fighting?
- What *choices* did individuals and governments make to meet those *constraints*?

The Civil War placed tremendous stress on American society, both North and South. As the men marched off to battle, women faced the task of caring for families and property alone. As casualties increased, the number of voluntary enlistments decreased. The armies consumed vast amounts of weapons, ammunition, food, clothing, and hardware. Government spending was enormous, hard currency was scarce, and inflation soared as both governments printed paper money to pay their debts. Society in both North and South changed to meet an array of *constraints* as individuals attempted to carry on their lives in the midst of the war's devastation.

Instituting the Draft

By the end of 1862, heavy casualties, massive desertion, and declining enlistments had depleted both armies. Although the North had a much larger population than the South, military fortunes sagged during 1862 and enlistments were low. Over a hundred thousand Union soldiers were absent without official leave. State drafts netted few replacements

Emancipating the Slaves

The Emancipation Proclamation

Entering into the Civil War, Abraham Lincoln repeatedly asserted that the Union's objective was nothing more than ending a rebellion against constitutional authority—the destruction or preservation of slavery was to play no role in the conflict. But in September 1862, Lincoln changed the course of the war—and the course of history—by choosing to issue the Emancipation Proclamation.

From the outset, Lincoln claimed that the proclamation was nothing more than a war measure. The phrasing of the document itself makes this clear: Lincoln was giving southerners one hundred days (from September 13, 1862, to January 1, 1863) to withdraw from the Confederacy and declare loyalty to the Union, or face a potential armed uprising among their slave population.

Newspaper editors, military figures, diplomats, and private citizens rallied around the president, praising Lincoln for what the New York Times *called a "revolution" in American attitudes about race and slavery. But just as many disagreed with the president's actions.*

That on the first day of January, in the year of our Lord one thousand eight hundred and sixty-three, all persons held as slaves within any State or designated part of a State, the people whereof shall then be in rebellion against the United States, shall be then, thenceforth, and forever free. . . .

That the Executive will, on the first day of January aforesaid, by proclamation, designate the States and parts of States, if any, in which the people thereof, respectively, shall then be in rebellion against the United States; and the fact that any State, or the people thereof, shall on that day be, in good faith, represented in the Congress of the United States by members chosen thereto at elections wherein a majority of the qualified voters of such State shall have participated, shall, in the absence of strong countervailing testimony, be deemed conclusive evidence that such State, and the people thereof, are not then in rebellion against the United States.

Now, therefor I, Abraham Lincoln, President of the United States, by virtue of the power in me vested as Commander-in-Chief of the Army and Navy of the United States in time of actual armed rebellion against the authority and government of the United States, and as a fit and necessary war measure for suppressing said rebellion, so, on

this first day of January, . . . and in accordance with my purpose to do so publicly proclaimed for the full period of one hundred days . . . order and designate as the States and parts of States wherein the people thereof respectively, are this day in rebellion against the United States. . . .

And . . . I do order and declare that all persons held as slaves within said designated States, and parts of States, are, and hence-forward shall be free; and that the Executive government of the United States, including the military and naval authorities thereof, will recognize and maintain the freedom of said persons.

And I hereby enjoin upon the people so declared to be free to abstain from all violence, unless in necessary self-defense; and I recommend to them that, in all cases when allowed, they labor faithfully for reasonable wages.

And I further declare and make known, that such persons of suitable condition, will be received into the armed service of the United States to garrison forts, positions, stations, and other places, and to man vessels of all sorts in said service.

And upon this act, sincerely believed to be an act of justice, warranted by the Constitution, upon military necessity, I invoke the considerate judgement of mankind, and the gracious favor of Almighty God.

Supporters Had This to Say

■ President Lincoln's proclamation . . . marks a new era in the history, not only of this war, but of this country and the world. It is not necessary to assume that it will set free instantly the enslaved blacks of the South, in order to ascribe to it the greatest and most permanent importance. Whatever may be its immediate results, it changes entirely the relations of the National Government to the institution of Slavery. Hitherto Slavery has been under the protection of the Government, henceforth it is under its ban. . . . This change of attitude is itself a revolution.   New York Times, *January 3, 1863*

■ President Lincoln has at last hurled against rebellion the bolt which he has so long held suspended. . . . no event in the history of this country since the Declaration of Independence itself has excited so profound attention either at home or abroad. *(Springfield)* Illinois State Journal, *September 24, 1862*

■ O dark, sad millions, patiently and dumb
Waiting for God, your hour, at last has come
And freedom's song
Breaks the long silence of your night of wrong!
John Greenleaf Whittier, "The Proclamation.," February 1863

Opponents Had This to Say

■ We may well leave it to the instincts of that common humanity . . . to pass judgment on a measure by which several millions of human beings of an inferior race, peaceful and contented laborers in their sphere, . . . are encouraged to a general assassination of their masters. . . . Our own detestation of those who have attempted the most execrable measure recorded in the history of guilty man is tempered by profound contempt for the impotent rage which it discloses.   *Jefferson Davis, speech to the Confederate Congress, January 12, 1863*

■ However we may inflate the emancipation balloon, it will never ascend among the constellations. The ugly fact cannot be concealed that it was done reluctantly and stintedly . . . and that no recognition of principles of justice or humanity surrounded the political act with a halo of moral glory.   *Lydia Maria Child, 1863*

■ Resolved: That the emancipation proclamation of the President of the United States is as unwarrantable in military as in civil law; a gigantic usurpation, at once converting the war . . . into the crusade for the sudden, unconditional and violent liberation of 3,000,000 Negro slaves, . . . consequences of which to both races cannot be contemplated. . . . *Resolutions of the Illinois State Legislature, January 7, 1863*

because the Democrats, who made tremendous political gains in 1862, at times refused to cooperate. In March 1863, Congress passed the **Conscription Act** to ensure enough manpower to continue the war. The law declared all single men between the ages of 20 and 45, and married men between 20 and 35, eligible to be drafted. Draftees were selected by a lottery.

The conscription law offered two ways for draftees to avoid military service. They could hire an "acceptable substitute" or pay a $300 fee to purchase exemption. In effect, the wealthy were exempt from the law. The burden of service thus fell on farmers and urban workers who were already suffering from high taxation and inflation. Together, conscription and emancipation, which touched on long-standing racial resentments, created a sense of alienation among the urban poor that exploded in the summer of 1863.

Some of the worst urban violence in American history began on July 13 in New York City. Armed demonstrators protesting unfair draft laws rioted for five days during which many blacks were beaten and six were lynched. Businesses owned by blacks and by people who employed blacks were ransacked. Thousands of poor Irish-Americans and other groups who competed for jobs with blacks joined in the riot.

The rioters vented their rage against Republican spokesmen and officials as well. They hanged Republican journalist **Horace Greeley** in **effigy** and sacked the homes of other prominent Republicans. After five days of chaos, federal troops put down the riot by pouring volleys into the mob. At least 105 people died in the riots. Fearful of more violence, the New York City Council voted to pay the $300 exemption fee for all poor draftees who *chose* not to serve in the army.

Conscription in the South similarly met with considerable resentment and resistance. Believing that slaves would not work unless directly overseen by masters, in 1862 Confederate officials exempted planters owning twenty or more slaves from military service. Like Union exemptions, the southern policy fostered the feeling that the poor were going off to fight while the rich stayed safely at home.

Confederate conscription laws also ran afoul of states' rights advocates. Southerners developed several forms of passive resistance to the draft laws. Thousands of draftees simply never showed up, and local officials, jealously guarding their political autonomy, made little effort to enforce the draft.

Wartime Economy in the North and South

Although riots, disorder, and social disruption plagued northern cities, the economy of the Union actually grew stronger as the war progressed. Manufacturers of war supplies benefited from government contracts. Textiles and shoemaking boomed as new labor-saving devices improved efficiency and increased production. Congress stimulated economic growth by means of railroad subsidies and land grants to support a transcontinental railroad and higher tariffs to aid manufacturing.

The South began the war without an industrial base and in desperate need of outside help if it was to have any chance of winning. In addition to lacking transportation, raw materials, and machines, the South lacked managers and skilled industrial workers. The Confederate government intervened more directly in the economy than did its Union counterpart, offering generous loans to companies that would produce war materials. Josiah Gorgas started government-owned production plants in Alabama, Georgia, and South Carolina. These innovative programs, however, could not compensate for inadequate industrialization.

The supply of money was another severe problem in the South. The South printed paper money, eventually issuing more than $1 billion in unbacked currency. The *outcome* was runaway inflation. By 1865 a pound of bacon cost $10.

Conscription Act   Law, passed by Congress in 1863, that established a draft but allowed wealthy people to escape it by hiring a substitute or paying the government a $300 fee.

Horace Greeley   Journalist and politician who helped found the Republican party; his newspaper the *New York Tribune* was known for its antislavery stance.

effigy   A likeness or image, usually three-dimensional.

Southern industrial shortcomings severely handicapped the military. Many Confederate soldiers went barefoot because shoes were in such short supply. Ordnance was always in demand. Northern plants could produce over five thousand muskets per day; Confederate production never exceeded three hundred. The most serious shortage, however, was food. Although the South was an agricultural region, most of its productive farmland was devoted to commercial agriculture. Supplies of corn and rice, the primary food products, were continually reduced by military campaigns and Union occupation. Southern cattle were range stock grown for hides and tallow rather than for food. Hog production suffered because of the war. Hunger became part of daily life for the Confederate armies. Before the war ended, many Union soldiers referred to their opponents as "scarecrows."

Southern civilians suffered from shortages as well. Distribution of goods became almost impossible as invading Union forces cut the few Confederate rail lines. The flow of cattle, horses, and food from the West diminished when Union forces gained control of the Mississippi. Although some blockade runners made it through, their number decreased as the war continued. The fall in 1862 of New Orleans, the South's major port, was devastating to the southern economy. Cities faced food shortages, newspapers were printed on wallpaper, clothes were made from carpet, and pins were made from dry thorns. Cut off from the outside world, the South consumed its existing resources and found no way to obtain more.

Women in Two Nations at War

Because the South had fewer men than the North, a larger proportion of southern families were left in the care of women. Some women worked farms, herded livestock, and supported their families. Others found themselves homeless. Some women tried to persuade their husbands to desert. The vast majority, however, fully supported the war effort despite the hardships at home. Women became responsible for much of the South's agricultural and industrial production.

Women in the North served in much the same capacity as their southern counterparts. They main-tained families and homes alone, working to provide income and raise children. Although they did not face the shortages of goods and ravages of battle, they did work in factories, run family businesses, teach school, and supply soldiers. Women assumed new roles that helped prepare them to become more involved in social and political life after the war.

Women from both sections actively participated in the war. Female nurses showed bravery and devotion. Often working under fire at the front, these volunteers nursed sick and wounded soldiers and offered as much comfort and help as they could. **Clara Barton,** a famous northern nurse, was known as the "Angel of the Battlefield." Most nurses, however, labored in obscurity.

Women on both sides served as scouts, **couriers,** and spies. More than four hundred disguised themselves as men and served as active soldiers until they were discovered (see Individual Choices: Private Lyons Wakeman). General William S. Rosecrans expressed dismay when one of his sergeants was delivered of "a bouncing baby boy." Army camps frequently included officers' wives, female camp employees, and camp followers. One black woman served the 33rd U.S. Colored Troops for years without pay. She taught the men to read and write and bound up their wounds.

Free Blacks, Slaves, and War

The Civil War opened new *choices* and imposed new *constraints* for African-Americans, both free and slave. At first, many free blacks attempted to enlist in the Union Army but were turned away. In 1861, General Benjamin F. Butler began using runaway slaves, called contrabands, as laborers. Several other northern commanders quickly adopted the practice.

After the Emancipation Proclamation, Union officials actively recruited former slaves, forming them

---

Clara Barton   Organizer of a volunteer service to aid sick and wounded Civil War soldiers; she later founded the American branch of the Red Cross.

courier   A messenger carrying official information, sometimes secretly.

Choosing to Volunteer

Private Lyons Wakeman

Different individuals had different motives for volunteering to serve in the Union Army during the Civil War. Like many, Lyons Wakeman's choice was partially economic—a signing bonus and regular army pay was attractive. But the desire for adventure was also an attractive feature. Wakeman overcame serious constraints to win adventure and economic independence, only to die before the war's end. Collection of Jackson K. Doane/Photo by Robert Burke.

Although protest against the Civil War was not uncommon and draft riots broke out in many areas, a large number of people *chose* to serve. Patriotism was the chief motivation of some. Hatred of slavery pushed others into Union uniforms. Not a few had economic motives. Times were hard in many areas of the North in the years leading into the war, and a signing bonus and promise of free meals had strong appeal. And some just hankered for adventure. For Lyons Wakeman, the *choice* to volunteer was influenced mostly by economic need and a daring, venturesome spirit.

Born in 1843 near Binghamton, New York, Wakeman was one of nine children in a farm family struggling for survival after the devastating Panic of 1837. Little is known about Wakeman's childhood except that educational opportunities were limited and Wakeman learned to read and write only passably well. Economic opportunities were scarce in Binghamton, so in 1862 Wakeman deserted farm and family. Writing back to report of being "tired of staying in that neighborhood," Wakeman took work as a canal boatman, *expecting* a life of adventure and perhaps a decent living.

Shortly after moving away from home, Wakeman caught "enlistment fever." Accepting a cash bounty, Wakeman signed up for a three-year hitch in the army and wrote back home that there was a possibility of getting an

into regiments known as the U.S. Colored Troops. Some northern state governments sought free blacks to fill state draft quotas. Agents offered generous bonuses to those who signed up. By the end of the war, about 180,000 African-Americans had enlisted in northern armies, and over 200,000 had served in the armed forces. By the end of the war, African-

Americans comprised about 10 percent of the Union's military manpower.

Army officials discriminated against African-American soldiers in many ways. Units were segregated, and until 1865, blacks were paid less than whites. All black regiments had white commanders, for the government refused to allow blacks to lead additional $800 for extending that enlistment if the war lasted and the newly inducted private survived. Death wasn't a major concern. "I don't fear the rebel bullets, nor I don't fear the cannon," Wakeman asserted in a letter home. "If it is God's will for me to be killed here, it is my will to die."

As the war dragged on, however, Wakeman began to wonder about the decision to join up. In a letter from the front, Wakeman reported, "It would make your hair stand out to be where I have been. How would you like to be in the front rank and have the rear rank load and fire their guns over your shoulder? I have been there myself." Wakeman also got homesick, writing to ask for care packages—"a box of apples and a bottle of cider" on one occasion and "a pair of knit gloves" on another. Wakeman also asked for stamps, so the flow of letters might continue.

Being away made the old farm in Binghamton seem less like a prison and more like a haven. Wakeman's letters nagged constantly for news of mundane things such as how much grain was harvested, how many hogs were slaughtered, and every detail about the new barn that was raised. Wakeman even began talking about buying a farm, though the private acknowledged, "I think I shall have to stay my three years in the Army."

Wakeman never got the chance to return to the farm in Binghamton. The New York Volunteers were assigned to the Red River expedition, an amphibious campaign to take Shreveport, Louisiana, in 1864. Wakeman was one of some twenty-seven thousand Union soldiers who marched 200 miles in just ten days. At Pleasant Hill, 60 miles south of Shreveport,

Wakeman's company fought a two-day engagement against Confederate forces. Writing from the front, Wakeman described the action: "There was heavy cannonading all day and a sharp firing of infantry . . . the next day I had to face the enemy bullets with my regiment. I was under fire about four hours and lay on the field of battle all night. There were three wounded in my company and one killed." Though not among the wounded, Wakeman did not survive the campaign. The private arrived back in New Orleans with violent diarrhea and after nearly a month of hospitalization died, one of some two hundred thousand Union soldiers who fell to disease rather than bullets.

Like so many others who *chose* to volunteer—whether for patriotic, idealistic, or economic reasons—Wakeman was buried in a simple grave far from home. A small stone in the Chalmette National Cemetery in New Orleans says simply "Lyons Wakeman—N.Y." Among the many things that might have been carved there was the one thing that made Wakeman different from all the men who volunteered and makes Wakeman's *choice* so worthy of note: Lyons Wakeman—born Rosetta Wakeman—was a woman.

blacks. Only one hundred were commissioned as officers, and no black soldier ever received a commission higher than major.

At first, African-American regiments were used as laborers or kept in the rear. But when finally sent into battle, black regiments performed so well that they won grudging respect. These men fought in

every theater of the war and had a casualty rate 35 percent higher than white soldiers. Still, acceptance by white troops was slow, and discrimination was the rule.

As the war progressed, the number of African-Americans in the Union Army increased dramatically. By 1865, almost two-thirds of Union troops in the Mississippi Valley were black. Some southerners violently resented the Union's use of these troops. Black soldiers suffered atrocities because some Confederate leaders refused to take black prisoners. At Fort Pillow, for example, Confederate soldiers massacred more than a hundred black soldiers who were trying to surrender.

Probably no other unit acquitted itself better than the **54th Massachusetts.** On July 18, 1863, it led a frontal assault on Confederate defenses at Charleston harbor. Despite sustaining heavy casualties, the black troops gained the parapet and held it for nearly an hour before being forced to retreat. Their conduct in battle had a large impact on changing attitudes toward black soldiers.

The war effort in the South relied heavily on the slave population, mostly as producers of food and as military laborers. Slaves constituted over half of the workforce in armament plants and military hospitals. The use of slave labor freed southern whites for battle.

Waging Total War

- What *expectations* contributed to military *choices* on both sides after 1862?
- What were the *outcomes* of those *choices*?

As the war entered its third year, Lincoln faced severe challenges on several fronts. The losses to Lee and Jackson in Virginia and the failure to catch Lee at Antietam had eroded public support. Many northerners resented the war, conscription, and abolitionism.

Lincoln's Generals and Northern Successes

Lincoln had replaced McClellan with Burnside, but the results had been disastrous. Lincoln then elevated General Joseph Hooker. Despite Hooker's reputation for bravery in battle, Lee soundly defeated "Fighting Joe" Hooker at **Chancellorsville** in May 1863 (see Map 14.3). Lincoln replaced Hooker with General George E. Meade.

Chancellorsville was a devastating loss for the North, but it was perhaps more devastating for the

Confederates. On the evening after the battle, Confederate troops mistook Stonewall Jackson's party for Union cavalry and opened fire, wounding Jackson. Doctors amputated Jackson's arm. "He has lost his left arm," said Lee, "but I have lost my right." Eight days later, Jackson died of pneumonia.

In the West, Union forces were mired during the first half of 1863. General Rosecrans was bogged down in a campaign to take Chattanooga, Tennessee. Grant had settled in for a long, drawn-out siege at Vicksburg. Nowhere did there seem to be a prospect for the dramatic victory Lincoln needed (see Map 14.2).

The summer of 1863, however, turned out to be a major turning point in the war. When Confederate leaders met in Richmond to weigh their options, Davis and his cabinet considered sending troops to relieve Vicksburg. Lee, however, advocated another major invasion of the North. Such a maneuver, he believed, would allow the Confederates to gather supplies and encourage the northern peace movement. Confederate leaders agreed and approved Lee's plan.

Confederates met only weak opposition as they marched into Maryland and Pennsylvania, where they seized livestock, supplies, food, clothing, and shoes (see Map 14.3). Then, on June 30, a Confederate brigade searching for shoes encountered a Union cavalry unit west of **Gettysburg,** Pennsylvania. Meade, who had been trailing behind Lee's army, moved his forces into Gettysburg. On July 1, Lee forced the Union army to fall back.

Meade took up an almost impregnable defensive position on Cemetery Ridge. The Confederates hammered both ends of the Union line on July 2 but

---

54th Massachusetts   Regiment of black troops from Massachusetts commanded by Robert Gould Shaw; it led an assault on Fort Wagner at Charleston harbor.

Chancellorsville   Site in Virginia where, in May 1863, Confederate troops led by Lee defeated a much larger Union force; Stonewall Jackson was mortally wounded in this battle.

Gettysburg   Site of a major battle that occurred in Pennsylvania in July 1863 when Lee led Confederate forces in an unsuccessful invasion of the North.

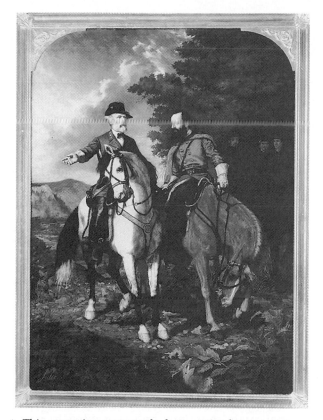

♦ This engraving captures the last meeting between two Confederate military giants, showing Robert E. Lee *(left)* and Thomas J. "Stonewall" Jackson on the eve of the Battle of Chancellorsville. Jackson's force defeated a Union army under General Joseph "Fighting Joe" Hooker, but Confederate troops mistook his returning soldiers for Union cavalry and fired on them, mortally wounding Jackson. Lee's Last Meeting with Jackson *(Chancellorsville) by E. B. D. Julio. Museum of the Confederacy.*

could gain no ground. On the third day, Lee ordered a major assault on the middle of the Union position. Over thirteen thousand men, led by Major General George E. Pickett, tried to cross open ground and take the hills held by Meade. Pickett's charge was one of the few tactical mistakes Lee made during the war. Meade's forces drove off the attack. The whole field was "dotted with our soldiers," wrote one Confederate officer. Losses on both sides were high, but Confederate casualties during the three-day battle exceeded twenty-eight thousand men, more than a third of Lee's army. Lee retreated, his invasion of the North a failure.

On the heels of Gettysburg came news from Mississippi that Vicksburg had finally fallen. Union forces had been shelling the city continuously for nearly seven weeks, driving residents into caves and shelters, but it was starvation and disease that finally laid waste to the city. On July 4, Vicksburg surrendered. Then on July 9, **Port Hudson** followed suit. The Mississippi River was now totally under Union control. The "Father of Waters," said Lincoln, "again goes unvexed to the sea."

The losses at Gettysburg and Vicksburg devastated the Confederates. Cut off from almost any hope of foreign intervention and low on food, munitions, uniforms, shoes, and weapons, Confederate morale plummeted. As Josiah Gorgas wrote in his diary after Gettysburg and Vicksburg, "The Confederacy totters to its destruction." But the Confederacy proved more resilient than many *expected* in the wake of Gettysburg and Vicksburg.

Meade, like McClellan, failed to pursue Lee and his retreating troops, allowing Lee to escape into Virginia. When he learned of Lee's escape, Lincoln grumbled, "Our Army held the war in the hollow of their hand and they would not close it."

Nor was General Meade Lincoln's only source of irritation. In Tennessee, Rosecrans had moved no closer toward Chattanooga. The war, which had appeared to be nearly over, was, in Lincoln's words, "prolonged indefinitely." Lincoln needed a general with killer instincts.

Grant, Sherman, and the Invention of Total War

Two generals rose to meet Lincoln's needs: Ulysses S. Grant and William Tecumseh Sherman. These two men invented a new type of warfare—**total war**—

Port Hudson   Confederate garrison on the Mississippi River that surrendered to Union forces in July 1863, thus giving the Union unrestricted control of the Mississippi.

total war   War waged not only against enemy troops but also against the civilian population in order to destroy morale and economic resources.

♦ Disliked by most of his fellow officers because of his usually unkempt appearance and ungentlemanly manner, Ulysses S. Grant, shown here in an 1863 photograph, had the right combination of daring, unconventionality, and heartlessness to finally defeat the Confederate Army. *Collection of Michael J. McAffee.*

that brought the South to its knees. Both were willing to wage war not only against the government and armed forces of the Confederacy but also against the civilian population. Their goal was to destroy the South's means and will to continue the struggle.

Lincoln placed Grant in charge of all Union forces in the West on October 13. Grant's immediate goal was to relieve Union forces that had captured Chattanooga but had then been besieged by Confederate forces under Braxton Bragg. Grant first relieved the pressure on Chattanooga by sending Sherman's troops there. Troops under Sherman and General George H. Thomas then stormed the Confederate strongholds that overlooked the city

and drove Bragg's forces out of south Tennessee. Confederate forces also withdrew from Knoxville in December, leaving the state under Union control. Delighted with Grant's successes, Lincoln promoted him again on March 10, 1864, this time to general-in-chief. Grant immediately left his command in the West to prepare an all-out attack on Lee and Virginia. He authorized Sherman to pursue a campaign into Georgia.

On May 4, 1864, Grant marched toward Richmond. The next day, Union and Confederate armies collided in a tangle of woods called **The Wilderness** near Chancellorsville. Two bloody days of fighting followed, broken by a night during which hundreds of wounded burned to death in brushfires between the two lines. Grant decided to skirt Lee's troops and head for Richmond, but Lee anticipated the maneuver and blocked Grant's route at Spotsylvania. Twelve more days of fighting brought neither side a victory.

Casualties on both sides at Spotsylvania were staggering, but Union losses were unimaginably horrible. As one Confederate officer put it, "We have met a man, this time, who either does not know when he is whipped, or who cares not if he loses his whole army."

Grant again withdrew and attempted to move around Lee, but again Lee anticipated Grant's approach. On June 1, the two armies met once again at **Cold Harbor,** Virginia. Grant ordered a series of frontal attacks against the entrenched Confederates. Lee's veteran troops waited patiently as Union soldiers marched toward them. Many of the young attackers had pinned their names on their shirts so that they might be identified after the battle. The Confederates fired volley after volley until dead

---

The Wilderness Densely wooded region of Virginia that was the site in May 1864 of a devastating but inconclusive battle between Union forces under Grant and Confederates under Lee.

Cold Harbor Area of Virginia, about 10 miles from Richmond, where Grant made an unsuccessful attempt to drive his forces through Lee's center and capture Richmond.

Union soldiers lay in piles. One southerner described Grant's assaults as "incredible butchery."

During the three campaigns, Grant lost sixty thousand troops, more than Lee's entire army. In a single day of frontal assaults at Cold Harbor, Grant lost twelve thousand men. Said Lee, "This is not war, this is murder." But Grant's seeming wantonness was calculated, for the Confederates lost over twenty-five thousand troops. And Grant knew, as did Lee, that the Union could afford the losses but the Confederacy could not. He also saw no other way to end the conflict. Despite diminished manpower and resources, Lee refused to surrender. And so the killing continued.

Now near Richmond, Grant guessed that Lee would *expect* him to assault the city. Instead, he swung south of Richmond and headed for Petersburg. His objective was to take the vital rail center and cut off the southern capital. Shaken by devastating losses, Grant's generals advanced cautiously, allowing Lee time to respond. Lee rapidly shifted the **vanguard** of his troops and occupied Petersburg. Grant bitterly regretted the indecision of his generals, feeling that he could have ended the war. Instead, the campaign settled into a siege.

The Election of 1864 and Sherman's March to the Sea

Lincoln was under fire from two directions. On May 31, 1864, a splinter group of Radical Republicans, concerned that Lincoln would be too soft on southerners after the war was over, nominated John C. Frémont as their presidential candidate. Lincoln's wing of the party, which began calling itself the Union party, renominated Lincoln in June. To attract Democrats who still favored fighting for a victory, Union party delegates dumped Vice President Hannibal Hamlin and *chose* **Andrew Johnson,** a southern Democrat, as Lincoln's running mate.

In August, the Democratic National Convention selected McClellan as its presidential candidate. The Democrats included a peace plank in their platform. Thus Lincoln sat squarely between one group that castigated him for pursuing the war and another group that rebuked him for failing to punish the South vigorously enough.

Confederate president Jefferson Davis also had political problems. As military losses mounted, resistance to the war effort increased. Several states refused to comply with the Confederate congress's call for a new draft. Governors in Georgia, North Carolina, and South Carolina kept troops at home and defied Davis to enforce conscription. Like Lincoln, Davis was under growing pressure to end the war.

The two sides did have several conversations about negotiating a settlement. Lincoln stated his terms: reunion, abolition, and amnesty for Confederates. Davis contended that "independence" or "extermination" was the only possible *outcome* for the South. Thus the fighting continued.

Sherman gave Lincoln the push he needed to win the election. During the summer of 1864 he advanced his army slowly toward Atlanta, one of the South's few remaining industrial centers (see Map 14.4). Only General Joseph E. Johnston's skillful retreats kept Sherman from annihilating his army. But the continuous retreats prompted President Davis to replace Johnston with the more aggressive John Bell Hood. Hood attacked, but Sherman inflicted such serious casualties that Hood had to retreat to Atlanta.

For days Sherman shelled the city. When a last-ditch southern attack failed, Hood evacuated Atlanta on September 1. Union troops occupied the city on the following day. This victory caused despair among Confederates and gave great momentum to Lincoln's re-election campaign.

Lincoln's re-election efforts were also given a boost by General Phil Sheridan's campaign in the Shenandoah Valley. In June, Confederate commander Jubal Early led a raid into Maryland. Sheridan headed off Early's offensive and then pursued him down the Shenandoah. Sheridan's men lived off the land and destroyed both military and civilian supplies whenever possible. Sheridan drove Early from

vanguard The foremost position in any army advancing into battle.

Andrew Johnson Tennessee senator who became Lincoln's running mate in 1864 and who succeeded to the presidency after Lincoln was killed.

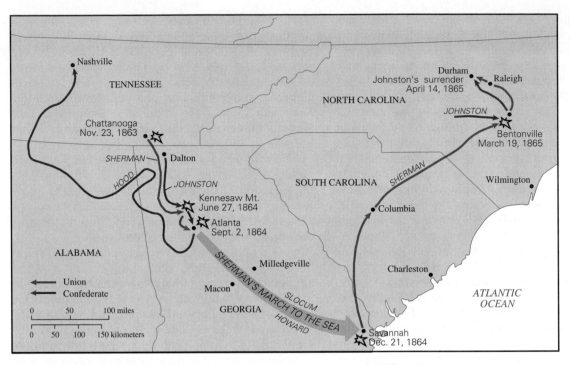

♦ **MAP 14.4 Sherman's Campaign in the South** This map shows how William Tecumseh Sherman's troops slashed through the South, destroying both civilian and military targets and reducing the South's will to continue the war.

the region in October and laid waste to much of Lee's food supplies.

These victories proved the decisive factor in the election of 1864. They defused McClellan's argument that Lincoln was not competent to direct the military fortunes of the North and quelled much antiwar sentiment in the North. These victories also caused the Frémont candidacy to disappear before election day. Lincoln defeated McClellan by half a million popular votes but won in the Electoral College by an overwhelming margin of 212 to 21.

The southern peace movement had viewed a Democratic victory as the last chance to reach a settlement. Now all hope of negotiation appeared lost. Despite the bleak prospects, Lee's forces still remained in Petersburg, as did Hood's in Georgia. Southern hopes were dimmed but not extinguished.

Sherman grew frustrated with the occupation of Atlanta and posed a bold plan to Grant. He wanted

to ignore Hood, leave the battered Confederates loose at his rear, go on the offensive, and "cut a swath through to the sea." "I can make Georgia howl," he promised. Despite some misgivings, Grant agreed and convinced Lincoln.

A week after the election, Sherman began preparing for his 300-mile **March to the Sea** (see Map 14.4). His intentions were clear. "We are not only fighting hostile armies, but a hostile people," he stated. By devastating the countryside and destroying the South's ability to conduct war, he intended to break down southerners' will to resist. "We cannot change

> **March to the Sea** Sherman's march from Atlanta to Savannah from November 16 to December 20, 1864, during which Union soldiers carried out orders to destroy everything in their path.

the hearts of those people of the South," he concluded, but we can "make them so sick of war that generations would pass away before they would again appeal to it." With that, he burned most of Atlanta and then set out for Savannah. His troops plundered and looted farms and towns on the way, foraging for food and supplies and destroying everything in their path.

When Sherman headed toward Savannah, Hood turned north toward General Thomas's Union troops at Nashville. Joined by cavalry leader Nathan Bedford Forrest, Hood attacked Union forces at Franklin, Tennessee, on November 30 and was shattered. The Confederate Army of Tennessee fragmented.

Sherman entered Savannah unopposed on December 20. The March to the Sea completed, Sherman turned north toward Columbia. Sherman's "bummers," so-called because they lived off the land, took special delight in ravaging the countryside in South Carolina, which they regarded as the seat of the rebellion. When they reached Columbia, flames engulfed the city. Whether Sherman's men or retreating Confederates started the blaze is not clear.

With the capital in flames, Confederate forces abandoned South Carolina and moved north to join Joseph E. Johnston's army in North Carolina. Union forces quickly moved into abandoned southern strongholds, including Charleston. Major Robert Anderson, who had commanded Fort Sumter in April 1861, returned to raise the Union flag over the fort that he had surrendered four years earlier.

The Fall of Lee and Lincoln

Sherman's marches were the centerpiece of a Union strategy that was a brutal variation of Winfield Scott's anaconda plan. In concert with Sherman's efforts, other Union armies attacked various southern strongholds. Admiral Farragut had already closed the port of Mobile, Alabama. The primary target, however, was Lee. Grant maintained the siege at Petersburg while Sherman moved north. His goal was to join Grant in defeating Lee and ending the war.

Hoping to keep the Confederacy alive, Lee made a desperate move in early April 1865. Fearing encir-

clement by Grant's forces, Lee advised Davis to evacuate Richmond. Lee then abandoned his stronghold in Petersburg and moved west as rapidly as possible, toward Lynchburg. From Lynchburg Lee hoped to use surviving rail lines to move his troops south to join Johnston's force in North Carolina.

Grant ordered an immediate assault as Lee's forces deserted Petersburg. Lee had little ammunition, almost no food, and only thirty-five thousand men. As they retreated westward, hundreds of Confederates collapsed from hunger and exhaustion. By April 9, Union forces had surrounded Lee's broken army. Saying, "There is nothing left for me to do but go and see General Grant, and I would rather die a thousand deaths," Lee sent a note offering surrender.

The two generals met at the courthouse in Appomattox, Virginia. Grant offered generous terms, allowing Confederate officers and men to go home "so long as they observe their paroles and the laws in force where they reside." This guaranteed them immunity from prosecution for treason and became the model for surrender. Grant sent the starving Confederates rations and allowed them to keep their horses.

On April 11, Lincoln addressed a crowd outside the White House about his hopes and plans for rebuilding the nation, urging a speedy reconciliation between the two sections. Three days later, Lincoln *chose* to relax by attending a play at Ford's Theater in Washington with his wife. At about ten o'clock, **John Wilkes Booth,** an actor and a southern sympathizer, entered the president's box and shot him behind the ear. Lincoln died the next morning.

Lee's surrender did not end the war. Joseph E. Johnston's forces did not surrender until April 18, at Durham Station, North Carolina. Even then, Jefferson Davis remained in hiding and called for continued resistance. But one by one, the Confederate officers surrendered to their Union

---

John Wilkes Booth   Actor and southern sympathizer who on April 14, 1865, five days after Lee's surrender, fatally shot President Lincoln at Ford's Theater in Washington.

opponents. On May 10, Davis and the Confederate postmaster general were captured near Irwinville, Georgia. The last Confederate general to lay down his arms was Cherokee leader Stand Watie, who surrendered on June 23, 1865.

The price of victory was high for both the winner and the loser. Over 360,000 Union soldiers were killed in action, and at least 260,000 Confederates died in the failed cause of southern independence. The war wrecked the economy of the South. Union military campaigns wiped out most southern rail lines, destroyed the South's manufacturing capacity, and severely reduced agricultural productivity. Both sides had faced rising inflation during the war,

but the Confederacy's actions had bled the South of most of its resources and money.

Soldiers and civilians on both sides had faced tremendous adversity. The war exacted a tremendous emotional toll on everyone, even on those who escaped physical injury. Perhaps General Carl Schurz, a Union general who fought at Chancellorsville, Gettysburg, and Chattanooga, best summed up the agony of the Civil War: "There are people who speak lightly of war as a mere heroic sport. They would hardly find it in their hearts to do so, had they ever witnessed scenes like these, and thought of the untold miseries connected with them that were spread all over the land."

SUMMARY

Both the Union and the Confederacy entered the war in 1861 with glowing *expectations*. Jefferson Davis *chose* to pursue a defensive strategy, certain that northerners would soon tire of war and let the South withdraw from the Union. Abraham Lincoln *chose* to use the superior human, economic, and natural resources of the North to strangle the South into submission. But many *constraints* frustrated both leaders during the first year of the war.

For Lincoln, the greatest *constraint* was military leadership. Union forces seemed unable to win any major battles despite their numerical superiority. Although Ulysses S. Grant scored victories in the Mississippi Valley, Robert E. Lee and "Stonewall" Jackson defeated every Union general that Lincoln sent to oppose them.

The war's nature and direction changed after the fall of 1862. Lee *chose* to invade Maryland and was defeated at Antietam. After that Union victory, Lincoln *chose* to issue the Emancipation Proclamation, *expecting* that it would undermine southern efforts and unify northern ones. After the proclamation, there could be no *choice* for either side but total victory or total defeat.

Union forces turned the tide in the war by defeating Lee's army at Gettysburg and by taking

E xpectations
C onstraints
C hoices
O utcomes

Vicksburg after a long siege. With an election drawing near, Lincoln spurred his generals to deal the death blow to the Confederacy, and two rose to the occasion. During the summer and fall of 1864, William Tecumseh Sherman made Georgia howl. And Grant, in a brutal campaign in northern Virginia, drove Lee into a defensive corner. In November, buoyed by Sherman's victories in Georgia, Lincoln was re-elected.

In the spring of 1865, Lee made a desperate *choice* to keep the Confederacy alive, racing to unify the last surviving remnants of the once-proud southern army. But Grant surrounded Lee's troops, forcing surrender. Lincoln's assassination a short time later left the nation in shock and a southern Democrat, Andrew Johnson, as president. In North and South, in April 1865, the *outcome* of the Civil War was uncertainty about what would follow.

SUGGESTED READINGS

Abel, Annie Heloise. *The Slaveholding Indians* (3 v., 1919–1925; reprint, 1992–1993).

This long-ignored classic work focuses on Indians as slaveholders, participants in the Civil War, and subjects of Reconstruction. Its three volumes have recently been updated by historians Theda Purdue and Michael Green. Each volume can stand on its own and will reward the patient reader.

Catton, Bruce. *This Hallowed Ground: The Story of the Union Side of the Civil War* (1956).

Catton is probably the best in the huge company of popular writers on the Civil War. This is his most comprehensive single-volume work. More detailed, but still very interesting, titles by Catton include *Glory Road: The Bloody Route from Fredericksburg to Gettysburg* (1952), *Mr. Lincoln's Army* (1962), *A Stillness at Appomattox* (1953), and *Grant Moves South* (1960).

Escott, Paul D. *After Secession: Jefferson Davis and the Failure of Confederate Nationalism* (1978).

An excellent overview of internal political problems in the Confederacy by a leading Civil War historian.

Josephy, Alvin M. *The Civil War in the American West* (1991).

An excellent overview of an often forgotten chapter in the Civil War. A former editor for *American Heritage,* Josephy writes an interesting and readable story.

McPherson, James. *Battle Cry of Freedom: The Civil War Era* (1988).

Hailed by many as the best single-volume history of the Civil War Era; comprehensive and very well written.

Thomas, Emory M. *The Confederate Nation* (1979).

A classic history of the Confederacy by an excellent southern historian.

Wills, Garry. *Lincoln at Gettysburg: The Words that Remade America* (1992).

A prizewinning look at Lincoln's rhetoric and the ways in which his speeches, especially his Gettysburg Address, recast American ideas about equality, freedom, and democracy. Exquisitely written by a master biographer.

Gettysburg

Ronald Maxwell directed this four-hour epic detailing one of the Civil War's most famous battles. Based on Michael Shaara's Pulitzer Prize winning novel *The Killer Angels,* this ambitious film seeks to capture not only the historical events, but the atmosphere and personalities of the era.

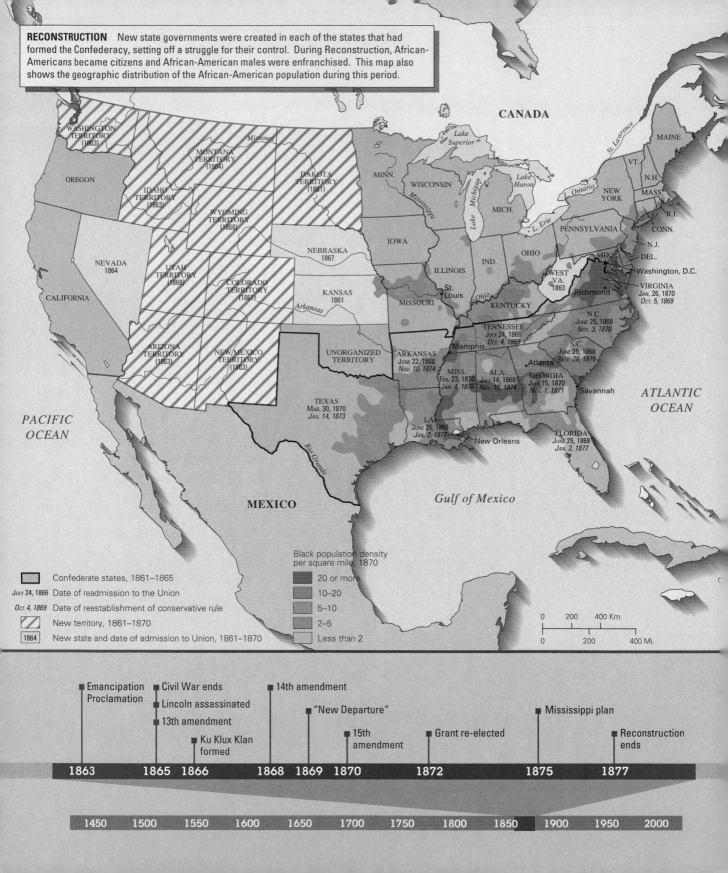

RECONSTRUCTION New state governments were created in each of the states that had formed the Confederacy, setting off a struggle for their control. During Reconstruction, African-Americans became citizens and African-American males were enfranchised. This map also shows the geographic distribution of the African-American population during this period.

CANADA

WASHINGTON TERRITORY (1863)

OREGON

MONTANA TERRITORY (1864)

IDAHO TERRITORY (1863)

Missouri

DAKOTA TERRITORY (1861)

MINN.

WISCONSIN

Lake Superior

L. Michigan

Lake Huron

MICH.

MAINE

VT.

N.H.

NEW YORK

MASS.

R.I.

CONN.

NEVADA 1864

WYOMING TERRITORY (1868)

UTAH TERRITORY (1868)

NEBRASKA 1867

IOWA

ILLINOIS

St. Louis

Ohio

OHIO

IND.

L. Erie

PENNSYLVANIA

N.J.

DEL.

MD.

Washington, D.C.

CALIFORNIA

COLORADO TERRITORY (1861)

KANSAS 1861

Arkansas

MISSOURI

KENTUCKY

WEST VA. 1863

Richmond

VIRGINIA
JAN. 26, 1870
OCT. 5, 1869

ARIZONA TERRITORY (1863)

NEW MEXICO TERRITORY (1863)

UNORGANIZED TERRITORY

ARKANSAS
JUNE 22, 1868
NOV. 10, 1874

TENNESSEE
JULY 24, 1866
OCT. 4, 1869

Memphis

N.C.
JUNE 25, 1868
NOV. 3, 1870

S.C.
JUNE 25, 1868
NOV. 28, 1876

TEXAS
MAR. 30, 1870
JAN. 14, 1873

MISS.
FEB. 23, 1870
JAN. 4, 1876

ALA.
JULY 14, 1868
NOV. 16, 1874

GEORGIA
JULY 15, 1870
NOV. 1, 1871

Atlanta

Savannah

ATLANTIC OCEAN

PACIFIC OCEAN

Rio Grande

LA.
JUNE 25, 1868
JAN. 2, 1877

New Orleans

FLORIDA
JUNE 25, 1868
JAN. 2, 1877

MEXICO

Gulf of Mexico

Black population density per square mile, 1870

	20 or more
	10–20
	5–10
	2–5
	Less than 2

Confederate states, 1861–1865

JULY 24, 1866 Date of readmission to the Union

OCT. 4, 1869 Date of reestablishment of conservative rule

New territory, 1861–1870

1864 New state and date of admission to Union, 1861–1870

0   200   400 Km.

0   200   400 Mi.

■ Emancipation Proclamation

■ Civil War ends

■ Lincoln assassinated

■ 14th amendment

■ "New Departure"

■ Mississippi plan

■ Reconstruction ends

■ 13th amendment

■ Ku Klux Klan formed

■ 15th amendment

■ Grant re-elected

1863   **1865**   **1866**   **1868**   **1869**   **1870**   **1872**   **1875**   **1877**

1450   1500   1550   1600   1650   1700   1750   1800   1850   1900   1950   2000

Reconstruction: High Hopes and Broken Dreams, 1865–1877

Presidential Reconstruction

- What did President Lincoln and President Johnson *expect* to accomplish through their Reconstruction plans?
- Why did each *choose* a lenient approach?

Freedom and the Legacy of Slavery

- What were freed people's *expectations* for freedom?
- What *constraints* on their freedom did African-Americans experience in the South during the first years of Reconstruction?

Congressional Reconstruction

- Why did Republicans in Congress *choose* to take control of Reconstruction?
- What did they *expect* to accomplish?

Black Reconstruction

- Who made up the Republican party in the South during Reconstruction?
- What important *choices* did Republican state administrations make during Reconstruction?
- Which *choices* brought the most lasting *outcomes*?

The End of Reconstruction

- How did the Mississippi Plan help to end Reconstruction?
- What were the final *outcomes* of Reconstruction?

INTRODUCTION

E xpectations
C onstraints
C hoices
O utcomes

By 1865, the war had touched the life of nearly every American. When the last Confederate military resistance collapsed, some 2.6 million men had served in the Union or Confederate army since 1861—about 40 percent of the male population aged 15 to 40 in 1860. More than a half-million had died. Women made important contributions to the war effort as civilians and even as soldiers.

Except for Gettysburg, the major battles in the Civil War had occurred in the South or the border states. Toward the end of the war, Union armies swept across the South, leaving devastation behind them: burned and shelled buildings, ravaged fields, twisted railroad tracks. This destruction, and the collapse of the region's financial system, posed significant *constraints* on economic revival in the South.

More devastating for many white southerners than the property damage and destruction was the emancipation of four million slaves. In 1861, fearful *expectations* about the future of slavery had caused the South to *choose* secession. The *outcome* of the war made those fears a reality. The end of slavery forced southerners of both races to reconsider their *expectations* and to make a series of *choices* about social, economic, and political relations between the races.

Reconstruction, the period between 1865 and 1877, was a time of physical rebuilding throughout the South. The term "Reconstruction," however, refers primarily to the rebuilding of the federal Union and to the political, economic, and social changes that came to the South after the war. Reconstruction involved *choices* about some of the most momentous questions in American history. How was the defeated South to be treated? What was to be the future of the former slaves? Were key decisions to be made in Washington or in the state capitals? Was Congress or the president to establish policies?

As the Republicans reconstructed the Union, they redefined the very nature of the Union. They made *choices* about the terms on which the South might rejoin the Union and about the rights of the former slaves. They also permanently changed the definition of American citizenship.

These changes conflicted with the *expectations* of most white southerners. *Choices* over the future of the South and of the freedmen also produced conflict between the president and Congress. A lasting *outcome* of these *choices* was a significant increase in the power of the federal government and new *constraints* on state governments. In the end, however, the *outcome* of Reconstruction failed to fulfill African-Americans' *expectations* for freedom and equality.

Presidential Reconstruction

• What did President Lincoln and President Johnson *expect* to accomplish through their Reconstruction plans?

• Why did each *choose* a lenient approach?

On New Year's Day 1863, President Abraham Lincoln began the process by which all people in the nation became free by signing the Emancipation Proclamation. Although the Proclamation abolished slavery only in territory under Confederate control, where it could not be enforced, every subsequent advance of a Union army brought the reality of **emancipation** to the Confederacy.

Republican War Aims

The Emancipation Proclamation established the destruction of slavery as a war aim second in importance only to preserving the Union. Freedom for the

emancipation   Release from bondage; freedom.

CHRONOLOGY

Reconstruction

1863	Emancipation Proclamation The Ten-Percent Plan
1864	Abraham Lincoln re-elected
1865	Freedmen's Bureau created Civil War ends Lincoln assassinated Johnson becomes president Thirteenth Amendment (abolishing slavery) ratified
1866	Ku Klux Klan formed Congress begins to assert control over Reconstruction Civil Rights Act of 1866 Riots by whites in Memphis and New Orleans
1867	Military Reconstruction Act Command of the Army Act Tenure of Office Act
1868	Impeachment of President Johnson Fourteenth Amendment (defining citizenship) ratified Ulysses S. Grant elected president

1869–1870	Victories of "New Departure" Democrats in some southern states
1870	Fifteenth Amendment (guaranteeing voting rights) ratified
1870–1871	Ku Klux Klan Acts
1872	Grant re-elected
1875	Civil Rights Act of 1875 Mississippi Plan ends Reconstruction in Mississippi
1876	Disputed presidential election: Hayes vs. Tilden
1877	Compromise of 1877 Hayes becomes president End of Reconstruction

slaves became a central concern in part because **abolitionists** were an influential element within the Republican party. This powerful Republican **faction** developed a third objective: citizenship for the former slaves and the equality of all citizens before the law. The people who held what were then considered extreme views on black rights were called Radical Republicans or simply **Radicals.**

Thaddeus Stevens, the Radical leader in the House of Representatives, had argued as early as 1838 that voting rights should be extended to Pennsylvania's free African-Americans. He became an uncompromising advocate of equal rights for African-Americans. So did Charles Sumner of Massachusetts, the leading Radical in the Senate. He had argued for **racial integration** of Massachusetts

schools in 1849 and won election to the U.S. Senate in 1851. A defender of slavery had caned Sumner

abolitionist   Someone who condemned slavery as morally wrong and believed that it should be abolished.

faction   A group of people with shared opinions and goals who split off from a larger group.

Radicals   A faction of the Republican party that advocated citizenship for former slaves; Radical Republicans believed the South should be forced to meet congressional goals for reform.

racial integration   The bringing together of people of different racial groups into unrestricted and equal association in a society or organization.

♦ This engraving celebrating the Emancipation Proclamation first appeared in 1863. While it places a white Union soldier in the center, it also portrays the important role of African-American troops and emphasizes the importance of education and literacy. *The Library Company of Philadelphia.*

severely on the Senate floor in 1856 because of his outspoken views against slavery.

Most Radicals demanded a drastic restructuring not only of the South's political system but also of its economy. They had opposed slavery on moral grounds, but they also believed that free labor was crucial to democracy itself. "The middling classes who own the soil, and work it with their own hands," Stevens once proclaimed, "are the main support of every free government." The Radicals concluded that free labor would have to be elevated to a position of honor for the South to be fully democratic.

Not all Republicans accepted the proposals of the Radicals. All Republicans had objected to slavery, but not all Republicans had been abolitionists, and not all Republicans wanted to extend citizenship rights to the former slaves. Some moderate Republicans were undecided about the proper course to take. Other **moderates** favored rapid restoration of the South so that the federal government could concentrate on stimulating economic growth and developing the West.

Lincoln's Approach to Reconstruction: "With Malice Toward None"

President Lincoln and congressional Radicals agreed that emancipation had to be a condition for the return of the South to the Union. However, major differences appeared over other terms for reunion when Lincoln issued a Proclamation of **Amnesty** and Reconstruction (the "Ten-Percent Plan") in December 1863.

The Proclamation offered a full pardon to those who swore their loyalty to the Union and accepted the abolition of slavery. Only high-ranking Confederate leaders were not eligible. When those who took the oath amounted to 10 percent of a state's voters in the 1860 presidential election, the pardoned voters were to write a new state constitution that abolished slavery. They were then to elect state officials. Lincoln hoped such leniency would encourage prominent southerners to abandon the Confederacy and to accept emancipation.

Many Republicans thought that Congress should be more involved in restoring the southern states to the Union. Two leading Radicals, Benjamin F. Wade and Henry W. Davis, proposed that 50 percent of a state's white males be required to swear loyalty to the Union before a new civil government could be

moderates Those whose views are midway between two more extreme positions; in this case, Republicans who favored some reforms but not all the Radicals' proposals.

amnesty A general pardon granted by a government, especially for political offenses.

formed. Congress passed the Wade-Davis bill in July 1864. Lincoln, however, killed it with a **pocket veto.**

Lincoln continued to hope that his Ten-Percent Plan might hasten the end of the war. New state governments were established in Arkansas, Louisiana, and Tennessee during 1864 and early 1865. In Louisiana, the new government denied voting rights to black males, and it maintained restrictions on plantation laborers. Radicals complained loudly, but Lincoln urged patience. The Radicals became convinced that freed people were unlikely to receive equitable treatment from state governments formed under the Ten-Percent Plan. Moderate Republicans moved toward the Radicals' position that only **suffrage** could protect the freedmen's rights and that only federal action could secure suffrage for blacks.

All Republicans could agree by 1865 that slavery had to be destroyed permanently. The Emancipation Proclamation had not affected slavery in states such as Delaware and Kentucky, where it remained legal. To destroy slavery forever throughout the Union, Congress in early 1865 approved the **Thirteenth Amendment.**

By December 1865, only nineteen of the twenty-five Union states had ratified the amendment; however, eight of the reconstructed southern states had ratified it, bringing the total to twenty-seven, the number needed for ratification. Thus the abolition of slavery was accomplished by reconstructed state governments in the South.

Andrew Johnson and Reconstruction

After the assassination of Lincoln in mid-April 1865, Vice President Andrew Johnson became president. A Tennessee Democrat who had been born into poverty, Johnson was the only southerner who did not resign from his U.S. Senate seat after **secession.** Lincoln had appointed him military governor of Tennessee early in the war. Johnson had harsh words for Tennessee secessionists, especially the wealthy planters whom he blamed for secession. Radical Republicans applauded Johnson's verbal assaults on these Confederates. He received the Republican nomination for vice president in 1864 because Lincoln wanted to appeal to Democrats and to Unionists in border states.

Radicals hoped that Johnson as president would join in their plans for transforming the South. Johnson, however, soon made it clear that he opposed the Radicals' plans. "White men alone must manage the South," Johnson told one visitor. He did recommend that a few freedmen be given limited political roles. But Johnson saw the major task of Reconstruction as empowering the region's white middle class and keeping the planters from regaining power.

In practice, Johnson's approach to Reconstruction differed little from Lincoln's. Like Lincoln, he relied on his power to grant pardons. Despite his bitterness toward the southern elite, he granted amnesty to most former Confederates who pledged loyalty to the Union and support for emancipation.

Johnson appointed provisional governors for the southern states that had not already been reconstructed and instructed them to call constitutional conventions. Some provisional governors, however, appointed former Confederates to state and local offices, outraging those who *expected* that Unionists would be appointed to these offices.

Johnson *expected* the state constitutional conventions to abolish slavery within each state, to ratify the Thirteenth Amendment, and to renounce secession and the state's war debts. The states were then to hold elections and resume their place in the Union. State conventions during the summer of 1865 usually complied with these provisions. Nearly all ratified the Thirteenth Amendment. They

---

pocket veto   The veto that occurs when Congress adjourns before the end of the ten-day period that the Constitution gives the president for considering whether to sign a bill and the president's decision is to "pocket"—that is, to not sign and let the bill expire.

suffrage   The right to vote.

Thirteenth Amendment   Constitutional amendment, ratified in 1865, that abolished slavery in the United States and its territories.

secession   The withdrawal of eleven southern states from the United States in 1860–1861, giving rise to the Civil War.

renounced secession. However, they all rejected black suffrage.

Freedom and the Legacy of Slavery

- What were freed people's *expectations* for freedom?
- What *constraints* on their freedom did African-Americans in the South experience during the first years of Reconstruction?

After the war, African-Americans throughout the South set about creating new, free lives for themselves. Slaves and most free blacks in the South had previously led lives tightly *constrained* by law and custom. They had been permitted few social organizations of their own. Now freed, they faced enormous changes in almost every aspect of their lives. They quickly developed *expectations* for a future free from the old *constraints.*

The central theme of the black response to emancipation was "a desire for independence from white control," historian Eric Foner observes. This desire for **autonomy** affected every aspect of life: family, churches, schools, newspapers, and a host of other social institutions.

Defining the Meaning of Freedom

Freedom was not something that Lincoln or the Union armies gave to enslaved blacks. It came, instead, when individual slaves stopped working for a master and claimed the right to be free. Nor did freedom come to all slaves at the same time. For some, freedom had come before the Emancipation Proclamation, when they had walked away from their owners, crossed into Union-held territory, and asserted their freedom. Toward the end of the war, many slaves simply declared their freedom and left their former masters. Owners were surprised when even their most favored slaves left them. For Kentucky slaves, freedom did not come until ratification of the Thirteenth Amendment.

Across the South, the approach of Yankee troops set off a joyous celebration that the slaves called a Jubilee. One Virginia woman remembered that "when they knew that they were free they, oh! baby! began to sing. . . . Such rejoicing and shouting you

never heard in your life." A man recalled that with the appearance of the Union soldiers, "We was all walking on golden clouds. Hallelujah!" Black historian **W. E. B. Du Bois** described it this way: "A great human sob shrieked in the wind, and tossed its tears on the sea,—free, free, free."

The freed people expressed their new freedom in many ways. Some *chose* new names. Many changed their style of dress. Some acquired guns. A significant benefit of freedom was the ability to travel without a pass. Many freed people took advantage of this new opportunity. Most, however, traveled only short distances to find work, to seek family members separated from them by slavery, or to return to homes that war had forced them to leave.

Many African-Americans felt they had to leave the site of their enslavement to experience full freedom. One woman explained that she left the plantation where she had been a slave because "if I stay here I'll never know I'm free." Many freed people did not return to their former homes because of the poor treatment they had suffered there.

The towns and cities of the South attracted many freed people. The presence of Union troops seemed to offer protection from the random violence that occurred in many rural areas. The cities and towns also offered black churches, schools, and other social institutions begun by free blacks before the war. Urban wages were usually better than those on the plantations. Cities and towns, however, had little housing for the influx of former slaves. Most crowded into black neighborhoods of hastily built shanties where sanitation was poor and disease common.

Creating Communities

During Reconstruction, African-Americans created their own communities with their own social insti-

---

autonomy   Self-government or the right of self-determination.

W. E. B. Du Bois   American historian and civil rights activist who helped found the National Association for the Advancement of Colored People and wrote several influential studies of black life in America.

◆ Churches were among the first social institutions created and controlled by African-Americans after Emancipation. Such churches became important elements in the development of African-American communities, and church leaders, such as this female minister, were usually influential community leaders. *Collection of William Gladstone.*

tutions. Freed people hoped to strengthen family ties. Some families were reunited after years of separation caused by the sale of children or spouses. Some spent years searching for lost family members.

The new freedom to conduct religious services without white supervision was centrally important. Churches became the most prominent social organization in African-American communities. Black ministers advised and helped to educate congregation members as they adjusted to the changes brought by freedom. Ministers emerged as important leaders within developing African-American communities.

Freed people understood the importance of education. Setting up a school, said one, was "the first proof" of independence. Many of the new schools were not just for children but also for adults who had previously been barred from learning by state laws. The desire to learn was widespread and intense. One freedman in Georgia wrote: "The Lord has sent books and teachers. We must not hesitate a moment, but go on and learn all we can."

Public school systems had not existed in much of the South before the war. In many places, freed people created the first public schools. The region faced a severe shortage of teachers, books, and schoolrooms. Northern reformers assisted the transition to freedom by focusing on education.

In March 1865, Congress created the **Freedmen's Bureau,** an agency run by the War Department to assist the freed people. The nation's first welfare agency, it helped them find employment or become farmers. Its most lasting contribution, however, was helping to establish a black educational system. Northern aid and missionary societies, together with the Freedmen's Bureau, also established schools to train black teachers. By 1870, the Bureau supervised more than 4,000 schools, with more than 9,000 teachers and 247,000 students. Still, in 1870, the schools had room for only one black child in ten.

African-Americans also developed political organizations. In politics, their first objective was recognition of their equal rights as citizens. Frederick Douglass insisted that "slavery is not abolished until the black man has the ballot." Political conventions of African-Americans in 1865 attracted hundreds of delegates. In calling for equality and voting rights, these conventions pointed to black contributions in the Civil War as evidence of patriotism and devotion. They also appealed to the Declaration of Independence's belief that "all men are created equal."

Land and Labor

Former slaveowners reacted to emancipation in a variety of ways. Some tried to keep their slaves from learning of their freedom. A very few, like Mary Chesnut of South Carolina, actually welcomed an end to slavery. Few provided any compensation to assist their former slaves. One freedman stated, "I do know some of dem old slave owners to be nice

---

Freedmen's Bureau   Agency established in 1865 to aid former slaves in their transition to freedom, especially by administering relief and sponsoring education.

enough to start der slaves off in freedom wid somethin' to live on . . . but dey wasn't in droves, I tell you."

Many freed people looked to Union troops for assistance. When General Sherman led his army through Georgia in 1864, thousands of African-Americans *chose* to follow the Yankee troops. They told Sherman that what they wanted most was to "reap the fruit of our own labor." In January 1865, Sherman responded by issuing Special Field Order No. 15. It set aside forty acres of land in the Sea Islands and coastal South Carolina and provided for the loan of an army mule for each family who settled there. By June, some forty thousand freed people had settled on 400,000 acres of "Sherman land."

Sherman's action encouraged many African-Americans to *expect* that the federal government would order a similar redistribution of land throughout the South. "Forty acres and a mule" became a rallying cry. Land, Thaddeus Stevens proclaimed, would give the freed people control of their own labor. "If we do not furnish them with homesteads," he once said, "we had better left them in bondage."

The Freedmen's Bureau took the lead in the efforts to assist the freed people toward landownership and free labor. At the end of the war, the Bureau controlled more than 850,000 acres of land abandoned by former owners or confiscated from leading Confederates. In July 1865, General Oliver O. Howard, head of the Bureau, directed Bureau agents to divide this land into 40-acre plots.

The widespread *expectation* of "forty acres and a mule" came to an end when President Johnson issued pardons to the former owners of the confiscated land and ordered Howard to return the land to them. Johnson's order displaced thousands of African-Americans who had already taken their 40 acres. They and others who had hoped for land now felt disappointed and betrayed. One recalled years later that they had *expected* "a heap from freedom dey didn't git."

Sharecropping slowly emerged across the South once *expectations* of **land redistribution** evaporated. Sharecropping grew out of the realities of the southern agricultural economy. Landowners owned large tracts but had no one to work them. Both black and white families wanted to raise their own crops but

♦ Sharecropping gave African-Americans more control over their labor than did labor contracts. But sharecropping also contributed to the South's dependence on one-crop agriculture and helped to perpetuate widespread rural poverty. Notice that the child standing on the right is holding her kitten, probably to be certain it is included in this family photograph. *Library of Congress.*

had no land, supplies, or money. The entire region was short of **capital.** Under sharecropping, an individual signed a contract with a landowner to rent land. The rent was typically a share of the annual harvest, ranging from a quarter to a third. If the landlord also provided mules, tools, seed, and fertilizer, however, the rent might be half or even two-thirds of the crop. Landowners preferred share-

---

sharecropping   Agricultural system in which tenant farmers give landlords a share of the crops as rent, rather than cash.

land redistribution   The division of land held by large landowners into small plots that are turned over to people without property.

capital   Money needed to start a commercial enterprise.

cropping because it encouraged tenants to be productive. Tenants preferred sharecropping to wage labor because they had more control over their work.

Sharecroppers nevertheless often found themselves in debt to a local merchant who had advanced supplies on credit until the harvest came. Many landlords required tenants to patronize the stores they ran. All too often, the debt owed the store exceeded the value of the tenant's share of the harvest. Many southerners, black and white alike, became trapped by sharecropping and debts.

The White South: Confronting Change

The slow spread of sharecropping was just one of many ways that the end of slavery transformed the lives of white southerners. For some white southerners, the changes were nearly as profound as for the freed people. With Confederate money worthless, savings vanished. Some found their homes and other buildings destroyed. Thousands sold their landholdings and left the South.

Southern whites were unprepared for the extent of change facing them. Their early response to emancipation suggests that they *expected* conditions to return to what they had been before the war. The newly reconstructed state legislatures passed **black codes** in 1865 to define the new legal status of African-Americans. Black codes placed significant restraints on the freedom of black people. They required all African-Americans to have an annual employment contract, restricted them from moving about the countryside without permission, forbade them from owning guns or carrying weapons, restricted ownership of land, and required those without a job to perform forced labor. The black codes clearly represented an effort by white southerners to define a legally subordinate place for African-Americans.

Other white southerners used violence to coerce the freedmen into accepting a subordinate status. Violence and terror became closely associated with the **Ku Klux Klan,** a secret organization formed in 1866. Most Klan members were small-scale farmers and workers, but the leaders were often prominent citizens. Former Confederate general Nathan

Bedford Forrest became a leader of the Klan. Klan groups throughout the South aimed to restore **white supremacy** and to end Republican rule.

Klan members covered their faces with hoods, wore white robes, and rode horses draped in white. So attired, they set out to intimidate leading black Republicans and their Radical white allies. Klan members also attacked African-Americans accused of not showing deference to whites. Night-riders burned black churches and schools. The Klan devastated Republican organizations in many communities.

In 1866, two events dramatized for the nation the violence routinely inflicted on African-Americans. In May, a three-day riot by whites in Memphis, Tennessee, left forty-five blacks and three whites dead. In New Orleans, some forty people died in July, most of them African-Americans attending a black suffrage convention, in an altercation with police. "It was not a riot," insisted General Philip Sheridan, the military commander of the district. "It was an absolute massacre by the police."

Congressional Reconstruction

- Why did Republicans in Congress *choose* to take control of Reconstruction?
- What did they *expect* to accomplish?

By early 1866, most congressional Republicans had concluded that Johnson's Reconstruction policies had encouraged the white South to *expect* that it would be able to govern the region as it saw fit. The

---

black codes   Laws passed by the southern states after the Civil War to limit the freedoms of African-Americans and force them to return to agricultural labor.

Ku Klux Klan   A secret society organized in the South after the Civil War to resurrect white supremacy by means of violence and intimidation.

white supremacy   The racist belief that whites are inherently superior to all other races and are therefore entitled to rule over them.

black codes, violence against freed people, and the failure of southern authorities to stem the violence turned opinion in Washington against the president's approach to Reconstruction. Increasing numbers of moderate Republicans now joined the Radicals in concluding that southern whites must be *constrained.*

Challenging Presidential Reconstruction

In December 1865, the Thirty-ninth Congress (elected in 1864) met for the first time. In both houses of Congress, Republicans outnumbered Democrats by more than three to one. The president's annual message proclaimed Reconstruction complete and the Union restored, but few Republicans agreed. Radical Republicans especially had been angered by Johnson's lack of support for black suffrage. To accomplish black suffrage, they needed to assert congressional power over Reconstruction. Most Republicans agreed with the Radicals' commitment to defining and protecting basic rights for the freed people. Most also agreed that Congress had the right to withhold representation from the South until state governments there met these conditions.

When the Thirty-ninth Congress first met, the newly elected congressmen from the South were excluded. Republicans were outraged that such high-ranking former Confederates as Alexander Stephens, the vice-president of the Confederacy, having been elected by his Georgia constituents, stood ready to take his place in Congress. Republicans set up a Joint Committee on Reconstruction to determine whether the southern states were entitled to representation. Thaddeus Stevens, head of the committee, announced that he intended to investigate the whole question of Reconstruction. While the committee worked, the former Confederate states were to have no representation in Congress.

At the same time, Republicans extended the life of the Freedmen's Bureau. Congress also passed a civil rights bill that gave citizenship to African-Americans and defined the rights of all citizens. Johnson vetoed both measures, but Congress passed them over his veto. Congress had asserted its control over Reconstruction.

The Civil Rights Act of 1866

The Civil Rights Act of 1866 defined all persons born in the United States (with the exception of certain Indians) as citizens. It also listed certain rights of all citizens, including the right to testify in court, own property, make contracts, bring lawsuits, and enjoy "full and equal benefit of all laws and proceedings for the security of person and property." It authorized federal officials to bring suit against violations of civil rights.

The Civil Rights Act of 1866 was the first effort to define some of the rights of American citizenship. It stipulated that the rights of national citizenship were to take precedence over the powers of the states. By expanding the power of the federal government in unprecedented ways, the law not only challenged traditional concepts of states' rights but did so on behalf of African-Americans.

When President Johnson vetoed the civil rights bill, he argued that it violated states' rights. Johnson may have hoped to generate enough political support to elect a more cooperative Congress in 1866. Instead, the veto led most moderate Republicans to give up all hope of cooperation with him. Congress's passage of the Civil Rights Act over Johnson's veto in April 1866 marked the first time that Congress had overridden a veto of major legislation.

Defining Citizenship: The Fourteenth Amendment

Leading Republicans worried that the Civil Rights Act could be repealed by a later Congress or declared unconstitutional by the Supreme Court. Only a constitutional amendment could permanently safeguard the freed people's rights as citizens.

The Fourteenth Amendment, approved by Congress in June 1866, defined American citizenship in much the same way as the Civil Rights Act of 1866. It then specified:

> *No State shall make or enforce any law which shall abridge the privileges or immunities of citizens of the United States; nor shall any State deprive any person of life, liberty, or property, without due process of law; nor deny to any person within its jurisdiction the equal protection of the laws.*

The Constitution and Bill of Rights prohibited federal interference with basic civil rights. The Fourteenth Amendment extended this protection against action by state governments. The amendment penalized states that did not **enfranchise** African-Americans by reducing their congressional and electoral representation.

Some provisions of the amendment stemmed from Republicans' fears that a restored South might try to undo the *outcome* of the war. One section barred from public office anyone who had sworn to uphold the federal Constitution but then "engaged in insurrection or rebellion against the same." Only a two-thirds vote of both houses of Congress could counteract this provision. (In 1872, Congress pardoned nearly all former Confederates.) The amendment also prohibited either federal or state governments from assuming any of the Confederate debt or compensating slaveowners.

Although Congress adjourned in the summer of 1866, the nation's attention remained fixed on Reconstruction. The bloody riots in Memphis and New Orleans kept northern attention focused on the South. Johnson, who opposed the Fourteenth Amendment, also undertook a speaking tour in which he urged voters to turn the fall election into a **referendum** on Reconstruction policies. His reckless tirades alienated many who heard him. Republicans swept the 1866 elections, outnumbering Democrats 143 to 49 in the new House of Representatives, and 42 to 11 in the Senate.

Radicals in Control: Impeachment of the President

By March 1867 it was clear that the Fourteenth Amendment had fallen short of ratification. The amendment had been rejected by twelve states: Delaware, Kentucky, and all the Confederate states except Tennessee. Moderates became more receptive to other proposals put forth by the Radicals.

The Military Reconstruction Act of 1867, passed on March 2 over Johnson's veto, divided the Confederate states (except Tennessee) into five military districts, each governed by a military commander (see Map 15.1). The act established a military occupation of the South—the only such episode in American history. The ten states were to hold constitutional conventions, and all adult male citizens

♦ Tickets such as these were in high demand, for they permitted the holder to watch the historic proceedings as the Radical leaders presented their evidence to justify removing Andrew Johnson from the presidency. *Collection of David J. and Janice L. Frent.*

were to vote, except former Confederates barred from office under the proposed Fourteenth Amendment. The constitutional conventions were to create new state governments that permitted black suffrage and that ratified the Fourteenth Amendment. Then, perhaps, Congress might recognize those state governments as valid.

On March 2 Congress also limited some of Johnson's constitutional powers. The Tenure of Office Act specified that officials appointed with the Senate's consent were to remain in office until the Senate approved a successor. This measure was intended to prevent Johnson from replacing federal officials who opposed his policies.

Some Radicals soon began to consider **impeaching** Johnson for his obstruction of their policies. The House Judiciary Committee initially found no convincing evidence of misconduct. Johnson, however, confronted Congress over the Tenure of Office Act by removing Edwin Stanton, a Lincoln appointee,

---

enfranchise   To grant the right to vote to a person or group of people.

referendum   The submission to the public for its approval or disapproval of a law passed or proposed by the legislature.

impeach   To formally charge a public official with improper conduct in office and bring the official to trial for that offense.

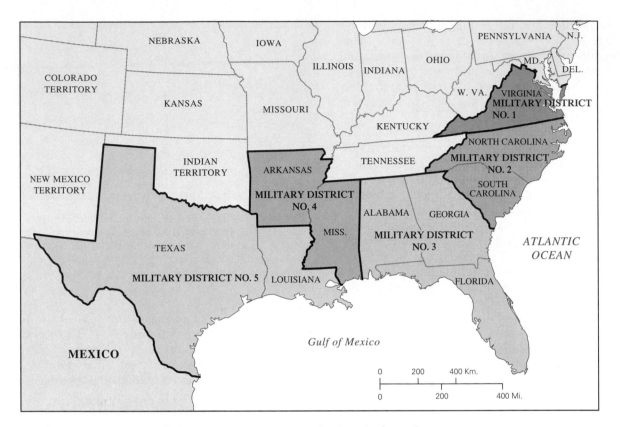

♦ **MAP 15.1 Reconstruction Military Districts**   This map displays the five military districts created when Congress approved the Reconstruction Act of 1867. Tennessee was exempted from military rule because it had been so quick to ratify the Fourteenth Amendment.

from his cabinet post as secretary of war. This action provided the Radicals with grounds for impeachment. On February 24, 1868, the House approved a recommendation for impeachment based on charges stemming from the Stanton affair. The actual motivation was that the Radicals disagreed with Johnson's actions and disliked him.

Johnson remained president after the Senate voted on his impeachment in May 1868 by the narrowest of margins. Thirty-five senators voted in favor of conviction, one vote short of the required two-thirds majority. Moderate Republicans who regarded the charges against Johnson as dubious thus saved his presidency (see Individual Choices: Lyman Trumbull).

Political Terrorism and the Election of 1868

Shortly after the impeachment vote, the Republicans nominated Ulysses S. Grant for president. Grant seemed the right person to end the conflict between the White House and Congress. During the war, he had fully supported Lincoln and Congress in implementing emancipation. By 1868, he had committed himself to the congressional view of Reconstruction. The Democrats nominated Horatio Seymour, a former governor of New York, and focused most of their campaign against Reconstruction.

In the South, the campaign stirred up fierce activity by the Ku Klux Klan and similar groups.

Terrorists assassinated an Arkansas congressman, three members of the South Carolina legislature, and several delegates to state constitutional conventions. Mobs attacked Republican newspaper offices and campaign meetings. Such coercion had its intended effect. In St. Landry Parish, Louisiana, where two hundred blacks were killed, not a single Republican vote was cast on election day.

Despite such violence, by election day many Americans probably *expected* a calmer political future. In June 1868, Congress had readmitted seven southern states that met its requirements, which included ratifying the Fourteenth Amendment. In July, the Fourteenth Amendment was declared ratified. In August, Thaddeus Stevens died. In November, Grant won the presidency, taking twenty-six of the thirty-four states and 53 percent of the vote.

Voting Rights and Civil Rights

Grant's election confirmed that Reconstruction was not likely to be overturned. Radical Republicans now addressed voting rights for all African-Americans. As of 1869, voting rights were still defined by the states, and only seven northern states allowed blacks to vote. To guarantee the voting rights of blacks everywhere, Congress approved the **Fifteenth Amendment** in February 1869. Widely considered to be the final step in Reconstruction, the amendment prohibited states from denying the right to vote because of a person's race. Democrats condemned the amendment as a "revolutionary" change in the rights of states.

Despite such opposition, within thirteen months the proposed amendment had been ratified by the states. Success came in part because Republicans who had been reluctant to impose black suffrage in the North recognized that the party's future success required black suffrage in the South.

The Fifteenth Amendment did nothing to reduce the violence that had become almost routine in the South. When Klan activity escalated in 1870, southern Republicans turned to Washington for support. In 1870 and 1871, Congress enacted the so-called Ku Klux Klan Acts to enforce the rights specified in the Fourteenth and Fifteenth amendments.

The prosecution of Klansmen began in 1871. Hundreds were indicted in North Carolina, and many were convicted. In Mississippi, federal officials indicted nearly seven hundred. In South Carolina, President Grant declared martial law and sent federal troops to occupy the region. Hundreds of arrests followed. By 1872, federal intervention had broken the strength of the Klan.

Congress passed one final Reconstruction measure, largely because of the persistence of Charles Sumner. Passed after Sumner's death, the Civil Rights Act of 1875 prohibited racial **discrimination** in the selection of juries and in public transportation and **public accommodations.**

Black Reconstruction

- Who made up the Republican party in the South during Reconstruction?
- What important *choices* did Republican state administrations make during Reconstruction?
- Which *choices* brought the most lasting *outcomes*?

Congressional Reconstruction set the stage for new developments throughout the South, as newly enfranchised black men organized for political action. The period when African-Americans participated prominently in state and local politics is usually called **Black Reconstruction.** It began with the

---

terrorists   Those who use threats and violence, often against innocent parties, to achieve ideological or political goals.

Fifteenth Amendment   Constitutional amendment, ratified in 1870, that prohibited states from denying the right to vote because of a person's race or because a person used to be a slave.

discrimination   Treatment based on class or racial category rather than on merit; prejudice.

public accommodations   Places such as hotels, bars and restaurants, and theaters set up to do business with anyone who can pay the price of admission.

Black Reconstruction   The period of Reconstruction when African-Americans took an active role in state and local government.

Choosing Principle Over Party

Lyman Trumbull

Lyman Trumbull, a former judge and chairman of the Senate Judiciary Committee, faced a choice between his party and his commitment to judicial principles when he had to vote on removing Andrew Johnson from presidency. Chicago Historical Society.

The sun was shining in Washington, D.C., on May 16, 1868, as a crowd swarmed around the entrance to the visitors' gallery of the Senate. Seats were in great demand, for at noon the Senate was to vote on the impeachment of President Andrew Johnson. Promptly at noon, Salmon P. Chase, Chief Justice of the Supreme Court, arrived to carry out his constitutionally mandated role of presiding over the proceedings. The roll call was delayed to permit the last of the 54 senators—weakened by a recent stroke—to take his seat.

Chase began to call the roll on the eleventh charge, the one considered most likely to be approved, asking each senator, "Is the respondent, Andrew Johnson, President of the United States, guilty or not guilty of a high misdemeanor, as charged in this article?" All Democrats voted not guilty. Nearly all Republicans voted guilty. Seven Republicans, however, made the difficult *choice* to break with their party, producing a final *outcome* of 35 for conviction and 19 opposed—one vote short of the two-thirds majority needed to convict Johnson and remove him from office.

Lyman Trumbull, chairman of the Senate Judiciary Committee and one of the leading Republicans in the Senate, had listened carefully to all the testimony on the case, sometimes bringing his young son Henry to observe the

efforts of African-Americans to take part in politics as early as 1865 and lasted until 1877.

The Republican Party in the South

Nearly all blacks who took an active part in politics did so as Republicans. Throughout Reconstruction,

they formed a large majority of the Republican party's supporters in the South. The southern wing of the party also included transplanted northerners and some native white southerners.

Suffrage made politics important in African-American communities. In Louisiana and South Carolina, more than half of the delegates to state historic proceedings. Trumbull, who had represented Illinois in the Senate for thirteen years, was one of the seven Republicans *choosing* to vote not guilty, despite the overwhelming majority of Republican leaders in his state who favored conviction. By his *choice*, he set himself not only against most of the leaders of his party and many of his friends, but even against his wife, Julia, described by a Chicago newspaper only nine days before the vote as "a warm impeacher."

Trumbull's *choice* reflected, in part, his *expectations* as a lawyer. As early as December 1866, he had called on Republicans to deal with the possibility of impeachment "coolly and deliberately" and not to be misled by "excited demagogues." As a former judge, Trumbull *expected* more proof of guilt than the leaders of the impeachment effort provided.

One of the important leaders of Congressional Reconstruction, Trumbull had little regard for Johnson, but had great respect for the constitutional separation of powers. Removing Johnson on flimsy evidence, he argued, would pose "far greater danger to the future of the country than can arise from leaving Mr. Johnson in office." Trumbull feared, too, that removal of Johnson would place a major *constraint* on all future presidents. "Once set an example of impeaching a President for what, when the excitement of the hour has subsided, will be regarded as insufficient causes," Trumbull warned the Senate, "and no future President will be safe who happens to differ with the majority of the House and two-thirds of the Senate."

Trumbull must have *expected* that his *choice* would bring harsh reprimands from Republicans in his home state. One Chicago newspaper even suggested that Trumbull was too unclean even to be touched by decent people. Long-time friendships were shattered by his action. One major Chicago newspaper defended his action, however, and he regained his high standing among the Republican leaders of the Senate.

For Trumbull, however, one *outcome* of the impeachment trial was that he began to rethink the constitutional issues involved in Reconstruction at the same time that he became more concerned about corruption. He grew more and more critical of the Radicals, the Black Reconstruction governments in southern states, and the Grant administration. In 1872, he joined the Liberal Republicans hoping to defeat Grant. Afterward he became a Democrat. He lost his bid for re-election to the Senate in 1873 and returned to the practice of law. His last major political appearance came in 1894 at the age of 81, when he condemned both the Republican and Democratic parties for failing to protect working people against the mighty industrial corporations and announced that he had become a Populist (see page 392).

constitutional conventions were black. With suffrage established, African-Americans began to be elected to public office. Between 1869 and 1877, fourteen black men served in the national House of Representatives and two in the U.S. Senate.

At the state level, blacks were most likely to be elected to the relatively unimportant offices of lieutenant governor and secretary of state. More than six hundred black men served in southern state legislatures during Reconstruction, three-quarters of them in just four states: South Carolina, Mississippi, Louisiana, and Alabama. Only in South Carolina did African-Americans ever have a majority in the state legislature.

Most African-American office-holders had some education and had been born free. Of the eighteen who served in statewide offices, only three had been slaves. Blanche K. Bruce was one of these. He had been educated, however, and after the war he attended Oberlin College in Ohio. He then moved to Mississippi, where he was elected U.S. senator in 1875.

Black Republicans achieved power only by securing at least some support from whites. Opponents referred to white Republicans as either **carpetbaggers** or **scalawags.** Both groups included idealists but also included some opportunists who hoped only to fatten their own purses.

Southern Democrats used the term "carpetbagger" to suggest that northerners who came to the South after the war were second-rate opportunists, with their belongings packed in a cheap bag made of carpet. In fact, most northerners who came south were well-educated people from middle-class backgrounds. Most men had served in the Union Army and moved South soon after the war to pursue financial opportunities, not politics. Some had left behind prominent roles in northern communities. Others hoped to transform the South by creating new institutions based on free labor and free schools. Carpetbaggers made up a sixth of the delegates to the state constitutional conventions but often took key roles in the conventions and the state legislatures.

Southern Democrats reserved their greatest contempt for scalawags—a term used to describe completely unscrupulous and worthless people. Scalawags were white southerners who became Republicans. Many had been political foes of the Democrats before the war. They made up the largest single category of delegates to the state constitutional conventions. Scalawags included many southern Unionists and others who thought the Republicans offered the best hope for economic recovery. Scalawags included small-town merchants, artisans, and professionals. Others were small-scale farmers from the backcountry, who had traditionally opposed the plantation owners. For them, Reconstruction promised an end to political domination by the plantation counties. Still others had been Whigs before the Civil War.

Despite differences, freedmen, carpetbaggers, and scalawags used the Republican party to inject new ideas into the South. Throughout the South, Republican governments extended the role of state and local government and expanded public institutions. They established or expanded schools, hospitals, orphanages, and penitentiaries.

Creating an Educational System and Fighting Discrimination

Free public education was perhaps the most permanent legacy of Black Reconstruction. Reconstruction constitutions required tax-supported public schools. Implementation, however, was expensive and proceeded slowly. By 1875, only half of southern children attended public schools.

The Reconstruction state governments debated whether white and black children should attend the same schools. Most blacks probably favored **integrated** schools. Southern whites, however, warned that integration would drive whites away. Only Louisiana and South Carolina did not mandate that schools be segregated. Most blacks probably agreed with Frederick Douglass that separate schools were "infinitely superior" to no public education.

Funding for the new schools was rarely adequate. The new schools had to be funded largely through **property taxes,** and property tax revenues declined during the 1870s as property values fell. Creating and operating two educational systems, one white and one black, was expensive. Black schools almost always received less support than white schools.

Reconstruction state governments moved toward equal rights in other areas. The new state constitutions prohibited discrimination and protected civil

---

carpetbagger Derogatory southern term for the northerners who came to the South after the Civil War to take part in Reconstruction.

scalawag Derogatory southern term for white southerners who aligned themselves with the Republican party.

integrated Open to people of all races and ethnic groups without restriction.

property taxes Taxes paid by property owners according to the value of their property; often used in the United States to provide funding for local schools.

♦ Howard University, Washington, D.C., was chartered by Congress in 1867 and quickly became the leading African-American university. Its first president and namesake was General Oliver O. Howard, former head of the Freedmen's Bureau. Over the years, the university has produced many of the nation's black leaders. *Collection of William Gladstone*

rights. Some states guaranteed **equal access** to public transportation and public accommodations. White Republicans, however, often opposed such laws. Such conflicts pointed up the internal divisions within the southern Republican party. Even when equal access laws were passed, they were often not enforced.

Railroad Development and Corruption

Republicans nationally sought to use the power of government to stimulate economic growth. They typically encouraged railroad construction. In the South, Reconstruction governments granted state lands to railroads, loaned them money, or helped to **underwrite** bonds. Sometimes they promoted railroads without finding out whether companies were financially sound. Such efforts often failed. During the 1870s, only 7,000 miles of new track were laid in the South, compared to 45,000 miles in the North.

Railroads sometimes tried to secure favorable treatment by bribing public officials, and all too many accepted their offers. The post–Civil War period saw the ethics of public officials reach a low point. From New York City to Mississippi, revelations and allegations of corruption became staples in political campaigning.

Conditions in the South were especially ripe for political corruption. Opportunities abounded for the ambitious and unscrupulous. Reconstruction governments included many whites and blacks who had only modest holdings but aspired to better things. One South Carolina legislator bluntly said: "I was pretty hard up, and I did not care who the candidate was if I got two hundred dollars." Corruption seemed especially prominent among Republicans only because they held the most important offices. Still, some Reconstruction Republicans remained scrupulously honest. In fact, Mississippi's government under Republican rule was far more honest than it had been under pre-war Democratic rule.

The End of Reconstruction

- How did the Mississippi Plan help to end Reconstruction?
- What were the final *outcomes* of Reconstruction?

Most white southerners resisted the new social order imposed on them. They created the black codes to maintain white supremacy and to restore elements of a bound labor system. They used terrorism against the advocates of black rights. Such resistance, however, had caused Congress to pass more severe terms for Reconstruction. This backlash drove some southern opponents of Reconstruction to rethink their strategy.

---

equal access The right of any group to use a public facility such as streetcars as freely as all other groups in the society.

underwrite To assume financial responsibility for; in this case, to guarantee the purchase of bonds so that a project can go forward.

The "New Departure"

By 1869, some leading southern Democrats had abandoned their resistance to change and had *chosen* instead to accept key Reconstruction measures. At the same time, they also tried to restore the political rights for former Confederates. The **New Departure** Democrats believed that continued resistance would only prolong federal intervention in state politics.

Sometimes southern Democrats supported conservative Republicans. The *outcome* of this strategy was to dilute Radical influence in state government. Democrats first tried this strategy in Virginia. There, William Mahone, a leading Democrat, forged a political **coalition** that accepted black suffrage. Mahone's organization then elected a northern-born Republican banker as governor. In this way, Virginia became the only Confederate state to avoid Radical Republican rule.

Similar coalitions won in Tennessee in 1869 and in Missouri in 1870. Leading Democrats elsewhere also endorsed the New Departure. They attacked Republicans more for raising taxes and increasing state spending than for their racial policies. Whenever possible, they added charges of corruption. Such campaigns brought a positive response from many taxpayers because southern tax rates had risen dramatically to support the new schools, subsidies for railroads, and other new programs.

The victories of New Departure Democrats coincided with terrorist activity aimed at Republicans. In Colfax, Louisiana, whites killed 280 African-Americans in 1872 in the bloodiest racial incident of the Reconstruction era. A few southern Republicans responded by proposing to create black militias. Most Republicans, however, feared that this might provoke a race war. In most of the South, the suppression of Klan terrorism came only with federal action.

The 1872 Election

The New Departure movement coincided with a division within the Republican party. The Liberal Republican movement began in 1870 as a revolt against corruption in the Grant administration. Liberal Republicans found allies among Democrats when they came out against the Radicals.

Horace Greeley, editor of the *New York Tribune*, won the Liberal nomination for president. Although Greeley had long opposed the Democrats, the Democrats also nominated him. The Liberal Republicans and Democrats were united almost solely by their opposition to Grant and the Radicals. Few Republicans found Greeley an attractive alternative to Grant, and Greeley alienated many northern Democrats by calling for the prohibition of alcohol. Grant won convincingly. He carried 56 percent of the vote and captured every northern state.

Redemption by Terror: The "Mississippi Plan"

After 1872, southern whites began to abandon the Republicans. The region polarized largely along racial lines, and the elections of 1874 proved disastrous for Republicans. Democrats won over two-thirds of the South's seats in the House of Representatives and "redeemed" Alabama, Arkansas, and Texas—meaning they regained political control of these states.

Republican candidates in 1874 lost in many parts of the North because of the economic **depression** that began in 1873. After the 1874 elections, Democrats outnumbered Republicans in the House by 169 to 109. Southern Republicans could thus no longer look to Congress for assistance.

Terrorism against black Republicans and their remaining white allies played a role in the victory of the **Redeemers** in 1874. The Klan had worn disguises and ridden at night, but Democrats now openly formed rifle companies and marched and

---

New Departure   A policy of cooperation with key Reconstruction measures that leading southern Democrats adopted in the hope of winning compromises favorable to their party.

coalition   An alliance, especially a temporary one of different people or groups.

depression   A period of drastic decline in a national or international economy, characterized by decreasing business activity, falling prices, and unemployment.

Redeemers   Southern Democrats who hoped to bring the Democratic party back into power and to suppress Black Reconstruction.

♦ *Harper's Weekly*, a leading northern periodical, used this cartoon in 1875 to argue that the presence of federal troops and federal law enforcement officials was necessary if African-Americans were to exercise equal rights in the South. *Library of Congress.*

The Compromise of 1877

In 1876, the nation stumbled through a potentially dangerous presidential election. As revelations of corruption grew nationally, the issue of reform took center stage. The Democratic party nominated Samuel J. Tilden, governor of New York, as its presidential candidate. Tilden had earned a reputation for reform by opposing the Tweed Ring, the corrupt Democratic political machine that ran New York City government. The Republicans also selected a reform candidate, Rutherford B. Hayes, a Civil War general and governor of Ohio. Hayes's unblemished reputation proved to be his greatest asset.

First election reports indicated a close victory for Tilden, who carried most of the South and crucial northern states such as New York and Indiana. But in South Carolina, Florida, and Louisiana, Republicans still controlled the counting of ballots. Republican election boards in those states rejected enough ballots to give Hayes those three states and thus a one-vote margin of victory in the Electoral College.

Democrats cried fraud. Some vowed to see Tilden inaugurated by force if necessary. For the first time, Congress had to face the problem of disputed electoral votes that could decide an election. To resolve the problem, Congress created a commission consisting of five senators, five representatives, and five Supreme Court justices. Eight Republicans and seven Democrats sat on the commission.

The nation braced itself for a potentially violent confrontation. However, as commission hearings droned on into February 1877, a series of informal discussions took place among leading Republicans and Democrats. The result was a series of informal agreements usually called the **Compromise of 1877.** Southern Democrats demanded **home rule,** by which they meant an end to federal intervention in

drilled in public. In some areas, armed whites prevented African-Americans from voting.

Political violence reached such an extreme in Mississippi in 1875 that the use of terror to overthrow Reconstruction became known as the Mississippi Plan. Democratic rifle clubs operated freely, attacking Republican leaders in broad daylight. When Mississippi's carpetbagger governor, Adelbert Ames, requested federal help, President Grant declined to give it. The president had grown weary of the continuing costs of Reconstruction and the seemingly endless bloodshed that it occasioned. The Democrats swept the Mississippi elections. When the legislature convened, it removed the black Republican lieutenant governor from office. The legislature then brought similar impeachment charges against Governor Ames. Ames resigned and left the state.

Compromise of 1877   Compromise in which southern Democrats agreed to allow the Republican candidate the victory in the disputed presidential election in return for the removal of federal troops from the South.

home rule   Self-government; in this case, an end to federal intervention in the South.

southern politics. They also called for federal subsidies for railroad construction and waterways in the South. In return, southern Democrats were willing to abandon Tilden's claim to the White House if the commission ruled for Hayes.

Most of the agreements that were part of the Compromise of 1877 were kept. By a straight party vote, the commission confirmed the election of Hayes. Soon after his peaceful inauguration, he ordered the last of the federal troops withdrawn from the South. The Radical era of a powerful federal government pledged to protect "equality before the law" for all citizens was over. Without federal protection, the last three Republican state governments fell in 1877. The party of white supremacy held sway in every southern state.

The Compromise of 1877 marked the end of Reconstruction. The war was more than ten years in the past, and the passions it had stirred had slowly cooled. Many who had yearned to punish the South for its treason turned to other matters. Some reformers concentrated on civil service or currency issues. A major depression in the mid-1870s, unemployment and labor disputes, the growth of industry, the emergence of big business, and the economic development of the West focused public attention on economic issues.

After Reconstruction

Southern Democrats read the events of 1877 as their permit to establish new systems of politics and race relations. Most Redeemers set out to reduce taxes, to dismantle Reconstruction legislation and agencies, to take political influence away from black citizens, and eventually to reshape the South's legal system to establish African-Americans as subordinate. They also began the process of turning the South into a one-party region.

Although voting and officeholding by African-Americans did not cease in 1877, the political context changed profoundly once they lost federal enforcement of their rights. The threat of violence from night-riders and the potential for economic retaliation sharply reduced independent action by African-Americans. Black political leaders increasingly recognized that efforts to mobilize black voters posed dangers to both candidates and voters. The public schools remained, segregated and underfunded, but important as both a symbol and a real opportunity to learn. Many Reconstruction-era laws remained on the books.

Not until the 1890s did black disfranchisement and thoroughgoing racial segregation become widely embedded in southern law (see pages 383–385). From the mid-1870s to the late 1890s, the South lived an uneasy compromise: African-Americans had certain constitutional rights, but blacks exercised their rights at the sufferance of the dominant whites. Such a compromise bore the seeds of future conflict.

For generations after 1877, Reconstruction was held up as a failure. The southern version of Reconstruction—that conniving carpetbaggers and scalawags had manipulated ignorant freedmen—appealed to the racial bias of many white Americans in the North and South alike, and it gained widespread acceptance among popular novelists, journalists, and historians. Thomas Dixon's popular novel *The Clansman* (1905) inspired the highly influential film *The Birth of a Nation* (1915). Historically inaccurate and luridly racist, the book and the movie portrayed Ku Klux Klan members as heroes who rescued the white South, and especially white southern women, from domination and debauchery at the hands of depraved freedmen and carpetbaggers. Although black historians such as W. E. B. Du Bois challenged this picture of Reconstruction, it was not until the civil rights movement of the 1950s and 1960s that large numbers of American historians began to reconsider Reconstruction.

Historians today recognize that Reconstruction was not the failure that had earlier been claimed. The creation of public schools was but one of the most important of the changes in southern life. At a federal level, the Fourteenth and Fifteenth amendments eventually were used to restore the principle of equality before the law. Historians also recognize that Reconstruction collapsed not so much because of internal flaws as because of the political terrorism that was unleashed in the South against blacks and Republicans.

SUMMARY

At the end of the Civil War, the nation faced difficult *choices* regarding the future of the defeated South and the future of the freed people. Committed to an end to slavery, President Lincoln *chose* a lenient approach to restoring states to the Union. When Johnson became president, he continued Lincoln's approach.

The end of slavery brought new *expectations* for all African-Americans. Taking advantage of the *choices* that freedom opened, they tried to create independent lives for themselves and developed social institutions that helped to define black communities. Few were able to acquire land of their own. Most became either wage laborers or sharecroppers. White southerners *expected* to keep African-Americans subordinate through black codes and violence.

In reaction against the black codes and violence, Congress *chose* to wrest control of Reconstruction from President Johnson. An attempt to remove Johnson from the presidency was unsuccessful. Reconstruction measures included the Fourteenth and Fifteenth amendments, the Civil Rights Act of 1866, and the Civil Rights Act of 1875. One *outcome* of these measures was to strengthen the federal government at the expense of the states.

Enfranchised freedmen, transplanted northerners, and some southern whites created a southern Republican party that governed most southern states for a time. The most lasting contribution of these state governments was the creation of public school systems. Like government officials elsewhere, however, some southerners fell prey to corruption.

In the late 1860s, many southern Democrats *chose* a "New Departure": they grudgingly accepted some features of Reconstruction and sought to recapture control of state governments. The 1876 presidential election was hotly disputed, but key Republicans and Democrats *chose* to compromise. The Compromise of 1877 permitted Hayes to take office and brought Reconstruction to an end. Without further federal protection for their civil rights, African-Americans faced severe *constraints* in exercising their rights. Sharecropping consigned most to a subordinate economic status. Terrorism, violence, and even death confronted those who *chose* to challenge their subordinate social role. The *outcome* of Reconstruction was white supremacy in politics, the economy, and social relations.

E xpectations
C onstraints
C hoices
O utcomes

SUGGESTED READINGS

Donald, David. *Charles Sumner and the Rights of Man* (1970).

A good account not just of this important Radical leader but of important Reconstruction issues.

Du Bois, W. E. B. *Black Reconstruction in America: An Essay Toward a History of the Part Which Black Folk Played in the Attempt to Reconstruct Democracy in America, 1860–1880* (1935; reprint, 1969).

Written more than a half-century ago, Du Bois's book is still useful for both information and insights.

Foner, Eric. *Reconstruction: America's Unfinished Revolution, 1863–1877* (1988).

The most thorough of recent treatments, incorporating insights from many historians who have written on the subject during the past forty years. Also available in a condensed version.

Litwack, Leon F. *Been in the Storm So Long: The Aftermath of Slavery* (1979).

Focuses especially on the experience of the freed people.

Woodward, C. Vann. *Reunion and Reaction: The Compromise of 1877 and the End of Reconstruction,* rev. ed. (1956).

The classic account of the Compromise of 1877.

Bibliography

Chapter 1 Making a "New" World, to 1588

Kenneth Andrews, *Trade, Plunder, and Settlement: Maritime Enterprise and the Genesis of the British Empire, 1480–1630* (1984); Fredi Chiapelli, *First Images of America: The Impact of the New World on the Old* (1976); Michael D. Coe, *Mexico*, rev. ed. (1984); Philip Curtin, *The Atlantic Slave Trade; A Census* (1969); Nigel Davies, *The Aztecs: A History* (1974); Henry F. Dobyns, "Estimating Aboriginal American Population," *Current Anthropology* (1966); Harry F. Dobyns, *Their Number Become Thinned: Native American Population Dynamics in Eastern North America* (1983); Harold E. Driver, *Indians of North America*, 2d ed. (1969); Brian M. Fagan, *The Great Journey: The Peopling of Ancient America* (1987); J. D. Fage, *An Introduction to the History of West Africa* (1969); Felipe Fernandez-Armesto, *Before Columbus: Exploration and Colonization from the Mediterranean to the Atlantic, 1229–1492* (1987); Charles Gallenkamp, *Maya: The Riddle and Rediscovery of a Lost Civilization*, 3d expanded ed. (1985); Charles Gibson, *Spain in America* (1966); Alvin M. Josephy, *America in 1492: The World of the Indian Peoples Before the Arrival of Columbus* (1992); Alfred L. Kroeber, "Native American Population," *American Anthropologist* (1934); Karen O. Kupperman, *Roanoke, The Abandoned Colony* (1984); Jerald T. Milanich, *First Encounters: Spanish Explorations in the Caribbean and the United States, 1492–1570* (1989); Samuel Eliot Morison, *The European Discovery of America: The Southern Voyages, 1492–1616* (1974); *The European Discovery of America: The Northern Voyages, 1500–1600* (1971); Roland Oliver, *A Short History of Africa*, 6th ed. (1988); J. H. Parry, *The Age of Reconnaissance: Discovery, Exploration, and Settlement, 1450–1650* (1963); William Phillips, *The Worlds of Christopher Columbus* (1992); David Beers Quinn, *North America from Earliest Discovery to First Settlements: The Norse Voyages to 1612* (1977); Kirkpatrick Sale, *The Conquest of Paradise: Christopher Columbus and the Columbian Legacy* (1990); Robert Silverberg, *Mound Builders of Ancient America: The Archaeology of a Myth* (1986); Dean Snow, *The Archaeology of North America: American Indians and Their Origins* (1976); Paolo Emilio Taviani, *Columbus, The Great Adventure: His Life, His Times, and His Voyages* (1991); David Weber, *The Spanish Frontier in North America* (1992); John Noble Wilford, *The Mysterious History of Columbus: An Exploration of the Man, the Myth, the Legacy* (1991); Eric Wolf, *Europe and the People Without History* (1983).

Chapter 2 English Entry into the New World, 1607–1752

Bernard Bailyn, *The New England Merchants in the Seventeenth Century* (1955); Patricia Bonomi, *A Factious People* (1971); Paul Boyer and Stephen Nissenbaum, *Salem Possessed: The Social Origins of Witchcraft* (1974); Timothy Breen, *Puritans and Adventurers* (1980); Timothy Breen, *Tobacco Culture* (1985); Jon Butler, *Awash in a Sea of Faith* (1990); Lois Carr and David Jordan, *Maryland's Revolution of Government, 1689–1692* (1974); William Cronon, *Changes in the Land: Indians, Colonists, and the Ecology of New England* (1983); Andrew Delbanco, *The Puritan Ordeal* (1989); John Demos, *Entertaining Satan* (1982); Philip Gura, *A Glimpse of Sion's Glory* (1984); David Hall, *Worlds of Wonder, Days of Judgment* (1990); Michael Kammen, *Colonial New York* (1975); Allan Kulikoff, *Tobacco and Slaves* (1986); James Lang, *Conquest and Commerce* (1975); Suzanne Lebsock, *A Share of Honor* (1984); James Lemmon, *The Best Poor Man's Country* (1972); Barry Levy, *Quakers and the American Family* (1988); H. T. Merrens, *Colonial North Carolina* (1964); Perry Miller, *Errand into the Wilderness* (1956); Edmund Morgan, *American Slavery, American Freedom* (1975); Oliver Rink, *Holland on Hudson* (1986); Frederick Siegel, *The Roots of Southern Distinctiveness* (1987); Kenneth Silverman, *The Life and Times of Cotton Mather* (1984); Harry Stout, *The New England Soul* (1986); Alan Tully, *William Penn's Legacy* (1977); Laurel Ulrich, *Goodwives: Image and Reality in the Lives of Women in Northern New England, 1650–1750* (1982); Robert Weir, *Colonial South Carolina* (1983).

Chapter 3 The British Colonies in the Eighteenth Century, 1700–1763

Bernard Bailyn, *The Origins of American Politics* (1968); Ira Berlin and Philip Morgan, eds., *Cultivation and Culture: Labor and the Shaping of Slave Life in the Americas* (1993); Patricia Bonomi, *Under the Cope of Heaven: Religion, Society, and Politics in Colonial America* (1986); Richard Bushman, *From Puritan to Yankee* (1967); Paul Clemens, *The Atlantic Economy and Colonial Maryland's Eastern Shore: From Tobacco to Grain* (1980); Jean Friedman, *The Enclosed Garden: Women and Community in the Evangelical South* (1985); Philip Greven, *The Protestant Temperament: Patterns of Childrearing, Religious Experience, and the Self in Early America* (1977); James Henretta, *The Evolution of American Society, 1700–1815* (1982); Rhys Isaac, *The Transformation of Virginia, 1740–1790* (1982); Francis Jennings, *Empire of Fortune* (1988); Joan Jensen, *Loosening the Bonds: Mid-Atlantic Farm Women, 1750–1850* (1986); Charles Joyner, *Down by the Riverside: A South Carolina Slave Community* (1984); Michael Kammen, *Spheres of Liberty: Changing Perceptions of Liberty in American Culture* (1986); Allan Kulikoff, *Tobacco and Slaves* (1986); Ned Landsman, *Scotland and Its First American Colony* (1985); Daniel Littlefield, *Rice and Slaves: Ethnicity and the Slave Trade in Colonial South Carolina* (1981); James Merrell, *The Indians' New World: Catawbas and Their Neighbors from European Contact Through the Era of Removal* (1989); Marcus Rediker, *Between* the Devil and the Deep Blue Sea (1985); Daniel Richter, *The Ordeal of the Longhouse* (1992); Sharon Salinger, *"To Serve Well and Faithfully": Labor and Indentured Servants in Pennsylvania, 1692–1800* (1987); Michael Sobel, *The World They Made Together: Black and White Values in Eighteenth Century Virginia* (1987); Laurel Ulrich, *Good Wives: Image and Reality in the Lives of Women in Northern New England, 1650–1850* (1982); Stephanie Wolf, *As Various as Their Land: The Everyday Lives of Eighteenth Century Americans* (1993).

Chapter 4 Deciding Where Loyalties Lie, 1763–1776

Bernard Bailyn, *The Ideological Origins of the American Revolution* (1967); Carol Berkin, *Jonathan Sewall: Odyssey of An American Loyalist* (1974); Edward Countryman, *The American Revolution* (1985); Thomas Doerflinger, *A Vigorous Spirit of Enterprise: Merchants and Economic Development in Revolutionary Philadelphia* (1986); Marc Egnal, *A Mighty Empire: The Origins of the American Revolution* (1988); Eric Foner, *Tom Paine and Revolutionary America* (1976); Paul Gilje, *The Road to Mobocracy: Popular Disorder in New York City, 1763–1834* (1987); Robert Gross, *The Minutemen and Their World* (1976); Francis Jennings, *Empire of Fortune: Crowns, Colonies and Tribes in the Seven Years War in America* (1988); Linda Kerber, *Women of the Republic: Intellect and Ideology in Revolutionary America* (1980); Pauline Maier, *From Resistance to Revolution* (1972); Mary Beth Norton, *Liberty's Daughters: The Revolutionary Experience of American Women, 1750–1800* (1980); Paul Rahle, *Republics Ancient and Modern: Republicanism and the American Revolution* (1992); Steven Rosswurm, *Arms, Country, and Class: The Philadelphia Militia and the "Lower Sort" During the American Revolution* (1987); Gordon Wood, *The Radicalism of the American Revolution* (1992).

Chapter 5 Recreating America: Independence and a New Nation, 1775–1783

Bernard Bailyn, *The Ordeal of Thomas Hutchinson* (1974); Carol Berkin, *Jonathan*

Sewall: Odyssey of an American Loyalist (1974); Ira Berlin and Ronald Hoffman, eds., *Slavery and Freedom in the Age of the American Revolution* (1983); Jeremy Black, *War for America* (1991); Colin Bonwick, *The American Revolution* (1991); Andrew Cayton, *The Frontier Republic* (1986); Edward Countryman, *The American Revolution* (1985); Edward Countryman, *A People in Revolution: The American Revolution and Political Society in New York, 1760–1790* (1981); Jeffrey Crow and Larry Tise, eds., *The Southern Experience in the American Revolution* (1978); John C. Dann, *The Revolution Remembered: Eyewitness Accounts of the War for Independence* (1980); James Flexner, *George Washington in the American Revolution* (1978); Jay Fliegelman, *Prodigals and Pilgrims* (1982); William Fowler and Wallace Coyle, eds., *The American Revolution: Changing Perspectives* (1979); Sylvia Frey, *Water from the Rock: Black Resistance in a Revolutionary Age* (1991); Barbara Graymont, *The Iroquois in the American Revolution* (1972); Robert Gross, *The Minutemen and Their World* (1976); Ronald Hoffman and Peter Albert, eds., *Women in the Age of the American Revolution* (1989); Michael Kammen, *A Season of Youth* (1978); Linda Kerber, *Women of the Republic: Intellect and Ideology in Revolutionary America* (1980); Duncan MacLeod, *Slavery, Race, and the American Revolution* (1974); Mary Beth Norton, *Liberty's Daughters* (1980); Mary Beth Norton, *The British-Americans* (1972); James O'Donnell, *Southern Indians in the American Revolution* (1973); Charles Royster, *A Revolutionary People at War: The Continental Army and American Character, 1775–1783* (1980); John Shy, *A People Numerous and Armed: Reflections on the Military Struggle for American Independence* (1976); James Walker, *The Black Loyalists* (1976).

Chapter 6 Competing Visions of a Virtuous Republic, 1776–1796

Joyce Appleby, *Capitalism and a New Social Order* (1984); Lance Banning, *The Jeffersonian Persuasion: The Evolution of a Party Ideology* (1978); Charles Beard, *An Economic Interpretation of the Constitution* (1913); Walker Bern, *Taking the Constitution Seriously* (1987); Richard Buel, Jr., *Securing*

the Revolution (1972); Thomas Curry, *The First Freedom* (1986); David B. Davis, *Slavery in the Age of Revolution* (1975); Stanley Elkins and Eric McKitrick, *The Federalist Era* (1993); Max Farrand, ed., *Records of the Federal Convention of 1787* (1911–1937); Richard Hofstadter, *The Idea of a Party System* (1970); Merrill Jensen, *The New Nation: A History of the United States During the Confederation, 1781–1789* (1950); Michael Kammen, *A Machine That Would Go of Itself: The Constitution and American Culture* (1986); Allan Kulikoff, *The Agrarian Origins of American Capitalism* (1992); Staughton Lynd, *Class Conflict, Slavery, and the United States Constitution* (1967); Jackson Turner Main, *The Antifederalists* (1961); Drew McCoy, *The Last of the Fathers: James Madison and the Republican Legacy* (1989); Forrest McDonald, *Novus Ordo Seclorum* (1985); William Miller, *The First Liberty: Religion and the American Republic* (1986); Edmund Morgan, *Inventing the People: The Rise of Popular Sovereignty in England and America* (1988); Thomas Pangle, *The Spirit of Modern Republicanism* (1988); Donald Robinson, *Slavery in the Structure of American Politics, 1765–1820* (1971); Barry Swartz, *George Washington: The Making of a Symbol* (1987); Gary Wills, *Explaining America* (1981); Gordon Wood, *The Radicalism of the American Revolution* (1992).

Chapter 7 The Early Republic, 1796–1804

Joyce Appleby, *Capitalism and the New Social Order: The Republican Vision of the 1790s* (1984); Alexander Balinky, *Albert Gallatin: Fiscal Theories and Policy* (1958); Lance Banning, *The Jeffersonian Persuasion: Evolution of a Party Ideology* (1978); John Boles, *The Great Revival, 1787–1805: The Origins of the Southern Evangelical Mind* (1972); Morton Borden, *Parties and Politics in the Early Republic, 1789–1815* (1967); Ralph Adams Brown, *The Presidency of John Adams* (1975); Richard Buel, Jr., *Securing the Revolution: Ideology in American Politics, 1789–1815* (1972); Robert Lowry Clinton, *Marbury v. Madison and Judicial Review* (1989); Noble E. Cunningham, *In Pursuit of Reason: The Life of Thomas Jefferson* (1987); *The Jeffersonian*

Republicans: The Formation of Party Organization, 1789–1801 (1957); Leonard P. Curry, *The Free Black in Urban America, 1800–1850: The Shadow of the Dream* (1981); Alexander Deconde, *The Quasi-War: Politics and Diplomacy of the Undeclared War with France, 1797–1801* (1966); *This Affair of Louisiana* (1976); Richard Ellis, *The Jeffersonian Crisis: Courts and Politics in the Young Republic* (1974); Richard Hofstadter, *The Idea of a Party System: The Rise of Legitimate Opposition in the United States, 1780–1840* (1969); Richard Kohn, *Eagle and Sword: The Federalists and the Creation of the Military Establishment in America, 1783–1802* (1975); Eugene P. Link, *Democratic-Republican Societies, 1790–1800* (1942); Richard P. McCormick, *The Presidential Game: The Origins of American Presidential Politics* (1982); Drew McCoy, *The Elusive Republic: Political Economy in Jeffersonian America* (1980); Forrest McDonald, *The Presidency of Thomas Jefferson* (1976); John C. Miller, *The Wolf by the Ears: Thomas Jefferson and Slavery* (1977); Gary B. Nash, *Forging Freedom; The Formation of Philadelphia's Black Community, 1720–1840* (1988); Bradford Perkins, *The First Rapprochement: England and the United States, 1795–1805* (1955); Merrill Peterson, *Thomas Jefferson and the New Nation: A Biography* (1970); Francis P. Prucha, *American Indian Policy in the Formative Years: The Indian Trade and Intercourse Acts, 1780–1834* (1967); James Ronda, *Lewis and Clark Among the Indians* (1984); Bernard W. Sheehan, *Seeds of Extinction: Jeffersonian Philanthropy and the American Indian* (1973); James Morton Smith, *Freedom's Fetters: The Alien and Sedition Laws and American Civil Liberties* (1956); William Stinchcombe, *The XYZ Affair* (1981); Julie Winch, *Philadelphia's Black Elite: Activism, Accommodation, and the Struggle for Autonomy, 1787–1848* (1988).

Chapter 8 Renewing Independence, 1805–1814

James M. Banner, *To the Hartford Convention: The Federalists and the Origins of Party Politics in Massachusetts, 1789–1815* (1970); Irving Brant, *James Madison and American Nationalism* (1968); Roger H. Brown, *The Republic in Peril: 1812* (1964); Harry L. Coles, *The War of 1812* (1965); Noble E. Cunningham, Jr., *The Jeffersonian Republicans in Power: Party Operations, 1801–1809* (1957); R. David Edmunds, *Tecumseh and the Quest for Indian Leadership* (1984); R. David Edmunds, *The Shawnee Prophet* (1983); Clifford L. Egan, *Neither Peace Nor War: Franco-American Relations, 1803–1812* (1983); David H. Fischer, *The Revolution of American Conservatism; The Federalist Party in the Era of Jeffersonian Democracy* (1965); William F. Fowler, Jr., *Jack Tars and Commodores: The American Navy, 1783–1815* (1984); Donald Hickey, *The War of 1812: A Forgotten Conflict* (1989); Reginald Horsman, *The Causes of the War of 1812* (1962); Reginald Horsman, *The War of 1812* (1969); Linda Kerber, *Federalists in Dissent: Imagery and Ideology in Jeffersonian America* (1970); Ralph Ketcham, *James Madison: A Biography* (1971); Shaw Livermore, *Twilight of Federalism: The Disintegration of the Federalist Party, 1815–1830* (1962); Milton Lomask, *Aaron Burr* (1979–1983); Drew R. McCoy, *The Last of the Fathers: James Madison and the Republican Legacy* (1989); Bradford Perkins, *Prologue to War: England and the United States, 1805–1812* (1968); Julius W. Pratt, *Expansionists of 1812* (1925); Robert A. Rutland, *Madison's Alternatives: The Jeffersonian Republicans and the Coming of War, 1805–1812* (1975); Robert Allen Rutland, *James Madison, The Founding Father* (1987); *The Presidency of James Madison* (1990); Marshall Smelser, *The Democratic Republic, 1801–1815* (1968); J. C. A. Stagg, *Mr. Madison's War: Politics, Diplomacy, and Warfare in the Early American Republic, 1783–1830* (1983); Robert W. Tucker, *Empire of Liberty: The Statecraft of Thomas Jefferson* (1990); Steven Watts, *The Republic Reborn: War and the Making of Liberal America, 1790–1820* (1987).

Chapter 9 The Rise of a New Nation, 1815–1819

Harry Ammon, *James Monroe: The Quest for National Identity* (1971); John Blassingame, *The Slave Community: Plantation Life in the Antebellum South* (1979); Bill Cecil-Fronsman, *Common Whites: Class and Culture in Antebellum North Carolina* (1992); Judith Wragg Chase, *Afro-American Art and Craft* (1971); Catherine Clinton, *The Plantation Mistress: Woman's World in the Old South* (1982); Clement Eaton, *The Growth of Southern Civilization, 1790–1860* (1961); Dena J. Epstein, *Sinful Tunes and Spirituals: Black Folk Music to the Civil War* (1977); Eugene D. Genovese, *Roll, Jordan, Roll: the World the Slaves Made* (1976); Charles G. Haines, *The Role of the Supreme Court in American Government and Politics, 1789–1835* (1944); Morton J. Horowitz, *The Transformation of American Law, 1780–1860* (1977); Nathan Huggins, *Black Odyssey: The Afro-American Ordeal in Slavery* (1977); Luther Porter Jackson, *Free Negro Labor and Property Holding in Virginia, 1830–1860* (1942); Charles Joyner, *Down by the Riverside: A South Carolina Slave Community* (1984); Suzanne Lebsock, *Free Women of Petersburg: Status and Culture in a Southern Town, 1784–1860* (1984); Lawrence Levine, *Black Culture and Black Consciousness: Afro-American Folk Thought from Slavery to Freedom* (1977); Ronald L. Lewis, *Coal, Iron, and Slaves: Industrial Slavery in Maryland and Virginia, 1715–1865* (1979); Ernest May, *The Making of the Monroe Doctrine* (1975); Sally McMillen, *Motherhood in the Old South: Pregnancy, Childbirth, and Infant Rearing* (1990); Nathan Miller, *Enterprise of a Free People: Aspects of Economic Development in New York State During the Canal Period, 1792–1838* (1962); James Oakes, *The Ruling Race: A History of American Slaveholders* (1982); Stephen B. Oates, *The Fires of Jubilee: Nat Turner's Fierce Rebellion* (1975); Dexter Perkins, *Hands Off: A History of the Monroe Doctrine* (1941); Albert J. Raboteau, *Slave Religion: The "Invisible Institution" in the Antebellum South* (1978); Robert V. Remini, *Henry Clay: Statesman for the Union* (1991); Todd L. Savitt, *Medicine and Slavery: The Diseases and Health Care of Blacks in Antebellum Virginia* (1978); Ronald E. Shaw, *Canals for a Nation: The Canal Era in the United States, 1790–1860* (1990); Michael Tadman, *Speculators and Slaves: Masters, Traders, and Slaves in the Old South* (1989); Richard C. Wade, *Slavery in the Cities, 1820–1860* (1964); Deborah Gray White, *Arn't I a Woman?: Female Slaves in the Plantation South* (1988); Gavin

Wright, *The Political Economy of the Cotton South: Households, Markets, and Wealth in the Nineteenth Century* (1978).

Chapter 10 Dynamic Growth and Its Consequences, 1820–1827

Ray Allen Billington, *The Protestant Crusade, 1800–1860: A Study of the Origins of American Nativism* (1964); Stuart M. Blumin, *The Emergence of the Middle Class: Social Experiences in the American City, 1760–1900* (1989); Priscilla J. Brewer, *Shaker Communities, Shaker Lives* (1986); Richard L. Bushman, *Joseph Smith and the Beginnings of Mormonism* (1984); Christopher Clark, *The Roots of Rural Capitalism: Western Massachusetts, 1780–1860* (1990); Robert F. Dalzell, Jr., *Enterprising Elite: The Boston Associates and the World They Made* (1987); Thomas Dublin, *Women at Work: The Transformation of Work and Community in Lowell, Massachusetts, 1826–1880* (1979); Barbara Leslie Epstein, *The Politics of Domesticity: Women, Evangelism, and Temperance in Nineteenth-Century America* (1981); Lawrence Foster, *Religion and Sexuality: Three American Communal Experiments of the Nineteenth Century* (1981); David A. Gerber, *The Making of an American Pluralism: Buffalo, New York, 1825–60* (1989); Lori D. Ginzberg, *Women and the Work of Benevolence: Morality, Politics, and Class in the Nineteenth-Century United States* (1990); Elliott J. Gorn, *The Manly Art: Bare-Knuckle Prize Fighting in America* (1986); Karen Halttunen, *Confidence Men and Painted Women: A Study of Middle-Class Culture in America, 1830–1870* (1982); Keith J. Hardman, *Charles Grandison Finney, 1792–1875: Revivalist and Reformer* (1987); Paul E. Johnson, *A Shopkeepers' Millennium: Society and Revivals in Rochester, New York, 1815–1837* (1978); Michael Katz, *The Irony of Early School Reform: Educational Innovation in Mid-19th Century Massachusetts* (1968); Bruce Laurie, *Working People of Philadelphia, 1800–1850* (1980); W. David Lewis, *From Newgate to Dannemora: The Rise of the Penitentiary in New York, 1796–1948* (1965); Kerby A. Miller, *Emigrants and Exiles: Ireland and the Irish Exodus to North America* (1985); Glover Moore, *The Missouri Compromise,*

1810–1821 (1967); Jonathan Prude, *The Coming of Industrial Order: Town and Factory Life in Rural Massachusetts, 1810–1860* (1983); Mary P. Ryan, *Cradle of the Middle Class: The Family in Oneida County, New York, 1790–1865* (1981); Merritt Roe Smith, *Harpers Ferry Armory and the New Technology: The Challenge of Change* (1977); Timothy L. Smith, *Revivalism and Social Reform in Mid-Nineteenth Century America* (1957); Ian Tyrrell, *Sobering Up: From Temperance to Prohibition in Antebellum America, 1800–1860* (1979); Anthony F. C. Wallace, *Rockdale: The Growth of an American Village in the Early Industrial Revolution* (1978); Ronald G. Walters, *American Reformers, 1815–1860* (1978); David Ward, *Cities and Immigrants: A Geography of Change in Nineteenth-Century America* (1971).

Chapter 11 Politics and Change in Jackson's America, 1828–1840

Jean Baker, *Affairs of Party: The Political Culture of Northern Democrats in the Mid-Nineteenth Century* (1983); John M. Belonlavek, *"Let the Eagle Soar!": The Foreign Policy of Andrew Jackson* (1985); Lee Benson, *The Concept of Jacksonian Democracy; New York as a Test Case* (1961); Donald B. Cole, *Martin Van Buren and the American Political System* (1984); Angie Debo, *And Still the Waters Run: The Betrayal of the Five Civilized Tribes* (1972); Richard Ellis, *The Union at Risk: Jacksonian Democracy, States Rights, and the Nullification Crisis* (1987); Roger A. Fischer, *Tippecanoe and Trinkets Too: The Material Culture of American Presidential Campaigns, 1828–1984* (1988); Grant Foreman, *Indian Removal: The Emigration of the Five Civilized Tribes of Indians* (1953); Ronald P. Formisano, *The Birth of Mass Political Parties: Michigan, 1827–1861* (1971); Paul Goodman, *Towards a Christian Republic: Antimasonry and the Great Transition in New England, 1826–1836* (1988); Michael D. Green, *The Politics of Indian Removal: Creek Government and Society in Crisis* (1982); Mary W. M. Hargreaves, *The Presidency of John Quincy Adams* (1985); Daniel Walker Howe, *The Political Culture of the American Whigs* (1979); Lawrence Frederick Kohl, *The Politics of*

Individualism: Parties and the American Character in the Jacksonian Era (1989); Richard P. McCormick, *The Second American Party System: Party Formations in the Jacksonian Era* (1966); William McLoughlin, *Cherokees and Missionaries, 1789–1839* (1984); *Cherokee Renascence in the New Republic* (1986); Marvin Meyers, *The Jacksonian Persuasion: Politics and Belief* (1957); John Niven, *Martin Van Buren: The Romantic Age of American Politics* (1983); Russel B. Nye, *Society and Culture in America, 1830–1860* (1974); Edward Pessen, *Jacksonian America: Society, Personality, and Politics* (1978); Merrill D. Peterson, *The Great Triumvirate: Webster, Clay, and Calhoun* (1987); Francis P. Prucha, *The Great Father: The United States Government and the American Indians* (1984); Robert V. Remini, *The Life of Andrew Jackson* (1988); Ronald N. Satz, *American Indian Policy in the Jacksonian Era* (1975); Charles G. Sellers, *The Market Revolution: Jacksonian America, 1815–1846* (1991); James Roger Sharp, *The Jacksonians Versus the Banks: Politics in the States After the Panic of 1837* (1970); William Preston Vaughn, *The Antimasonic Party in the United States, 1826–1843* (1983).

Chapter 12 Westward Expansion and Manifest Destiny, 1841–1849

Leonard J. Arrington, *The Mormon Experience: A History of the Latter-Day Saints* (1979); Lois Banner, *Elizabeth Cady Stanton, A Radical for Women's Rights* (1980); Barbara Berg, *The Remembered Gate; Barbara Berg, Origins of American Feminism: The Woman and the City, 1800–1860* (1978); Paul Bergeron, *The Presidency of James K. Polk* (1987); Ray Allen Billington, *The Far Western Frontier, 1830–1860* (1956); Ruth Bloch, *Visionary Republic: Millennial Themes in American Thought, 1756–1800* (1985); William A. Bowen, *The Willamette Valley: Migration and Settlement on the Oregon Frontier* (1978); Joan E. Cashin, *A Family Venture: Men and Women on the Southern Frontier* (1991); Clarence Danhof, *Change in Agriculture: The Northern United States, 1820–1870* (1969); Arnoldo DeLeon, *The Tejano Community, 1836–1900* (1982); Don Harrison Doyle, *The Social Order of a Frontier Community: Jacksonville, Illinois,*

1825–1870 (1978); John Mack Faragher, *Women and Men on the Overland Trail* (1979); Norman Graebner, *Empire on the Pacific: A Study in American Continental Expansion* (1955); Richard Griswold del Castillo, *The Treaty of Guadalupe Hidalgo: A Legacy of Conflict* (1990); Neal Harlow, *California Conquered: The Annexation of a Mexican Province, 1846–1850* (1982); Reginald Horsman, *Race and Manifest Destiny: The Origins of American Racial Anglo-Saxonism* (1981); Edward C. Kendall, *John Deere's Steel Plow* (1959); Earnest M. Lander, Jr., *Reluctant Imperialists: Calhoun, the South Carolinians, and the Mexican War* (1980); Robert E. May, *The Southern Dream of a Caribbean Empire, 1854–1861* (1973); Frederick Merk, *Manifest Destiny and Mission in American History: A Reinterpretation* (1963); Sandra Myres, *Westering Women and the Frontier Experience, 1800–1915* (1982); Norman Lois Peterson, *The Presidencies of William Henry Harrison and John Tyler* (1989); Leonard Pitt, *The Decline of the Californios: A Social History of the Spanish-Speaking Californians, 1846–1890* (1970); David Pletcher, *The Diplomacy of Annexation: Texas, Oregon, and the Mexican War* (1973); Mary P. Ryan, *Women in Public: Between Banners and Ballots, 1825–1880* (1990); John H. Schroeder, *Mr. Polk's War: American Opposition and Dissent, 1846–1848* (1973); Henry Nash Smith, *Virgin Land: The American West as Symbol and Myth* (1950); David J. Weber, *The Mexican Frontier, 1821–1846: The American Southwest Under Mexico* (1982).

Chapter 13 Sectional Conflict and Shattered Union, 1850–1860

Tyler Anbinder, *Nativism and Slavery: The Northern Know Nothings and the Politics of the 1850s* (1992); Eugene H. Berwanger, *The Frontier Against Slavery: Western Anti-Negro Prejudice and the Slavery Extension Controversy* (1967); Frederick J. Blue, *The Free Soilers: Third Party Politics, 1848–1854* (1973); Gerald Capers, *Stephen A. Douglas, Defender of the Union* (1959); Avery O. Craven, *The Growth of Southern Nationalism, 1848–1861* (1953); Daniel W. Crofts, *Reluctant Confederates: Upper South Unionists in the Secession Crisis* (1989); Merton L. Dillon, *Slavery Attacked:*

Southern Slaves and their Allies, 1619–1865 (1991); David Donald, *Charles Sumner and the Coming of the Civil War* (1960); Louis Filler, *The Crusade Against Slavery, 1830–1860* (1960); Eric Foner, *Free Soil, Free Labor, Free Men: The Ideology of the Republican Party Before the Civil War* (1970); Lacy K. Ford, Jr., *Origins of Southern Radicalism: The South Carolina Upcountry, 1800–1860* (1988); William W. Freehling, *The Road to Disunion* (1990); Lawrence J. Friedman, *Gregarious Saints: Self and Community in American Abolitionism, 1830–1870* (1982); William Gienapp, *Origins of the Republican Party, 1852–1856* (1987); Holman Hamilton, *Prologue to Conflict: The Crisis and Compromise of 1850* (1966); Robert W. Johannsen, *Stephen Douglas* (1973); Paul Kleppner, *The Third Electoral System, 1853–1892: Parties, Voters, and Political Cultures* (1979); Stephen Oates, *With Malice Toward None: The Life of Abraham Lincoln* (1977); William H. Pease, *They Who Would Be Free: Blacks' Search for Freedom, 1830–1861* (1974); Benjamin Quarles, *Black Abolitionists* (1969); James A. Rawley, *Race & Politics: "Bleeding Kansas" and the Coming of the Civil War* (1969); Richard Sewell, *Ballots for Freedom: Antislavery Politics in the United States, 1837–1865* (1976); James Brewer Steward, *Holy Warriors: The Abolitionists and American Slavery* (1976); John L. Thomas, *The Liberator, William Lloyd Garrison, a Biography* (1963); Larry E. Tise, *Proslavery: A History of the Defense of Slavery in America, 1701–1840* (1987); Ronald G. Walters, *The Antislavery Appeal: American Abolitionism After 1830* (1976); James A. Ward, *Railroads and the Character of America, 1820–1887* (1986); Gerald W. Wolff, *The Kansas-Nebraska Bill: Party, Section, and the Coming of the Civil War* (1977).

Chapter 14 A Violent Solution: Civil War, 1861–1865

Nancy Scott Anderson, *The Generals: Ulysses S. Grant and Robert E. Lee* (1987); Dudley Taylor Cornish, *The Sable Arm: Negro Troops in the Union Army, 1861–1865* (1966); David P. Crook, *The North, The South, and the Powers, 1861–1865* (1974); Charles P. Cullop, *Confederate Propaganda in Europe, 1861–1865* (1969); Leonard P.

Curry, *Blueprint for Modern America: Non-Military Legislation of the First Civil War Congress* (1968); William C. Davis, *Jefferson Davis: The Man and His Hour* (1991); Robert F. Durden, *The Gray and the Black: The Confederate Debate on Emancipation* (1972); James W. Geary, *We Need Men: The Northern Draft in the Civil War* (1991); Joseph T. Glatthaar, *Forged in Battle: The Civil War Alliance, Black Soldiers and White Officers* (1990); *The March to the Sea and Beyond: Sherman's Troops in the Savannah and Carolinas Campaigns* (1985); Randall C. Jimerson, *The Private Civil War: Popular Thought During the Sectional Conflict* (1988); Frank L. Klement, *The Copperheads in the Middle West* (1960); Gerlad F. Linderman, *Embattled Courage: The Experience of Combat in the American Civil War* (1989); Mary Elizabeth Massey, *Bonnet Brigades* (1966); James M. McPherson, *The Negro's Civil War: How American Negroes Felt and Acted* (1965); James M. McPherson, *Abraham Lincoln and the Second American Revolution* (1990); Grady McWhiney, *Attack and Die: Civil War Military Tactics and the Southern Heritage* (1982); James H. Moorhead, *American Apocalypse: Yankee Protestants and the Civil War, 1860–1869* (1978); Larry E. Nelson, *Bullets, Ballots, and Rhetoric: Confederate Policy for the United States Presidential Contest of 1864* (1980); Frank L. Owsley, *States' Rights in the Confederacy* (1925); *King Cotton Diplomacy: Foreign Relations of the Confederate States of America* (1959); Philip Paludan, *A People's Contest: The Union and the Civil War, 1861–1865* (1988); Benjamin Quarles, *The Negro in the Civil War* (1953); Charles Royster, *The Destructive War: William Tecumseh Sherman, Stonewall Jackson, and the Americans* (1991); Joel Silbey, *A Respectable Minority: The Democratic Party in the Civil War Era* (1977); Emory M. Thomas, *The Confederacy as a Revolutionary Experience* (1971); *Bold Dragoon: The Life of J. E. B. Stuart* (1987); Hans L. Trefousse, *The Radical Republicans: Lincoln's Vanguard for Racial Justice* (1969); Gordon H. Warren, *Fountain of Discontent: The Trent Affair and Freedom of the Seas* (1981); Bell Irvin Wiley, *The Life of Johnny Reb, The Common Soldier of the Confederacy* (1943); Bell Irvin Wiley, *The Plain People of the Confederacy* (1944); Bell Irvin Wiley, *The Life of Billy Yank, The*

Common Soldier of the Union (1952); T. Harry Williams, *Lincoln and the Radicals* (1941); Agatha Young, *Women and the Crisis: Women of the North in the Civil War* (1959).

Chapter 15 Reconstruction: High Hopes and Broken Dreams, 1865–1877

Herman Belz, *Emancipation and Equal Rights: Politics and Constitutionalism in the Civil War Era* (1978); Michael Les Benedict, *The Impeachment and Trial of Andrew Johnson* (1973); David Warren Bowen, *Andrew Johnson and the Negro* (1989); Albert E. Castel, *The Presidency of Andrew Johnson* (1979); Vincent P. DeSantis, *Republicans Face the Southern Question* (1959); John Hope Franklin, *Reconstruction: After the Civil War* (1961); John Hope Franklin and Alfred A. Moss, Jr., *From Slavery to Freedom: A History of Negro Americans*, 6th ed. (1988); Herbert G. Gutman, *The Black Family in Slavery and Freedom* (1976); Harold M. Hyman and William M. Wiecek, *Equal Justice Under Law: Constitutional Development, 1835–1875* (1982); Jacqueline Jones, *Labor of Love, Labor of Sorrow: Black Women, Work and the Family, from Slavery to the Present* (1985); Mark Krug, *Lyman Trumbull: Conservative Radical* (1965); William S. McFeely, *Grant: A Biography* (1981); Martin E. Mantell, *Johnson, Grant, and the Politics of Reconstruction* (1973); Eric L. McKitrick, *Andrew Johnson and Reconstruction* (1960; reprint, 1988); James M. McPherson, *Ordeal by Fire: Reconstruction* (1982); Milton Meltzer, *Thaddeus Stevens and the Fight for Negro Rights* (1967); David Montgomery, *Beyond Equality: Labor and the Radical Republicans, 1862–1872* (1967); Michael Perman, *Reunion Without Compromise: The South and Reconstruction, 1865–1868* (1973); Keith I. Polakoff, *The Politics of Inertia: The Election of 1876 and the End of Reconstruction* (1973); Roger L. Ransom and Richard Sutch, *One Kind of Freedom: The Economic Consequences of Emancipation* (1977); Kenneth M. Stampp, *The Era of Reconstruction, 1865–1877* (1965); Hans Louis Trefousse, *Andrew Johnson: A Biography* (1989); Hans Louis Trefousse, *Impeachment of a President: Andrew Johnson, the Blacks, and Reconstruction* (1975); Allen W. Trelease, *White Terror: The Ku Klux Klan Conspiracy and Southern Reconstruction* (1971); Vernon Lane Wharton, *The Negro in Mississippi: 1865–1890* (1965; reprint, 1974); Forrest G. Wood, *The Era of Reconstruction, 1863–1877* (1975); C. Vann Woodward, *Reunion and Reaction: The Compromise of 1877 and the End of Reconstruction*, rev. ed. (1956); C. Vann Woodward, *Origins of the New South, 1877–1913* (1951).

Documents

Declaration of Independence in Congress, July 4, 1776

When, in the course of human events, it becomes necessary for one people to dissolve the political bonds which have connected them with another, and to assume, among the powers of the earth, the separate and equal station to which the laws of nature and of nature's God entitle them, a decent respect to the opinions of mankind requires that they should declare the causes which impel them to the separation.

We hold these truths to be self-evident: That all men are created equal; that they are endowed by their Creator with certain unalienable rights; that among these are life, liberty, and the pursuit of happiness; that, to secure these rights, governments are instituted among men, deriving their just powers from the consent of the governed; that whenever any form of government becomes destructive of these ends, it is the right of the people to alter or to abolish it, and to institute new government, laying its foundation on such principles, and organizing its powers in such form, as to them shall seem most likely to effect their safety and happiness. Prudence, indeed, will dictate that governments long established should not be changed for light and transient causes; and accordingly all experience hath shown that mankind are more disposed to suffer, while evils are sufferable, than to right themselves by abolishing the forms to which they are accustomed. But when a long train of abuses and usurpations, pursuing invariably the same object, evinces a design to reduce them under absolute despotism, it is their right, it is their duty, to throw off such government, and to provide new guards for their future security. Such has been the patient sufferance of these colonies; and such is now the necessity which constrains them to alter their former systems of government. The history of the present King of Great Britain is a history of repeated injuries and usurpations, all having in direct object the establishment of an absolute tyranny over these states. To prove this, let facts be submitted to a candid world.

He has refused his assent to laws, the most wholesome and necessary for the public good.

He has forbidden his governors to pass laws of immediate and pressing importance, unless suspended in their operation till his assent should be obtained; and, when so suspended, he has utterly neglected to attend to them.

He has refused to pass other laws for the accommodation of large districts of people, unless those people would relinquish the right of representation in the legislature, a right inestimable to them, and formidable to tyrants only.

He has called together legislative bodies at places unusual, uncomfortable, and distant from the depository of their public records, for the sole purpose of fatiguing them into compliance with his measures.

He has dissolved representative houses repeatedly, for opposing, with manly firmness, his invasions on the rights of the people.

He has refused for a long time, after such dissolutions, to cause others to be elected; whereby the legislative powers, incapable of annihilation, have returned to the people at large for their exercise; the state remaining, in the mean time, exposed to all the dangers of invasions from without and convulsions within.

He has endeavored to prevent the population of these states; for that purpose obstructing the laws for naturalization of foreigners; refusing to pass others to encourage their migration hither, and raising the conditions of new appropriations of lands.

He has obstructed the administration of justice, by refusing his assent to laws for establishing judiciary powers.

He has made judges dependent on his will alone, for the tenure of their offices, and the amount and payment of their salaries.

He has erected a multitude of new offices, and sent hither swarms of officers to harass our people and eat out their substance.

He has kept among us, in times of peace, standing armies, without the consent of our legislatures.

He has affected to render the military independent of, and superior to, the civil power.

He has combined with others to subject us to a jurisdiction foreign to our constitution, and unacknowledged by our laws, giving his assent to their acts of pretended legislation:

For quartering large bodies of armed troops among us;

For protecting them, by a mock trial, from punishment for any murders which they should commit on the inhabitants of these states;

For cutting off our trade with all parts of the world;

For imposing taxes on us without our consent;

For depriving us, in many cases, of the benefits of trial by jury;

For transporting us beyond seas, to be tried for pretended offenses;

For abolishing the free system of English laws in a neighboring province, establishing therein an arbitrary government, and enlarging its boundaries, so as to render it at once an example and fit instrument for introducing the same absolute rule into these colonies;

For taking away our charters, abolishing our most valuable laws, and altering fundamentally the forms of our governments;

For suspending our own legislatures, and declaring themselves invested with power to legislate for us in all cases whatsoever.

He has abdicated government here, by declaring us out of his protection and waging war against us.

He has plundered our seas, ravaged our coasts, burned our towns, and destroyed the lives of our people.

He is at this time transporting large armies of foreign mercenaries to complete the works of death, desolation, and tyranny already begun with circumstances of cruelty and perfidy scarcely paralleled in the most barbarous ages, and totally unworthy the head of a civilized nation.

He has constrained our fellow-citizens, taken captive on the high seas, to bear arms against their country, to become the executioners of their friends and brethren, or to fall themselves by their hands.

He has excited domestic insurrection among us, and has endeavored to bring on the inhabitants of our frontiers the merciless Indian savages, whose known rule of warfare is an undistinguished destruction of all ages, sexes, and conditions.

In every stage of these oppressions we have petitioned for redress in the most humble terms; our repeated petitions have been answered only by repeated injury. A prince, whose character is thus marked by every act which may define a tyrant, is unfit to be the ruler of a free people.

Nor have we been wanting in our attentions to our British brethren. We have warned them, from time to time, of attempts by their legislature to extend an unwarrantable jurisdiction over us. We have reminded them of the circumstances of our emigration and settlement here. We have appealed to their native justice and magnanimity; and we have conjured them, by the ties of our common kindred, to disavow these usurpations, which would inevitably interrupt our connections and correspondence. They, too, have been deaf to the voice of justice and of consanguinity. We must, therefore, acquiesce in the necessity which denounces our separation, and hold them, as we hold the rest of mankind, enemies in war, in peace friends.

We, therefore, the representatives of the United States of America, in General Congress assembled, appealing to the Supreme Judge of the world for the rectitude of our intentions, do, in the name and by the authority of the good people of these colonies, solemnly publish and declare, that these United Colonies are, and of right ought to be, FREE AND INDEPENDENT STATES; that they are absolved from all allegiance to the British crown, and that all political connection between them and the state of Great Britain is, and ought to be, totally dissolved; and that, as free and independent states, they have full power to levy war, conclude peace, contract alliances, establish commerce, and do all other acts and things which independent states may of right do. And for the support of this declaration, with a firm reliance on the protection of Divine Providence, we mutually pledge to each other our lives, our fortunes, and our sacred honor.

JOHN HANCOCK
and fifty-five others

Constitution of the United States of America and Amendments*

Preamble

We the people of the United States, in order to form a more perfect union, establish justice, insure domestic tranquillity, provide for the common defense, promote the general welfare, and secure the blessings of liberty to ourselves and our posterity, do ordain and establish this Constitution for the United States of America.

Article I

Section 1   All legislative powers herein granted shall be vested in a Congress of the United States, which shall consist of a Senate and a House of Representatives.

Section 2   The House of Representatives shall be composed of members chosen every second year by the people of the several States, and the electors in each State shall have the qualifications requisite for electors of the most numerous branch of the State Legislature.

No person shall be a Representative who shall not have attained to the age of twenty-five years, and been seven years a citizen of the United States, and who shall not, when elected, be an inhabitant of that State in which he shall be chosen.

Representatives and direct taxes shall be apportioned among the several States which may be included within this Union, according to their respective numbers, *which shall be determined by adding to the whole number of free persons, including those bound to service for a term of years and excluding Indians not taxed, three-fifths of all other persons.* The actual enumeration shall be made within three years after the first meeting of the Congress of the United States,

---

* Passages no longer in effect are printed in italic type.

and within every subsequent term of ten years, in such manner as they shall by law direct. The number of Representatives shall not exceed one for every thirty thousand, but each State shall have at least one Representative, *and until such enumeration shall be made, the State of New Hampshire shall be entitled to choose three, Massachusetts eight, Rhode Island and Providence Plantations one, Connecticut five, New York six, New Jersey four, Pennsylvania eight, Delaware one, Maryland six, Virginia ten, North Carolina five, South Carolina five, and Georgia three.*

When vacancies happen in the representation from any State, the Executive authority thereof shall issue writs of election to fill such vacancies.

The House of Representatives shall choose their Speaker and other officers; and shall have the sole power of impeachment.

Section 3 The Senate of the United States shall be composed of two Senators from each State, *chosen by the legislature thereof,* for six years; and each Senator shall have one vote.

Immediately after they shall be assembled in consequence of the first election, they shall be divided as equally as may be into three classes. The seats of the Senators of the first class shall be vacated at the expiration of the second year, of the second class at the expiration of the fourth year, and of the third class at the expiration of the sixth year, so that one-third may be chosen every second year; *and if vacancies happen by resignation or otherwise, during the recess of the legislature of any State, the Executive thereof may make temporary appointments until the next meeting of the legislature, which shall then fill such vacancies.*

No person shall be a Senator who shall not have attained to the age of thirty years, and been nine years a citizen of the United States, and who shall not, when elected, be an inhabitant of that State for which he shall be chosen.

The Vice-President of the United States shall be President of the Senate, but shall have no vote, unless they be equally divided.

The Senate shall choose their other officers, and also a President *pro tempore,* in the absence of the Vice-President, or when he shall exercise the office of President of the United States.

The Senate shall have the sole power to try all impeachments. When sitting for that purpose, they shall be on oath or affirmation. When the President of the United States is tried, the Chief Justice shall preside: and no person shall be convicted without the concurrence of two-thirds of the members present.

Judgment in cases of impeachment shall not extend further than to removal from the office, and disqualification to hold and enjoy any office of honor, trust or profit under the United States; but the party convicted shall nev-ertheless be liable and subject to indictment, trial, judgment and punishment, according to law.

Section 4 The times, places and manner of holding elections for Senators and Representatives shall be prescribed in each State by the legislature thereof; but the Congress may at any time by law make or alter such regulations, except as to the places of choosing Senators.

The Congress shall assemble at least once in every year, and such meeting *shall be on the first Monday in December, unless they shall by law appoint a different day.*

Section 5 Each house shall be the judge of the elections, returns and qualifications of its own members, and a majority of each shall constitute a quorum to do business; but a smaller number may adjourn from day to day, and may be authorized to compel the attendance of absent members, in such manner, and under such penalties, as each house may provide.

Each house may determine the rules of its proceedings, punish its members for disorderly behavior, and with the concurrence of two-thirds, expel a member.

Each house shall keep a journal of its proceedings, and from time to time publish the same, excepting such parts as may in their judgment require secrecy; and the yeas and nays of the members of either house on any question shall, at the desire of one-fifth of those present, be entered on the journal.

Neither house, during the session of Congress, shall, without the consent of the other, adjourn for more than three days, nor to any other place than that in which the two houses shall be sitting.

Section 6 The Senators and Representatives shall receive a compensation for their services, to be ascertained by law and paid out of the treasury of the United States. They shall in all cases except treason, felony and breach of the peace, be privileged from arrest during their attendance at the session of their respective houses, and in going to and returning from the same; and for any speech or debate in either house, they shall not be questioned in any other place.

No Senator or Representative shall, during the time for which he was elected, be appointed to any civil office under the authority of the United States, which shall have been created, or the emoluments whereof shall have been increased, during such time; and no person holding any office under the United States shall be a member of either house during his continuance in office.

Section 7 All bills for raising revenue shall originate in the House of Representatives; but the Senate may propose or concur with amendments as on other bills.

Every bill which shall have passed the House of Representatives and the Senate, shall, before it become a law, be presented to the President of the United States; if he approve he shall sign it, but if not he shall return it with objections to that house in which it originated, who shall enter the objections at large on their journal, and proceed to reconsider it. If after such reconsideration two-thirds of that house shall agree to pass the bill, it shall be sent, together with the objections, to the other house, by which it shall likewise be reconsidered, and, if approved by two-thirds of that house, it shall become a law. But in all such cases the votes of both houses shall be determined by yeas and nays, and the names of the persons voting for and against the bill shall be entered on the journal of each house respectively. If any bill shall not be returned by the President within ten days (Sundays excepted) after it shall have been presented to him, the same shall be a law, in like manner as if he had signed it, unless the Congress by their adjournment prevent its return, in which case it shall not be a law.

Every order, resolution, or vote to which the concurrence of the Senate and House of Representatives may be necessary (except on a question of adjournment) shall be presented to the President of the United States; and before the same shall take effect, shall be approved by him, or being disapproved by him, shall be repassed by two-thirds of the Senate and House of Representatives, according to the rules and limitations prescribed in the case of a bill.

Section 8   The Congress shall have power

To lay and collect taxes, duties, imposts, and excises, to pay the debts and provide for the common defense and general welfare of the United States; but all duties, imposts and excises shall be uniform throughout the United States;

To borrow money on the credit of the United States;

To regulate commerce with foreign nations, and among the several States, and with the Indian tribes;

To establish an uniform rule of naturalization, and uniform laws on the subject of bankruptcies throughout the United States;

To coin money, regulate the value thereof, and of foreign coin, and fix the standard of weights and measures;

To provide for the punishment of counterfeiting the securities and current coin of the United States;

To establish post offices and post roads;

To promote the progress of science and useful arts by securing for limited times to authors and inventors the exclusive right to their respective writings and discoveries;

To constitute tribunals inferior to the Supreme Court;

To define and punish piracies and felonies committed on the high seas and offenses against the law of nations;

To declare war, grant letters of marque and reprisal, and make rules concerning captures on land and water;

To raise and support armies, but no appropriation of money to that use shall be for a longer term than two years;

To provide and maintain a navy;

To make rules for the government and regulation of the land and naval forces;

To provide for calling forth the militia to execute the laws of the Union, suppress insurrections, and repel invasions;

To provide for organizing, arming, and disciplining the militia, and for governing such part of them as may be employed in the service of the United States, reserving to the States respectively the appointment of the officers, and the authority of training the militia according to the discipline prescribed by Congress;

To exercise exclusive legislation in all cases whatsoever, over such district (not exceeding ten miles square) as may, by cession of particular States, and the acceptance of Congress, become the seat of government of the United States, and to exercise like authority over all places purchased by the consent of the legislature of the State, in which the same shall be, for erection of forts, magazines, arsenals, dockyards, and other needful buildings; — and

To make all laws which shall be necessary and proper for carrying into execution the foregoing powers, and all other powers vested by this Constitution in the government of the United States, or in any department or officer thereof.

Section 9   *The migration or importation of such persons as any of the States now existing shall think proper to admit shall not be prohibited by the Congress prior to the year 1808; but a tax or duty may be imposed on such importation, not exceeding $10 for each person.*

The privilege of the writ of habeas corpus shall not be suspended, unless when in cases of rebellion or invasion the public safety may require it.

No bill of attainder or ex post facto law shall be passed.

No capitation, or other direct, tax shall be laid, unless in proportion to the census or enumeration herein before directed to be taken.

No tax or duty shall be laid on articles exported from any State.

No preference shall be given by any regulation of commerce or revenue to the ports of one State over those of another; nor shall vessels bound to, or from, one State, be obliged to enter, clear, or pay duties in another.

No money shall be drawn from the treasury, but in consequence of appropriations made by law; and a regular statement and account of the receipts and expenditures of all public money shall be published from time to time.

No title of nobility shall be granted by the United States: and no person holding any office of profit or trust under them, shall, without the consent of the Congress, accept of any present, emolument, office, or title, of any kind whatever, from any king, prince, or foreign state.

Section 10   No State shall enter into any treaty, alliance, or confederation; grant letters of marque and reprisal; coin money; emit bills of credit; make anything but gold and silver coin a tender in payment of debts; pass any bill of attainder, ex post facto law, or law impairing the obligation of contracts, or grant any title of nobility.

No State shall, without the consent of Congress, lay any imposts or duties on imports or exports, except what may be absolutely necessary for executing its inspection laws: and the net produce of all duties and imposts, laid by any State on imports or exports, shall be for the use of the treasury of the United States; and all such laws shall be subject to the revision and control of the Congress.

No State shall, without the consent of Congress, lay any duty of tonnage, keep troops or ships of war in time of peace, enter into any agreement or compact with another State, or with a foreign power, or engage in war, unless actually invaded, or in such imminent danger as will not admit of delay.

Article II

Section 1   The executive power shall be vested in a President of the United States of America. He shall hold his office during the term of four years, and, together with the Vice-President, chosen for the same term, be elected as follows:

Each State shall appoint, in such manner as the legislature thereof may direct, a number of electors, equal to the whole number of Senators and Representatives to which the State may be entitled in the Congress; but no Senator or Representative, or person holding an office of trust or profit under the United States, shall be appointed an elector.

The electors shall meet in their respective States, and vote by ballot for two persons, of whom one at least shall not be an inhabitant of the same State with themselves. And they shall make a list of all the persons voted for, and of the number of votes for each; which list they shall sign and certify, and transmit sealed to the seat of government of the United States, directed to the President of the Senate. The President of the Senate shall, in the presence of the Senate and House of Representatives, open all the certificates, and the votes shall then be counted. The person having the greatest number of votes shall be the President, if such number be a majority of the whole number of electors appointed; and if there be more than one who have such majority, and have an equal number of votes, then the House of Representatives shall immediately choose by ballot one of them for President; and if no person have a majority, then from the five highest on the list said house shall in like manner choose the President. But in choosing the President the votes shall be taken by States, the representation from each State having one vote; a

quorum for this purpose shall consist of a member or members from two-thirds of the States, and a majority of all the States shall be necessary to a choice. In every case, after the choice of the President, the person having the greatest number of votes of the electors shall be the Vice-President. But if there should remain two or more who have equal votes, the Senate shall choose from them by ballot the Vice-President.

The Congress may determine the time of choosing the electors and the day on which they shall give their votes; which day shall be the same throughout the United States.

No person except a natural-born citizen, *or a citizen of the United States at the time of the adoption of this Constitution,* shall be eligible to the office of President; neither shall any person be eligible to that office who shall not have attained to the age of thirty-five years, and been fourteen years a resident within the United States.

In cases of the removal of the President from office or of his death, resignation, or inability to discharge the powers and duties of the said office, the same shall devolve on the Vice-President, and the Congress may by law provide for the case of removal, death, resignation, or inability, both of the President and Vice-President, declaring what officer shall then act as President, and such officer shall act accordingly, until the disability be removed, or a President shall be elected.

The President shall, at stated times, receive for his services a compensation, which shall neither be increased nor diminished during the period for which he shall have been elected, and he shall not receive within that period any other emolument from the United States, or any of them.

Before he enter on the execution of his office, he shall take the following oath or affirmation:—"I do solemnly swear (or affirm) that I will faithfully execute the office of the President of the United States, and will to the best of my ability preserve, protect and defend the Constitution of the United States."

Section 2   The President shall be commander in chief of the army and navy of the United States, and of the militia of the several States, when called into the actual service of the United States; he may require the opinion, in writing, of the principal officer in each of the executive departments, upon any subject relating to the duties of their respective offices, and he shall have power to grant reprieves and pardons for offenses against the United States, except in cases of impeachment.

He shall have power, by and with the advice and consent of the Senate, to make treaties, provided two-thirds of the Senators present concur; and he shall nominate, and by and with the advice and consent of the Senate, shall appoint ambassadors, other public ministers and consuls, judges of the Supreme Court, and all other officers of the United States, whose appointments are not herein otherwise provided for, and which shall be established by law: but Congress may by law vest the appointment of such inferior officers, as they think proper, in the President alone, in the courts of law, or in the heads of departments.

The President shall have power to fill up all vacancies that may happen during the recess of the Senate, by granting commissions which shall expire at the end of their next session.

Section 3   He shall from time to time give to the Congress information of the state of the Union, and recommend to their consideration such measures as he shall judge necessary and expedient; he may, on extraordinary occasions, convene both houses, or either of them, and in case of disagreement between them, with respect to the time of adjournment, he may adjourn them to such time as he shall think proper; he shall receive ambassadors and other public ministers; he shall take care that the laws be faithfully executed, and shall commission all the officers of the United States.

Section 4   The President, Vice-President and all civil officers of the United States shall be removed from office on impeachment for, and on conviction of, treason, bribery, or other high crimes and misdemeanors.

Article III

Section 1   The judicial power of the United States shall be vested in one Supreme Court, and in such inferior courts as the Congress may from time to time ordain and establish. The judges, both of the Supreme and inferior courts, shall hold their offices during good behavior, and shall, at stated times, receive for their services a compensation which shall not be diminished during their continuance in office.

Section 2   The judicial power shall extend to all cases, in law and equity, arising under this Constitution, the laws of the United States, and treaties made, or which shall be made, under their authority;—to all cases affecting ambassadors, other public ministers and consuls;—to all cases of admiralty and maritime jurisdiction;—to controversies to which the United States shall be a party;—to controversies between two or more States;—*between a State and citizens of another State;*—between citizens of different States;—between citizens of the same State claiming lands under grants of different States, and between a State, or the citizens thereof, and foreign states, citizens or subjects.

In all cases affecting ambassadors, other public ministers and consuls, and those in which a State shall be party, the Supreme Court shall have original jurisdiction. In all the other cases before mentioned, the Supreme Court shall have appellate jurisdiction, both as to law and fact, with such exceptions, and under such regulations, as the Congress shall make.

The trial of all crimes, except in cases of impeachment, shall be by jury; and such trial shall be held in the State where said crimes shall have been committed; but when not committed within any State, the trial shall be at such place or places as the Congress may by law have directed.

Section 3   Treason against the United States shall consist only in levying war against them, or in adhering to their enemies, giving them aid and comfort. No person shall be convicted of treason unless on the testimony of two witnesses to the same overt act, or on confession in open court.

The Congress shall have power to declare the punishment of treason, but no attainder of treason shall work corruption of blood, or forfeiture except during the life of the person attainted.

Article IV

Section 1   Full faith and credit shall be given in each State to the public acts, records, and judicial proceedings of every other State. And the Congress may by general laws prescribe the manner in which such acts, records, and proceedings shall be proved, and the effect thereof.

Section 2   The citizens of each State shall be entitled to all privileges and immunities of citizens in the several States.

A person charged in any State with treason, felony, or other crime, who shall flee from justice, and be found in another State, shall on demand of the executive authority of the State from which he fled, be delivered up, to be removed to the State having jurisdiction of the crime.

No person held to service or labor in one State, under the laws thereof, escaping into another, shall, in consequence of any law or regulation therein, be discharged from such service or labor, but shall be delivered up on claim of the party to whom such service or labor may be due.

Section 3   New States may be admitted by the Congress into this Union; but no new State shall be formed or erected within the jurisdiction of any other State; nor any State be formed by the junction of two or more States, or parts of States, without the consent of the legislatures of the States concerned as well as of the Congress.

The Congress shall have power to dispose of and make all needful rules and regulations respecting the territory or other property belonging to the United States; and nothing in this Constitution shall be so construed as to prejudice any claims of the United States, or of any particular State.

Section 4   The United States shall guarantee to every State in this Union a republican form of government, and shall protect each of them against invasion; and on application of the legislature, or of the executive (when the legislature cannot be convened), against domestic violence.

Article V

The Congress, whenever two-thirds of both houses shall deem it necessary, shall propose amendments to this Constitution, or, on the application of the legislatures of two-thirds of the several States, shall call a convention for proposing amendments, which, in either case, shall be valid to all intents and purposes, as part of this Constitution, when ratified by the legislatures of three-fourths of the several States, or by conventions in three-fourths thereof, as the one or the other mode of ratification may be proposed by the Congress; provided *that no amendments which may be made prior to the year one thousand eight hundred and eight shall in any manner affect the first and fourth clauses in the ninth section of the first article;* and that no State, without its consent, shall be deprived of its equal suffrage in the Senate.

Article VI

All debts contracted and engagements entered into, before the adoption of this Constitution, shall be as valid against the United States under this Constitution, as under the Confederation.

This Constitution, and the laws of the United States which shall be made in pursuance thereof; and all treaties made, or which shall be made, under the authority of the United States, shall be the supreme law of the land; and the judges in every State shall be bound thereby, anything in the Constitution or laws of any State to the contrary notwithstanding.

The Senators and Representatives before mentioned, and the members of the several State legislatures, and all executive and judicial officers, both of the United States and of the several States, shall be bound by oath or affirmation to support this Constitution; but no religious test shall ever be required as a qualification to any office or public trust under the United States.

Article VII

The ratification of the conventions of nine States shall be sufficient for the establishment of this Constitution between the States so ratifying the same.

Done in Convention by the unanimous consent of the States present, the seventeenth day of September in the year of our Lord one thousand seven hundred and eighty-seven and of the Independence of the United States of America the twelfth. In witness whereof we have hereunto subscribed our names.

GEORGE WASHINGTON
and thirty-seven others

Amendments to the Constitution*

Amendment I

Congress shall make no law respecting an establishment of religion, or prohibiting the free exercise thereof; or abridging the freedom of speech, or of the press; or the right of the people peaceably to assemble, and to petition the government for a redress of grievances.

Amendment II

A well-regulated militia being necessary to the security of a free State, the right of the people to keep and bear arms shall not be infringed.

Amendment III

No soldier shall, in time of peace, be quartered in any house without the consent of the owner, nor in time of war, but in a manner to be prescribed by law.

Amendment IV

The right of the people to be secure in their persons, houses, papers, and effects, against unreasonable searches and seizures, shall not be violated, and no warrants shall issue but upon probable cause, supported by oath or affirmation, and particularly describing the place to be searched, and the persons or things to be seized.

Amendment V

No person shall be held to answer for a capital, or otherwise infamous crime, unless on a presentment or indictment of a grand jury, except in cases arising in the land or naval forces, or in the militia, when in actual service in time of war or public danger; nor shall any person be subject for the same offense to be twice put in jeopardy of life or limb; nor shall be compelled in any criminal case to be a witness against himself, nor be deprived of life, liberty, or property, without due process of law; nor shall private property be taken for public use without just compensation.

Amendment VI

In all criminal prosecutions, the accused shall enjoy the right to a speedy and public trial, by an impartial jury of the State and district wherein the crime shall have been committed, which district shall have been previously ascertained by law, and to be informed of the nature and cause of the accusation; to be confronted with the witnesses against him; to have compulsory process for obtaining witnesses in his favor, and to have the assistance of counsel for his defense.

* The first ten Amendments (the Bill of Rights) were adopted in 1791.

Amendment VII

In suits at common law, where the value in controversy shall exceed twenty dollars, the right of trial by jury shall be preserved, and no fact tried by a jury shall be otherwise reexamined in any court of the United States, than according to the rules of the common law.

Amendment VIII

Excessive bail shall not be required, nor excessive fines imposed, nor cruel and unusual punishments inflicted.

Amendment IX

The enumeration in the Constitution, of certain rights, shall not be construed to deny or disparage others retained by the people.

Amendment X

The powers not delegated to the United States by the Constitution, nor prohibited by it to the States, are reserved to the States respectively, or to the people.

Amendment XI

[Adopted 1798]

The judicial power of the United States shall not be construed to extend to any suit in law or equity, commenced or prosecuted against one of the United States by citizens of another State, or by citizens or subjects of any foreign state.

Amendment XII

[Adopted 1804]

The electors shall meet in their respective States, and vote by ballot for President and Vice-President, one of whom, at least, shall not be an inhabitant of the same State with themselves; they shall name in their ballots the person voted for as President, and in distinct ballots the person voted for as Vice-President, and they shall make distinct lists of all persons voted for as President, and of all persons voted for as Vice-President, and of the number of votes for each, which lists they shall sign and certify, and transmit sealed to the seat of government of the United States, directed to the President of the Senate;—the President of the Senate shall, in the presence of the Senate and House of Representatives, open all the certificates and the votes shall then be counted;—the person having the greatest number of votes for President shall be the President, if such number be a majority of the whole number of electors appointed; and if no person have such majority, then from the persons having the highest numbers not exceeding three on the list of those voted for as President, the House of Representatives shall choose immediately, by ballot, the President. But in choosing the President, the votes shall be taken by States, the representation from each State having one vote; a quorum for this purpose shall consist of a member or members from two-thirds of the States, and a majority of all the States shall be necessary to a choice. And if the House of Representatives shall not choose a President whenever the right of choice shall devolve upon them, before *the fourth day of March* next following, then the Vice-President shall act as President, as in the case of the death or other constitutional disability of the President.

The person having the greatest number of votes as Vice-President shall be the Vice-President, if such number be a majority of the whole number of electors appointed; and if no person have a majority, then from the two highest numbers on the list the Senate shall choose the Vice-President; a quorum for the purpose shall consist of two-thirds of the whole number of Senators, and a majority of the whole number shall be necessary to a choice. But no person constitutionally ineligible to the office of President shall be eligible to that of Vice-President of the United States.

Amendment XIII

[Adopted 1865]

Section 1 Neither slavery nor involuntary servitude, except as a punishment for crime whereof the party shall have been duly convicted, shall exist within the United States, or any place subject to their jurisdiction.

Section 2 Congress shall have power to enforce this article by appropriate legislation.

Amendment XIV

[Adopted 1868]

Section 1 All persons born or naturalized in the United States, and subject to the jurisdiction thereof, are citizens of the United States and of the State wherein they reside. No State shall make or enforce any law which shall abridge the privileges or immunities of citizens of the United States; nor shall any State deprive any person of life, liberty, or property, without due process of law; nor deny to any person within its jurisdiction the equal protection of the laws.

Section 2 Representatives shall be apportioned among the several States according to their respective numbers, counting the whole number of persons in each State, excluding Indians not taxed. But when the right to vote at any election for the choice of Electors for President and Vice-President of the United States, Representatives in Congress, the executive and judicial officers of a State, or the members of the legislature thereof, is denied to any of the male inhabitants of such State, being twenty-one years of age and citizens of the United States, or in any way abridged, except for participation in rebellion, or other crime, the basis of representation therein shall be reduced in the proportion which the number of such male citizens shall bear to the whole number of male citizens twenty-one years of age in such State.

Section 3 No person shall be a Senator or Representative in Congress, or Elector of President and Vice-President, or hold any office, civil or military, under the United States, or under any State, who, having previously taken an oath, as a member of Congress, or as an officer of the United States, or as a member of any State legislature, or as an executive or judicial officer of any State, to support the Constitution of the United States, shall have engaged in insurrection or rebellion against the same, or given aid or comfort to the enemies thereof. Congress may, by a vote of two-thirds of each house, remove such disability.

Section 4 The validity of the public debt of the United States, authorized by law, including debts incurred for payment of pensions and bounties for services in suppressing insurrection or rebellion, shall not be questioned. But neither the United States nor any State shall assume or pay any debt or obligation incurred in aid of insurrection or rebellion against the United States, or any claim for the loss or emancipation of any slave; but all such debts, obligations, and claims shall be held illegal and void.

Section 5 The Congress shall have power to enforce, by appropriate legislation, the provisions of this article.

Amendment XV
[Adopted 1870]

Section 1 The right of citizens of the United States to vote shall not be denied or abridged by the United States or by any State on account of race, color, or previous condition of servitude.

Section 2 The Congress shall have power to enforce this article by appropriate legislation.

Amendment XVI
[Adopted 1913]

The Congress shall have power to lay and collect taxes on incomes, from whatever source derived, without apportionment among the several States, and without regard to any census or enumeration.

Amendment XVII
[Adopted 1913]

Section 1 The Senate of the United States shall be composed of two Senators from each State, elected by the people thereof, for six years; and each Senator shall have one vote. The electors in each State shall have the qualifications requisite for electors of [voters for] the most numerous branch of the State legislatures.

Section 2 When vacancies happen in the representation of any State in the Senate, the executive authority of such State shall issue writs of election to fill such vacancies: Provided, that the Legislature of any State may empower the executive thereof to make temporary appointments until the people fill the vacancies by election as the Legislature may direct.

Section 3 This amendment shall not be so construed as to affect the election or term of any Senator chosen before it becomes valid as part of the Constitution.

Amendment XVIII
[Adopted 1919; Repealed 1933]

Section 1 After one year from the ratification of this article the manufacture, sale, or transportation of intoxicating liquors within, the importation thereof into, or the exportation thereof from the United States and all territory subject to the jurisdiction thereof, for beverage purposes, is hereby prohibited.

Section 2 The Congress and the several States shall have concurrent power to enforce this article by appropriate legislation.

Section 3 This article shall be inoperative unless it shall have been ratified as an amendment to the Constitution by the legislatures of the several States, as provided by the Constitution, within seven years from the date of the submission thereof to the States by the Congress.

Amendment XIX
[Adopted 1920]

Section 1 The right of citizens of the United States to vote shall not be denied or abridged by the United States or by any State on account of sex.

Section 2 The Congress shall have power to enforce this article by appropriate legislation.

Amendment XX
[Adopted 1933]

Section 1 The terms of the President and Vice-President shall end at noon on the 20th day of January, and the terms of Senators and Representatives at noon on the 3rd day of January, of the years in which such terms would have ended if this article had not been ratified; and the terms of their successors shall then begin.

Section 2 The Congress shall assemble at least once in every year, and such meeting shall begin at noon on the 3d day of January, unless they shall by law appoint a different day.

Section 3 If, at the time fixed for the beginning of the term of the President, the President-elect shall have died, the Vice-President-elect shall become President. If a President shall not have been chosen before the time fixed for the beginning of his term, or if the President-elect shall have failed to qualify, then the Vice-President-elect shall act as President until a President shall have qualified; and the Congress may by law provide for the case wherein neither a President-elect nor a Vice-President-elect shall have qualified, declaring who shall then act as President, or the manner in which one who is to act shall be selected, and such persons shall act accordingly until a President or Vice-President shall have qualified.

Section 4 The Congress may by law provide for the case of the death of any of the persons from whom the House of Representatives may choose a President whenever the right of choice shall have devolved upon them, and for the case of the death of any of the persons from whom the Senate may choose a Vice-President whenever the right of choice shall have devolved upon them.

Section 5 Sections 1 and 2 shall take effect on the 15th day of October following the ratification of this article.

Section 6 This article shall be inoperative unless it shall have been ratified as an amendment to the Constitution by the Legislatures of three-fourths of the several States within seven years from the date of its submission.

Amendment XXI

[Adopted 1933]

Section 1 The eighteenth article of amendment to the Constitution of the United States is hereby repealed.

Section 2 The transportation or importation into any State, Territory, or Possession of the United States for delivery or use therein of intoxicating liquors, in violation of the laws thereof, is hereby prohibited.

Section 3 This article shall be inoperative unless it shall have been ratified as an amendment to the Constitution by conventions in the several States, as provided in the Constitution, within seven years from the date of submission thereof to the States by the Congress.

Amendment XXII

[Adopted 1951]

Section 1 No person shall be elected to the office of President more than twice, and no person who has held the office of President, or acted as President, for more than two years of a term to which some other person was elected President shall be elected to the office of President

more than once. But this article shall not apply to any person holding the office of President when this article was proposed by the Congress, and shall not prevent any person who may be holding the office of President, or acting as President, during the term within which this article becomes operative from holding the office of President or acting as President during the remainder of such term.

Section 2 This article shall be inoperative unless it shall have been ratified as an amendment to the Constitution by the legislatures of three-fourths of the several States within seven years from the date of its submission to the States by the Congress.

Amendment XXIII

[Adopted 1961]

Section 1 The District constituting the seat of Government of the United States shall appoint in such manner as the Congress may direct:

A number of electors of President and Vice-President equal to the whole number of Senators and Representatives in Congress to which the District would be entitled if it were a State, but in no event more than the least populous State; they shall be in addition to those appointed by the States, but they shall be considered for the purposes of the election of President and Vice-President, to be electors appointed by a State; and they shall meet in the District and perform such duties as provided by the twelfth article of amendment.

Section 2 The Congress shall have the power to enforce this article by appropriate legislation.

Amendment XXIV

[Adopted 1964]

Section 1 The right of citizens of the United States to vote in any primary or other election for President or Vice-President, for electors for President or Vice-President, or for Senator or Representative in Congress, shall not be denied or abridged by the United States or any State by reason of failure to pay any poll tax or other tax.

Section 2 The Congress shall have the power to enforce this article by appropriate legislation.

Amendment XXV

[Adopted 1967]

Section 1 In case of the removal of the President from office or of his death or resignation, the Vice-President shall become President.

Section 2 Whenever there is a vacancy in the office of the Vice-President, the President shall nominate a Vice-President who shall take office upon confirmation by a majority vote of both Houses of Congress.

Section 3 Whenever the President transmits to the President pro tempore of the Senate and the Speaker of the House of Representatives his written declaration that he is unable to discharge the powers and duties of his office, and until he transmits to them a written declaration to the contrary, such powers and duties shall be discharged by the Vice-President as Acting President.

Section 4 Whenever the Vice-President and a majority of either the principal officers of the executive departments or of such other body as Congress may by law provide, transmit to the President pro tempore of the Senate and the Speaker of the House of Representatives their written declaration that the President is unable to discharge the powers and duties of his office, the Vice-President shall immediately assume the powers and duties of the office as Acting President.

Thereafter, when the President transmits to the President pro tempore of the Senate and the Speaker of the House of Representatives his written declaration that no inability exists, he shall resume the powers and duties of his office unless the Vice-President and a majority of either the principal officers of the executive department[s] or of such other body as Congress may by law provide, transmit within four days to the President pro tempore of the Senate and the Speaker of the House of Representatives their written declaration that the President is unable to discharge the powers and duties of his office. Thereupon Congress shall decide the issue, assembling within forty-eight hours for that purpose if not in session. If the Congress, within twenty-one days after receipt of the latter written declaration, or, if Congress is not in session, within twenty-one days after Congress is required to assemble, determines by two-thirds vote of both Houses that the President is unable to discharge the powers and duties of his office, the Vice-President shall continue to discharge the same as Acting President; otherwise, the President shall resume the powers and duties of his office.

Amendment XXVI

[Adopted 1971]

Section 1 The right of citizens of the United States, who are eighteen years of age or older, to vote shall not be denied or abridged by the United States or by any State on account of age.

Section 2 The Congress shall have power to enforce this article by appropriate legislation.

Amendment XXVII

[Adopted 1992]

No law, varying the compensation for the services of the Senators and Representatives, shall take effect, until an election of Representatives shall have intervened.

Tables

Territorial Expansion of the United States

Territory	Date Acquired	Square Miles	How Acquired
Original states and territories	1783	888,685	Treaty with Great Britain
Louisiana Purchase	1803	827,192	Purchase from France
Florida	1819	72,003	Treaty with Spain
Texas	1845	390,143	Annexation of independent nation
Oregon	1846	285,580	Treaty with Great Britain
Mexican Cession	1848	529,017	Conquest from Mexico
Gadsden Purchase	1853	29,640	Purchase from Mexico
Alaska	1867	589,757	Purchase from Russia
Hawaii	1898	6,450	Annexation of independent nation
The Philippines	1899	115,600	Conquest from Spain (granted independence in 1946)
Puerto Rico	1899	3,435	Conquest from Spain
Guam	1899	212	Conquest from Spain
American Samoa	1900	76	Treaty with Germany and Great Britain
Panama Canal Zone	1904	553	Treaty with Panama (returned to Panama by treaty in 1978)
Corn Islands	1914	4	Treaty with Nicaragua (returned to Nicaragua by treaty in 1971)
Virgin Islands	1917	133	Purchase from Denmark
Pacific Islands Trust (Micronesia)	1947	8,489	Trusteeship under United Nations (some granted independence)
All others (Midway, Wake, and other islands)		42	

Admission of States into the Union

	State	Date of Admission		State	Date of Admission
1.	Delaware	December 7, 1787	26.	Michigan	January 26, 1837
2.	Pennsylvania	December 12, 1787	27.	Florida	March 3, 1845
3.	New Jersey	December 18, 1787	28.	Texas	December 29, 1845
4.	Georgia	January 2, 1788	29.	Iowa	December 28, 1846
5.	Connecticut	January 9, 1788	30.	Wisconsin	May 29, 1848
6.	Massachusetts	February 6, 1788	31.	California	September 9, 1850
7.	Maryland	April 28, 1788	32.	Minnesota	May 11, 1858
8.	South Carolina	May 23, 1788	33.	Oregon	February 14, 1859
9.	New Hampshire	June 21, 1788	34.	Kansas	January 29, 1861
10.	Virginia	June 25, 1788	35.	West Virginia	June 20, 1863
11.	New York	July 26, 1788	36.	Nevada	October 31, 1864
12.	North Carolina	November 21, 1789	37.	Nebraska	March 1, 1867
13.	Rhode Island	May 29, 1790	38.	Colorado	August 1, 1876
14.	Vermont	March 4, 1791	39.	North Dakota	November 2, 1889
15.	Kentucky	June 1, 1792	40.	South Dakota	November 2, 1889
16.	Tennessee	June 1, 1796	41.	Montana	November 8, 1889
17.	Ohio	March 1, 1803	42.	Washington	November 11, 1889
18.	Louisiana	April 30, 1812	43.	Idaho	July 3, 1890
19.	Indiana	December 11, 1816	44.	Wyoming	July 10, 1890
20.	Mississippi	December 10, 1817	45.	Utah	January 4, 1896
21.	Illinois	December 3, 1818	46.	Oklahoma	November 16, 1907
22.	Alabama	December 14, 1819	47.	New Mexico	January 6, 1912
23.	Maine	March 15, 1820	48.	Arizona	February 14, 1912
24.	Missouri	August 10, 1821	49.	Alaska	January 3, 1959
25.	Arkansas	June 15, 1836	50.	Hawaii	August 21, 1959

Presidential Elections

Year	Number of States	Candidates	Parties	Popular Vote	% of Popular Vote	Electoral Vote	% Voter Participation[b]
1789	11	**George Washington**	No party			69	
		John Adams	designations			34	
		Other candidates				35	
1792	15	**George Washington**	No party			132	
		John Adams	designations			77	
		George Clinton				50	
		Other candidates				5	
1796	16	**John Adams**	Federalist			71	
		Thomas Jefferson	Democratic-Republican			68	
		Thomas Pinckney	Federalist			59	
		Aaron Burr	Democratic-Republican			30	
		Other candidates				48	
1800	16	**Thomas Jefferson**	Democratic-Republican			73	
		Aaron Burr	Democratic-Republican			73	
		John Adams	Federalist			65	
		Charles C. Pinckney	Federalist			64	
		John Jay	Federalist			1	
1804	17	**Thomas Jefferson**	Democratic-Republican			162	
		Charles C. Pinckney	Federalist			14	
1808	17	**James Madison**	Democratic-Republican			122	
		Charles C. Pinckney	Federalist			47	
		George Clinton	Democratic-Republican			6	
1812	18	**James Madison**	Democratic-Republican			128	
		DeWitt Clinton	Federalist			89	
1816	19	**James Monroe**	Democratic-Republican			183	
		Rufus King	Federalist			34	
1820	24	**James Monroe**	Democratic-Republican			231	
		John Quincy Adams	Independent-Republican			1	
1824	24	**John Quincy Adams**	Democratic-Republican	108,740	30.5	84	26.9

Presidential Elections, *Continued*

Year	Number of States	Candidates	Parties	Popular Vote	% of Popular Vote	Electoral Vote	% Voter Participation[b]
		Andrew Jackson	Democratic-Republican	153,544	43.1	99	
		Henry Clay	Democratic-Republican	47,136	13.2	37	
		William H. Crawford	Democratic-Republican	46,618	13.1	41	
1828	24	**Andrew Jackson**	Democratic	647,286	56.0	178	57.6
		John Quincy Adams	National Republican	508,064	44.0	83	
1832	24	**Andrew Jackson**	Democratic	688,242	54.5	219	55.4
		Henry Clay	National Republican	473,462	37.5	49	
		William Wirt	Anti-Masonic	101,051	8.0	7	
		John Floyd	Democratic			11	
1836	26	**Martin Van Buren**	Democratic	765,483	50.9	170	57.8
		William H. Harrison	Whig			73	
		Hugh L. White	Whig			26	
		Daniel Webster	Whig	739,795	49.1	14	
		W. P. Mangum	Whig			11	
1840	26	**William H. Harrison**	Whig	1,274,624	53.1	234	80.2
		Martin Van Buren	Democratic	1,127,781	46.9	60	
1844	26	**James K. Polk**	Democratic	1,338,464	49.6	170	78.9
		Henry Clay	Whig	1,300,097	48.1	105	
		James G. Birney	Liberty	62,300	2.3		
1848	30	**Zachary Taylor**	Whig	1,360,967	47.4	163	72.7
		Lewis Cass	Democratic	1,222,342	42.5	127	
		Martin Van Buren	Free Soil	291,263	10.1		
1852	31	**Franklin Pierce**	Democratic	1,601,117	50.9	254	69.6
		Winfield Scott	Whig	1,385,453	44.1	42	
		John P. Hale	Free Soil	155,825	5.0		
1856	31	**James Buchanan**	Democratic	1,832,955	45.3	174	78.9
		John C. Frémont	Republican	1,339,932	33.1	114	
		Millard Fillmore	American	871,731	21.6	8	
1860	33	**Abraham Lincoln**	Republican	1,865,593	39.8	180	81.2
		Stephen A. Douglas	Democratic	1,382,713	29.5	12	
		John C. Breckinridge	Democratic	848,356	18.1	72	
		John Bell	Constitutional Union	592,906	12.6	39	
1864	36	**Abraham Lincoln**	Republican	2,206,938	55.0	212	73.8
		George B. McClellan	Democratic	1,803,787	45.0	21	
1868	37	**Ulysses S. Grant**	Republican	3,013,421	52.7	214	78.1
		Horatio Seymour	Democratic	2,706,829	47.3	80	

Presidential Elections, *Continued*

Year	Number of States	Candidates	Parties	Popular Vote	% of Popular Vote	Electoral Vote	% Voter Partici- pation[b]
1872	37	**Ulysses S. Grant**	Republican	3,596,745	55.6	286	71.3
		Horace Greeley	Democratic	2,843,446	43.9	a	
1876	38	**Rutherford B. Hayes**	Republican	4,036,572	48.0	185	81.8
		Samuel J. Tilden	Democratic	4,284,020	51.0	184	
1880	38	**James A. Garfield**	Republican	4,453,295	48.5	214	79.4
		Winfield S. Hancock	Democratic	4,414,082	48.1	155	
		James B. Weaver	Greenback-Labor	308,578	3.4		
1884	38	**Grover Cleveland**	Democratic	4,879,507	48.5	219	77.5
		James G. Blaine	Republican	4,850,293	48.2	182	
		Benjamin F. Butler	Greenback-Labor	175,370	1.8		
		John P. St. John	Prohibition	150,369	1.5		
1888	38	**Benjamin Harrison**	Republican	5,477,129	47.9	233	79.3
		Grover Cleveland	Democratic	5,537,857	48.6	168	
		Clinton B. Fisk	Prohibition	249,506	2.2		
		Anson J. Streeter	Union Labor	146,935	1.3		
1892	44	**Grover Cleveland**	Democratic	5,555,426	46.1	277	74.7
		Benjamin Harrison	Republican	5,182,690	43.0	145	
		James B. Weaver	People's	1,029,846	8.5	22	
		John Bidwell	Prohibition	264,133	2.2		
1896	45	**William McKinley**	Republican	7,102,246	51.1	271	79.3
		William J. Bryan	Democratic	6,492,559	47.7	176	
1900	45	**William McKinley**	Republican	7,218,491	51.7	292	73.2
		William J. Bryan	Democratic; Populist	6,356,734	45.5	155	
		John C. Wooley	Prohibition	208,914	1.5		
1904	45	**Theodore Roosevelt**	Republican	7,628,461	57.4	336	65.2
		Alton B. Parker	Democratic	5,084,223	37.6	140	
		Eugene V. Debs	Socialist	402,283	3.0		
		Silas C. Swallow	Prohibition	258,536	1.9		
1908	46	**William H. Taft**	Republican	7,675,320	51.6	321	65.4
		William J. Bryan	Democratic	6,412,294	43.1	162	
		Eugene V. Debs	Socialist	420,793	2.8		
		Eugene W. Chafin	Prohibition	253,840	1.7		
1912	48	**Woodrow Wilson**	Democratic	6,296,547	41.9	435	58.8
		Theodore Roosevelt	Progressive	4,118,571	27.4	88	
		William H. Taft	Republican	3,486,720	23.2	8	
		Eugene V. Debs	Socialist	900,672	6.0		
		Eugene W. Chafin	Prohibition	206,275	1.4		
1916	48	**Woodrow Wilson**	Democratic	9,127,695	49.4	277	61.6
		Charles E. Hughes	Republican	8,533,507	46.2	254	

Presidential Elections, *Continued*

Year	Number of States	Candidates	Parties	Popular Vote	% of Popular Vote	Electoral Vote	% Voter Participation[b]
		A. L. Benson	Socialist	585,113	3.2		
		J. Frank Hanly	Prohibition	220,506	1.2		
1920	48	**Warren G. Harding**	Republican	16,143,407	60.4	404	49.2
		James M. Cox	Democratic	9,130,328	34.2	127	
		Eugene V. Debs	Socialist	919,799	3.4		
		P. P. Christensen	Farmer-Labor	265,411	1.0		
1924	48	**Calvin Coolidge**	Republican	15,718,211	54.0	382	48.9
		John W. Davis	Democratic	8,385,283	28.8	136	
		Robert M. La Follette	Progressive	4,831,289	16.6	13	
1928	48	**Herbert C. Hoover**	Republican	21,391,993	58.2	444	56.9
		Alfred E. Smith	Democratic	15,016,169	40.9	87	
1932	48	**Franklin D. Roosevelt**	Democratic	22,809,638	57.4	472	56.9
		Herbert C. Hoover	Republican	15,758,901	39.7	59	
		Norman Thomas	Socialist	881,951	2.2		
1936	48	**Franklin D. Roosevelt**	Democratic	27,752,869	60.8	523	61.0
		Alfred M. Landon	Republican	16,674,665	36.5	8	
		William Lemke	Union	882,479	1.9		
1940	48	**Franklin D. Roosevelt**	Democratic	27,307,819	54.8	449	62.5
		Wendell L. Wilkie	Republican	22,321,018	44.8	82	
1944	48	**Franklin D. Roosevelt**	Democratic	25,606,585	53.5	432	55.9
		Thomas E. Dewey	Republican	22,014,745	46.0	99	
1948	48	**Harry S Truman**	Democratic	24,179,345	49.6	303	53.0
		Thomas E. Dewey	Republican	21,991,291	45.1	189	
		J. Strom Thurmond	States' Rights	1,176,125	2.4	39	
		Henry A. Wallace	Progressive	1,157,326	2.4		
1952	48	**Dwight D. Eisenhower**	Republican	33,936,234	55.1	442	63.3
		Adlai E. Stevenson	Democratic	27,314,992	44.4	89	
1956	48	**Dwight D. Eisenhower**	Republican	35,590,472	57.6	457	60.6
		Adlai E. Stevenson	Democratic	26,022,752	42.1	73	
1960	50	**John F. Kennedy**	Democratic	34,226,731	49.7	303	62.8
		Richard M. Nixon	Republican	34,108,157	49.5	219	
1964	50	**Lyndon B. Johnson**	Democratic	43,129,566	61.1	486	61.7
		Barry M. Goldwater	Republican	27,178,188	38.5	52	
1968	50	**Richard M. Nixon**	Republican	31,785,480	43.4	301	60.6
		Hubert H. Humphrey	Democratic	31,275,166	42.7	191	
		George C. Wallace	American Independent	9,906,473	13.5	46	
1972	50	**Richard M. Nixon**	Republican	47,169,911	60.7	520	55.2
		George S. McGovern	Democratic	29,170,383	37.5	17	
		John G. Schmitz	American	1,099,482	1.4		
1976	50	**Jimmy Carter**	Democratic	40,830,763	50.1	297	53.5
		Gerald R. Ford	Republican	39,147,793	48.0	240	

Presidential Elections, *Continued*

Year	Number of States	Candidates	Parties	Popular Vote	% of Popular Vote	Electoral Vote	% Voter Participation[b]
1980	50	**Ronald Reagan**	Republican	43,899,248	50.8	489	52.6
		Jimmy Carter	Democratic	35,481,432	41.0	49	
		John B. Anderson	Independent	5,719,437	6.6	0	
		Ed Clark	Libertarian	920,859	1.1	0	
1984	50	**Ronald Reagan**	Republican	54,455,075	58.8	525	53.1
		Walter Mondale	Democratic	37,577,185	40.6	13	
1988	50	**George Bush**	Republican	48,901,046	53.4	426	50.2
		Michael Dukakis	Democratic	41,809,030	45.6	111[c]	
1992		**Bill Clinton**	Democratic	44,908,233	43.0	370	55.0
		George Bush	Republican	39,102,282	37.4	168	
		Ross Perot	Reform	19,741,048	18.9	0	
1996[d]	50	**Bill Clinton**	Democratic	47,130,000	49.2	379	48.8
		Bob Dole	Republican	39,086,000	40.8	159	
		Ross Perot	Reform	8,143,000	8.5	0	

Candidates receiving less than 1 percent of the popular vote have been omitted. Thus the percentage of popular vote given for any election year may not total 100 percent.

Before the passage of the Twelfth Amendment in 1804, the Electoral College voted for two presidential candidates; the runner-up became vice president. Before 1824, most presidential electors were chosen by state legislatures, not by popular vote.

[a] Greeley died shortly after the election; the electors supporting him then divided their votes among minor candidates.

[b] Percent of voting-age population casting ballots.

[c] One elector from West Virginia cast her Electoral College presidential ballot for Lloyd Bentsen, the Democratic party's vice-presidential candidate.

[d] Election figures for 1996 are based on preliminary returns.

Index